THE CAMBRIDGE HISTORY OF AMERICAN LITERATURE

The Cambridge History of American Literature addresses the broad spectrum of new and established directions in all branches of American writing and includes the work of scholars and critics who have shaped, and who continue to shape, what has become a major area of literary scholarship. The authors span three decades of achievement in American literary criticism, thereby speaking for the continuities as well as the disruptions sustained between generations of scholarship. Generously proportioned narratives allow at once for a broader vision and sweep of American literary history than has been possible previously, and while the voice of traditional criticism forms a background for these narratives, it joins forces with the diversity of interests that characterize contemporary literary studies.

The *History* offers wide-ranging, interdisciplinary accounts of American genres and periods. Generated partly by the recent unearthing of previously neglected texts, the expansion of material in American literature coincides with a dramatic increase in the number and variety of approaches to that material. The multifaceted scholarly and critical enterprise embodied in *The Cambridge History of American Literature* addresses these multiplicities – the social, the cultural, the intellectual, and the aesthetic – and demonstrates a richer concept of authority in literary studies than is found in earlier accounts.

This volume is the first complete narrative history of nineteenth-century American poetry, ranging from the revolutionary period through the Civil War and the surging pluralism and emerging mass society at the turn of the century. Barbara Packer explores the riches of the neoclassical and satiric forms mastered by the early Federalist poets; the creative reaches of once-celebrated, and still compelling, poets such as Philip Freneau, John Greenleaf Whittier, and the distinctive lyric forms developed by Ralph Waldo Emerson and the Transcendentalists. Shira Wolosky provides a new perspective on the achievement of female poets of the period, as well as a close appreciation of African-American poets, including the collective folk authors of the Negro spirituals. She reveals the virtuosity and historical force of the "genteel poets," from Oliver Wendell Holmes, Sr. to George Santayana. And she offers a fresh and illuminating analysis of the major works of the period, from Poe through Melville and Crane, to the poetic giants of the century, Walt Whitman and Emily Dickinson. The authors of this volume discuss this extraordinary literary achievement in both formal terms and in its sustained engagement with changing social and cultural conditions. In doing so they recover and elucidate American poetry of the nineteenth century for our twenty-first-century pleasure, profit, and renewed study.

THE CAMBRIDGE HISTORY OF
AMERICAN LITERATURE

Volume 4

1800–1910

THE CAMBRIDGE
HISTORY OF
AMERICAN LITERATURE

Volume 4
Nineteenth-Century Poetry
1800–1910

General Editor

SACVAN BERCOVITCH
Harvard University

CAMBRIDGE
UNIVERSITY PRESS

PUBLISHED BY THE PRESS SYNDICATE OF THE UNIVERSITY OF CAMBRIDGE
The Pitt Building, Trumpington Street, Cambridge, United Kingdom

CAMBRIDGE UNIVERSITY PRESS
The Edinburgh Building, Cambridge, CB2 2RU, UK
40 West 20th Street, New York, NY 10011–4211, USA
477 Williamstown Road, Port Melbourne, VIC 3207, Australia
Ruiz de Alarcón 13, 28014 Madrid, Spain
Dock House, The Waterfront, Cape Town 8001, South Africa

http://www.cambridge.org

© Cambridge University Press 2004

First published 2004

Printed in the United Kingdom at the University Press, Cambridge

Typeface Garamond 3 11/13 pt.   *System* LaTeX 2ε {TB}

A catalogue record for this book is available from the British Library

ISBN 0 521 30108 4 hardback

CONTENTS

ACKNOWLEDGMENTS

FROM THE GENERAL EDITOR

My thanks to Harvard University for support of this project and to Ray Ryan of Cambridge University Press for his editorial guidance. I am grateful once again to Peter Buttigieg, my superb research assistant. On a personal note: my abiding gratitude and love to my sister, Ninel Segal, and my brother-in-law, Charles Segal.

Here as in several previous volumes, the Introduction is divided into two parts. The first part (pp. 1–5), describing the design and aims of this multi-volume project as a whole, was written by me. The second part (pp. 5–8), describing the organization and contents of this particular volume, was a collaborative effort, written jointly by me and by an outstanding representative of the current generation of Americanists – representative, that is, of the type of reader for whom this *History* is ideally intended. I was most fortunate to enlist Neal Dolan (now an Assistant Professor at the University of Toronto) for this task. He turned out to be the main author in our collaboration, and I am grateful to him for all he did, both in this matter and in his compiling of the Chronology.

Sacvan Bercovitch
Harvard University

AMERICAN VERSE TRADITIONS, 1800–1855

I wish to thank the UCLA Academic Senate Committee on Research for grants supporting this project. A fellowship year at the Center for Advanced Study in the Behavioral Sciences at Stanford gave me time to begin the work, and sabbatical leaves from UCLA helped me complete it. I am grateful to my UCLA colleagues Paul Sheats and Thomas Wortham for their willingness to discuss nineteenth-century English and American poetry with me. John Hollander and David Bromwich were correspondents generous with their time and information. I was helped by two talented research assistants, Anne Shee-han and Martin Griffin. And Sacvan Bercovitch served as critic, encourager, and advisor throughout the writing of the text.

Barbara Packer
University of California, Los Angeles

POETRY AND PUBLIC DISCOURSE, 1820–1910

I wish to thank first and last Sacvan Bercovitch. Working with him has been an extraordinary experience among the many adventures of this project. I wish to thank Harold Bloom, who has been and remains a guiding figure in my experience of poetry. I wish to thank my former teachers and colleagues in the study of poetry and culture: Emory Elliott, Robert Fagles, Joseph Frank, Geoffrey Hartman, John Hollander, A. Walton Litz, Alan Trachtenberg. I wish to thank for their suggestions, encouragement, and the delight of their com-pany in my work on this volume, Shuli Barzilai, Sandy and Emily Budick, Tova Halbertal, Beverly Haviland, Michael Kramer, Cristanne Miller, Ilana Pardes, Jeffrey Perl. I wish to thank the Israel Academy of Arts and Sciences for fellow-ship support, and the Hebrew University of Jerusalem for generous Sabbatical time. I wish to honor the memory of my brother, Gary Wolosky, and to give heartfelt thanks to my parents, Blanche and David Wolosky; my sisters, Leslie Wolosky and Rickey Wolosky Palkovitz; and to my husband, Ariel Weiss. I dedicate this section of the volume to my children, Talya, Elazar, Tamar, and Nomi.

Versions of material in this volume have been published as:
"An American-Jewish Typology: Emma Lazarus and the Figure of Christ," *Prooftexts* 16: 2, May 1996, 113–25.
"Santayana and Harvard Formalism," *Raritan* 18:4, Spring 1999, 51–67.
"Women's Bibles," *Feminist Studies*, 28: 1, Spring 2002.
"The Claims of Rhetoric: Towards an Historical Poetics," *American Literary History*, 15:1, Spring 2003, 14–22.
"Being in the Body," *The Cambridge Companion to Emily Dickinson*, ed. Wendy Martin, Cambridge University Press, New York: Cambridge University Press, 2002, 129–41.

Emily Dickinson's poetry is reprinted by permission of the publishers and the Trustees of Amherst College from *The Poems of Emily Dickinson*, 3 volumes, ed. Thomas H. Johnson, Cambridge, MA: Harvard University Press. Copy-right 1951, 1955, 1979 by the President and Fellows of Harvard College; and *The Poems of Emily Dickinson*, ed. Ralph W. Franklin, Cambridge, MA: The

Shira Wolosky
Hebrew University of Jerusalem

INTRODUCTION

This multi-volume *History* marks a new beginning in the study of American literature. The first *Cambridge History of American Literature* (1917) helped introduce a new branch of English writing. The *Literary History of the United States*, assembled thirty years later under the aegis of Robert E. Spiller, helped establish a new field of academic study. This *History* embodies the work of a generation of Americanists who have redrawn the boundaries of the field. Trained in the 1960s and early 1970s, representing the broad spectrum of both new and established directions in all branches of American writing, these scholars and critics have shaped, and continue to shape, what has become a major area of modern literary scholarship.

Over the past three decades, Americanist literary criticism has expanded from a border province into a center of humanist studies. The vitality of the field is reflected in the rising interest in American literature nationally and globally, in the scope of scholarly activity, and in the polemical intensity of debate. Significantly, American texts have come to provide a major focus for inter- and cross-disciplinary investigation. Gender studies, ethnic studies, and popular-culture studies, among others, have penetrated to all corners of the profession, but perhaps their single largest base is American literature. The same is true with regard to controversies over multiculturalism and canon formation: the issues are transhistorical and transcultural, but the debates themselves have often turned on American books.

However we situate ourselves in these debates, it seems clear that the activity they have generated has provided a source of intellectual revitalization and new research, involving a massive recovery of neglected and undervalued bodies of writing. We know far more than ever about what some have termed (in the plural) "American literatures," a term grounded in the persistence in the United States of different traditions, different kinds of aesthetics, even different notions of the literary.

These developments have enlarged the meanings as well as the materials of American literature. For this generation of critics and scholars, American literary history is no longer the history of a certain, agreed-upon group of

American masterworks. Nor is it any longer based upon a certain, agreed-upon historical perspective on American writing. The quests for certainty and agreement continue, as they should, but they proceed now within a climate of critical decentralization – of controversy, sectarianism, and, at best, dialogue among different schools of explanation.

This scene of conflict signals a shift in structures of academic authority. The practice of all literary history hitherto, from its inception in the eighteenth century, has depended upon an established consensus about the essence or nature of its subject. Today the invocation of consensus sounds rather like an appeal for compromise, or like nostalgia. The study of American literary history now defines itself in the plural, as a multivocal, multifaceted scholarly, critical, and pedagogic enterprise. Authority in this context is a function of disparate but connected bodies of knowledge. We might call it the authority of difference. It resides in part in the energies of heterogeneity: a variety of contending constituencies, bodies of materials, and sets of authorities. In part the authority of difference lies in the critic's capacity to connect: to turn the particularity of his or her approach into a form of challenge and engagement, so that it actually gains substance and depth in relation to other, sometimes complementary, sometimes conflicting, modes of explanation.

This new *Cambridge History of American Literature* claims authority on both counts, contentious and collaborative. In a sense, this makes it representative of the specialized, processual, marketplace culture it describes. Our *History* is fundamentally pluralist: a federated histories of American literatures. But it is worth noting that in large measure this representative quality is adversarial. Our *History* is an expression of ongoing debates within the profession about cultural patterns and values. Some of these narratives may be termed celebratory, insofar as they uncover correlations between social and aesthetic achievement. Others are explicitly oppositional, sometimes to the point of turning literary analysis into a critique of liberal pluralism. Oppositionalism, however, stands in a complex relation here to advocacy. Indeed it may be said to mark the *History*'s most traditional aspect. The high moral stance that oppositional criticism assumes – literary analysis as the occasion for resistance and alternative vision – is grounded in the very definition of art we have inherited from the Romantic era. The earlier, genteel view of literature upheld the universality of ideals embodied in great books. By implication, therefore, as in the declared autonomy of art, and often by direct assault upon social norms and practices, especially those of Western capitalism, it fostered a broad ethical-aesthetic antinomianism – a celebration of literature (in Matthew Arnold's words) as the criticism of life. By midcentury that criticism had issued, on the one hand, in the New Critics' assault on industrial society, and, on the other hand, in the neo-Marxist theories of praxis.

The relation here between oppositional and nonoppositional approaches makes for a problematic perspective on nationality. It is a problem that invites many sorts of resolution, including a post-national (or post-American) perspective. Some of these prospective revisions are implicit in these volumes, perhaps as shadows or images of literary histories to come. But by and large "America" here designates the United States, or the territories that were to become part of the United States. Although several of our contributors adopt a comparatist transatlantic or pan-American framework, and although several of them discuss works in other languages, mainly their concerns center upon writing in English in this country – "American literature" as it has been (and still is) commonly understood in its national implications. This restriction marks a deliberate choice on our part. To some extent, no doubt, it reflects limitations of time, space, training, and available materials; but it must be added that our contributors have made the most of their limitations. They have taken advantage of time, space, training, and newly available materials to turn nationality itself into a *question of literary* history. Precisely because of their focus on English-language literatures in the United States, the term "America" for them is neither a narrative *donnée* – an assumed or inevitable or natural premise – nor an objective background (*the* national history). Quite the contrary: it is the contested site of many sorts of literary-historical inquiry. What had presented itself as a neutral territory, hospitable to all authorized parties, turns out upon examination to be, and to have always been, a volatile combat-zone.

"America" in these volumes is a historical entity, the United States of America. It is also a declaration of community, a people constituted and sustained by verbal fiat, a set of universal principles, a strategy of social cohesion, a summons to social protest, a prophecy, a dream, an aesthetic ideal, a trope of the modern ("progress," "opportunity," "the new"), a semiotics of inclusion ("melting pot," "patchwork quilt," "nation of nations"), and a semiotics of exclusion, closing out not only the Old World but all other countries of the Americas, north and south, as well as large groups within the United States. A nationality so conceived is a rhetorical battleground. "America" in these volumes is a shifting, many-sided focal point for exploring the historicity of the text and the textuality of history.

Not coincidentally, these are the two most vexed issues today in literary studies. At no time in literary studies has theorizing about history been more acute and pervasive. It is hardly too much to say that what joins all the special interests in the field, all factions in our current dissensus, is an overriding interest in history: as the ground and texture of ideas, metaphors, and myths; as the substance of the texts we read and the spirit in which we interpret them. Even if we acknowledge that great books, a few configurations of language raised to an extraordinary pitch of intensity, have transcended their time and place (and even if we believe that their enduring power offers a recurrent source of opposition), it is evident upon reflection that concepts of aesthetic transcendence are themselves timebound. Like other claims to the absolute, from the hermeneutics of faith to scientific objectivity, aesthetic claims about high art are shaped by history. We grasp their particular forms of beyondness (the aesthetics of divine inspiration, the aesthetics of ambiguity, subversion, and indeterminacy) through an identifiably historical consciousness.

The same recognition of contingency extends to the writing of history. Some histories are truer than others; a few histories are invested for a time with the grandeur of being "definitive" and "comprehensive"; but all are narrative conditioned by their historical moments. So are these. Our intention here is to make limitations a source of open-endedness. All previous histories of American literature have been either totalizing or encyclopedic. They have offered either the magisterial sweep of a single vision or a multitude of terse accounts that come to seem just as totalizing, if only because the genre of the brief, expert synthesis precludes the development of authorial voice. Here, in contrast, American literary history unfolds through a polyphony of large-scale narratives. Because the number of contributors is limited, each of them has the scope to elaborate distinctive views (premises, arguments, analyses); each of their narratives, therefore, is persuasive by demonstration, rather than by assertion; and each is related to the others (in spite of difference) through themes and concerns, anxieties and aspirations, that are common to *this* generation of Americanists.

The contributors were selected first for the excellence of their scholarship and then for the significance of the critical communities informing their work. Together, they demonstrate the achievements of Americanist literary criticism over the past three decades. Their contributions to these volumes show links as well as gaps between generations. They give voice to the extraordinary range of materials now subsumed under the heading of American literature. They express the distinctive sorts of excitement and commitment that have led to the remarkable expansion of the field. And they reflect the diversity of interests that constitutes literary studies in our time as well as the ethnographic diversity that has come to characterize our universities, faculty and students alike, since World War II, and especially since the 1960s.

The same qualities inform this *History*'s organizational principles. Its flexibility of structure is meant to accommodate the varieties of American literary history. Some major writers appear in more than one volume, because they belong to more than one age. Some texts are discussed in several narratives within a volume, because they are important to different realms of cultural experience. Sometimes the story of a certain movement is retold from different perspectives, because the story requires a plural focus: as pertaining, for example, to the margins as well as to the mainstream, or as being equally the culmination of one era and the beginning of another. Such overlap was not planned, but it was encouraged from the start, and the resulting diversity of perspectives corresponds to the sheer plenitude of literary and historical materials. It also makes for a richer, more intricate account of particulars (writers, texts, movements) than that available in any previous history of American literature.

Sacvan Bercovitch

Every volume in this *History* displays these strengths in its own ways. This volume does so by emphasizing the complex, conflicted engagement of nineteenth-century American poets with the governing patterns of thought and belief of the culture, among these the ideology of high culture. The achievement of many of these poets has been eclipsed by the success of literary modernism. When Pound and Eliot rejected the Romantic idiom of Wordsworth and Tennyson as sentimental, stilted, and rhetorically inflated, they implicitly passed negative judgment on most of the verse published in the US from 1800 to 1910. The authors of this volume provide a long-overdue corrective by giving close attention to a wide range of nineteenth-century poets, South as well as North, black as well as white, female as well as male. Their approach is both formalist and historical. They note the many pleasures still available in that body of poetry to contemporary readers – not just in the now-canonical works of Walt Whitman and Emily Dickinson, but (among others) in the once-famous works of Henry Wadsworth Longfellow and John Greenleaf Whittier, and in such lesser but interesting figures as Lydia Sigourney and Emma Lazarus. They also detail the rich historical context within, through, and against which these poets wrote.

Barbara Packer takes on a formidable challenge in attempting to refresh our appreciation of the neoclassical poetry of the first half of the century. She contends not only against modernist aesthetic preferences, but equally against a Romantic-nationalist narrative according to which American literature only becomes mature when it ceases to imitate foreign models. American poets of this period, Packer reminds us, tended to be anxious about their provincialism. Mastery of classical and English forms affirmed membership in a larger European tradition. In the early nineteenth century, even a politically radical poet like Joel Barlow employed decorous neoclassical couplets to proclaim the advent of an Enlightenment millennium in America. Packer finds both wit and lyrical beauty in his poetry, as well as in the Augustan-influenced satirical stanzas of John Trumbull, John Quincy Adams, Hugh Henry Brackenridge, Philip Freneau, Joseph Rodman Drake, and Fitz-Greene Halleck. Even in the Romantically oriented lyrical poems of the era, which in most respects owe a large debt to Wordsworth, Packer finds a persistent effort to contain the wild American landscape within pre-Wordsworthian metrical and rhetorical structures.

Emerson's poetry provides the most intricate example of this tension between British forms and American materials. His discovery of Wordsworth and Coleridge in the early 1830s transformed his sensibility; and in a few fine poems such as "Hamtreya" and "Musketaquid" he successfully adopts the blank verse of (say) "Tintern Abbey." But most of his poems, Packer shows, take shape as idiosyncratic hybrids of Romantic themes articulated in neoclassical couplets and seventeenth-century quatrains, derived from Herbert, Milton, Jonson, and Marvell. The Sage of Concord could celebrate Walt Whitman's free verse, but retained his own commitment to regular verbal patterning. His influence on Whitman was philosophical and inspirational, not formal. In this sense, his most direct heir was Emily Dickinson, whose poems display not only the Transcendentalist preoccupation with the boundaries of the self, but also something of Emerson's gnomic, compressed, almost abrasive rhyming style. Never has this period of American literary history, from the Federalist poets through Emerson and Whittier, been more vividly evoked or more authoritatively analyzed.

Packer's literary focus reveals historical continuity and change. Shira Wolosky illuminates the poetry of the second half of the century through an emphasis on broad matters of social engagement. She sees her poets as everywhere involved in rhetorical negotiation with prevailing cultural norms. Especially important in this regard are the efforts of women poets in this period to recast feminine obligations to modesty and the private sphere. In the work of a broad range of now-forgotten or under-appreciated female poets —Julia Ward Howe, Frances Harper, Helen Hunt Jackson, Ellen Wheeler Wilcox, Charlotte Perkins Gilman, Lucy Larcom, Alice and Phoebe Cary, and others — Wolosky traces a subtle dialectic of self-assertion through revisionary submission. Authority in the private sphere, she points out, was nonetheless a form of authority, and the assertion of modesty was nonetheless an assertion. These poets managed to achieve a public voice in the paradoxical act of publicly avow-ing the private-sphere values of domesticity and modesty. None exploited this paradox more fiercely than Emily Dickinson. Wolosky finds in the histrionic privacy of her life and her poems an infinitely volatile enactment of "explosive compliance."

The strongest male poets of the period were no less complexly engaged with the culture at large. The era's deepest cultural conflict, between South and North, was reflected in Poe's morbid hostility towards Longfellow's com-placent moral didacticism. Both poets, Wolosky points out, convey profound disappointment with the marginal place of poetry in a commercial society, but they do so in regionally distinctive ways. A gentle tone of elegiac patri-cian futility pervades Longfellow's evocations of dead or dying cultures of the past, while Poe's tortured social and intellectual marginality finds expression in a poetics of negation. Wolosky brilliantly identifies several variants of these opposed strategies – nostalgic and proto-modernist – in the subsequent fig-ures she treats. Where "genteel" writers such as Oliver Wendell Holmes, James Russell Lowell, and George Santayana attempted to dissociate poetic language from the surging pluralism of an emerging mass society, Herman Melville, Stephen Crane, and Paul Lawrence Dunbar fashioned lastingly painful poems out of stark confrontations with this society's fractures, paradoxes, dualities, and alienations. The collective folk authors of the Negro spirituals voiced resis-tance to the cruelest form of capitalist exploitation in a poetry of apocalyptic hope. And in Whitman, Wolosky finds a sustained effort to figuratively over-come what was (and remains) perhaps the central conflict of social and political life in America – the conflict between "negative" individualist liberty on one hand, and the felt need for communal bonds on the other. At his best, she sug-gests, Whitman, like many of the women poets treated earlier in the volume, finds a kind of civic-communal counterbalance to liberal individualism in a poetry of intimate sentiment, including (as in the elegy to Lincoln) the socially binding sentiment of mourning.

Both critics and champions of liberal-individualist principles have often worried about the affective sustenance of societies governed by them. Both sides should find much to reflect upon here. If poetry is, as Wordsworth sug-gested, "the history of feeling," we have here an elucidation of human feeling as it formally confronts the conditions of experience in an ever-increasingly liberal-individualistic society. The ambivalent post-colonial relationship to the cultural parent; the difficult negotiation of the highly charged bound-ary between the public and the private spheres; the self-discovery and self-assertion of minorities and women; the exhilarations of nationalism; the alienations of capitalism and the search for countervailing values; the multiple identifications of pluralism and the accompanying nostalgia for more easily knowable communities: these and other problematics of what might be called social feeling are richly and accessibly articulated in nineteenth-century American poetry, and they are richly and accessibly commented upon in this volume. Packer locates these principally in her poets' choices of genre and form, whereas Wolosky finds them principally in her poets' accommodations of prevailing cultural rhetorics. But both agree in seeing the poetry as everywhere engaged in its historical settings, and in doing so they recover and elucidate American poetry of the nineteenth century for our twenty-first century pleasure, profit, and renewed study.

Neal Dolan
University of Toronto

Sacvan Bercovitch
Harvard University

American verse traditions, 1800–1855

Barbara Packer

PREFACE: REVERENCE AND AMBITION

In an 1854 lecture entitled "Poetry and English Poetry," Ralph Waldo Emerson introduced a familiar subject. "The question is often asked, Why no poet appears in America? Other nations in their early, expanding periods, in their war for existence, have shot forth the flowers of verse, and created mythology which continued to charm the imagination of after-men. But we have all manner of ability, except this: we are brave, victorious; we legislate, trade, plant, build, sail, and combine as well as any others, but we have no imagination, no constructive mind, no affirmative books." Seventeen years earlier, in "The American Scholar," his criticism had sounded more hopeful. "Perhaps the time is already come . . . when the sluggard intellect of this continent will look from under its iron lids and fill the postponed expectation of the world with something better than the exertions of mechanical skill." But the iron lids of the continent had stayed closed, despite the best efforts of Bryant, Longfellow, Whittier, Poe, and Emerson himself (whose *Poems* had appeared in 1846) to pry them open.

The complaint was freely sounded even in books meant to appeal to national pride. When the New York editor Rufus Griswold (1815–57) published *The Poets and Poetry of America* in 1842, he cautioned that the United States could be said to have only the beginnings of a national literature. He had chosen the best poems he could find from the five hundred volumes of "rhythmical compositions" that had been published in America since the earliest days of European settlement. But he warned his readers not to expect too much. "A high degree of excellence, especially in poetry, is attained only by constant and quiet study and cultivation," he noted. "Our poets have generally written with too little preparation, and too hastily, to win enduring reputations." There were several reasons for this haste. Lack of "a just system of copyright" in the United States made it more profitable for publishers to pirate the works of famous British poets than to publish American poems. Magazine and newspaper editors would sometimes pay for verses, but even then, Griswold noted, "the rewards of literary exertion are so precarious that but a small number can give their exclusive attention to literature." American poets were ministers, lawyers, doctors, journalists, politicians; wives with improvident husbands or widows with many children. John Quincy Adams managed to write his poems and translations while serving as United States minister to the Netherlands, to Berlin, to Russia, and to the Court of St. James; as Boylston Professor of Rhetoric and Oratory at Harvard; as United States Senator, Secretary of State, President, and (for the last seventeen years of his life) Congressman from Massachusetts.

Griswold found something else to regret about American poetry. Too few of his authors were free "from that vassalage of opinion and style which is produced by a constant study of the literature of the country from which we inherit our language, our taste, and our manners." This was Emerson's complaint as well. "Our poetry reminds me of the catbird who sings so affectedly & vaingloriously to me near Walden," he observed. "Very sweet & musical! very various! fine execution! but so conscious, & such a *performer! not a note is his own*, except at last, *miow miow.*" But the poets themselves did not seem to think of themselves as vassals, unless (like Emerson) they were also cultural critics. The poems, letters, and memoirs of American poets suggest instead that they looked upon the British poets as friends, companions, models, and even liberators. Before the Connecticut poet Joel Barlow (1754–1812) was expelled from England for subversive activity in 1792, he found time to pay a visit to Pope's grotto at Twickenham in order to pay tribute to the poet who had inspired all his own verse. Washington Allston not only wrote a sonnet in praise of his friend Samuel Taylor Coleridge, he painted two portraits of him. When Fitz-Greene Halleck was a Connecticut schoolboy his prized possessions were two volumes by Scottish poets: a copy of Robert Burns's poems and Thomas Campbell's *Pleasures of Hope* (1799). After Halleck had moved to New York City he happened to mention to a new acquaintance that his idea of heaven would be to "swing on a rainbow and read Tom Campbell." The new acquaintance, Joseph Rodman Drake, impulsively seized Halleck by the hand to signify his heartfelt agreement. The two men at once became close friends and literary collaborators. William Cullen Bryant recalled that when he first read the *Lyrical Ballads* (as a friend later remembered) "a thousand springs seemed to gush up at once into his heart, and the face of Nature, of a sudden, to change into a strange freshness and life."

American poets already loved Shakespeare, Milton, Dryden, Pope, Thomson, Collins, Gray, Young, Cowper, and Burns; they were hungry for new poems by Sir Walter Scott, and Campbell, and Byron. Eventually (though this took longer) they learned to read and admire Wordsworth, Coleridge, Keats, and Shelley. Americans of this era were indefatigable translators. John Quincy Adams translated the satires of Juvenal; later, as a way of teaching himself German when he was serving as minister to Russia, he translated Wieland's

Oberon into Spenserian stanzas. William Cullen Bryant translated the *Iliad* and *Odyssey*; the Transcendentalist poet Christopher Pearce Cranch translated the *Aeneid*. Emerson translated Persian poetry from the German translations of Joseph von Hammer; Thoreau translated Aeschylus and Anacreon. In 1845 Henry Wadsworth Longfellow published a large collection of his own translations from ten European languages, *The Poets and Poetry of Europe*; his even more famous translation of *The Divine Comedy* appeared in 1867. If American poets of this period could choose a collective motto, it might be the quotation from Milton's *History of Britain* that Margaret Fuller printed as the epigraph to her translation of Eckerman's *Conversations with Goethe*: "As wine and oil are imported to us from abroad, so must ripe understanding, and many civil virtues, be imported into our minds from foreign writings."

Americans were enthusiastic importers of poems, but their national history, short as it was, altered their reception of these poems. The literary styles popular during the era of the Revolution were those of the English Augustan age. Because they were connected with the first effervescence of national spirit and the dawn of republican hopes, they retained the affection of Americans long after British writers had abandoned them. The French Revolution was at first a source of mild rejoicing in America, when it seemed as if France might follow the transatlantic Republic she had helped to establish into popular government. But there was nothing in the United States to correspond to the excitement prompted by the French Revolution in the generous youth of England or to the disillusionment that followed its failure. When English Romanticism reaches American shores, then, it tends to be stripped of its political references. Emerson often quoted two lines from Wordsworth's *Excursion*, in which the Wanderer reminds the Solitary that it is "the most difficult of tasks to keep / Heights which the soul is competent to gain." The lines expressed perfectly to Emerson the instability of the soul's exalted moments. Yet he never alluded to the context of the speech, which concerns the Solitary's despondency after the failure of the French Revolution. From time to time an American poet who had read Shelley would try to portray some President as a fiend-like oppressor, as James Gates Percival did with Andrew Jackson, though the charge was hard to make credible in a nation where fiend-like oppressors were limited by custom to two terms in office. The one class of Americans who might have protested with convincing fury against repression were the slaves, but except in spirituals – where wrath can communicate through Biblical allusions – poems written for white readers might speak longingly of freedom but not of rebelliousness.

Romanticism first appealed to American poets as a species of exoticism, a welcome change from the satiric or philosophic verse favored by poets of the Revolutionary era. They wrote poems of Fancy (as Coleridge put it) rather than poems of the Imagination: tales about fairies who haunted the villages on the Hudson River; dream-visions involving sylphs; steamy Oriental romances (complete with learned footnotes) involving angels in love with mortal maidens. Most of these poems now seem gingerbready, though the distinction they draw between their own world and the world of "Mammon's slaves" suggests that what looks now like dilettantism had strong ideological appeal. As if mindful of foreign sneers that the mercantile spirit prevailed in the United States, American poets tried to create poems whose uselessness vouched for their innocence. At the same time, there were more serious experiments in sensation and perception, like Washington Allston's extraordinary sequence of sonnets on paintings by the great masters, or James Gates Percival's lengthy descriptions of the effects of sunlight and moonlight on mist and water.

Surprisingly, poets in the United States did not at first show much interest in Romantic nature-poetry, despite the spectacular scenery that foreign travelers had already made famous. Bryant had grown up in a wild, beautiful region on the western Massachusetts border, and his mature poetry reveals a deep love of nature, yet it took Wordsworth's *Lyrical Ballads* to show him something in his own surroundings that he had never seen. Wordsworth had the same effect upon Emerson, Longfellow, and Whitman, whose *Leaves of Grass* (1855) everywhere shows its debt to Wordsworth's great autobiographical epic *The Prelude* (1850). Wordsworth appealed to American poets because he was the Romantic poet most in love with bleakness as well as with natural sublimity, commodities which the United States had in abundance. Very early in the century poets began to write about the real landscape of their States. The poet John Brainard (1796–1828) wrote about the Connecticut countryside in language that anticipates the spareness of Robert Frost.

> The dead leaves strew the forest walk,
> And withered are the pale wild flowers;
> The frost hangs blackening on the stalk,
> And dew-drops fall in frozen showers.
>
> ("Stanzas")

Brainard also could delight in the colors of a New England autumn, when "man enjoys the breeze that sweeps along / The bright, blue, sky above him, and that bends / Magnificently all the forest's pride." Slowly, poets began to stake out claims to bits of the American landscape. James Hillhouse (1789–1841) celebrated the beauties of New Haven's reddish dolomite bluffs, East Rock and West Rock. Fitz-Greene Halleck (1790–1867) described the distant glitter of romantic Manhattan ("Tall spires, and glittering roof, and battlement") as seen from the cliffs of Weehauken across the Hudson, while his friend Rodman

Drake sang of the "bonny Bronx" (the Bronx River) and the pastoral beauty of his family's farm at nearby Hunter's Point.

This transmission of ideas and styles, however, faced an obstacle no American poet really knew how to surmount. In an essay on "American Poetry," W. H. Auden noted that "even the most formal and elevated styles of poetry are more conditioned by the spoken tongue, the language really used by men of that country, than anything else." Beyond obvious differences in the pronunciation of individual words, British and American English speech patterns differ in noticeable ways. Auden confessed:

What the secret of the difference is, I cannot put my finger on; William Carlos Williams, who has thought more than most about this problem, says that "Pace is one of its most important manifestations," and to this one might add another, Pitch. If undefinable, the difference is, however, immediately recognizable by the ear, even in verse where the formal conventions are the same.

Poetic lines written in traditional meters naturally sound "English" to an American ear, no matter which side of the Atlantic they come from.

Most American poets of the nineteenth century had not yet learned to accommodate the rhythms of the language they actually spoke to metrical schemes they had inherited. Except in comic verse, which often conveys a sense of colloquial raciness and swing, they gave the impression of exiling themselves from their own tongue when they attempted serious verse. American poets might substitute Monadnock or Mt. Shasta for Helvellyn or write poems to the Swannanoa instead of the River Duddon, but they could not so easily write poetry in traditional meters that sounded wholly natural to their readers' ears. Yet very few poets wanted to abandon meter and rhyme altogether, as Whitman did in *Leaves of Grass*.

What sustained the poets of the early Republic in their little-known and ill-rewarded labors? Perhaps the special hope of beginning a national literary tradition that inspired Joseph Rodman Drake's juvenile poem "The Mocking-Bird." The mocking-bird is an American bird, insouciant and irrepressible. Each mocking-bird's song is an original composition fabricated entirely of thefts. Yet his thrilling notes are more beautiful than the nightingale's, and he ends by silencing the birds whose songs he has stolen.

> Low and soft the song began;
> Scarce I caught it, as it ran
> Through the melancholy trill
> Of the pensive whippoorwill.
> Twittering sparrow, cat-bird's cry,
> Red-bird's whistle, robin's sigh,
> Black-bird, blue-bird, swallow, lark;

Each his native song must mark.
Burst at length the finished song,
Loud and clear it poured along.
All the choir in silence heard,
Hushed before the wondrous bird.

Drake found in the glorious mockingbird an "emblem of the rhyming race." Poets, too, learn only by imitation; their precursors are the strings they must learn to sweep before they can sing their own song.

Soft and low each note they sing,
Soft they tune each varied string;
Till each power is tried and known
Then the kindling spark is blown.
Thus, perchance, has Maro sung;
Thus, his harp has Milton strung;
Thus, immortal Avon's child;
Thus, O Scott! thy witch-notes wild;
Thus, has Pope's melodious lyre
Rung each note with Homer's fire;
Thus did Campbell's war-blast roar
Round the cliffs of Elsinore;
Thus, he dug the soldier's grave,
Iser! by thy purpled wave.

The poets of the early nineteenth century in the United States do not form a continuous tradition. They were more like small Fourth-of-July rockets going off at intervals against the blackness of the night sky. Still, they were participating in a great national experiment. Was it possible to write poetry in a sprawling and thinly populated Republic? If so, what should the poetry sound like? Like the poetry of Byron or the poetry of Pope? Should it mock like the *Anti-Jacobin* or soothe and sweeten like the lyricism of Moore? American poets tried their hands at many different genres during the first half of the nineteenth century. Their experiments communicate the freshness of discovery, and their best poems still have power to charm.

✿

NEOCLASSICISM: COMIC AND SATIRIC VERSE

The architecture of the Federal period is still admired in the United States; the prose of the Founding Fathers is widely praised as the best the country has ever produced. But the poetry that was part of the same culture has come to seem more alien than the neo-Latin poetry of the Puritans. The high gloss and urbanity of neoclassical verse seems inherently at odds with the prosaic realities of American life. Yet the poets who were writing neoclassical poetry at the turn of the nineteenth century were quite inventive in shaping imported conventions to fit their own purposes. The radiant self-satisfaction that beams through every couplet of Barlow's ten-book *Columbiad* will not attain such intensity again until the first edition of *Leaves of Grass*, and the reader who wants to understand Whitman's rewriting of European tradition would do well to examine Barlow's epic first.

Behind the enduring appeal of neoclassical conventions in the United States lay an educational system still devoted to the study of classical languages and literatures. When the hero of Washington Allston's novella *The Hypochondriac* wickedly suggested that the only reason people profess to value the classics is that they refuse to admit that their educations have been thrown away, he was assuming such an identification, which lasted well into the nineteenth century. Admission to a college demanded a reading knowledge of Latin and Greek, and the first two years of study were largely taken up with linguistic exercises. Such an education was very far from worthless to men who wished to take part in public affairs, where writing and speaking with power were still necessary skills. Other readers praised the classics because they embodied what Henry David Thoreau called "the noblest recorded thoughts of man." In the "Reading" chapter of *Walden* (1854) he argued that if the vernacular is our mother tongue, then a classical language is our father tongue, "a reserved and select expression, too significant to be heard by the ear, which we must be born again in order to speak."

For those who lacked the time or the inclination for learning Latin and Greek, the great English translations of the seventeenth and eighteenth century – Dryden's Virgil, Pope's Homer – made the classical epics available to anyone who could read. At the same time these translations strengthened the connection in people's minds between the classicism of Greece and Rome and the stylistic conventions of English Augustan poetry. Writing in pentameter couplets came to seem as natural as breathing and remained so through at least the 1820s. Neoclassical couplets conveyed a meaning beyond the meanings they contained. They signified urbanity and authority, London and Rome. They were civilizing gestures, an assertion of membership in European culture. They assuaged the two worst fears of the provincial imagination – the fears of being marginal and of being belated. Conventions which had come to seem like shackles to English Romantic writers were to American poets stays against confusion, and when the changing literary fashions had finally made neoclassicism seem outmoded even in the United States, poets were at first left with nothing to put in its place.

Neoclassical poetry was public and political, suited to panegyric and satire. Tocqueville was amused by the "pompous name" (the Capitol) chosen by the citizens of the new republic for the building that housed their Congress, but for the citizens themselves the intended parallels between their nation and Rome were a source of considerable pride. The destiny of the United States, they hoped, would be to unite the austere virtues of Republican Rome with the wealth and power of the Roman Empire. Every President, since he relinquished to his successor control of the government, could be praised as a Cincinnatus; every new administration (to its supporters, anyway) could be expected to begin a Golden Age and woo the goddess Astraea back to earth. The Pennsylvania poet Hugh Henry Brackenridge (1748–1816) celebrates Thomas Jefferson's inauguration this way in "To Jefferson, in Imitation of Virgil's Pollio." Jefferson's repeal of the Alien and Sedition acts is an invitation to "Virgin Justice" to descend from her heaven, while his plan to slash the army's budget and get rid of the navy seems to promise the beginning of a reign of universal peace and to guarantee that kind of golden age particularly dear to the American heart ("An age of gold in private coffers felt"). In similar language, Philip Freneau (1752–1832), Brackenridge's friend and Princeton classmate, praises Jefferson at the end of his second term in office as a Cincinnatus. Jefferson has joined that rare company of sages who, "in their country's cause, / Exert their valour, or enforce its laws, / And, late retiring, every wrong redress'd, / Give their last days to solitude and rest." At Monticello he can oversee his farm and shelter his slaves from woe, while with his pen he labors "To illume the statesmen of the time to come, / With the bold spirit of primeval Rome." From this happy retreat Jefferson can "look, with pity, on the cares of kings" while he rejoices in the peace and prosperity his administration has secured to his countrymen: "While smiling plenty decks the abundant plain / And hails Astraea to the world again."

Two criticisms of this sanguine view of things are possible, one from the left, one from the right. Joel Barlow (1754–1812) reserved half a book of his *Columbiad* (1807) to denounce slavery as inconsistent with the beliefs Americans profess, that "Equality of Right is nature's plan / And following nature is the march of man." Of all peoples Americans ought to be least tolerant of slavery, since it is part of that "whole crude system that torments this earth / Of rank, privation, privilege of birth" – the aristocratic and monarchial system that Jefferson devoted his life to fighting. Barlow warned us to remember what happened to the Romans when they forsook their republican simplicity for conquest.

> See Rome's rude sires, with autocratic gait,
> Tread down their tyrant and erect their state;
> Their state secured, they deem it wise and brave,
> That every freeman should command a slave,
> And, flusht with franchise of his camp and town,
> Rove through the world and hunt the nations down;
> Master and man the same vile spirit gains,
> Rome chains the world and wears herself the chains.

Barlow castigated Jefferson's revolution, in other words, for not going far enough. Jefferson's Federalist opponents, on the other hand, saw his visionary attempt to govern as if universal peace were at hand – while Napoleon menaced on one hand and the British on the other – as a folly that threatened the very existence of the country. Jefferson's hope of an enlightened polity seemed to his opponents a delusion and a snare. In 1801 John Quincy Adams (1767–1848), still bitter from the recent election that had defeated his father, sent a translation of Juvenal's Thirteenth Satire to the Philadelphia *Port Folio*, a new magazine edited by his friend Joseph Dennie. The age portrayed by Juvenal is anything but golden:

> Such are the horrors of our modern times,
> They bleach the blackness of all former crimes,
> The age of iron has long since been past,
> And four besides, each blacker than the last;
> A ninth succeeds, compared with which, of old,
> The age of iron was an age of gold;
> An age, which nature does not even name,
> Nor yields a metal to express its shame.

If virtue ever existed, it belongs to the far-off age before Saturn was ejected from his throne:

> Before he laid his diadem aside,
> And in the rustic sickle took a pride,
> While Ida's caves were yet the haunts of Jove,
> Nor virgin Juno, conscious of his love.
>   . . .
>
> No gloomy Pluto ruled the realms of shade
> Nor yet had ravished the Sicilian maid,
> Hell then no wheel, no rock, no furies bore,
> No vulture's pounces dripped with ghostly gore.

Neoclassical models existed for much more than satire or panegyric. American poets tried their hands at georgic, mock-epic, and that American invention known as the "rising glory" poem – in which the poet, surveying the new nation from a mount of vision, foretells the rising glory of America. Finally, there was the epic, that crowning glory without which no people could be said to have achieved admission to the company of civilized nations. The best way to get a sense of the full range of neoclassical possibilities in American verse is to look at the career of Joel Barlow, whose epic, *The Columbiad*, was intended (as its Preface asserts) both "to inculcate the love of rational liberty" in the citizens of the United States and to confer on the new nation the poetic dignity it lacked.

Barlow was born in rural Connecticut in 1754. He attended Yale College, where he studied poetry with the elder Joseph Buckminster and with Timothy Dwight. From them he acquired that love of formal rhetoric and reverence for the great English neoclassical poets that survived unchanged through all the political and religious upheavals of his maturity. Admiration for the English Augustan age was, indeed, widespread in America during the period immediately following the Revolutionary War – itself "almost as much a civil war as it had been a revolution," as one scholar has noted. England under Queen Anne and the first two Georges provided a model that Americans wished to emulate. This idealized England was the England of Pope's "Windsor-Forest," Barlow's favorite poem. It served as the template for everything from his early Yale commencement poem "The Prospect of Peace" (1778), written during Revolutionary War, to the mighty *Columbiad* itself, brought to completion in the anxious decade when Thomas Jefferson still hoped to persuade the world that free trade and political liberty were the surest guarantors of human felicity. Pope himself had prophesied such an age at the end of "Windsor-Forest," in a passage that seemed at once to license and require an answering energy from the other side of the Atlantic.

> The time shall come, when free as seas or wind
> Unbounded Thames shall flow for all mankind,
> Whole nations enter with each swelling tide,
> And seas but join the regions they divide;
> Earth's distant ends our glory shall behold,
> And the new world launch forth to seek the old.
>   . . .
> O stretch thy reign, fair Peace! from shore to shore,
> Till Conquest cease, and Slavery be no more.

Pope's vision of a paradise of justice and free trade animates the happy jumble of Barlow's commencement poem, where he prophesied (with more optimism than accuracy) a speedy end to the war with Britain and looked forward to the arrival of Peace at her new dwelling-place in America, where she "Bids long, calm years adorn the happy clime / And roll down blessings to remotest time." Barlow followed this prophecy with a list of the good things to come in an earthly paradise of enlightened activity and social justice. The slaves would be freed, commercial navies would fill the seas, women poets would arise to sing with "Sapphic sweetness," meteorologists would probe the mysteries of rain clouds, feudal exploitation would be forbidden ("No grasping lord shall grind the neighboring poor") and metaphysicians would "soar with Edwards to the clouds of light."

Barlow would later renounce the orthodox Christianity that Yale's former President Jonathan Edwards exemplified, and he came to resent Yale itself because he was denied a tutorship he thought he deserved. But he clung to the vision of felicity he first expressed in "The Prospect of Peace," and the years of his maturity were spent trying to persuade others to realize it. During the Revolutionary War, while serving an unlikely stint as chaplain to the Revolutionary Army ("On Thursday evening I began to open my mouth, which is none of the smallest, and out of it there went a noise which the brigade received as the duty of my office," he wrote of his first sermon), he found time to work on the first version of his epic, *The Vision of Columbus* (1787). At one point in it, Columbus, permitted to view the future by an angel (like Adam in *Paradise Lost*, though with a secular and American twist), is permitted to see the gradual unification of mankind through international trade.

> See, thro' the whole, the same progressive plan,
> That draws, for mutual succor, man to man,
> From friends to tribes, from tribes to realms ascend,
> Their powers, their interests, and their passions blend.

Sea-captains, international traders, will link "each remotest realm" in a chain of friendship that binds the human family, "Till tribes and states and empires find their place, / And one wide interest sways the human race."

"Interest" has for us a vaguely sinister sound, but Barlow followed an influential school of eighteenth-century political thought in seeing the "interests" –
the needs and desires of individual human beings – as counterweights to the
social forces that drive human beings into isolation or hostility. Our interests make society possible; without them we should roam the wild places like
solitary beasts. In a poem written for delivery at another Yale commencement in 1781 Barlow had described the era of universal peace he expected
shortly. Reason will displace war, good sense will displace military bravado,
till "mutual interest fix the mutual friend." The perfect union of self-interest
and mutual interest is the only sure foundation for a lasting peace, because it
does not require a transformation of human nature to produce it.

The sheer romance of international commerce intoxicated Barlow. Christian
apocalyptics had loved to imagine the ingathering of the nations as a harvest, a
bringing-in of sheaves. Barlow imagined the millennium as the launching of a
thousand merchant ships. "Russian forests to the deep advance," and ships from
all nations join the happy procession: "At once in gathering squadrons, from
the north, / The mingling streamers lead the nations forth; / From different
shores unnumbered masts arise; / And wave their peaceful curtains to the
skies." They are joined by more and more ships in a white procession, "Till far
as pole from pole, the cloudlike train / Skirts the dim heavens and shades the
whitening main."

In *The Vision of Columbus* this conviction that the world might be fully and
naturally redeemed prompted Barlow to append a sprawling footnote to the
final book of the poem. He begins by quoting Richard Price's assertion (in
"Observations on the American Revolution") that the human race is continually improving, so that we can expect "an improved and happy state of affairs"
to take place "before the final consummation of all things." Barlow agrees: "It
has long been the opinion of the Author, that such a state of peace and happiness as is foretold in scripture and commonly called the millennial period,
may be rationally expected to be introduced without a miracle." He lists three
preconditions for such a state. The world must be "considerably peopled"; its
different nations must be known to one another; and "their imaginary wants
must be increased, in order to inspire a passion for commerce." Traditional
moralists might see "imaginary wants" as the root of all corruption in society,
but for Barlow they are the indispensable agents of world unification. Trade
in mere necessaries – corn, hides, lumber – can never be lucrative enough to
inspire that commerce whose beneficent influence makes "the ports unfold,
the glimmering navies dance." Only imaginary wants can tempt merchants to
risk their lives to bring the kinds of luxuries Pope found mingled on Belinda's
dressing-table, the altar of Barlow's new religion:

This Casket *India's* glowing gems unlocks,
And all *Arabia* breathes from yonder Box.
The Tortoise here and Elephant unite,
Transformed to combs, the speckled and the white.
                    (*The Rape of the Lock*, Canto 1)

Barlow got a chance to put into practice his theories of world unification through commerce in 1788, when he set sail for France as the agent of a company set up to sell shares in Ohio land to would-be French emigrants. The company later collapsed and the shares proved worthless, but Barlow was apparently innocent of the fraud, and he remained in France on good terms with his hosts. By then he had become caught up in events far more interesting. To his wife Ruth, who had remained behind in the United States, he sent a letter on 20 July 1789, in hopes of conveying some sense of his own pride and excitement: "All the true things which you see published, however horrible, however noble, memorable, and important in their consequences, have passed under my eye, and it is really no small gratification to me to have seen two complete revolutions in favor of liberty."

The conviction that he was in the vanguard of historical change that would soon sweep the civilized world fills the prose works he wrote during an extended stay in England from 1790 to 1792. The first of these, "Advice to the Privileged Orders" (1792), is like the many responses to Burke's *Reflections on the Revolution in France* written by Barlow's English friends. But its polemical purpose is quickly swallowed up in millennial glee, as Barlow warns the "privileged orders" to prepare to yield gracefully to the "republican principle," which he defines as "the great simplicity of nature applied to the organization of society." He offers a thumbnail sketch of European history since the fall of Rome that identifies three dominant historical spirits: Hierarchy, Chivalry, and Commerce. All three may be used by unscrupulous governments to forge instruments of oppression. But commerce by its very nature tends to subvert the chauvinism natural to ages of hierarchy or chivalry. In the act of trading we find that the hated foreigners are really beings like ourselves, and realize too that their existence and their prosperity are as necessary to us as ours is to them. The spirit of commerce cannot abolish war, but it can reveal war's futility. No nations are natural enemies, and hatreds stirred up between them are fatal deceptions "perpetually imposed upon each nation, by its own government, for the private benefit of its administrators."

"Advice to the Privileged Orders" had been directed at an English audience. In 1792 Barlow also had an opportunity to offer advice to his revolutionary comrades. The French Assembly had decided to revise the constitution it had hastily drawn up in 1791. Barlow addressed a "Letter to the National

Convention of France" to the delegates of that assembly, pointing out some defects in their original scheme and proposing remedies. As everyone has noticed, Barlow's suggestions were intended to move the French constitution in the direction of the American one, as when he advocated abolition of the monarchy and of a state church. What is more remarkable is the tone of the pamphlet. "Advice to the Privileged Orders" had been pugnacious, insolent, satirical. "Letter to the National Convention" was serene. Barlow suddenly realized that the French Revolution had transformed the United States from the world's newest nation to the world's oldest living republic, on whose happy model other aspiring republics might fashion their constitution and their laws. (The French delegates do not appear to have taken any of Barlow's advice; still, they were so pleased with his "Address" that they made him an honorary citizen of France.)

This rare mood of balance, this sense of being the middleman between Old World and New, pervades Barlow's one undisputed poetic masterpiece, the famous *Hasty-Pudding* of 1793. Barlow, having decided to campaign for election to the French Assembly from the newly annexed territory of Savoy, was served in an inn at Chambery a dish of polenta, which he recognized as the "hasty-pudding" of his Connecticut youth. Traditional accounts of the poem usually ignore its frankly political setting, from the mention of the "Gallic flags, that o'er their heights unfurl'd, / Bear death to kings, and freedom to the world," through its sneer at British paranoia (a footnote reminds us that "a certain king, at the time when this was written, was publishing proclamations to prevent American principles from being propagated in his country"), to its ultimate celebration of the prolific and egalitarian "Yankey" whose "abundant feast, / With simples furnished, and with plainness drest, / A numerous offspring gathers round the board, / And cheers alike the servant and the lord." But these are incidental decorations compared with the dominant theme of the poem. The poem celebrates the happy commerce established when the raw material of the New World (here, Indian corn) met the whole system of poetic tropes (imaginary wants) painstakingly elaborated by the Old. So Barlow invokes the Muse to help him trace the origin of corn-meal:

> Assist me first with pious toil to trace
> Thro' wrecks of time thy lineage and thy race;
> Declare what lovely squaw in days of yore,
> (Ere great Columbus sought thy native shore)
> First gave thee to the world; her works of fame,
> Have liv'd indeed, but liv'd without a name.

If Europe is first in poetry, America is first in corn-meal; and Barlow chose from the moving toy-shop of neoclassical convention precisely those tropes best suited to unite agrarian innocence and courtly polish. So perfect is the counterfeiting that one of the best set-pieces in the poem sounds as if it might have been lifted directly from Dryden's translation of the *Georgics*:

> Slow springs the blade, while check'd by chilling rains,
> Ere yet the sun the seat of Cancer gains;
> But when his fiercest fires emblaze the land,
> Then start the juices, then the roots expand;
> Then like a column of Corinthian mould,
> The stalk struts upward, and the leaves unfold;
> The bushy branches all the ridges fill,
> Entwine their arms, and kiss from hill to hill.

As an American Barlow was spared the conflict between revolutionary sentiment and patriotism that tormented so many English poets of the same era. The Terror in France affected him only as an illustration of the principle that centuries of oppression breed barbarism. France's betrayal of her own revolution was another matter, and Barlow refers to it ruefully in several letters of 1802. He reports an invitation he had received from a Polish lady to celebrate the anniversary of the Polish Constitution, which, he observes, "has long since ceased to exist." And he adds, "I suppose next Vendemiaire we shall be called upon to celebrate the anniversary of the French Republic, which has never existed at all." Upon finding a mouse in a bag of corn-meal he announces his intention to order his cook to save the rest by making him "a polenta, as the barbarous, conceited coxcombs of the great nation call it, who know as little about a hasty-pudding as they do about a republic." Later that year he grumbled about the fuss being made for the birthday of Napoleon. "The bells are ringing and cannon firing ever since sunrise – enough to deafen one; high mass and Te Deum all over France; more powder burnt than would serve to conquer half Europe. And this is to conquer the French people!" Napoleon's rise to power finally helped dislodge Barlow from Europe and made him willing to return to America, less optimistic about the chances for world revolution than he had been in 1793, perhaps, but for that reason all the more devoted to the only Republic who had preserved her principles in innocence. He brought with him all sorts of mechanical gadgets, agricultural implements, promising plant species, and the completed manuscript of the great epic with which he hoped to confirm America's entry into the company of civilized nations.

The Columbiad has been ridiculed more often than Horatio Greenough's statue of a half-naked Washington seated in the pose of Phidias' Zeus. Certainly, many of the charges lodged against Barlow's poem are true. The long historical sections are dreary, the diction frigid, the conceits strained. Still, the formidable Francis Jeffrey, who reviewed the poem for the *Edinburgh Review* in 1809 and who was one of the last critics able to take the poem seriously on its own terms, found things to praise as well as mock. Jeffrey began by making fun of Barlow for being an American bourgeois trying to sound like an aristocrat; he pointed out that Barlow's real poetic affinities were not with Homer (even Pope's Homer) but with Erasmus Darwin. Yet he praised Barlow as a "philosophical poet" and even went so far as to say that Barlow was the best in this kind since Milton.

The reader who plunges into *The Columbiad* at the ninth book will see what Jeffrey meant. Barlow there sets out to tell the story of creation from the moment when Nature first forced our world from the "black breast" of Chaos to the unimaginably distant moment when her last-evolved creature, man, takes intellectual dominion over that world, and "earth is fill'd with happiness and peace." What lies in between are the painfully slow accretions of natural history ("Millions of generations toil'd and died / To crust her coral and to salt her tide") and the even more painful writhings of the human spirit in the series of wrecks that make up human history. Barlow had translated his friend Volney's *Les Ruines, ou méditations sur les révolutions des empires*, and from that work he derives many of the details of his melancholy survey of human pride and folly. How many empires, he wonders, have "promis'd o'er the world to rise, / Spouse of the sun, eternal as the skies," only to join Babylon and Nineveh in the dust. Yet Barlow shares Volney's faith that the general direction of human history is nevertheless upward, that the world can be united in peace and joy as soon as it frees itself from the twin self-deceptions of monarchy and priestcraft. From this pinnacle, this "bright eminence" (as Barlow wickedly calls it, thumbing his nose at Milton) man will look back in astonishment at his wanderings in error and misery. *The Columbiad* ends with a joyous ceremony in which the symbols of religious and political hegemony are willingly sacrificed by representatives of the nations.

> Beneath the footstool all destructive things,
> The mask of priesthood and the mace of kings
> Lie trampled in the dust; for here at last
> Fraud, folly, error all their emblems cast.
> Each envoy here unloads his wearied hand
> Of some old idol from his native land;
> One flings a pagod on the mingled heap,
> One lays a crescent, one a cross to sleep.

Barlow took special care to have this scene illustrated and engraved as one of the plates published with the poem. Of course it got him into endless trouble in the nation he was attempting to glorify. His old friend Noah Webster was so upset by Barlow's descent into "atheism" that he refused to review the poem;

and the popular press reviled Barlow as an infidel. When the Bishop of Blois, a friend of Barlow's from their revolutionary days in France, addressed an open letter to him praising the poem but remonstrating with him for his insult to the Christian religion, Barlow blandly replied that he was merely continuing the iconoclastic tradition of his Protestant forebears, who had always degraded the symbol in favor of the thing symbolized.

Barlow perished in the service of the international commerce he had so long praised. President Madison called him from retirement on his Washington estate in 1811 to serve as minister to France. France had been seizing American vessels engaged in the British trade and harassing Americans trading in French ports. The previous American minister had complained repeatedly, to no avail. In one last attempt to avoid war with France, Madison had decided to try negotiation, and Barlow's known diplomatic skills with fickle dictators (he had once succeeded in ransoming a group of captive American seamen from the mercurial Dey of Algiers) made him the logical choice to approach the Emperor whom he privately despised.

Barlow reached France in September of 1811, but Napoleon, then engaged in planning his invasion of Russia, had little interest in negotiations with the United States. A year had passed without progress when Barlow received word that the Emperor, then in Moscow, would finally meet with him in the eastern city of Wilna. Barlow set off for Wilna on 25 October 1812, accompanied by his nephew. They arrived in Wilna on 18 November to find it filled with sick and wounded soldiers. Napoleon, so they now heard, had been forced to evacuate Moscow. They hoped he might retreat to Wilna and winter there, but on 4 December a courier brought the news that the Emperor had been defeated at the battle of Beresina and was now in full flight back to Paris. Barlow and his nephew tried to return to the west in a carriage that took them across a devastated Poland, littered with the bodies of men and horses frozen so solidly that even the scavenger birds could not eat them. They managed to reach Warsaw, but as they headed southwest again Barlow developed pneumonia in the bitter cold. He died on Christmas Eve in the little Polish village of Zarnowiec, where he was buried.

Before he died he found time to write one final poem, savage in its bitterness. "Advice to a Raven in Russia" pretends to offer friendly advice to the miserable ravens pecking the frozen corpses. "Black fool, why winter here?" Barlow asks. Go south, go south; you need not fear a shortage of prey. The earth is full of Napoleon's slaughter. The French armies "taint the breeze with every nation's gore, / Iberian, Lussian, British widely strown, / But still more wide and copious flows their own." In lines of disturbing beauty he describes the transformation of dying soldiers into fallen statues of ice. Napoleon's "tentless troops are

marbled through with frost / And change to crystal when the breath is lost."
He then explains to the ravens in gruesome detail why the dead in Poland
make such bad dinners:

> . . . from their visual sockets, as they lie
> With beak and claws you cannot pluck an eye.
> The frozen orb, preserving still its form,
> Defies your talons as it braves the storm.
> But stands and stares to God, as if to know
> In what curs'd hands he leaves the world below.

In one of the bitterest jokes against himself Barlow defines the relationship
between Napoleon and his Imperial Scavengers as that perfect symbiosis of
interest he had so long championed as the basis for a lasting international
peace. "For see what mutual benefits you lend! / (The surest way to fix the
mutual friend) / While on his slaughtered troops your tribes are fed / You
cleanse his camp and carry off his dead." Only when "men resume their souls"
and hurl the Emperor from his throne of blood will this partnership of raven
and slaughterer end, and the "prostrate world" rise up again in dignity and
peace.

A tradition of comic verse had always existed side by side with serious
satire in America and had enjoyed a wider popularity. John Trumbull's satire,
M'Fingal (1775), remained the most popular poem in America throughout
the first half of the nineteenth century, and was reprinted in Britain as well.
Comic poetry was usually topical, and this fact explained some of its initial
appeal. But the imagery of comic poems often remains memorable long after
the targets of its wrath have disappeared. The hapless Tory squire M'Fingal,
tarred and feathered by a Revolutionary mob, suddenly becomes an object of
strangeness and beauty when the tarry icicles that drip from his beard glitter in
the rays of the setting sun, making him look "Like sleet-bound trees in wintry
skies / Or Lapland idol carved in ice." Fitz-Greene Halleck's best images of
old age occur during a tribute to an aging New York political hack, who, like
the poet himself, is

> Ripened like summer's cradled sheaf
> Faded like autumn's falling leaf –
> And nearing, sail and signal spread,
> The quiet anchorage of the dead.
> ("The Recorder")

Even more remarkable is the metrical fluency of comic verse. One has only
to compare the stiffness of Emerson's tetrameters with the conversational ease
of Trumbull's or Brackenridge's to see how much grace could be attained by

forgetting the obligation to be gnomic. Comic poetry could be liberating in other ways, too. Contrasting Old World culture with New World rawness was usually a depressing exercise. But comic poets are able to make cultural dissonance the subject of the poem. What would Robert Burns have said of the homesteads on the western Pennsylvania frontier? What would Byron have thought of Wall Street? Out of some forgotten political squabble in a provincial newspaper come stanzas whose melody and sense of assurance will hardly be heard in American poetry again before the twentieth century.

Consider the Scots poems of Hugh Henry Brackenridge, the man who had sent Jefferson the stiff little imitation of Virgil's Fourth Eclogue. Born in Scotland, Brackenridge had emigrated with his parents to the Pennsylvania frontier when he was five. In the late 1790s and early 1800s he became involved in an exchange of poems – first of compliments, later (when political differences intervened) of abuses – with a fellow Scottish immigrant named David Bruce. The exchange was carried out at first in the newspapers, though both men later collected their poems for separate publication in book form. They both express intense nostalgia for Scotland and see their new land as gloomy, uncivilized, and grim. In these verses the western frontier is where things peter out, not where they open up. At first Brackenridge claims to see in Bruce a reincarnation of the Scottish poet Allan Ramsay, his favorite poet. Then honesty forces him to qualify that praise:

> But ah! your sang is nae sae shrill
>   Nor pipe sae soft:
> The voice ye had, as clear's a bell,
>   'S a weething dowff'd.

Everything suffers attenuation at the edge of the Western world. Even the long summer twilights of Scotland are cut short in the latitude of Pennsylvania. No wonder poets cannot write.

> What's mair expect'd here i' the west,
> Sae near where night taks off his vest
> And his gray breeks, and gaes to rest,
>   And the lang day
> Is dock'd o' several hours at best,
>   Sic as on Tay.

Bruce agrees wholeheartedly. Who can write poetry in this miserable landscape? In place of shepherds and flocks and "bony braes" there is nothing to please the eye, nothing but "great lang trees." No wonder the poet falls silent.

> At morn nae lav'rock tunes his whistle,
> Nor i' the bush is heard the throstle,
> There's naething but a skreek and rustle
>   Amang i' the leaves. –
> The musie sweer her sangs to cuzle
>   She dwines and grieves.

The best of Brackenridge's Scots poems concerned this silence of the muses. The poem first appeared in a Pittsburgh newspaper under the title "To the Scots Irishman." The two immigrants had become public enemies in the years of bitterness preceding Jefferson's election, and their interchange of compliments had turned into a flyting. But with Jefferson's election secure, Brackenridge was in a conciliatory mood, and managed to tease his rival without malice during the course of a "Dogrel" that is also a charming piece of autobiography. The poem, in tetrameter couplets, records the three chief disappointments the young immigrant had suffered in the New World. The first was the rude surprise administered by the glossy black animal with the white stripe down its back that he had made the mistake of trying to stroke. Next was his disappointment at being unable to find any of the mythological creatures his Latin schoolbooks described. Finally, there was his mature distress at finding his boyhood mishap repeated in the quarrel with his one-time friend: he took Bruce for a friendly animal and reached down to pet him, only to be drenched with the "assa-fetid" of party slander. The poem is refreshing in its naturalism and gentle humor, particularly in its portrait of the boy's curiosity in his new landscape, and of his understandable puzzlement at finding no trace of the gods and nymphs his schoolbooks describe anywhere in the landscape around him. He finally decides that the absence of Pennsylvania dryads must be attributable to the frantic pace of settlement on the western frontier:

> Soon after this, I gaed to Latin,
> And read a buke, I kenna what in
> That talked o' things that whir in bushes,
> Dryads, Hamadryads, Muses,
> On tops o' hills wad sing like Mavies
> And in the shady woods and cavies.
> Thought I, it maun be this vile clearing,
> And grubbing up the trees, and bleering,
> That scares these things out o' their senses,
> And drives them frae our fields and patches.
> For who sees any, now or catches,
> A moor-land deity or Nymphy,
> That roosts in trees or wades in lymphy?

Brackenridge's disappointment in the landscape around him was often expressed even by poets who were born in the New World and had never left it. Laments over the impossibility of writing poetry in a landscape devoid of everything poetic would be heard again and again in American poetry. Neoclassicism had offered a defense against this sense of deprivation. Access to its system of generalized description promised to free the provincial writer from isolation. Like the Romes and Ithacas and Syracuses incongruously planted in the American wilderness, the conventions of literary neoclassicism linked the uncivilized present to the civilized past in a single universe of discourse. But neoclassicism had finally died a lingering death, and the future of Scots poetry in the United States was limited to ceremonial occasions like the "St. Andrew's Anniversary" celebrated by the Pittsburgh Inhabitants of Scottish Descent, for whose meeting Brackenridge had been moved to write the first of his Scots poems. Still, if Brackenridge's Scots poems are an end-point and not a beginning, they are a witty and tender evocation of the immigrant's experience, with all its longing and confusion.

That indestructible writer Philip Freneau (1752–1832) was still vigorous enough in 1815 to produce another volume of poetry. The recent war with Britain had provoked an abundance of patriotic verse, including, of course, Francis Scott Key's "The Defense of Fort McHenry." Freneau saw in the unsuccessful British naval attack upon a Connecticut seaside town the opportunity for a native version of the British broadside ballad, crude and vigorous. "The Battle of Stonington," as the note attached to the poem tells us, recorded the attempt by three armed British ships to take the town of Stonington, defended only by its citizen militia and "a small fort of two guns." Every stanza ends with the flinty and resolute name of the town, and Freneau delights both in the miserable aim of the British guns –

> The bombardiers with bomb and ball,
> Soon made a farmer's barrack fall,
> And did a cow-house sadly maul
>   That stood a mile from Stonington.

– and the pounding given the invincible British navy by the two Yankee cannon. Each ship advances in turn to fire on the fort but has to sneak away "crippled, riddled," and "forlorn." The ballad ends with a taunt Yankees found deeply satisfying:

> But some assert, on certain grounds,
> (Besides the damage and the wounds)
> It cost the king ten thousand pounds
>   To have a dash at Stonington.

It is hard to remember that Presidents once wrote poetry; but John Quincy Adams (1767–1848) wrote original verse of which he was quite proud. Two of the pieces published in his posthumous collection of poems (1848) are at once surprising and delightful. "To Sally" takes as its epigraph the famous opening lines from the ode of Horace – "Integer vitae, scelerisque purus / Non eget Mauris jaculis, neque arcu" – of which Adams's poem is a wildly free imitation. To get an idea of what Adams is parodying, consider the schoolboy translation of the same ode by the young William Cullen Bryant. Here are its first two stanzas:

> The man whose life, devoid of guile,
> Is pure from crimes and passions vile;
> Needs not the aid of Moorish art,
> The bow, the shaft, and venom'd dart,
>
> Whether he tempt the scorching blast,
> Through Lybian sands, a trackless waste:
> Rude frosty Caucasus explores,
> Or treads Hydaspes' golden shores.

Adams's "To Sally" begins innocently enough. "The man in righteousness arrayed / A pure and blameless liver" sounds like a village psalmist's version of Horace, with its thumping iambic rhythms and its unfortunate rhyme on "liver." But as the poem proceeds we come to realize that "To Sally," like Lewis Carroll's parodies of Isaac Watts, glories in its badness. Adams has a fondness for Latinate coinages; and he is as determined as Barlow to get New World place names into his poem.

> What though he plough the billowy deep
>   By lunar light, or solar,
> Meet the resistless Simoon's sweep,
>   Or iceberg circumpolar.
> In bog or quagmire deep and dank,
>   His foot shall never settle;
> He mounts the summit of Mont Blanc
>   Or Popocatapetl.

Decades of poetic inversions reached their hapless end in Adams's boast that the wolf he frightened away with a clap of his hands was more ravenous than "the fell constrictor boa."

A different kind of humor appears in "The Wants of Man," a poem in twenty-five numbered stanzas, each written on a separate sheet of paper (so the story goes) to satisfy the request of several young ladies for his autograph. It too begins with an epigraph, this time from Goldsmith: "Man wants but little here below / Nor wants that little long." But Adams quotes Goldsmith's lines only to differ from them. "Tis not with ME exactly so," he says, and then proceeds to explain just how extensive his wants are.

> What first I want is daily bread,
>   And canvas backs and wine;
> And all the realm of nature spread
>   Before me when I dine.

These "wants" proceed to multiply in stanzas that seem to flow from his pen as easily as desires proliferate in his heart. What were the modest wants of Adams? Nightly banquets, jewels, fine clothes, mansions, rich furnishings, gold and silver plate, horses, servants, famous paintings, a virtuous wife, exemplary children, loyal friends, a great career, uninterrupted health, acknowledged genius, the gratitude of his country, and eternal fame:

> I want the voice of honest praise
>   To follow me behind,
> And to be thought in future days
>   The friend of human kind;
> That after ages, as they rise,
>   Exulting may proclaim,
> In choral union to the skies,
>   Their blessings to my name.

Adams's facility in describing his desires gives a new twist to the old rhetorical ideal of copia, and seems designed to illustrate the truth of Emerson's remark that "every man woke in the morning with an appetite that could eat the solar system like a cake." The complacent speaker of "The Wants of Man" is a staple of English and American comedy: the man of sense, the thoroughly reasonable being whose composure can never be disturbed by his own hubris or the madness of the world around him.

A different sort of wit – the irreverence and cynicism of the urban *flâneur* – begins to emerge in the poems of two young New Yorkers born in the decade after Adams. Joseph Rodman Drake (1795–1820) was born in New York City; his friend Fitz-Greene Halleck (1790–1867) arrived there from Connecticut in his early twenties. Both tried to combine a passion for poetry with the necessity of making a living in a city newly conscious of its sophistication. Their "serious" poetry was modeled on the Romantic lyrics and narratives of Scott, of Moore, of Thomas Campbell.

But some comic verses Drake sent home from Scotland in a letter to Halleck were in a lighter key. They are worth noticing not only because they reveal a gift for literary parody but because they form so neat a contrast to the Scots poems of Brackenridge. Like every American reader of Scottish poetry, Drake had formed romantic ideas about Scotland. But the real Scotland seemed very far from the imagined one. Drake confected a kind of pidgin Scots out of scraps of remembered Burns poems to abuse the stunted trees, "cauld and reekie skies," and miserable brooks:

> For streams ye'll find a puny puddle
> That wouldn't float a skulebairn's coble;
> A cripple still might near hand hobble
>   Dry bauchled over;
> Some whinestone crags to make it buble,
>   And there's a river.

After Drake returned to New York, he and Halleck decided one Sunday morning in 1819 to send some comic verses on current events to William Coleman, editor of the *New York Post*. They called their poetic partnership "Croaker & Co." after a character in one of Goldsmith's comedies. To their delight, Coleman printed the verses, and Drake and Halleck soon found that the Croaker poems were talked of all over New York. (When Halleck sent copies to his sister Maria in Connecticut, he warned her: "The subjects are, many of them, purely local, and will, of course, be unintelligible to you. They are well understood here, however.")

Drake had always been able to write verses quickly, and fifteen of the first twenty-two "Croaker" poems are by Drake alone. Many of the subjects are too local to have more than historical interest now: the consternation produced at a Tammany Hall dinner when their distinguished guest, General Jackson, proposed a toast to their mortal enemy, Governor Clinton; the ridiculous lengths to which the Surgeon-General of New York went in trying to define the words "militia" and "grog" in his annual report; but when Drake's subject was literary or artistic his wit could still bite. James Kirke Paulding (1779–1860) had been unfortunate enough to decorate his patriotic narrative poem, *The Backwoodsman* (1818), with a simile that quickly became notorious:

> So have I seen in garden rich and gay
> A stately cabbage waxing fat each day
> Unlike the lively foliage of the trees,
> Its stubborn leaves ne'er wave in summer breeze.

Paulding's cabbages were one favorite target of Drake's ridicule; he also loved to poke fun at Samuel Woodworth, author of the popular poem "The Bucket" (now usually called "The Old Oaken Bucket"). Drake mocked both poets in a poem inscribed to another forgotten poetaster, John Minshull, then traveling in England.

> Oh! bard of the West, hasten back from Great Britain,
>   Our harp-strings are silent, they droop on the tree;
> What poet among us is worthy to sit in
>   That chair whose fair cushion was hallowed by thee?
> In vain the wild clouds o'er our mountain-tops hover,
>   Our rivers flow sadly, our groves are bereft;
> They have lost, and forever, their poet, their lover!
>   And Woodworth and Paulding are all we have left.
>   ("To John Minshull, Esq.")

Another kind of humor emerges in a poem originally titled "The Declaration of Independence," the title of the famous painting by John Trumbull that Drake detested. Coleman rejected the poem as too vindictive for publication, but a rival editor quickly printed it under the title "The National Painting." Here Drake attacks both the ideology and the execution of Trumbull's attempt to crowd the heads of all the signers of the Declaration into the painting he designed for the Capitol Rotunda. Whatever its virtues as a political principle, equality is disaster in art, and Trumbull's evident determination to make all the seated figures in the room the same height (together with his inability to render facial expression) makes the signers look like a row of boiled peas. "How smooth the hair on every pate! / How vacant each immortal face!"

Vacuousness is also the subject of a poem written jointly by Drake and Halleck: "Ode to Simeon DeWitt, Esq., Surveyor-General of the State of New York," lampooning DeWitt for bestowing pompous classical names like "Rome" and "Ithaca" on the fledgling towns of western New York State.

> Godfather of the christened West!
>   Thy wonder-working power
> Has called from their eternal rest
> The poets and the chiefs who blest
>   Old Europe in her happier hour.
> Thou givest to the buried great
> A citizen's certificate;
> And, aliens now no more,
> The children of each classic town,
> Shall emulate their sires' renown
> In science, wisdom, or in war.

The last of the original series of "Croaker" poems appeared on 17 July 1819. Drake died of tuberculosis the next year, and was commemorated by his friend in "Verses on the Death of Joseph Rodman Drake": "Green be the turf above thee, / Friend of my better days! / None knew thee but to love thee, / Nor named thee but to praise." In subsequent years Halleck went on writing

Croaker-like poems from time to time, which he then included in a collected
and annotated edition of "The Croakers" he prepared for publication by New
York's Bradford Club in 1859. Many of these supplementary "Croakers" were
written to celebrate particular events, and in them Halleck loved to mock the
national penchant for long-winded self-congratulation. At ceremonies marking the opening of the new Park Theatre in 1821 (the old had been destroyed
by fire), Halleck offered to supply the only thing lacking – a laudatory speech,
that "modern mode of winning hearts, / And power, and fame, in politics
and arts." How do we know that our nation is "wise, learned, and happy?"
Dr. Mitchill, the Surgeon-General of the State of New York, has said so in his
Phi Beta Kappa address. Who has "convinced the world that we have men /
First with the sword, the chisel, and the pen"? Mr. Adams, in his Fourth of
July Speech. In fact, as Governor DeWitt Clinton (1769–1828) pointed out
in his interminable speech at the opening of the New York Legislature in
January of 1825, the peculiar blessings of our social condition can hardly be
overestimated.

> It seems, by general admission,
>   That, as a nation, we are thriving:
> Settled in excellent condition,
>   Bargaining, building, and beehiving;
> That each one fearlessly reclines
>   Beneath his "fig-tree and his vines."
> (The dream of philosophic man),
>   And all is quiet as a Sunday,
> From Orleans to the Bay of Fundy,
>   From Beersheba to Dan.
>   ("Governor Clinton's Speech")

A closer look at how fortunes are really made and lost on Wall Street suggests
some shading in this general picture of prosperity. A little over five years
earlier, in December of 1819, Halleck had published *Fanny*, a narrative poem
tracing the rise and sudden fall of a New York merchant and his ambitious
daughter as they make their way from the obscurity of Chatham Street to
the splendor of a Broadway mansion, only to see their dreams vanish as his
credit collapses in a crash of bad debts. Like the "Croaker" poems, *Fanny*
was published anonymously; like them, it quickly became required reading
for *le tout New York*. Indeed, its fame quickly spread as far as Albany, where
Halleck had the pleasure of hearing his poem read aloud by Governor Lewis
to the company at the hotel where he happened to be staying. When a Senator
who knew Halleck voiced his suspicions that Halleck was the author of both

Fanny and the "Croaker" poems, Halleck found that he had become suddenly famous.

What made *Fanny* seem so striking at the time was Halleck's discovery that the stanza of Byron's *Beppo* could be employed in a poem about New York's financial world and the fortunes of those connected to it. Byron's frankness, his irreverence, his occasional tenderness, offered Halleck a varied series of inflections for suggesting the sophistication – and the pathos – of the American commercial capital. At the beginning of the story, our heroine's father, a widower, is the owner of a humdrum dry-goods store in Chatham Street. By carefully nursing his "little earnings," he is able finally to move to Pearl Street and set up business in Hanover Square. Already he feels the transforming power that money possesses, for the very people who once called him a "dull, / Good, honest man" – a "cabbage-head," in fact – discover "brilliant traits of mind, / And genius, clear, and countless as the dyes / Upon the peacock's plumage" in him when he moves uptown. At this point in her life young Fanny is simply a "castle-builder," hearing the distant sounds of music from fashionable parties as she sits by her "lone plebeian hearth," dreaming of the day when her father's wealth might make her a belle. Such happy moments in life, the narrator tells us, "come upon the mind like some wild air / Of distant music," and "their power / Though brief, is boundless." From then on the dream of wealth shapes Fanny's life. And after all, her ambition is no wilder than the hopes of the throng of political schemers who seek to rise with the "huge balloon / Of party" to positions of wealth and power at the State capital in Albany. For Fanny's father really does have the money to "'buy out' the one-half / Of Fashion's glittering train," who frequent New York's evening parties: "Gay as the Brussels carpeting they tread on, / And sapient as the oysters they are fed on."

A few years pass. Fanny's father is now the director of a bank and six insurance offices, a "planetary star" at the Stock Exchange, that brotherhood where "each exerts his intellectual force / To cheat his neighbor – Legally, of course." He is "circled around by lesser orbs," who borrow not only his light but his money, something he does not mind as long as they shower praises in his willing ear. Alas! Not content with this degree of glory, he falls prey to the temptations of the "jade Ambition," who visits him in a dream wearing the emblems of Tammany Hall: "Her brow was turbaned with a bucktail wreath, / A brooch of terrapin her bosom wore." Despite his lack of formal education (he has never acquired "that sort of knowledge / Taught so profoundly at Columbia College"), Fanny's father really does begin to think "that Nature / had formed him for an alderman at least" – perhaps even a member of the Legislature. He learns all the tricks of Tammany Hall ("when to clap and when to vote") and finally is invited to one of their famous turtle soup suppers in Hoboken. The next morning, inflated with a sense of his own coming greatness, he engages a mansion on Broadway, buys a carriage and horses, and fills his rooms "with servants, and whatever, / Is necessary for a 'genteel liver.'"

Fanny, meanwhile, has become a fashionable belle who aspires "to reign a fairy queen in fairy land" – Broadway or Park Place. And, in anticipation of that hour,

> Her star of hope, her paradise of thought,
> She's had as many masters as the power
>   Of riches could bestow; and had been taught
> The thousand nameless graces that adorn
> The daughters of the wealthy and high-born.

She has studied singing, and dancing, and foreign languages (each twice a week for two months); she has skimmed the latest novels and read the Croakers "when they were in fashion"; she attends the popular lectures on science, where "in rainbow groups" the maids and matrons of New York learn words like "hydraulics, hydrostatics, and pneumatics," and where they find out "why frogs, for want of air, expire; / And how to set the Tappan Sea on fire!" If she seems to have in her beautiful face a look "a little like effrontery," if the innocence of her earlier manner has been replaced with a studied self-consciousness of gesture, that is only because she wants "to be admired by all she met" – no mean feat in a city where the dandies are as self-centered as the belles, and come to evening parties not to pay chivalrous homage to Beauty but "To lounge in graceful attitudes – be stared / Upon, the while, by every fair one's eye."

Fanny carelessly rejects offers of marriage made by "men of the middle ranks." Is not her father now "a Croesus among men"? He mingles with those "within whose veins the blood ran pure – the magnates of the land" (that is, merchants whose fortunes are slightly older than his own). He becomes a patron of the arts and a philanthropist. He "spread to the liberal air his silken sails / And lavished guineas like the Prince of Wales." She can hardly believe it when he confesses to her one day that he is beginning to be worried about his solvency. She asks, astonished: "How can a man be in the path to ruin / When all the bankers are his bosom friends?" If his creditors are becoming importunate, she tells him, the thing to do is "give a 'party' – and astonish them."

So Fanny finally gets the "midnight rout" she has been dreaming of since Chatham Street. Carpets are rolled up; artists called in to chalk flowers on the floor. The "blackest fiddlers" of the day are "Placed like their sire, Timotheus, on high." The best society is invited – belles, dandies, officers of the militia, everyone "from the head / Down to the very toe of our nobility."

> And when the thousand lights of spermaceti
> > Streamed like a shower of sunbeams – and free tresses
> Wild as the heads that waved them – and a pretty
> > Collection of the latest Paris dresses
> Wandered about the room like things divine,
> It was, as I was told, extremely fine.

Just at the moment when money seems to achieve pure transcendence in creating the illusion of its own solidity, there is a horrible crash. A huge chandelier falls to the ground; guests and musicians flee affrighted. The next morning finds Fanny alone with her father again.

> The desolate relief of free complaining
> > Came with the morn, and with it came bad weather;
> The wind was east-northeast, and it was raining
> > Throughout the day, which, take it altogether,
> Was one whose memory clings to us for life,
> Just like a suit in Chancery, or a wife.

When a notary arrives with a note on which Fanny's father has stopped payment, the greater "crash" takes place – the ruin of their fortunes. The town talks of it two days, and forgets it by the third. As for Fanny, the narrator claims to have seen her recently on the street, fighting back tears, wearing a cheap shawl. Their Broadway mansion is now "to let," and Fanny and her father have been banished to that limbo inhabited by the poor and proud. The father has recently been seen strolling down Broadway in that "withering bitterness of soul, / Quaintly denominated the 'blue devils'." He thinks of the mighty who have fallen before him – "Bonaparte and Belisarius, / Pompey, and Colonel Burr, and Caius Marius." Sadly, he pays a shilling to look through a showman's telescope at Jupiter, and for a brief moment fancies that he hears the music of the spheres. But the sound turns out to be only that of a nearby band playing "Yankee Doodle." Fanny's father composes his own sad little ballad about the transience of earthly hopes and joys, and with it the poem ends.

To give only the plot of *Fanny* without the high-spirited digressions that once made it famous – digressions on American culture, politics, and pretensions – is to do it an injustice. *Fanny* is a comic poem, whose digressions are more in the insouciant spirit of the "Croakers" than of the poem's closing lament. Most of them are as irreverent as the stanza in which Halleck calls the

Ancients "an ignorant set of men at best" and explains why we no longer need
to read them.

> Twas their misfortune to be born too soon,
>   By centuries, and in the wrong place too,
> They never saw a steamboat, or balloon,
>   Velocipede, or Quarterly Review;
> Or wore a pair of Baehr's black satin breeches,
> Or read an Almanac, or Clinton's speeches.

These digressions now require as many footnotes to make them intelligible as
Pope's jokes in the *Dunciad* about "great Cibber's brainless, brazen brothers" or
"slashing Bentley with his desp'rate hook." Is it worth it? For the last edition
of his poems done in his lifetime, Halleck prepared notes to "The Croakers,"
Fanny, and "The Recorder" (the longest and best of his political poems). The
mocking epigraph he adapted for "The Recorder" from the *Dunciad* – "Live in
Settle's numbers one day more!" – leaves it up to us whether to place him on
the spectrum of topical poets closer to Pope or to Elkanah Settle.

As it happens, "Thomas Castaly," the city poet in "The Recorder" who
presents his petition to Richard Riker (then the Recorder, afterwards Mayor,
of New York City), really is a kind of American Elkanah Settle: he is one of
the thirty-seven or so city poets who inhabit the fourteen wards of New York
City. Castaly wants to be crowned laureate of the entire city, and it is only
natural that he should apply for the job to that prince of all political patrons,
"Dicky" Riker, "For whose contractors' jobs we pay / Our last dear sixpences
for taxes, / As freely as in Sylla's day / Rome bled beneath his lictor's axes." As
he feels his bark drawing closer to that great "shoreless, sleepless sea" Castaly
admits that he is increasingly willing to trade immortal fame for that more
immediately gratifying variety of renown Halleck had defined, in one of the
"Croaker" poems, as "Notoriety": "The death-dirge is sung o'er the warrior's
tomb, / Ere the world to his valor its homage will give, / But the feathers
that form Notoriety's plume, / Are plucked in the sunshine, and live while we
live." Castaly therefore concludes his petition by expressing his willingness to
trade fame for present honors:

> I rhyme not for posterity
> Though pleasant to my heirs might be
>   The incense of its praise,
> When I, their ancestor have gone,
> And paid the debt, the only one
>   A poet ever pays.

❦

EARLY NARRATIVE AND LYRIC

Although comic verses were widely reprinted in newspapers, and neoclassical verse was still used regularly on ceremonial occasions – college commencement exercises, Phi Beta Kappa Society meetings – most serious American poets in the early nineteenth century wrote narratives, lyrics, or contemplative verses: religious poems of praise or confession in the style of Herbert's "Temple" or Donne's Holy Sonnets; elegiac quatrains modeled on Gray's; hymns in the style of Cowper; blank-verse meditations like *Night Thoughts* or like *Tintern Abbey*. The size of the United States and the primitive state of its transportation system meant that poets often wrote in isolation from one another and were chiefly influenced by whatever books their family, college, or town libraries happened to supply. Although many young writers eagerly read reviews of new books of poetry in the great British quarterlies, to which college literary societies often subscribed, obtaining the books themselves was difficult. A bookseller in Philadelphia might issue a pirated edition of Wordsworth, but how would a poet in western Massachusetts learn of its existence, except by chance? An edition of Shelley's poems might be picked up by a young minister in Boston and reviewed in the magazine he edited in Louisville, but Carolinians or Georgians would be none the wiser. Cultural life in the United States was haphazard, random, a matter of luck and chance encounters – though for that reason still full of excitement that residents of British or European cities might never know. Stumbling upon a single book could change a life, and giving or lending books to someone else was a sign of high esteem. (When Ralph Waldo Emerson met an intelligent young matron named Emily Mervine Drury on a Mississippi steamboat during his first midwestern lecture tour, he sent her a copy of the *Bhagavadgita* as soon as he got home; when he met John Muir in California in 1871, he gave him a copy of Sampson Reed's *The Growth of the Mind*.)

For these reasons, American poets who were born a year apart and lived within fifty miles of one another often appeared to live in entirely different eras of literary history. Any survey of the poets who wrote during the early nineteenth century must necessarily be organized on a principle drawn from some discipline other than poetry itself. What follows, then, is a survey of American poets born in the last decades of the eighteenth century who began writing poetry in the early decades of the nineteenth. The survey begins in the northern and western regions of New England before turning to the chief northern ports, Boston and New York, which (like Edinburgh and London) naturally drew to them the most ambitious poetic experimenters.

The northern and western regions of New England, still close to wild forests and sparsely settled, tended to produce poets in whom the heritage of Puritanism was still clearly visible. Manoah Bodman (1765–1850) was born in the village of Sunderland, Massachusetts, and moved when he was young to Williamsburg, a village seven miles west of the Connecticut River, a place still so wild and remote that (according to his biographer) only a bridle-path through a swampy region connected it to the next settlement. Bodman was trained as a lawyer, like so many poets of the early Republic, but the four *Orations* he published have nothing to do with the law. Instead they reflect that intense spirituality which the Connecticut River valley seemed peculiarly to foster. The longest of them, the 300-page *Oration on Death, and the Happiness of the Separate State, or the Pleasures of Paradise* (1817), a prose treatise with a few intercalated poems, grew out of the special revelations Bodman began to experience in 1789. Bodman was already "converted," that is, he felt that he had received assurance that his sins had been forgiven and that he would inherit eternal life. Other people might be persuaded to desire salvation more earnestly, he believed, if the manifold joys of the future life could be made real to them. Fire-and-brimstone preachers were forever asking people to imagine the pains of hell. Bodman encourages his readers to put themselves in the place of the angel who enjoys the ecstasies of heaven:

> Awake, arise, shake off your fears,
>   In sweeter thoughts recount,
> What the bold Seraph hourly hears
>   On Zion's awful mount.
>
> He soars aloft in endless seas,
>   And flies in bliss away;
> In total labyrinths of peace
>   And floods of endless day.

Bodman reminds his readers that

God the Creator, hath seemed to delight himself in a rich variety of productions in all his worlds . . . Let us make a pause here, and stand still and survey the overflowing riches of his wisdom which are laid out on this little spot of his vast dominions, this earthly globe on which we treat; and we may imagine the same variety and riches overspreading all those upper worlds which we call planets or stars.

Those religious writers who have imagined heaven as a place of dreary sameness, with ranks of angels endlessly chanting the identical words of praise, cannot be right. A deity whose earth reveals his delight in difference will surely foster it in heaven as well. Bodman follows this argument with the best of his intercalated poems, which seems to blend something of George Herbert's intricacy with the visionary sweetness of Christopher Smart.

> What rich profusion here,
>   Is scatter'd all abroad,
> To make us love and fear,
>   Obey and worship God.
>   And sound his praise,
>   Through every clime,
>   In constant lays,
>   Till end of time.
>
> The huge leviathan,
>   The oyster and the eel,
> The lion and the lamb,
>   Each in their nature feel.
>   And go abroad
>   In quest of food,
>   Depend on God,
>   For every good.
>
> These shining crumbs of clay,
>   With yellow, green, and gold,
> March on their lucid way,
>   And day in night unfold.
>   And shine so bright,
>   And please themselves,
>   And fill'd with light
>   They quit their cells.

The glowworm, like the Seraph, is self-delighting as well as self-illuminating, and its nightly dispersal of light mimics the way God's benevolence spreads throughout creation.

Benevolence was the favorite theme of another deeply religious New England poet, Carlos Wilcox (1794–1827). Although Wilcox published his first poem only five years after Bodman's *Oration on Death*, the nearly thirty years that separate the births of the two poets seem to carry us directly from the seventeenth century into the Age of Sensibility. Wilcox was born in 1794 in Newport, New Hampshire. His father, a prosperous farmer, moved the family to Orville in western Vermont, near the southern end of Lake Champlain, some time late in the 1790s. A serious injury when he was nine left him unsuited to farming and affected his health for life. Since he had already shown an interest in books, his parents decided to give him a liberal education. He entered Middlebury College in Vermont in 1809 at the age of fifteen. A historian of the college points out that although it had no formal denominational tie, its early presidents and most of its faculty were Congregational ministers, and 40 percent of its early graduates went into the ministry.

Wilcox entered Middlebury College with no thoughts of entering the church. He had already begun to write poetry and he was eager to pursue his classical studies. As he later recalled, "I felt desirous of an immense stock of earthly knowledge, and my heart glowed with fervent anxiety for worldly honours and emoluments." When a religious revival swept through the college during his first year he kept apart from it. Though he sometimes had fears for his salvation, he had decided to put conversion off to "a more convenient opportunity" – though he also worried that such procrastination might provoke Divine wrath. He decided to return home to Orville for a few weeks, an absence that required the permission of the college authorities. But the professor he sought out to obtain this permission began to ask probing questions about the state of his soul, and after receiving unsatisfactory answers told him that he would let Wilcox go home two weeks hence only if he would declare then that he "had resolved to persist in the ways of sin, and at last go down to destruction." Startled, Wilcox returned to his room to look up two Bible verses that suddenly came to his mind: Deuteronomy 32:35 ("To me belongeth vengeance, and recompense: their foot shall slide in due time: for the day of their calamity is at hand, and the things that shall come upon them make haste") and Proverbs 1:25 ("Because I have called, and ye refused; I have stretched out my hand, and no man regarded").

Now he earnestly desired salvation, but found that all his efforts to overcome his own rebellious heart were unavailing. Finally he surrendered himself wholly to his Savior, confessed his helplessness, and solicited protection. He went to pray in chapel, and found that for the first time he had "a heart to pray. My burden was gone." In the joy and gratitude that overflowed him now, he wrote: "It now seems to me that if there is any happiness in life, it is in living near God." He announced to his parents that he wished to enter the clergy. After graduating from Middlebury in 1813, he spent some time with an uncle in Georgia (a trip that let him see slavery at close range), then returned in 1814 to begin the study of theology at Andover Theological Seminary in Massachusetts.

Andover had been established to defend New England orthodoxy from the theological liberalism that (in view of its founders) had hopelessly corrupted Harvard. During his studies there Wilcox suffered repeated attacks of ill health and episodes of severe depression. He was in debt to Middlebury for the cost of his education and saw little way of repaying what he owed; he had "a deep feeling of indescribable wretchedness" and a "disheartening consciousness" of his unfitness for the ministry. He wrote: "My mind is unstrung, relaxed till it has almost lost the power of reaction; every little labour, seems an Herculean task, every little obstacle, a mountain of difficulty." Like his poetic and spiritual model William Cowper, he sought relief from depression in long walks and the close study of nature, filling a commonplace book with descriptions of what he had seen. A *Memoir* of his life published in 1828 observes of this book:

It is filled with descriptions of a great variety of objects, so minute and graphic, that they cannot be read without a conviction, that he looked on nature, with an eye observant of all her varities, and a heart alive to all her power. He seemed to have stored in this repository, every thing which which he met, that ever might be of use to him as a writer, and especially, as a writer of poetry.

By 1817, his last year at Andover, he had already begun an ambitious poem in blank verse, *The Age of Benevolence*, whose first book was published in New Haven in 1822. Fragments of Books II, III, and IV appeared only in the volume of literary *Remains* (1828) published after his death.

The Age of Benevolence is a theodicy drawing its arguments chiefly from Books III and VII of *Paradise Lost*. Wilcox's Calvinist professors at Middlebury and Andover were doubtless pleased not only with their student's general orthodoxy but with his occasional digs at the liberal religion of Boston ("O how false the friendship, that unites / Preacher and hearer in the ruinous work / Of mutual flattery!") Yet nothing could be farther from the angry vindictiveness of Milton's Deity than the God of Wilcox's poem, who delights in creating variety and joy as the purest manifestation of his glory, and whose kindness is manifested in the happiness of his whole creation, which is felt even at the microscopic level:

> Look where it may, the opened eye of faith
> Beholds the fullness of benevolence,
> And oft its overflowing, as in showers
> Falling on seas, on barren rocks and sands; –
> In wholesome fruit within the wilderness,
> Growing each year, and perishing uncropt; –
> In myriads of living atoms, found
> In every turf, and leaf, and breath of air,
> Too small indeed for unassisted sight,
> But not too small to feel the good they have.

The Christian scheme of salvation is merely the highest expression of God's benevolence, and the "Triumph of Benevolence" with which the poem was to have ended is the conclusion of that plan:

> Love was its source in the eternal mind,
> And its accomplishment was wrought by love.
> Love made the covenant ere time began,
> And love fulfilled it at the destined hour.

The God who sustains the universe and directs history still considers tenderly his creatures' welfare: "His hand, while holding oceans in its palm, / And compassing the skies, surrounds my life, / Guards the poor rush-light from the blast of death."

Long passages in Books I and II of *The Age of Benevolence* seek to trace God's benevolence in the features of the landscape. Rufus Griswold published excerpts from these books in *The Poets and Poetry of America* under titles like "Spring in New England" or "A Summer Noon," as if Wilcox were a sort of American Thomson. Certainly Wilcox delighted in dwelling upon what made the climate and fauna of his native region distinctive as well as beautiful. He portrays the blinding swiftness of spring's arrival in New England, which takes place during a single week in which the bare woods are first filled with light and then darkened again by rapidly expanding leaves:

> On the first morn, light as an open plain
> Is all the woodland, filled with sunbeams, poured
> Through the bare tops, on yellow leaves below,
> With strong reflection: on the last, 'tis dark
> With full-grown foliage, shading all within.
> In one short week the orchard buds and blooms.

New birds arrive every day: "the lonely snipe" who flies in the dusky air, "Invisible, but with faint, tremulous tones, / Hovering or playing o'er the listener's head"; the night-hawk, whose dark wings suddenly reveal a single white feather when upturned against a sunset sky; the haunting whip-poor-will, "her name her only song," who comes to the edge of the grove as soon as children draw near. In summer, stillness hangs over the landscape: fields are ripe with stalks that support heavy heads of grain "as motionless as oaks," and the air is full of softly descending thistledown. Equally enticing to the pensive man is September, "soft twilight of the slow-declining year," when reflections of "the yellow, red, and purple of the trees" surround the boat on which he glides downstream, and the surrounding woods are silent save for "the sound of nut-shells by the squirrel dropt / From some tall beech fast falling through the leaves."

But the love of nature "feasted high and long / Without controlling faith" can lead to indolence, profligacy, even to skepticism, Wilcox warns in "The Religion of Taste," a poem in 207 Spenserian stanzas read to the Phi Beta

Kappa society at Yale in 1824. The "piety of faith" reads natural beauty as a sign of God's love, while the "piety of taste" finds pleasure chiefly in scenes of sublimity, "Where power in bright pre-eminence is seen":

> In heaven's clear blue and earth's contrasted green,
> In mountain-tops and clouds around them driven,
> In boundless seas, high stars, and night's pale queen,
> In all the hues and notes of morn and even.

The true lover of God must move from contemplation to action, from feelings of benevolence to acts of goodness. In haunting stanzas Wilcox recounts a dream in which he finds himself alighting on the shores of the blessed kingdom with a bright throng of redeemed spirits who seek out the friends who have helped them find the way to heaven. He alone has no one to meet, and his very isolation is a terrible reproach: "It seemed that I was brought to heaven to dwell / That conscience might alone do all the work of hell." Awakened from this dream, relieved to be still alive and capable of change, he vows to live so as to secure the bliss of fellowship, and he encourages the young men of Yale to do likewise: "Do something – do it soon – with all thy might; / An angel's wing would droop if long at rest, / And God himself inactive were no longer blest."

Throughout the early 1820s Wilcox had no permanent home. He lived with various friends in Connecticut, working on his poetry, preaching in various churches when his health permitted it, hoping for a permanent settlement. A call finally came from the North Church in Hartford, Connecticut, where he had been ordained in 1824. His sermons were carefully prepared, eloquent, and full of feeling, but his frail health could not support the demands of his position, and he was forced to resign it in the spring of 1826. Efforts to recover his health through rest and travel were partly successful, and by the fall of 1826 he was well enough to accept a call from a church in Danbury, Connecticut. But by the following spring his health again failed, and he died on 29 May 1827.

The Age of Benevolence remained unfinished at his death, but fragments of Book III, on the "Need of Benevolence in our world," were published in his *Remains*. Various well-known forms of cruelty and sin are there discussed, though Wilcox prefers singing the joys of repentance to threatening the stiff-necked. Only when he comes to the subject of American slavery does real anger suffuse his poem. He is outraged by those who loudly proclaim liberty and equality for all in a nation where "one man in five is born and dies a slave." The anger is mixed with sadness, because Wilcox really does believe that his own era is intended as an age of benevolence, whereas the retrograde cruelties of slavery drag "the happy land" of America backwards into barbarism. Every time noisy patriots gather to celebrate the nation's birthday, their toasts mock the woes of the slaves who sit mutely by, "thinking defiance which they dare not speak." What, after all, are the sufferings of the colonists who rebelled against King George compared to the scourgings and mutilations that slaves must daily endure without complaint? Slaves are "taxed" of every penny their labor is worth; and if they were to lift a hand against their oppressors their punishment would be death. To the common objection that the slaves cannot be "safely" emancipated Wilcox brusquely responds:

> Done it should be; with safety if it can,
> With danger if it must. It ill becomes
> Our name to shrink from suffering in our turn,
> We who have reaped the profits of their fall
> Selfish in all, shall we expect to make
> Their rise our gain?

Emancipation of the slaves will at last make the bloodstained and bedraggled "Columbia" the true daughter of the skies, and the whole nation will enjoy "the smiles of freedom, equal, common, as the air." Can anyone really wish to postpone such happiness, or wish it to come *gradually*? "At such a prospect, who, that has a heart / With one remaining spark of generous fire, / Feels not an inward glowing of delight?"

The poets of Connecticut shared many of the enthusiasms of their Massachusetts neighbors, but their styles and poetic aims were more various. John Brainard (1796–1828) was born in New London, where the Thames River enters the sea. The son of a justice of the Connecticut Supreme Court, Brainard entered Yale in 1815 and took up the study of law. He was admitted to the bar and moved to Middletown, intending to start a practice there. But the daydreaming and indolence that had plagued him in college made him an indifferent lawyer at best. As John Greenleaf Whittier later noted: "His friends were always welcome, save when they came as clients." In 1822 he gave up his practice to move to Hartford and take up the editorship of the *Connecticut Mirror*, in which he published many of his own poems. He collected some of them into a volume published in 1825, and prefaced it with an address informing the reader with refreshing candor that publication had been undertaken *not* at the request of friends but from the vanity of the author and his hopes of profit. The book was well received and he was encouraged to embark on a longer work. But in 1827 he began to show symptoms of tuberculosis. He resigned from his editorship and returned to New London, where he died the next year.

Brainard's chief attraction for his contemporaries – aside from the grace of his lyrics and the occasional vigor of some of his martial poems – lay in his determination to use native settings and native traditions in his verse. As Whittier noted, Brainard is "wholly American ... He does not talk of the palms and cypress where he should describe the rough oak and sombre hemlock. He prefers the lowliest blossom of Yankee-land to the gorgeous magnolia and the orange bower of another clime." Whittier is here alluding to Brainard's best poem, the "Stanzas," beginning "The dead leaves strew the forest walk," where the poet, with splendid panache, refuses the temptation to escape the coming winter. He loves the New England climate not in spite of but because of its harshness. Others might seek the warm southern climate with its buds and flowers, but Brainard cannot imagine loving a landscape where

> No forest tree stands stript and bare,
> No stream beneath the ice is dead,
> No mountain top with sleety hair
> Bends o'er the snow its reverend head.

To friends who depart for the South each winter Brainard bids a firm farewell:

> Go there, with all the birds, – and seek
> A happier clime, with livelier flight,
> Kiss, with the sun, the evening's cheek,
> And leave me lonely with the night.

The happiest of the Connecticut poets was James Hillhouse (1789–1841). Born in New Haven, he was the son of a Revolutionary War captain who later served as United States senator, commissioner of the state school fund, and treasurer of Yale (whose coffers he managed substantially to enrich). After graduating from Yale in 1808, James Hillhouse lived in Boston for two or three years before returning to New Haven. A short career as a businessman in New York City ended when he married the daughter of a wealthy New York merchant. The next year he retired to New Haven, where he led the life – rare for an American poet – of a leisured man of letters. He spent the winters in New York City, the rest of the year on his New Haven estate, Highwood.

In 1836, he read a speech to the Brooklyn Lyceum entitled "On the Relations of Literature to a Republican Government." Like most speakers on this topic, Hillhouse deplores the lack of American cultural achievement.

Where is the library in this powerful Empire ... that a sixpenny German palatine would honor with the name? – Where are the archives in a single State, from which its own history could be written? – Where are our observatories? – Where are our fellowships? – Where are the sums paid out for exploration and discovery? What national care or favor, as a people, have we extended to any *high* department of knowledge?

He argues for the necessity of creating a cultured leisure class in America, made up of the sons of men who have already earned their fortunes. Such a class could perform the cultural functions of an aristocracy without its "intolerable appendages." Creating the culture the nation presently lacks would give a meaningful task to the sons of rich men, who tended to feel useless in a society that honors the amassing of wealth much more than the possession of it. (Auden noted a similar scale of values operating in the twentieth century. In "The Almighty Dollar" he argues that "what an American values . . . is not the possession of money as such, but the power to make it as a proof of his manhood; once he has proved himself by making it, it has served its function and can be lost or given away. In no society in history have rich men given away so large a part of their fortunes.")

Towards the end of his life Hillhouse wrote a genial poem about Highwood. In the poem, he proposes to rename the estate "Sachem's Wood" to honor the memory of his father, who had been nicknamed "the Sachem" for his sagacity as well as for the strongly Indian cast of his features. But the estate is not all that Hillhouse proposes to rename. The poem was published in 1838, the two hundredth anniversary of New Haven's founding, and Hillhouse suggests renaming the city's two most imposing natural features – East Rock and West Rock – after important figures from New Haven's history. East Rock he proposes to call Sassacus, after the last of the Pequot chiefs, and West Rock "the Regicide," because a cave in its base is said to have sheltered two of the regicide judges (William Goffe and Edward Whalley) who fled England for the colonies after the Restoration. The city lies surrounded by these twin emblems of courage, which change their aspects as the sun passes over them.

> See! how its guardian Giants tower
> Changing their aspect with the hour! –
> There Sassacus in shade or glow,
> Hot with the noon, or white with snow,
> Dark in the dawn, at evening red
> Or rolling vapors round his head
> A type of grandeur ever stands,
> From God's benignant, graceful hands!
>
> In the soft west, as day declines,
> The REGICIDE, his rival, shines,
> Whose noble outline, on the sky
> Draws, and detains, the enamored eye,
> For floating there, the steeds of eve,
> Flakes from their ruddy nostrils leave.

In striking contrast to the complacency of Hillhouse was the lifelong anguish of his fellow Yale graduate, James Gates Percival (1795–1856). Born in Berlin,

Connecticut in 1795, he decided to follow his father into the medical profession, and after graduating from Yale College in 1810 took his M.D. degree there in 1815. But he made only feeble attempts to practice his profession. A severe case of typhoid fever in childhood had left him with a laryngeal deformity that rendered him unable to speak above a whisper. Intensely shy, morbidly sensitive, he several times attempted suicide. A few poems he had published in a New Haven medical magazine aroused so much favorable interest that in 1821 he published at his own expense a small volume of poems, which in turn attracted so much favorable attention that he quickly followed it by three more volumes in 1822.

The flourishing of his poetic reputation seemed only to depress him further. As James Onderdonk noted in his *History of American Verse* (1901), Percival "was determined to write, and when people read and rather liked his poetry, he vowed that he would write no more." By the age of thirty he had become a recluse, supporting himself by various literary and editorial tasks. During the late 1820s and early 1830s he began a study of foreign languages and literatures, translating foreign poems into English, experimenting with foreign meters, and writing original poems in German, French, and Italian. The last volume of poetry he published, *The Dream of a Day and Other Poems* (1843), collected the fruits of his experiments in these foreign meters and stanza forms, all far removed from the endlessly concatenated blank verse of his early poetry.

The excitement aroused by that earlier verse among Percival's contemporaries now seems puzzling. His poetry is mostly a pastiche of passages from Wordsworth, Shelley, or Byron. His interminable blank verse paragraphs avoid end-stopped lines with a single-mindedness that leaves the reader feeling giddy. Yet that very intoxication had a kind of decadent fascination for a generation only recently weaned from the closed pentameter couplet. Percival's best poems are purely descriptive, like "Morning among the Hills" or "To Seneca Lake" or the curious and lovely portrait of an undersea reef, "The Coral Grove."

> Deep in the wave is a coral grove,
> Where the purple mullet and gold-fish rove;
> Where the sea-flower spreads its leaves of blue,
> That never are wet with falling dew,
> But in bright and changeful beauty shine,
> Far down in the green and glassy brine.
> . . .
> There with a light and easy motion,
> The fan-coral sweeps through the clear deep sea;
> And the yellow and scarlet tufts of ocean,
> Are bending like corn on the upland lea.

His favorite scenes involve complicated atmospheric effects – the sun rising over a sea of mist and creating a momentary river of gold upon the mist as it begins to disperse it, the light reflected in a lake:

> How sweet, at set of sun, to view
>   Thy golden mirror spreading wide,
> And see the mist of mantling blue
>   Float round the distant mountain's side.
>   ("To Seneca Lake")

Percival's insistence that poetry was more than rhyme or meter, that it was "a mysterious feeling, which combines / Man with the world around him, in a chain / Woven of flowers" ("Prevalence of Poetry") endeared his writing to poets attempting to find in British or Continental Romanticism an alternative to drearily didactic verse.

The two major port cities of the North, Boston and New York, offered poets easy access to publishers, periodicals, and audiences; they also provided intellectual and cultural opportunities impossible to obtain in smaller cities or country villages. Poets migrated to the Boston area or to New York City to escape the limitations of village life and to find the intellectual companionship that provincial cities denied them. Once there, they often became thoroughly identified with their adopted cities. (Bryant, who edited an influential newspaper in New York City for fifty years, first suggested the idea that the city needed a great central park within its boundaries. He took an active part in the successful campaign to persuade the New York State Legislature to set aside land for its creation.)

Washington Allston (1779–1843) was a painter and art theorist who also wrote poetry, a poet whose best poems concern the puzzles of representation in visual art. Born in South Carolina to a prominent plantation family, he was educated in the North: first in Newport, Rhode Island, where he became the friend of William Ellery Channing, later at Harvard. He had begun drawing and painting at an early age: he loved to paint gloomy landscapes dotted with banditti, just as he loved to read Gothic romances and tales of the supernatural. In poetry he admired Thomson's *Seasons* (he later would paint "Damon and Musidora," after characters in the poem); Charles Churchill, an eighteenth-century English satirist much admired for his "manly" roughness; and Robert Southey, whose epic *Joan of Arc* helped fuel his ambition to become a history painter.

If history painting was then thought to be the noblest of genres, it was also the most poorly paid. No market for such works existed in the United States: the only American artists who could hope to make a living were portrait painters like John Copley or Gilbert Stuart. If Allston wished to study history painting or find patrons for his canvases he would have to leave home. In 1801, therefore, he set sail for London (having sold his Carolina patrimony to obtain funds for the journey), where he applied to become a student at the Royal Academy and was immediately accepted. For three years he studied painting under its director Benjamin West, another expatriate American, to whose generous encouragement Allston later would pay tribute in a sonnet entitled "To My Venerable Friend, the President of the Royal Academy." (West is also the subject of one of Allston's best portraits, a study of "vigorous powers" imparting youthful freshness to old age.)

In 1803 Allston and a friend left London and traveled through the Low Countries to Paris, where they found the Louvre and Luxembourg galleries newly full of Napoleon's artistic plunder. Allston admired the work of the great Venetian colorists Titian and Tintoretto and set himself to try to learn the secrets of their colors and glazes. By 1804 he was ready to leave Paris for Rome, where he continued his study of Titian and added to it a reverence for the serenity of Raphael and the miraculous draftsmanship of Michelangelo. He also formed lasting friendships with literary men then residing in Rome, most notably with Washington Irving and with Coleridge, who had arrived in Rome from Malta on the last day of the year 1805.

Coleridge, then thirty-three, had reached one of the lowest points in his life by the time of his arrival in Rome. Estranged from his wife, in poor health, addicted to opium, he was unable to support himself or his family. He had left Malta after angering his only benefactor there. Allston, on the other hand, was a generous and talented man of twenty-six, whose career seemed all before him, though in fact he was far closer to Coleridge in temperament than then appeared. Allston was cursed with a talent for procrastination that developed into the full-fledged misery of his twenty years' work on the great canvas he left unfinished at his death, "Belshazzar's Feast." But to Coleridge in 1806 he seemed a godsend, at once a version of Coleridge's younger self and a responsive friend to take the place of Wordsworth.

Allston loved to talk about the theory of art – he was clearly, as Coleridge said, "a man of genius," but his main interest was in painting, not poetry. Coleridge could act as an intellectual benefactor without feeling the "little ugly Touchlets of pain & little Shrinkings Back at the Heart" he confessed he felt when he discovered that Wordsworth had used one of his suggestions to write a new poem. The two men roamed the city together during the winter and early spring of 1806: at one point they took a three-week trip into the Roman Campagna together. In 1805 Allston had painted a "Self-Portrait" showing himself as a strikingly handsome young man in dark clothing gazing directly at the viewer with an enigmatic yet somehow challenging stare. He now began a portrait of Coleridge so similar in setting, tone, and expression that Allston's modern interpreter has suggested that the two paintings should be thought of as "pendants, a commemoration of a newly formed but already intense personal relationship." The relationship was interrupted (and the Coleridge portrait left unfinished) when Coleridge left Rome abruptly in May of 1806. But the friendship had already left a profound impression upon both men. Allston later declared that he owed more to Coleridge "intellectually" than to any other man, a truth which Allston's posthumously published "Discourses on Art" bear out. For his part, Coleridge told Allston that "of all people I love you best next to Wordsworth: if I had not known him I should have loved you best."

When Allston returned from Europe in 1808 to marry his patient fiancée, Ann Channing, to whom he had been engaged eight years before, he brought with him news of the Lake poets to a Boston still largely entrenched in the eighteenth century. Romantics like Scott, Burns, Campbell, and Moore had become popular all over the United States. But Wordsworth and Coleridge were a different matter. Difficult, obscure, metaphysical, or else (by neoclassical standards) alternately mawkish and bathetic, they were ridiculed by the critics. Allston's relationships with the prominent literary men of Boston helped introduce Coleridge and Wordsworth there several years before the rest of the country had accepted them.

He had begun work upon a volume of poems before leaving Boston again in 1813 for England. His visit home had been pleasant enough, but the impossibility of getting buyers for the kind of pictures he wanted to paint in the United States (where portrait painters alone could hope to survive) made him return to London with Ann. There, in 1813, *The Sylphs of the Seasons* was first published (an American edition followed the same year). The narrative poem that gives the volume its title takes the form of a dream-vision. Speaking in a tone of light self-mockery also employed in Allston's prose tale "The Hypochondriack," the poet boasts of his indolent superiority to the "slave of Mammon" who is vulgar enough to ask what profit his labors have ever produced. Secure in the knowledge that the man who has "a World within his mind" needs no external solace, the poet then falls asleep.

Suddenly the scene shifts to a visionary plain with caverns, castles, gates, blinding lights, and voices. Led to the throne he will someday inherit and introduced to the "Four Damsels . . . of the Faery race" who compete for his affections, he listens to each remind him of the pleasures she has brought to him. The sensuous imagery each Season displays changes quickly into boasting of a more transcendental sort. Thus Summer rests her case not on the languorous pleasures in her gift but on her "genial influence, / Which made the body's indolence / The vigor of the mind." But Winter, who can offer both the terror of the icy blast that freezes the ocean's waves "Like bending sheaves by harvest hind / Erect in icy death" and the beauty of the afternoon sun turning the ice-encrusted branches into a rainbow of colors, asserts that only she can confer the "nobler power" that is "the soul's creative might." Spring, Summer, and Fall reach the mind through the senses, and so can claim a share of "Fancy's hallow'd power." But in the still of night and the blankness of snow Winter summons up the images from the whole preceding year and teaches the poet to work them "with rare combining skill," filling the mighty void of space with new worlds through a creative power like Nature's own. Forced to choose between the Faeries who have offered him such riches, the poet pleads his helpless indecision and is rescued from his plight by a pain that breaks the frame of the dream: "When lo! there pour'd a flood of light / So fiercely on my aching sight, / I fell beneath the vision bright / And with the pain awoke."

"The Sylph of the Seasons," like Joseph Rodman Drake's later "The Culprit Fay," is so innocent that it now seems gauzy. Yet both poems were once highly esteemed for their skill at imagining ideal realms and peopling them with creatures of the imagination. "The Culprit Fay" continued to be reprinted throughout the nineteenth century, often in small illustrated editions meant to be used as gift books for young readers. In their profusion of images (often borrowed from *A Midsummer Night's Dream* and *The Tempest* or from *The Faerie Queene*) they are poems of the Fancy. They testify to a surprised, delighted awareness that the country was finally rich enough to afford language whose only function was to give pleasure. It may be true, as Wordsworth noted, that Fancy was given only "to quicken and beguile the temporal part of our nature," but he hastened to add that Fancy "as she is an active, is also, under her own laws and in her own spirit a creative faculty." Moreover, since the creative power of Fancy reflects the desires of the individual ego in a way that Imagination does not, even the slightest poems of the Fancy manifest that individual liberty Emerson would later call "Whim."

The relation between sensuous and imaginative reality continued to fascinate Allston throughout his life as a painter and theorist of visual art. During the 1830s he wrote five "Lectures on Art," distinguished by their Coleridgean insistence on treating familiar topics like "Form" and "Composition" from a point of view resolutely idealistic, yet informed throughout by a detailed sense of how aesthetic perception functions. Describing the travels of the eye through the intricacies of composition in a great painting allowed Allston to speculate on the point of intersection between the formal decisions of the artist and the aesthetic experience of the viewer. Theorists since the Renaissance have speculated on the mysteries of perspective in painting, which let two-dimensional sketches suggest three-dimensional realities. Allston wanted to know how painters manage to suggest concepts even more resistant to representation. He made these meditations the subject of a series of remarkable sonnets published in *The Sylphs of the Seasons*.

The sequence begins with a sonnet titled "On a Falling Group in the Last Judgment of Michael Angelo, in the Capella Sistina." What interests Allston is the way the falling forms created by the artist suggest the terrifying idea of "space interminable" to the viewer, as the "giant hand" of the artist (here taking the place of the Deity whose wrath it represents) hurls the "human forms, with all their mortal weight / Down the dread void" in a free fall "as endless as their fate." What we can actually see on the wall of the Sistine Chapel is a group of forms immobilized in an instant of time. But the imagination of the viewer is stimulated to create a temporal sequence stretching before as well as after: "Already now they seem from world to world / For ages thrown" in a fall whose endlessness fills the mind with the pathos and terror of eternal damnation more effectively than any portrayal of hellish torments could do.

A different kind of mystery is explored in "On the Group of Three Angels before the Tent of Abraham, by Raffaelle, in the Vatican." If Michelangelo suggests a sequence of perceptions stretching out into infinite space, Raphael creates an infinity concentered upon itself in a triune unity as mysterious as that of the Divinity of which it is a type.

> O, now I feel as though another sense,
> From Heaven descending, had inform'd my soul:
> I feel the pleasurable, full control
> Of Grace, harmonious, boundless, and intense.
> In thee, celestial Group, embodied lives
> The subtle mystery; that speaking gives
> Itself resolv'd: the essences combin'd
> Of Motion ceaseless, Unity complete.
> Born like a leaf by some soft eddying wind,
> Mine eyes, impell'd as by enchantment sweet,
> From part to part with circling motion rove,
> Yet seem unconscious of the power to move;
> From line to line through endless changes run
> O'er countless shapes, yet seem to gaze on One.

In the "Lectures on Art" Allston would describe the descent of grace which is our experience of artistic unity as a kind of ecstasy engendered by repetition. Standing before a great picture, "silently passing through all its harmonious transitions without the movement of a muscle, and hardly conscious of action," we finally return to the point where our journey through the images began. "Then it was, – 'as if we had no eyes till then' – that the magic whole poured in upon us, and vouched for its truth in an ecstasy of rapture." The "motion ceaseless" by which Allston's gaze is "borne like a leaf" around the lines of Raphael's painting sounds at first like the circulation of the damned in the fifth canto of Dante's *Inferno* or the ceaseless fall of Michelangelo's doomed sinners. But the unity of Raphael's design overpowers Allston's soul in a rapture that recalls instead the end of the *Paradiso*, where Dante's Will and Reason become one with the love that moves the sun and the other stars. "I feel the pleasurable, full control / Of Grace, harmonious, boundless and intense."

The three artists Allston considers next present experiences less overwhelming to the viewer. Yet each points up a different paradox suggested by the nature of representation. "On Seeing the Picture of Aeolus by Pellegrino Tibaldi, in the Institute at Bologna" praises Tibaldi as a true inheritor of Michelangelo's influence.

> 'Twas thine, deciph'ring Nature's mystick leaves,
> To hold strange converse with the viewless wind;
> To see the Spirits, in embodied forms,
> Of gales and whirlwinds, hurricanes and storms.
> For lo! obedient to thy bidding, teems
> Fierce into shape their stern, relentless Lord.

Far stranger are the two succeeding sonnets. "On Rembrandt: Occasioned by his Picture of Jacob's Dream" was occasioned by a picture now known to be by one of Rembrandt's pupils, Aert de Gelder. Bequeathed in 1811 to the Dulwich Picture Gallery in London as part of the immense collection of Sir Peter Francis Bourgeois, it quickly became one of the most popular paintings in the gallery. Allston himself would later (in 1817) paint his own "Jacob's Dream," but his heavily populated canvas, with symmetrical choirs of angels receding upwards into what he called "space immeasurable," differs in every way from the simplicity and obscurity of de Gelder's painting. A dark canvas shows Jacob sleeping while two angels (one on a cloud, one descending) are suffused with intense light. Its simplicity of composition, the ease with which it blends the homely and the celestial, reminds Allston of the age of faith that produced it, "When all beyond the narrow grasp of mind / Seemed fraught with meanings of supernal kind," and great scientists who studied the secrets of the universe still "listened with reverence to the changeling's tale." So far Allston's sonnet is a familiar Romantic lament for the age before the dissociation of sensibility. What follows next is startling.

> E'en so, thou strangest of all beings strange!
> E'en so thy visionary scenes I hail;
> That, like the rambling of an idiot's speech,
> No image giving of a thing on earth,

> No thought significant in Reason's reach,
> Yet in their random shadowings give birth
> To thoughts and things from other worlds that come,
> And fill the soul, and strike the reason dumb.

The tonal monotony of de Gelder's painting, its stark contrasts between light and shade, stands in sharp contrast to the brilliant color and luminous glazing Allston admired in the Italian masters and imitated in his own paintings. His initial distaste for de Gelder's painting is evident both in the ugliness of his simile (the painting is like an idiot's speech) and in his repeated insistence that de Gelder's painting represents no image and no thought. Yet this very refusal of imagery in fact allows de Gelder to "shadow forth" things ordinary painters cannot represent – "thoughts and words from other worlds that come." Like the fools in Shakespeare, de Gelder achieves transcendence through incoherence, and defeats criticism through astonishment.

After the intensity of the "Jacob's Dream" sonnet it is a relief to pass to the affectionate wit of the sonnet "On the Luxembourg Gallery," where Allston offers Rubens one of the shrewdest compliments any painter has ever paid to another. This sonnet, like the previous one, concerns a struggle between judgment and admiration, though the conflict is not between transcendence and rationality but between vulgarity and secret admiration. In the octave of the sonnet the struggle is represented as something taking place between Rubens and the viewer, as Rubens's "seductive charm" holds the will of the "struggling gazer" powerless until his reason lies vanquished. The sestet, more boldly, compares a Rubens painting to the ocean in stormy weather. Each impetuous wave threatens to flood the land as it crashes over the high rocks, but at the last moment the ebb draws the surges back to sea.

> Thy lawless style, from timid systems free,
> Impetuous rolling like a troubled sea,
> High o'er the rocks of reason's lofty verge
> Impending hangs; yet, ere the foaming surge
> Breaks o'er the bound, the refluent ebb of taste
> Back from the shore impels the wat'ry waste.

A graceful tribute to Benjamin West, who aided younger artists without envy and who loved art for its own sake, closes the sonnet sequence.

The famous portrait of Coleridge painted by Allston in 1814, which now hangs in England's National Gallery, stands not only as a tribute to their friendship but as a kind of summary of this period in Allston's life, when poetry, painting, theory stimulated one another to luxuriant growth. But Allston's career was soon overtaken by tragedy. His wife Ann died suddenly in

1815. The grief he felt soon deepened into near-madness. He was tormented by "horrible thoughts," and felt "diabolical imprecations" force themselves into his mind. Coleridge, who had suffered much with similar demons, was able to console Allston during his worst agony by persuading him that the mere presence in the mind of an evil thought does not constitute sin, so long as the will does not consent to it. But Allston's depression lingered until one evening when he found himself walking the London streets on a dim night in November. "The fog enveloped the lamps, so that each looked like a huge bundle of cotton-wool; the air was comfortless; my own spirit was even drearier than the outward scene; a heavy weight was on my heart and in my brain." What he most feared was the horrible sense of "imprisonment in my own self forever." He felt "a sense that it would be a relief to get out of such a dungeon, even into the cold, raw, wretched air." Suddenly a train of thought in verse came to him as if it had been "whispered by a spirit objective to mine."

This unpremeditated verse became Allston's poem, "The Atonement." In it he proclaims his conversion to a fully Trinitarian belief in Christ's saving power, a belief he acted upon by undergoing confirmation in the English church. "The Atonement" is in places so elliptical as to constitute a private code. (The poem was never published in Allston's lifetime. Together with the other poems written after *The Sylphs of the Seasons*, it appeared in the volume of his writings published in 1850.) The poem reflects Allston's deep fear of the "horrid thoughts" that had tormented him. If the "self" Allston calls the "Ever-conscious I" has no existence apart from the "thoughts that herald forth the Will," and if these thoughts (including the blasphemous ones) are immortal, how can the self ever be freed from them? On the very brink of the grave wicked thoughts may recur and link themselves to "the living chain of self, self-wrought / Which binds the soul." Allston fears the resurgence of what he had recanted, like Satan in Book IV of *Paradise Lost*. ("But say I could repent and could obtain / By act of grace my former state: how soon / Would highth recall high thoughts, how soon unsay / What feign'd submission swore.") Satan rules out any thought of repentance, but in "The Atonement" Allston turns this compulsive tendency to repeat into the strongest argument for the necessity of a Redeemer. He implores Christ to intervene to stop this compulsive forging of mind-forged manacles. He confesses that he cannot entirely explain *how* Christ's suffering on the cross could take away the sins of the human race. "Yet who shall make me doubt a truth I *need?*" The peace offered by traditional Christianity freed Allston for a time from the agonies of grief and guilt. His first major painting after the illness – "The Angel Liberating St. Paul from Prison" – may be read both as personal allegory and an offering of thanks.

Although he continued to paint and exhibit successfully in England, where he attracted important patrons and was spoken of as a likely successor to Benjamin West as President of the Royal Academy, Allston decided to return to the United States. His friends warned him that such a decision meant the end of his career as a painter of historical and religious subjects. He nevertheless set sail for Boston in 1818, taking with him the rolled-up canvas of a large painting upon which he had already begun work. "Belshazzar's Feast" was probably a dangerous subject for any painter with demanding aesthetic standards, a tendency towards self-reproach, and habits of procrastination. The story lends itself all too easily to personal application. As Emily Dickinson would later tell the story:

> Belshazzar had a letter –
> He never had but one –
> Belshazzar's correspondent
> Concluded and begun
> In that immortal copy
> The Conscience of us all
> Can read without its Glasses
> On Revelation's Wall –

Still, the huge canvas (16 by 20 feet) was nearly complete when Allston unveiled it before a few friends in September 1820. Gilbert Stuart, the portrait painter, made some criticisms of the perspective, which Allston agreed was faulty and needed fixing.

What happened then is one of the strangest and saddest tales in American cultural history. Allston began work on revising "Belshazzar" almost immediately. He would work obsessively for months, refusing other commissions, even accepting a subscription of $10,000 collected by wealthy Boston art lovers to free him from debt and financial worry while he worked on his masterpiece. Then for years at a time the canvas would lie rolled up in his studio. Even after he had married for a second time (his second wife, Martha, was the sister of the poet Richard Henry Dana, Sr.) and moved to Cambridgeport in order to obtain a better studio, he could not bear to hear the painting mentioned. He always kept it veiled when visitors were in the studio. One of his biographers noted that "he smoked incessantly, became nervous, and was haunted by fears that his great picture would not come up to the standard of his high reputation." And yet he could never abandon it. He was still at work on the painting less than seven hours before his death in 1843.

When a little group of friends and relatives assembled after his funeral to enter the studio where "Belshazzar's Feast" stood behind its veil, they felt as if they were breaking the seal on a sacred prophecy. The younger Richard Henry

Dana later recalled that he could hardly bring himself to turn the key to the studio. "An awe had been upon my mind as though I were about to enter a sacred and mysterious place." They tried to prepare themselves for the worst, but they were still shocked by what they saw. "There before us was spread out the great sheet of painted canvas, – but dimmed, almost obscured by dust and marks and lines of chalk. The eye ran across the picture for the main figures. Daniel stood erect. The queen was there. But where the king should have been, where Daniel's eyes were fixed, was a shroud, a thickly painted coat, effectually blotting out the whole picture." They stood for a while in silence. Then the elder Dana said, "That is his shroud." Allston's executors later hired a restorer to remove the thick layer of paint that covered the king, so that the painting, which now hangs in the Detroit Museum of Art, does not contain the large black blot that greeted Dana's eyes in 1843. All of the major figures are at least visible, if incomplete. But the canvas bears the marks of a series of endless revisions, shifts of perspective and scale, that seem to justify Dana in his belief that the studio had become a place of torment for Allston: "The agonies he had endured here no tongue can tell!"

Even the beautiful serenity of Allston's "Lectures on Art," read aloud to a small circle of friends but never delivered publicly, only makes the thought of Allston's own sense of failure more painful. What he had hoped to accomplish may be deduced from some beautiful lines he wrote about the "noble Tuscan" whose works he had studied with such reverence in Rome. Michelangelo's representation of "forms unseen of man, unknown to Earth" makes him a true prophet – a seer himself, and the cause of vision in others: "So, through Elisha's faith, the Hebrew Youth / Beheld the thin blue air to fiery chariots grow."

Richard Henry Dana, Sr. (1787–1879), Allston's friend and brother-in-law, was a far less talented poet than Allston, but for that reason his poems are almost more useful in studying how the English Romantic tradition altered when it reached the New World. Dana often warped what he read in bizarre and revealing ways. Born in Cambridge, Dana moved to Newport, Rhode Island during his boyhood and remained there until he entered Harvard. After leaving college in 1807, he spent two additional years studying Latin language and literature, then moved to Baltimore to read law in the office of General R. G. Harper. He returned to Cambridge to open a law office there, and even became a member of the state legislature. But he eventually gave up his law practice and political career to devote himself to literature. He began writing essays for the recently founded *North American Review* (whose readers he shocked by suggesting that Wordsworth and Coleridge were to be preferred to Johnson and Pope), and by contributing poetry to a number of periodicals in New England and New York.

In 1821, disappointed and angered because he was not offered the editorship of the *North American Review* when the post fell vacant, he began his own short-lived periodical, *The Idle Man*. In 1827 the poems he had written were collected and published in a volume entitled *The Buccaneer and Other Poems*; this book was followed in 1833 by *Poems and Prose Writings*, which included some new poems as well as the short stories and essays Dana had written to fill the pages of his periodical. His longest poem, the bloodstained romance entitled *The Buccaneer*, was once much admired – a British reviewer called it "the most powerful and original of American poetical compositions" – but it now seems a bizarre hybrid, one-third Coleridge ("The Rime of the Ancient Mariner"), one-third Crabbe (the tale of Peter Grimes), and one-third Byron (*The Corsair*). Its hero is a buccaneer with the incongruously Wordsworthian name of Matthew Lee, who robs and murders on both coasts of the Atlantic until a Spirit Horse (the ghost of a Spanish charger Lee drove from his ship into the ocean) arrives to carry him off to an eternity of torment. There are some memorable images, mostly in passages describing the sea. And there are some unintentionally funny moments – as when Lee briefly decides to turn from pirate to merchant, apparently seeing little difference between the two callings. But for the most part this tale of slaughter and attempted rape is interesting in showing the dark side of the New England imagination, the repressed violence and guilt that made Dana see the inner life as something fearsome.

Most of his poetry, fortunately, is calmer, and heavily indebted to Wordsworth. Poems and essays are often decorated by two or three epigraphs from Wordsworth, the sound of whose blank verse echoes throughout Dana's lines. Wordsworth's picture of childhood forms the basis for several pages in Dana's essay "Domestic Life" (1833). At one point in that essay Dana quotes the line "Heaven lies about us in our infancy" as a way of reminding his readers how differently children experience time.

When children are lying about seemingly idle and dull, we, who have become case hardened by time and satiety, forget that they are all sensation, that their outstretched bodies are drinking in from the common sun and air, that every sound is taken note of by the ear, that every floating shadow and passing form come and touch at the sleepy eye, and that the little circumstances and the material world about them make their best school.

This note – the happiness of pure sensation – is rare in Dana's poetry. His endless recollections of "Tintern Abbey" and the Immortality Ode are usually invoked in support of testimony about loss, never about the "abundant recompense" Wordsworth tells us that he also received. In a long poem Dana entitled "The Changes of Home," he describes a visit to the vale in which he was born. But he finds there only human decay and a natural beauty that torments him by its contrast to "the dull, still desert of the mind." Only when he remembers the happy season of youth as it concentrated toward love "in strange, yet pleasing strife / Filling the quickened mind with visions fair" does the poem escape for a moment from the overpowering melancholy that weighs the rest of it down. But love leads to loss, and loss can lead to madness. Dana's grief when his wife Ruth died in 1822 had been as extreme as Allston's after the death of his first wife, Ann. His son later remembered that no description he had read "of agony short of madness" could equal it. In "The Changes of Home" this suffering is split between two figures – the poet, who remembers his terrible grief after the death of the girl he loved when he was young ("Benumbing grief and horrors filled my breast: / Dark death, and sorrow dark, and terror blind"), and a mad woman who has lost her lover to the sea, and who now wanders inconsolably around the hills: "A grief there is of deeper, withering power, / That feels death lurking in the springing flower – / That stands beneath the sun, yet circled round / By a strange darkness –." Even death itself is merciful compared to this "dread, living blight." The quiet valley has become a tomb, and the exercise of memory only a valediction: "These old, familiar things, where'er I tread / Are round me like the mansions of the dead." Ignoring the pleas of an old man that he take up residence in the valley again, the poet decides to leave once more for the sea, and the poem ends.

In another poem, entitled "Thoughts on the Soul," Dana carries even further the obsessiveness of Allston's "The Atonement." Wordsworth and Coleridge had celebrated (and warned of) the mind's power over the universe it perceives, but Dana speaks as if the mind were really like a spirit in a Swedenborgian heaven or hell, perpetually generating the reality it perceives. This generative power is something the soul is born with, and something it cannot recall – "it *must* create." If the soul is happy, the world will reflect joy like a lake. But if not, then it finds itself surrounded by a hell of its own creation: "All must be, / Like thy dread self, one dread eternity." Dana mocks those who think that death can put an end to this process, or absorb the soul back into some kind of comforting Whole. Death will only make plainer the passions that ordinary life keeps hidden: "Bursting to life, thy dominant desire / Shall upward flame, like a fierce forest fire: / Then, like a sea of fire, heave, roar, and dash – / Roll up its lowest depths in waves, and flash / A wild disaster round, like its own woe." The only escape from this inner hell lies in the saving power of Christ. "Come lowly; he will help thee." Dana's need for a Redeemer was as pressing as Allston's had been, and led him to the same conclusion. During the controversy that divided the Unitarians from the Trinitarians in the Congregational churches of New England, he sided firmly with the Trinitarians. He eventually joined the Episcopal Church.

Still, Dana may have had more in common with the Transcendentalists he denounced than he realized. "Thoughts on the Soul," after its pious advocacy of submission to Christ, goes on to a bizarre coda in which Dana begins to indulge thoughts of what it will be like to share eternity with God, to send one's thoughts wandering through eternity. He catches himself in a thought that (he admits) borders on blasphemy: "I, like God, shall ever *be*." He closes with an apostrophe to Man scarcely less ecstatic than the myth of the Orphic poet that ended Emerson's *Nature* (1836):

> Creature all grandeur, son of truth and light,
> Up from the dust! the last great day is bright,
> Bright on the Holy Mountain, round the Throne
> Bright where in borrowed light the far stars shone,
> Look Down! the Depths are bright!

"Thoughts on the Soul" tries to achieve submission and ends up coveting power, begins in fear and ends in celebration of human majesty.

Dana's style rose to something like eloquence only when he was treating one subject rare in American poetry: happily consummated heterosexual love. His wife had died after only nine years of marriage. He remained a widower until his death at the age of ninety-two. His memories of love provide almost the only happy moments in a poem like "The Changes of Home," as when he suddenly asserts that only those people who are truly in love can be said to be alive: "And life it is, when a soft, inward sense / Pervades our being, when we draw from hence / Delights unutterable, thoughts that throw / Unearthly brightness round this world below." Even an apparently mournful poem like "The Husband and Wife's Grave" becomes a celebration of sensuous union, as the silence of the grave is compared to the radiant silence of the marriage bed "in which ye rested once / Most happy, – silence eloquent, when heart / With heart held speech, and your mysterious frames / Harmonious, sensitive, at every beat / Touched the soft notes of love." Dana imagines the pair in heaven, blending into one another (like Milton's angels), enjoying "sensation all, / And thought, pervading, mingling sense and thought!" To be so alive, "wrapped in a consciousness / Twofold, yet single" is a mystery Dana delights in contemplating and hoping for – "this is love! this life!" – a faith that makes him unusual in a literary tradition where the most ecstatic intercourse tends to take place between the Me and the Me Myself.

If Allston found a license for imaginative voluptuousness in studying European works of art, another poet from the Boston area, Maria Gowen Brooks

(1794–1845), found sensuous delight in two unlikely places – a coffee plantation in Cuba, and the Dartmouth College Library. She was born the daughter
of a prosperous goldsmith in Medford, Massachusetts. The Harvard professors
among her father's friends encouraged her in her love of learning; by the age
of nine she had already committed to memory passages from Milton's *Comus*
and Addison's *Cato*. But this happy rural childhood ended abruptly when her
father's business failed and he died bankrupt in 1809. She was immediately
betrothed, at the age of fourteen, to her deceased sister's husband, a Boston
merchant nearly three times her age. He paid for her education and married
her before she was sixteen; she bore him two sons. (What she thought of such
early marriages may be guessed from a footnote to her long narrative poem
Zophiël, where she notes that the Spartans forbade women to marry before
the age of twenty, a policy to which they owed "the strength and beauty of
the race.") The marriage, never happy, was made less so when financial losses
caused her husband to retire to Portland, Maine. Cut off from the intellectual
life of the Boston area, linked to a husband whose faults seemed to increase as
his fortunes declined, she turned to the writing of poetry to assuage her loneliness and express her anger. When she was nineteen she wrote her first metrical
romance, a poem in seven cantos, which was never published and which has
not survived. In 1820, when she was twenty-six, she collected some of her
poems into a small volume, entitled *Judith, Esther, and Other Poems, by a Lover
of the Arts*. Her interest in Biblical heroines whose courage or submissiveness
were alike fatal to their enemies indicated the direction her mature poetry was
to take. Judith's beheading of the drunken Holofernes in his tent is described
with a relish impossible to mistake:

> Mid the warm gush she smote him yet again,
> And when the quivering visage severed lay,
> Wiped from her ivory arms the steaming stain,
> And took the costly canopy away.
> · · ·
> Then Judith's voice awoke the silent night:
> "Descend, O watch, and Praise the great divine!
> Weeping Judea, arm thee in his might!
> Arise! Arise! The enemy is thine!"

Her husband's death in the summer of 1823 liberated her from exile in
Maine. A maternal uncle invited her to make her home with him on his coffee
plantation in Cuba. In the preface she wrote to *Idomen*, an autobiographical
novel published in the 1840s, Brooks remembered what this sudden change
was like: "A stranger newly transported from the snows of the north, and
placed in a piazza not far from the shores of Cuba, becomes, if he has not the

least sensibility, inebriate with warmth and fragrance." Like Wallace Stevens in Florida, Brooks suddenly found herself in the sort of paradise New Englanders thought had been lost with Adam's banishment. There, in a vine-covered summer house on the coffee plantation, she completed the first canto of *Zophiël*, a mythological epic in the style of Robert Southey's *Curse of Kehama* or *Thalaba the Destroyer*. This canto was published in Boston in 1825. Shortly afterwards her wealthy planter uncle died, leaving her his estate. She returned to the United States to be near her son, who was studying at Dartmouth. She used the Dartmouth College Library to gain access to scholarship about the history and religions of the ancient world. If Cuba had awakened her passions, Dartmouth encouraged her intellectual daring. The many learned footnotes in *Zophiël* having to do with subjects like ritual prostitution and heterodox religions were written there, and they quietly advance her claim to an intellectual freedom rarely enjoyed by women. Like a more celebrated American poet a generation later, Brooks always dressed in white; but she added to her costume a single passion flower in her blonde hair. In 1831 she traveled to London and the Lake District, where she met Robert Southey, who was charmed by her and who assisted her in publishing the now-completed six-canto version of *Zophiël*.

The plot of *Zophiël, or The Bride of Seven* is drawn from an incident in the apocryphal Book of Tobit, where a maiden who has lost seven husbands on the bridal night to a jealous demon lover named Asmodeus is finally rescued by a youth who, acting on the advice of the archangel Raphael, burns the heart and liver of a fish in the bridal chamber and so drives the demon lover away. Asmodeus becomes Brooks's Zophiël (the name is taken from one of Milton's fallen angels) in a narrative whose baroque complications allow Brooks to comment upon matters from battlefield rape to the motivation of the rank-and-file fallen angel (of one such character she says "Within the vortex of rebellion drawn / He joined the shining ranks *as others did*").

Part of the poem's power to shock comes from its sensuality, which is indeed so frank that Miss Catherine Bowles, to whom Southey had sent a copy of the poem, reminded him that he had informed its author of the necessity of "cooling" her poem in some parts. "Now if you have effected this refrigerating process," Miss Bowles wanted to know, "for Heavens's sake at what degree of temperature did it stand previously?" *Zophiël* also shocks by its heterodox rewriting of *Paradise Lost*. It gives us Milton's poem as it might have been related by Eve and Belial rather than by Milton, Adam, and God. Brooks made the challenge explicit in her invocation: "Spirits, who hovered o'er Euphrates' stream / When the first beauteous mother of our race / First oped her mild eyes to the new light-beam, / And in the lucid wave first saw her own fair face . . ." The "false sky" of the pool in which Milton's Eve sees her face in

Book IV of *Paradise Lost* has become Brooks's "lucid wave," and in Brooks's tender recollection of the moment of human origin there is no mention of Adam or God. Her sparring with Milton goes on throughout the poem. In the "drear song of woe" to "wild ambition" sung by Zophiël early in the poem, Eve is listed right after the angels as the chief human victim of ambition: "Darting through all her veins the subtle fire, / The world's fair mistress first inhaled thy breath." That judgment is Miltonic enough. But Brooks goes on to make Eve the ancestor of all ambitious artists and discoverers. Milton compares Eve to Pandora; Brooks suggests that Eve is closer to Prometheus, since without her "Fame ne'er had roused, nor song her records kept; / The gem, the ore, the marble breathing life, / The pencil's colors, all in earth had slept."

Brooks's powers of invention are perpetually surprising; her narrative verse is lively; and the learned footnotes that follow each canto allow her an impressive display of erudition. She can sometimes be bitter – her use of Aristophanes' myth from Plato's *Phaedrus* to explain the reasons for unhappiness in marriage is a striking anticipation of Melville's "After the Pleasure Party," and may have suggested it – but more often her attitude is one of delight and curiosity. A sense of daring pervades the poem, as the author asks us to admire the richness of her sensuous particulars and the sober authority of her learned footnotes. In the fifth canto she has an episode describing the various emotions of young Syrian women led to the temple of Mylitta to engage in the required act of ritual prostitution. A footnote, instead of denouncing the practice with horror, calmly refers us for more information to Herodotus and to the "very full and amusing account" of the same subject given in "Les Voyages d'Antenor."

The learned footnote is a genre with a long history, and by Brooks's time it had achieved nuances of expression that emphasized its subversive intent. The eighteenth-century German scholars who had annotated Biblical texts by noting resemblances between Jewish narratives and ritual practices and those of surrounding peoples may have intended originally to shed light on what was obscure in the Sacred Text, but in so doing they undermined orthodox belief in the uniqueness of the Scriptures, reducing them (as one scholar has observed) to examples of Oriental literature. It did not take long for imaginative writers to exploit the possibilities in this new hybrid genre, the Oriental poem with learned footnotes. In Southey's 1801 epic *Thalaba the Destroyer* the tale itself indulges the mythologizing imagination to the fullest while the skeptical footnotes debunk it. Yet if the footnotes are subversive to the text they are flattering to the reader, who is addressed as a progressive, one who finds the superstitions of all primitive peoples stimulating to the imagination but repugnant to the intellect. The annotated Oriental tale – the genre to which *Zophiël*, like *Thalaba*, belongs – aims to provide both the thrills of credulity and the satisfactions of enlightenment. But Brooks did even more with her footnotes than Southey had done with his. She often used them to point out the resemblance between Cuba and the ancient Near East, or else to comment upon the graciousness of Spanish culture when compared to the barbarous customs of New England. She noted that Biblical names, which sound so ugly in English, are melodious in both Hebrew and Spanish. (Friends remembered that she always gave the word "Cuba" the correct Spanish pronunciation.)

One of her best lyrics, "Composed at the Request of a Lady, and Descriptive of Her Feelings," bears the ominous subtitle: "She Returned to the North, and Died Soon After." It concerns the unhappiness of a Northern lady called to return to her "native snows." On her Cuban plantation, every prospect pleases, every breeze is full of fragrance and song. The scarlet flowers of the pomegranate glow in the "jetty hair" of the island's dark-eyed women; the "light seguidilla" sung by the muleteer riding home in the evening repeats his mistress's name throughout the verses. A grove of orange trees overtopped with blooming vines sounds like the garden in the Song of Solomon:

> The orange-tree has fruit and flowers;
> The grenadilla, in its bloom,
> Hangs o'er its high, luxuriant bowers,
> Like fringes from a Tyrian loom.

The plantation whose beauty Brooks had celebrated was not without its own terrors, however, and the tropical fever endemic to Cuba claimed the lives of a son and stepson before she succumbed to it herself in 1845. At the time of her death she had achieved what seemed like a secure place in American literary history. John Quincy Adams admired her poems; Rufus Griswold devoted a large chunk of his *Female Poets of America* (1856) to them. He said there: "It may be doubted whether, in the long catalogue of those whose works illustrate and vindicate the intellectual character and position of women, there are many names that will shine with a clearer, steadier, and more enduring lustre, than that of *Maria del Occidente*" (the pen name she always used, supposed to have been conferred on her by Southey).

The poets who were born in, or gravitated towards, New York City, are far less gloomy than their New England contemporaries, though none of them displayed the sensuality of the transplanted Brooks. Description interested them less than melody. The river addressed in Joseph Rodman Drake's poem *Bronx* might be any romantic stream (though it is hard for the modern reader to modify the word "Bronx" with "romantic," the landscape was then still pastoral), and even the opening of Drake's long poem of the Fancy, *The Culprit Fay*, does little to identify the scene of its action (the Hudson River near

West Point) beyond the lines naming a nearby mountain: "The moon looks down on old Cronest / She mellows the shades of his shaggy breast." Drake's comic verse-letters to Halleck from Scotland show that he was capable of vivid description when he cared to write it. But his serious poems are often more fluent than memorable.

Halleck's best descriptive poems usually incorporate some element of irony or burlesque, and the artistry with which the blend is managed determines whether the resulting poem seems sophisticated or merely irritating. Edgar Allan Poe, who always strove after purity of aesthetic sensation, hated these poems written in mixed styles. In a review of Halleck's poems for the 1836 *Southern Literary Messenger* he argues that any attempt to link "the low burlesque with the ideal" produces an effect of "incongruity" and "profanation." But in a poem like "Alnwick Castle," incongruity and profanation are the themes of the poem. Halleck has visited the traditional home of the Percy family hoping to find the castle of his imagination. His first sight of the castle seems to live up to his expectations:

> A gentle hill its side inclines
>   Lovely in England's fadeless green,
> To meet the quiet stream which winds
>   Through this romantic scene,
> As silently and sweetly still,
> As when, at evening, on that hill
>   When summer's wind blew soft and low,
> Seated by gallant Hotspur's side,
> His Katherine was a happy bride,
>   A thousand years ago.

To his chagrin, he soon discovers that the noble families of England have been turned into merchants or debtors:

> Lord Stafford mines for coal and salt,
> The Duke of Norfolk deals in malt,
>   The Douglass in red herrings;
> And noble name and cultured land,
> Palace and park and vassal-band,
>   Are powerless to the notes of hand
>   Of Rothschild or the Barings.

Alnwick Castle has become a place where visitors are bowed through the rooms by an obsequious servant "for ten-and-sixpence sterling."

A similar mixing of tones takes place in Halleck's two meditations on American subjects: "Red Jacket," inspired by a contemporary painting, and "Connecticut," left unfinished at his death. In these poems the interweaving of seriousness with irony makes for a texture of surprising complexity. Red Jacket was a famous Chief of the Tuscaroras, the subject of a romanticized portrait by the painter Benjamin Weir. The opening of an exhibition to display Weir's portrait gave Halleck a fine opportunity to comment upon the tendency of American writers and artists to portray all Indians as impossibly noble savages: "as tall, as sinewy, as strong / As earth's first kings." Halleck could guess what the real Red Jacket would have thought about being pressed into service by palefaces desperate for heroic "ancestors." He was a ferocious warrior who hated with all his heart the race of "missionaries and cold water," the white men who stole his land.

In "Connecticut" Halleck turns a similar historical skepticism upon the legends and histories written in his native state. The poem begins with an affectionate tribute to Connecticut's proud history and its notoriously stiff-necked citizens. Connecticut is a land "where none kneel, save when to Heaven they pray, / Nor even then, unless in their own way." But the tone changes when Halleck turns his attention to the works of New England's most famous historian. At first he treats Cotton Mather as a kind of naive Romantic allegorist, weaving "his forest dreams into quaint prose, / Our sires his heroes." But Mather's *Magnalia* records episodes of brutality that seem to earn for the Pilgrims an honorable place among the world's mass murderers.

> Herod of Galilee's babe-butchering deed
> Lives not on history's blushing page alone,
> Our skies, it seems, have seen like victims bleed,
> And our own Ramahs echoed groan for groan.

If the Pilgrims – those defenders of the faith, those fierce champions of personal freedom – butchered the Indians as indiscriminately as Mather says, how can we honor them? But if they were monsters, why is the state they founded as happy and virtuous as it appears to be? Upon this rock the poem splits, and Halleck tries (rather oddly) to dismiss Mather's tale of conquest as "a brain-born dream of rain and hail," a fit of bad temper like Milton's divorce tracts or Dante's liberally vented spleen. To conclude your reading of history by denying the reality of the events described is a desperate strategy, but Halleck adopts it, as he urges us to forgive the Pilgrims: "Forget their story's cruelty and wrong; / Forget their story-teller; or but deem / His facts the fictions of a minstrel's song." It is far better to think of the beauties of present-day Connecticut: "Hers are not Tempe's nor Arcadia's spring, / Nor the long Summer of Cathayan vales." Still, the rigors of her winters and summers bring health, and "in the autumn-time / Earth has no purer and no lovelier clime."

William Cullen Bryant (1795–1878), like Fitz-Greene Halleck, came to New York from New England and remained there throughout a long and distinguished career. At the time of his death, he was regarded as one of America's foremost literary figures. When Charles Dickens visited New York in 1842, he sent Bryant this invitation to come join him for breakfast: "I have a thumbed book at home, so well worn that it has nothing upon the back but one gilt 'B' and the remotest possible traces of a 'y.' My credentials are in my earnest admiration of its beautiful contents." Many years later, when Bryant traveled to Mexico City from Vera Cruz (braving the risk that bandits then posed to stagecoach travelers), he was honored at a reception attended by high government ministers, justices of the supreme court, and literary men. President Benito Juárez, who received him the following day, provided his party with a military escort back to Vera Cruz. Bryant had been a lifelong admirer and translator of Spanish literature; the last poem he wrote, "Cervantes," was designed for a festival held by the Spanish residents of New York City to honor Cervantes's birthday. He translated Provençal, Portuguese, and German poetry in addition to his translations of the *Iliad* (1870) and *Odyssey* (1871). He was a vigorous walker as well as a frequent and adventurous traveler, who in 1845 rode in a birch-bark canoe piloted by Indians down foaming, mile-long rapids near Sault Ste. Marie, and in 1853 he made a twenty-day trip by camel from a village near Cairo to Jerusalem.

He was born in the tiny western Massachusetts village of Cummington on the Westfield River, one of the tributaries of the Connecticut. His mother taught him to read the Scriptures and repeat Watts's hymns and moral poems for children. His father was a doctor who played the violin and admired Alexander Pope. Dr. Bryant brought elements of urbanity to his rural family, sometimes in unusual ways. The failure of an investment that he had made with borrowed money made him flee his home to avoid debtors' prison. He signed on as ship's surgeon on a vessel sailing from New York to Mozambique, hoping to earn enough money to pay his debts. The vessel was captured by the French, and Dr. Bryant was detained for a year on the island of Mauritius, where he worked in the island's hospital. He returned home a year later, still penniless, but now French-speaking. Restored to solvency through the kindness of his father-in-law (money he eventually repaid), he was elected as Hampshire County's representative to the Massachusetts state assembly, which met in Boston. His visits there helped him to collect a good library, books eagerly read by his sons on firelit winter evenings. In Boston Dr. Bryant became a convert to Unitarianism. At home he attended the regular Sunday services at his local Congregational church but remained seated when the congregation rose to sing the Doxology.

Dr. Bryant encouraged his son's early poetic efforts, although he was a severe critic of anything he considered doggerel or bombast. When Cullen wrote a 244-line satire attacking Thomas Jefferson's 1807 Embargo Act (hated in New England, whose economy relied heavily upon foreign trade), Dr. Bryant approved of it enough to show it to friends in the state legislature, and with their aid revised it for publication in February 1808 as a twelve-page booklet. *The Embargo* proved so popular that it was reissued the next year in an enlarged version, together with other poems and translations by the now fourteen-year-old author, one of which was a poem entitled "The Spanish Revolution," praising the Spanish uprising against Joseph Bonaparte.

At the end of 1809 Bryant was sent from Cummington to the home of his maternal uncle, the Rev. Thomas Snell of North Brookfield, Massachusetts, to begin the study of Latin in order to prepare him for college. After years spent in a village school, Bryant was fascinated by the Latin language and made rapid progress. The Rev. Snell, noticing his quickness, advanced him rapidly from grammatical exercises to reading Horace and Virgil. After a brief return to Cummington the next summer to work on the family farm, Bryant traveled to Plainfield to begin Greek with another tutor, the Rev. Moses Hallock, who charged a dollar a week to feed his pupils on milk and bread while he set them to studying Greek and mathematics. Bryant did so well under this austere regimen that he was judged ready to enter the sophomore class at Williams College in Williamstown, Massachusetts, in the fall of 1810.

But the preparation his tutors had given him turned out to be better than the instruction offered at the college, then at a low point in its fortunes. During the brief time that he was there, Bryant, like most American undergraduates of the time, turned for solace from the dull classroom recitations to the lively meetings of the student-run literary societies (the Philologian and Philotechnian), for whose meetings he composed verses. He translated an ode of Anacreon and a chorus of *Oedipus Tyrannus*; he wrote a comic poem abusing muddy Williamstown and its disheveled college, which he portrayed as a Gothic dungeon of suffering:

> Where through the horror-breathing hall
> The pale-faced, moping students crawl,
>   Like spectral monuments of woe
> Or studious seek the unwholesome cell,
> Where dust, and gloom, and cobwebs dwell,
>   Dark, dirty, dank, and low.
>
>   (*Descriptio Gulielmpolis*)

He asked his father for permission to withdraw from Williams and return home to prepare himself for the entrance examinations at Yale. He spent the summer of 1811 studying mathematics and performing chemistry experiments with the equipment his father used to compound drugs. He delved into Linnean botany and read poetry. This happy interval came to an end when his father had to confess that he could not find enough money to send him to Yale. At the age of sixteen, his formal education over, Bryant left Cummington to read law in the offices of Samuel Howe, a friend of his father's. A few years later he moved to Bridgewater to continue his education as the assistant of a well-known lawyer and member of Congress, William Baylies, who left Bryant to run his office when Congress was in session. Baylies was aware of Bryant's poetical ambitions, but warned him: "Poetry is a commodity, I know, not suited to the American market. It will neither help a man to wealth nor office."

Bryant knew that Baylies was right to warn him that poets in America were likely to starve in obscurity, but his poetic ambitions were not easy to renounce. When he was only eight or nine, he later remembered, he had included in his prayers a plea that he "might receive the gift of poetic genius, and write verses that might endure." As a boy he had imitated the models his culture approved: Milton, Watts, Pope, the English poets of Sensibility. Later he had translated poetry by Horace, Virgil, Simonides, Anacreon, and Sophocles. And during the years of his legal apprenticeship his poetry also began to reflect the influence of the *Lyrical Ballads*. (Samuel Howe, his first instructor in law, caught him reading the book one day and told him to stop wasting his time.) The influence of Wordsworth's blank verse can be felt in some untitled lines that Bryant wrote in 1813. The forty-nine line fragment begins abruptly, as a voice stops the passer-by and delivers this reminder:

>   – Yet a few days
> And thee the all-beholding sun will see no more,
> In all his course; nor yet in the cold ground,
> Where thy pale form was laid with many tears,
> Nor in the embrace of ocean, shall exist
> Thy image. Earth, that nourished thee, shall claim
> Thy growth, to be resolved to earth again,
> And, lost each human trace, surrendering up
> Thine individual being, shalt thou go
> To mix forever with the elements,
> To be a brother to the insensible rock
> And to the sluggish clod, which the rude swain
> Turns with his share, and treads upon. The oak
> Shall send his roots abroad, and pierce thy mold.

Four years later, when Bryant had moved to Great Barrington, Massachusetts to start his own legal practice, his father found the fragment among his papers and sent it, with a handful of other poems, to acquaintances who were founding a new journal in Boston, the *North American Review*. Edward T. Channing, one of the journal's editors, read the verses aloud to Richard Henry Dana, who thought they were a hoax – some scrap of contemporary British poetry passed off as the work of a local poet. As he told Channing: "That was never written on this side of the water."

It is easy to see why Dana was skeptical about the poem's provenance. American blank verse rarely moved with such assurance. And American poems about death (when they did not aim to terrify with visions of Judgment) were usually pious and consolatory. Nowhere in Bryant's fragment is there any mention of an afterlife. As for our immortal souls, Bryant never mentions them. Instead of promising us immortality the poet asks us to take comfort from the beauty of our common sepulcher:

> The hills
> Rock-ribbed and ancient as the sun; the vales
> Stretching in pensive quietness between;
> The venerable woods; rivers that move
> In majesty, and the complaining brooks
> That make the meadows green; and, poured round
> Old ocean's grey and melancholy waste, –
> Are but the solemn decorations all
> Of the great tomb of man.

Lacking a title for this fragment, the *North American Review* editors called it "Thanatopsis" when they published it along with several other Bryant poems and translations in their September 1817 issue. Bryant, whose titles are usually simple, would probably not have approved it. But the poem achieved notoriety from the moment of its first publication, and Bryant kept the title given by the editors when he republished the poem in his *Poems* of 1821. There he introduced his fragmentary meditation on death with sixteen-and-a-half lines written to make his *siste viator* seem the voice of Nature herself, and he added a conclusion suggesting that the thought of our common mortality should help us face death with dignity and without fear. But he still declined to make any mention of life after death, an omission which caused one reviewer to denounce the poem as an example of doctrines "which lead at last to atheism and annihilation."

He had grown up in a country village whose virtues indeed allowed him to survive to a vigorous old age in the rough-and-tumble world of New York journalism. (When he was in his eighties he still walked three miles to the building that housed the *Evening Post*, ignoring the elevator to walk up ten flights of stairs to the newspaper office.) His schooling had been intermittent; his hopes of escaping the hinterlands for the coast had been frustrated by his father's poverty; and he had been forced to choose a profession he did not much like. But he still loved the western Massachusetts landscape, as he made clear in two poems published in the *North American Review* in 1817 and 1818. "The Yellow Violet" praises a small flower hardy enough to bloom next to snowbanks and colorful enough to make "the woods of April bright."

> Ere russet fields their green resume,
> Sweet flower, I love, in forest bare,
> To meet thee, when thy faint perfume
> Alone is in the virgin air.

"The Yellow Violet" is suffused with tenderness. Bryant's most famous lyric, "To a Waterfowl," on the other hand, involves darker emotions – fear, perplexity, loss. The sight of a solitary waterfowl against the evening sky reminds Bryant at once of the bird's vulnerability and of the instincts nature has given it to survive its enemies.

> Whither, 'midst falling dew,
> While glow the heavens with the last steps of day,
> Far, through their rosy depths, dost thou pursue
> Thy solitary way?
>
> Vainly the fowler's eye
> Might mark thy distant flight to do thee wrong,
> As, darkly seen against the crimson sky,
> Thy figure floats along.

He tries to encourage the bird to stay aloft by reminding it of its destination, where the loneliness of migration will terminate in social joy: "Soon shalt thou find a summer home and rest, / And scream among thy fellows; reeds shall bend, / Soon, o'er thy sheltered nest." Enviously, he notes that the waterfowl's lonely flight through "the desert and illimitable air" is guided by a Power whose care means the bird is "lone wandering, but not lost." As the figure of the bird disappeares in the heavens, the poet draws comfort from the thought that something in him corresponds to the instinct that guides the bird, and that the Power watches over him as well:

> He who, from zone to zone,
> Guides through the boundless sky thy certain flight,
> In the long way that I must tread alone,
> Will lead my steps aright.

Bryant did not invent the stanza form of "To a Waterfowl," which he found in Southey's poem, "Hope." But he uses it here to advantage. The slightly offbeat effect created by overlaying an *abba* metrical scheme with an *abab* rhyme scheme suits the poem's uneasy mixture of anxiety and reassurance, even as the metrical scheme itself, billowing outward from trimeter to pentameter and then folding itself down to trimeter again, seems like an anxious migration returning to the firm ground of trust.

Great Barrington, where Bryant set up his legal practice, lies on the Housatonic River, near the western border of Massachusetts. The Green River flows into the Housatonic, and in 1819 Bryant wrote a poem about it using a meter he had defended in an essay published the same year, "On the Use of Trisyllabic Feet in Iambic Verse." An iambic meter varied by occasional anapests, he argues, produces a vigorous swinging rhythm that Sir Walter Scott found perfect for verse narratives like *The Lay of the Last Minstrel*. In Bryant's "Green River" it is most effective where exuberance is the poet's theme:

> Oh loveliest there the spring days come,
> With blossoms, and birds, and wild bees' hum;
> The flowers of summer are fairest there,
> And freshest the breath of the summer air;
> And sweetest the golden autumn day
> In silence and sunshine glides away.

From the grimness of his legal practice, which forces him to "scrawl strange words with the barbarous pen" and mingle with the "sons of strife," he returns to the "lonely and lovely stream" that casts back an image of the peace his heart desires.

His poems in the *North American Review* had attracted so much interest that he was invited to deliver the Phi Beta Kappa poem at the Harvard Commencement festivities in 1821. He wrote for the occasion a survey of human history in Spenserian stanzas, "The Ages." He placed it first in a small volume of *Poems* his new Boston acquaintances from the *North American Review* helped him publish in 1821. In addition to "The Ages," "To A Waterfowl," "The Yellow Violet," "Green River," and "Thanatopsis," the forty-four-page book contained his youthful "Translation of a Fragment of Simonides," a "Song," and an "Inscription for the Entrance to a Wood," which reminds us that although the world is fallen,

>   . . . these shades
> Are still the abode of gladness, the thick roof
> Of green and stirring branches is alive
> And musical with birds, that sing and sport
> In wantonness of spirit.
>   . . .

> Throngs of insects in the shade
> Try their thin wings and dance in the warm beam
> That waked them into life. Even the green trees

> Partake the deep contentment; as they bend
> To the soft winds, the sun from the blue sky
> Looks in and sheds a blessing on the scene.

Even the dark causeway formed by "the old and ponderous trunks of prostrate trees" suggests tranquillity rather than decay, while the rivulet, "leaping down the rocks, / Seems with continuous laughter, to rejoice / In its own being." If we could learn to tread softly enough not to scare the wren who comes to drink in the stream, Bryant promises us a gentle reward:

> The cool wind,
> That stirs the stream in play, shall come to thee
> Like one that loves thee nor will let thee pass
> Ungreeted, and shall give its light embrace.

Bryant's 1821 *Poems*, now considered one of the most important first volumes of poetry in American literary history, did not even pay the full cost of its publication. Preoccupied with the demands of his legal practice, he gave up poetry for almost two years. Then the editor of a new journal to be based in Boston, the *United States Literary Gazette*, offered him 200 dollars a year to produce one hundred lines of poetry a month for the magazine. To a struggling lawyer whose practice at best yielded $500 a year, this stimulus to production proved irresistible, though only a few of the poems written for the *Gazette* turned out to be memorable. "Summer Wind," which portrays a heat-stricken rural landscape, is full of vivid details like this image of the piled-up white cumulus clouds above a New England forest:

> . . . far in the fierce sunshine tower the hills,
> With all their growth of woods, silent and stern,
> As if the scorching heat and dazzling light
> Were but an element they loved. Bright clouds,
> Motionless pillars of the brazen heaven; –
> Their bases on the mountains – their white tops
> Shining in the far ether – fire the air
> With a reflected radiance.

In "An Indian at the Burying-Place of His Fathers," one of several poems on Indian themes, Bryant challenges the way that descendants of white settlers saw New World history – a tale of progress in which fruitful, cultivated plains displace gloomy woods and useless swamps. The poem is spoken in the voice of an Indian who much prefers the untamed wilderness his ancestors knew. The white man likes to boast that Nature has been made subservient to human wishes, but the Indian sees in this instinct for domination only looming ecological disaster. Before the trees were cut down and the fields tilled, the woods were filled with the music of numberless brooks. But now

> Those grateful sounds are heard no more,
> The springs are silent in the sun,
> The rivers, by the blackened shore,
> With lessening current run.

The Indian warns his white conquerors that unless they change their ways their victory over the native tribes may prove to be Pyrrhic: "The realms our tribes are crushed to get / May be a blackening desert yet."

Writing on contract for the *United States Literary Gazette* helped Bryant "keep his hand in" (as he told Dana) at a time when he had almost given up composing verse. He began to consider leaving his provincial law practice for some other life more closely suited to his talents and interests. Of course he did not expect that writing poetry would ever be able to support him and his wife and daughter. But friends encouraged him to think that he might make a living doing literary journalism in New York City, perhaps as the editor of a new journal. The journal he and his friends started after he moved there in 1825, the *New York Review and Athenaeum Magazine*, began with high ambitions. The "review" section was to survey recent books; the "magazine," to provide poems, stories, letters, and notes. Bryant's biographer notes that for one issue Bryant wrote a critical article of more than 8,500 words on the recent reissue of a sixteenth-century French book on the troubadour poets. (Bryant translated all the Provençal poetry he quoted in the review.) Perhaps predictably, the *New York Review and Athenaeum Magazine* failed after eight issues. Grimly, Bryant took out a license that would allow him to practice law in New York. Then, in July 1826, William Coleman, the editor of the New York *Evening Post*, was thrown from his gig and seriously injured. Bryant accepted what he thought would be temporary employment with the paper. When Coleman died in 1829, Bryant assumed the editorship of the paper, a post he held until his own death in 1878.

The task of writing editorials for a daily paper did not completely end his career as a poet and translator, but after 1829 journalism necessarily took most of his time. In 1831 he issued the first collected edition of his poetry. Editions that followed usually contained only a few new poems and translations to accompany the early poems upon which his fame chiefly rested. One of the best of these later poems, "The Prairies," records Bryant's impressions on his first trip in 1832 to Illinois, where his brothers had emigrated. There he saw for the first time the "awful solitudes" and "boundless wastes" (as he described them in a letter to his wife) that visitors from the eastern states often found unnerving – the broad, grassy, treeless plain, stretching out in all directions to the horizon. The opening lines of "The Prairies" record both Bryant's exhilaration in this strange landscape and his bewilderment at trying to represent it.

> These are the Gardens of the Desert, these
> The unshorn fields, boundless and beautiful,
> For which the speech of England has no name –
> The Prairies. I behold them for the first,
> And my heart swells, while the dilated sight
> Takes in the encircling vastness. Lo! they stretch
> In airy undulations, far away,
> As if the ocean, in his gentlest swell,
> Stood still, with all his rounded billows fixed,
> And motionless for ever. – Motionless? –
> No – they are all unchained again. The clouds
> Sweep over with their shadows, and beneath,
> The surface rolls and fluctuates to the eye.

The features of this landscape were designed by "the hand that built the firmament." Yet the absence of human presence from this vast Eden only makes it dearer to the sky:

> The great heavens
> Seem to stoop down upon the scene in love, –
> A nearer vault, and of a tenderer blue,
> Than that which bends above the eastern hills.

Auden once observed that American poets differed from European ones because they could easily imagine what the earth would look like if it were uninhabited by human beings. He might have been thinking of these lines from "The Prairies," or of similar ones from Bryant's sonnet of 1830, "To Cole, the Painter, Departing for Europe." Thomas Cole, a poet and landscape painter, intended to go abroad to study European art. Bryant approves, but reminds him that even among Europe's most beautiful landscapes Cole will always bear within him "a living image of our own bright land":

> Lone lakes – savannahs where the bison roves –
> Rocks rich with summer garlands – solemn streams –
> Skies, where the desert eagle wheels and screams –
> Spring bloom and autumn blaze of boundless groves.

Europe has woods and mountains too, but from her lowest glens to the fierce Alpine air one can never escape "the trace of men." To know what the earth looks like without that trace is the American artist's special gift, the "earlier, wilder image" Bryant reminds Cole to keep bright in his heart.

Bryant became a great public literary intellectual, introducing European and Latin American literature to his countrymen, making the American wilderness familiar to foreign readers. His greatest service to his contemporaries came from his half-century of courageous journalism – campaigning for free trade and the rights of working men, fighting against the expansion of slavery, arguing for emancipation and then for the extension of the franchise to former slaves. The respect he enjoyed as a poet and translator only added to his fame, though his later poems are more often graceful than deeply imaginative. In a handful of early poems, however, he was as important as that prehistoric genius who began the agricultural revolution by finding amid "the grasses of the field / That spring beneath our careless feet" those "shining stems that yield / The grains of life-sustaining wheat" ("Dante").

From the beginning, poetry written in the American South was marked by the high value it placed on melody. If Northern poets wanted to write like Thomson or Wordsworth, Southern poets wanted to write like Byron or Thomas Moore, and their best poems are songs. Richard Henry Wilde (1789–1847) was a poet and translator whose most famous lyric, "The Lament of the Captive," was set to music by several well-known composers. Wilde, who had been born in Ireland, came with his family to the United States in 1796, first to Baltimore and then to Augusta, Georgia. His father's early death in 1802 meant that Wilde had little time for formal education, obliged as he was to help the family out by working in various stores. The owner of one store kept a shelf of lawbooks next to his ordinary wares: cotton and silk hose, cigars, tobacco, and gunpowder. Wilde studied the lawbooks for five hours each night. Later, he read law with a prominent lawyer whose partner he would become. At nineteen he survived a three-day examination to win admission to the Georgia bar. By 1811 he had become Solicitor General of Georgia's middle circuit, and so, *ex officio*, Attorney General of the State. Subsequently he was elected to five terms in the United States Congress (1815–17; 1827–35). With a later law partner, Joseph M. White, Wilde became part-owner of a Florida sugar-cane plantation.

Over six feet in height, he impressed one onlooker as "cheerful in his disposition, dignified and yet affable in his address, brimful of anecdote, eloquent in speech, impressive in action, and quick at repartee." In 1813 or 1814 he began several fragments of an "epic" meant to amuse a military brother who had fought against the Seminoles in Florida. In the fourth fragment, based upon an episode in Garcilasso de la Vega's *Historia de la Florida*, an unnamed Indian recalls the single white man spared during a raid provoked by the greed of the invading whites: "Among the false he only had been true – /And much we loved this man of single mind, / And ever while he lived to him were kind." The Indians strive to cheer him, but he cannot be comforted. He sits looking out at the sea that separates him from his native land, and he feels keenly his exclusion from the sympathy that nature grants even to the most transient of her phenomena – blossoms, leaves, and footprints on the seashore:

> My life is like the summer rose
> > That opens to the morning sky,
> And, ere the shades of evening close,
> > Is scattered on the ground to die;
> Yet on that rose's humble bed
> The softest dews of night are shed;
> As if she wept such waste to see –
> But none shall drop a tear for me!

Although Wilde never published "Lament of the Captive," he gave copies to friends, and the poem quickly found its way into print as early as 1815 or 1816. There it took on a life of its own. An Irish poet named Patrick O'Kelly changed Wilde's reference to "Tampa's desert strand" into "Lehinch's desert strand" and claimed that he had written the poem "on the beautiful beach of Lehinch, in the county of Clare." A New York weekly, *The Catholic Register and Diary*, proudly announced that it wished "to pluck the stolen laurels from the Honorable Plagiarist of Georgia" and bestow them on O'Kelly. Wilde bore that accusation in silence, but he felt obliged to reply to an accusation arising from quite a different source. One day in 1834, Alexander Barclay, British consul to Savannah, entertained some American friends at his house. The subject of Wilde's alleged "plagiarism" came up. One of Barclay's guests, a local pastor, thought he remembered some Greek verses that resembled Wilde's poem. Later that evening, Barclay made a rough translation of Wilde's lines into Greek prose, arranging the phrases on the page to look like verses. He contrived that a manuscript of this Greek "original" should fall into the hands of the innocent pastor, who then announced confidently that "Lament of the Captive" was certainly a translation from Alcaeus. The pastor even submitted a copy of Barclay's translation to the President of the University of Georgia, who pronounced the Greek "pure and ancient." Wilde now found himself obliged to deny in public the charge of having plagiarized his best-known poem from a Greek source. He wrote a good-natured letter to Barclay, then in New York, explaining what had happened and asking him to acknowledge the authorship of the Greek version, if he were indeed its author. Barclay willingly acknowledged his authorship, and expressed surprise that his "crude translation" in prose could ever have been mistaken for verse. He regretted the "indiscreet publication" of his joke. The two letters were published in the *New-York Mirror* in 1835.

By the end of his final Congressional term Wilde had grown weary of political life. He decided to travel abroad, where he lived for the next six years, mostly in Florence. He had been interested in Romance literatures long before he emigrated to Italy. As Washington Allston had found inspiration in the figures and glazes of the fifteenth-century painters, Wilde found in the lyric poetry of Portugal, Spain, and above all Italy, the strength and sweetness he wished to impart to his own original poetry. He found the same qualities in the English poets of the sixteenth century. His translation of a sonnet by Camoëns, "They say the swan, though mute his whole life long," appeared over the name "Surrey" in the *Augusta Chronicle* on 12 November 1821. Surrey and Camoëns were contemporaries, but Wilde's choice of a pen name probably suggested a deeper sense of identification. (Later, in his long narrative poem, *Hesperia*, he would complain that American literature hadn't even had its Surrey yet – Surrey, the morning-star of English literature.)

While he lived in Florence, he devoted himself to the study of Italian literature. His only published work from the period was a scholarly study of Torquato Tasso's imprisonment (*Conjectures and Researches Concerning the Love, Madness, and Imprisonment of Torquato Tasso*, 2 vols., New York, 1842). He had also projected an ambitious work to be called *The Italian Lyric Poets*, containing short biographies and translations from a number of Italian lyric poets. He never finished the project, but the surviving manuscript shows that on occasion Wilde could be a translator of great skill. His translations of Petrarch and Tasso are perhaps his best. He was obviously attracted by the mixture of strength and passion the Italian poems displayed, but the poems he selected to translate also hint at another reason for his fascination with Italian literary culture. The very interconnectedness of the culture – where Dante invites Cavalcanti to sail away to an enchanted isle, where Tasso denounces Guarini, where Boccaccio mourns Petrarch's death, or writes a sonnet in which Dante is made to speak his own epitaph – had a powerful appeal to a poet whose contemporaries were strung out along a coastline that stretched a thousand miles. Wilde did make the acquaintance of prominent Americans like Edward Everett, Horatio Greenough, Henry Wadsworth Longfellow, but he met them in Italy, or as a result of friendships formed there.

When he returned to Augusta in 1841, he found that the plantation he owned was failing and that his chances of earning a living by practicing law in Augusta were slim. A New Orleans friend encouraged him to hope that opportunities would be better in Louisiana. Wilde moved to New Orleans in 1843, selling twenty-two of his slaves to finance the trip. There he practiced law and became a prominent citizen, helping to found the law school at Tulane University. But his fortunes declined towards the end of his life; and his few remaining slaves made what money they could for him during the day and slept on the floor of his law offices at night. In 1847 he succumbed to yellow fever, a common disease in mosquito-plagued New Orleans. He left behind the manuscript of a long poem entitled *Hesperia*. It consists of four cantos, each devoted to a different large region of the North American continent. (His son edited the poem and published it in 1867.) At least one passage seems to reflect the influence of Bryant:

> Across the Prairie's silent waste I stray,
> A fertile, verdant, woodless, boundless plain;
> Shadeless it lies beneath the glare of day,
> But gentle breezes sweep the grassy main,
> Over whose surface, as they rest or play,
> The waving billows sink or rise again;
> While some far distant lonely hut or tree
> Looms like a solitary sail at sea!
>
> (Canto IV)

Themes of exile are also prominent in the work of another Southern poet, Samuel Henry Dickson (1798–1872), a physician who made significant contributions to American medicine. Born in Charleston, South Carolina, he earned his bachelor's degree from Yale and his medical degree from the University of Pennsylvania. He helped to found the Medical College of South Carolina, and taught there from 1824 until 1858, when he moved to Philadelphia to accept a position at Jefferson Medical College. Thirty-four of his poems were collected in a privately printed volume in 1844. The next year his best-loved poem, "Song – Written at the North," was printed in William Gilmore Simms's anthology *The Charleston Book* (1845).

> I sigh for the land of Cypress and Pine,
> Where the Jessamine blooms, and the gay Woodbine;
> Where the moss droops low from the green Oak tree,
> Oh! that sunbright land is the land for me.
>
> . . .
>
> There the echoes ring through the livelong day,
> With the Mockbird's changeful roundelay,
> And at night when the scene is calm and still,
> With the moan of the plaintive Whip-poor-Will.

Dickson, like Bryant, uses trisyllabic feet with particular skill, balancing anapestic rhythms – "Where the Jessamine blows" – against lines full of accented monosyllables like "moss droops low" and "green Oak tree." Like

Wilde's "My Life is Like a Summer Rose," Dickson's poem was set to music and became well known as a song.

Dickson's fellow Charlestonian William Gilmore Simms (1806–70) was a prolific poet, novelist, and editor eager to foster Southern literature. In his *Charleston Miscellany* he printed an essay by Daniel K. Whittaker entitled "The Necessity of a Southern Literature," which argued that "the South as well as the North, belongs to the country, and the light of her genius and scholarship is yet to shed its rays, like the sun in the firmament, over every part of our wide-spread union." Some of his poems praise familiar forms of natural beauty, like the "lively Swanannoa," bounding like a schoolboy on its path beneath the silent mountains. Or else they sing the glories of the Southern climate, which rivals that of Italy or southern France: "Our skies look down in tenderness / From out their realms of blue." Such delicious softness and freshness persuades dwellers in Southern latitudes that "We have our Eden here." Of course Eden, we remember, hung far above a vast realm of darkness, a landscape of monstrosities that Milton's devils in *Paradise Lost* encounter on their exploring expedition:

> A Universe of death, which God by curse
> Created evil, for evil only good,
> Where all life dies, death lives, and nature breeds,
> Perverse, all monstrous, all prodigious things . . .

The Carolinian Eden also borders on such a realm, which Simms describes with relish in "The Edge of the Swamp." In this blighted spot no bird sings, and rank growths taint with poisonous dews the "thoughtless hand" that penetrates them.

> Wild, ragged trees,
> That look like felon spectres – fetid shrubs
> That taint the gloomy atmosphere – dusk shades,
> That gather, half a cloud, and half a fiend.

At the edge of the swamp is its bad eminence, the cayman, who

> Slumbers, half-buried in the sedgy grass.
> Beside the green ooze where he shelters him,
> A whooping crane erects his skeleton form,
> And shrieks in flight.

Startled by the presence of the travelers, the cayman "Crawls slowly to his slimy, green abode, / Which straightaway receives him." Only his head appears on the surface of the stream, but even that disappears when the cayman suddenly goes down, causing a startled butterfly who had lighted on his brow (as Milton's sailor moored in the side of Leviathan) to soil its bright wings in the fetid water. Wisely, the travelers decide to seek lodging among sweeter scenes.

Sometimes the conventional forms of Anglo-American verse were used by black Southerners who hoped to earn their freedom with their songs. George Moses Horton (1797?–1883?) was born a slave on the North Carolina tobacco farm of one William Horton. Early in life he learned to read and write, teaching himself on Sundays with the help of a tattered spelling book, reading by rushlight or barklight far into the night. In 1814 William Horton died, willing George to his son. George Moses Horton began taking long walks to the Chapel Hill campus of the University of North Carolina to sell fruit to the students, who soon discovered his accomplishments and urged him to deliver orations for them. Horton soon realized that a more profitable way of capitalizing on their interest in him was to sell them love-poems to give to their sweethearts; he charged twenty-five cents a verse. Now his education began in earnest. The students gave him books; the university President took an interest in him; the novelist Caroline Lee Hentz (a professor's wife) tutored him in prosody and transcribed his poems. As part of an effort to earn enough money to buy his freedom from a reluctant master, Horton's friends printed a small pamphlet of twenty-one poems entitled *The Hope of Liberty* in 1829. "The Slave's Complaint" sounds a good deal like one of Wilde's lyrics or translations from Tasso, but the "rugged tide" of misfortune it laments is real, and the bondage more than a pleasing fiction. In "On Hearing of the Intention of a Gentleman to Purchase the Poet's Freedom," Horton tells how he recovered his early delight in poetry when hearing that he might become free. His hopeless condition of bondage left him as silent as the Israelites in Babylon; now that freedom is near his song once again revives. In Psalm 137, "By the rivers of Babylon," the Israelites had hung their harps upon the willows rather than sing the song that their Babylonian masters ordered them to sing. Horton's tongue is unlocked by the promise of freedom, and the harp, taken down from the willows, is once more tuned:

> The silent harp which on the osiers hung,
> Was then attuned, and manumission sung;
> Away by hope the clouds of fear were driven,
> And music breathed my gratitude to Heaven.

But Horton's master was unwilling to sell, even when the Governor of North Carolina offered to buy the poet's freedom. Then a change in the political climate placed manumission even farther out of reach. Shortly after *The Hope of Liberty* appeared, Nat Turner's 1831 slave rebellion triggered a wave of repressive legislation that made manumission unpopular if not illegal. Horton worked at the university for another thirty years, not winning freedom until the Union troops occupied Raleigh in 1865. A sympathetic captain in the Union army helped the newly emancipated poet to publish a new collection of his poetry under the title *Naked Genius*. Some of the poems were taken from an intermediate volume Horton had published in 1845, but most were new. In the best of them, "George Moses Horton, Myself," he speaks wistfully of the cruel system that imprisoned his powers by keeping him away from the ancient wisdom he longed to possess:

> My genius from a boy,
> Has fluttered like a bird within my heart;
> But I could not thus confined her powers employ,
> Impatient to depart.

3

❦

TRANSCENDENTALISM

American poets who were born during the first two decades of the nineteenth century differ in certain ways from their slightly older compatriots, though they still had to earn their living in some other way than writing verse. The provincial backwardness of earlier decades began to dissipate; poetry published in the 1830s and 1840s increasingly showed the influence of Wordsworth and Tennyson as well as that of Thomson, Cowper, and Burns. If American poets were finally beginning to discover the writings of living English poets, they were also engaged in an earnest recovery of seventeenth-century English writing, which seemed to them to possess a vigor and morning freshness that later English writing had lost. The seventeenth-century poets were valuable both as models of style and character to American writers who felt out of place in a society devoted to money-making and untroubled by any consciousness of higher truths. Oliver Wendell Holmes called Emerson's 1837 Phi Beta Kappa Address at Harvard "America's declaration of literary independence." But Emerson's Address also contains this estimate of contemporary American society: "Public and private avarice make the air we breathe thick and fat. The scholar is decent, indolent, complaisant. See already the tragic consequence. The mind of this country taught to aim at low objects, eats upon itself." (Contemporary British society was little better, as Americans learned from reading Carlyle.) The young writers of New England turned to the English seventeenth century for better sources of inspiration. Emerson's favorites were Herbert, Milton, and Bacon, but he took pride in having introduced Margaret Fuller to a host of other seventeenth-century writers as well: Chapman, John Ford, Beaumont and Fletcher, and Sir Thomas Browne. Fuller herself translated the Latin poetry of Lord Herbert of Cherbury, George Herbert's older brother, and wrote an imaginary dialogue between the two concerning the relative merits of the active and contemplative life. Thoreau, who spent three years after he got out of college working on a planned history of English poetry, filled his notebook with quotations from masques of Ben Jonson and Thomas Carew, which he later wove into his *A Week on the Concord and Merrimack* (1849) and *Walden* (1854). The mystical sonnets of Jones Very recall both the *Silex Scintillans* of Vaughan and the Holy Sonnets of Donne.

This poetry of meditation, of religious intensity, suffused by a new appreciation of natural beauty, was written during a period that witnessed both the wild efflorescence of utopian hopes and the growing bitterness of sectional strife. Beginning with the debate over the annexation of Texas, growing more intense during the Mexican War, erupting into open hatred with the passage of the Fugitive Slave Law in 1850, writers began to caricature one another with a vitriol ordinarily reserved for hereditary enemies. In Northern poems we meet the planter with his bloodstained lash; in Southern poems we meet the Northern hypocrite who bewails the wickedness of slavery while he lets his ragged factory workers starve. Should poets take part in this battle? Or would poetry be ruined by being dragged down into an arena dominated by "the priest's cant / And the statesman's rant," as Emerson warned? Poetry devoted to inwardness and beauty risked sounding irrelevant in a political climate marked by violence and hatred; on the other hand, newspaper verses about the latest political outrage or human atrocity seemed to participate in the ugliness they mocked. In happier times Drake and Halleck could switch back and forth between comic and serious verse at will. But as the middle of the century approached, any decision about what kind of poetry to write could leave poets feeling chagrined. Popular satirists and political writers knew that their poems were by definition ephemeral, very far from the solid "tower of song with lofty parapet" that Longfellow admitted he once hoped to build. Serious narratives and lyrics, on the other hand, seemed to offer readers only the contemptible pleasures of escape. Fortunately, the poets who wrote during the middle decades of the century were not always plagued by scruples; there are sunny and peaceful poems as well as sad or anguished ones. But the poetry of the period is often haunted by a melancholy its authors were themselves hard pressed to explain.

The century had begun in hope, not in doubt or despair. At the age of eleven Ralph Waldo Emerson (1803–82) wrote a hymn in tetrameter couplets that combines praise of God with delight in the soul's centrality:

> My soul O look around and see
> How many things are made for thee
> For thee the fields are cover'd o'er,
> For thee the harvest yields its store,
>
> . . . .
>
> God's praise is sung by every rill
> O then let not my tongue be still.

Praise for such efforts left him with an abiding wish to be a poet. In his senior year at Harvard he entered a competition with a poem in pentameter couplets on the assigned theme of "Indian Superstition." The poem he produced was a dutiful specimen of what might be called Gothic Orientalism, with hideous idols, the temple of Juggernaut (where the vultures, reported one traveler, were "shockingly tame"), and suttee. Still, the exercise (besides winning him ten dollars) got him to read Teignmouth's *Life of Sir William Jones* and Robert Southey's *The Curse of Kehama*. Southey's epic about a virtuous man laid under a curse that water should never flow to him, nor fire burn him, impressed Emerson so deeply that in "Experience" (1844) he made the ill-fated Indian "a type of us all." And in the long quotations from the *Bhagavadgita* quoted in Southey's learned footnotes he discovered an alternative to the dualistic theology of the West. Another Indian tradition that impressed him, or so he wrote in his journal, was the doctrine of "Eye-fascination." He used the word to explain his attraction to one Martin Gay, a young man his own age who entered Harvard's freshman class when Emerson was a junior. In a manuscript poem headed "Dedication," whose Virgilian epigraph expresses longing more openly than does the poem itself ("Quem fugit? Aut te nostris complexibus arcet?"), he recalls meeting the young man's "cold encountering eyes" for an exchange of "deeply thrilling" glances, and offers his own dedication in lines more glowing than grammatical:

> By all which you have felt and feel
> My eager gaze returning
> I offer to this silent zeal
> On youthful altars burning.
> (*Journals*, 19 November 1821)

He never actually worked up the courage to exchange more than a dozen words with Gay, and their meetings on campus turned into an elaborate dance of "chance" near-meetings and last-minute evasions. The seventeen-year-old Emerson could see that his fascination grew as much out of imagination as of desire. In a passage full of cancellations, with a blank space left for the name of the friend, he admitted:

Before I ever saw him, I wished my *friend* to be different from any individual I had seen. I invested him with a solemn cast of mind, full of poetic feeling, & an idolater of friendship, & possessing a vein of rich sober thought. When I saw [   ]'s pale but expressive face & large eye, I instantly invested him with the complete character which fancy had formed.

He would later note in himself "a fondness for particular casts of feature perchance like the doting of old King James" whose serial infatuations with male favorites had brought "misery to self & seed." This tendency to invest new friends with imagined perfections continued to mark Emerson's relationships later in life.

After Emerson's death in 1882 one of his closest friends, Samuel Gray Ward, explained to James Elliot Cabot why he had preferred to keep some distance from Emerson, although they maintained a long and intimate correspondence: "He carried me off my feet & absorbed me to such an extent that had I been much with him I could not have lived my own life . . . & you know the passion of friendship with which he idealized the latent abilities of his young men."

Life after Harvard turned Emerson into a "hopeless Schoolmaster," toiling at a profession in which he had no interest and little skill. Ill health plagued him; poverty and the awkwardness it brought made him feel farther than ever from the fame he wanted to win. He finally began study at Harvard's new Divinity School, only to have his course of study interrupted by eye trouble; his Aunt Mary Moody Emerson tried to console him by reminding him that blindness might make him another Milton. When he had finished his course of studies and was approbated to preach, he developed both a rheumatic hip and alarming symptoms of pulmonary disease. A sympathetic uncle gave him the money for a trip southward, first to Charleston, then to St. Augustine. The blank-verse poem he wrote, however, makes the voyage sound like an expedition rather than an invalid's retreat.

> For fifteen winter days
> I sailed upon the deep, & turned my back
> Upon the Northern lights, & burning Bear,
> On the twin Bears fast tethered to the Pole
> And the cold orbs that hang by them in heaven,
> Till star by star they sank into the sea.
>   ("St. Augustine")

In the city of "orange groves & citron bowers" even the "rude sea" is friendly, "and pours warm billows up the beach of shells." But grateful as Emerson was for St. Augustine's healing warmth, he was eager to return to New England and to the clerical career that awaited him if his health permitted it. When he returned he traveled first to his family's ancestral village, Concord. He spent most of the summer weekdays there; on Sundays he preached in various western Massachusetts towns. The blank-verse poem he wrote to celebrate his return testifies to his sense of growth and loss at once. "Awed I behold once more / My old familiar haunts," he begins, marveling that the same Concord stream he admired as a child should still be here: "Look, here he is unaltered, save that now / He hath broke his banks & flooded all the vales / With his redundant waves." That the quiet Concord River (or Musketaquid, to use the Indian name Emerson later favored) should have broken its banks to flood the surrounding valleys seems an image of power. But the unchanging landscape, with its rocks, flowers, fields, and overhanging boughs serves only to remind him of his mortality.

> They know me as their son, for side by side,
> They were coeval with my ancestors,
> Adorned with them my country's primitive times,
> And soon may give my dust their funeral shade.

This poem is significant not only because it reveals Emerson's attachment to the village he would one day make his home. It also reveals his growing fascination with Wordsworth, of whom he had not always been an admirer. "I have thirsted lately to abuse the poetical character of Mr. Wordsworth whose poems have just been read to me," he wrote while he was in college. "He is the poet of pismires. His inspirations are spent light." Wordsworth, unlike Byron, had confused faithfulness to nature with "mere fidelity of representation." Still, certain lines from Wordsworth began to haunt Emerson, and by 1824 he filled several pages of his journal with quotations from a four-volume edition of *The Poetical Works of William Wordsworth* (1824) recently published in Boston. At this point he seemed chiefly attracted to the spiritually elevated Wordsworth — to the Immortality Ode, "Lines: Left upon a Seat in a Yew-Tree," "Dion," and *The White Doe of Rylestone*. The publication in 1831 of James Marsh's American edition of Coleridge's *The Friend*, with its quotations from Wordworth's unpublished poem on his own life, introduced Emerson to a new side of Wordsworth. The poet's ability to make everyday occurrences the symbol of his thought and his dogged refusal to conform to anyone else's notions of style now won Emerson's frank admiration. Of the ice-skating scene (later published in Book 1 of the *Prelude*) he wrote: "How much self reliance it implies to write a true description of anything[.] For example Wordsworth's picture of skating; that leaning back on your heels & stopping in mid-career. So simple a fact no common man would have trusted himself to detach as a thought."

On Christmas Day 1827 Emerson met Ellen Tucker, the pretty young stepsister of a Harvard friend who had invited him to preach in Concord, New Hampshire. Emerson was still only a candidate for the ministry, preaching in towns all over New England, waiting for his sermon-barrel to fill. His health was far from robust. Still, his prospects at Boston's prestigious Second Church, where he had preached on several occasions, looked promising. In December 1828 he became engaged to Ellen. The following March he was ordained as junior pastor at the Second Church; in July became its pastor at the very generous salary of $1,200 a year. He married Ellen in September 1829. When he had announced his engagement to his brother William he wrote that he was "now as happy as it is safe in life to be." For a time the young couple was indeed happy. But even before her marriage Ellen had shown symptoms of tuberculosis, and after a new onset of the illness her decline was rapid. On 8 February 1831 she died in their house in Boston. She was nineteen when she died; he was twenty-seven. Despite her promises to remain with him in spirit, which had sustained him through the first weeks of mourning, he felt increasingly bereft. The poems he tried to write to her trailed off into terrible cries of pain.

He distracted himself by reading new books – a lifelong pattern that explains why major intellectual expansions in his life so often followed personal losses. He began Victor Cousin's *Cours de l'histoire de la philosophie*, whose sympathetic treatment of Indian philosophy and religion gave him far better knowledge than he had acquired while doing hurried research for "Indian Superstition." His dissatisfaction with the Unitarian church, and with Christianity itself, had been growing for some time. Christianity erred by looking for God everywhere but in the soul – in a heaven, or in the Scriptures, or in the miracles performed by Jesus. Far better was a religion founded on immanence and intuitive certainty, as in this passage from the *Bhagavadgita*: "The soul itself is its own witness; the soul itself it its own refuge; offend not thy conscious soul, the supreme internal witness of men!" Again: "O friend to virtue! that supreme Spirit, which thou believest one and the same with thyself, resides in thy bosom perpetually, and is an all-knowing inspector of thy goodness or thy wickedness."

In July 1831 he wrote an irregular poem in his journal celebrating the dawning of a new sense of conviction within him. He called it "*Gnothi Seauton*." It is an exhortation to himself (and to his reader) to discover the "clouded & shrouded" form of "the Infinite" who dwells in every person:

> If thou canst bear
> Strong meat of simple truth
> If thou durst my words compare
> With what thou thinkest in the soul's free youth
> Then take this fact unto thy soul –
> God dwells in thee.–

. . .

> Thou art the *law*;
> The *gospel* has no revelation
> Of peace or hope until there is response
> From the deep chambers of thy mind thereto

In the radiance of this vision the whole world hastens back to its divine source:

> There is nothing else but God
> Where e'er I look
> All things hasten back to him
> Light is but his shadow dim

He resigned his pastorate at the Second Church the following year. After a year of travel abroad to recover from an illness that had debilitated him, he returned to take up a profession newly made available by the rapid growth of an adult education movment in the United States: lyceum lecturer. He still preached in Unitarian pulpits as a "supply" preacher, but increasingly he saw himself as an explorer of the universe for the secular congregations of the country lyceum or city lecture hall. This new freedom was exhilarating, yet at the same time it made him aware how much he owed to the discipline his upbringing had instilled in him. In a short poem entitled "Grace" he pays tribute to the forces of restraint whose overthrow he had recently been preaching. In form and tone it recalls the poetry of George Herbert, Emerson's favorite among the seventeenth-century poets.

> How much, Preventing God! how much I owe
> To the defenses thou hast round me set:
> Example, custom, fear, occasion slow, –
> These scorned bonsdmen were my parapet.
> I dare not peep over this parapet
> To gauge with glance the roaring gulf below,
> The depths of sin to which I had descended,
> Had not these me against myself defended.

In 1834 Emerson moved to Concord, whose rural beauties he quickly learned to celebrate. "The Rhodora" describes the sudden meeting of poet and wild-flower in a damp nook where "The purple petals, fallen in the pool, / Made the black water with their beauty gay." If the rhodora should be asked to explain why she wastes her beauty on a spot where few can see it, the poet tells the flower to reply that "Beauty is its own excuse for being." Concord's winter landscape was as beautiful for its concealments as its springtime ponds were for their revelations. In "The Snow-Storm" Emerson celebrates the artistry of a New England blizzard, which first "veils the farm-house at the garden's end" in "whited air," then imposes its own absolute rule upon the human inhabitants of the village:

> The shed and traveler stopped, the courier's feet
> Delayed, all friends shut out, the housemates sit
> Around the radiant fireplace, enclosed
> In a tumultuous privacy of storm.

The next morning the housemates awake to a landscape transformed:

> Come see the north wind's masonry.
> Out of an unseen quarry evermore.
>
> . . .
>
> Furnished with tile, the fierce artificer
> Curves his white bastions with projected roof
> Round every windward stake, or tree, or door.

With a kind of mockery, the snow-storm decks a coop or kennel with a wreath of purest marble, makes a thorn-bush into a swan, fills up the lane from wall to wall, and then miraculously vanishes, leaving

> . . . astonished Art
> To mimic in slow structures, stone by stone,
> Built in an age, the mad wind's night-work,
> The frolic architecture of the snow.

In 1835 Emerson proposed marriage to Lydia Jackson, a woman he had met when he lectured in her home town of Plymouth. She was reluctant to leave her home and friends, but he quietly declared his attachment to Concord in a letter he sent shortly after they became engaged. "Under this morning's severe yet beautiful light I thought dear friend that hardly should I get away from Concord. I must win you to love it." And he added:

I am born a poet, of a low class without doubt yet a poet. That is my nature & vocation. My singing be sure is very "husky," & is for the most part in prose. Still I am a poet in the sense of a perceiver & dear lover of the harmonies that are in the soul & in matter, & specially of the correspondences between these & those. A sunset, a forest, a snow storm, a certain river-view, are more to me than many friends & do ordinarily divide my day with my books. Wherever I go therefore I guard my study & my rambling propensities with a care that is ridiculous to people, but to me is the care of my high calling.

He bought a house on the outskirts of Concord, whose citizens asked him to deliver an oration at the town's bicentennial celebration on 12 September 1835. The long and carefully researched "Historical Discourse" Emerson prepared for the occasion traced the settlement from its origins all the way up to the

Concord Fight of 19 April 1775. A few aged veterans of that fight were present to hear his thanks for having secured the liberties that everyone in the country now enjoyed. Yet their frailty also reminded everyone that the Revolutionary generation was quickly passing away. To preserve the memory a little longer was the aim of the Battle Monument dedicated on 4 July 1837. Emerson had promised to write a hymn for the occasion, though he could not be on hand to hear it sung. "Hymn Sung at the Completion of the Concord Monument," now known as the "Concord Hymn," contains the most famous stanza he ever wrote:

> By the rude bridge that arched the flood,
> Their flag to April's green unfurled,
> Here once th'embattled farmers stood,
> And fired the shot heard round the world.

People who know only the poem's first stanza are likely to be surprised at the quiet stanzas that follow, which emphasize not man's defiance but time's victory:

> The foe long since in silence slept,
> Alike the conqueror silent sleeps,
> And time the ruined bridge hath swept
> Down the dark stream that seaward creeps.

The Battle Monument offers a momentary stay against oblivion. Yet it too is subject to the same forces that have swept away the ruined bridge. Emerson closes his hymn with a prayer to the only force that can outlive time and change:

> Spirit, that made these heroes dare
> To die and leave their children free,
> Bid time and nature gently spare,
> The shaft we raise to them and thee.

Between 1836 and 1850 Emerson was chiefly engaged in writing the public addresses and books of essays that made him famous. Nearly every winter he delivered a new course of lectures, then later incorporated parts of the lectures into published books. During these years his major published books and addresses included *Nature* (1836); "The American Scholar" (1837); the Divinity School Address (1838); *Essays* (1841); *Essays: Second Series* (1844); "Emancipation in the British West Indies" (1844); and *Representative Men* (1850). He gave courses of lectures on "The Philosophy of History" (1836–7); "Human Culture" (1837–8); "Human Life" (1838–9); "The Present Age" (1839–40); "The Times" (1841–2); "New England" (1843–4);

"Representative Men" (1845–6); and "Mind and Manners of the Nineteenth Century" (1848–9).

Throughout these busy years he continued to write poetry. The Boston edition of his *Poems* was published on Christmas Day in 1846; a London edition appeared soon after. The book contained fifty-seven original poems and two translations from Hafiz, the fourteenth-century Persian poet whose works (in a two-volume German translation) Emerson had discovered that spring in Elizabeth Peabody's bookstore. *Poems* began with the notoriously inscrutable poem "The Sphinx" and ended with the Concord Hymn – as if he had decided to winnow his potential readers first and reward them with familiar material only after they had proved their hardihood.

Emerson experimented with different meters and poetic forms throughout the volume, which included poems written as long ago as the early 1830s and as recently as summer 1846. A number of short love poems in rhymed stanzas were written to his first wife, Ellen. In "Thine Eyes Still Shined," the lover finds his beloved's presence everywhere, in the mist and dew of a hillside or a startling flash of color: "When the redbird spread his sable wing / And showed his side of flame." The lover of "The Amulet" first playfully wishes for love-tokens that might "keep intelligence" with the beloved's changing moods, and not, like her picture and letter, keep saying the same thing over and over. The final stanza then lets us glimpse the insecurity that really lies behind the lover's request:

> Alas! that neither bonds nor vows
> Can certify possession;
> Torments me still the fear that love
> Died in its last expression.

In a poem entitled "The House," Emerson anticipates Emily Dickinson's poems-about-poetry. "The House" represents the Muse as an architect who searches through continents for everlasting materials to frame her everlasting structures:

> Slow and warily to choose
> Rafters of immortal pine,
> Or cedar incorruptible,
> Worthy her design.
>   . . .
> She ransacks mines and ledges
> And quarries every rock,
> To hew the famous adamant
> For each eternal block.

Other poems in the 1846 volume were written in blank-verse lines or pentameter couplets. Emerson included his early poems "The Rhodora" and "The Snow-Storm" and added to them several interesting new experiments. The speaker of "Xenophanes" (one of Emerson's favorite pre-Socratic philosophers) complains that Nature's wealth of individual objects conceals a monotonous sameness. But he draws from this evidence of replication a faith in the dialectical method: "To know one element, explore another, / And in the second reappears the first." In "Blight" Emerson laments the replacement of an older, generous, unity-seeking science by the confident young scholars who give Latin names to the plants they pluck but never discover their "sweet affinities to human flesh." The aggressive gaze we turn on nature makes the very elements reject us: "And haughtily return us stare for stare."

> Therefore to our sick eyes,
> The stunted trees look sick, the summer short,
> Clouds shade the sun, which will not tan our hay,
> And nothing strives to reach its natural term.

Immediately following "Blight," and clearly intended as its antidote, is "Musketaquid," Emerson's affectionate tribute to the notoriously slow-flowing Concord River and to the leisurely life he lives by its banks:

> Because I was content with these poor fields,
> Low, open meads, slender and sluggish streams,
> And found a home in haunts which others scorned,
> The partial wood-gods overpaid my love,
> And granted me the freedom of their state.

The moon and planets shoot rays of thought and tenderness through his solitude; the chilly glories of a New England spring surround him:

> For me, in showers, in sweeping showers, the spring
> Visits the valley; – break away the clouds, –
> I bathe in morning's soft and silvered air.

His own garden teaches him to be happy with little, for "the cordial quality of pear or plum" ascends in a single tree as happily as "in broad orchards resonant with bees." Best of all is the sense of "true liberty" he finds "in the glad home plain-dealing nature gave."

The poem "Hamatreya" contains Emerson's version of a dialogue between Vishnu and Maitreya in the *Vishnu Purana*, in which Vishnu repeats the chants of the earth triumphing over the greed and folly of princes. In Emerson's version the princes have become Concord farmers – "Minott, Lee, Willard, Hosmer, Meriam, Flint" – whose names, monosyllabic or accented on the first syllable, dig into the iambic line like so many plowshares. The crops they proudly raise have names just as blunt: "Hay, corn, roots, hemp, flax, apples, wool, and wood." Yet these homely Saxon farmers become lyrical when they chant the joys of possession they believe themselves to enjoy:

> "How sweet the west wind sounds in my own trees!
> How graceful climb those shadows on my hill!
> I fancy these pure waters and the flags
> Know me, as does my dog; we sympathize;
> And, I affirm, my actions smack of the soil."

But the self-satisfied farmers are deaf to the "Earth-Song" of the ineluctable goddess who lies in wait for them:

> Earth laughs in flowers, to see her boastful boys
> Earth-proud, proud of the earth which is not theirs;
> Who steer the plough, but cannot steer their feet
> Clear of the grave.

The earth's song is written in short lines that sound like charms or runes:

> Mine and yours;
> Mine, not yours.
> Earth endures;
> Stars abide –
> Shine down in the old sea.

The earth remains, but farmers, lawyers, and heirs have all vanished, swept clean from the landscape "like the flood's foam." At the conclusion of the "Earth-Song" Emerson attaches four lines of his own, in tone neither quite like the sympathetic ironies of the blank-verse narrative nor the eerie menace of the "Earth-Song":

> When I heard the Earth-song,
> I was no longer brave;
> My avarice cooled
> Like lust in the chill of the grave.

Emerson rarely convicted himself of deadly sins: "If I am the Devil's child, I will live from the Devil," he says in "Self-Reliance." Yet here the traditional language is accurate. Unlike ordinary lust, land-fever does not wane with age – indeed, the traditional avarice of old age only increases a man's hunger for land. "Hamatreya" reminds us that the boldest buyer of real estate will find himself at last asleep beneath his grounds, while a stranger plows new furrows over him.

The irregular lines of the "Earth-Song" link it to another group of important poems: "The Sphinx," "Bacchus," "Saadi," the two "Merlin" poems, and the "Ode: Inscribed to W. H. Channing." The verse-paragraphs of these poems contain lines of varying lengths (tetrameter, trimeter, dimeter, even monometer), usually iambic, though sometimes headless and hence trochaic in effect. The poems rhyme, though the rhyme scheme that obtains in one verse-paragraph may be discarded by the next. That Emerson cast some of his most important poetic, political, and theological statements in this verse form indicates that he found it suppler and more expressive than either regular stanzaic poetry or blank verse.

"The Sphinx," which sits at the entrance to Emerson's *Poems* challenging brave readers to solve its riddle, is the most regular of these poems. Fourteen of its seventeen eight-line stanzas are written in iambic-anapestic dimeter; the remaining three stanzas and the four-line coda are trimeter lines.

> The fiend that man harries
>   Is the love of the Best;
> Yawns the pit of the Dragon,
>   Lit by rays from the Blest.
> The Lethe of nature
>   Can't trance him again,
> Whose soul seeks the perfect,
>   Which his eyes seek in vain.

The riddle of the Sphinx, as the earlier stanzas have told us, is man's apparent exclusion from the universal happiness of nature. But as this stanza makes clear, the poet answers the Sphinx by asserting that what harries man is his "love of the Best." The hunger for perfection will, it is true, keep human beings permanently discontented: "Have I a lover / Who is noble and free? — / I would he were nobler / Than to love me." But it also means that the ceaseless alternation of joy and sorrow in life is part of Love's plan: "Eterne alternation / Now follows, now flies; / Under pain, pleasure, — / Under pleasure, pain lies." However unhappy we are, we remain convinced that "Love works at the centre" of this universe of change, sending its "strong pulses / To the border of day." The Sphinx's response to this expression of contempt for her riddle is unexpected: instead of precipitating herself down the slope to her death (like the Sphinx whose riddle Oedipus solved) she suddenly assumes a thousand beautiful shapes:

> Uprose the merry Sphinx,
>   And crouched no more in stone;
> She melted into purple cloud,
>   She silvered in the moon;
> She spired into a yellow flame;
>   She flowered in blossoms red;
> She flowed into a foaming wave;
>   She stood Monadnoc's head.

She leaves us with this final message: "Who telleth one of my meanings, / Is master of all that I am."

Many of the poems named after mythological, legendary, or historical characters – "Bacchus," "Saadi," and "Merlin" – concern the writing of poetry. "Bacchus" links the writing of poetry to divine intoxication.

> Bring me wine, but wine which never grew
> In the belly of the grape,
> Or grew on vine whose tap-roots, reaching through
> Under the Andes to the Cape,
> Suffered no savor of the earth to scape.
>   . . .
> Wine that is shed
> Like the torrents of the sun
> Up the horizon walls,
> Or like the Atlantic streams, which run
> When the South Sea calls.

So inspired, the poet will leave behind the ashes and diluted wine his culture offers in place of true sustenance. The poem closes with a formal invocation to the god, asking for a renovation in which nature herself might share:

> Pour, Bacchus! the remembering wine;
> Retrieve the loss of me and mine!
>   . . .
> Refresh the faded tints,
> Recut the aged prints,
> And write my old adventures with the pen
> Which on the first day drew,
> Upon the tablets blue,
> The dancing Pleiads and eternal men.

The seven Pleiades, daughters of Atlas and Pleïone, are transformed into a constellation with one "invisible" star: Merope, who hid her light in shame at having given her love to a mortal man. The myth of the missing Pleiad appealed to Emerson, for whom it symbolized the loss of mental powers. "Every poet has on the hills counted the Pleiads, & mourned his lost star. Ah the decays of memory, of fancy, of the saliency of thought!"

Were there ways of obtaining access to lost inspiration? In April 1846 Emerson had bought a copy of Joseph von Hammer's two-volume German edition of the Persian poet Hafiz: *Der Diwan von Mohammed Schemsed-din Hafis* (1812–13). Soon he was fascinated with the fourteenth-century mystical poet. He began to translate into English von Hammer's German translations from the Persian, eventually filling a 250-page notebook with translations from Hafiz and other poets he discovered in von Hammer's history of Persian poetry (*Geschichte der schönen Redekünste Persiens*, 1818). Two of these translations appeared in his 1847 *Poems*. Like the poet of "Bacchus," Emerson's Hafiz is a seeker of inspiration and visionary power:

> Butler, fetch the ruby wine
> Which with sudden greatness fills us;
> Pour for me, who in my spirit
> Fail in courage and performance.
>   . . .
> Haste, that by thy means I open
> All the doors of luck and life.
> Bring to me the liquid fire
> Zoroaster sought in dust:
>   . . .
> Bring it me, that through its force
> I, as Jamschid, see through worlds.
>   ("From the Persian of Hafiz")

Jamschid, a mythical king of Persia, possessed a magic cup that reflected the whole world in its depths; in Emerson's rendering he becomes a type of the poet who (as he says in the essay "Poetry and Imagination") "turns the world to glass, and shows us things in their right series and progression." Another Persian poet, Saadi, earns Emerson's praise for resolutely declining to drink the wormwood offered him by the "sad-eyed Fakirs" who sing "endless dirges to decay," instead preferring the wisdom that comes from joy: "Sunshine in his heart transferred / Lighted each transparent word" ("Saadi").

Emerson's two poems about Merlin, the powerful magician of King Arthur's court, are darker in mood than his Persian poems. They express a desire to assert individuality rather than dissipate it into ecstasies or absorb it into the natural world. The magician of the first "Merlin" poem wants to strike blows of fate with his rhymes, which should chime "with the gasp and moan / Of the ice-imprisoned flood" and resound with the "cannonade of wars." Yet Merlin's

powerful rhymes still require the kind of self-abandonment that Hafiz sought
in his drafts of mystical wine:

> Pass in, pass in, the angels say,
> In to the upper doors,
> Nor count compartments of the floors
> But mount to paradise
> By the stairway of surprise.

Even in these hymns to wild freedom Emerson's mythic bards never completely
forgo meter and rhyme, though his delighted response to Whitman's 1855
Leaves of Grass shows that he was perfectly willing to see someone else do so.
Rhyme for Emerson had metaphysical meanings, for (as the second "Merlin"
poem explains) "balance-loving Nature / Made all things in pairs." The universe
itself is symmetrical: "Perfect-paired as eagle's wings, / Justice is the rhyme
of things." Even Nemesis is a god of rhyme and symmetry: he sends to the
wrongdoer a punishment that "fills the just period / And finishes the song."

"Uriel" resembles the other mythological poems in general style, though
after its introductory quatrain it is written in regular tetrameter couplets.
Uriel, the archangel whom Milton's Satan saw standing in the sun, becomes
in Emerson's poem an angel who makes the mistake of speaking his mind.
As the "young deities" of heaven discuss "Laws of form, and metre just, /
Orb, quintessence, and sunbeams, / What subsisteth, and what seems," Uriel
interposes his own opinion:

> Line in nature is not found;
> Unit and universe are round;
> In vain produced, all rays return;
> Evil will bless, and ice will burn.

The notion that no good is without unintended consequences and no evil
without benefits (the message of Emerson's essay "Compensation") threatens
to confound traditional schemes of eternal punishment and reward.

> Seemed to the holy festival
> The rash word boded ill to all;
> The balance-beam of Fate was bent;
> The bounds of good and ill were rent.

The "stern old war-gods" shake their heads while all slides to confusion around
them. But Uriel, the instigator of all this woe, is damaged by the chaos he has
unleashed:

> A sad self-knowledge, withering, fell
> On the beauty of Uriel;

> In heaven once eminent, the god
> Withdrew, that hour, into his cloud.

Uriel's truth-telling "voice of cherub scorn" now reaches us only from the swift changes of the natural world: "shrilling from the solar course, / Or from fruit of chemic force." This voice of "cherub scorn," however hidden or disguised, still has power to make the clouds blush and the old war-gods shake on their thrones. If "Uriel" is, as most commentators think, an allegory of Emerson's response to the controversy that followed his Divinity School Address, it expresses both defiance and loss. Like his own Uriel, Emerson never recanted, but the "sad self-knowledge" he has acquired ended the fine innocence that allowed him to speak without awareness of consequences.

As its title suggests, the "Ode: Inscribed to W. H. Channing" is meant to recall the English Pindaric odes of the seventeenth and eighteenth centuries, with their rapid shifts of tone and mood. The Ode refers to a specific event: the beginning of the Mexican War, which Emerson (like the abolitionist minister to whom the Ode is inscribed), regarded as a slaveholder's war of aggression. "Behold the famous States / Harrying Mexico / With rifle and with knife!" Yet Emerson cannot agree with W. H. Channing and the Garrisonian abolitionists that the free states should secede from the slave states, though his reluctance has nothing to do with sentimental attachment to the Union. Instead it stems from a cynical assurance that even in a Northern confederation purged from the taint of slavery, "Boston Bay and Bunker Hill / Would serve things still; — Things are of the snake."

> 'Tis the day of the chattel,
> Web to weave and corn to grind;
> Things are in the saddle,
> And ride mankind.

Rather than trying to meddle with events, the wise will leave these problems to be solved by an "over-god" who behaves like the Nemesis of "Merlin" (II).

> Sex to sex, and even to odd; —
> The over-god
> Who marries Right to Might,
> Who peoples, unpeoples, —
> He who exterminates
> Races by stronger races,
> Black by white faces, —
> Knows how to bring honey
> Out of the lion;
> Grafts gentlest scion
> On pirate and Turk.

Are these lines an apology for genocide or a defense of miscegenation? Emerson's increasingly desperate hope in 1846 was that the over-god would find some way to bring honey out of the carcass of history, but he was certain than the process would be bloodier than pacifists like Channing imagined and hoped.

Most of the remaining poems in the 1846 volume are rambling collections of tetrameter couplets, a form for which Emerson lacked the necessary fluency. But on occasion he could achieve eloquence even here. The final lines of "The Visit," where an impatient host wishes he could get rid of a caller, end in a memorable distich: "If Love his moment overstay, / Hatred's swift repulsions play." And lines from "The Problem" about the faith that inspired the great Christian churches recall the great seventeenth-century masters Emerson admired: Milton, Jonson, Marvell.

> The hand that rounded Peter's dome,
> And groined the aisles of Christian Rome,
> Wrought in a sad sincerity;
> Himself from God he could not free;
> He builded better than he knew; –
> The conscious stone to beauty grew.

The penultimate poem in the 1846 volume was "Threnody," Emerson's elegy for his first-born son, who had died in 1842. The poem combines passages of varying line-lengths with long stretches of tetrameter couplets. Expressions of grief are given lines of varying lengths:

> O child of paradise,
> Boy who made dear his father's home
> In whose deep eyes
> Men read the welfare of the times to come,
> I am too much bereft.

The "deep Heart," on the other hand, rebukes Emerson's sorrow in relentless tetrameter couplets: The Heart reminds him: "I taught thy heart beyond the reach / Of ritual, bible, or of speech." Will he now repay the loan of this small Messiah with "the blasphemy of grief"? The Maker's world is always transitory.

> "Not of adamant and gold
> Built he heaven stark and cold;
> No, but a nest of bending reeds,
> Flowering grass and scented weeds;
> Or like a traveller's fleeing tent,
> Or bow above the tempest bent."

The rushing Lord plants the seeds of worlds to come amid the "ruined systems" of mortal lives and loves. "House and tenant go to ground, / Lost in God, in Godhead found."

Emerson continued to write and publish poetry throughout the 1840s and 1850s, although he would not publish another complete volume of poems until *May-Day and Other Pieces* in 1867. He had begun to write verse mottoes for individual essays in 1844, with the publication of *Essays: Second Series*. He wrote mottoes for an 1847 reprint of his 1841 *Essays* as well as for the essays in the 1860 book, *The Conduct of Life*. These mottoes have the kind of gnomic compression he had come to esteem in the Persian poetry of Hafiz. Affixed to one of the essays, they allowed Emerson to play both roles: oracle and interpreter. He included thirteen of these mottoes in *May-Day and Other Pieces* (1867). The first of a pair of mottoes written for "Compensation" (*Essays: First Series*) reminds us that natural objects obey the same economic laws that torment human beings:

> Mountain tall and ocean deep
> Trembling balance duly keep.
> In changing moon and tidal wave
> Glows the feud of Want and Have.

The second motto whispers encouragement to a human subject who needs to be reminded wealth and success will cleave to enterprise as vine clings to elm: "Man's the elm, and Wealth, the vine; / Stanch and strong the tendrils twine." Yet all this wealth cannot purchase happiness for an individual or for a state, as the motto to "Politics" warns, "Fear, Craft, and Avarice / Cannot rear a State."

The politicians at Washington whose greed for land had led to the Mexican War paid little heed to Emerson's warnings, and even before the war was over they were quarreling about whether slavery would be prohibited in the territory they hoped to detach from Mexico. Proposing to tear land from another country and then infecting it with slavery seemed to bring American politics to a new low. After writing a couplet that would become part of a new manuscript poem in his poetry notebooks – "As the bird trims himself to the gale / So I trim myself to the tempest of time" – Emerson followed it with a clause in prose, as if his disgust were too great to wait for the inspiration of rhyme and meter. He wrote: "And I shall find something pleasant in my last throb that I am getting out of mean politics." The new poem he was working on would eventually be published as "Terminus" in the January 1867 issue of *The Atlantic Monthly* and subsequently reprinted in *May-Day*. The drafts of "Terminus" are sandwiched in between drafts of poems sent to the publisher between 1846 and 1850, and the first lines of "Terminus" follow immediately after the only manuscript copy we have of the poem "Bacchus" (published in 1846). In other words, Emerson's well-known poem about old age may have been begun when he was only forty-three. "Bacchus" had called for renovation through ecstasy; in "Terminus" Emerson receives a command from a different god:

> It is time to be old,
> To take in sail: –
> The god of bounds,
> Who sets to seas a shore,
> Came to me in his fatal rounds,
> And said: "No more!"

The poet's failing life-force must now be husbanded. Resentfully, the poet first blames his ancestors, who have left him with "a legacy of ebbing veins, / Inconstant heat and nerveless reins" and thus rendered him unfit for either poetry or politics: "Amid the Muses, left thee deaf and dumb, / Amid the gladiators, halt and numb."

Emerson's sense of frustration at having to stand on the sidelines grew as gladiators better fitted by nature for public strife bowed down before iniquity. In the summer of 1852 he wrote in his journal an angry epigram about Daniel Webster, once his hero, now an enthusiastic supporter of the Fugitive Slave Law: "Why did all manly gifts in Webster fail? / He wrote on Nature's grandest brow, For Sale." Bostonians who defended Webster came in for similar ridicule. In a scrap of manuscript verse from the 1850s Emerson addressed his native city this way:

> O Boston city lecture-hearing,
> O unitarian God-fearing.
> But more, I fear, bad men-revering;
>
> . . .
> Thy fault is much civility,
> Thy bane, respectability.

He wrote, then canceled, the names of Winthrop and Everett as examples of the way an excess of civility can lead to compromise with the forces of evil. When the Civil War broke out he rejected even his own earlier suggestion in "American Slavery" (1855) that slavery be peacefully ended by the purchase of all the slaves. In a famous stanza of the "Boston Hymn" read in the Music Hall on the day of Emancipation, 1 January 1863, he urged his fellow-citizens to "Pay ransom to the owner / And fill the bag to the brim." But the slaveowner is not the one to be compensated: "Who is the owner? The slave is owner, / And ever was. Pay him."

May-Day and Other Pieces, Emerson's second volume of poetry, appeared in 1867. The title poem begins with an evocation of village May-Day celebrations in which "girls are peeling the sweet willow" and boys fill the air with joyous whoops. But "May-Day" quickly turns into something else, as it tracks the floods of returning warmth working miracles on the frozen New England landscape. Emerson's passionate ode to heat begins to sound like a Sufi hymn:

> What fiery force the earth renews,
> The wealth of forms, the flush of hues,
> Joy shed in rosy waves abroad
> Flows from the heart of Love, the Lord.

"The Adirondacks," a blank-verse narrative that follows "May-Day," is in another key entirely, yet it too celebrates the renovating powers of nature. Ten scholars (among them Emerson) went off with guides in August of 1858 to a well-planned vacation in the Adirondacks. The guides did all the heavy work: rowing, pitching camp, cooking, supervising the scholars as they took turns firing rifles or gathering natural specimens. For all its feeling of childish play-acting, the vacation actually exhilarated the campers: "We seemed the dwellers of the zodiac, / So pure the Alpine element we breathed, / So light, so lofty, pictures came and went." The men relished their distance from all civilized cares, yet when they received word from the outside world that the Atlantic cable had finally reached the shores of North America, they greeted the news with "loud, exulting cries." Why are they so happy? Is it because lightning, "masterless too long," has now been made to serve human purposes, "spelling with guided tongue man's messages / Shot through the weltering pit of the salt sea"? Possibly. Or is nature herself, that fearsome waylayer of travelers, happy to have her mysteries deciphered, as Emerson had suggested in "The Sphinx"? As they leave the wilderness,

> . . . Nature, the inscrutable and mute,
> Permitted on her infinite repose
> Almost a smile to steal to cheer her sons,
> As if one riddle of the Sphinx were guessed.

Among the *May-Day* poems included under the heading "Nature and Life" is a touching poem of farewell written by Emerson's brilliant, handsome younger brother Edward, who had died at the age of twenty-nine. "The Last Farewell" was written (as the headnote informs us) while its author was "sailing out of Boston Harbor, bound for the island of Porto Rico, in 1832." Ostensibly he was seeking a warmer climate in hopes of recovering his health, but he knew perfectly well that he would never return:

> Farewell, ye lofty spires
> That cheered the holy light!
> Farewell, domestic fires
> That broke the gloom of night!
> Too soon those spires are lost,
> Too fast we leave the bay,
> Too soon by ocean tost
> From hearth and home away.
>   Far away, far away.

Emerson followed this poem with one intended to celebrate his "brother of the brief but blazing star!" "In Memoriam, E. B. E." begins with Emerson mourning upon the Concord battlefield – though not for the "angry farmers" who came "in sloven dress and broken rank" to oppose the invading British troops. Now his attention is caught by the "stern head-stone" erected to mark the "friendless grave" of the enemy dead. The pathos of this unvisited grave makes him think of his brother's grave in distant Puerto Rico. Yet the sun shines on the Concord monument that guards the British dead, and the "endless smile / of Nature" beams on the place where Edward lies.

> What matter how, or from what ground,
> The freed soul its Creator found?
> Alike thy memory embalms
> That orange-grove, that isle of palms,
> And these loved banks, whose oak-boughs bold
> Root in the blood of heroes old.

Emerson's poetry constitutes only a part, though an important one, of his contributions to the growth of an American literary tradition. Beginning in 1836, when he wrote the preface to a Boston edition of Carlyle's *Sartor Resartus* (its first appearance in book form), he embarked upon a second career as publisher, editor, translator, literary impresario, and patron-of-last-resort. His efforts to publish Carlyle's works in authorized American editions involved him in every aspect of the publishing business – negotiating contracts, canvassing for subscriptions, editing texts, bargaining with paper sellers and bookbinders, dealing with printers, proofreading, finding ways to get books to distant booksellers, casting up accounts, and negotiating with bankers – for Carlyle's royalties had to be converted from dollars to pounds and transported from the United States to England.

In serving as Carlyle's self-appointed and unpaid American literary agent, Emerson had discovered a new vocation for which he had talent and time. Since resigning as pastor of Boston's Second Church in 1832, he had cobbled together a satisfying rural life as a lyceum lecturer, Unitarian supply preacher, author, and Concord householder. (Like all newly married men he was elected village hog-reeve in 1836, charged with levying fines on the owners of marauding swine.) But more strenuous activity on behalf of other people seemed necessary. In "The American Scholar" (1837) he had said: "Action is with the scholar subordinate, but it is essential. Without it, he is not yet man . . . The preamble of thought, the transition through which it passes from the unconscious to the conscious, is action." Yet in the late 1830s Emerson shed obligations faster than he acquired them. In the spring of 1838 he ended his relationship with the East Lexington congregation whose pulpit he had been supplying; in the summer he delivered his notorious Address to the graduating class at Harvard Divinity School, which closed the university to him for thirty years.

The editorial labors he undertook almost by accident for Carlyle in 1836 began a new phase in his life, during which he served as the unofficial center for a new congregation of writers who turned to him for encouragement, advice, help finding publishers – and sometimes for employment or money. A letter he wrote from New York City to Margaret Fuller in 1842 shows how important this role was to him. The sight of busy New Yorkers only confirmed his belief in the importance of poets: "The air of Wall Street, the expression of the faces of the male & female crowd in Broadway, the endless rustle of newspapers all make me feel not the value of their classes but of my own class – the supreme need of the few worshippers of the Muse – wild & sacred – as a counteraction to this world of material & ephemeral interest." In "Self-Reliance" he had said proudly: "There is a class of persons to whom by all spiritual affinity I am bought and sold; for them I will go to prison, if need be." Trying to help other writers never got him imprisoned, but it did make demands upon his time, his sympathy, and his funds.

The first of these mentoring relationships was the strangest. In 1837 Elizabeth Peabody, author, educator, and friend of Alcott and Emerson, heard a young man named Jones Very (1813–80) deliver a lecture at the Salem Lyceum. Very, a native of Salem, had graduated from Harvard in 1836, and now was serving as Greek tutor there while he studied divinity. "Why There Cannot Be Another Epic Poem" struck Peabody as remarkable, and she suggested to Emerson that the Concord Lyceum might want to hear it too. Emerson sent word to Peabody that he had duly asked the curator of the Concord Lyceum to ask Very to speak, and that the curator had "promised his good offices" to bring the affair about. After Very's 4 April lecture in Concord, the Emersons had him to dinner at their home. Emerson seems to have been impressed with the intense young man; his journal for 19 April 1838 mentions Very as one of the young men who made him begin to "conceive hopes of the Republic." In September, however, came distressing news, which Emerson immediately passed onto Margaret Fuller: "Have you heard of the calamity of poor Very, the tutor at Cambridge? He is at the Charlestown Asylum & his case tho't a very unpromising one."

Although Emerson did not know it, Very had been in the midst of a prolonged spiritual struggle. In 1836 he had undergone a conversion experience, a change of heart that brought him a sense of God's presence and mercy. Convinced that only his individual will kept him separated from God, Very set about to eradicate his will, to submit himself entirely to the will of God. By the autumn of 1838, Very felt that his individual will had been extirpated and his "identification with Christ" made finally complete. On 18 September he walked unannounced into the study of Henry Ware, Jr., professor at the Divinity School. Ware was talking to a group of students. Very broke in, offering what one of the students later remembered as a "spiritual" interpretation of Matthew 24, Jesus' prophecy to his disciples of the world's approaching end. The next day, Very told his undergraduate students to "flee to the mountains, for the end of all things is at hand." When word of this behavior reached Josiah Quincy, Harvard's President, he quickly relieved Very of his duties and summoned Very's brother to remove him from the university and take him home to Salem.

Very wanted to stop in Concord to speak with Emerson. He was prevented from making the visit, but was permitted to send Emerson a manuscript essay and a letter announcing the glad tidings: "The gathering time has come and the harvest is now reaping from the wide plains of earth. Here, even here the will of the Father begins to be done as in heaven. My friend I tell you these things as they are told me." Very had been an eager reader of Emerson's millennial prophecies in *Nature* (1836), as his heavily underlined copy of the book makes clear. He had also been present when Emerson delivered his Divinity School Address (15 July 1838), urging the graduates to cast tradition behind them and "acquaint men at first hand with the Deity." In fact Henry Ware, Jr., was engaged in completing a major sermon ("The Personality of the Deity") in reply to Emerson's Address when Very burst into his study and gave his impromptu exegesis of Matthew 24.

Emerson's Address was held by many to be blasphemous; now people began holding it responsible for Very's derangement as well. The way Very behaved when he reached Salem did not help matters. He called on Elizabeth Peabody, placed his hand on her head, and solemnly told her that he came to baptize her "with the Holy Ghost and fire." He called for a Bible and announced: "I am the Second Coming." She was frightened but managed to keep her composure until he left peacefully. That evening he returned to give her what she described as "a monstrous folio sheet of paper, on which there were four double columns of Sonnets – which he said the Spirit had enabled him to write, and these he left with me to read as the utterances of the Holy Ghost."

The Salem ministers whom Very tried to baptize in this fashion were not so tolerant; they insisted that he be committed to McLean Asylum. After a peaceful month there he was released. He had renounced none of his beliefs, but the physicians concluded that he posed no danger to himself or anyone else. A week later he arrived in Concord for a five-day visit with the Emersons. Why would the Emersons have been willing to entertain such an extraordinary house-guest? Emerson had experience in dealing with temporary insanity. Ten years earlier his brother Edward had suffered a fit of derangement so severe that he had to be taken in closed carriage, bound with a strap, to the same asylum from which Very had just been released. (Edward eventually recovered his sanity, though not his health: he died of tuberculosis in 1834.)

What did Very want? As Emerson later recalled it: "He seemed to expect from me a full acknowledgment of his mission and a participation of the same." This he could not give, though he admired Very's absolute self-trust, and he found himself confiding in his guest as he did in few other people.

I told J[ones]. V[ery], that I had never suffered, & that I could scarce bring myself to feel a concern for the safety & life of my nearest friends that would satisfy them: that I saw clearly that if my wife, my child, my mother, should be taken from me, I should still remain whole with the same capacity of cheap enjoyment from all things. I should not grieve enough, although I love them.

Still angered by some of the attacks he was receiving from ministers scandalized by his Divinity School Address, Emerson was delighted when Very confronted the presiding minister at a teachers' meeting at Concord and "bid him wonder at the Love which suffered him to speak there in his chair, of things he knew nothing of." After Very left, Emerson wrote to Elizabeth Peabody:

I wish the whole world were as mad as he. He discredits himself I may say by a certain violence of thought & speech; but it is quite superficial; he is profoundly sane, & as soon as his thoughts subside from their present excited to a more natural state, I think, he will make all people sensible of it. If it shall prove that his peculiarities are fixed, it can never alter the truth & illumination he communicates, if you deal with him with perfect sincerity.

Very was not satisfied with Emerson's approval; he wanted complete assent. With a sincerity that charmed them, he told his host and hostess at one point that he hated them, that it was a "day of hate" with him, that he discerned the bad element in every one he met. On the other hand, he impressed Emerson as "one who had the manners of a man." Very thought it an honor to wash his face, "being as it was the temple of the Spirit." When his visit was over, Emerson carried him part way to Cambridge, where he hoped to win reinstatement at Harvard. The authorities there declined to offer him his old position, and Very withdrew to Salem, where he went into virtual seclusion in the family home. He continued to write sonnets, publishing some in the Salem *Observer*. He sent clippings to Emerson.

Impressed by the quality of the sonnets, Emerson urged him keep writing and to think about publishing a volume of his work. "I love them," he wrote back, "and read them to all who have ears to hear." Very, in turn, urged Emerson to embrace the Spirit unconditionally: "You must pass out of that world in which you are, naked (that is, willess) as you came in . . . You must not even wish where you are, but be happy in absolute nakedness." Six months later he sent a packet containing all the poems and essays he had written, leaving to Emerson the task of deciding what to publish. In a letter of 9 July 1839 Emerson announced to Margaret Fuller: "I am editing Very's little book. Three Essays; & verses. Out of two hundred poems, I have selected sixty-six that really possess rare merit." *Essays and Poems by Jones Very* was published in Boston by Charles C. Little and James Brown in September 1839. Though it did not attract much public attention, it was noticed and praised by poets: by the senior Richard Henry Dana, by William Cullen Bryant, by Margaret Fuller, and by James Russell Lowell (who noted in his copy of the book that Very's poetry was better than any yet published in America). Rufus Griswold reprinted eleven of the poems in his influential anthology *Poets and Poetry of America* (1842), with a biographical headnote for which Emerson supplied most of the information. (It mentions his "religious enthusiasm" but not his stay at McLean Asylum.)

It is not hard to see why Very's sonnets attracted such praise from other poets. Even as a young man, writing poems in the style of Goldsmith, Thomson, Collins, or Burns, Very could write with a fluency and lightness uncommon in American verse. Most of his early poems are in pentameter couplets, blank verse, or stanzas of varying shapes. In 1837, however, he began to experiment with sonnets – joyous poems about trees and flowers like "The Sabbatia" (modeled on Emerson's "The Rhodora") or "The Columbine," in which the poet longs to gaze on the flower until he takes root by its side in friendly companionship:

> Upon this craggy hill our life should pass,
> A life of summer days and summer joys,
> Nodding our honey bells mid pliant grass

In which the bee half hid his time employs;
And here we'll drink with thirsty pores the rain,
And turn dew-sprinkled to the rising sun,
And look when in the flaming west again
His orb across the heaven its path has run.

In September 1838, as he began to feel a strong surge of religious exaltation, his sonnets changed markedly. Some describe what it feels like to experience spiritual rebirth, an experience in which ecstasy seems mingled with terror:

'Tis a new life – thoughts move not as they did
With slow uncertain steps across my mind,
In thronging haste fast pressing on they bid
The portals open to the viewless wind;
That comes not, save when in the dust is laid
The crown of pride that gilds each mortal brow,
And before man's vision melting fade
The heavens and earth – Their walls are falling now –
Fast crowding on each thought claims utterance strong,
Storm-lifted waves swift rushing to the shore
On from the sea they send their shouts along,
Back through the cave-worn rocks their thunders roar,
And I a child of God by Christ made free
Start from death's slumbers to eternity.

("The New Birth")

As the speaker moves from uncertainty to assurance, heaven and earth seem to dissolve in his sight. Yet his thoughts move into speech like a series of waves beating on the shore – until the speaker awakes at once both from the death-in-life that preceded his rebirth and from the sonnet itself. The world he now sees around him is wholly transfigured.

Father! I bless thy name that I do live
And in each motion am made rich with thee
That when a glance is all that I can give
It is a kingdom's wealth, if I but see.
("In him we live, & move, & have our being")

His glance is returned by a responsive world: "The flowers I pass have eyes that look at me / The birds have ears that hear my spirit's voice." He now has a new relation of reciprocal love to the natural world:

The bubbling brook doth leap when I come by,
Because my feet find measure with its call;
The birds know when the friend they love is nigh,
For I am known to them both great and small;
The flowers, which on the lovely hill-side grow,

Expect me there, when Spring their bloom has given;
And many a bush and tree my wanderings know,
And e'en the clouds and silent stars of heaven.
For he, who with his Maker walks aright,
Shall be their lord, as Adam was before;
His ear shall catch each sound with new delight,
Each object wear the dress that then it wore;
And he, as when erect in soul he stood,
Hear from his Father's lips that all is good.

("Nature")

Even his solitary Salem room becomes radiant with God's love, as his few belongings take on the aspect of Milton's serviceable angels.

I sit within my room and joy to find
That thou who always loves art with me here,
That I am never left by Thee behind,
But by Thyself Thou keepst me ever near;
The fire burns brighter when with Thee I look,
And seems a kinder servant sent to me;
With gladder heart I read thy holy book,
Because Thou art the eyes by which I see;
This aged chair, that table, watch, and door
Around in ready service ever wait;
Nor can I ask of Thee a menial more
To fill the measure of my large estate,
For Thou Thyself, with all a Father's care,
Where'er I turn, art ever with me there.

("The Presence")

To bring the tidings of this great joy to his fellow men was Very's prophetic mission:

Father! I wait thy word – the sun doth stand,
Beneath the mingling line of night and day,
A listening servant waiting thy command
To roll rejoycing on its silent way;
The tongue of time abides the appointed hour
Till on our ear its solemn warnings fall;
The heavy cloud withholds the pelting shower,
Then every drop speeds onward at thy call;
The bird reposes on the yielding bough
With breast unswollen by the tide of song;
So does my spirit wait thy presence now
To pour thy praise in quickening life along
Chiding with voice divine man's lengthened sleep,
While round the Unuttered Word and Love their vigils keep.

("The Son")

Yet the world refused to hear his message. Harvard expelled him, the ministers of Salem committed him to an asylum, and even in the Emerson household he found only kindness and patience rather than joyous reception. In a sonnet entitled "The Morning Watch," Very likens those who will not hear his message to the sleepy inhabitants of a New England village, unable or unwilling to admit that daylight has broken through their windows.

> 'Tis near the morning watch, the dim lamp burns
> But scarcely shows how dark the slumbering street;
> No sound of life the silent mart returns;
> No friends from house to house their neighbors greet;
> It is the sleep of death; a deeper sleep
> Than e'er before on mortal eyelids fell;
> No stars above the gloom their places keep;
> No faithful watchmen of the morning tell;
> Yet still they slumber on, though rising day
> Hath through their windows poured the awakening light;
> Or, turning in their sluggard trances, say –
> "There are yet many hours to fill the night;"
> They rise not yet; while on the bridegroom goes
> 'Till he the day's bright gates forever on them close!

The bridegroom in Jesus' parable arrives at midnight; Very's New England bridegroom arrives at dawn, eager to awaken the slothful before the gates of redemption close for ever. Still, "The Morning Watch" offers the possibility of redemption. In other poems, however, the unregenerate appear damned, hopeless, a terminally denuded grove: "Dry, leafless trees no autumn wind laid bare":

> No sap doth through their clattering branches flow,
> Whence springing leaves and blossoms bright appear;
> Their hearts the living God have ceased to know,
> Who gives the springtime to th'expectant year.
> ("The Dead")

To prophesy to the multitudes was pointless unless the hearers were willing to undergo a rebirth like Very's. No one could apprehend the truth of his doctrine without an emptying of self as radical as his own: "I cannot show thee that for which I live," he says in a poem called "The Holy of Holies":

> Go, cleanse thy soul, blot out the secret sin,
> Put off thy shoes for this is holy ground;
> And thou shalt see the kingdom come within,
> And in its holy precincts too be found.

God himself offers divine sonship to anyone who can drive false idols from the temple of the heart.

> Awake, thou hast long filled the holy place
> With idols that thy heart has lifted high,
> From My pure temple every daemon chase,
> Then to thy spirit will My soul draw nigh;
> And thou shalt be my sun, and I thy God
> To lead thee in the way thy master trod.
> > ("The Holy of Holies")

God's voice is also heard in "The Promise" ("I come the rushing wind that shook the place / Where those once sat who spake with tongues of fire") and in "The Creation."

> I said of old when darkness brooded long
> Upon the waste of waters Be thou light
> And forthwith sprang the son rejoicing strong
> To chase away the mystery of the night.

This assurance of intimacy with God amid a world of darkness and sin inspires what may be Very's strangest and most beautiful poem, "The Garden."

> I saw the spot where our first parents dwelt;
> And yet it wore to me no face of change,
> For while amid its fields and groves I felt
> As if I had not sinned, nor thought it strange;
> My eye seemed but a part of every sight,
> My ear heard music in each sound that rose,
> Each sense forever found a new delight,
> Such as the spirit's vision only knows;
> Each act some new and ever-varying joy
> Did by my Father's love for me prepare;
> To dress the spot my ever fresh employ,
> And in the glorious whole with Him to share;
> No more without the flaming gate to stray,
> No more for sin's dark stain the debt of death to pay.

The poet enters Paradise in a waking dream, as Adam did. The "sweet gardening labour" that Milton shows the unfallen Adam and Eve discussing in *Paradise Lost* is Very's "ever fresh employ," just as the solitary delights named in the sonnet recall Adam's morning song to Eve about a world in which gazing is entertainment enough:

> Awake, the morning shines, and the fresh field
> Calls us, we lose the prime, to mark how spring
> Our tended plants, how blows the citron grove,
> What drops the myrrh, and what the balmy reed,
> How nature paints her colors, how the bee
> Sits on the bloom extracting liquid sweet.

Other details in Very's sonnet are less Miltonic. In *Paradise Lost* Adam's request for someone to share his joy is an essential first test of his humanity. He asks God a rhetorical question: "In solitude / What happiness, who can enjoy alone / Or all enjoying, what contentment find?" In Very's sonnet God's love is a closed circuit of divine love and human gratitude, a solitude that seeks no fellowship and no mate. Then, too, if Very's Garden really wears "no face of change," why are its gates described as "flaming"? At the end of *Paradise Lost*, Adam and Eve look back to see the eastern side of Paradise "waved over by that flaming brand, the gate / With dreadful faces thronged and fiery arms." But this fiery transformation of the gates is a consequence of their sin, not a pre-existing state of affairs. If Very cannot help imagining the world outside the gates of Paradise as a world of sin and death, then even a sonnet meant to celebrate unfallen joy suggests that the Garden has already changed irrevocably.

Between 1838 and 1840 Very spoke urgently to anyone who would listen to him: to members of the Transcendental Club, whose meetings he some-times attended; to William Ellery Channing, the great Unitarian minister; to Wendell Phillips, the abolitionist; to Lidian Emerson, whose sympathy for Very's doctrine of submission to God's will was greater than her husband's. Yet none of these intelligent people wished to follow him into the kingdom. Their polite rejection was, he now realized, the agony he had to bear on earth.

> I cannot tell the sorrows that I feel
> By the night's darkness, by the prison's gloom;
> There is no sight that can the death reveal,
> The spirit suffers in earth's living tomb.
> ("He Was Acquainted With Grief")

What consoled him now was promise of an eternal rest instituted by a God whose creation of a Sabbath he himself did not need was the final gesture of benevolence in the week of Creation:

> Thou needst not rest, the shining spheres are thine,
> That roll perpetual on their silent way;
> And thou dost breathe in me a voice divine,
> That tells more sure of thine Eternal sway;
> Thine the first starting of the early leaf,
> The gathering green, the changing autumn hue;
> To Thee the world's long years are but as brief,
> As the fresh tints the spring will still renew;
> Thou needest not man's little life of years,
> Save that he gather wisdom from them all;
> That in thy fear he lose all other fears,
> And in thy calling heed no other call;

Then shall he be thy child to know thy care,
And in thy glorious self the eternal sabbath share.
("Labor and Rest")

Sometime during the spring of 1840, the religious exaltation that had sustained Very for nearly two years gradually ebbed. The Spirit ceased to speak to him directly, though for a time he still tried to assume its tones of authority. He stopped writing poetry. When he resumed, the poems he wrote were (like his early poems) graceful but not visionary. He wrote poems about nature, like "The Wild Rose of Plymouth" and "The Woodwax"; political sonnets indignantly attacking slavery and the political encroachments of slavery; hymns; pious mediations; elegies; and occasional verses. His faith in God remained unwavering; indeed, he became a supply preacher in local Unitarian pulpits. But he never again tried to speak as the directly inspired messenger of God's word.

Emerson had already found a new object for his attention and editorial concern. In 1837 he had met Henry David Thoreau (1817–62), a Concord resident recently graduated from Harvard College and now trying to earn his living by teaching school and working in his father's pencil factory. The first entry in Thoreau's journal – a project that eventually ran to almost two million words – records a question that may have been asked by Emerson: "'What are you doing now?' he asked. 'Do you keep a journal?' – So I make my first entry today." Early in 1838 Emerson mentions taking a walk with Thoreau. Their friendship grew throughout the spring. Emerson wrote of Nature in the philosophical or universal sense; Thoreau introduced Emerson to the local beauties of the Concord woods. "This afternoon in a very thick grove where H[enry]. D[avid]. Thoreau showed me the bush of mountain laurel, the first I have seen in Concord, the stems of pine & hemlock & oak almost gleamed like steel upon the excited eye." In 1841 Emerson invited Thoreau to move from his family's house into the Emerson house, where he would serve as gardener and handyman and be compensated by peace, quiet, and time to write. He remained with the Emersons until April 1843, when he left to become tutor to Emerson's nephew on Staten Island.

During these years Thoreau filled his journal with drafts of poems and paragraphs of prose on subjects like "Despondency" or "Bravery": "There is nowhere any apology for despondency. Always there is life – which, rightly lived, implies a divine satisfaction"; "We do all stand in the front ranks of the battle every moment of our lives; where there is a brave man there is the thickest of the fight – there the post of honor –." Unlike Emerson, who usually copied passages from his journals into lecture or essay manuscripts, leaving

the journals themselves intact, Thoreau removed pages bodily from his journal
to insert into new compositions. And he often winnowed his early journals
by copying extracts from them into new notebooks, discarding the originals.
Even so, enough material from this period remains to convey an impression
of the young man who wrote it. Like Milton, Thoreau was ambitious, already
worried in his early twenties by his failure to have produced any poem of
lasting worth. Thoreau's version of "How soon hath Time, the subtle thief of
youth" occurs in the 1840 journal:

> Two years and twenty now have flown —
> Their meanness time away has flung,
> These limbs to man's estate have grown,
> But cannot claim a manly tongue.
>
> Amidst such boundless wealth without
> I only still am poor within;
> The birds have sung their summer out,
> But still my spring does not begin.

Nothing in Nature is delayed or unripe; even the smallest bird knows by
instinct how to sing and to create. Why then must the poet alone be artless
and mute?

> The sparrow sings at earliest dawn
> Building her nest without delay;
> All things are ripe to hear her song,
> And now arrives the perfect day.
>
> Shall I then wait the Autumn wind
> Compelled to seek a milder ray,
> And leave no empty nest behind,
> No wood still echoing to my lay?

Self-reproach was only one mood in Thoreau's early journals, and not the
dominant one. "A wave of happiness flows over us like sunshine over a field,"
he wrote, and added, "Society is fragrant." He translated into unrhymed verse
three poems ascribed to Anacreon: "To Spring," "To Love," and the delightful
"Ode to the Cicada": "We pronounce thee happy, Cicada, / For on the tops of
the trees, / Sipping a little dew / Like any king thou singest." The muses love
the cicada, and Phoebus himself has bestowed upon it a shrill song: "Age does
not wrack thee, / Thou skillful — earth-born — song-loving, / Unsuffering —
bloodless one; Almost thou art like the gods" (later incorporated into "The
Natural History of Massachusetts"). He found reason for happiness in every
season. When a February thaw raised the Concord River so high that the
muskrats who lived in holes along its banks were driven out, Thoreau noted

that "the wind from over the meadows is laden with a strong scent of musk, and by its racy freshness advertises us of an unexplored wildness." He turned the experience into a poem (later incorporated into "The Natural History of Massachusetts"):

> The river swelleth more and more,
> Like some sweet influence stealing o'er
> The passive town; and for awhile
> Each tussuck makes a tiny isle,
> Where, on some friendly Ararat,
> Resteth the weary waterrat.

The flood transformed Concord into a landscape of romance:

> Our village shows a rural Venice,
> Its broad lagunes where yonder fen is,
> Far lovelier than the Bay of Naples
> Yon placid cove amid the maples,
> And in my neighbor's field of corn
> I recognize the Golden Horn.

Like beauty, love seemed to be everywhere in the landscape Thoreau saw: "Love is the burden of all natures odes – the song of the birds is an epithalamium – a hymeneal. The marriage of the flowers spots the meadows and fringes the hedges with pearls and diamonds." He tried his hand at New England Anacreontics to smoke, to haze, and to fog. The swiftly rising smoke from his morning fire became "Light-winged smoke, Icarian bird, / Melting thy pinions in thy upward flight, / Lark without song, and messenger of dawn." Summer haze was the "Aerial surf upon the shores of earth, / Etherial estuary, frith of light, / Breakers of air, billows of heat, / Fine summer spray on inland seas." Even the melancholy fog that collects in the river bottoms and marshes was praised as a "Protean god" and addressed with admiration: "Thou wind-blown meadow of the air."

If perception offered one sort of delight, memory heightened the joys of perception. In an untitled blank-verse poem ("Within the circuit of this plodding life") begun in the 1840 journal and later published in the *Dial* and in "The Natural History of Massachusetts," Thoreau explains how the beauty of a scene perceived can be heightened by memories of a different season:

> I have remembered, when the winter came,
> High in my chamber in the frosty nights,
> When in the still light of the cheerful moon,
> On every twig and rail and jutting spout,
> The icy spears were adding to their length

> Against the arrows of the coming sun,
> How in the shimmering noon of summer past
> Some unrecorded beam slanted across
> The upland pastures where the Johnswort grew.

The frozen brook reminds him of the purling sound it made when flowing. The blank fields, buried deep "beneath a thick integument of snow," remind him of how the new-plowed furrows shone in the spring sunshine as fieldfares pecked the earth behind the plowman. And so, "by God's cheap economy made rich again," Thoreau finds strength to go upon his winter's task again.

He also wrote poems about nature in a different tone, full of playfulness and quiet humor. In his journal he described "a rill released by the noonday sun from its frosty fetters – while the icicles were melting upon the apple trees, and the ever present chic-a-dee – and nuthatch flitted about." Immediately following these sentences are twenty stanzas of dimeter lines – the first group dealing with early spring, the second with the winter preceding it. "Simplicity is exuberance," Thoreau observed in his journal. These lines suggest how much exuberance he had already learned to see and hear all around him.

> Now melts the snow
>   In this warm sun
> The meadows flow
>   The streamlets run.
>   . . .
> The apples thaw
> The ravens caw
> The squirrels gnaw
>   The frozen fruit.
>
> To their retreat
> I track the feet
> Of mice that eat
>   The apples root.
>   . . .
> The snow dust falls
> The otter crawls
> The partridge calls
>   Far in the wood
>
> The traveller dreams
> The tree-ice gleams
> The blue-jay screams
>   In angry mood
>   . . .
> The axe resounds
> And bay of hounds

> And tinkling sounds
> Of wintry fame.
>
> The hunter's horn
> Awakes the dawn
> On field forlorn
> And frights the game.
>
> The tinkling air
> Doth echo bear
> To rabbit's lair
> With dreadful din
>
> She scents the air
> And far doth fare
> Returning where
> She did begin.

In the first stanza of another short lyric, "Salmon Brook," also written in autumn 1842, Thoreau speaks of his longing to return (if only in memory) to two New Hampshire brooks whose names rhyme pleasingly across linguistic barriers.

> Salmon Brook,
> Penichook,
> Ye sweet waters of my brain,
> When shall I look,
> Or cast the hook,
> In your waves again?

Thoreau had visited the brooks during his two-week boating and hiking trip to the White Mountains in 1839 with his brother John, a trip he later memorialized in his first published book, *A Week on the Concord and Merrimack Rivers* (1849). But John had died in January of 1842, and the sweet waters of Thoreau's brain were inaccessible now for reasons other than geographical distance.

It is a measure of Thoreau's seriousness about poetry that neither John's death nor his own serious illness following shortly after could long dissuade him from a project he had embarked on in 1841: a projected history of English poetry. He left the Emerson house in November 1841 to move in with an old friend in Cambridge to be closer to the Harvard library. Beginning with the Saxon poetry, which seemed to him "of a more philosophical cast than any that can be called English," he worked his way through the corpus of English and Scottish poetry as far as the seventeenth century: metrical romances, ballads, Chaucer, Gower, Dunbar, Gavin Douglas, King James I, Lydgate, Daniel, Sidney, Spenser, Raleigh, Marlowe, Peele, Shakespeare, Jonson, Herbert, Marvell, Carew, Quarles, Donne, and Lovelace. He was not much concerned with balance or proportion; he devoted as much space to Gower as to Chaucer, much more to Quarles than to Herbert or Donne. What interested him were the moments in which some strong poetic virtue – descriptive power, candor, or just strong common sense – abolished all historical distance between poet and reader. "To hear the sunset described by the Old Scotch Poet Douglas – as I have seen it – repays me for many weary pages of antiquated Scotch. Nothing so restores and humanizes antiquity – and makes it blithe – as the discovery of some natural sympathy between it and the present." So Quarles attracted him by the "strong unaffected sense" of his poems: "The words he speaks are made of the very breath which he lives, and not of some passing wind for any artful purpose. They are a vital breath . . . It is delightful to hear with what sound and relish he utters his words. Such sturdiness must be forever respectable."

His judgments of individual poets are often acute, and his comments about English poetry in general can be startling. Reading Herbert made him realize "how rarely in our English tongue do we find expressed any affection for God. No sentiment is so rare as love of God – universal love. Herbert is almost the only exception." Thoreau never finished this study of English poetry, though fragments of several seventeenth-century masques by Jonson and Carew made their way into *Walden* (1854). The real value of this intensive study of English poetry lay in its stimulus to thinking about imaginative activity in general and about his own writing in particular. Throughout the journals of the period one can trace a pattern: Thoreau's commentary on an English poet is surrounded by aphorisms on poetry or the imagination, as well as by original poems or paragraphs of descriptive prose. In an 1842 journal, for instance, Thoreau had discussed the fourteenth-century poet John Gower at some length:

Gower writes like a man of common sense with good parts who had undertaken with steady rather than high purpose to do narrative with rhyme . . . He narrates what Chaucer sometimes sings. With a fair understanding of the original he tells his story – and sometimes it gains a little in directness and point – or perhaps I should say in blunt plainness, in his hands.

What follows this discussion of Gower is a paragraph on the poet's stance: "The poet is partaker of a repose which is akin to the central law of the universe – no excitement is in the mode in which he acts – he is perfectly poised, and rests as it were on the axis of the universe." A discussion of Chaucer's *Prioress's Tale* and *Nun's Priest's Tale* passes directly into the poem "Within the circuit of this plodding life." The next day Thoreau wrote sentences about the joys of reading natural history in wintertime that would soon become the opening of "The Natural History of Massachusetts." Reading the English poets invigorated him, and he used his energy in fresh creation.

Moreover, the sixteenth- and seventeenth-century poets – with their playful-ness, love of paradox, and complex treatment of human passion – gave Thoreau a way of talking about his inner life more congenial to his temperament than any his immediate poetic predecessors could offer. In an early poem entitled "Sympathy" he expresses his sadness that mutual reserve prevented a deeper union with a "gentle boy, / Whose features all were cast in Virtue's mold":

> Each moment, as we nearer drew to each,
> A stern respect withheld us farther yet,
> So that we seemed beyond each other's reach,
> And less acquainted than when first we met.

Now that the boy has departed, Thoreau is left to bewail his missed chances as if he were the singer of a pastoral elegy:

> Make haste and celebrate my tragedy;
> With fitting strain resound ye woods and fields;
> Sorrow is dearer in such case to me
> Than all the joys other occasion yields.

Though he longed for love, and talked about it endlessly in his journal, Thoreau's sense of inner poverty was at times acute. "The most I can do for my friend is simply to be his friend. I have no wealth to bestow on him – If he knows that I am happy loving in him – he will want no other reward," he wrote in 1841. He felt awkward, ill-assorted: "My soul and body have tottered along together of late tripping and hindering oneanother [*sic*] like unpractised Siamese twins," he noted ruefully. In "I am a parcel of vain strivings tied," a poem first printed in the July 1841 *Dial* and later in the Friday chapter of *A Week on the Concord and Merrimack Rivers*, he likens himself to a nosegay of small flowers and herbs tied together by straw:

> I am a parcel of vain strivings tied
>   By a chance bond together,
> Dangling this way and that, their links
>   Were made so loose and wide,
>   Methinks,
>   For wilder weather.
>
> A bunch of violets without their roots,
>   And sorrel intermixed,
> Encircled by a wisp of straw
>   Once coiled about their shoots,
>   The law
>   By which I'm fixed.
>
>   . . .

> And here I bloom for a short hour unseen,
>   Drinking my juices up,
> With no root in the land
>   To keep my branches green,
>   But stand
>   In a bare cup.

Here, the seventeenth-century complexity of the stanza form tempers pathos with wit, and the speaker's disunity is made the occasion for self-deprecation. But the helplessness of "I am a parcel of vain strivings tied" is not Thoreau's only erotic posture. A poem published in the October 1841 *Dial* imagines a noble masculine friendship so laced with hostility that it verges on the murderous – as if one tent should cover, not Achilles and Patroclus, but Achilles and Agamemnon. Under an epigraph expanded from Shakespeare – "Friends, Romans, Countrymen, and Lovers" – Thoreau utters this strange prayer for an ideal love:

> Let such pure hate still underprop
> Our love, that we may be
> Each other's conscience,
> And have our sympathy
> Mainly from thence.
>
> We'll treat one another like gods,
> And all the faith we have
> In virtue and in truth, bestow
> On either, and suspicion leave
> To gods below.

He printed the poem in the Wednesday chapter of *A Week on the Concord and Merrimack Rivers*, where it reprises his long discussion of friendship – a tribute both to his dead brother John, who had been his companion on the 1839 river excursion, and to Emerson, who had urged him to write an account of the trip. "There are passages of affection in our intercourse with mortal men and women, such as no prophecy has taught us to expect, which transcend our earthly life, and anticipate Heaven for us," Thoreau wrote. "Our life without love is coke and ashes." But he also warned: "If I can see my Friend's virtues more distinctly than another's his faults too are made more conspicuous by contrast. We have not so good a right to hate any as our Friend." If the true Friend is "flesh of my flesh, bone of my bone," then any quarrel between us will be "fatal and everlasting." Friends are "fatally late when they undertake to explain and treat with one another like foes . . . The necessity itself for explanation, – what explanation will atone for that?"

In the early 1850s, when he had become for a time estranged from Emerson, Thoreau speculated in his journal about the bond that had now become a source of anguish: "Here I have been on what the world would call friendly terms with one fourteen years, have pleased my imagination with loving him; and yet our hate is stronger than our love. Why are we related, thus unsatisfactorily?" In a series of painful journal poems he records both a hate "that would fain annihilate" its object and a love that recurs even against his will. The meetings Emerson and Thoreau held to try to resolve their grievances seemed to him like the endless legislative strife between North and South:

> The vessel of love, the vessel of state
> Each is ballasted with hate.
> Every Congress that we hold
> Means the union is dissolved.
> (Journal, September 1852)

The rift between them, though it ended the intense intimacy that had marked the first years of their friendship, did not end their association for ever. By the mid 1850s Emerson's journals again contain accounts of their walks:

Yesterday to the Sawmill Brook with Henry. He was in search of yellow violet (pubescens) and menyanthes which he waded into the water for & which he concluded, on examination, had been out five days. Having found his flowers, he drew out of his breast pocket his diary & read the names of all the plants that should bloom on this day, 20 May, whereof he keeps account as a banker when his notes fall due.

A walk again with Henry, & found *Solidago Odora*, pellucid points on the leaves: found two polygalas with checkerberry scent . . . But I was taken with the aspects of the forest, & thought to Nero advertising for a luxury a walk in the woods should have been offered. 'Tis one of the secrets for dodging old age.

Emerson had another regular partner for healthful and luxurious walks, a poet who was also Thoreau's close friend. William Ellery Channing (1818–1901), the son of a prosperous merchant and the nephew of the famous Unitarian minister, wrote poetry that impressed Emerson as revealing "a highly poetical temperament & a sunny sweetness of tho't & feeling." He had been shown Channing's poems by Ward, a friend of Channing's. To Channing himself (whom he had not yet met) Emerson wrote:

I have seen no verses written in America that have such inward inspiration. Certainly I prize finished verses, which yours are not, and like best, poetry which satisfies eye, ear, heart, & mind. Yet I prize at such a dear rate the poetic soul, that where that is present, I can easily forgive the license & negligence the absence of which makes the merit of mediocre verses.

Emerson wrote an article on "New Poetry" for the October 1840 *Dial* incorporating twelve of Channing's poems. He had tried to persuade Channing to let him correct their punctuation, smooth out their meter, and remove instances of bad grammar, but had found the poet obdurate. He was exasperated (as he told a friend) that Channing seemed to think his "bad grammar and his nonsense" were all "consecrated by his true *afflatus*. Is the poetic inspiration amber to embalm and enhance flies and spiders?" But in the *Dial* itself he defended Channing's lapses in a sentence that offended more than one reader: "The writer was not afraid to write ill; he had a great meaning too much at heart to stand for trifles, and wrote lordly for his peers alone."

When Channing (with Emerson's editorial assistance and Sam Ward's money) published a small volume of *Poems* in 1843, the book came under the scrutiny of a critic who did not belong to Boston or Concord and who regarded Emerson's attempt to puff Channing's poems as an example of the pernicious effects of literary nationalism upon critical good sense. Edgar Allan Poe reviewed Channing's *Poems* in the August 1843 issue of *Graham's Magazine* under the contemptuous title: "Our Amateur Poets." He set out to demonstrate that Channing's poems were objectively wretched – ungrammatical, unmetrical; full of fustian and empty of sense. He is particularly contemptuous of Channing's inability to write a line that scans.

The utter *abandon* – the charming *negligé* – the perfect looseness (to use a western phrase) of his rhythm, is one of Mr. C's most noticeable, and certainly one of his most refreshing traits. It would be quite a pleasure to hear him read or scan, or to hear any body else read or scan, such a line as this, at p. 3, for example:
        Masculine, almost though softly carv'd in grace,
where "masculine" has to be read as a trochee, and "almost" as an iambus . . . or this, at p. 18:
        I leave thee, *the* maid spoke to *the* true youth,
where both "thes" demand a strong accent to preserve the iambic rhythm . . . or this, at p. 32:
        The *se*rene azure *the* keen stars are now
or this, on the same page:
        Some*time* of sorrow, joy to *thy* Fu*ture*.

But Channing's limping meter is only part of his problem. His sentiments are fatuous where they are not incomprehensible, and Poe cannot resist puncturing them with mocking asides. When Channing looks at his sleeping mistress and asks himself rhetorically: "Would it not, O! comfort thee, / If thou couldst nightly go to rest / By that virgin chastity?" Poe replies: "Yes, we think, upon the whole, it would." When Channing declares that it is "Better to be forgotten / Than lose equipoise," Poe agrees: "It is better to be forgotten, for instance, than lose one's equipoise on top of a shot tower."

Emerson's praise of bad poetry seemed to Poe an egregious example of a national tendency he had often deplored: overpraising American authors just because they were American. Such partisanship guaranteed continued mediocrity in the nation's literature. To make excuses for poets who could not observe the rules of grammar or meter was to confess one's belief that American poets could really do no better. Literary nationalism led to literary incompetence. James Russell Lowell came to a similar conclusion when he surveyed the meager results produced by seventy years of attempting to will an American literary tradition into being. "The feeling that it was absolutely necessary to our respectability that we should have a literature, has been a material injury to such as we have had."

Undaunted by Poe's criticism, Emerson continued his efforts to help Channing. When he became editor of the *Dial* in 1843 he published batches of Channing's poems – so many, indeed, that Channing had more pieces published in the *Dial* than did any other contributor. When Channing's second series of *Poems* (1847) was in press, Emerson sent an advance copy to Longfellow hinting that a few friendly lines in the *Boston Courier* might help the book's chances. Longfellow responded with a polite refusal: "I am not blind to its many beauties but it does not command the spontaneous admiration which I like so much to feel."

What did Emerson see in Channing? He once confessed that he was particularly susceptible to the "witchcraft" of incantatory lines in poetry. And Channing had a gift for writing lines that appealed to him. "I have woven shrouds of air / In a loom of hurrying light"; "Silent companions of the blinded earth, / Day's recollection, enemies of time"; "I flow between the shores of this large life"; "If my bark sinks, 'tis to another sea." He scattered Channing's lines throughout his essays, and even made the line about the sinking bark the concluding sentence in his essay "Montaigne" (1850).

Isolated lines were hardly enough to establish Channing's claim to serious consideration as a poet, even in Emerson's generous eyes, and the 1843 *Poems* deserved all the scorn Poe heaped on on it. But Channing, who rarely stuck to any bargain or completed any project, did work seriously on his poetic technique in subsequent years, learning to write lines that scanned and finding new subjects and styles better suited to his talents than the pseudo-Shelley lyricism of his first failed volume. His next three volumes of poetry contained much better poems, the best of them devoted to a consideration of New England's landscape and inhabitants. These low-keyed narratives in pentameter lines, rhymed or unrhymed, reflect Channing's love for the New England countryside in which he took daily walks, often as Thoreau's companion or Emerson's.

The poems also reflect his wise decision to look for imaginative material close at hand.

"The Sexton's Story," in *Poems: Second Series* (1847), concerns a woodchopper who also serves as the village sexton, making coffins and digging graves. One bitterly cold winter afternoon he sets out with a cheerful heart to deliver a newly made coffin. He is neither callous nor oblivious to the sufferings of the bereaved, but long acquaintanceship with death has made it seem familiar. "The Sexton had forgotten what Death was, / And graves he dealt in, as some deal in Farms." As he makes ready to cross a deep but narrow brook the sudden glow of the fields makes him turn to see the setting sun:

> He turned when near the Bridge, for such a flush
> Of crimson wandered o'er the snow, the fields,
> So glowed as if with Summer's fire, his heart
> Bounded to meet that last gold glance of Day.

He delivers his coffin to the grieving family. As he begins his return journey, the air is suddenly filled with whirling wreaths of snow and the trees with the sound of storm wind:

> From the soft hills that hem the Meadows in,
> The Sexton heard the music of the Pines,
> A sudden gush of sounds, as when a flock
> Of startled Birds are beating through the air,
> And tossing off the light from their quick wings.

The snow has filled up the road and obliterated all landmarks, but the Sexton tells himself that he has endured worse. He breasts the drifts, beats his arms across his chest to warm himself, and tries to find the small footbridge in the white blur. Suddenly his foot goes through the snow to something slippery. It is the brook's glassy surface. Before he can recover his balance, he slides across the brook and sinks down on the farther shore, terrified and wailing aloud for help. A nearby farm family hears him and rescues him from the bankside drifts. The next day, the chastened Sexton retraces his route and discovers that "the spanning frost" had thrown only a single arch of ice across the running brook, the surface upon which he had crossed.

Two more poems from the 1847 volume describe Channing's own encounters with the New England landscape. "The Lonely Road" begins with a walk past an abandoned homestead – a cellar hole with a fruit tree growing out of it, an ancient apple orchard surrounding a smaller garden:

> A little wall half falling bounds a square
> Where choicer fruit-trees showed the Garden's pride,
> Now crimsoned by the Sumach, whose red cones
> Displace the colors of the cultured growth.

The complete desolation of such spots tarries with the poet even after he has long left them behind, though the sadness he feels comes from the abandonment of a way of life rather than a tragedy. Thinking of the vibrant past, the poet raises an imaginary house and peoples it with imaginary children, then realizes that in just such weavings of the Fancy "all this that we call life abides." He leaves with a prayer that the "dim and silent spot" will be visited only by "men to Contemplation vowed, / Still as ourselves, creators of the Past."

"Wachusett," the longest poem in the 1847 volume, is written in relaxed pentameter couplets, with rhymes that sometimes demand New England pronunciation, as when "before" rhymes with "Noah" or "adorn" with "Lawn." Mt. Wachusett is not very tall as mountains go; modern atlases reckon it as slightly more than two thousand feet high. (Channing says that Wachusett is "not as flat level as a Salem beach, / And yet within a feeble body's reach.") If it lacks the grandeur of the White Hills or the cataracts and silver rills of the Catskills, it offers views of a settled landscape studded with small, agreeable villages. As Thoreau noticed when he climbed the same mountain: "On every side, the eye ranged over successive circles of towns, rising one above another, like the terraces, till they were lost in the horizon." Channing notes with amusement that there are three spires at least to every village in his sight: "Baptist, Methodist, and Orthodox," and sometimes a Unitarian spire as well. The doctrinal differences of such interest to the villagers mean little to Channing, who sees the same truth in every creed, but the sight is still pleasing to his eye:

> But I love dearly to look down on them
> In rocky landscapes like Jerusalem.
> The villages gleam out painted with white,
> Like paper castles are the houses light,
> And every gust that o'er the valley blows,
> May scatter them perchance like drifting snows.

The landscape is rural but hardly pastoral, since Yankees see in every body of water merely a source of energy:

> The little streams that thread the valleys small,
> Make scythes or axes, driving factories all,
> The ponds are damned, and e'en the petty brooks
> Convert to sluices swell the River's crooks.

This industrious landscape reflects the temper of its inhabitants, who every day test their wits against the stinginess of nature and the keenness of their neighbors' wits in that mystic strife called "competition," the modern substitute for chivalric warfare. As a younger man Channing had been quick to heap scorn on Mammon's slaves, but now he sees something more honorable in the hard judgments of village life: "He who has craft, he gets respect from all, / He who has none, by his deserts doth fall / To his true level." This strict accounting makes the busy villages, with their cattle shows and lending libraries, still the sites of an innocent plenty: "Sweet bread, rich milk, and apples weight the board." Nor does the landscape want magnificence of its own in the Indian summer air, when frost has given the oak-leaves a color "like wine, / That ripens red on warm Madeira's line" and a ray of the departing sun makes a lake momentarily flash out "like Saladin's bright blade." Is this cold, drear, inhospitable New England? Or the warm coast of Africa? In the molten glory of the sunset it is hard to tell: "'Tis Tangiers yonder, and dark Atlas' height; / Or Mauritania, with her sable skins, / And gold-dust rivers, elephants and kings."

In the 1849 volume entitled *The Woodman and Other Poems* is a short but lovely poem entitled "The Sunset Lakes," describing a walk Channing had taken through an unfamiliar landscape on a cloudy day through scenes of wild beauty. Each stage of his journey revealed a new lake. He thanks Nature for making "three lakes, thrice to rejoice my eyes / The careless eyes that slowly seek the good."

> And as I mused, upon the yielding moss,
> A flashing beam of day's last glory fell
> In unexpected splendor, through the gloom,
> Slanting across the silent, lonely hills,
> Until the place seemed social in this fire.

Channing's own lonely life was a sad chronicle of opportunities wasted and duties neglected, but he continued to find in nature evidence of "the fresh, the fair, the ever-living grace" offered to every human being. In "Near Home" (1858) he urges his readers to go forth before dawn to see the daily birth of the world. They may then find joy on every hand, as they watch the morning mist withdraw from the meadows, listen to the loon's cry, or lean over the side of a rowboat to watch the water-insects "weave their continual circles o'er the pool / With their dusk boat-like bodies, things of joy." Best of all is the late-summer hunt for New England's ambrosial fruit, the blueberry, whose upland bushes are the end of every quest:

> Here, be gardens of Hesperian mould,
> Recesses rare, temples of birch and fern,
> Preserves of light-green Sumac, Ivy thick,
> And old stone-fences tottering to their fall.

Other poets in the Transcendental circle published in the *Dial* as well. Caroline Sturgis (later Mrs. William Tappan [1819–88]), the daughter of a wealthy Boston merchant, had been introduced to Emerson in 1836 by Margaret Fuller. Charmed by Sturgis's impetuosity, her apparent scorn for convention, and her dark good looks, he began an epistolary flirtation with her that over time deepened into genuine friendship. Like all of the Transcendentalists, she argued for the importance of poetry and art in an age preoccupied by various movements of social reform. In a poem entitled "The Hero" she argues that culture is as essential to human dignity as the work of reformers: "Toil not to free the slave from chains, / Think not to give the laborer rest; / Unless rich beauty fills the plains / The free man wanders still unblest." Her older sister Ellen Sturgis Hooper (1815–48) contributed eleven poems to the *Dial*, three of which Emerson later included in his anthology *Parnassus* (1874). Hooper's poem "To R. W. E." reveals an ambivalence common among Emerson's acquaintances, who were often inspired by his nobility yet frustrated by his aloofness. The poem begins by praising Emerson as both a mount of vision to his friends and the sheltering sky arching over them: "Thou art the deep and crystal winter sky, / Where noiseless, one by one, bright stars appear." But the third stanza hints that Emerson's otherworldly calm was the sign of a deficiency, an absence of passion:

> It may be Bacchus, at thy birth, forgot
>   That drop from out the purple grape to press
> Which is his gift to man, and so thy blood
>   Doth miss the heat which ofttimes breeds excess.

Ellen Hooper's impatience with Emerson was only part of a larger indictment she drew up against a society content with freezing out human impulses in the name of virtue. "Better a sin which purposed wrong to none / Than this still wintry coldness at the heart," she wrote. Sin without malice would be better than virtue without humanity; the God "who framed this stern New-England land, / Its clear cold waters, and its clear, cold soul," also created "tropic climes and youthful hearts." If the poet should fail in her attempt to teach her soul patience, then she would rather be among the abandoned than among the Pharisees: "Let me sin deep so I may cast no stone."

If Christopher Pearse Cranch (1813–92), who began as a Unitarian minister but left the pulpit to become a landscape painter, felt any ambivalence towards Emerson, he confined it to the series of pen-and-ink caricatures he drew when he was in Louisville helping James Freeman Clarke edit *The Western Messenger*. Emerson was not the only target of Cranch's pen; Ellery Channing, Theodore Parker, and George Ripley each get one caricature apiece. But Emerson's writings are lovingly explored and copiously illustrated. The caricatures inspired by *Nature* alone show Emerson as a giant treetrunk in a sympathetic pumpkin patch; as a huge eyeball on legs; as a large melon expanding in the genial sun; and as a calm philosopher watching assorted vermin, prisons and madhouses-on-feet fleeing before the influx of the spirit. After returning to Boston, Cranch attended meetings of the Transcendental club and sent poems to the *Dial*. "Correspondences," which appeared in the January 1841 *Dial*, explains a central tenet of Transcendentalist thought: the doctrine of correspondence. As Emerson said in *Nature*: "Every natural fact is a symbol of some spiritual fact. Every appearance in nature corresponds to some state of the mind." Cranch's "Correspondences" expands upon the idea in unrhymed dactylic hexameter lines whose alternating masculine and feminine endings suggest elegiac distichs: "All things in Nature are beautiful types to the soul that can read them; / Nothing exists upon earth, but for unspeakable ends." Before sin came into the world, everything "stood as a letter or word of a language familiar." Now only the angels can read God's language clearly. Human beings try painfully to discern here and there a letter, unaware of the one form of unconscious wisdom we still possess – the figures of speech we unconsciously use every moment, which bear within them clues to the symbolic nature of reality: "Gleams of the mystery fall on us still, though much is forgotten, / And through our commonest speech, illumine the path of our thoughts."

> Thus do the sparkling waters flow, giving joy to the desert,
> And the great Fountain of Life opens itself to the thirst.
> Thus does the word of God distil like the rain and the dew-drops,
> Thus does the warm wind breathe like to the Spirit of God,
> And the green grass and flowers are signs of regeneration.

Cranch's poem is theologically more orthodox than Emerson's *Nature* in the conclusions it draws from correspondences. To Emerson's Orphic poet, correspondences are the sign that we have fallen away from our own divinity, leaving the vast shell of nature surrounding us. To Cranch, they are messages from the Creator, fragments of that meaning once transparent "when Adam lived sinless in Eden." Only in figures of speech do we sense the manifold meaning of the symbolic world we inhabit.

> O thou Spirit of Truth; visit our minds once more,
> Give us to read in letters of light the language celestial

> Written all over the earth, written all over the sky –
> Thus we may bring our hearts once more to know our Creator,
> Seeing in all things around, types of the Infinite Mind.

"Correspondences" ends on a joyous note, like Blake's *The Four Zoas*, imagining a redeemed human race in a transparent world. But Cranch also suffered from recurrent depressions that left him sitting mute even among his friends. In a poem entitled "Enosis," the Greek word for "communion," he portrayed the obstacles that prevent even the closest of souls from coming together.

> Thought is deeper than all speech,
>   Feeling deeper than all thought;
> Souls to souls can never teach
>   What unto themselves was taught.
>
> We are spirits clad in veils;
>   Man by man was never seen;
> All our deep communing fails
>   To remove the shadowy screen.
>
> Heart to heart was never known;
>   Mind with mind did never meet;
> We are columns left alone
>   Of a temple once complete.

The headless tetrameters, with their trochaic rhythms, add an air of finality to Cranch's negations: man by man was *never* seen, mind with mind did *never* meet. Our vaunted individuality is the product of an earlier collapse. Is there any hope that selves so sundered might ever reunite? Love alone can melt "the scattered stars of thought."

> Only when our souls are fed
>   By the Fount which gave them birth,
> And by inspiration led,
>   Which they never drew from earth,
>
> We like parted drops of rain,
>   Swelling till they meet and run,
> Shall be all absorbed again,
>   Melting, flowing into one.

Margaret Fuller, the editor of the *Dial* from 1840 to 1842, was already moving away from Transcendentalist circles and literary forms even before Emerson let the magazine expire with the April 1844 number. In May 1843 she seized the opportunity to escape New England when a friend offered to finance her trip to see the Great Lakes region, a trip that took her past Niagara Falls, through Chicago to the Illinois prairie, and as far west as Milwaukee.

When she returned she wrote a book about her experiences – not a conventional travel book, but a series of observations extrapolated from the notes and letters she had written during the trip. *Summer on the Lakes in 1843* blends accounts of travel, literary sketches, and original poems. A beautiful estate on the bend of Illinois' Rock River, where pigeons in flocks came sweeping every afternoon across the lawn, draws from Fuller this tribute:

> Blest be the kindly genius of the scene;
> The river, bending in unbroken grace,
> The stately thickets, with their pathways green,
> Fair lonely trees, each in its fittest place.
> Those thickets haunted by the deer and fawn;
> Those cloudlike flights of birds across the lawn.

On 4 July, still on the Rock River, she composed a poem "on the height called the Eagle's Nest," as the epigraph to "Ganymede to his Eagle" informs us. Her letters make clear that she saw herself in Ganymede, who longs for the eagle's flight that will carry him once again to Jove's court. Ganymede recalls that even in youth he sought to question nature about his parentage. The mountains and sky ignored him, but in storms he found clues to his identity:

> But, from the violet of lower air,
> Sometimes an answer to my wishing came,
> Those lightning births my nature seemed to share,
> They told the secrets of its fiery frame,
> The sudden messengers of hate and love,
> The thunderbolts that arm the hand of Jove,
> And sometimes strike the sacred spire, and strike the sacred grove.
>
> Come in a moment, in a moment gone,
> They answered me, then left me still more lone.

At the end of the poem Ganymede is still waiting with his cup bearing waters from the spring whose waters celestial poets are to drink, praying that he may be allowed to bring his "pure draught" heavenwards before night falls.

When Fuller and her companions returned to Chicago from the countryside she learned that Washington Allston had died. At her first meeting with him four and a half years before she had been fascinated with his "smile of genius" and the way he spoke of his art, flaming up into "a galaxy of Platonism." For the first number of the *Dial* she had written "A Record of Impressions Produced by the Exhibition of Mr. Allston's Pictures in the Summer of 1839." Her own best sonnet, "Flaxman," addressed to the Romantic sculptor and artist famous for his classical bas-reliefs and engravings, is modeled on Allston's ekphrastic sonnets to Michelangelo, Raphael, and Rubens. The sunset that evening in

Chicago "was of a splendor and calmness beyond any we saw in the West." It seemed an appropriate setting for hearing the news that "the American Titian"(as Allston was called) had passed from earth. Though Allston's Trinitarian Christianity filled him with horror at Transcendentalism's apostasies, many Transcendentalists were moved by his lifetime of devotion to art and by the sufferings that his unfinished masterpiece, *Belshazzar's Feast*, had cost him. Fuller prayed that Allston's spirit is now in a place where "Love will free him from the grasp of Fear."

Returning to New England after the freedom and exhilaration of the western trip left Fuller with a feeling of depression. Though Emerson had encouraged her to write *Summer on the Lakes* and had helped find a publisher for it, she felt out of sorts with him, weary with playing her appointed role as sibyl or muse, impatient with the cultural limitations of New England. Her journal for 1844, which contains the last poetry she wrote, also contains an account of a visit she paid to Concord that summer. There Emerson read her the new essay he had composed: then called "Life," later published as "Experience" (*Essays, Second Series*). "He read me his essay on Life. How beautiful, and full and grand. But oh, how cold. Nothing but Truth in the Universe, no love, and no various realities," she wrote. Then she caught herself. "Yet how foolish with me to be grieved at him for showing towards me what exists toward all." In a letter to Emerson himself written two days later, she explained the difference between them simply: "You are intellect, I am life." She wanted a larger and more various world than Concord, attentions more passionate than letters from a brilliant scholar. In a poem called "Sistrum," addressed to the rattle used in ceremonies of the goddess Isis, she declares her need to attain inner harmony without sacrificing the energy that sustained her: "Life-flow of my natal hour / I will not weary of thy power / Till in the changes of thy sound / A chord's three parts distinct are found." Six years later, now a veteran of the brief but glorious Roman revolution and the mother of a young son, she wrote a letter to her friend Marcus Spring from a ship quarantined in Gibraltar harbor. She had boarded the brig *Elizabeth* in Florence with her husband and child, but their intended voyage to America had been halted by an outbreak of smallpox that had killed the *Elizabeth*'s captain. She described the beauty and pathos of the captain's burial at sea – the ships at sea with their banners flying, the stern pillar of Hercules shrouded in roseate vapor. But a sense of foreboding made her add: "Yes! it was beautiful, but how dear a price we pay for the poems of this world."

4

JOHN GREENLEAF WHITTIER

When John Greenleaf Whittier (1807–92) published his first poem in 1826, Carlos Wilcox and John Brainard were still alive; when he published his last poem in 1892, Robert Frost was in high school and Ezra Pound was seven years old. No other poet of the American nineteenth century spans such distances or wrote in such varied styles. Whittier was a lover of New England landscape and traditional lore; he was a political activist, whose poems were meant to awaken consciences; he was an exuberant satirist; he was a Quaker whose verse spoke of forbearance and faith. For more than thirty years he was involved in the struggle against slavery, as an active member of both local and national anti-slavery parties. The events of the day kept him well supplied with topics for verse – sometimes the cruelties of slaveholders, more often the collusion of the Northern businessmen with the anti-abolition mobs who pelted him and his friends with rotten eggs, sticks, and light missiles when they tried to hold public meetings to discuss slavery. He could write about the rotten eggs with amusement, but not about the menace to civil liberties offered by the 1835 pro-slavery meeting in Boston's Faneuil Hall, where (to use Whittier's words) "a demand was made for the suppression of free speech, lest it should endanger the foundations of commercial society," or by Governor Edward Everett's inaugural message in 1836, which urged citizens to abstain from any discussion of slavery. This address drew from Whittier an outraged question addressed to Everett in the *Haverhill Gazette*: "Is this the advice of a republican magistrate to a community of freemen?" Or, as he put it in "Stanzas for the Times" (1835), must the Yankee farmer "be told, beside his plough, / What he must speak, and when, and how?"

His boyhood on a New England farm had given him delight in nature; a sympathetic schoolmaster had introduced him to the intoxication of poetry by lending him a volume of Robert Burns. His formal schooling had ended with two terms at the local Haverhill Academy, but he continued to read poetry and write it copiously as he worked on newspapers in different New England cities. He met Lydia Sigourney when he was editing the *New England Weekly Review* in Hartford, and he continued to write to her even after ill-health had forced him to resign his editorship and return to his birthplace. "The truth is, I love poetry, with a love as warm, as fervent, as sincere, as any of the more gifted worshippers at the temple of the Muses," he confessed. He quoted with entire approval Halleck's lines against posthumous fame:

> Will it avail me aught that men
> Tell to the world with lip and pen,
>   That I have lived and died? –
> *No* – if a garland for my brow,
> Is growing – let me have it *now*
>   While I am live to wear it.
>   ("Notoriety")

By the end of 1832 Whittier had already published over two hundred poems in newspapers and journals, poems heavily influenced by Byron, Scott, Burns, Richard Henry Dana, Felicia Hemans, and Sigourney herself. He had dabbled in politics as an editor and had thought of entering politics himself. During this early period of his life he could hardly be classed as an abolitionist, if we can judge by a letter he wrote in 1831 about an incident in Hartford:

We had a frightful row here on Friday night. At about eleven o'clock a band of negroes paraded our streets, knocking down every white man who made his appearance. Eight or ten were injured – and two it is feared will not recover. I hate these negroes, and would think favorably of John Randolph's proposition of shooting them without ceremony.

Yearly Quaker meetings where slavery was discussed helped change his heart, as did reading issues of Benjamin Lundy's abolitionist newspaper, *The Genius of Universal Emancipation*. Lundy's protegé, William Lloyd Garrison, converted him to active abolitionism. Garrison had been one of the first to notice Whittier's talents; in 1826 he had published seventeen of Whittier's poems in his paper, the *Newburyport Free Press*. By 1833 Garrison had moved to Boston, founded the *Liberator*, announcing in it the doctrine of immediate emancipation. Hearing that Whittier had resigned his Hartford editorship and was at loose ends, Garrison sent him a letter appealing to him to join the new movement: "Whittier, enlist! – Your talents, zeal, influence – all are needed!" (22 March 1833). By May 1833 Whittier had written an anti-slavery pamphlet, *Justice and Expediency*, and in December he attended the initial meeting of the American Anti-Slavery Society in Philadelphia, where, with Garrison and Samuel May, he helped to draft its declaration of principles. In subsequent years he helped edit abolitionist papers in New York and Philadelphia (where his newspaper office was burnt by an anti-abolitionist mob intent on destroying the hall in which it was housed). When recurrent ill health finally forced him to give up editorial work and return to Massachussetts, he continued to contribute anti-slavery poems and articles to sympathetic periodicals. In a poem written to celebrate the world anti-slavery convention in London, he celebrated the modern press's power to multiply its prophecies by the thousands: "Its wizard leaves the Press shall fling / Unceasing from its iron wing."

Robert Penn Warren thought that Whittier's career as an anti-slavery polemicist had rescued him from the vapid diffuseness of his early verse. Writing editorials and blasting opponents in public letters taught him to shape an argument; polemical intent gave his verse concision and sting. Using verse to advance the cause of emancipation also licensed the release of aggression, and showed that Whittier had read more of Byron than *Manfred* or *Childe Harold*. Whittier's best anti-slavery verses are rollicking, like "The Hunters of Men," with its fox-hunting, anapestic gallop. (He wrote the poem in 1834 to mock the Colonization Society's opposing emancipation unless freed slaves were sent to Africa; it achieved a new and horrible appropriateness after 1850, when Congress passed the Fugitive Slave Act making slavecatching a federal obligation even in the free states.)

> Have ye heard of our hunting, o'er mountain and glen,
> Through cane-brake and forest, – the hunting of men?
> The lords of our land to this hunting have gone,
> And the fox-hunter follows the sound of the horn.
>   . . .
> Oh, goodly and grand is our hunting to see,
> In this "land of the brave and the home of the free."
> Priest, warrior, and statesman, from Georgia to Maine,
> All mounting the saddle, all grasping the rein;
> Right merrily hunting the black man, whose sin
> Is the curl of his hair and the hue of his skin!

Whittier's quotation from Francis Scott Key's "Defense of Fort McHenry" took on new ironies the next year, when Key (then District Attorney for Washington, DC) prosecuted a young Quaker doctor named Reuben Crandall for lending a copy of Whittier's *Justice and Expediency* to a friend. Crandall was eventually acquitted, but died from the tuberculosis he had contracted during the eight months he had spent in prison awaiting trial. Whittier would later remember Crandall as one who suffered "For uttering simple words of mine, / And loving freedom all too well."

What provoked Whittier's strongest contempt were moments of hypocrisy or spinelessness from Northerners who ought to be defending liberty but were instead trying to stamp out free speech. In 1837 the Congregational ministers of Massachusetts, worried by the growing contentiousness of the anti-slavery debate and scandalized by the recent anti-slavery lectures of the Grimké sisters, met at Brookfield and issued a pastoral letter urging pastors to avoid "perplexed and agitating subjects" and warning women not to speak in public. Whittier mocks them in "The Pastoral Letter" both for their feebleness and for their historical amnesia:

> So, this is all – the utmost reach
> > Of priestly power the mind to fetter!
> When laymen think, when women preach,
> > A war of words, a "Pastoral Letter!"
> Now, shame upon ye, parish Popes!
> > Was it thus with those, your predecessors,
> Who sealed with racks, and fire, and ropes
> > Their loving-kindness to transgressors?

The Grimké sisters should be hailed as prophetesses, like Miriam and Deborah, not shooed back to the parlor by clergymen too frightened to hear (much less speak) the truth. Whittier addresses these unworthy pastors in a fiery stanza as the poem draws towards its close:

> And what are ye who strive with God
> > Against the ark of His salvation
> Moved by the breath of prayer abroad
> > With blessings for a dying nation?
> What, but the stubble and the hay
> > To perish, even as flax consuming,
> With all that bars His glorious way,
> > Before the brightness of His coming?

Fortunately, the virtues of New England lay not in the tremors of her clergymen but in the courage of her ordinary citizens. The arrest in Boston of a fugitive slave named George Latimer in 1842 provoked demands from Virginia that he be returned to his master. The Friends of Liberty held meetings all over Massachusetts trying to prevent it. For one of these meetings Whittier wrote "Massachusetts to Virginia," in which the Northern state reminds her Southern sister of their shared Revolutionary past but scorns to cower before her current bluster.

> Wild are the waves which lash the reefs along St. George's bank;
> Cold on the shores of Labrador the fog lies white and dank;
> Though storm, and wave, and flinding mist, stout are the hearts which man
> The fishing-smacks of Marblehead, the seaboats of Cape Ann.

> The cold north light and wintry sun glare on their icy forms,
> Bent grimly o'er their straining lines or wrestling with the storms;
> Free as the winds they drive before, rough as the waves they roam,
> They laugh to scorn the slaver's threat against their rocky home.

In these poems and others like them, Whittier could blend dedication to the cause of abolition with love for his native region. But the task of writing so much satire sometimes wearied him, as he admitted in the coda to a long political poem entitled "The Panorama" (1856):

> Oh, not of choice, for themes of public wrong
> I leave the green and pleasant paths of song,
> The mild, sweet words which soften and adorn,
> For sharp rebuke and bitter laugh of scorn.
> More dear to me some song of private worth,
> Some homely idyl of my native North,
> Some summer pastoral of her inland vales,
> Or, grim and weird, her winter fireside tales
> Haunted by ghosts of unreturning sails,
> Lost barks at parting hung from stem to helm
> With prayers of love like dreams on Virgil's elm.

He found some time to write such poems even during the busy 1840s and 1850s. A narrative poem about a seventeenth-century Indian wedding, entitled "The Bridal of Pennacook" (1844–5), is framed by a story of contemporary New Englanders traveling for pleasure through a landscape still glorious with Indian names, whose formidable polysyllables Whittier accommodates to blank-verse lines as skillfully as Wordsworth had done with Loughrigg, Skiddaw, and Glaramara:

> . . . We had tracked
> The winding Pemigewasset, overhung
> By beechen shadows, whitening down its rocks,
> Or lazily gliding through its intervals,
> From waving rye-fields sending up the gleam
> Of sunlit waters. We had seen the moon
> Rising behind Umbagog's eastern pines,
> Like a great Indian camp-fire; and its beams
> At midnight spanning with a bridge of silver
> The Merrimac by Uncanoonuc's falls.

The bridal-narrative itself gives him the opportunity to describe the New England winter landscape in all its frightening beauty. When Weetamoo, daughter of Bashaba of Pennacook, marries Winnepurkit of Saugus, she finds a landscape of surpassing bleakness:

> A wild and broken landscape, spiked with firs,
> Roughening the bleak horizon's northern edge;
> Steep, cavernous hillsides, where black hemlock spurs
> And sharp, gray splinters of the windswept ledge
> Pierced the thin-glazed ice, or bristling rose
> Where the cold rim of the sky sunk down upon the snows.

> And eastward cold, wide marshes stretched away,
> Dull, dreary flats without a bush or tree,
> O'er-crossed by icy creeks, where twice a day
> Gurgled the waters of the moon-struck sea;
> And faint with distance came the stifled roar,
> The melancholy lapse of waves on that low shore.

Snow, ice, and fir-trees; marsh, mud, and tides – these were the poetic subjects to which Whittier's mind instinctively turned. In a poem of 1840, "The Exiles," he praises William Macy, one of the first white settlers on Nantucket, not only for the moral courage that had inspired him to defend a wandering Quaker from the wrath of the Massachusetts Puritans, but for choosing an island refuge that was "Free as the winds that winnow / Her shrubless hills of sand, / Free as the waves that batter / Along her yielding land." In "The Prophecy of Samuel Sewall" (1859) he surveys with evident pleasure the shore that had greeted Justice Sewall's eyes over a century before.

> Long and low, with dwarf trees crowned,
> Plum Island lies, like a whale aground,
> A stone's toss over the narrow sound.
> Inland, as far as the eye can go
> The hills curve round like a bended bow.

Whittier's native gift for description found its greatest outlet in *Snow-Bound*, published the year after the Civil War ended. Its portrait of a New England farm family in the 1820s, cut off by a blizzard from the outside world, made Whittier, to his surprise, suddenly famous (it sold twenty thousand copies in the first few months). With a fluency few American poets could match, his tetrameter couplets describe the coming storm:

> The sun that brief December day
> Rose cheerless over hills of gray,
> And, darkly circled, gave at noon,
> A sadder light than waning moon.
> Slow tracing down the thickening sky
> Its mute and ominous prophecy.

Inside, the boys and their father build a huge fire that makes "the old, rude-furnished room / Burst flower-like into rosy bloom" to wait out the snow-storm's fury. When it finally passes they look out upon a night landscape full of "coldness visible":

> The moon above the eastern wood
> Shone at its full; the hill-range stood
> Transfigured in the silver flood,

> Its blown snows flashing cold and keen,
> Dead white, save where some sharp ravine
> Took shadow, or the sombre green
> Of hemlocks turned to pitchy black.

No matter how forbidding the scene, the family and friends gathered around the "great throat of the chimney" fear neither the night nor the raving of the hearth-wind, as they repeat old family stories, play games, recite anti-slavery poems, or listen to the young village schoolmaster who is boarding with the family tell comic versions of the legends of Greece and Rome. But "Time and Change" have done what the snow-storm could not, as Whittier sadly acknowledges, scattering the family circle to death, exile, and old age. And the itinerant schoolmasters of 1866 must go out upon their wanderings following in "War's bloody trail." It is significant that this brief allusion to the Civil War (the only one in the poem) occurs as Whittier discusses the nation's need for teachers who can "uplift the black and white alike." For even in the New England of his boyhood there had been many households not so fortunate as his own had been, many slatternly, weedy homesteads full of "shrill, querulous women, sour and sullen men," as he says in the Prelude to *Among the Hills* (1869). Frightened of Judgment but deaf to the voice of charity, these unhappy people never saw the divine love that surrounded them everywhere: the may-flowers underneath their feet, the voice of the song-sparrow, the gold and crimson splendors of New England's annual "sacramental mystery." To awaken his countrymen, to "Invite the eye to see and heart to feel / The beauty and the joy within their reach," must once again be the task of poetry, its civilizing mission: "Finding its late fulfillment in a change, / Slow as the oak's growth, lifting manhood up / Through broader culture, finer manners, love." The faith that had sustained Whittier through the abolition movement and the Civil War gave him confidence that this private work of Reconstruction could also succeed. In an 1865 poem ("The Grave by the Lake") he asserts that true faith will not doubt that salvation might extend to those buried in an Indian mound beside a lake:

> Not with hatred's undertow
> Doth the Love eternal flow;
> Every chain that spirits wear
> Crumbles in the breath of prayer;
> And the penitent's desire
> Opens every gate of fire.

A faith like Whittier's in the civilizing powers of imagination had sustained American poetry from its beginnings. It inspired Joel Barlow's belief in the eventual triumph of Reason, Jones Very's trust that sonnets might inspire conversions, and Ralph Waldo Emerson's unshakeable conviction that the individual mind contains all divinity within it. But faith in imagination also inspires John Quincy Adams's playfulness, Fitz-Greene Halleck's urbanity, Maria Gowen Brooks's fearlessness, Washington Allston's reverence for Rubens as well as for Raphael, and Henry Thoreau's tenderness towards the small excellences of the landscape. Other American poets were already combining these qualities in new and surprising ways.

Poetry and public discourse, 1820–1910

Shira Wolosky

PREFACE: THE CLAIMS OF RHETORIC

Rhetoric is the art of making claims. As such, it has often been suspected of being narrowly strategic and interested, if not distorting. But it can also be claimed that, instead of only putting forward some particular argument, rhetoric broadly structures experience in so far as this is mediated by language and expressed through language. To study rhetoric is then to study fundamental patterns in a culture, as made evident and pursued through its varied discourses. In this sense, rhetoric provides a site where literature intersects with other forms of discourse, and not least public ones. The rhetorical modes of a culture penetrate literary representation, while literature derives its materials through such rhetorical matrices, but in ways that are more self-conscious, self-reflective, and directed to its own ends.

The study of nineteenth-century American poetry confirms the mutual reference between literary work and other modes of rhetoric. In the nineteenth century, poetry had a vibrant and active role within ongoing discussions defining America and its cultural directions. The notion of poetry as a self-enclosed aesthetic realm; constituted as a formal object to be approached through more or less exclusively specified categories of formal analysis; conceived as meta-historically transcendent; and deploying a distinct and poetically "pure" language: these notions seem only to begin to emerge at the end of the nineteenth century, in a process which is itself peculiarly shaped in response to social and historical no less than aesthetic trends. Within the course of the nineteenth century itself, such an enclosed poetic realm seems not to have been assumed, except as an anxiety and as a looming threat within American culture itself. Instead, poetry directly participated in and addressed the pressing issues facing the new nation.

The second part of this book, "Poetry and Public Discourse," approaches poetry as a distinctive formal field on which the rhetorics of nineteenth-century American culture finds intensified expression, concentration, reflection, and command. The literary force, not to say genius, of a writer often entails a mastery of the rhetorical constructions widely available in his or her surrounding culture. Poetic representation reflects, but also gives a heightened definition and self-consciousness to general rhetorical constructions, in ways that may both reinforce and critique them. It is one argument of this study that poetry gains not only historical grounding but also aesthetic coherence and illumination through study of its transformative relationship to the rhetorics that surround it. This is not to collapse or deny all aesthetic difference. Distinctions remain between greater and lesser poetic mastery, itself illuminated through an investigation of how each situates the other and provides a necessary matrix for reading the other. Nor is it to reduce literature to historical or ideological reproduction of social experience. It is rather to claim that literature has its origins and its reference in a broad range of historical and cultural experiences, as mediated through rhetorical practices among other factors. Values, attitudes, interests, and cultural directions at large in the society are expressed through rhetorical tropes, which in turn reemerge in poetry, marking such specifically poetic structures as voice, imagery, setting, self-representation, and address. Conversely, poetic representation foregrounds and sharpens the terms of a culture's rhetorical configurations. Thus, far from negating the specifically literary nature of a poetic text, rhetorical context illuminates and affirms poetry's cultural importance and aesthetic power.

Walt Whitman of course figures as the outstanding example of poetry as participating in American public and cultural life. But he is only the greatest exemplar of a fundamental impulse in nineteenth-century poetic enterprise. At the same time, anxiety over the place of art within evolving American cultural commitments is a recurrent pressure on many of the writers of the period, as a feared deformation of American promise. In the face of this pressure, poets offer a range of responses. These invariably, however, devote poetic vision to political, social, religious, and moral, as well as aesthetic concerns. Poetry is conceived as actively participating in the national life; and this also profoundly shapes the poet's conception of himself and herself and his and her role in society.

In this study, rhetoric provides a site where literature intersects with various public discourses. I have focused on a set of rhetorical topics that cross literary and cultural-historical forces. In each case, a vital American concern is approached through a rhetorical mode shared by both poetry and its surrounding social worlds. The first topic investigates the rhetoric of modesty as this situates nineteenth-century American women poets. It is a given of much nineteenth-century historical and literary study that women's lives were circumscribed within a domestic world, in ways that extended into almost every aspect of their social roles and personal definitions. The gendered division between public and private is therefore seen to be stark, enforced through many of the norms controlling political, social, and personal conduct – as expressed specifically in the burgeoning literature of conduct-books through-out the period, instructing ladies on appropriate manners in a world of extreme social change where these were becoming increasingly unclear.

Yet the poetry produced by women undermines and complicates the division between public and private as these categories have been applied to female (and male) experience. A large number of the poems written by women address public issues. Indeed, the very conception of what is public and what private is challenged in light of the work of women poets, as these categories apply to both women and men. In this, the poetry reflects historical ambiguities that complicate the accepted paradigm of women's lives as private. In historical terms, women were in fact widely engaged in activities and issues beyond their domestic spaces. These activities have been generally conceptualized as extensions of the woman's sphere, rather than as challenges to it. Yet, even while some activities women conducted outside the home were rather like those performed within it – care for the sick, the elderly, the poor, immigrants, children – other activities were not. These include direct political activism in abolition, Indian rights, urban-planning, sanitation, and women's suffrage. Indeed, throughout the century, most social services (as we would call them) were performed by women. Calling this "private" while reserving the term "public" for the activities of men – who were overwhelmingly engaged in economic pursuits that, while taking place outside the home, ultimately served personal interests and private economic ends – is a use of the terms "public" and "private" in ways that are already gendered. That is, it is only because and when women performed certain activities and community services that these are categorized as private. It is only because men were engaged in and controlling economic production that these are categorized as public.

These public engagements are reflected in women's verse. Besides the many verses addressed to social concerns, including care of children (which can itself be seen as a social and not merely private commitment), a good deal of verse explicitly concerns public issues and political disputes. And poetry particularly served as an important avenue for women to address issues and events of central cultural importance – a role, it can be argued, that poetry has never simply abandoned in any case. At its best, this women's poetry is one of rhetorical reflection, capturing and structuring the languages and rhetorical patterns around it. Often these rhetorics appear as gendered voices, interestingly posed against each other, as figures for those cultural values each is shown to represent in their increasing alienation or disturbance. The poetic topics are often those of women's activism: slavery, poverty, prostitution. More broadly, they engage overarching questions facing American society as, through the course of the century, economic interests increasingly seemed to challenge, and curtail, the earlier call to republican commitments and the value of community as against private concerns. There is in this women's verse a pressing sense of a double standard – itself a recurrent image in the sexual sense, but also as a broad figure of America's bifurcating worlds and conflicting values.

This poetry is valuable as representations of women's lives, but also raises aesthetic issues that need not be merely dismissed. Much of this women's poetry is no worse than minor male poetry that remained continuously in circulation – anthologized, reprinted, and included in literary histories. While the poetry often does not offer self-reflective language and self-conscious forms (as also most male poetry does not), what it does powerfully do is re-present, expose, and manipulate the rhetorics of its surrounding culture, bringing them to view and to self-consciousness. These poems belong more to literary history than to monumental art. But this is to say – as is the case with minor male poets also – that they reveal the conditions, in both language and history, which shaped the aesthetic and cultural experience of their period.

Women's verse is not unique in this participation of poetry in wider cultural discourses. Religious rhetoric stands as another field in which poetry crosses with public expression, where religious discourse addresses not only theological but also political and sectional, gendered and ethnic interests. In poetry, as in speeches, sermons, fictions, and newspapers, nineteenth-century America's efforts at self-definition took shape through religious claims and counter-claims. The Bible, as a foundational text of American national identity, provided terms for articulating and arguing many different aspects of American commitments. Here the outstanding feature is the way the Bible in particular, but also a variety of religious traditions and understandings, became a rhetorical base shared even by quite violently opposing interests. Among a very wide range of disputants, each asserts its own contrasting visions and claims against the others within a religious rhetoric that remained nonetheless common. In one sense, this mutually contrastive deployment of Biblical and religious justification made the intensity of disputation more severe. However, in another sense religious rhetoric permitted diverse viewpoints and even violent disagreements to confront each other in a common language, out of a shared cultural inheritance. Religious language similarly penetrates the poetry of the period, fashioning it into a territory of claim and counter-claim, where words pull in conflicting, yet also common directions understood by all: conservative and liberal, religious and secular, South and North, white and black. To a remarkable degree, religious impulses in America take their place within a tradition of open discourse and anti-authoritarian individualism, making religion part of a cultural heritage that retains varieties of liberal experience. As a mode of poetic expression, religious language comes to register diverse meanings: in slave spirituals, in women's poetry, and even, as in the work of Herman Melville, as a mode of refusal to claim absolute certainties altogether.

This diversity of meanings within a common language is strongly felt in poetry written by men throughout the century – a poetry in many ways focused upon the very question of what an American poetic language might be, what claims it can make, on the one hand, against England whose language it fundamentally shared, and on the other, in a society apparently concerned with practical and not aesthetic production. Here sectional strife, but also cultural division is strongly registered, with the question of American identity itself highly unsettled. This is the case both in the North and the South. The poetry of these regions almost hauntingly provides an image of the divided nation, as each inherits a revolutionary discourse that each then claims in contradictory ways. But both before and after the Civil War, in the poetry of Henry Wadsworth Longfellow, Edgar Allan Poe, and Stephen Crane, the question of an American poetic language is seen in anxious contest against the materialist-commercial trends emerging with increasing stridency. Poe in particular constructs a poetic of negation directed against the conditions of America (as of reality in general), a poetic of extremity showing the obverse side of American possibility. By the century's end, a fearful distrust and sense of displacement by the riotous turn to material prosperity as the defining American value becomes the basis for a new aesthetic, centered at Harvard and especially in the figure of George Santayana, bent on defending poetry from public space. The redrawing of poetic lines as a boundary against the active world, such that the poem comes to be defined as a self-enclosed aesthetic object, finds its origins in an emerging turn-of-the-century formalist aesthetics.

The post-Civil War world witnesses new senses of identity and new poetics engaging, expressing, and shaping them. As in fiction, there emerges a poetry of regional and ethnic diversity, as these reflect and attempt to formulate shifts in the relationships between geographic distribution and federal definition. A new sense of post-war geographic, ethnic, racial, and religious pluralism can be felt, alongside gender identity. Women's writing is not in fact a separate subgroup more or less marginal to American literature, but an integral part of America's poetic enterprise, even while gender introduces specific textual questions and expressions. At issue in this poetry are both new conceptions of America as a national framework and new conceptions of the individual's place within it. Yet, rather than emphasizing group identifications as determinative, with pluralism measured through the interactions between groups, this poetry suggests a possibility of multiple participations in a number of groups, with a relatively high degree of voluntarism and permeability. Identity in this sense itself becomes multiple. The self represents a site where different associations may be variously negotiated. In poetry, what becomes of central structural importance is how several different identities achieve expression, emerging textually as an orchestration of voices. Differentiated senses of the self are invoked and deployed in mutual relation and collision, with dialect, region, gender, ethnicity, and social class all significant factors. The text itself becomes a pluralist site, and pluralism becomes a mode of negotiating not only between diverse groups, but between diverse elements, identities, and commitments within the individual as he and she participates in a larger, complex polity.

Walt Whitman and Emily Dickinson emerge from the nineteenth-century's cultural and rhetorical matrices as the two master figures: yet in ways that seem dramatically opposed. For these two seem to be, and in some ways are, the most public and private of poets. Regarding Whitman, my argument questions readings that emphasize enormities of the self, and instead situates Whitmanian selfhood within a vision of political individualism that Whitman himself rigorously explored. In this model, the individual remains a founding site; and Whitman's greatness as an American poet surely inheres not least in his passionate devotion to the individual's endless possibility, creative energy, infinite potential, and pursuit of happiness. Whitman calls to each reader to recognize and actualize these resources of the self – which would be, in his project, to call to each reader to himself and herself become a poet. Yet Whitman does not do so as a solipsistic, self-directed apotheosis of unlimited individuality. He, on the contrary, insists on individual self-realization as inextricably connected to, and grounded upon, a sense of place in an ongoing political and social realization. Without the contribution of each individual, without the active commitment and participation of each towards creating a polity in which just such individual potential can be realized, the American experiment will founder. Both poet and reader serve as a figure of the potential citizen, where, however, the poet summons other citizens to this right and responsibility, in a role of service that itself truly defines leadership.

The imagined possibility of such a community of individuals is for Whitman the figure of America and the promise of America. If America is to him the greatest poem, it is because it represents that creative individual potential which can find expression on every level of experience, yet whose multiplicities intersect in a common venture. Whitman inscribes such multiple levels of meaning in his own poetic conduct, which offers intensely complex figures for the variety of experiences, individual and communal. Whitman, however, is also deeply disturbed by the obvious failures of America to be true to its own promise. His poetry is born from, and reflects, a profound misgiving and alarm at the dissolution of America's varied constitutive forces: most explosively in the Civil War, and in the slavery which contradicts the American commitment to freedom, but subsequently in the War's aftermath, as American promise threatens to shrink to a narrow, flat, and restrictive material prosperity and exclusionary self-interest.

Emily Dickinson in uncanny ways presents an obverse face to Whitman. This does not mean that her concerns are restricted to a private world. On the contrary, Dickinson gives strong voice to Whitman's anxieties and suspicions regarding the fulfillment of an American promise. Her work, like his, reflects back on diverse elements of the American experience. These include gender, religion, history, and economic orders. Dickinson's peculiar poetic posits and challenges the variant claims of each of these spheres. Under her scrupulous investigation, the cultural assumption that these differing spheres are concordant and mutually supporting becomes undermined if not exploded. Her texts become a site for the confrontation and often the conflict between orders of experience that prove to be contradictory rather than mutually affirming. This confrontation can be described in terms of her own identities, which similarly contradict or subvert each other. Her roles as woman, as poet, within religious tradition, and as American each finds expression in her work, but in ways that open and dramatize fissures between them. Particularly her status as woman complicates her possibilities of participation in American culture. The very privacy of her work – unpublished in a lifetime spent largely in reclusion and structured through obscurity – is a critical reflection on the options open to women and the expectations of them within her society. Here, the work of other women's poetry becomes a vital context for interpreting the high art of Emily Dickinson, not only in terms of women's domestic confinement, as has been mainly emphasized, but also in terms of women's distinctive voices in critique of the fantasies of autonomy and self-reliance increasingly commensurate with American identity itself – models of identity that Dickinson's work at once deploys and disrupts. In Dickinson's poetry, the cultural norm of modesty acquires intensified and eruptive expression, exposing models of both male and female selfhood. The result is a critique of many fundamental American assumptions, undertaken in a densely figured language whose multiple meanings and implications collide with complex and explosive force.

Throughout this study, poetry retains its specific status and is interpreted through its own characteristic structures, its language uses, and its self-reflective impulses. Yet, I treat these literary modes as they order, shape, and give expression to the vital concerns of culture, through intersecting rhetorics which poetry then addresses, employs, critiques, and transforms. Literature as an art and a discipline itself thus participates in, and reflects, history as it has been shaped by rhetoric, and rhetoric as it has been shaped by history. Within the body of nineteenth-century verse, I pursue poetry as it represents and reflects such cultural norms and concerns as gender structures; religious commitments and national identity as these mutually inform each other; ethnic and regional conflicts and claims; and claims to the national heritage. My subject is poetry's role in the nineteenth century of investigating and articulating, within its own unique terms and through its own unique modes of self-reflection, issues fundamental to the definition of American life.

MODEST CLAIMS

WRITING ETIQUETTE

Anne Bradstreet inaugurated American poetry with a disclaimer. In the "Prologue" to her work she concedes that, as a woman poet, she may be "obnoxious" to the many readers eager to cast "despite . . . on female wits." But, she goes on, while hers will always and only be an "unrefined ore" in contrast against male "glistring gold," all she is seeking is a crown of kitchen herbs suitable to her station: "Give thyme and parsley wreath, I ask no bays."

On this meek note she launched not only her own poetically ambitious project, but a rhetoric that is pursued by women writers through the next centuries. In a feminization of the classical *apologia* – apology in defense or justification – Bradstreet modestly denies her abilities. In doing so, however, she asserts her right to speak against those who would not even grant her that much. Reassuring her readers that she will not exceed her proper place, she enables herself, at least within these confines, to exercise her powers. But this in turn becomes a method and avenue exactly for broadening the narrow strictures allotted to her.

Modesty, then, serves as an image of confinement, restriction, and boundary. Yet it also represents the instability of that boundary, its revision and even transgression as a feminine mode of entry into a wider world. In this double sense, modesty emerges as a central topos and stance of female writing. (There are comparable topoi for men, especially in the discourses of religious humility. Nevertheless, I would claim that there are distinctions of gender within the uses of these topoi. In general, male humility is theological; men are willing to humble themselves before God or his representatives within an ecclesiastical hierarchy. For women, modesty has been more socialized, and more centrally defining. Women are taught to humble themselves before other human beings, i.e. men.) Women's poetry of the nineteenth century has until recently been more or less omitted from American literary history. Even in recent discussions, it is at times lamented as offering on the whole a sentimental verse characterized by lack of ambition, fear of fame, and images of powerlessness, while modesty is treated almost entirely as a mark of female submission. The modesty topos, however, is not merely a negative stance. It also reflects the efforts of women to speak for and to female experience, to find a literary voice that will accord with their sense of themselves as women, and even to articulate distinctive values and commitments. Instead of being viewed only as negative self-effacement in polar opposition to positive self-assertion, modesty, within nineteenth-century female culture, can be said to represent a dialectical negotiation between these two poles towards the redefinition of both of them. Neither stark self-denial nor unlimited self-assertion represents for these women the ideal for personal or communal life. Modesty, in various guises, marks their efforts to define a selfhood between these oppositions threatening to fragment them not only as women, but as Americans. Asserted repeatedly through female poetic writing in America from the colonial poetry of Anne Bradstreet to such twentieth-century poets as Marianne Moore and Elizabeth Bishop, modesty within the nineteenth century frames the work of women poets both popular and elite, accomplished and minor. Among these, it takes on different roles and carries differing degrees of force. Lydia Sigourney and Emily Dickinson invoke modesty in ways that vary greatly. Despite differences, however, modesty provides a lens for seeing into the diverse poetry produced by nineteenth-century women, as well as linking literary production to social conditions and cultural paradigms.

For modesty, of course, is not only a literary stance. Perhaps more than any other quality, it has traditionally defined the quintessence of womanhood. Cotton Mather, in his *Ornaments for the Daughters of Zion*, names it as an indispensable adornment in the ideal female daily dress of "the Silk of Piety, the Satin of Sanctity, and the Purple of Modesty." As an early advice book puts it, modesty "is a very general and comprehensive quality. It extends to everything where a woman is concerned: conversation, books, pictures, attitude, gesture, pronunciation." Indeed, through the myriad etiquette books published from the late eighteenth and into the nineteenth centuries, modesty comes to extend well beyond an exclusive concern with female sexual behavior "to cover," as one advice book puts it, "the whole of experience." It "prescribes you a perfect rule of direction, how to behave yourselves in your whole course or conversation: In your very motion, gesture, and gate, observe modesty." As "the most indispensable requisite of a woman," it is urged as the quality most "essential and natural to the sex"; encompassing "your looks, your speech, and the course of your whole behavior, [which] should own an humble distrust of your selves."

Modesty may be said peculiarly to mark the complex structure of the "separate spheres" and the "Cult of True Womanhood" which in many ways shaped gender roles and relations in nineteenth-century America. Within this construction, the lives of women and men were distinguished and assigned: the one to the private and domestic; the other to the public, political, and economic domains. Enforcing this division of social life were legal and political restrictions denying to (married) women the right to inherit and indeed to own property, even their personal and household belongings; to have bank accounts and sign checks (hence treasurers of female societies had to be single or widowed); to hold office or to vote. Extra-legal social norms reinforced legal ones, making it unseemly, for example, to speak publicly in mixed ("promiscuous") company, or even to go out into public spaces unchaperoned or improperly dressed. Such norms established restrictions perhaps no less potent than legal ones because they were not only imposed but internalized. In these senses, the modest demeanor, status, and possibilities demanded of women served to enclose and subordinate them.

And yet, modesty acted not only as a barrier but also as a gateway of the women's sphere. While undoubtedly serving to keep women the prisoners (called "guardians") of the domestic hearth, modesty served as well to mediate between and bridge private and public worlds. Its restrictive senses did not prevent it from becoming, in the hands of women writers at least, an avenue also leading out of the private domestic circle into the broader space of public and published expression. Modesty as a literary topos thus stands in complex relation to its social uses. Indeed, it serves as a manner not only of self-effacement but of self-presentation and self-representation in both social and literary intercourse, which could be exploited to enlarge or intensify self-expression. This is what occurs in the hands of literary artists.

Modesty, then, is not just a mode of self- and social enclosure. It also defines parameters for expression, for venturing forth into the world. And the boundaries separating the domestic from the non-domestic, privacy from publicity, are neither as absolute nor as fixed as the ideology of the woman's sphere asserts. Norms of behavior, far from being self-evident and assured, were particularly vulnerable and uncertain through the nineteenth century – as the explosion of etiquette manuals itself suggests. People required so much instruction exactly because they were unsure what behavior was expected or acceptable. Nineteenth-century America was a period of extraordinary dynamism, transformation, and indeed rupture on almost every level, including demographic and economic as well as social and political structures. Urbanization, industrialization, and democratization all more or less radically changed the rules of conduct no less than the organization of work and financing, home-life, class divisions, and civic and political developments. Migrations to cities replaced the familiar intimacy of village life with the anonymity, mobility, production, and consumption of urban spaces. Life among multitudes of strangers required new norms of behavior for establishing and avoiding acquaintanceships, with a strong sense of (and desire for) social status mediating relations in both the world of business and the drawing room. The gentility that had been traditionally defined through social differentiations of inherited rank and titles, became in industrializing America the aspiration of a middle class. Defining proper behavior thus became an urgent need, as new social situations and roles generated uncertainty as to the forms of genteel conduct as well as the desire to master them. At the same time, new technologies in communication, transport, material production, and publishing provided the means for disseminating a literature with instructions for doing so.

Etiquette books, mass produced, rushed in to service this new demand for respectability. Gentlemen and gentlewomen, educators, editors, and journalists, all were happy to inform middle-class young ladies at what hours, with what companions; in what clothes, with what tones of voice and topics of conversation it was suitable for them to present themselves to what was called the World. As the much reprinted *Lady's New Year's Gift* explained, venturing "out of your house into the world" is

> "a dangerous" step: where your vertue alone will not secure you, except it is attended with a great deal of Prudence. You must have both for your guard, and not stir without them. The Enemy is abroad, and you are sure to be taken if you are found struggling. Your behavior is therefore to incline strongly toward the Reserv'd part . . . The Extravagances of the Age have made Caution more necessary . . . A Close behavior is the fittest to receive Vertue for its constant Guest.

Besides offering what amounts to self-advertisement, this advice images the double face of modesty. Warning against the unknown "abroad," urging Prudence and Reserve and "Close behavior," it nevertheless also outlines, within accepted social norms, how to negotiate the world's dangers. This delicate balance is reenacted through the many available guides to manners. Strictures on modest dress – "never showy," writes Sarah J. Hale, and in keeping with the "prevailing fashion" so as to be "less conspicuous," warnings against loud talk or laughter in company ("a young lady should never make herself conspicuous in public assembly" writes Eliza Ware Farrar in her popular *Young Lady's Friend*), also implicitly acknowledge new contexts and new opportunities for women to appear in public. Whereas women had before been largely circumscribed by household spaces, city streets offered new avenues for outings, although their movements continued to be carefully overseen by specially demarcated semi-public places and many ordinances guarding public order. If women were officially restricted from venturing forth in the city streets unattended by chaperones, they were nevertheless granted a certain, albeit circumscribed, leeway. This was especially the case with regard to the specific middle-class female contribution to the domestic economy, i.e. shopping. Department stores, a new creation of metropolitan space, generated in turn a "Ladies Mile" of shops in downtown New York, wherein it was permissible to walk, even alone. Eliza Farrar's is therefore a double message when she continues: "Always remember that a store is a public place; that you are speaking before and often to strangers, and therefore, there should be a certain degree of reserve, in all you do and say . . . dispatch your business in a quiet and polite manner, equally removed from haughtiness and familiarity."

Such genteel behavior in public was intended not least to distinguish women of the middle class from their working-class sisters, to say nothing of prostitutes. And behavioral codes remained restrictive. Still, American middle-class women enjoyed much more freedom of movement than did their counterparts in Europe, as De Tocqueville comments (one need only recall Daisy Miller, who dies in Italy of a bad reputation). While falling far short of the women's rights envisioned and fought for by "ultraist" feminist political activists, middle-class social roles also, it has been increasingly argued, strengthened female identity and enlarged female activity and power. The dual face of modesty as both suppressive and expressive in some sense mirrors an ambiguity, or perhaps instability, within the structure of the separate spheres themselves. For the woman's sphere, despite its ideological and indeed actual circumscription of female activity, also framed activities that made possible its own subversion. Feminist historians see the development of a specifically separate female sphere as constituting a distinctive culture in which nineteenth-century women shared events and intimate, highly supportive relationships. Within the early nineteenth-century home, women developed not only new female companionships but also gained new recognition and new power. The domestic sphere as properly women's own gave women one area of authority at least. A general increase in control over and within the family structure is visible, measured by such factors as limitation in family size, in what has been called "domestic feminism." The family in this sense becomes a scene of social change and not only of resistance to it. Nineteenth-century domestic confinement similarly frames the intense female friendships attested in letters and diaries, which in turn become one resource for female literary practices.

What is more, the intensification of the domestic sphere paradoxically also became the basis for involvement in activities beyond it. Even as the separation of spheres heightened gender-group identification and asserted limits on what was proper for women, it also militated against such strict boundaries, serving as a ground from which women could pursue worldly careers. There was, so to speak, a public side to domesticity, enacted through the extensive participation of nineteenth-century American women in societies and associations devoted to a wide range of social and political goals. These included mission work, poor relief, hospital service, education, temperance, and, at the more radical extreme, abolition and legal reforms for the rights of women. Such women's organizations marked a penetration into areas of public life from which women were ostensibly debarred. Besides setting up often elaborate business administration including fund-raising, wages, incorporation, and distribution of benefits, the women "volunteers" also engaged in direct political activity such as lobbying, petitioning, and financing and contributing to campaigns.

These economic and political activities were justified as extensions, not revisions, of acceptable gender roles. Women were not so much liberated from the domestic sphere as enabled to enter social territories seen to derive in it. Social and political activities were viewed not as assaulting the whole (gendered) distinction of public/private, but rather as based within it. New ventures and rights remained extensions of the traditional domestic roles of wife and mother and not alternatives to them. The achievement of new economic roles, the rise in women's education, as well as the increasingly public social roles associated with various reform projects were essentially based in, and applications of, home values. Female education was justified as enabling women to educate children and to provide husbands with more fit companions. Social action was mainly directed towards improving the material and moral conditions of the poor, the immigrant groups, the family farm, and perhaps above all, the men: agitation against drink, prostitution, and gambling included attacks on the saloon, not only as the site of these nefarious activities but as a man's world away from his domestic obligations.

Women could present these social programs as intended to safeguard the home against evil, even if doing so led out of the home into the world. Female social action remained, moreover, concordant with the female figure as nurturing, self-sacrificing, and morally high and pure. The essentially conservative element in these reform projects can be measured as well by the relative unpopularity of more radical feminist goals such as the suffrage, which posed a much greater threat to the separate spheres by implicitly defining women as individuals, rather than as members of a household. Even abolition was a less popular cause than, say, temperance, and was often justified in the name of the destructive effects of slavery on the family.

Still, if education, economic rights, and social reform began as extensions of the domestic sphere, they nevertheless instituted changes often unforeseen by their initiators. To take one prominent example, Catherine Beecher's devotion to female education and other gendered issues such as health, dress, and domestic economy was firmly rooted in her sense of the home as a private domain of moral value away from the marketplace. Nevertheless, Beecher's programs and writings, though committed to domestic identity as the basis for a special role for women, finally exceeded and indeed unraveled it. By strengthening female identity, insisting on the need for and right to education and remuneration, and establishing the authority of women over issues before given to men, even if only within the home, Beecher ultimately challenged the perimeters of the domicile and the domestic restraints on female autonomy. As her father, Lyman Beecher, instructively complained, her public advocacy could only be at the cost "of that female delicacy, which is above all price." Thus, although attacked as conservative by contemporary feminist suffragists, Beecher's has come to be seen as another avenue of development for women's rights.

Similarly, Sarah J. Hale – author of the unruly "Mary Had a Little Lamb" and the editor of the wildly successful magazine *Godey's Lady's Book* – held a basically conservative outlook on what was permissible for women. This in part explains her popularity. Conservative values, however, became her ground for arguments in support of female education, property rights, athletic prowess, and moral power. Thus, her "Advice to a Daughter" urges young ladies to "modestly accept any attentions which propriety warrants" while discouraging any unacceptably forward behavior or "artful insinuations" towards the opposite sex. She boldly supports new property laws granting to married women continued control of "all estate, real and personal, belonging to a woman at the time of her marriage." In her own advice book published in 1862, she denounces the "premature ladyism" that unduly restricts women from "healthy, innocent sports." And, in the name of properly fulfilling their profession of "Domestic Science" (a term Hale carefully enforced in order to elevate housework), women deserve an ambitious program of education: "Is it not time to begin the experience of fitting woman for her own work? Among these duties, there must be some of importance to the public weal. Do not the daughters of the Republic require more in their culture than the elementary education of the common schools? Medical science belongs as surely to women as to men."

Hale's position is finally in favor of an indirect influence as against a direct one, although Hale herself (like Beecher) preferred the career of giving this advice to one of taking it. She thus grants to women only "the controlling power over their homes, children, and social life" – a modest role in which "Greatness is most perfect when it acts with the least reference to the self; power is most efficient when moving the will [of men] through the heart."

What remains controversial is the extent to which such indirect influence, and the paradoxes of the woman's sphere generally, were finally socially transforming or self-defeating. Urging indirect influence rather than direct economic, professional, or political opportunity may trade off more power than it gains. Restricting women's effective power, even rhetorically, to a moral, interior, private appeal rather than to concerted, public, organized pressure may only reaffirm the problems and divisions it sets out to overcome. In the specific realm of literature, representations of private selves may similarly be no more than a sentimental substitution of genuine historical consciousness for personal intimacy. But feminine modesty broadly conceived served as well as an apology for new strength. Combining an increased sense of power with promises to limit it, modest claims may serve less to betray than to safeguard identity and autonomy. And they play a vital role in what can retrospectively be seen as an ongoing process of renegotiating private/public spaces and roles.

This renegotiation is particularly dramatic with regard to publishing. A manner of appearing in public, publishing was explicitly seen as an issue of modesty. Thus, one Puritan contemporary of Anne Bradstreet wrote in condemnation of his own sister's venture into publishing, "Your printing of a Book beyond the Custom of your Sex, doth rankly smell." Bradstreet's own insistence that her poems were published against her will and without her knowledge is (even if true) quite standard, both during her period and after it. Denials of responsibility along with concealments of authorship under pseudonyms or anonymity reflected proper sensibility of publishing as immodest exposure, not to mention the danger of being so accused. One preface to a book of poems explains that the young lady author would have been named "had not her modesty absolutely forbid it." The female author of *An Essay in Defence of the Female Sex* (1696) states that nothing could "induce me to bring my name upon the public stage of the world . . . The tenderness of reputation in our sex . . . made me very cautious, how I exposed mine to such poisonous vapours."

This caution against public printing in fact extends to more general restrictions against speaking at all. Richard Allestree begins what was probably the most influential seventeenth-century conduct-book, *The Ladies Calling*, with a section "Of Modesty." He there issues warnings against a young girl "too forward and confident in her talk." Instead, "modesty prescribes the manner, so does it also the measure of speaking, [and] restrains all excessive talkativeness." Or, as Richard Brathwaite sums up in *The English Gentlewoman*, a woman's "modest disposition" urges the lady in public "to observe rather than discourse."

Modesty here verges into repressive silencing, an extreme which women writers by definition resist. What is interesting is the way they not only circumvent restrictions, but exploit them, incorporating them into complex literary personae, styles, motifs, and ventures. Lydia Sigourney, for example, began her publishing career anonymously, as did many women novelists and authors of advice books. Hidden authorship, however, often initiated little dramas of "discovery," betraying women not only to fame but to profit. For Sigourney, this was a matter of explicit calculation. "I wish," she dutifully writes, "to avoid notoriety." But, she explains, "this would be disagreeable to those whom it is my duty to conciliate," i.e. the publishers who urged the market value of her name. With this plea, she cheerfully moved from anonymity to advertising; and she did not hesitate through her career fully to exploit the commercial value of her name. Julia Ward Howe similarly calculated discovery, writing to one New York friend about a recently published volume of verse: "The authorship is of course a secret now, and you had best talk openly of it all of you, as it may help the sale of the book in New York."

At issue is not hypocrisy – an especially Protestant concern with "true inner" modesty as opposed to a merely "external" appearance of it – on which some recent discussions have focused. Modesty is, both in society and in literature, above all a convention, whose display constitutes its very existence and measure. That is, modesty occurs as a mode of presentation, of appearing before the self and others, within a system of social or literary encoding. As such, distinctions between interiority and exteriority are much less relevant than are questions of conformity, manipulation, and transgression. Nor is reticence, if this is taken to mean invisibility and silence, exclusively at work. Modesty is multiply constituted, and cannot be reduced simply to self-erasure, submission, powerlessness, or sexual chastity for that matter. If chastity correlates in Victorian America with "passionlessness," modesty in contradistinction remains a sexual mode, in which partial concealment suggests partial exposure with erotic effect. Similarly, the modesty topos as a literary event does not reduce to invisibility and submission, but rather also works as a vehicle of assertion: of deploying such public opportunity as was available to women within specific cultural norms. As has been claimed more generally of the "separate spheres," modesty must be multiply constructed: as an ideology imposed on women, but also as a culture created by women; as a repressive and limiting condition, but also as a scene of female values, activities, and identity. Modesty retains these dual aspects, and especially in literature, contributes to a complex composition of female personae, style, images, and strategies.

Modest self-representation in literature in effect renegotiates the boundaries and definitions of public and private spaces. It demarcates a special arena in which private crosses with public, concession frames assertion, disclaimer launches claim. Encompassing textual units both large and small, it amounts to a complex rhetorical mode. As such, it is a stance not just imposed but also deployed: a self-insisting claim that makes voluble its own reticence, an appropriation of demure strictures against writing in order to write, an assertive call to expose one's own concealment, and also, finally, a value genuinely informing female identity in ways that direct energy towards communal responsibility and indeed public activity, and away from purely self-interested self-assertion. It is in this sense that Addison and Steele define modesty as "the virtue which makes Men prefer the Publick to their Private interest."

Modesty emerges, then, both as a barrier to be negotiated and as an avenue to self-expression; as a challenge, but also a medium, for female representation. Nor is this entirely, or always, a matter of calculation and strategy. As part of nineteenth-century female self-definition, modest representations may genuinely assert feminine values often critical of the broader society, as part of an authentic voice for an historically constituted female identity. Instead of a stark opposition between submission and assertion in feminine identity, especially that of writers, modesty offers ways of negotiating between these two poles, in critical redefinition of each of them. Although modesty embodied society's restrictive pressures on women, it also came to serve as a mode for developing and expressing a complex feminine voice.

THE FEMALE WORLD OF LYDIA SIGOURNEY

Lydia Sigourney's biography reads like one of the plots so popular in nineteenth-century women's fiction. Born a poor girl in 1791 in Norwich, Connecticut, she came to the attention of the wealthy Mrs. Lathrop, who employed Lydia's father as a gardener and handyman. She was educated and then sponsored by this patrician family in her first publishing efforts, in her career as teacher in a female seminary in Hartford, and finally in her marriage to a Hartford businessman and into the middle class. This last triumph, however, rather undermined the earlier ones. Her new husband did not wish for her to parade his name in publication. As she wrote upon marrying: "Thou too, my harp! and can it be / That I must bid adieu to thee?" But failure came to her aid. As with many women writers of the nineteenth century, the impetus to a literary career came from financial need. When her husband's business declined, Sigourney began to provide for the family by publishing her works: first anonymously, and then with increasingly lucrative publicity (besides fantastic sales of her own books, Sigourney was paid top dollar for features given to magazines, and finally sold her name for use in Sarah J. Hale's *Godey's Lady's Book* until a quarrel ended this financial arrangement). The tensions her work created in her marriage were finally resolved with her entry into a protracted and satisfactory widowhood, lovingly surrounded by former students, and hailed as the Sweet Singer of Hartford until her death in 1865.

Despite her immense popularity during her own lifetime, Sigourney's writings have since been all but erased from American literary consciousness. Even some recent discussions have only promoted her from total eclipse to bland dismissal as a sentimental and cloying writer – "valueless and trite" – with a fondness for dead people approaching necrophilia. Others, however, have begun to urge Sigourney's recognition not only as significant within her historical context but as herself a historian who constructs a view of the public sphere and aggressively comments on it. Sigourney in fact succeeded in becoming, with Longfellow, what to us seems almost an oxymoron: a bestseller poet. She is perhaps best placed in the context of the similarly popular women novelists, also dismissed as sentimental – Hawthorne's mob of scribbling women. Sigourney, like them, was able to articulate the values of her middle-class readership, and to reflect the social norms and images of her period. In spite of poetry's relative lack of apparent context compared to the novel, Sigourney's elegies and death scenes, as well as her domestic, descriptive, social, and didactic verses, often yield complex and intricate representations of the female culture that women's historians of the nineteenth century are increasingly uncovering. And even as literary art, the poems deploy more levels than at first may appear. Sigourney's is neither a full-fledged feminism, nor a sustained, structured irony. Still, there is often a further, excessive meaning beyond the surface, with revealing configurations of gender and society and a lurking critical reflection on them.

Sigourney's poetry, to begin with, is rich in domestic tropes and feminized figures. Her tribute to "The Mother of Washington" pictures Nature as a housekeeper, "spreading her vernal tissue," while, conversely, good mothers set out to "sow good seed" in their children. The heavens, instead of reigning in classical indifference to sublunar life, become a domestic sky-world, where planets dance around the stars "as children round the hearth-stone" ("The Stars") and stars gaze on mountains as "some babe might gaze with brow of timid innocence" ("Sunset on the Alleghany"). Death, too, has a domestic side, attending the infant's "polished brow" and binding "the silken fringes" of the eyes' "curtaining lids" ("Death of an Infant"). "The Lonely Church," with its "slender turrets pointing where man's heart should oftener turn," serves as a mirror image for the solitary "poor mourning mother" in its yard, just as, in another poem, the church is a maternal "nurse of holy thought." "Winter," like the domestic female, spends its "lengthened eve . . . full of fireside joys, and deathless linking of warm heart to heart."

These are the sort of images which made Edgar Allan Poe complain that Sigourney "the woman rather than the authoress wrote her poems" and that "the domestic note is heard again and again" (while her didacticism presumably compromised even his own favorite subject, dead women). Nevertheless, there are poems, such as "To a Shred of Linen," which not only reflect on domestic space with wit and self-conscious artistry, but open it to historical and social meditation rendered through multiple viewpoints:

> . . . Here's a littering shred
> of linen left behind – a vile reproach
> To all good housewifery. Right glad am I,
> That no neat lady, train'd in ancient times
> Of pudding making, and of sampler-work,
> And speckless sanctity of household care,
> Hath happened here, to spy thee. She, no doubt,
> Keen through looking through her spectacles, would say,
> "This comes of reading books:" – or some spruce beau,
> Essenc'd and lily-handed, had he chanc'd
> To scan thy slight superfices, 'twould be
> "This comes of writing poetry."

This poem poses Sigourney's own hard-won and precarious literary opportunities against the traditional role of women, represented on the one hand by the disapproving lady "train'd in ancient times," and on the other by the "spruce beau" left free to be "lily-handed" and condescending to the women whose labor so releases him. The shred of linen continues through the poem to mediate Sigourney's historical consciousness about her current place and aspirations, including the history of its own production. It becomes a feminized bed-linen supporting the birth of infants and the nursing of the ill. Finally, the linen is remade by "the paper-mill," to emerge a "fair page" tracing "wisdom and truth." It has become the material ground as well as the topic of a female poetic composition.

Indeed, the linen emerges as a trope for "the thread of discourse" of Sigourney's own poetic activity, and in this marks at once an evolution in female roles even as it registers their continued confinement. The result is a complex structure of mockery. Far from being another trivial moment of Sigourney's "gemmy" world in which "inanimate objects busy themselves with every sort of domestic activity," as Sigourney's biographer describes it, the poem is a highly crafted reflection on its own status as this in turn represents wider women's issues. As such, it is essentially ambivalent, although in a comic mode. Ridiculing both those who would confine the poet to menial household tasks but also her own aspirations beyond them, the poem registers at once acquiesence and critique, defiance and compliance, increased opportunity and its limits. These double impulses are collected into the poem's final gesture of modesty, in which the poet wishes the linen-paper an "end better than thy birth" in the hands of a "worthier bard" than herself.

"To a Shred of Linen" is unusual in the degree of self-consciousness with which it represents Sigourney's dilemma as a female writer within her culture. But the ambivalence it records is present widely through her work. Sigourney's writing generally reflects the contradictory aspects of the "separate spheres" in whose culture it is deeply embedded. Sigourney was indeed conservative regarding the doctrine of the woman's sphere; she was one of its national champions. The popularity of her work, both in verse and prose, is due in part to its role as a handbook of domesticity. And Sigourney essentially accepts the traditional female roles and occupations consistent with the woman's sphere. But she claims for them a special dignity and significance in opposition against the other, masculine sphere, the "world." Moreover, her interests reach beyond the house walls into public concerns such as social welfare, moral and social reform, and policy issues, especially regarding the fate of the native American Indian. Yet these ventures, for Sigourney as generally for women during the period, also remain limited within the gender roles established through domesticity. Thus, Sigourney's poetry enacts the fundamental instability in the boundaries drawn by the ideology of the woman's sphere. The world it encloses increasingly speaks for a viewpoint, value system, and identity which spill from the privacy of the home into the public domain, yet without directly challenging the basic ideology of female against male, domestic against public divisions.

Sigourney's domestic scenes can be said generally to implicate the world beyond them. There are, for example, many poems which indirectly mirror or portray the changing economic conditions of nineteenth-century America. Sentimental verses ("The Mother," "The Sea-Boy," "Filial Claims") in which mothers are consumed with anxiety and grief over sons who have abandoned them reflect the new economic forces which sent sons much sooner from home to the west or the city or the sea in search of a livelihood the parental place could no longer provide. The family so cherished in verse acts as a counter-image to the social mobility whose obverse side was insecurity derived from urban, industrial pressures on traditional family structures. Sigourney's stylized home scenes often implicitly critique the outer world of the market and the danger of its insidious forces penetrating the home sanctum. The values founded by "The Fathers of New England" are threatened "should Mammon cling too close around your heart, or wealth beget that bloated luxury." The literal and figurative forests of national values are likewise endangered, as "Death among the Trees" results from man's thirst for "sordid gain." This market-contagion threatens even the devoted mother, who only in tending "The Sick Child" realizes the dangers of "fashion's joy" and the "gay flambeau" and "merry viol" of idle balls.

Nevertheless, Sigourney's critique of the market is hardly radical. It accepts the home as the refuge from an increasingly competitive industrial society, but stops short of direct contest in explicit economic or political terms against the values from which it retreats. As in "A Cottage Scene," Sigourney's homes provide escape and refreshment "from weary commerce with the heartless world." Sigourney in this shares the basic ethos of reform: that change would come, not by political action, but rather by way of an inward improvement of morals and manners, effected principally through the home and the home's guide, the wife and mother. Hers is a poetry of the Female Benevolent Society. There are many poems whose subjects are contemporary events and public issues; Sigourney's handling of them, however, remains decidedly unpolitical. Like the volunteer associations through which women of her time and class undertook many different social projects, Sigourney's topical poetry allows her an interest and even intervention into public issues and causes. But it does so by pressing outward the boundaries of the home, rather than crossing them to enter the public world directly.

Thus, if Sigourney writes about the nation's westward expansion, or slavery and the civil strife it was causing, her justification for doing so remains domestic. Poems such as "The Western Emigrant" and "Death of the Emigrant" imagine the dislocations and challenges of new settlement through tender conversations, illnesses, and deaths within isolated families. Sigourney's Unionism pictures the nation as a "Thriving Family," and she objects to factional strife as the "shame 'twould be to part / So fine a family." "To the First Slave Ship" personalizes the slave's suffering in "the childless mother's pang severe, the orphan's misery." War, and the male attraction to it, is denounced as anti-family. "The Volunteer" interestingly portrays the battlefield as a male world where rough companions "share such pleasures" as "the stirring drum, the pomp of measur'd march, the pride of uniform." But such indulgence in manly pursuits leaves the family to suffer and starve.

Sigourney's benevolent interests, like those of many nineteenth-century ladies, are multiple. She writes poems on temperance, such as "Only This Once" about how one drink is one too many; poems in "Appeal of the Blind"; and she generally praises "Benevolence" as the best investment, giving "the famished food, the prisoner liberty, light to the darkened mind, to the lost soul a place in heaven." Her particular cause remained the Indians, to whom she devoted tracts and prose works as well as the full epic *Pocahontas* and various short lyrics. Her intense lobbying efforts to protect Indian rights and lands were, of course, unsuccessful. But the extent to which she made poetry a vehicle for expressing such social/political positions at least suggests a different sense of women's and also poetry's place and purpose than the aesthetic which later refused her recognition. It further illustrates how, for Sigourney, the personal sphere extends into the public one. The "Meeting of the Susquehanna with the Lackawanna" reads the American landscape politically, but also domestically, portraying the two rivers as representing the hope of harmony between the white and Indian peoples in an imagery of marriage with "vows" and "nuptial songs." In "Funeral of Mazeen," the betrayal of the Indians betrays the white man's own Christian values, pitting political culture against the inner, religious world. And an "Indian Girl's Burial" presents the mother mourning her daughter as a figure for both Indian nobility and white indifference.

Sigourney's benevolent-society poetry remains poised between social and domestic roles. It is a balance, however, that is often unsteady. Sigourney basically assumes and accepts the doctrine of women as wielding an indirect influence only, as when she writes in one of her many advice books that "the strength of woman, lies not in resisting, but in yielding" (*The Wedding Gift*). The only political role for women that she sanctions is the increasingly recognized one of providing education so that children may learn properly to exercise their democratic rights and powers. The domestic objects that clutter Sigourney's poems often represent the mother in this role as home-educator. Each object teaches its lesson, usually on the vanity of material things (even as the many precious objects attest to their allure). "The Ancient Family Clock," "The Broken Vase," "The Faithful Dog" each makes its instructive appearance. The poems themselves in a sense serve to convey the "Mother's Counsels" they also thematize, themselves the maternal "Book Divine" urging piety, humility, and devotion.

While deriving her representations from such interior spaces and states, however, Sigourney also valorizes them, and even proposes them as defining human culture in its truer, more authentic commitments. "We are accused," Sigourney writes in her *Letters to Young Ladies*, "of 'being discomposed by trifles.' Our business is among trifles. Household occupations, to men engrossed by the sublime science, seem a tissue of trifles. Yet trifles make the sum of human things." Conceding the trivial nature of everyday tasks, Sigourney also claims them as life's genuine sum, with a sideswipe at a male "sublime" realm that, however, may prove no greater. Her vision of the nation as one large family, with each historical concern or event figured as within a domestic scene, on the one hand retreats from political structures. On the other, it establishes a female domestic realm as the truly defining one, feminizing political and national life. This familial vision is most ornately sustained in Sigourney's poem "On the Admission of Michigan into the Union."

> Come in, little sister, so healthful and fair,
> Come take in our father's best parlor a share,
> You've been kept long enough at the nurse's, I trow,
> Where the angry lakes roar and the northern winds blow;
> Come in, we've a pretty large household, 'tis true,
> But the twenty-five children can make room for you.
> Those ladies who sit on the sofa so high,
> Are the stateliest dames of our family,
> Your thirteen old sisters, don't treat them with scorn,
> They were notable spinsters before you were born,
> Many stories they know, most instructive to hear,
> Go, make them a curtsy, 'twill please them, my dear.

This poem elaborately recasts the politics of admission in terms drawn from etiquette manuals. Michigan is figured as the "little sister," graduating from her "nurse" to enter "our father's best parlor," and bringing with her a rich "dowry" of natural beauty and "cupboard" of towns. She is enjoined, however, to pay full respect to "the stateliest dames of our family, your thirteen old sisters," who remain somewhat jealous of their position as the original founders of the nation. This twist of the Founding Fathers into "proud and old" spinster sisters recalls the tendency of the ladies' societies to feminize male organizations, refounding, for instance, the George Washington Union in female counterpart as the Martha Washington Union. In this witty poem, the effect is less one of a ladies' auxiliary than of an inversion and even displacement of norms. Here domesticity becomes the arena, not the retreat from politics, with national life at large reconceived through feminized images and relationships.

Sigourney's most stereotypically feminine and aesthetically resistant verses remain her consolation poetry – the kind of mortuary verse that Mark Twain mocks through *Huckleberry Finn*'s Emmeline, the gentlewoman poet of obituary verse who died because the undertaker got there first. To us, Sigourney's tender, maudlin death scenes are as uncompelling as are her inevitable gestures to heavenly refuge. Death, however, functions as a complex trope for anxieties and commitments generated by changing social conditions both in general and specifically within nineteenth-century female culture. The poems of mourning, first, directly represent the infant mortality that remained an all

too common experience (Sigourney herself lost three babies) and the female
role of nursing, which continued on the whole to be undertaken at home,
hospitals not yet having been widely established in this function. Their affect
further reflects a generally intensified family life, with a new sense of emotion
and attention lavished on children as the number of offspring declined and as
women increasingly took on the role of educator previously assumed by the
father. And their popularity attests broadly to new literary interest in portraying such feminized experience, among both women writers and their female
readership.

But the death scenes also serve as tropes for anxieties and values, points
of view and events that exceed the immediate events they portray. Like
Sigourney's feminized imagery in general, the poems of consolation evoke the
peculiarly female world inhabited by women in the period. Disputes remain
among historians regarding how extreme the gendering of social life may have
been. But female daily life in many senses was conducted primarily among
women: mothers, daughters, sisters, friends, living and acting together at
home, as well as in female seminaries, ladies' church circles, and ladies' reform
associations. Sigourney's mourning poems evoke this intimate female world,
not least in terms of various threats against it, in which death often acts as
an image for other forms of separation, vulnerability, and conflict. Sigourney's
mourner-figures are by far mostly female, as are most of those who are mourned
(excluding genderless infants). Poetic dead daughters, sisters, schoolfriends,
and mothers come in close behind dead babies in Sigourney's verse. As is the
case of much female letter writing, in such poems Sigourney speaks of intimate female relationships in the most extravagant terms: "The Lost Darling"
("she was my idol"); "Rose to the Dead" ("the last poor symbol of a love that
cannot fade away"); "The Bride" ("even triflers felt how strong and beautiful is
woman's love"). "The Knell" is devoted to a feminized "beloved" whose "soft
blue eye . . . snowy hand . . . and ruby lip" are longed for, and without whom "I
am now but a divided being." Sigourney's commemorative verse may generally
be seen in the aspect of public elegy and memorial. On a figural level, these
poems often seem to mourn just such divisions: not only lost relationships,
but lost parts of the self, lost possibilities, and inner conflicts. What is at
issue is the break-up of the family and incursions into its largely feminized
structure, conflicts within the cherished domestic ideal, and a whole register of
ambivalence regarding the changing conditions and status of women through
the century.

It is remarkable, for example, that the same images and tropes refer either
to death or to marriage, so that it is often difficult to tell which event the poem
is commemorating. "To an Absent Daughter" presents such a case:

Where art thou, bird of song?
   Brightest one and dearest?
Other groves among,
   Other nests thou cheerest;
Sweet thy warbling skill
   To each ear that heard thee,
But 'twas sweetest still
   To the heart that rear'd thee.

Lamb, where dost thou rest?
   On stranger-bosoms lying?
Flowers, thy path that drest,
   All uncropp'd are dying;
Streams where thou didst roam
   Murmur on without thee.
Lov'st thou still thy home?
   Can thy mother doubt thee?

Seek thy Savior's flock,
   To his blest fold going,
Seek that smitten rock
   Whence our peace is flowing;
Still should Love rejoice,
   Whatsoe'er betide thee,
If that Shepherd's voice
   Evermore might guide thee.

It is almost impossible to be sure here whether the daughter has departed to the "other nests" of the Afterworld or to her own new family; whether the "Savior's flock" which she is commended to "seek" at the poem's end implies salvation in the next world or guidance within this one. In either case, death and marriage are tropes for one another, at least from the mother's point of view. Either way, the home has been shadowed with loss, with its flowers dying "all uncropp'd" and its streams an emblem of the daughter's absence. And either way, the sustained ambiguity of the text dramatizes this odd mutual implication of marriage and death with considerable literary craft.

This mutual imaging of marriage and death persists into other poems, even when ambiguity is resolved. "Forgotten Flowers to a Bride," for example, is concerned with bridal, rather than funeral flowers. But death imagery continues to govern the poem. The flowers, personified as a lady and representing the bereft mother, undergo a long, terrifying journey among strangers, finally to arrive at the daughter's new home. There they die, a sign of the bereft mother's "benison kiss." "The Bride" is even starker. "I came, but she was gone" is its grim opening, followed by a list of all the now abandoned familiar belongings. Although the poem then portrays not a death-scene, but an altar, its imagery is more mortuary than celebratory. The bride is led away by the husband, "the stranger," who "brings forgetfulness of all beside." The "mother's lip turn[s] ghastly pale" and finally commends the bride to the "ministry of Death."

Death in Sigourney's work acts as a trope for female ventures besides marriage. "On the Death of a Sister while Absent at School" portrays grief not only at the sister's death, but at her removal from home to school. The "stranger's pillow" of the distant school suggests its rivalry with traditional family life and loyalty, and ultimately projects an ambivalence about daring to cultivate the self apart from family. However committed Sigourney was to female education – and she was a devoted school teacher at the eminent Hartford Female Seminary – her verse registers the anxieties such new opportunities and self-definition represented. "To the Memory of a Young Lady" commemorates a girl "brilliant and beautiful," with talent, wit, and intellect "lofty and bright." The girl's death then seems to figure the mixed feelings of those many who "feared the splendor" of her "high gifts," although these were mollified by her "respect to woman's noiseless duties, sweetly bow'd." Similarly mixed is the "School of Young Ladies," which opens with praises for the blossoming girls at last admitted to "Learning's sacred fen." Yet the poem at once warns that this, like all earthly things, is a "bubble" that will finally burst with life's "unceasing toil, unpitied care, cold treachery's serpent moan." Some sense of the hard lot of women seems at work here, as well as a fear to trust too much in educational opportunities that may challenge traditional Christian and female values. Thus the poem concludes with "woman's deep, enduring love" and "steadfast faith" ultimately trusting only the world above.

"The Mourning Daughter" offers a variation, in that it is the father who is ostensibly mourned – although the mother's earlier death sets the stage. The poem, however, centers less on the father's memory, than on the position and predicament of the daughter-mourner. For one thing, she was (again) away at school, "distant far . . . toil [ing] for the fruits of knowledge," and thus arrived at the bedside only when "'twas too late." This conflict between self-realization and filial attachment is intensified in that the father's death also threatens loss of her social place.

> The deadly calmness of that mourner's brow
> Was a deep riddle to the lawless thought
> Of whispering gossips . . . Bold they gaz'd
> Upon her tearless cheek, and, murmuring, said,
> "How strange that he should be so lightly mourn'd."
> Oh woman, oft misconstrued! the pure pearls
> Lie all too deep in thy heart's secret well,
> For the unpausing and impatient hand

> To win them forth. In that meek maiden's breast
> Sorrow and loneliness sank darkly down,
> Though the blanch'd lips breath'd out no boisterous plaint
> Of common grief.

The daughter's reticence here works against her, misinterpreted as an unfeminine indifference to her father's death. This is a no-win situation: Sigourney construes modesty here as strength, which then, however, fails to fulfill its feminine social function. The daughter is left at the end the prey of "whispering gossips," almost a social outcast as her private grief is "misconstrued" by an unsympathetic throng of "curious villagers" and "cold worldly men."

Female experience, with its strengths and limitations, is finally Sigourney's primary literary subject. It is portrayed in fundamental ways as private. Privacy in its various forms of unostentation, humility, and restraint appears again and again as an essential aspect of female representation in Sigourney's work. In conformity with the prevailing ethos of modesty, Sigourney ladies are characteristically meek, bow'd, and silent. They are "blest laborers in [a] humble sphere," working with "humble" "unambitious mind," with "chastened cheerfulness," and "chasten'd heart to heal another's wound." Ever selfless, their "delight" is to "seek another's good." But, as with "The Mourning Daughter," modesty can carry complex implication in Sigourney's work. Far from fulfilling a stereotype of sentimentality, reticence in the poem bespeaks strength and self-command, as the daughter stands "in deadly calmness" like a "marble statue." That is, she both fulfills and resists social expectations of her. Yet for this she pays a heavy price. She is misunderstood and suspected exactly because her "meek maiden's breast" makes no outward display of its "sorrow and loneliness," her "blanch'd lips breath[ing] out no boisterous plaint of common grief."

Such contradictory reflection on modest norms is finally integral to Sigourney's own self-representation and indeed the conduct of her career as a writer. Sigourney's husband had complained that in publishing her work she had thrown off "that mantle of modesty, with which the female character should ever be shrouded." Her success as a writer in the end depended on an ability at once to sustain and contest the modest expectations of her. Only as a meek lady was she acceptable to her publishers. As Sarah J. Hale put it, "The path of poetry, like every other path of life, is to the tread of woman exceedingly circumscribed. She may not revel in the luxuriance of fancies, images, and thoughts, or indulge in the license of choosing themes at will, like the Lords of creation." Certainly this is the path demanded by critics with the power to promote writers or to bury them. Rufus Griswold is careful to claim little for the writers he anthologizes in his *Female Poets of America*, warning in his preface against mistaking women's "natural craving of affections" with the male's true "mental superiority." Sigourney herself he compliments for her "modest title of Moral Pieces" which, while fine as "little instructive pieces" show "no capability for the highest attainments." With this confined assessment Sigourney in many ways concurred. In her verse, she repeatedly concedes that her place in the "scale of being [is] light and low," that "it seems scarce lawful, with our erring lips to talk familiarly" of sublime things, and urges the need to seek divine favor only "in humble silence." Her *Letters of Life* offers in apology for her poetry, that "its literary pretensions might be slender, [but] its moral and religious tone was accepted as a redeeming quality."

Yet, this very accommodation suggests self-conscious assessment of the opportunities available to her, and often can verge into critical irony. Sigourney writes: "If there is any kitchen in Parnassus, my muse has surely officiated there as a woman of all work, and an aproned writer." This is to know one's place with a small vengeance, reshaping the figure of the Muse herself in the image of the housewife divided among many devotions. Here as elsewhere, the private feminine domain becomes the topic for public, artistic expression, not in self-contradiction, but in self-assertion. Modesty acts as mediator between the sequestered woman's world and her new opportunities as a woman writer. And some of the values Sigourney seems to support she also quietly criticizes, while a female value structure is often implied, at odds with an increasingly ascendant American ethos of power and competition. Even Sigourney's pious gestures to the heavenly world at times come with an anguish that almost raises questions about what will seem to Emily Dickinson a penurious divine economy: "And yet I wish I had not seen the pang that wrung her features, nor the ghastly white settling around her lips" ("The Lost Darling"). In a poem on "Poetry," there is almost a suggestion that earthly art is a "holy thing" not less than the life in the world to come.

More incisive, if not less indirect, are a series of remarks which condescend to men as proud and elevate women as modest. Though "green-house patricians" may frown on simple "wild flowers," divine justice finally "heeds the lowly and humbles the proud." When Sigourney writes: "Man seeketh homage. He exacteth fear from those who serve him. His proud spirit loves the quick observance of an abject eye and cowering brow," "Man" seems a gendered rather than universal term.

Like the "Young Lady" she commemorates, Sigourney remained "sweetly bow'd and tempered [her] gifts" in deference to those who may have "feared their splendor." And yet, like the young lady, she commanded her own "subtle shaft of wit." None of this adds up to a modern critique of society, an ambitious feminism, or Dickinsonian irony. Sigourney's poetry mirrors rather than transforms the paradoxes of female socialization of her period. Nevertheless, her writing contains elements of a female aesthetic and a female irony that will resurface in other women poets. In the work of a bolder, starker writer such as Emily Dickinson, the modest irony of Sigourney intensifies to become dramatic and explosive.

PUBLIC AND PRIVATE: RECONSIDERED

Women's verse of the nineteenth century is a poetry placed in an awkward position. Bounded by the private sphere to which middle-class, urban women were officially relegated, it nevertheless addresses a public sphere into which women were also making their way. Much women's verse continues to be devoted to topics considered seemly for the female. Women poets often had to insist – both to themselves and to others – that their literary ventures faithfully reflected their domestic roles. Their writing to some extent retains as its framework the separate personal life of each. It is in many ways a poetry akin to the "indirect influence" which each woman was called upon to exercise in isolation, forming an aggregate of private efforts rather than a collective action through political association. And the image of the woman poet continues to be modest and retiring, reflecting a degree of uncertainty regarding the right of women to speak and modes for doing so, a deeply rooted difficulty in finding their own voices.

And yet, the characteristic images of women's writing also register dynamic shifts in identity and opportunity. Domestic settings are not merely self-contradictory instances of women revealing in public their private lives, and the poets' modest figures represent more than powerlessness of various kinds. Privacy and modesty serve instead as multivalent and complex tropes through which women negotiated rapidly changing historical circumstances. Indeed, through the course of the century, the balance between public and private spheres does not remain fixed, either socially or aesthetically. The mere fact of addressing an audience gives even women's intimate verse a public side. However private her settings, the woman poet was speaking within a community, voicing experiences, conditions, and dissatisfactions shared by the many readers of lady's magazines, yearbook collections, and domestic poetry. Publishing itself was historically consequential, as women writers addressed women readers, creating a professional role for themselves and a shared cultural territory with their audience.

Within verse, boundaries between personal issues and public affairs are shifting and permeable. Intimate social relations and domestic roles become the means through which women's poetry reaches out to larger issues. Inner home and outer world are mutually reflecting; a modest mien serves as a public persona; and domestic subjects and subplots employ language that is public. But public subjects are also themselves directly addressed. It is striking, in this regard, that (with the ever complicated exception of Emily Dickinson) the few women poets to achieve any enduring literary fame did so through verse that went public. This is the case with Julia Ward Howe, whose *Passion Flowers* never commanded the attention she desired but whose "Battle Hymn of the Republic" is known to all; and with Emma Lazarus, who, bitter over Emerson's failure to include her in his *Parnassus* anthology of poets, became herself a monument with her "New Colossus."

Nineteenth-century women's poetry is engaged with social and political issues to a surprising degree. A review of the poetry of nineteenth-century women yields results that contest not only its enclosure in any simply private sphere, but challenges the topography of the public and private altogether. Indeed, this women's poetry does not support the distinction between public and private that has largely governed analysis not only of women's writing, but of nineteenth-century women's history and political theorizing as well. This is not to question the historical fact that women's activities have been proscribed in cultural and political discourse as belonging to the private domain, indeed long before the nineteenth century. The distinction between public and private, and the assignment of women to the latter, reaches far back in political and social history. Moreover, nineteenth-century women themselves did largely adopt the distinction, conceiving and describing their situation within its terms. Nevertheless, the poetry shows the public/private distinction to be highly unstable, open to revision and reconfiguration. The boundaries of each domain emerge in this verse as far from fixed. The poetry raises questions regarding just what the private, as opposed to the public, demarcates. And it calls into question presumed alignments between male and female, public and private, in terms of social, political, economic, and civic distributions. Each of these categories in actuality projects areas of activity that intercross, and which do not necessarily correspond with the gendered opposition between male and female. Women's poetry, rather than programmatically fulfilling public/private distinctions, calls them, and their gendering, into question.

Recent discussion has reopened and reexamined the question of sentimental fiction – which is to say, largely, women's fiction – contesting its status as domestic and emotional in purely private senses. Instead, the sentimental has come to be seen as an ideological and even radical mode for critiquing American society and attempting to transform its social forms. These arguments about fiction bear closely on nineteenth-century women's poetry as well. The sentimental emerges, in this verse, not as simple withdrawal from the public into a private realm of emotion. Sentimentalism instead attempts to address public issues, which remain its focus. That is, although framed in private settings and through emotional experiences, this poetry often addresses issues that can only be described as public: appeals for reform; for education; for the blind, deaf, orphaned; the poor; the slave. The intent is public, but the method is to move the audience through personal sympathy and identification.

Whether or not sentimentalism is finally successful as a tactic, whether the appeal to emotion does powerful ideological work or betrays it, it is clear that sentimental verse cannot be described as merely private. Sentimental appeals seem to share the paradoxes that generally characterize action taken within the ideology of the separate spheres, of upholding certain gender roles even while extending them. In terms of effect, the power of private appeal is limited in its rejection of collective, political action in favor of individual moral awakening, in the mode of female moral reform. But this is to say that what the domestic or sentimental mode lacks is power, not public intention. The poetry not only is decidedly public, it reflects upon this very split between certain kinds of public involvement and power itself. What may be called for is a redrawing of the geographies of public and private altogether. Women's poetry redefines, or reconceives, the "public" sphere itself, in terms different from its increasing identification through the course of the century with economic pursuits. Women's writing, including poetry, is steadfastly critical of the reduction of life to economic relationships, goals, and values. What this women's poetry suggests is that economic ventures, based in self-interest, are in fact a form of private pursuit, as the term private enterprise would confirm. Conversely, women's own activities, both in the home and outside it, address shared and communal, which is to say public, interests of the wider community. In these senses, it is the women who pursue and speak for public causes and the public good. What their concerns lack is not public interest, but political and economic power.

Through almost all the verse written by women, the modesty topos remains central. And yet it takes on many different guises, often within the body of work of a single author. This is not merely a question of advance and regression. Modesty is not a static stance. Its rhetoric expresses more than simple acquiescence to repressive female stereotypes and social pressures, or even conflict between the status of woman and that of poet. Much women's verse remains traditionally gendered, as writers negotiate the need to accommodate inherited social identities while developing newly independent viewpoints – a tension with both topical and structural importance. In this effort, the modest persona, rather than signaling abject acquiescence, serves a pivotal role in the negotiation between traditionally female characteristics as they undergo transformation. A form of concealment, modesty registers a conformity to female restrictions which remain all too real, but it also serves as a persona for expressing feminized and often critical viewpoints. Through its terms, women are able to emerge into self-expression, in a shifting self-representation that both undergoes and registers changes in identity-structures as the period unfolds. It marks the attempts of women to assess, redefine, and integrate different senses of themselves, in their lives, their art, and their society. An integral part of the representation of women, modesty emerges as a complex and dynamic term.

Julia Ward Howe (1819–1910) is a case in point. *Passion Flowers* (1854), Howe's first volume of poetry, in effect reads like one, long, agonized modesty topos. Whatever the particular subject, verse after verse is devoted to apologizing for its own existence. This begins with the opening "Salutatory," where Howe presents herself to her fellow poets as a mere "pilgrim" of "untutored strain" who, as she keeps assuring, is "not too greedy of men's praise":

> Better to sit at humble hearths
> Where simple souls confide their all,
> Than stand and knock at the groined gate
> To crave a hearing in the hall.

This abject note (although groined could have a "gendered" sense) is sustained through various pleas to a "Master" (one thinks of Emily Dickinson) from whom Howe begs, in one poem, no greater "boon" than "thine approving hand upon my head" and the words, "modest but glorious . . . 'Thou hast done well'." In another, she deplores her "straggling measure" and concludes that her best tribute to her master ("I to thee am so beholden") would be her own silencing. If she writes at all, "not a word I breathe is mine"; it is, rather, her master who has come, with his "whisper and his nod." Or, he comes as a "Royal Guest," while she remains "slow and difficult of speech" but ever oh so true:

> Bethink thee, then, whene'er thou coms't to me
> From high emprise and noble toil to rest
> My thoughts are weak and trivial matched with thine
> But the poor mansion offers thee its best.

The groveling in these poems is enough to make one gag. This still may be distinguished from male humility. Men, too, especially within religious conventions, humble themselves and deny their worthiness. But they mainly do this only before God. Among women, modesty is a social norm (although certainly reinforced by religion). Men bow, not to other men (or women) but to the Almighty. Women bow to men. In Howe's work, her debasement intensifies whenever poems are addressed to male figures, conforming to a clear and distinct distribution of power. "Gretchen to Goethe" knows well "thou'rt far above me" but pledges to him her "grateful heart." Howe writes to her brother as "a beggar," "the lowliest tenant . . . of the high precincts of [his] house." But there are other poems in which the distribution of power shifts. "The Seaward Window" presents a feminized moon that shows "the sun she, too, can shine" and recalls a female friendship in which the "two souls met / and vows of earnest import made." "The Mill-Stream" enacts overt revolt, as the female river reacts in fury at the miller's attempts to dam her: "And fragments of the Miller's work / Threw in the Miller's face." In the "Sibyl," "The Joy of Poesy," and "Stanzas," Howe pays homage to the positive power of poetry, even as she continues to register inner conflict about claiming it for herself. Thus, we are assured that while the Sibyl's "head is wild with books," nevertheless her "heart is good and kind." The Sibyl remains a source of poetic power above the poet, as in the male-muse "Master" poems. But, as "maternal saint," the Sibyl shares this power with the poet, so that, though "human by nature," she is "made by the Sibyl half-divine."

What seems to be at work, and will be developed in Howe's *Later Lyrics* (1866), is a general, if inchoate, rethinking of feminine poetic identity. Most *Passion Flower* poems are set within the poet's private chambers, as records of her intimate thoughts in the mode of private diaries or correspondence. This generic setting places Howe, however, in a predicament. She finds it problematic to speak when speaking only for herself, as her disclaimers testify. Yet, she has not yet discovered a resource or foundation for her voice beyond herself. She herself, however, is aware of this. *Passion Flowers* is first set in Italy, where Howe had more or less fled after the first years of marriage, leaving her husband and older children behind in Boston. In this foreign setting, she begins to reflect on public American events and issues, and especially the looming war over slavery. The aptest signal of what is to come is perhaps the poem called "Apology," in which she apologizes for her own immodesty in daring to speak at all. This is indeed a difficult feat "for one bred up in Modesty," who is, as she pleads, unable to "bring the trained weapon of the mind" to her aid. Nevertheless, she forsakes "the smile of courtesy" in her anger at injustice and the grief she feels at "my country and my race."

Howe continues to forsake courtesy in *Later Lyrics*, whose poems display a genuine effort to break out of the closed chamber into a broader world. There is, it is true, a section called "A Lyrical Romance" which brings humility close to humiliation (in "Waiting," the poet folds her "meek hands" and, like a fountain, waits to "gush" when her lord "drawest nigh"). But alongside it are "Poems of the War" – which includes the "Battle-Hymn" – and "Lyrics of the Street." These last, though hampered by a ladylike diction, show glimpses of an unstable urban world in which strangers see and then lose each other in crowds ("At a Corner"). Old men visit "sons of pain in prison cells." And the charitable lady walks out into the city's "bewildering alley," a world of cursing and brawling, drunkenness and child abuse, whose vivid description goes beyond set-piece benevolence imagery. Tragedies abound, but they are more sordid than genteel.

Howe has not renounced modesty as a central female identity. And yet, it is undergoing redefinition. In *Later Lyrics*, Howe no longer apologizes for her assertions, even when she is urging humility. And humility is not necessarily the same as unalloyed female subordination. It can also represent a complex effort to reconcile modes of self-realization with her sense of herself as a (nineteenth-century) woman, including familial and community commitments. This effort at a revitalized and harmonious self is hinted in images of art. The poet for Howe stands less in contest against her status as woman, than as a mode for balancing her various energies. "A Visit to C.H." is an interesting poem in this regard. It is set in a female world that crosses class and perhaps ethnic divisions. The poet calls on a "sister" who sits by a "scanty rag-carpet" in "calico garment and rough-twisted hair." But instead of charity condescension, the visit turns out to be to the Muse herself: a muse whose powers derive exactly from the experiences of feminine life. The poem is almost a roster of topics in women's poetry – a poetry produced while dreaming over the "wash tub" or in grief over a dead child, "when you lay down the needle, and take up the pen." The poem pays homage, then, to the lives of women in their devotion to others and to each other. But it is not a poem of self-erasure. Howe instead comes seeking her "poet sister," in order "to claim [her] kinship."

Julia Ward Howe's career marks a mid-century transition for women and women's poetry. Heiress to a prominent New York banker, she enjoyed a girlhood of independent, elegant, and cultured life in the milieu of fancy New York City townhouses. She benefited from new opportunities for women in education through private tutoring at home and elite girls' schools. She also personally lived the issue of women's property rights. She married Dr. Samuel (Chev) Gridley Howe in 1843, before the 1848 New York Bill granted independent inheritance rights to married women. She thus lost control over her extensive property holdings in upper Manhattan, which her husband sold off as worthless real estate. Not until she became widowed in 1875 did she regain control of her much reduced fortune, as well as her personal freedom to write and lecture – activities of which her husband had, through years of passionate but stormy marriage, fiercely disapproved. A charismatic and overbearing man, Samuel Howe's commitments to various reform movements and radical politics (he headed an institute for the blind and supported John Brown's extreme abolitionism) stopped short when it came to women's rights and his own domestic arrangements. As Julia remarked, "If he had been engaged to Florence Nightingale, and had loved her ever so dearly, he would have given her up as soon as she commenced her career as a public woman." Regarding her own efforts to write, publish, lecture, and eventually preach (she was active in the Unitarian ministry), she observed that "in twenty-two years of marriage, my husband had never approved of one act that I valued." Some of her early verses make concrete and personal the analogy between marriage and death which runs through women's poetry of the period: "Hope died as I was led / Unto my marriage bed," she writes in an 1844 poem she calls "The Darkest Moment." Or, as she wrote in 1846, "Marriage, like Death, is a debt we owe to nature." At first hesitant about a political commitment to women's rights, Howe became an activist after attending her first suffrage meeting in 1868 ("I am with you!"), going on to serve as president of the New England chapter. Yet, in her lectures she continued to insist that "Women are the natural guardians of social morals," that the "Duty of Women" continues to be based on a woman's role as "mother of the race, guardian of its helpless infancy, its earliest teacher, most zealous champion, the home maker."

Howe's verse, like her biography, reflects a tension between resistance and accommodation to conventional female paradigms. This tension emerges as fundamental to women's poetry throughout the century. To some extent, the concern is with personal achievement. Poems abound which take fame, ambition, opportunity, aspiration as their subject. These are often ambivalent, continuing to be structured through double-pointing modesty tropes. Alice Carey's (1820–70) "Fame" on the one hand accuses fame of "dragging this or that man down" even while it "will not raise you the higher," yet ends with a call to "clear the bright wake of geniuses, / Then steadily steer out." Adah Isaacs Menken's (1839?–68) "Aspiration" reproaches the "impious Soul" for its "high hopes," but finally does so in recognition that the star above is already its "own reflection in Eternity." In her poem "Ambition," Henrietta Cordelia Ray (1850?–1916) denounces it as "unrest, defeat" but also concedes its lure: "fair, illusive, sweet." Her poem "Aspiration" similarly denies that any "inner jar of conflict bids us with our quest to part" and condemns that quest to defeat in "coming gloom." Helen Hunt Jackson's poem on "Opportunity" is about the failure to realize it, with its vision of "golden gates" suddenly opening in rock, only to slam shut again before she can go through. Her "Memoir of a Queen" presents a fable of feminine power greater than the "False grasping powers" of male regimes. Yet the Queen's name remains unknown, and her great and blessed reign is recorded on no "written page or stone." Ella Wheeler Wilcox seems in her poem "Opportunity" to be promising it to those able, with "heart's desire, [to] work and wait." But the poem "Retrospection" clarifies that the way to "ambitions" is "the rugged road Duty," while the "Hostess" in the poem "The House of Life" directs the way to Happiness through Duty, Toil, Pain, and Faith. In Emma Lazarus's "Success," the prototype is "The bold, significant, successful man." The ambivalence, at once internal to these women writers and responding to the norms of their culture, is perhaps epitomized in the *No Name Series*, a collection of writings published anonymously (and whose editor, Helen Hunt Jackson, repeatedly and unsuccessfully solicited Emily Dickinson's contribution).

But even these ambivalent reflections on ambition implicate more than personal concerns and sensibility. At issue are very broad social structures, within the context of American values and their realization in American institutions. And the modesty which on one hand acts as a constraint on female aspiration, on the other hand serves as an avenue of critique, and not simply against the social restriction of women. Modesty is not only a negative value, but a positive one directed against developments of culture that women were among the first to recognize, deplore, and protest. Women's protests against the limits of their sphere did not necessarily mean endorsing the male "world" or sphere in which ambition was fast becoming the defining and paramount value. Instead, they portray that world as unbridled competition, felt increasingly as corruption, exploitation, and impoverishment in American life.

This critique of American life as betraying its own truest promise is in some sense shared by both conservative and radical women, where these two ends of the political spectrum can make common cause. Howe, for example, writes in protest against the middle-class feminine world of visiting, fashion, and parties, rejecting frivolity and vanity as false and limited feminine activities. This is done, however, in the name of an older self-sacrificing, maternal ideal, as well as towards a fuller view of woman as an individual that resists her reduction to a commodity within an order where all value has become economic. Thus, in one poem Howe derides the ballroom mannequin's "marble face," but calls on her to don the "garb of penitence" worn in "glad humility" ("Contrasts"). In a poem anthologized by Rufus Griswold in his *Female Poets of America*, she denounces woman as "Beautiful Statue," "Devoid of sense, / Buried in thine own beauty, speechless, pale." In "Woman," another Griswold selection which offers a compendium of True Womanhood, Howe disengages herself from the

"Vestal priestess, proudly pure, / But of a meek and quiet spirit" (at the end she calls this a "childish dream" and admits that she is not this Woman). However, the figures Howe offers in its stead remain shadowy, and shadowed by set feminine expectations. Howe thus remains unclear just how radical she is willing to be. These confusions are especially pronounced in "The Tea-Party." The poem denounces women who merely visit and gossip together: "My life has striven for a broader scope than yours." Yet the poem also distances itself from a more radical "woman's standard, new-unfurled," warning: "keep your limits, – do not rule the world."

Any hesitation regarding the need for active, political organization disappears in the work of Frances Harper (1825–1911). Yet Harper also often represents her public concerns in terms taken from the private and domestic worlds, in sentimental ways. Born to free black parents in Baltimore, Harper enjoyed unusual educational opportunities. After her parents' death when she was three, she went to live with an uncle who headed an academy for free blacks, where she studied. Already writing poems and articles in the 1840s, she was precipitated into activism in the Underground Railroad by the story of a free Maryland black who was kidnapped and sold into slavery. In 1854 she published her first volume of *Poems on Miscellaneous Subjects*, which went through 20 editions and sold 50,000 copies in the next two decades. Frances Harper devoted her adult life to the causes of abolition and women's rights, actively speaking in both the North and the South except during the brief period of her marriage (1860–4); on the death of her husband, she returned to lecturing. She brought out further volumes of poetry in 1871 (*Poems*) and 1872 (*The Martyrs of Alabama and Other Poems*), as well as a long narrative poem called *Moses: A Story of the Nile*.

Harper's poems, taken together, portray a dark side of public America. As in Frederick Douglass's famous oration asking "What to the Slave is the Fourth of July?" Harper shows the double meanings of American celebrations and rhetoric for slaves as opposed to free whites. Harper invokes slogans of the American self-image, showing how these fail and are betrayed in actual history. Slavery makes American freedom an oxymoron – a "proud country's shame" – as the star-spangled "banner in mockery waves" over the fugitive mother, hunted as she flees ("Eliza Harris"). In a poem called "Free Labor," Harper exposes free labor as nothing more than an inverse image of the slave labor that grounds whole areas of American production: "no toiling slave / wept tears of hopeless anguish"; "no cry to God," "no stain of tears and blood." The "Eden" and "Zion" of American promise are smothered by "Slavery's scorching lava-tide" ("Lines") and vitiated by the right "to bind with galling chains the weak and poor" and "hunt the slave" ("The Dismissal of Tyng"). Harper picks up the language of American mission – "Build me a nation, said the Lord" – but then shows it to be a scene of betrayal: "Men grasped the prize, grew proud and strong / and cursed the land with crime and wrong" ("Then and Now"). In her mouth, "Bury me in a Free Land" makes that American epithet ironic, while her willingness to be buried anywhere and however humbly still excludes American soil: "Make it among earth's humblest graves, but . . . bury me not in a land of slaves."

Frances Harper's work challenges given categories and the distinctions on which they are based. As often occurs in sentimental writing – and indeed, in the abolitionist movement itself – the horrors of slavery in Harper's work are portrayed through its assault on the integrity of the family. Many poems on slavery are thus cast in "domestic" terms, through its destruction of personal ties and family relationships. Scenes of auction, of escape, of floggings, of imprisonment all are filtered through the emotional wrenching they impose on loved ones. In "The Slave Auction," young girls are "defenseless in their wretchedness" while "mothers stood with streaming eyes / And saw their dearest children sold." In her own recasting of *Uncle Tom's Cabin*, Harper presents the escaping "Eliza Harris" as "a mother – her child is a slave – And she'll give him his freedom, or find him a grave!" "The Slave Mother" opens with a "shriek" and a "heart breaking in despair," as "her boy clings to her side."

But Harper's very representation of the slave family in sentimental terms makes a radical political claim. To be a chattel slave was by definition to be reduced to an economic status governed by economic forces. Harper's insistence on the private and personal status, feelings of sentiment, and family devotion among slaves is already to deny their reduction to economy and property, and to assert their status as cultural beings with human rights. That is, to describe the slaves' domesticity *as* family, as a private and domestic realm, is already a political act claiming for them a human status which slavery tries to deny. When Harper insists: "She is a mother, pale with fear," her granting to the slave mother a domestic, private status is already a political statement, exposing the slave's economic reduction as human distortion: "He is not hers, although she bore / For him a mother's pain."

Harper's tactic of aligning the anti-slavery cause with the sanctity of family life and defense of sexual morality was general to reform workers and writers, including Harriet Beecher Stowe herself. Genteel, white, middle-class women, and also anti-slavery male poets such as Longfellow, Whittier, and James Russell Lowell, all wrote sentimental reform verse. Maria White Lowell (James

Russell's wife) wrote a poem on "The Slave Mother," and Julia Ward Howe's work includes such domestic anti-slavery poems as "The Question" and "The Death of Slave Lewis." This shared rhetoric has raised questions regarding Harper, who has been accused of accommodating herself to genteel norms of the white middle-class in its conservative commitment to inner virtue, proper thoughts, feelings, sentiments, refinement, and self-restraint. But while Harper's work to some extent continues to respect white middle-class female norms, it shows their potential complexity, and how they can be brought into critical relation to society. Her verse, for example, includes many of the devotional poems that help make nineteenth-century women's poetry so alien today. Her treatment of American Christianity, however, as opposed to her faith in Christ, shows the same critical stance she extends to the American mythology of freedom. America's failure to live by its supposed Christian values runs as a bass chord through many texts. "The Martyr of Alabama" tells the story of a black boy who is lynched for refusing to dance in front of a church. "The Dismissal of Tyng" mocks a missionizing America that sends Bibles to far "heathen lands" while failing in its own Christian commitments. Nor are benevolent society women spared. "An Appeal to My Country Women" shows them to be more concerned with the exotic "sad-eyed Armenian" and "exile of Russia" than with slavery in their own nation, and to stop short of concrete action. To "sigh," "mourn," "pity," and "sorrow" in "gentle compassion" is not enough, and risks bringing down "God's retribution."

Harper's work reflects the way reform movements served women as springboards into wider social issues and yet also continued to limit them within a genteel sensibility and to methods of moral suasion. But this dilemma involves more than questions of tactics or of failure to contest social norms with sufficient radicalism. Rather, it reflects broadly on divisions within American society that extend well beyond women's issues. The acceptance of separate spheres includes not only the assignment to women of domestic functions, but of morality itself. What women's writing demonstrates is how the demarcation of separate spheres is problematic in ways deeply consequential for America at large. For it dramatizes how morality as such was becoming increasingly excluded from the public realm, not only in the sense of personal comportment, but of responsibility for the sick, the poor, the immigrant, the minority. If women are concerned with morality, this is not merely a private, but a social engagement. Indeed, categorizing moral concerns as private is part of the problem. For what does it imply about public life? If woman's sphere is moral, then what is man's?

Such a question is indirectly posed even by so moderate a woman as Helen Fiske Hunt Jackson (1830–85). Jackson distanced herself throughout her life from the cause of women's suffrage, although she did become a crusader for Indian rights in the 1880s. Born in Amherst the same year as Emily Dickinson, Jackson did not begin her writing career until 1865, after the death of her first husband and their two children forced her to consider the problem of sustaining herself, both financially and psychologically (it was a condition of her second marriage that her new husband agree to her continuing her career; this apparently led to a good deal of marital strain). Mostly known as a writer of prose sketches, stories, and also novels, she published *Verses* in 1870. *Sonnets and Lyrics* (1886) and *Poems* (1891) were brought out posthumously.

Helen Hunt Jackson's verse includes conventional meditations on nature, the seasons, and faith in an afterlife. Quite often, however, they take a gendered turn, and show a world quite divided. Jackson makes women her subjects, in direct or implicit opposition to a male point of view or frame of reference. In "In Time of Famine" she defends a woman against those who claim "she has no heart," asserting instead her secret strength and inner integrity. This subtly contests traditional images of what is feminine, casting female virtue as heroic fortitude. This becomes an expressed if doomed defiance in a poem whose title – "A Woman's Battle" – makes its gendering clear and central. The speaker knows that "thou'll win the fight / I know thou hast the stronger bark." But she will not show her "dear foe" either her wounds or her distress. Conceding defeat, she shows defiance:

> Fate steers us, – me to deeper night,
> And thee to brighter seas and suns;
> But thou'lt not dream that I am dying,
> As I sail by with colors flying!

Opposition deepens until male and female seem to be inhabiting two separate worlds and speaking two separate languages. In the poem "Two Truths," the man's assurance "I never meant to hurt you" is met by the woman's: "Forgive my selfish tears." But

> All the same, deep in her heart
> Rankled this thought, and rankles yet
> "When love is at its best, one loves
> So much that he cannot forget."

Here, as so often throughout women's verses, the mere recovery of a hidden or suppressed woman's view or voice becomes a central project. But gender is not the only issue. It is allied to a whole vision of warring values and power struggle. "A Rose Leaf" denounces a tyrannical king who arbitrarily puts his queen to death. "The Prince is Dead," however, makes its opposition not between male and female, but rather between palace and hovel, and indeed, public and private:

> A room in the palace is shut. The king
> And queen are sitting in black.
> All day weeping servants will run and bring
> But the heart of the queen will lack
> All things; and the eyes of the king will swim
> With tears which must not be shed . . .
> And dumbly writhes while the courtiers read
> How all the nations his sorrow heed.
> 　The Prince is dead.
>
> The hut has a door, but the hinge is weak,
> And to-day the wind blows it back;
> There are two sitting here who do not speak;
> They have begged a few rags of black.
> They are hard at work, though their eyes are wet
> With tears which must not be shed;
> They dare not look where the cradle is set . . .
> They feel as if they were turning to stone,
> They wish their neighbors would leave them alone.
> 　　The Prince is dead.

In this text, the typical women's poetry of dead babies undergoes transformation, or perhaps examination. The experience of mourning unites the two families. But the social order divides them, and the poem dramatizes how the experience of one is dwarfed and made to seem invisible by the other, even as it protests this erasure by asserting their equal dignity and significance. Personal grief thus becomes a context for examining social divisions, with the relation between the personal and social itself addressed in the text, as the child of royalty is publicly mourned while death for the poor remains their private affair. The whole boundary between domestic and public worlds shifts. In some sense, "The Prince is Dead" is about the relationship between domestic poetry and public issues. Social orders penetrate the domestic realm; domestic concerns obtrude into the public domain.

"The Prince is Dead" in its uses of rank seems removed from the American context. But Jackson's "The Money-Seeker" brings its lesson closer to home:

> What has he in this glorious world's domain?
> Unreckoned loss which he counts up for gain,
> Unreckoned shame, of which he feels no stain,
> Unreckoned dead he does not know where slain.

The subject is money, and the way it has begun to chart and define the American world. This concern is widespread among women poets. In Alice Cary's (1820–71) "Growing Rich," the man's prosperity is vitiated by the woman's continued attachment to the family she has left behind and which remains impoverished – to "brother Phil" who still works in the "coal pit" and Molly whose hand "was cut off in the mill." The cost of American production and expansion is recognized and portrayed. Alice Cary ("The West Country"), Frances Harper ("Going East"), and Lydia Sigourney ("The Western Emigrant") all have poems on the difficult lives of women on the western frontier. Poems of the city show "The Homeless" (Alice Cary) wandering "Alone in the populous city," or follow a "Charitable Visitor" (Julia Ward Howe) as she leaves her "city palace" to enter "a bewildering alley, with ashes and dust thrown out," populated by beaten children, drunken men, and hungry, angry wives. In Harper's "The Revel," the dead haunt the "brilliant lights," the "wines" and "viands" of gay balls in their material display.

The image of divided worlds – male and female, but also privileged and poor, public and private, in ways that complicate these categories and their mutual relationships – recurs in the work of Ella Wheeler Wilcox (1850–1919). Wilcox, writing later in the century, directly registers shifting paradigms of femininity. Scandalous in her time for a poetry of outspoken passion, Wilcox has been praised and blamed for a new, bold expression of female sensuality, which, however, is not bold enough for some. Born in Wisconsin on a farm, Wilcox attended public schools and then the University of Wisconsin. She began publishing at the age of fifteen. Her *Poems of Passion* (1883) sold 60,000 copies in two years after (because of) being rejected by a publisher as obscene. She went on to publish forty-six books. She married in 1884, and some contemporary readers seem unable to forgive either her conventional marriage, or her "continued ideal of renunciation and self-sacrifice." But it is just this mixture of the conventional alongside changing norms that is her subject. In many ways a New Woman, Wilcox also remains an old one. Focusing only on the erotic poems which first gained her notoriety tends to obscure the degree to which her work (including the poems of passion) faces outward towards socio-cultural concerns. Her first published book, *Drops of Water* (1872), was devoted to temperance. Later volumes, and especially *Poems of Progress*, portray a world of women leading separate lives in different terms and with different terms of discourse from those of men. In the poem "A Holiday," wife and husband talk past each other. The wife urges the husband to join the family for a holiday ("The gardener should come, methinks, / And walk among his bowers"), preferring his company to any Christmas gift his "toil" will buy. The husband replies:

> Impossible! You women do not know
> The toil it takes to make a business grow . . .
>
> Of course I love you, and the children too:
> Be sensible, my dear; it is for you
> I work so hard to make my business pay.
> There now, run home; enjoy your holiday.

This is still a poem of separate spheres. But here the woman's sphere is less restrictive than aggressive. Wilcox intends it as critique of a men's world in which, as she writes in her own, ironic "Hymn of the Republic," "I have seen the money-getters pass unheeding on the way . . . And I marveled, and I wondered, at the cold dull ear of greed." Wilcox's work can veer towards a sort of thinnish moralism, although the old virtues of duty and work take on different meanings in new social and economic contexts. But her thinking can be bolder. In "Lord, Speak Again" she suggests that God made some fundamental errors when He created the world. According to this revised creation story, God specifically appoints "Motherhood" to represent Him, "to go forth throughout all time . . . And make my world what I would have it be." But things have gone "wrong" with the world, and the "Motherhood, for which it was begun" now must change its role in order to fulfill "its holiest purpose."

As is characteristic, this "holiest purpose" does not abandon the vision of woman as moral guardian. If Wilcox is willing to challenge women's roles, she is yet suspicious of replacing them with what she sees as problematic male values. In the poem "The Cost," a woman rebels against her sphere to enter, successfully, the man's world:

> She wept no more. By new ambition stirred
> Her ways led out, to regions strange and vast . . .
> Still on and up, from sphere to widening sphere,
> Till thorny paths bloomed with the rose of fame . . .
> She stood triumphant in that radiant hour,
> Man's mental equal, and competitor.

But the poem then takes a strange turn. Instead of gladly praising this transformation, it suddenly runs up against "the cost":

> But ah, the cost! from out the heart of her
> Had gone love's motive power –
> Love's all compelling power.

The economic term is not accidental. What the woman has earned is also the price she must pay, the reduction of self to monetary measures.

Ella Wheeler Wilcox's is a poetry of conflict against social strictures, but also within the female self. Her work begins to exhibit increasingly complex desires and options, which cannot be easily reconciled and which implicate the general social order well beyond women's issues narrowly defined. In many poems, conflicts of identity focus in imagery of writing itself, where the vocation of poet or artist threatens female identity and vice versa. In the poem "Individuality," the speaker on the one hand declares she loves her "king, my master" "Better than I love my beloved art." But she also adds: "I feel an exaltation as I know / I have not made you a complete surrender." There remains the "rare essence [of] my art's alone . . . you cannot grasp it; 'tis mine own." In "Music in the Flat," her domestic circumstances make it impossible for her to play her music. But in "Burdened," the saddest fate is to "be burdened so that you can not / Sit down contented with the common lot / Of happy mother and devoted wife." Wilcox then goes on to reject, even as she records, her "fever" to hear "A loud-voiced public boldly mouth your name." In the poem "A Sculptor," the artwork under construction is the artist herself. But the poem weirdly directs this imagery of self-creation to the destruction of "selfishness," "ill-temper," "silly pride" in the female self. The "ambitious sculptor" creates herself, but as a traditional woman remote from artistic ambition.

The sense of conflict that becomes more urgent or overt in Wilcox's work is to some extent present throughout nineteenth-century women's poetry, and indeed lives. In terms of poetry, a difficulty in integrating different roles may account in part for the weaknesses in minor women's verses, as it becomes a difficulty in defining a speaking self, of finding a voice of one's own. Much interesting work, however, makes this problem an explicit topic. Women poets seem consciously intent, at the very least, in speaking for and as women, representing women's lives, experiences, and not least values. Helen Hunt Jackson's poems on women often turn on just this sense of speaking as a woman, on recovering her own and other women's voices from oblivion. They insist on her female poetic power to record what has been erased, to speak for those who cannot, so that her own "words might become a two-edged sword" ("In Time of Famine"). At issue is certainly private experience, which, however, is represented as heroic and courageous adventure, as in her poem on a woman "Found Frozen." Beyond recovering the hidden and silent life and death of a woman invisible to those (men) around her, the poem ends with the proud declaration that only her poetic "I, who loved her first, and last, and best" can write her adequate record. This is, then, to enter private story into historical record. And a poem such as "Memoir of a Queen" is explicitly about public records: their suppression and their recovery, as she, the poet, supplies the "written page" of the nameless queen which is missing from history.

The recovery of women's history and voices turns in Wilcox's work to questions of sexual self-expression, which, in the poem "Forbidden Speech" becomes congruent with verbal expression: "The passion you forbade my lips to utter / Will not be silenced." More than only erotic liberty is at stake. Her poem "The Tiger" is an accomplished, complex text explosive with implicit meanings, telling a tale of aroused passion that turns back on the hunter who awakens it:

> In the still jungle of the senses lay
> A tiger soundly sleeping, till one day
> A bold young hunter chanced to come that way.
>
> "How calm," he said, "that splendid creature lies,
> I long to rouse him into swift surprise!" . . .
> And lo! the tiger rouses up and turns . . .
>
> Once having tasted human flesh, ah! then
> Woe, woe unto the whole rash world of men,
> The wakened tiger will not sleep again.

Often taken as a poem of female eroticism, this may instead be one of gender rage. It would then speak less of female sensuality than of female anger. Or, given the poem's peculiar gendering that makes the tiger as well as the hunter male, it may speak of unconscious lusts and urges which men unleash on the world, to its and their destruction. While recognizing the power of inner forces, it would still recognize the need for their proper, moral restraint.

The sexuality in Wilcox's work is in one sense innovative, introducing new possibilities to female self-expression. But the sexuality Wilcox treats in terms of personal sensibility had been in another sense a recurrent concern of women's verse throughout the century, not as it points inwards to individual sensibility but as it points outwards to broad social and economic structures. Sexuality in fact received wide treatment throughout the century: not as a new freedom for women but as their betrayal, through seduction, ruined social status, and prostitution. That is, women throughout the century were concerned with sexuality as a site where the so-called "private" world of morality and the "public" world of economic system intersect. Their focus centered on the double standard which, as Keith Thomas demonstrates, is deeply rooted in a long legal and economic history treating female chastity as the property rights of the woman's father or husband. This battle against a double standard which restrains female but not male sexual behavior, took specific form as social action in the Social Purity movements of the 1830s and then Moral Reform movements later in the century. These campaigns were immediately directed against prostitution, which had reached new levels due to urbanization, immigration, and industrialization. As such, the Reform movements retained a strong conservative element, trying to legislate sexual morality while continuing to assert the ideology of the separate spheres. They defined women as moral guardians and justified public intervention in the name of protecting the sanctity of the home. This conservative reassertion of traditional gender divisions ultimately weakened the effectiveness of these campaigns; its legislative successes were few and often empty.

But, as recurs through much nineteenth-century women's activism, conservative elements conjoined with radical ones. The agitation for moral reform played an important role in women's political emergence through the century, as an avenue for their participation in public discussion and legislative activities. It became a base for activism towards women's rights in employment, which would offer alternatives to prostitution for the destitute and desperate. In legal terms, the radical implications of the Moral Reform program emerged in its insistence that not only prostitutes, but their patrons, be prosecuted. But most fundamentally, the Reform movements raised broad questions concerning not only the sexual double standard, but the wider gendering of social powers of which it is one expression. Their work began to explore and expose ways in which sexual codes involved not only a personal, moral condition but also the social and economic status of women generally. And it raised questions concerning social and economic inequalities in American life, as betraying America's own promise and its own older senses of public responsibility and the public good.

In terms of verse, many poems on the sexual double standard explore its economic implications, opposing not only the fallen woman against the fancy-free seducer, but also dependence against independence and poverty against wealth. These poems dramatizing seduction, betrayal, and prostitution provide one striking arena for a critical attack on society in the name of feminine values. Julia Ward Howe's "The Soul-Hunter" pictures a lurid hunter, haunting the night, setting a "Devil's bait" for the as yet "sinless" maiden. In Howe's "Outside the Party," a girl hovers, looking in

> At yon clear window, light-opened before me,
> Glances the face I have worshipped so well:
> There's the fine gentleman, grand in his glory

who dances blithely away with "fair ladies," while she holds at her bosom a baby "akin to him, shunned and forsaken." Alice Cary treats the theme within the Gothic-balladic conventions she favors. Her "Spectre Woman" endlessly haunts the churchyard in grave clothes, mourning her seducer while she "bend[s] down fondly, but without a mother's pride / Over something in her bosom that her tresses can not hide." Frances Harper's "The Contrast" juxtaposes the "wrecked and ruined" girl whose fate is irremediable:

> They scorned her for her sinning,
> Spoke harshly of her fall,
> Nor lent the hand of mercy
> To break her hated thrall

against "he, who sullied / Her once unspotted name" but now

> Through the halls of wealth and fashion
> In gaity and pride,
> He was leading to the altar
> A fair and lovely bride.

In her poem "A Double Standard," Harper pursues this nexus of sin and seduction into its consequences in prostitution. The poem, written in the first person in a move that might bring its middle-class readers into greater sympathy with its speaker, is constructed as a series of accusatory questions against her accusers. The fallen girl, who did not see "Beneath his burning kiss / The serpent's wiles" pointedly asks:

> Can you blame me that my heart grew cold
> That the tempted, tempter turned;
> When he was feted and caressed
> And I was coldly spurned?

These seduction poems largely belong to the tradition of the melodramatic and sentimental in women's writing, but in this they shed light on the parameters of the sentimental itself. Like sentimental work generally, they approach civic, social, and political issues through private experience. But this does not negate their representation of the social order, and specifically as one increasingly being emptied of morality and community commitment; an order that reduces women, but also all Americans, to social exploitation and indifference. Social life as portrayed here seems increasingly to betray basic tenets of the American promise. This betrayal was by no means the exclusive concern of women. It is equally central to works as different as *Walden* and *The Education of Henry Adams*. In women's poetry, however, it becomes specifically gendered. The separate spheres become spatial configurations for general bifurcations within American culture. Double standards between men and women represent not only sexual discrimination, but the division of economic and political life from moral responsibility and communal commitments.

These issues are directly posed in the openly ideological poetry of Charlotte Perkins Gilman (1860–1935). Best known today for her story "The Yellow Wallpaper" and its painful exploration of domestic confinement as imprisonment and indeed a form of madness, Gilman in her own time was most famous for her tract *Women and Economics*. There she traces the connections between gender roles, economics, and their broader social consequences, arguing that the current relationship between men and women is an economic one where "woman's economic profit comes through the power of sex-attraction." This makes the "open market of vice" only relatively different from marriage, the "same economic relation made permanent, established by law, sanctioned and sanctified by religion, covered with flowers and incense and all accumulated sentiment." Female economic dependence culminates in "the full flower of the sexuo-economic relation, – prostitution." *Women and Economics* begins with a "Proem," where she rewrites the story of Creation and Fall. Like other poems Gilman wrote (collected in *In This Our World*, 1893), it rehearses and attacks conventional gender roles. In Gilman's work, these betray both women and men to sexual, psychological, and social bondage. The "Proem" shows the Fall to have been into economic exploitation and gender division, making all "blind and crippled, all astray."

Gilman's central poetic technique is one of a rhetorical control of voices. She characteristically represents the dominant voices of society in ways that expose and then undercut their positions. Or, she represents the suppressed, muted voices of women, giving expression to their lives in a public poetic record, and yet also recording the extent to which they themselves have internalized the view which dominates and subordinates them. The poem "Unmentionable" mimes its topic by refusing to mention prostitution, except by recording evasions of it:

> There is a thing of which I fain would speak,
> Yet shun the deed;
> Lest hot disgust flush the averted cheek
> Of those who read.
>
> And yet it is as common in our sight
> As dust or grass;
> Loathed by the lifted skirt, the tiptoe light,
> Of those who pass.

In Gilman's poem "Homes: A Sestina," a full rhetoric of the separate spheres itself speaks, with the "Homes" voicing their complacent assignments. Regarding women, the Home says:

> And are we not the woman's perfect world,
> Prescribed by nature and ordained of God,
> Beyond which she can have no right desires
> No need for service other than in homes?

At the same time, men have no other need in life

> Than to go forth and labor in the world,
> And struggle sore with other men therein?
> Not to serve other men, nor yet his God,
> But to maintain these comfortable homes?

The spheres, by way of their own rhetoric, are shown to split apart both society and individual person. They are a reduction and betrayal of each, and destructive to the society as a whole. Society becomes bifurcated between lives sacrificed to others and lives selfishly consumed – a configuration that is gendered but also economic. And Gilman's solutions are economic and social. Poems such as "Unsexed" and "Females" insist that only full participation in economic life can reform and transform women and men. Yet her goal remains a vision of social participation, not private gain. Her poem "Nationalism" pledges itself to a vision that encapsulates individual participation in a republic that is quintessentially Jeffersonian. What America requires is

> the sum of all our citizens,
> Requires the product of our common toil . . .
> Our liberty belongs to each of us;
> The nation guarantees it; in return
> We serve the nation, serving so ourselves.

Charlotte Perkins Gilman is extreme in her rejection of women's domestic role, which in her own case resulted in the mental breakdown she records in "The Yellow Wallpaper." After hesitating for some years to marry (in a private journal entry, she asks: "O God I wish to do / My highest and best in life! . . . And can I also be a wife?") she did so, only to crash into depression. She herself found cure for her "hysteria" as gender role by abandoning and then divorcing her husband. Devoting herself completely to women's rights' causes, she remarried only under condition that she have no domestic duties, no children, and retain her freedom to travel, lecture, and write. Her decision to give custody of her child to her ex-husband when he married her own best friend, caused scandalous gossip during her lifetime. In some sense, Gilman merely radicalizes conflicts between domestic and professional commitments apparent in the lives of other nineteenth-century women. One cannot help but notice the inverse relation between marriage and creative writing among the best-known women poets: Alice and Phoebe Cary, Emily Dickinson, Lucy Larcom, Lizette Reeze,

Louise Imogen Guiney, and Emma Lazarus did not marry. Of those poets who did marry, most wrote either in defiance of their husbands, or as widows. Nevertheless, within a nineteenth-century context, terms of conflict such as Adrienne Rich, for example, describes in "Of Woman Born" do not really apply. Rich envisions a "womanly splitting of the self" between "the unfree woman, the martyr" as against a self-image that is "individuated and free." But nineteenth-century women's senses of self neither simply dismiss service as martyrdom, nor simply elevate pure individual freedom. For nineteenth-century women, as expressed in their writing, fundamental senses of identity entailed a connection to family, to community. Even a Wilcox poem such as "Woman," which rejects the model of gracious "lady" as appropriate for "lackeys," offers as authentic "Woman" – "full of fine force, strong, beautiful and firm, / Fit for the noblest use of tongue or pen" – the terms "Mother, Wife, and Sister." This commitment to community and family is something these women would want not only to retain, but to defend. Indeed, it is part of their critique of a society that they see as increasingly commercial and morally empty. Their insistence on values of responsibility for and to others, as opposed to unmitigated competition between isolated individuals vying with each other for economic gain, transforms their traditional self-definition into an attack on the evolving American industrial, urban, and political culture.

Mary Wollstonecraft devoted one section of her *Vindication of the Rights of Woman* to "Modesty Comprehensively Considered and Not as a Sexual Virtue," which she intended as a refutation to advice-book rules of comportment. There, Wollstonecraft distinguishes modesty first from chastity; then from humility (which is a "kind of self-abasement"); then from bashfulness, timidity, innocence, and ignorance. Modesty instead represents for her "the reserve of reason," the ability to conceive "a great plan and tenaciously adhere to it, conscious of [one's] own strength," and in sum: "a simplicity of character that leads us to form a just opinion of ourselves, equally distant from vanity or presumption, though by no means incompatible with a lofty consciousness of our own dignity." Wollstonecraft here attempts to transform modesty from an emblem of female restriction to a powerful self-definition, which would oppose unrestrained self-assertion no less than self-abasement. At issue is no longer a specific and restrictive female virtue, but a general moral stance closely tied to what, in political history, may be called civic virtue. Viewed from this angle, the social involvements, reform movements, charity work, and other social services undertaken by nineteenth-century women do not merely represent an extension of private, domestic roles into a public sphere. Instead, these activities by women can be seen as communal, and indeed public work, in the tradition of disinterested public virtue associated with America's Revolutionary ideology.

It may be argued that it was nineteenth-century women who inherited this tradition, while men increasingly through the century came to pursue an economic interest which can properly be called private. The inheritance by women of civic virtue also signals, however, the relative devaluation of social and communal concerns in an America increasingly devoted to economic values and private material gain.

The career of Emma Lazarus in many ways traces and encapsulates the complex and changing relationship between private and public concerns within women's writing. Her early work shows characteristic modesty regarding her status as a woman poet. A poem such as "Echoes" concedes that she as poet is "Late-born and woman-souled . . . veiled and screened by womanhood." Even in this poem, however, disclaimer verges towards claim. She cannot command "the might of manly, modern passion," and retreats instead to the enclosed, almost domestically rendered setting of "some lake-floored cave." But the "echoes" her poetry offers show a love of "solitude and song" which suggests a romanticist, figural richness perhaps greater than "the strong-armed warriors . . . dangers, wounds, and triumphs of the fight."

This casting of restraint as strength and of modesty as claim becomes central to Lazarus's Statue of Liberty sonnet, "The New Colossus," which in many ways stands as a compendium of nineteenth-century female imaging and as the modesty topos's grandest emblem and transformation. The sonnet's opening octave repudiates an immodest, European pomposity in the name of a feminized America. The Statue stands

> Not like the brazen giant of Greek fame,
> With conquering limbs astride from land to land

but as

> A mighty woman with a torch, whose flame
> Is the imprisoned lighting, and her name
> Mother of Exiles. From her beacon-hand
> Glows world-wide welcome; her mild eyes command
> The air bridged harbor that twin cities frame.

This woman's power is structured through a deeply gendered rhetoric of oxymoron, a "mighty woman" whose flame is imprisoned, who commands through "mild eyes." Against Europe's arrogant "fame," she "cries" with "silent lips," at once asserting her voice and yet also muting it, in an image of both her presence and of her devotion.

The "name" she does adopt is "Mother of Exiles," offering a "world-wide welcome," in an overarching gesture of American domesticity and service.

The sonnet's famous ending – "Give me your tired, your poor, / Your huddled masses yearning to breathe free . . . Send these, the homeless, tempest-tost to me" – brings to its epitome the century-long female involvement in social affairs. This image of America as welcoming hostess is not only a powerful figure of womanhood in public service, but a vision of a national life defined through the civic value of community.

2

❧

CLAIMING THE BIBLE

Although slave-songs reach far back into slave history, the Civil War in many ways marks their birth into national consciousness. Civil division serves as well as a powerful backdrop for interpreting the spirituals, and especially their language and imagery. The music of the spirituals has generally attracted first attention and appreciation. But the texts are no less important registers of cultural forces effecting both the development of a black literary tradition and its place within American culture. While clearly a product of African enslavement in Protestant America, the spirituals present a complex interaction between multiple and crossing impulses: African and white American aesthetic as well as Christian religious forms; sacral and secular functions and meanings; with theological and social/political commitments.

The Bible is central to interpreting these interacting and competing elements, both in the spirituals themselves and in terms of their placement within American culture. Here, two related but distinct issues emerge: the treatment of the Bible within the spirituals, but also the question of access to the Bible by the spiritual singers. In its broadest implications, the spirituals' modes of Biblical engagement dramatize the ways in which interpreting the Bible carries powerful political implications within American culture, involving claims to American identity, even as such claims complicate just what that identity may be.

Many questions remain regarding the history and constitution of the spirituals: their development, their authorships, and establishing the texts themselves, as well as their religious and political implications. Textual analysis of slave spirituals is complicated by their production, transmission, and transcription. The versions which are available often result from painstaking work in collecting and collating variant forms, through such pivotal projects as musical arrangements and performances by the Fiske Jubilee Singers during the 1870s, and into oral histories of former slaves undertaken in the early twentieth century. Historians vividly describe the difficulties confronting attempts to recover the early slave songs, given the dearth of written record. The collective production of the songs, as well as their highly improvisational character, makes any transcription in some sense provisional. The slave spirituals, moreover, generally reflect the syncretist nature of Afro-American culture, described by W. E. B. Du Bois as evolving through African, Afro-American, and Americanized modes. Recent discussion has increasingly underscored such Afro-American hybridity, as African ancestral beliefs and practices evolved in dynamic relation to Anglo-American ones. The two cultures are increasingly recognized as interpenetrating, requiring that each be interpreted through their mutual reflection. Syncretism in this sense penetrates not only the production and transcription of the spirituals, but also their performance as involving cross-cultural encounters. The interpretation of the texts, as of the music, requires recognition of contending cultural systems and the mutual adjustment, rather than imposition, of interpretive paradigms.

Such syncretism has long been recognized in the music of the spirituals, whose distinctive features such as antiphonal structure and improvisational character are seen as closer to the musical styles and performances of West Africa than to the musical style of Western Europe. But in regard to the texts, these same features have been mainly judged derivative, accidental, and formless. Texts generally have been considered as secondary – "dictated," as one commentator puts it, "more by a logic of rhythm and sound than of verbal meaning." The choral exchanges and repetitions have been judged as having a "lack of logical coherence . . . a patchwork, scissors-and-paste quality" with little "continuity of thought between the various lines of a stanza, between stanza and refrain, or between the various stanzas." This seeming incoherence finally extends to the spirituals' major thematic engagement, the Bible. As Thomas Wentworth Higginson was among the first to notice, the spirituals are not only selective in their Biblical references – exhibiting a strong preference for Old Testament figures and the Book of Revelations "with no Jesus narrative in between"; they also appear to present these texts as "a vast bewildered chaos of Jewish history and biography" in which "most of the great events of the past, down to the period of the American Revolution, they instinctively attribute to Moses." The spirituals have accordingly been described as drawing "without regard for biblical chronology or even accuracy on the whole Bible story, conflating the New Testament with the Old, and the Old with the New." Thus James Weldon Johnson speaks of the "misconstruction or misapprehension of the facts of [the] source of material, generally the Bible."

The spirituals' uses of the Bible, however, reflect major traditions of exegesis within American Biblical traditions, which are then given unique directions in what can be called an African-American typology. The combination

of motifs in "Go Down Moses" can be taken as exemplary. What is striking and not so easily accounted for in this song's full elaboration is the high
degree of sophistication and command it exhibits in its structuring of Biblical texts. First published as "The Song of the Contraband" black slaves
who had escaped to the Northern soldiers at Fort Monroe, this was the first
spiritual to reach a wide American audience. Its full text as printed in the
National Anti-Slavery Standard of December 1861 is an elaborate, detailed representation of Biblical events that goes well beyond a general identification
with the plight of the ancient Hebrew slaves. The Exodus story is intensely
imagined, with special emphasis at the outset on the vengeance of the Lord
against the Egyptians and the appropriation of their wealth by the newly freed
slaves:

> Thus saith the Lord bold Moses said, (Let my people go)
> If not, I'll smite your first born dead (Let my people go)
>
> No more shall they in bondage toil, (Let my people go)
> Let them come out with Egypt's spoil (Let my people go).

These verses seem to have immediate historical reference, especially in terms
of the hopes and aims of the Civil War itself. But the song also continues
into a future, at once historical and prophetic, of spiritual guidance, providential intervention, Christian salvation, and finally triumphant judgment.
Thus, its terms move from Moses crossing the Red Sea (and duly drowning
"Pharoah and his host") to the sojourn into the wilderness, and then onward,
through Old Testament history, across the Jordan, to Joshua before the walls
of Jericho. It ultimately moves into a New Testament vision of salvation in
Christ, culminating in the close of history in Apocalypse:

> You'll not get lost in the wilderness (Let my people go)
> With a lighted candle in your breast (Let my people go)
>
> Jordan shall stand up like a wall (Let my people go)
> And the walls of Jericho shall fall (Let my people go)
>
> Your foe shall not before you stand (Let my people go)
> And you'll possess fair Canaan's land (Let my people go)
>
> 'Twas just about in harvest time, (Let my people go)
> When Joshua led his host Divine (Let my people go)
>
> O let us all from bondage flee (Let my people go)
> And let us all in Christ be free (Let my people go)
>
> We need not always weep and mourn (Let my people go)
> And wear these Slavery chains forlorn (Let my people go)

This world's a wilderness of woe (Let my people go)
O let us on to Canaan go (Let my people go)

What a beautiful morning that will be! (Let my people go)
When time breaks up in eternity (Let my people go).

What this text quite elaborately projects is a vision of history stretching from Biblical through present times into a promised future. Throughout, immediate reference is sustained to the concrete historical present of slavery, and also to the constant spiritual experience of salvation. The Biblical wilderness is therefore at once a historical and a spiritual scene, with the divine guide of "fire by night" become "a lighted candle in your breast"; even as it remains an eternally present experience in this world's "wilderness of woe." The redemption from slavery is equally a multi-temporal process, at once historical, spiritual, and prophetic, to be attained fully only in a still distant future morning "When time breaks up in eternity."

This complex and carefully constructed historical scheme can be precisely situated within traditions of Biblical typological interpretation especially powerful in American culture. But the very access of the slave singers to this tradition, and indeed to the Bible itself, raises historical questions. The slave experience of Christianity generally, as well as access to the Biblical text, was fraught with complexities. Christian mission to the slaves was complicated by white planters reluctant to concede that their slaves had souls. Fears that slaves once baptized could claim the legal right to emancipation had been hurriedly settled with legislation explicitly denying that conversion required manumission. But resistance to religious expression by the slaves remained. Slaveholders suspected religious activity would undermine slave servitude. The fundamental conditions of slavery itself, including the destabilizing of family life through sexual assault and slave markets, obviously opposed the fundamental tenets of Christianity. A general religious indifference on the part of the slaveholders, the dispersion of the slave community across large plantations, and the lack of clergy in the South, compounded the obstacles to Christian mission, which was generally tied in the South to slave-politics. Despite these efforts at suppression, American Christianity can itself be seen as influenced by interactions between white and black communities, and the history of black religion shows a variety of church configurations. These ranged from "bush" or arbor meetings for worship kept secret and away from the eyes of masters, to all-black churches, to black churches under white leadership and supervision, to mixed churches attended by both blacks and whites. In each of these, African and European religious forms intercrossed and mutually shaped each other to varying degrees, with Southern Christian experience a new mixed culture resulting from their interplay. Still, to the extent that slavery framed the development of black Christianity, a political atmosphere of domination and restriction continued to be felt. This had consequences both in attempts to control and limit worship, and in the attitudes of what has been described as a "white theology" intent on forcing its domination upon black life.

The problem of literacy further complicates the slaves' reception of the Bible. Frederick Douglass tells the story of the Class Leaders of the Church "who ferociously rushed in upon my Sabbath School" and "forbade our meeting again, on pain of having our backs made bloody by the lash" (for, "if the slaves learned to read, they would learn something else, and something worse"). This is no mere anecdote. It finds its place in the attempts on the part of slaveowners to prevent the black population from learning to read and write, as against resistance by the blacks to these repressive measures. On the side of repression, a comprehensive legal system against literacy was in place in the South, beginning with the 1654 and 1723 ordinances forbidding assembly, through the 1740 Slave Act forbidding teaching slaves to read, through the South Carolina law of 1800 forbidding Negroes to assemble from sunset to sunrise "for the purpose of mental instruction or religious worship." As one North Carolina law declared, it is a "crime to teach, or attempt to teach any slave to read or write . . . [which] has a tendency to excite dissatisfaction in their minds and to produce insurrection and rebellion." Slave accounts report punishments such as having the "forefinger cut from his right hand" for any slave caught writing.

These prohibitions have implications beyond literacy, extending into symbolic and political claims regarding the African, and indeed his and her very status as a full human being. Just how successful repressive measures were in preventing literacy remains a subject of investigation. While exact figures are still difficult to determine, a considerable body of slave testimony portrays not only the difficulty of learning letters, but also the success, despite all, in attaining it. W. E. B. Du Bois uses the figure of 5 percent, and assessments range from 5 to 10 percent literacy. Legal restrictions, however brutal, were not uniformly instituted or applied; and the achievement of literacy is impressive in the face of dangers and difficulties.

What all accounts do attest is the religious context in which the drive to literacy took place. Both the pursuit of literacy, and to some extent the opposition against it, centered in the Bible. Slaveowners attempted to edit the Bible, with emphasis on texts that promoted what John Blassingame has called the Slave Beatitudes: "Blessed are the patient, the faithful, the cheerful, submissive, hardworking, and above all, the obedient." Howard Thurman describes his ex-slave grandmother's enduring antipathy to selected Pauline texts such as "Let every man abide in the same calling"; "Servants, be subject to your masters with all fear"; or "Servants, obey in all things your masters according to the flesh." Other slave testimonials report similar typical sermon texts: "Servants obey our masters." Against such attempts to control Scripture, blacks themselves considered learning to read almost a religious act. Those who succeeded often assumed positions of leadership, providing a core of preachers able to communicate the Biblical message to their communities.

The problem of illiteracy was circumvented in other ways as well. Illiteracy had presented obstacles to the conversion of the slaves, especially in the earlier efforts by the Church of England's Society for the Propagation of the Gospel (SPG). Its strong orientation towards catechetical instruction relied on written texts, which made it difficult to reach an illiterate population. With the Great Awakening, however, and the spread of Baptist and Methodist preaching in camp-meetings, a new participation by blacks became possible, as did new forms of American Christianity through interracial contacts. The evangelical shift from instruction to conversion; from catechism to the drama of sin and salvation; from strict hierarchy to the democratization of preaching; all appealed to the bondmen and welcomed them. And against increasing opposition against black literacy, a new method of oral instruction – "religion without letters" – was adopted, relying heavily on simplified catechisms, repetition of question and answer, and, of greatest significance for the spirituals, hymn-singing.

The hymns finally provide one central link between the black community at large and the Biblical heritage, although black preaching remains an important context. This link to the hymns by no means reasserts old, discredited claims that the spirituals are merely derived from white Gospel songs. White and black forms of worship generally influenced each other in the biracial Revivalist context, with song in particular a medium bringing white confessions to blacks but also making the experience of worship more emotional and improvisational for whites. The hymns almost at once underwent such syncretist transformation. As Thomas Higginson reports, the newly freed slaves sang only reluctantly "the long and short metres of their hymn-books, always gladly yielding to the more potent excitement of their own 'spirituals.'"

The significance of the hymnal-link lies not in questions of imitation or derivation, but of source material and cultural exchange. The hymns provide exposure to Christian structures and particularly exegetical methods to which the slaves otherwise had very limited access. They help to fill the gap left by the absence of written records for tracing the spirituals in their development and evolution. Above all, they provide a link between the slave community and sophisticated structures of Biblical interpretation through which the slaves then constructed their own scriptural American history and identity.

Mission records repeatedly refer to the hymnal as one of the earliest and most effective means for reaching a population who could not read, but could sing with extraordinary talent. Charles C. Jones reports in his history of *The Religious Instruction of the Negroes in the United States*, the importance of deaconing or "lining-out" hymns for participation among congregants without access to the written text, where the preacher would sing and the congregation would respond line by line. The Reverend Samuel Davies, in an early Presbyterian mission to the slaves of Virginia, writes that "books were all very acceptable, but none more so than the Psalms and Hymns, which enable them to gratify their peculiar taste for hymnody." The hymnal, perhaps more than any other written text, played a central role in bringing Christian culture to the African-American. Records further show that the most widely disseminated hymnal for this purpose was the *Hymns and Spiritual Songs* of Isaac Watts. Reverend Davies, for example, goes on to request specifically a supply of Bibles and Watts Hymns. Charles Colcock Jones, a leading figure in the mission to the slaves, recommends Watts's first and second catechism and above all, since they "are extravagantly fond of music . . . Watts will furnish a great number of suitable psalms and hymns." Paul Petrovich Svinin records in his 1811 travel notes how holy writ was disseminated in the form of "Watt's Psalms of David Imitated" which were read out line by line ("lined-out"), allowing the congregation to sing the text they could not read. Other slave testimonials describe the service of a pre-war church as one where "the hymns were sung with unusual fervour . . . The hymns were mostly Isaac Watts." This widespread importance of Watts holds throughout the Great Awakening for both blacks and whites, as one of the many modes of mutual interpenetration of culture.

The popularity of the Watts hymnal has special significance. Watts provides a connection and point of comparison between the slave-songs and a New England heritage reaching not only back to the Puritans, but also laterally to other contemporary uses. It is this very Watts hymnal that Emily Dickinson took as a basis for her prosody, tropes, images, and even texts, with her own strong twists and improvisations. Watts for generations reigned in the New England churches as the primary song liturgy. Finally, Watts provides a concrete basis for studying the transmission of Biblical history to the slaves and their reworking of it in the spirituals.

Unlike the Wesley Methodist hymns which tend to dramatize the inward call to salvation, Watts centrally focuses on Biblical history. Watts offers a large group of verse translations of Psalms, alongside many Biblically based hymns. Moreover, the exegetical form he explicitly follows, and at times explains, is that of typology: a mode especially potent within Puritan culture as it established itself in America. Far more than an interpretive method of texts, typology offers a comprehensive historical vision, with far-reaching social and political implications. As a reading of Biblical history, it takes its place within the wider context of the role of the Bible in shaping American identities. This begins, in North America, with the Puritans. The New England Fathers' Errand into the Wilderness was declared by them to be an Exodus. They, the New Israel, had been divinely chosen to cross the Atlantic Ocean/Red Sea, and, under the leadership of Winthrop/Moses, to escape the slavery of Pharaonic England in order to found the New Jerusalem in the New World. At work here is not just a vague correspondence or general metaphor, but the rigorous exegetical method of Biblical typology, as specifically adopted and elaborated by the Puritan community. In this highly structured reading of prediction and fulfillment inherited from the Catholic tradition, events of the Old Testament, while fully historical as actual occurrences, find their true meaning as prefigurations of events to come in the New Testament. In particular, the life of Christ – his passion, death, and resurrection – provides the pattern without which the meaning of the earlier event remains veiled and hidden. Only in light of New Testament revelation, do Old Testament events emerge into their full significance.

In Puritan America, this ancient exegetical method underwent further and particular developments. The model had, through early and medieval Christianity, been elaborated to apply not only to relations between the Old and New Testament, but also to the inner life of each Christian as it conforms to Christ's sacrifice and resurrection (the tropological level); and to the end of time, when the whole world will be immolated and reborn in apocalypse (the anagogic level). The medieval tradition, that is, generally turned the force of the Biblical model inward and upward, away from historical events towards the inner spiritual life or the heavenly afterworld. The Protestant Puritans, in their handling of typology, reintroduce a radical historical element. Not just the inner life of the individual, but the social life of the community come to be read in light of the Biblical patterns, Old and New. Not only the end of time, but the historical present, is understood through the predictive patterns which God, in his Providence, had revealed through Scripture. This is the founding visionary stone of the Puritan City on the Hill. What it amounts to is the transformation of a mode of textual interpretation and spiritual introspection into a full fledged historical and political vision, with accompanying claims to mission, power, and legitimacy.

Typology as the founding ethos of the Puritan mission to America became in time one of America's founding paradoxes. As the country expanded both in territory and in population, each emergent or arriving group made its own claim to the Biblical authorization. The Puritan symbol offers a model for all who would be American. Exodus becomes a central American theme, with Benjamin Franklin even proposing the division of the Red Sea for the Official Seal. Each ethnic group claims its own ordination as God's chosen ones. On the one hand, adopting the Exodus theme thus signals the assimilation of diverse groups into a central American mythology. On the other, it gives rise to divergent and even conflicting usages, with shifts in emphasis and in the basic structure of interpretation as each group makes its claim against the others. Different groups, that is, lay claim to Biblical authority in order to assert their own special place in an unfolding American society. The exegetical practices for construing the Bible and applying its lessons thus emerge as a form of cultural politics with profound resonance and ramification.

What this makes possible is the Bible as a common discourse between divergent American groups, but also as a scene of conflicting claims and visions. This potential for conflictual Biblical claims is unsurprisingly and intensely realized through the ante-bellum period, as it becomes increasingly riven by competing ideological positions. Divergent readings of Scripture pose one denomination against the other, North against South both outside and within church institutions, and finally culminates in church schisms that prefigure the greater national crisis. Not least among these competing Biblical engagements stands black against white; with the drama of evolving Biblical claims and counter-claims especially charged in the emergence of the slave-songs. The spirituals themselves represent a powerful vehicle of counter-claim for a black Biblical authorization against white interpretations, in all their political-economic implications. Slaves enter into the battle for the Bible, undertaken through the reception, selection, and re-presentation of Biblical material among blacks. The spirituals thus register both difference and continuity within an American culture where Biblical interpretation constitutes a major dynamic of political identity.

The Watts hymnal stands as one specific historical link and entry of the black community into this perhaps peculiarly American mode of identity formation. Typology in turn clarifies the spirituals' own textual structure, as well as the specific historical vision projected by them. Watts's *Hymns and Spiritual Songs* throughout offer parallels between Biblical heroes from Adam through Christ, in historical sweeps reaching from creation to apocalypse. As occurs no less in the spirituals, multiple historical references appear together in single texts. But this is not due to confusion. Rather, it projects the intimate union between these different moments within a divine, eternal pattern. Watts links

Christ to Moses as Redeemer; to the first Adam as his anti-type antidote; to Aaron as priest; to the Passover Lamb as sacrifice. Babel parallels Egypt parallels Babylon; Noah's flood parallels apocalypse; the Old Testament Law prefigures the Gospel. The *Hymns and Spiritual Songs* even offer footnotes explaining, for example, how Moses' law and Aaron's priesthood must give way as "Joshua leads . . . your tribes to rest," such that "Joshua [is the] same as Jesus, and signifies a Saviour"; or expressly declaring Old Testament figures to be "Shadow[s] of [Christ the] Son." Within hymns as well Watts directly employs such terms as "types" or "shadows." Christ appears as "the true Messiah" before whom "the types are all withdrawn," just as "fly the shadows and the stars / Before the rising dawn." The "types and figures" of the Old Testament in Watts Select Hymn 7 are the "glass" for viewing Jesus as the "paschal sacrifice," the priestly "lamb and dove," the "scape-goat" – each a "type, well understood." Throughout, New Testament events are seen as already revealed, indeed as taking part, within Israelite history. Multiple figures are incorporated, placed in careful parallels and asserting together a unity of divine purpose and divine will.

With Watts in mind, the composites of figures in many spirituals become not accidental jumbles but rather significant expressions of a black Biblical/ historical vision. It is striking from the start how the spirituals repeatedly introduce strings of linked figures. These linkages may be more or less elaborate. Yet even apparently incidental references, such as the many invocations of the River Jordan, remain deeply embedded in a broad understanding and conceptual scheme, affording a glimpse through to a large and complex vision. In "We am clim'in Jacob's Ladder, Soldiers of de Cross" cross and ladder are simply posed as versions of each other. But such figures can find extension elsewhere. In "To See God's Bleeding Lam'" the Christic lamb is seen coming down "Jacob's ladder" with the angels, giving way in turn to an apocalyptic "Sheet of blood all mingled wid fire." Here, Old and New Testaments are interpolated, intercrossing with anagogic visions of the End of Time and concluding with a return to the present of the spiritual itself: "Den raise yo' voice up higher / An' you jine dat heab'nly choir."

There are many spirituals, even under the constraints of incomplete renderings of all the verses in variant versions, which exhibit a quite systematic and complex typological architecture. "Didn't Old Pharaoh Get Los'" for example, directly juxtaposes Isaac, infant Moses, Joseph, and Samuel:

> Isaac a ransom while he lay upon an alter bound;
> Moses an infant cast away, by Pharaoh's daughter found.
> Joseph by his false brethren sold, God raised above them all;
> To Hannah's child the Lord foretold how Eli's house should fall.

Each of these Old Testament figures is of course a type of Christ, each reenacting (before the event) Christ's passion of suffering and his glorious redemption. The parallels are, however, remarkably articulated not only through this general correlation but also in terms of that range of roles finally gathered into the Christic antitype. Isaac evokes sacrifice. Moses represents both priesthood and kingship, as does Joseph, although here each is cast in his most vulnerable moments – as infant and sold slave – such that miraculous rescue is underscored, a type of Christian salvation. And Samuel, Hannah's child, specifically invokes prophecy. The song then pursues a fuller course, through added verses, focusing on Moses's confrontation with Pharaoh – including an again very specified type of "hidden manna," making the Biblical bread also the spiritual body of Christ – and concluding, as the spiritual's title and refrain promises, with how "Old Pharaoh an' his host / Got los' in de Red Sea."

It is of course no accident that Pharaoh's defeat should emerge center stage. Of all the Biblical histories, the story of Hebrew slavery and deliverance would have deepest resonance. Nevertheless, even this almost self-evident point of connection projects specific differences in the African-American treatment of shared symbols, as well as distinctive historical structures and the African-American relationship to them. The sharpest contrast lies in the dramatic fact that the roles of the types have been thoroughly reversed. This has, first, historical force. The Africans are unique in that their coming to America was not by their own choice, and brought no deliverance from bondage into freedom. Rather, it was a forced voyage into enslavement. As against the Puritan tradition claiming America as the promised land, a tradition inherited (with differences) by both North and South, in the spirituals, the South is not the New Israel, but rather Egypt. America is the land of the Pharaohs. There is a stark and systematic reassignment of typological roles, which shape the choice and treatment of favorite figures and events claimed by the slaves. Daniel, for example, recurs frequently, in conjunction with a range of other figures and events:

> Didn't my Lord deliver Daniel
> And why not every man
> He delivered Daniel f'om de lion's den,
> Jonah f'om de belly of de whale,
> An' de Hebrew chillun f'om de fiery furnace
> An' why not every man.

The deliverance from the lion's den dramatizes the desperation felt by, and the enormous odds against, the chosen one. Just so is Jonah delivered from the hopeless circumstances of the whale, and the Hebrew children, in a cross-image, not from Egypt but the fiery furnace – of wrath, of Hell. The strong contrasts between entrapment and release serve as expressions of the slave's own remoteness from, yet hope for rescue. And, it is the slave who is represented by Daniel, Jonah, the Hebrew chillun – the prophets and chosen ones of the Lord – as against the white Protestant masters, who are now relegated to lion, whale, and furnace: not the chosen figures, but the monstrous, the satanic ones.

Neither does the spiritual fail to carry forward the lessons of Biblical history into its own time. As was done to Daniel, Jonah, the Hebrews, why not to every black slave? Often singing itself marks this historical immediacy:

> Lit'le David play on yo' harp, Hallelu-lu
> Lit'le David was a shepherd boy,
> He kill'd Golia an' shouted fo' joy – Hallelu-lu
> Joshua was de son of Nun, He never would quit
> Till his work was done – Hallelu.

Role reversals again function to assign David, the singer, to represent blacks, while Goliath, the giant force of evil, represents white Americans. The claim is, at once, historical and prophetic, individual and communal. Not just David alone, but the whole of Israel is, through his kingship, hereby redeemed. Not just Joshua triumphs, but the whole city of the foe is brought down through prophetic power, for all its formidable walls.

It may be too much to claim, as some African-American theologians have done, that such differences amount to a "reversal of meanings of terms" and even a separate Christianity. Yet there are genuine distinctions in the Bible as it is received, interpreted, and projected through the specific interests of the African-American community. And typology further provides a theoretical framework for many of the spirituals' contested features. Arguments over whether spirituals are sacred or secular, this-worldly or other-worldly, political or theological, African or American, can be reframed in terms of typology. African religious sensibility has often been associated with the spirituals' deep sense of continuity between sacred and secular realms, earthly experience and divine presence, between past, present, and future experience. But these are also characteristic of typology, and find ready form in typological correlations. The mundane becomes an arena for divine concern and manifestation in both the spirituals and early Puritan typologies of events. The divine hand is seen in the most ordinary circumstances, as when the railroad becomes a gospel train. Spirituals characteristically cross immediate conditions with ultimate concerns, attempting, as does typology, to negotiate the distance between them. Meanings sweep from present life into sacred realms. This is reflected not only within the texts of individual spirituals, but in the fluid transitions between songs of work and songs of worship – a distinction apparently more assignable to song collectors than to practitioners.

To connect daily activity with eternal reality through Biblical patterning does more, however, than deepen the spirituality of everyday existence. Establishing ties that reach from this world into the next is equally a political act, claiming theological sanction and power for current undertakings. The Bible then offers an appeal to the past in order to validate the present and empower the future. This is the case with the whole Puritan venture. Within African-American history, it can be seen most dramatically in instances of slave rebellion. White fears against disseminating the Bible to slaves were pretty much affirmed by such slave revolts as the Stono Rebellion of 1739, Gabriel's Rebellion of 1800, and then by rebellions led by Denmark Vesey and Nat Turner. In each case, the leaders claimed to enact Biblical paradigms and figures, as when Gabriel claimed that with his people, as the Israelites, "Five shall conquer one hundred." Nat Turner aligned himself with Moses, Zachariah, and Joshua, declaring "Behold the day of the Lord cometh." It was in the wake of just these rebellions that anti-literacy laws were redrafted with ever greater stringency.

The overt politics of slave revolt underscores the political configurations more generally implicit in the work of Biblical hermeneutic. And the specific political circumstances of the black community accordingly introduced fundamental shifts in the structure of black typological interpretation, in the relationships operating between past, present, and future, and in the function of the paradigms within the communal life of the spiritual singers. Their different interpretations posed participants and audience against, and often in contrast with, other competing interpretive communities, as well as differently situating each interpretive community relative to the prophetic histories it claims. The difference is, not least, one of power. The social and political position of the slave community was profoundly different from, for example, that of the seventeenth-century Puritans; and this is reflected in the basic typological structures each group constructs. The Puritans, at least in New England, early established themselves as the ruling group. It was the Puritans who defined the terms of settlement, both economically and religiously, to which other groups conformed. And within the rhetoric of typology, despite Jeremiad warnings of divine chastisement, there was an underlying sense of continuity between present conditions and future fulfillments. Prophetic promises were already, at least to some extent, felt and evident in present providences.

But the slave community was without political control of economic, religious, and even personal circumstances. This difference in situation significantly shifts the balance between the poles that typology mediates. Compared with the medieval Catholic tradition's emphasis on interiority and eschatology, the Puritans made typology far more worldly and historical. The Puritan emphasis on specific mundane events of their own history in a sense introduced a new, contemporary literalist level. This turn-to-history extended the pattern of Christian living from an interior spiritual experience to an exterior, social/political one. Not only the individual, but the community was to follow in the path of Christ. The carefully distinguished territories of inner and final spiritual experience as against outer history and politics – Augustine's City of God as against his City of Man – became, for the Puritans, conflated together. The pattern of conformation to divine plan is now visibly revealed in the history and politics of the Puritan colonies. This shift to history did not eliminate the anagogic level pointing beyond it. Rather, the one was in a sense incorporated into the other. Puritan politics can claim to realize Biblical pattern exactly because God's Plan, in them, was approaching its final fulfillment. The Puritan City on the Hill is not only an event within history; it is also the final fulfillment of the divine plan as history's End.

Black typology asserts a still more radical turn to history, where history is, however, experienced in far more disjunctive ways. There is, first, an emphatic sense of the literal level of historical events, often recognized as an unusually immediate "identification," "parallel," "correspondence," or "literalization" in the spirituals between present and Biblical history (although this identification is generally seen as based in "obvious parallels" in experience rather than a Biblical hermeneutic). The past is more immediate: it is felt not only as interpretive paradigm, but as present, lived experience. Slavery is both image and reality.

What occurs, then, is a collapse of the typological present and past. At the same time, a stark discontinuity looms between immediate conditions and dreams of redemption structured through Biblical promise. The distinction is not so much white identification with the "new Israel" against black identification with the "old Israel"; new Israel and old are, in typological terms, aspects of each other. What is different is the severity of strain in negotiating from one to the other. The past is more immediately present. And yet its relation to the overarching pattern is more problematic. Present history appeals to, but also challenges, a redemptive pattern not yet manifest. The different typological levels are in this sense discontinuous. The immediate present in slavery asserts itself in all its tragic power, against a future deliverance that penetrates in faith. But its promise has not yet been fulfilled, and the present has not been visibly incorporated into redemptive pattern. Such future promise is not, that is, actually evident in present circumstances, but is rather severely remote from and contradictory to them. It is this strain that serves to confirm the reality of history, its present conditions, even while passionately referring to a divine plan that remains, for now, tragically remote. History is read in light of future fulfillment; but, despite faith in the triumphant outcome, history retains its immediate and terrible presence. What emerges, rather than a continuous world reaching from present to future by way of the past, is instead an explosive and ultimately apocalyptic appeal to the future, in the name of the past, not only to shape the present but to abolish it.

Such historical disjunctions haunt a spiritual such as "He's Jus' De Same Today":

> When Moses an' his soldiers, f'om Egypt's lan did flee,
> His enemies were behin' him, an' in front of him de sea.
> God raised de waters like a wall, and opened up de way,
> An' de God dat lived in Moses' time is jus de same today.
>
> When Daniel faithful to his God, would not bow down to men,
> An' by God's enemies he was hurled into de lion's den,
> God locked de lion's jaw we read an' robbed him of his prey,
> An' de God dat lived in Daniel's time is jus de same today.

The immeasurable odds against Moses and Daniel give way to the miraculous deliverance which overturns those in power against them. Each of these Biblical events thus reflects the other, revealing an eternal pattern at work through all time and hence also "today." But when exactly is this "today"? It is not, alas, the here and now of the spiritual's creation, which remains rather caught between enemies and the sea. Indeed, although "today" remains a reenactment of past sorrows, it is not yet a participation in future redemption. It is promise, but not yet fulfillment. In the spiritual "Who'll Be a Witness for My Lord," a series of Biblical witnesses are cited, from Methusaleh through Samson through Daniel, each as model and image of the present-day soul. But the deliverance they witnessed remains undisclosed in present history. Such spirituals, on the one hand, bring the promise of rescue into the present as its true paradigm; but, on the other hand, redemption remains quite remote from the continued actual enslavement that has not yet met its end.

Typology as practiced here verges into apocalyptic. And it is striking how many spirituals introduce scenes of judgment and of trumpets, of falling stars and world immolation, when, as in the conclusion of "Didn't my Lord Deliver Daniel," the pattern is carried forward from Daniel and Jonah to King Jesus. He appears as the "moon run down in a purple stream, De sun forbear to shine, and every star disappear" and the historical world undergoes its final throes. "My Lord What a Mornin'" celebrates that dawn "when de stars begin to fall . . . / When ye hear de trumpet sound . . . / To wake de nations under ground." "O Rocks Don't Fall On Me" bids rocks and mountains to fall, as with "Jericho's walls," only on sinners, as "De trumpet shall soun' / And de dead shall rise." In such songs, the focus of energy fastens on past and future, with the present of slavery elided. And yet slavery remains the painful, defining term in all its historical force. Immediate present history is both absent, unmentioned, and yet the controlling center of the asserted pattern. In this way, the slaves' political condition generates an interpretive mode. Vulnerability in political position makes the Biblical past less a set paradigm for the slaves than a crisis and drama as yet unresolved. History, though interpreted in light of an encompassing pattern, is nevertheless reaffirmed in all its painfully discontinuous process. Slavery and redemption point as much away from as towards each other, requiring less a fulfillment than an erasure of the present by the future. This tension multiplies the relationships between parallel events cited within the spiritual texts. It calls for more radical acts of interpretation, with stark tensions and jumps, implying not only a claim to a chosen redemption, but also a counter-claim, especially against their immediate Biblical-historical competitors, the slaveholders.

It is ultimately this political context that shapes slave adaptations of typological tradition, requiring sharp transfers of meaning and discontinuities of language in a truly dynamic, communal production. Here another much discussed feature of the spirituals finds its place. The spirituals have often been called coded messages, in which apparently religious images take on specific, concrete reference. Such dual meanings are attested from the earliest accounts, as when Frederick Douglass glosses that "the north was our Canaan." Higginson similarly reports a black soldier as explaining: "Dey tink de Lord mean for say de Yankees." The need for encoded messages is conversely met by decodings by masters. As one ex-slave explained, when they were singing "Ride on King Jesus, No man can hinder Thee," the "padderollers told them to stop or they would show him whether they could be hindered or not."

But all typology is in some sense a code. Each exegetical level always points beyond itself to another, with the balance between them kept in relational play. In the most fundamental sense, the whole business of typology is to mediate between an immediate history and a pattern encompassing and directing it. In its multiple structures, typology is devoted to asserting connections between secular venture and sacred vision, communal destiny and individual salvation, history and eternity, the present and an eternal plan extending into past and future. This it continues to do in the spirituals, whose "codes" remain mutually referring. They can finally be resolved neither into a purely political and this-worldly meaning, nor into an exclusively other-worldly longing.

Rather, multivalent meanings operate throughout, in ways that typology helps illuminate.

The interplay within black typology does, however, remain distinctive – and does so in ways that look forward to later black literary practices. If traditional typology finally points away from history to eternal pattern, African-American typology both insists on and radically contests present history. History, that is, does not function as mere signifier to be subsumed into the signified of eternity's plan. Within black typology, the direction of the signifier/signified relationship is destabilized, so that the literal force of history strains in radical distance from the eventual triumph also radically asserted. This destabilization operates not only within the typological structures of the spirituals, but also in their complex relationship to other Biblical interpretations. The slave-songs above all wrest from the surrounding culture a version of the Bible against the one propagated by the white masters. As with other African-American literary practices, they both double and displace elements from the surrounding culture, in special transformation within their own community.

The unique features of black typology finally amount to distinctive and competitive claims to the Bible as a potent center of authority and power in America. The spirituals mark the battle between the slave community and their masters over which Biblical texts should be cited as models – those preaching obedience as against those preaching deliverance; what theological interpretation should be given to them – a purely inward and other-worldly one, or an assertion of redemption reaching from past to future but with immediate historical reference; and ultimately, which community can look forward to divine reward, and which to damnation.

Typology thus emerges not as a fixed set of practices but as a dynamic, interactive, and multiple political-textual mode. A founding form for both American historical consciousness and American literary practice, it comes to reflect the changing conditions of an American society undergoing rapid trans-formation. Rather than functioning as a stable reference generating clear or unitary prophecies, typology moves back and forth between groups in mutual reflection and competition in a highly syncretist fashion, as each group seeks its own reflection in the magic mirror of the Bible, trying to project its chosen future in the images and texts of its past.

WOMEN'S BIBLES

In 1895, Elizabeth Cady Stanton published *The Woman's Bible*, dedicated to contesting the "idea of women's subordination [as] reiterated times without number from Genesis to Revelation." Stanton's *Woman's Bible* was too radical even for the progressive National-American Woman's Suffrage Association, which repudiated it. But it was nonetheless widely read, and stands as a culmination to a century of Biblical controversy in religion, in scholarship, and in politics. Such Biblical controversy extends into many nineteenth-century American communities, and is by no means restricted to women's issues. But Stanton's feminist understanding of the Bible as an authority implicating political, legal, and social powers, has specific relevance for nineteenth-century women writers, and not least poets. In nineteenth-century American women's poetry, Biblical revision constitutes a distinctive subgenre. Even without Stanton's express political program ("an entire revolution in all existing institutions is inevitable" she writes), many women poets display an acute awareness of the Bible's power to define models, morals, and social strictures. Their exploration of Biblical texts reflects and informs their understanding of their status and place in society.

The women poets engaged in projects of Biblical exegesis represent a wide range of religious, social, and political commitments. They could be pious or skeptical; conservative or radical; with varying combinations of these impulses. Different women had different degrees of religiosity and different relations to established institutions, both secular and religious. These varying positions translated into a variety of literary methods. Commonly cited stories and persons could be reread with different emphases, even if a specifically female viewpoint remained muted. Standard, authoritative texts may be read from a specifically female point of view. Or, attention may focus on neglected or suppressed texts, especially those involving female figures generally passed over in official church culture (Elizabeth Cady Stanton complained, "We never hear sermons pointing women to the heroic virtues of Deborah as worthy of their imitation"). Such attention to neglected texts in itself implies different values than those usually urged; and this is especially the case when accompanied by overtly feminist positions. Intentions may thus be actively feminist and religiously liberal; or they may remain conservative and devout; with feminized viewpoints sometimes overt, sometimes hidden; or perhaps asserting themselves against and despite a conservative framework.

The very entry of women into the field of exegesis, however, already carried with it implications for their rights as women, both with regard to the constitution of religious authority and in terms of the political roles these carried in nineteenth-century America. Such a politics of exegesis is implicit in women's literary strategies, and extends beyond the content of any particular reading. Specific textual explication represents only one element in a complex series of decisions and commitments. Explication itself is framed, first, by the decision as to which texts should be selected for interpretation: which actors, which events, which images will receive interpretive attention. But, second, this selection implies a prior decision as to which figures are to be taken as models for behavior, prooftexts for argument, or illustrations of principles. That is, the selection of texts already privileges specific values and behaviors as exemplary. And this, third, in turn derives from fundamental understandings of what the Bible teaches – a vision of the Bible's central message which the preferred passages are then adduced to demonstrate.

Broadly speaking, there emerged, particularly around the issues of both slavery and women's rights, two opposing understandings as to the Bible's central and fundamental teaching. On the one hand, a 'subordinationist' reading regarded the Bible as a book of hierarchical authority, extending from the text to the church, and urging patient acceptance of one's lot as ordained by God within a fixed order. Such a reading asserted the divine sovereignty of God, ruling over the world through His church institutions, and authorizing hierarchical structures in which, for example, men governed women and masters governed slaves. In contrast stood what may be generally called a liberal interpretation, which defined the Bible's central teaching as the principles of freedom, liberation, individual conscience, and the sacred integrity of every soul created equally by God.

Finally, inseparably linked to these broad principles of understanding is the question of who has the power to do the interpreting. The principle of subordination or liberality implicates not only the Biblical message but also the right to interpret it. If the Bible declares both sexes equal, then Scripture itself allows women, and not only the established, male, white clergy – such as those who denounced Stanton's Bible as "the work of women and the devil" – the power of exegesis. The issues of Biblical exegesis thus extended from the content of a given interpretation to questions regarding which Biblical texts should be emphasized; which figures should be adopted as exemplary models; which criteria should guide interpretation; and who possessed the right to do the interpreting.

The exegesis of the Bible by women takes its place within a wider scene of pluralist interpretation, which has in America many different sources, and in which both centripetal and centrifugal forces intercross in Biblical discourse. From the outset, American religious history had undermined the establishment of any single, controlling religious authority. The failure of any church to establish itself to the exclusion of others; the Protestant emphasis on inner voice or conscience as the site of ultimate religious experience; the lack of rigorous hierarchy in most American churches, intensified through the relative anarchy of territorial expansion; and the competition between denominations in an open religious market, without any state-sanctioned power, all worked to multiply American religious experience and authority. This tendency was strengthened by Protestant traditions of the Bible, emphasizing personal encounters with the text and deemphasizing catechismal or priestly discipline such as persisted in the High Churches. The Higher Criticism then further splintered notions of the text and methods for its understanding. Its historicist, *Wissenschaft* orientation approached the Bible not as an ahistorical revelation, but rather as a set of documents written, transcribed, and redacted under varying historical circumstances by divergent authors and groups.

This variegated background of Biblical dissemination frames the participation of nineteenth-century American women, including poets, in the project of interpreting Scripture. The poetry further underscores the mixture of opposing commitments which characterized Biblical exegesis. On the one hand, multiple and feminized interpretations raised questions about traditional readings and exclusive claims to religious authority. On the other, they continued to accord to the Bible a central power of reference. This mixture can be seen in Stanton herself. Stanton denounces the traditional place of the Bible in church discourse as political and repressive. Hers is a work of exposure. "From the inauguration of the movement for women's emancipation," she declares, "the Bible has been used to hold her in the 'divinely ordained sphere' prescribed in the Old and New Testaments." At the same time, Stanton does not simply dismiss the Bible as irrelevant. Her very desire to recast the Bible from a woman's viewpoint, to engage and indeed enlist it with regard to the question of woman's rights, acknowledges its continuing power. As she herself remarks, "So long as tens of thousands of Bibles are printed every year, and circulated over the whole habitable globe, and the masses in all English-speaking nations revere it as the word of God, it is vain to belittle its influence." But these contradictory elements themselves underscore the ways in which the Bible provided a common discourse in America, even for warring camps. Whatever the disagreements of purpose and dissent of opinions taking place, the interpretive project in women's poetry reaffirms a shared Biblical discourse as fundamental to both personal identity and American cultural community. It demonstrates the way Biblical interpretation both reasserted tradition and acted as an arena of disagreement and protest. Even radical disagreement was in this sense conducted within the frame of a common discourse. The Bible could thus serve interests both traditional and radical, conservative and reforming, emerging as a common ground upon which opposing ideologies could clash and yet each continue to participate in a joint American community.

Lydia Sigourney (1791–1865) provides an example of a conservative treatment of the Bible. Sigourney's piety and conformity with expected feminine roles made her as immensely popular in her own day as she is today dismissed for sentimental hack work. Nevertheless, she introduces a female perspective through a female voice. In the poem "The Ark and Dove," Sigourney offers a characteristic scene of female domestic instruction: a mother is asked by her daughter ("my little girl") to tell a bedtime story. At first, the gendering in the poem is subtle. The Ark appears as an idyllic Sigourney domicile, in which husband, wife, children, and all the animal couples "in their quiet vessel dwelt secure." Instead of featuring Noah, however, the poem turns to the "meek dove," on whom the fate of all depends. This dove is not only "gentle," but also adventurous and courageous, setting out on her own (in this version, unlike the Bible's, she escapes from the Ark), "her lonely pinion" confronting the flood's desolation in solitary, heroic venture, while her mate, staying behind, "with sad moans had wondered at her absence."

Sigourney has indeed made Noah and the Flood into, as the daughter comes to call it, a story of "The Ark and Dove." And the dove is not the only hero(ine). The poem interpolates into the Biblical tale the story of its telling, with mother initiating daughter into a female line of sacred wisdom. She thereby offers a model for both the girl's own future life, when she, "Like that exploring dove," will sometime "dare the billows of the world"; and for the mother herself as guide. The mother, in fact, becomes the central figure in the poem's implicit typology. If Noah retains the role of "righteous man" who receives the "wandering dove" in the Old Testament version, the poem's conclusion in the corresponding present focuses on Noah's antitype, who is no less than the mother herself. The poem concludes:

> Mothers can tell how oft
> In the heart's eloquence, the prayer goes up
> From a sealed lip: and tenderly hath blent
> With the warm teaching of the sacred tale
> A voiceless wish, that when that timid soul,
> New in the rosy mesh of infancy,
> Fast bound, shall dare the billows of the world,
> Like that exploring dove, and find no rest,
> A pierced, a pitying, a redeeming hand
> May gently guide it to the ark of peace.

Christ is the ultimate redeemer. Yet, as pitying, gentle guide, he appears more as Mother than male, with the mother/poet made in his/her image.

In Sigourney's text, female nature continues to be described as "timid," just as the dove herself is "meek." But this, almost despite the poem's governing premises, also becomes the basis for daring and exploring, at least in the interest of protecting domestic arks – and also of writing about them. Although the poet describes her "wish" for her daughter as "voiceless," her own lips are hardly sealed. Although written in the name of domesticity and female timidity, Sigourney as poet is not voiceless. Conservative in intention, faithful both to religious tradition and to the woman's sphere, Sigourney yet takes the Bible into her own interpretive hands, and speaks for female experience and redemptive power.

Thus, even texts committed to conservative Christian and social values introduce more progressive features in the very fact of new, women interpreters, speaking in their own voices and from their own experiences. Often texts represent volatile combinations of interests, configured through different orientations, in ways that may also be incompatible. Such a complex intersection of forces is in part what makes Julia Ward Howe's "Battle Hymn of the Republic" such a powerful American text. Its visionary rhetoric is situated within the deployment of Biblical energies so central to American political history, and indeed as these were often placed in contest against each other. Howe displays an almost technical virtuosity in her command of Biblical pattern, with the poem a typological tour de force. The "Battle Hymn" is based on verses from Revelation 14, 19, and 20, as these in turn rework the books of Daniel, Joel, Isaiah, and Ezekiel. It then makes all four levels of Scripture into one, as history unfolds from Old to New Testament, into contemporary events, within the ultimate prophetic structure of American apocalypse. The glory that is seen is now, then, and final. And the end serves both as judgment and as history's conclusion. That harvest of wrath prophesied (Joel 3:1 / Revelation 14:19) as the lightning of the Second Coming (Revelation 19:15), is now revealed and taking place in the military present of the "watch-fires" and "dews and damps" of the Civil War camps.

As in all exegetical undertakings, interpretation here is not neutral, either in its assignment of roles or in its working principles. As a white, Northern Unitarian, Julia Ward Howe distributes the forces of revelation in accordance with her allegiances:

> I have read a fiery gospel writ in burnished rows of steel,
> As ye deal with my contemners, so with you my grace shall deal;
> Let the Hero, born of woman, crush the serpent with his heel,
>   Since God is marching on.

The "Battle Hymn" gathers and concentrates the several features characteristically defining apocalyptic rhetoric. Immediate and particular events become universal, cosmic drama, in which absolute Evil confronts absolute Good. All this comes to its Final End, both as Judgment and as the End of history, when time stops forever in eschatological fulfillment. Thus, here, the "burnished rows of steel" of historical guns write a "fiery gospel" in which the Hero

(North) crushes the serpent (South) in present and eternal time. God marches on through American history.

There is little overt gendering in the "Battle Hymn." The Hero "born of woman" reminds us, perhaps, that the sex said to have brought sin into the world will also bring its redemption. "The beauty of the lilies" where Christ was born may also imply some feminization. Other poems of war do show Julia Ward Howe to be more directly concerned with gender than she is here. "Our Orders" calls women away from making silk dresses to making silk flags and "homely garments" – with which to cover the dead, and clothe their orphans. This also converts the war effort from military to social services, with art itself enlisted to address its "offices" to the courage of destiny. The poem's title is itself a complex pun. Women take up "orders" not to enlist but to salvage, in what may imply a feminized reordering of the world.

But despite the lack of specific gendering in the "Battle Hymn," the status of the speaker is extravagantly highlighted. The action of the poem is not contained only in the apocalyptic patterning of current events. It dramatizes no less the act of interpretation itself, the prophetic action of witness. "Mine eyes have seen," "I have seen," "I can read his righteous sentence by the dim and flaring lamps," "I have read a fiery gospel writ in burnished rows of steel." Howe underscores her own visionary powers. At the dramatic center of events when God is "sifting out the hearts of men" for judgment, she herself is called: "Be swift my soul to answer him." The text finally proclaims not only the divine power unfolding before her, but also her own power to see into the world's events and unveil their ultimate and eternal meanings. Without direct reference to her gender, she nevertheless asserts her power to read history in all its political force.

That authority to interpret is as implicitly explosive as the apocalyptic vision it records. It brings into the text a cross-section of American cultural impulses, in ways that reveal both their collaboration and their potential collisions. The poem is, on the one hand, traditional, even conservative, in its nationalist fervor, expressed through its faith in America as the ultimate stage of divine will and divine care. The "Battle Hymn" aligns itself firmly with American political/religious discourse at large. Its apocalyptic language was generally characteristic of Civil War rhetoric: in sermons and newspapers, as well as an immense amount of patriotic verse. In this sense, Howe seems to have been seized less by a higher power, as she claimed, than by the period's overwhelming rhetoric.

Yet, the poem makes its religious/patriotic claims in the name of that ideological liberalism which is also traditional in America – such that even conservative impulses defend themselves within the terms of an American political individualism which is essentially liberal. It is this peculiarly American formation that the poem enacts. Its creed is a version of the American civil religion that takes as its center the liberal truths:

> In the beauty of the lilies Christ was born across the sea,
> With a glory in his bosom that transfigures you and me.
> As he died to make men holy, let us die to make men free,
>   While God is marching on.

The sacred integrity of every individual soul transfigured in Christ, with freedom itself the image of holiness, is declared here to be the true American faith. The poem asserts the voice of individual conscience, in its own speaking and as calling to each soul to be swift in answer. But this in turn implies the right of each to his or her own version of events and assignment of values; yet does so in the language, and out of the ethos, of communal values and a social redemption beyond individual salvations. Finally, the voice here is also that of a woman, taking on herself the role of prophet of the American Way: a status at once within and outside the liberal ethos, which had not yet incorporated women, while also addressing the communal arena from which women remained officially excluded but within which they in fact moved, worked, and served.

How far America's shared discourse could contain the competing claims conducted within it, is a question dramatized by the war itself. From the viewpoint of the history of women's poetry, what is especially striking is the poem's decidedly and self-evidently public concern, and not least in its Biblical engagement. The poem, simply in engaging in exegesis, already contests restrictions against women's participation in public and indeed political activity. This power of Biblical discourse within the public and political arena had been recognized by radical and conservative women alike. Already at the 1837 Anti-Slavery Convention of American Women, a resolution had passed explicitly associating Biblical interpretation with women's access to power: "Woman has too long rested satisfied in the circumscribed customs that a perverted application of the Scriptures have marked out for her, and that it is time she should move in the enlarged sphere which her great Creator has assigned her." Even Frances Willard, president of the essentially conservative Women's Christian Temperance Union, called in *Woman in the Pulpit* for "women commentators to bring out the women's side of the Bible."

The political power of the Bible, its complex positioning between radical and conservative as well as religious commitments, and its uses in enabling the participation of women in public life, comes to center stage in the writing of Frances Ellen Watkins Harper (1825–1911). Harper's work powerfully projects the radical potential of religious piety. Probably the most radical woman poet of the century, Harper was the daughter of free blacks, was educated in her uncle's school in Baltimore, and then grew up to be an activist for both abolition and women's rights. Her poetry is specifically situated in the context of these movements, whose debates over slavery and suffrage were often conducted through Biblical reference and on Biblical terrain, with both sides blandishing texts as central weapons.

At issue was Biblical interpretation, and the specific uses to which it could be put; although this distinction was perhaps rarely conscious on the part of the contestants. On the one hand, established interests invoked the Bible as the basis of their own hegemony. Prooftexts were brought by conservatives not only as God-given evidence of their own legitimacy, but also to attack those who contested their position, accusing them of rebellion against both men and God. On the other hand, as Lydia Child observed, "sects called evangelical were the first agitators of the woman question," even if their activities went against the intention of a clergy who had lost control of their female crusaders. Abolitionists and suffragists accordingly marshaled counter-citations of Biblical prooftexts against conservative authorities. Angelina Grimke, for example, in her *Appeal to the Christian Women of the South*, urged Southern women to "read the Bible" in the fight to overthrow slavery: "it contains the words of Jesus . . . Judge for yourselves whether he sanctioned such a system of oppression and crime." Her sister, Sarah Grimke, extended the principle to the rights of women. In her *Letters on the Equality of the Sexes and the Condition of Woman* she similarly declares: "I shall depend solely on the Bible to designate the sphere of woman," thus contesting what she calls "the perverted interpretation of Holy Writ" as it has been used to defend corrupt institutions that betray the Bible's message. Instead, she asserts a liberal interpretation of the Bible as a text of deliverance. Thus, she denounces the "anti-Christian traditions of men which are taught instead of the commandments of God: Men and women were CREATED EQUAL: they are both moral and accountable beings, and whatever is right for men to do, is right for women."

Harper participated in white women's organizations and therefore was engaged with such debates. But her combination of political involvement with profound Christian piety specifically, as well as her close ties to black women's organizations, connect her to discourses within the black Christian community, and especially to the emergence of black women preachers and activists. The democratizing, populist, egalitarian elements of evangelical religion sowed unintended seeds among women participants, who found themselves called – indeed, as they themselves vehemently insist, irresistibly summoned against any intention or assertion of their own – to preach the

Lord's Word to the unconverted. Autobiographical accounts, such as those by Jarena Lee, Zilpha Elaw, and Julia Foote, exhibit fascinating and destabilizing features in ways that recall Lydia Sigourney's, declaring a heartfelt humility even while, in the name of a divine authority, they feel impelled to transgress earthly strictures. Their radicalization is oddly reluctant, imposed upon them by an overriding higher power, and with profound struggles to balance their accepted gender roles against a higher command to defy them. Nevertheless, they self-consciously reflect on the gender and racial egalitarianism revealed in God's power to call them, in a deeply committed liberal reading of religious principles and Biblical texts. The often implicit radicalization in these preachers becomes explicitly political and indeed militant in the speeches of Maria Stewart, the first woman in America, black or white, to speak in public before a "promiscuous" mixed audience of men and women. Stewart is perhaps closest to Frances Harper's own political consciousness. And like Harper, her political radicalism is inextricably founded in her sense of religious calling, where religion itself becomes the central and necessary foundation for a near revolutionary political activism.

Harper's work directly addresses Bible interpretation as an instrument of power. Her "Bible Defense of Slavery" makes this its explicit subject. The official spokesmen of the white Church "insult . . . God's majestic throne / with th' mockery of praise."

> A "reverend" man, whose light should be
> The guide of age and youth,
> Brings to the shrine of Slavery
> The sacrifice of Truth.
>
> For the direst wrong by man imposed,
> Since Sodom's fearful cry,
> The word of life has been unclosed
> To give your God the lie.

In a controlled pattern of inversion, the altars of Christianity are themselves betrayed to become the site of a Sodomic wickedness. Christian truth is made to serve the lie of slave interest, until white Christians themselves are exposed, at the poem's end, as the true "heathens."

Harper represents one combination of piety and radicalism. She does not subscribe to the Higher Criticism, with its challenge to textual authority and inerrancy that opened Scripture not only to new readings, but also to a different status. Here she differs from Elizabeth Cady Stanton, who regarded the Biblical texts as "wholly human in their origin and inspired by the natural love of domination in the historians." To Stanton it seems obvious that both the "Word of God" (the quotations are always hers) and its interpretations are the products of human history and agency. Accordingly, its teachings must be reviewed in light of the interests of a given interpretive community. Speaking against the "fetish" by which Bible-readers, including women, have accepted every Biblical word uncritically, thereby "gloss[ing] over the most objectionable features of the various books," she contests that notion of "apostolic authority" which excludes women from "any public participation in the affairs of the Church" and "State." Thus, Stanton commits herself without hesitation to liberalizing movements in Biblical reception that had been gaining ground throughout the nineteenth century, undermining any unitary Biblical authority. Her own point in undertaking *The Woman's Bible*, in which she specifically enlisted Biblical critics as well as consulting midrashic and other sources from a broad range of exegetical traditions, is "to read [the Bible] as we do all other books, accepting the good and rejecting the evil it teaches." In this, however, she claimed a higher fidelity to divine truth. The Revising Committee, "in denying divine inspiration for such demoralizing ideas, shows a more worshipful reverence for the great Spirit of All Good than does the Church."

Harper concurs with Stanton's guiding interpretive light as the egalitarian "ideal great first cause that . . . holds the land, the sea, the planets . . . each in its own elliptic, with millions of stars in harmony all singing together." But Harper works from a different position. To her the "Word of God" is "unique and pre-eminent, wonderful in its construction, admirable in its adaptation, [containing] truths that a child may comprehend," as she writes in her epilogue to *Poems on Miscellaneous Subjects* (1891). Even the abuse of the Bible to defend slavery does not compromise its status as divine truth. It remains in the poem "the word of life" which has been "unclosed to give your God the lie." Her own duty is merely to "unclose" this true word against its wicked misappropriation.

Harper's work has close ties to the spiritual tradition. In her poem "Deliverance," she in effect writes a spiritual of her own, not only in her use of the Exodus story but in her skillful mastery of a complex typological structure connecting that story to the story of her people. The poem works back and forth, from the Biblical events of the Passover sacrifice as a type for the New Testament sacrifice in Christ as Lamb; to the founding of the feast of deliverance for all the future "unborn years" when children will be taught these past events; then leaping forward to this future vantage point from which she again looks back, with an apocalyptic image of "jubilee" suspended between past redemption and its still awaited future fulfillment.

In such poems as "Bible Defense of Slavery" and "Deliverance," Harper's racial identity takes precedence over gender. Other texts display other balances.

Her mastery of typological schema is most fully apparent in her long narrative poem based on the Exodus story, *Moses: A Story of the Nile*. It is, like her better-known novel, *Iola Leroy*, a narrative of passing: Moses, initially passing for Egyptian, chooses instead to rejoin his slave brethren, quite explicitly depicted in Southern slave cabins, harvesting Southern crops. In its typological structure, Moses compares his own sacrifice to those of Abraham, Isaac, and Christ, and his birthright to that of Jacob and Joseph.

This Biblical lore he learned from his mother. The poem, in this as in other ways, oddly shifts attention away from its male hero, lavishing imaginative energy instead on Pharaoh's daughter, who tells her own story of finding the Hebrew baby as her rebirth into motherhood; and then on Moses' mother. The figure of Moses is in fact mediated through the viewpoints of these two women, to whom he recounts his decisions and intentions. An honored place is also given to Miriam, Moses' sister, who sings her distinctive Song of Triumph on crossing the Red Sea.

Harper's exegetical readings explicitly assert a liberal understanding of the Bible's message. In *Moses*, she makes the Revelation at Sinai one that declares "the one universal principle, the unity of God," as this "link[s] us with our fellow man [in] peace and freedom . . . instead of bondage, whips and chains." Her radical egalitarianism moves her to include and redeem in her own work Biblical models, and especially women, traditionally neglected or cast as negative figures. The poem *Moses* focuses on Pharaoh's daughter and Yocheved. Harper's "Dedication Poem" features Hagar, as against Sarah, as the type illustrating God's power to uplift the outcast in redemptive grace. It is Hagar, Abraham's disinherited concubine, who incarnates the image of the "heavy hearted, sorrow stricken" mother caring for her child; Hagar for whom a fountain springs up in the desert through divine care; and thus Hagar who serves as prophetic witness of "the fountains of refreshment / ever springing by our way" still today.

Harper here does not contest the Bible's claim to authority. On the contrary, she appeals to it. Nevertheless, by offering her own versions of Biblical events she takes part in a proliferation of exegetical practices that implicitly challenged Biblical authority. Her work displays that ambivalence which seems deeply embedded through the entire evolution of women's self-representation in the nineteenth century. She remains, on the one hand, traditional regarding Scripture's sacred status, and even appears genteel in some of her assumptions about Christianity and woman's sphere. In her epilogue, for example, she reaffirms the Christian faith as "a system uniform, exalted and pure" which "has nerved the frail and shrinking heart of woman for high and holy deeds." Nevertheless, in practice her commitment to the rights of blacks and women led her to untraditional emphases, with potentially disruptive implications.

These various and contesting elements come together with particular resonance in the figure of Vashti, who not only Harper, but a remarkable number of nineteenth-century women poets each treat in turn. Vashti, the first wife whose elimination makes way for Esther's providential appointment as Ahasveros' next queen, tends to be treated somewhere between a harlot and a witch in traditional readings. Her refusal of the king's summons to present herself unveiled (in some commentaries, undressed) before a drunken party launches, in the *Scroll of Esther* itself, a diatribe against rebellious wives as a threat to the fundamental orders of the kingdom. It is therefore gripping that Vashti becomes not only prominent, but positively heroic in a broad cross-section of nineteenth-century women's discourses. Elizabeth Cady Stanton singles her out (along with Miriam, Deborah, and Huldah, and against Sarah, Rebecca, and Rachel) for special commendation: "Huldah and Vashti added new glory to their day and generation – one by her learning and the other by her disobedience." Anna Howard Shaw similarly praises Vashti in an article entitled "God's Women," as does Lucinda Chandler, for whom Vashti is the symbol of "that point in human development when womanliness asserts itself and begins to revolt and throw off the yoke of sensualism and of tyranny." What is striking about Vashti is that her rebellion is made in the name of modesty, which in many ways made up the heart of the cult of domesticity and of female definition. Vashti is womanly, upholding specifically female virtues; but also defiant, making those virtues the basis of self-assertion and autonomy.

Harper's poem, "Vashti," highlights this radical, or perhaps paradoxical potential within the cult of womanhood. Bidden by the king's decree to "unveil her lovely face" amid the lordly (and drunken) men feasting with him, Vashti "proudly" answers:

> I'll take the crown from off my head
> And tread it 'neath my feet,
> Before their rude and careless gaze
> My shrinking eyes shall meet.

Through an image system centered in patterns of inversion and exposures, Vashti treads underfoot the crown which represents in the poem both her economic possession and her derived social status as queen; refusing her own self-exposure and thus reversing modesty as a marker of submission to one of self-declaration. "Shrinking eyes" here then answeringly "meet" the rude and presumably lascivious "gaze" of the men. Defying a decree which would bring her "shame," she instead exposes the king's behavior as shameful. The poem also emphasizes the threat, or sexual fear, of Vashti's rebellion, to the whole order of male authority and power:

> The women, restive 'neath our rule,
>   Would learn to scorn our name,
> And from her deed to us would come
>   Reproach and burning shame.

This imagery of the "name" is carefully woven through the text. Vashti before had refused to make her own name scandalous. At the last, she claims for herself an independent social status as woman rather than queen, leaving "her high estate / Strong in her earnest womanhood." She thus establishes her own "spotless name," asserting both her female purity and her independence, for which self-naming is a powerful trope.

These same conflicts and transformations, where modesty is both submissive and assertive, recur in Helen Hunt Jackson's rendering of "Vashti." Her queen, too, is "pure and loyal-souled as fair" in characteristically gendered imagery. But "love" makes her "bold to dare / Refuse the shame which madmen would compel." Citing both her married and her independent status – "I am his queen; I come of king's descent" – it is Vashti who asserts proper royal standards. The issue of defining the self autonomously, as against a social structure of obligations, is introduced as well in Jackson's companion sonnet "Esther." In this pair of sonnets, Vashti, traditionally viewed as defective, is praised; while Esther, the traditional heroine, is viewed critically.

> Yet thoughtful hearts, that ponder slow and deep,
> Find doubtful reverence at last for thee;
> Thou heldest thy race too dear, thyself too cheap;
> Honor no second place for truth can keep.

In this liberal critique, Esther remains too defined by her obligations to her "race" and moves too far towards traditional self-abnegation ("honor") at the expense of self-development ("truth"). As Stanton wrote, "our motto is: self-development is a higher duty than self-sacrifice." Yet even Stanton, while making Vashti a type of rebellion, imagines her response to the chamberlain's to be: "Go tell the king I will not come; dignity and modesty alike forbid." Modesty and defiance, restriction and rebellion, remain in not entirely stable relationship.

Yet another extended treatment of "The Revolt of Vashti" was undertaken by Ella Wheeler Wilcox in her rewriting of the *Scroll of Esther*. This text is patently feminist. Wilcox's Vashti will not only "loose my veil" but also "loose

my tongue!" making modesty, as well as the economic, social, and sexual status
of women, the very topic to be exposed:

> I am no more than yonder dancing girl
> Who struts and smirks before a royal court!
> But I will loose my veil and loose my tongue!
> Now listen, sire – my master and my king:
> And let thy princes and the court give ear!
> 'Tis time all heard how Vashti feels her shame.

Vashti's "shame" here is her reduction to king's concubine and possession,
which she brings to public notice in the name of proper modesty – in what
amounts to a political speech delivered before the court. And she goes on
to claim her own self-definition and self-evaluation outside the hierarchical
gendered order – that is, to name herself:

> I was a princess ere I was a queen.
> And worthy of a better fate than this!
> There lies the crown that made me queen in name!
> Here stands the woman – wife in name alone!
> Now, no more queen – nor wife – but woman still –
> Aye, and a woman strong enough to be
> Her own avenger.

Here again images of naming, and a rejection of the dependent titles of "queen"
and "wife" for "woman," mark Vashti's accession to her own self-identity and
strength.

Vashti is a figure of particular interest in the way she projects contradictory
impulses within female definition. She, however, is only one of a number of
figures from the Bible who undergo transformation, with each representation
implying different combinations of feminine attributes according to the differing and complex combinations of intentions in their authors. Maria Gowen
Brooks (1794–1865) is best known for her long, narrative poem *Zophiël* (1833),
a rewriting of the book of Tobit which remains, however, only tangentially
tied to the original text, introducing instead her own characters and events in
what is in many ways an erotic fantasy. This work is given special attention
in Rufus Griswold's 1848 *Female Poets of America* anthology – an essentially
conservative collection which includes a wide range of verse-types: descriptive,
commemorative, balladic, domestic, funerary, aesthetic; but with strikingly
little verse dedicated to Biblical topics. But Brooks had published an earlier
work, *Judith, Esther, and Other Poems* (1820), fully situated in Biblical material.
Both the portraits of Esther and of Judith remain essentially traditional. Yet
in each, if modesty is explicitly made the central, defining attribute, it is also a

mode of heroic strength and courage. Thus, although Esther is "gentle, meek, and mild," she remains the focus of the story's retelling. And by penetrating into Esther's fears and ambivalence, Brooks projects a female heroism and explores a female figure's interiority. She also offers a feminized critique of the treatment of Vashti, who despite "all her beauty" was dishonored "for one slight offense." Brooks's Judith is similarly presented as "proudly meek." But she is also wily and courageous, with a heavy emphasis on erotic power that becomes, in the end, communal leadership as Judith calls to the "Weeping Judea: arm thee in his might / Arise, Arise, the enemy is thine."

Brooks offers conventional heroines whose traditional virtues are given a different cast. Ella Wheeler Wilcox, in contrast, prefers unconventional heroines, with clear intention to displace traditional female virtues by assertive and transgressive ones. She wrote, for example, a poem called "Delilah," a woman whom even Elizabeth Cady Stanton found wicked. This poem switches voices, giving Samson the speaking role. Yet this only underscores how Delilah's image – Delilah as image – has been culturally produced, without her own voice or consent (Delilah here is "indolent," a figment of Samson's desire). This may not recover Delilah's viewpoint, but it does expose at least this occlusion.

Here, an untraditional heroine becomes the figure for a very untraditional subject. In other instances, conventional heroines are redefined in unconventional ways. Adah Isaacs Menken, like Maria Brooks, retells the story of "Judith." But she pretty thoroughly redefines what makes her heroic. Menken was notorious in her day for scandalous love affairs and marriages (she claimed there were six); changes of identity (probably born in New Orleans in 1839 to free black parents, she converted to Judaism on marrying Alexander Isaacs Menken, and claimed Jewish ancestry); her many places of residence in both America and Europe; and her sensational professional career as an actress. After reading her poem on Judith, what comes to seem strange is how the iconographic tradition could ever have represented this dauntless and deceptive woman as embodying the victory of chastity and humility over lust and pride. Menken's Judith is wild warrior and contentious prophet, aggressive both in flesh and spirit. Menken is selective, even fragmentary, in her presentation of story elements. Instead of the narrative of Judith as attracting, feting, and then decapitating Holofernes, the general who has laid siege to Bethulia in the wars of Nebuchadnezzar, the poem shows Judith primarily engaged in acts of prophetic speech. Menken is one of the few nineteenth-century women poets to break free of traditional metric and stanzaic form, in a verse clearly influenced by Whitman. Judith speaks in the poem in the loose, rhythmic cries of the Psalms, calling on the "God of Battles" as her guide and claiming the visionary "sword of the mouth" of Revelation. Her theme, indeed, is "the advent of power" of both word and sword in apocalyptic intensity ("Power that will unseal the thunders! Power that will give voice to graves!") The poem's final section glorifies Judith herself in self-proclaimed identity and self-naming: "I am Judith! . . . Oh forget not that I am Judith!"

Judith is somewhat gruesome in her blood lust, with Holofernes' murder a frenzy of sensual passion. These excesses, however, seem purposely directed against the female types Menken is repudiating: "I am no Magdalene waiting to kiss the hem of your garment." There seems generally through this verse a preference for rewriting Old Testament rather than New Testament figures. Submission is cast off, to be replaced by anger. Judith is become a Woman of Desires, not of Sorrows. And what emerges as central is the imagery of voice itself: the dead Holofernes' "great mouth" opens vainly "in search of voice"; but Judith calls to speech the living and the dead, "each as their voices shall be loosed." In Menken's "Judith," both battle and prophecy are ultimately those of poetic power and identity.

This central place of voice and its assertion, of self-naming and identity, can be seen throughout women's interpretation of Biblical materials, with all that this implies concerning public roles and political definition. Indeed, women's poetry of Biblical interpretation generally raises questions regarding the demarcation of women's lives as within private as against public spheres. This division, under continuous negotiation during the nineteenth century itself, is decidedly complicated by nineteenth-century women's poetry, and not least poetry of Biblical revision or invocation. In most women's poetry, publicity and privacy, the desire to speak and inhibitions against doing so, remain in a tension which Biblical figures at once mediate and reenact. And yet, Biblical reference and rhetoric in itself casts a public light, invoking and entering a realm of communal reference and authority. This is the case through a range of attitudes, from, as we shall see, Emma Lazarus, who openly and self-consciously takes on the mantle of the public prophet, to even so private a poet as Emily Dickinson in her often contradictory uses of the Bible.

Women's Biblical poetry, exhibiting a complex range of stances, occupies a near contradictory position of both containment by tradition and challenge against it. To some extent, this is characteristic of the discourse of American Biblical politics generally, where conservative and liberal elements intercross. Radical commitments are conducted in terms of traditional Biblical boundaries, while conservative intentions take place in the context of American diversity and individualist assertion. But for women, at issue is the right to participate at all, both in Biblical discourse and in the American polity. Whatever their intentions, and through all their variations, issues of achieving their own voice and of naming themselves structure women's exegetical interpretations: from Lydia Sigourney's hesitant balancing between voicing and being voiceless; through Julia Ward Howe's "Battle Hymn"; Frances Harper's radical politics of Christian piety; the various unveilings and declarations of Vashti; the prophetic, and violent, self-namings of Judith; the public polemics of Emma Lazarus; and the withheld, agonistic confrontations of Emily Dickinson. In an America relatively naked of institutions, the Bible remained a central reference for any attempt at self-definition: religious, political, or social. Women poets, by taking part in Biblical discourse, are not only exploring their personal or religious identities, but their place within the American political community. At stake in this poetry is their very right to speak, which itself becomes a central poetic subject, and which in turn implicates their right to participate within the American polity.

FRACTURED RHETORIC IN *BATTLE-PIECES*

Melville's *Battle-Pieces* is an intractable work, and this is not accidental. Indeed, it is even more difficult to construe the poems, than it is to appreciate them. Melville was driven to poetry in discouragement. Despite his breakneck production of ten novels in ten years, Melville's career through the 1850s traces a course of failure to find a mode of writing pleasing both to himself and to a paying public. The initial success of his South-Sea adventure stories gradually deteriorated into the financial disasters of *Pierre* and *The Confidence Man*. With this final defeat of his hopes to support himself by writing, Melville resorted to the post of Inspector of Customs (no. 75) for the Port of New York, and to writing a poetry he himself called "eminently adapted to unpopularity." This poetry, from *Battle-Pieces* (1866) through "Clarel" (1876), "John Marr" (1888), and "Timoleon" (1891), has never enjoyed the recovery of reputation since accorded to his prose.

It is not, however, a lack of literary virtuosity that makes *Battle-Pieces* so impenetrable. Rather, it is the specific ends Melville undertook, within the contexts that impelled him, that shape his verse in its inaccessible directions. Melville intended *Battle-Pieces* to address and participate in a common discourse. The volume takes its place beside an immense outpouring of Civil War verse, and indeed of Civil War writing generally: in newspaper reports, sermons, and speeches. But Melville's book was a complete commercial failure, selling less than 500 copies in a market where volumes of poetry could reach sales of many thousands. And yet, this failure itself is a measure of the poems' weight. Their outstanding feature is their resistance to interpretation. As a fierce encounter with contemporary culture, the poems place at their center not only history, but the effort to construe it. Interpretation is at the crux: the compulsion towards it, and beyond even its impossibility, its endless pitfalls.

It has long been known that Melville's basic reference source in constructing *Battle-Pieces* was the *Rebellion Record*, a compilation of newspaper writings already collected and published during the war years. This compilation provided him with the source material – the dates, sites, names of participants, and scenes of action – out of which he composes his poems. Indeed, he scrupulously and insistently marks each poem in terms of a specific historical event, including in its title or subtitle the place and date he takes as his subject. But it is a mistake to suppose, as has often been the case, that the volume is intended as some summary presentation of the history of the war, in verse conventions more or less inadequate to this narrative task. To take *Battle-Pieces* as "a chronicle of patriotic feelings of an anxious middle-aged non-combatant as, day by day, he reads the bulletins from the front" as Edmund Wilson does is indeed to condemn it as "some of the emptiest verse that exists."

Yet neither are the poems fully explained through an appeal to their "themes," as illuminating Melville's stances regarding philosophical, moral, and political issues in a narrow sense. Certainly the poems propose such issues as have been ascribed to them, such as the conflict between order and anarchy; or between law and empire; or cycles of law and evil; or between political idealism and moral and metaphysical realism; or the tragic need for action in a world of ambiguity. But such attempts to systematize the poems into a testament of Melville's political views on slavery and Union, democracy and American destiny (and almost all commentators do this) underestimate the role of rhetoric as such in the volume. *Battle-Pieces* provides less a historical or philosophical record than a rhetorical one. Melville's suspicions of radical evil, as well as his attitudes towards slavery, Union, and democracy, are engaged through the languages that had shaped America's conception of itself and through which Americans continued to express, seek, and contest their identity. The Civil War, as *Battle-Pieces* represents it, emerges as an explosion of language patterns deployed in the rhetorical enactment of American identity. It displays, on the one hand, the importance of rhetoric in constructing and shaping national claims, especially with regard to historical mission. On the other, it traces the courses through which national rhetoric, instead of binding the Union in a unifying historical interpretation, became both a means and field for dissolution into fratricidal conflict.

It is in terms of such rhetorical contest that *Battle-Pieces* – and the title is surely a pun on fragmentation – must be read. The central engagement of the volume is the power of language to assume and assert interpretive paradigms, as displayed through the course and the discourses of the war.

And this is the material which Melville took from the *Rebellion Record*. The *Rebellion Record* provides a completely different experience from that of reading the reports of any individual newspaper. What the *Record* does is bring together and starkly juxtapose accounts from the widest range of journals, of both the North and the South: *The New York World* and *New York Times*, *Boston Transcript* and *Philadelphia Enquirer*, alongside *The Richmond Enquirer*, *Charleston Courier*, *Baltimore Sun*, and *Louisville Democrat*, to name a few. These accounts are often starkly contrasting. Even basic facts, such as descriptions of battles, are presented through wildly diverging angles of vision and ideological interests. The *Record* also includes political speeches and sermons. Abraham Lincoln and Jefferson Davis each appears, with each one calling, for example, for national fasts in the service of each one's cause. Religious exhortations are, side by side, delivered against each other by ministers of identical denominations, in churches recently split through the sectional strife and become schismatic. Not least, each volume concludes with an extensive collection of topical verse, Northern and Southern, each equally patriotic and devoted. Among them is a whole panoply of Battle Hymns, a widely popular poetic genre which bear special relationship to Melville's own efforts.

At issue, then, is not merely the historical sources of Melville's *Battle-Pieces* in newspaper accounts, but contemporary rhetoric and interpretive paradigms as these shape and impel experience. Melville's long poem "Donelson (February, 1862)" directly dramatizes just this question of rhetoric. The poem mimics the format of a report filed from the front. Sections are organized through bulletin-like announcements: "IMPORTANT," "LATER FROM THE FRONT," "FURTHER." Headlines are incorporated: "GLORIOUS VICTORY OF THE FLEET!" "WE SILENCED EVERY GUN." This format, and the conventions of newspaper reporting and reception, are the poem's subject no less (indeed more) than the battle of its title. As the poem slyly remarks, "(Our own reporter a dispatch compiles / As best he may, from varied sources)." And it opens with a scene of "anxious people" crowding around a "bulletin-board." At issue is less historical information than the attempt to shape out of historical incident a meaningful poetic or political design. And this finally reflects back on the source material itself.

"Donelson" is unusual in its overt stylization of newspaper sources; but questions of historical account and interpretation underwrite almost every poem. In particular, Melville is fascinated by the web of projection and retrospection, in which outcomes are unknown, forecast is negated by event, and interpretation is refracted by the contradictory interests of the competing sides. A number of poems – "The March into Virginia," "Ball's Bluff," "On the Slain Collegians" – turn on the particular drama of young soldiers marching into foredoomed futures, cast in a viewpoint they themselves never share, since, with the exception of "The College Colonel," they do not march back again. Markers of temporal irony recur throughout *Battle-Pieces*, in such words as "doom," "forebode," "forecast," "decree," which Melville deploys with almost breathtaking calculation: yet always to the defeat or retraction of the predictive power such terms imply. "The March into Virginia" offers just such masterful and tortuous rhetorical undoings:

> Did all the lets and bars appear
>   To every just or larger end,
> Whence should come the trust and cheer?
>   Youth must its ignorant impulse lend– . . .
> The champions and enthusiasts of the state:
>   Turbid ardors and vain joys
>   Not barrenly abate –
> Stimulants to the power mature,
>   Preparatives of fate.
>
> Who here forecasteth the event?
> What heart but spurns at precedent
> And warnings of the wise,
> Contemned foreclosures of surprise? . . .
>
> In Bacchic glee they file toward Fate,
> Moloch's uninitiate;
> Expectancy, and glad surmise
> Of battle's unknown mysteries.

The poem opens with the question of how events are to "appear" in terms of some "just or larger end." It then proceeds through a veritable labyrinth of words of prescription: "fate," "forecast," "precedent," "warning," "foreclosures," "expectancy," "surmise." In each case, however, Melville so situates his fateful terms as to confute, unravel, and defeat any claim they may make to validity, either as prediction or even as immediate description. "Foreclosures" are "contemned." "Expectancy" faces "unknown mysteries." "Champions and enthusiasts of the state" eagerly assert their own actions as "Preparatives of fate," but they do so in such contradictory phrases, negations, and contorted syntax as: "Turbid ardors and vain joys / Not barrenly abate." Vanity in fact is a recurrent image throughout *Battle-Pieces*, applied in turn to Jackson, Lyon, the Swamp Angel, as well as these Marchers into Virginia. "The Conflict of Convictions" in its final lines underscores the specific sense of emptiness which vanity is given in Ecclesiastes: "Wisdom is Vain, and Prophesy."

"Who here forecasteth the event?" "The March into Virginia: Ending the First Manassas (July, 1861)" commemorates one of the first Northern invasions into Virginia. Seen in the South as the "desecration" of "the sacred soil of Virginia . . . by the hostile tread of an armed enemy," it was first celebrated in the North in "total confidence, the march resembl[ing] a picnic more than a military operation" with sightseers, politicians, and ladies along to enjoy the victory. Instead, after intense confusion, the battle turned into a complete rout to the North, with army and spectators fleeing back to Washington (a reversal that would recur, as Melville reminds in the poem's final lines, in a "Second Manassas" fought again at Bull Run). Melville's textual confusions register historical ones. *Battle-Pieces* repeatedly features battles marked by indecision, confusion, reversal, or accident, such as "In the Turret," "A Utilitarian View of the Monitor's Fight," "Shiloh," "Battle of Stone River," "Sheridan at Cedar Creek," or "Stonewall Jackson" where the General is killed by friendly fire. Civil War battles were, through the first years at least, notoriously indecisive, not only in outcome, but in an almost incredible lack of control, planning, foresight, or grasp of what was taking place during their enactments, by either soldier participants or commanders. It is this inchoate history that Melville commemorates. The gnomic memorial verses which conclude the book inten-sify in its language such arbitrary changes of direction. Retreat becomes a mode of victory, and victory of defeat, as homage is paid to the war dead who have "built retreat" ("On the Home Guard"). The "Inscription" "erect[s]" a stone for participants "where they were overthrown." "The Fortitude of the North" is shown "through retreat."

Nevertheless, Melville's central engagement is not with historical courses, but the way they implicate interpretive design. And for Melville, what stands at the center of interpretive design is the Bible. This does not mean, of course, that the Bible is his only interpretive model – or, rather, is not Melville's only model for interpretive defeat. Melville generously introduces a whole range of promising patterns which then prove false, including references and analogies from literary (especially Miltonic), religious, and political history. A misguided sense of "Bacchic glee" can appear alongside their ignorance as "Moloch's uninitiate" for the Marchers into Virginia. But the Bible retains a privileged status in the (mis-)interpretation of historical design. Raised in the Calvinist Orthodoxy of the Dutch Reformed Church, Melville was perhaps particularly situated to appreciate his culture's vision of the Bible as interpretive key. From earliest childhood, the Bible had cast its prophetic shadow over him as with a strong net. The exegetical apparatus of Biblical prophecy mediated his, as it did the nation's, experience of history. Melville is only too conscious of the patterns of American mission, unfolding from the Puritan exodus into the American promised land, through the millennial harvests of the Great Awakening and the Revolution and then impelling the nineteenth century's vision of expansion as Manifest Destiny. The events of the Civil War, inheriting this full typology of American history, in turn were seen not only as human and temporal but also as cosmic, elect, and divine. Their meaning unfolded not merely in their relation to each other but in terms of the divine plan which, conversely, finds realization in them. The power of textual interpretation thus becomes the power of historical claim, based in the Bible but extending from text to experience, and issuing finally in a pervasive and compelling national rhetoric.

For Melville, however, the ante-bellum context and then the war itself underscored the schismatic rather than cohesive powers of this interpretive design. The contrary uses of Biblical prophecy itself becomes his subject, as they not only contest each other but ultimately undermine the general validity of prophetic claims. "The Portent (1859)," the opening poem of the collection, itself stands as an ominous warning of the counter-designs the book will engage:

> Hanging from the beam,
>   Slowly swaying (such the law),
> Gaunt the shadow on your green,
>   Shenandoah!
> The cut is on the crown
>   (Lo, John Brown),
> And the stabs shall heal no more.
>
> Hidden in the cap
>   Is the anguish none can draw;
> So your future veils its face,
>   Shenandoah!
> But the streaming beard is shown
>   (Weird John Brown),
> The meteor of the war.

Here, as often in *Battle-Pieces*, the Biblical presence is oblique but penetrating. Melville situates this poem at the very center of all Christian typology, the Crucifixion, the pivotal moment around which all sacred history takes shape. John Brown, stabbed, cut, and hanged from the beam, inevitably is posed as a Christ figure. But Brown's figure, while certainly portentous, is presented as precisely unclear. Though punished through the (old) law against insurrection, it is far from certain whether his is a redemptive martyrdom inaugurating any (new) order of love. If "shadow on your green" recalls the 23rd Psalm's green pastures and valley of the shadow of death, it does so as against the Psalm's security in faith, and also the devastation of the Shenandoah valley in the final campaigns of the Civil War, when it was burned to the sea. Brown's face remains hidden by the hangman's cap; just so his significance within any broader scheme remains fearfully enigmatic. And if Brown's beard streams, like a meteor's, in weird omen seeming to project this moment onto cosmic stage, still, all that is "shown" is a veiled future.

This poem is at once deeply typological and anti-prophetic. Even as it invokes overarching designs, it does so in the name of the impossibility of prediction by reference to them. As is true for all of *Battle-Pieces*, the careful dating of the text in historical time subtly opposes the date of its composition against its publication at the war's end. The poet is writing of foresight from the vantage point of hindsight, knowing that John Brown's hanging brought no redemption – and despite Emerson's extravagant claim, in a rhetoric fully contemporary, that Brown had made the gallows glorious as the cross. For Melville, the portent points not towards reconciliation but disintegration. But at issue is not any specific prediction; it is the collapse of predictability as such. In direct opposition to normal typological interpretations, what finally occurs is not the placement of historical event into prophetic pattern, but the collapse of prophecy into brute history. With regard to prediction and fulfillment, time future proves the ultimate irony.

The Biblical paradigm thus asserts itself in the poem, beyond any specific reference, most forcefully through the implicit shape events are meant to, but do not take; and through the language that wishes to assert such prophetic claims. This is the case through the remainder of the volume. When battles are represented through Biblical types, this in no way mitigates their historical havoc. "The Battle for the Mississippi (1862)" is cast in terms of "Israel camping by Midgol hoar" as witness to "Pharaoh's crew" drowning in the great River Nile. But the river battle in fact consumed all sides in confused conflagration. "The Armies of the Wilderness (1863–4)" are cast "as in ages long ago," in the image of such wildernesses as "Paran," the "plain" of "the city of Cain," and the Sinai desert of the "Pillar of Smoke." But this engagement at the Wilderness, a large forest south of the Rapidan River in Spotsylvania County, Virginia, was prolonged, bitter, and inconclusive. "Gettysburg (1863)" is a palimpsest recalling the first Gettysburg encounter the year before, as well as Lincoln's own dedication of the site as a "warrior-monument." This victory cost the Union 23,000 casualties, more than one-quarter of its army; while the South had 28,000 men killed, wounded, or missing, more than a third of Lee's army. The Northern generals, moreover, failed, as was repeatedly the case, to take the opportunity to pursue and destroy Lee's retreating army for conclusive victory. The war would continue two more years. Melville registers these vicissitudes in his often noted imagery of storm, gale, and sea. Here, as elsewhere in Melville, the sea serves as antithetical Wilderness that defies all consecrating Errand. The "three waves" of ocean-like troops "in flashed advance / Surged, but were met, and back they set." Tides and tempests image the impossibility of any final directional turn or resolution. The battle-scene is become

> a beach
> Which wild September gales have strown
> With havoc on wreck, and dashed therewith
> Pale crews unknown –
> Men, arms, and steeds. The evening sun
> Died on the face of each lifeless one.

This "havoc on wreck" is not mitigated by the Biblical comparison of the North to "the ark of our holy cause" before which the "Dagon" South falls, "Dagon foredoomed."

What seems at work here is an incipient structure of typological levels, joining Old Testament to New Testament to Civil War by way of other historical events, with final reference to the apocalypse. But these levels work at cross-purposes. They give broad structure to the mutually deflating false analogies so characteristic of *Battle-Pieces*, with the falsest analogy history itself. Melville's battles seem to disclose nothing more than history at an impasse, repeatedly set against prophetic paradigm and defeating it. And typology amounts to a historical short circuit. It is circular in every sense. It is flawed philosophical reasoning, with its only confirmation the fulfillments already molded according to the predictions they are supposed to confirm. But it is also historical stalemate and interpretive deadlock. Historical time is not a progressive line. Neither is it an advancing spiral with each event at once repetition and further fulfillment, confirming above all the pattern's validity and direction. The century's sacral-secular faith in the onward march of American destiny from election through millennial promise realizing itself on American soil becomes a series of military marches that dissolve into self-negating tropes.

Such self-defeating tropes emerge as the peculiar field of Melville's poetic genius. *Battle-Pieces* is an exercise in linguistic self-retraction, which, while not likely to win Melville a wider audience, nevertheless attests to his craft. In a sustained control of linguistic unraveling that reminds of nothing so much as Samuel Beckett's late prose works, *Battle-Pieces* pursues a language of self-undoing: through strained diction, abrupt meter, tortuous syntax, with tautology, negation, and oxymoron the central rhetorical figures. Into such tropes of impasse Melville converts analogical figures such as allusion, simile, and metaphor, and generally, any rhetoric of advancement. Melville's almost perverse decision to use what are often metrically impossible Hebrew and Indian words (Shiloh, Shenandoah) or surnames (McClellan, Lyon) as pivotal rhymes or repeated refrains, intensifies the sense of historical event as inassimilable into controlled poetic design. On almost every level, textures of analogy prove delusive, with typology as temporal analogy the falsest of all. Thus, "Battle of Stone River, Tennessee (1863)" would compare the Civil War to the War of the Roses' "Yorkist and Lancastrian"; but also to Christ's life, each side battling with "Passion," "sacred fervor," each under a "broidered cross." Yet here the "crossing blades profaned the sign." "Apathy and Enthusiasm" would compare, as was often done in the North, the War of Secession to Milton's War in Heaven (itself Biblical commentary on Milton's own Civil War) come down to American soil. "Michael" is duly cast against the "Arch-Fiend," and the winter of 1860–1 marked through the Christian calendar from Lent to Easter. But this only intensifies its "foreboding" of defeat. "Lyon" is proposed as a "prophetic" figure, combining the crusader-spirit of Richard the "Lyon"-hearted with an apocalyptic "swift sharp sword," and at last ascending, in a flourish of hyperbole and bombast, "up to Zion, / where prophets now and armies greet brave Lyon." The "Armies of the Wilderness" give shape only to the question: "Has time gone back?"

Into this fearsome circle of collapsed analogy as reverse doom, the figure of Lincoln falls. Melville calls his poem on Lincoln "The Martyr," adding as subtitle: "Indicative of the Passion of the People on the 15th Day of April, 1865"; and reminding in the first line that Lincoln had the peculiar fortune to be assassinated on "Good Friday." The poem seems to join the Christic apotheosis which Lincoln's death launched and which found voice in a veritable outpouring of contemporary verse. In Julia Ward Howe's poem "Requittal," to take one example, Lincoln is he who "died beneath the uplifted thong / Who spared for us a thousand lives . . . Sweet Christ, with flagellations brought / To thine immortal martyrdom." But Melville's poem is an extraordinary performance of revocation. Though Lincoln himself represents the "Forgiver," his redemptive power is aborted rather than realized through his death. Furthermore, not a single assassin, but an encompassing "they" are the killers "from behind." In a backward gesture, what this corporate body destroys is the possibility for "clemency and calm" that Lincoln had promised, substituting for it "the iron hand." Thus, the very people who mourn Lincoln with "passion" defeat his Christic promise of redemptive history.

The rhetorical complexities of Melville's simultaneous invocations and retractions are most intensely focused in the poem called "The Conflict of Convictions." This poem stands almost as a synecdoche for the volume as a whole, in its juxtaposition and confrontation between multiple and discordant understandings of the events it addresses. The temptation to read it as a coherent debate between stable although opposing viewpoints should be resisted. Its dizzying variety of assertions makes such schematization impossible. Nor can Melville's "true" philosophical or political position be determined. The text is more productively seen as an ingathering of rhetorical specimens, a display of the ways in which the formulae and figures for describing events already shape the expectations we have of them.

> On starry heights
>   A bugle wails the long recall;
> Derision stirs the deep abyss,
>   Heaven's ominous silence over all.
> Return, return O eager Hope
>   And face man's latter fall.
> Events, they make the dreamers quail;
> Satan's old age is strong and hale,
> A disciplined captain, gray in skill,
> And Raphael, a white enthusiast still;
> Dashed aims, whereat Christ's martyrs pale,
> Shall Mammon's slaves fulfill?

Starry heights and deep abyss situate this as a landscape that is both cosmic and apocalyptic, and immediate and historical. As with typology in general, each rhetorical moment takes on multiple historicities: the "bugle" points at once to Biblical and apocalyptic judgments, as well as to the immediate war and to inward trials. But the invocation of such overarching design is crossed by its inaccessibility, misapplication, self-contradiction, and/or revocation. "Dreamers" indeed must "quail" before events, and not least those who would see Satan and Raphael in the contest before them. Almost every word here swallows itself like a chinese box. "Heaven" is felt only as "ominous silence," a phrase which, like "Dashed aims," is made to border on oxymoron. Most disturbing is Melville's peculiar unconversion of Ezekiel's prophetic call to "Return, return" (Ezekiel 33:11). One of the Bible's most powerful summons to the possibility of spiritual and historical recovery, Melville reduces it to repetition, doom, and a backwards motion reiterating "man's latter fall." The bugle's "recall" points only back to history as iron circle – "Iron Dome," as Melville says later in the poem, which, as an image of the Capitol, revokes the specifically American promise of political salvation. America is cast not as typological and Christic witness, but as a nation where "Christ's martyrs pale" before "Mammon's slaves."

"The Conflict of Convictions" questions more than the assignment of roles within prophetic patterns. Its disintegrative rhetoric implicates the patterns themselves. The concluding stanza appears to offer two arguments or interpretations of American destiny – a "YAY" and "NAY," with God's "MIDDLE WAY" promising some kind of synthesis between them. But the poem absorbs these into its echo chamber of pieces of language without anchor in any systematic viewpoint. In it, invocations to American providential history resist rather than reveal history – "The terrors of truth and dart of death / To faith alike are vain." They point nowhere except to their own doomed tautological circle – "The poor old Past / The Future's slave, / She dredged through pain and crime . . . Age after age shall be / As age after age has been." Pattern dissolves into oxymoron. Signs – "In the cloud a sword is girded on" – only disclose "the hid event." "The wind in purpose strong" only "spins against the way it drives." It is, indeed, impossible here to distinguish a voice of progress from one of pessimistic reversion. At most there are voices of pained assertion and distressed denial. Reference to the past gives birth not to future vision but only to a repeating sense of uncertainty: "The cloistered doubt / Of olden times / Is blurted out."

Images of a consecrated America thus only heighten the poem's disorientation. And none of the voices fully escapes it. The retraction of typological structure by no means frees Melville from it. Not least among *Battle-Pieces'* tremendous challenges is the problem of locating Melville's own voice within the disintegrative rhetorics he deploys. Even his cryptic counter-rhetoric of typology mirrors and is to that extent determined by the discourse of the war period. The discourses surrounding him enter the work still more directly in the form of cliché, whose pressure is felt throughout the volume as its least mediated rhetoric. Often the same poems that deflate the war as the Armageddon of American mission also bombastically assert it as "Truth's sacred cause" ("On the Slain Collegians"); "the fight for the Right" ("Armies of the Wilderness"); such that "Faith in America never dies" and "Heaven shall the end ordained fulfill" ("Lee at the Capitol"). "A Canticle" is particularly troubling. Opening in metaphysical hyperbole that makes sublime landscape into the scene of historical "Fall," glorifying battle against "The Giant of the Pool" as the Evil One incarnate, the poem manages to put into verse the most overblown language of American prophetic confidence:

> The Generations pouring
>   From times of endless date,
> In their going, in their flowing
>   Ever form the steadfast State;
> And Humanity is growing
>   Toward the fullness of her fate.
> Thou Lord of hosts victorious,
>   Fulfill the end designed;
> By a wondrous way and glorious
>   A passage Thou dost find –
>   A passage Thou dost find;
> Hosanna to the Lord of Hosts,
>   The hosts of human kind.

Does this war-hymn represent Melville's personal sentiments? Melville's intractable language, where each word is nearly crushed under the burden of its uses, comes closest here to masquerading as the transparent, topical nineteenth-century verse in which guise he hoped to market it. Comparison is instructive. The *Rebellion Record*, Volume III, includes poems on "Lyon," "Ball's Bluff," and a "Hymn for our Country" by Elizbeth Oakes Smith: "God bless our country / . . . She standeth like a bride / Upheld by God's almighty hand / How fair art thou, O Native land." Volume II includes "A Psalm of Freedom": "It is our nation's judgment Day / That makes her stars to fall, / And all the dead start from their graves / At freedom's trumpet call." It also includes a "Battle Hymn" by Rev. Woodbury Fernall:

> When Israel's foes, a numerous host
> > Through years of conflict pressed their cause
> Thy powerful arm was all their boast
> > Confederate revels owned her laws . . .
>
> Thine is the battle, mighty Lord
> > The skill, the wisdom all are thine
> The fire that lit the sacred Word
> > Shall flash from out our battle line.

Volume IV includes "A Thanksgiving Hymn" by Park Benjamin, of the *Atlantic Monthly* circle, who had written in a negative review of *Mardi* that "Every page fairly reeks with the smoke of the lamp":

> O God of Battles! By whose hand
> Uplifted to protect the Right
> Are led the armies of our land
> To be triumphant in the fight . . .
>
> Accept and let thy mercy crown
> This contest, Holy in thy sight
> And Thine be all the vast renown
> And ours the victory of Right.

But it would be foolhardy to assume that Melville represents in "A Canticle" anything like his own position. The poem's full subtitle explicitly announces its rhetorical framework: "Significant of the National Exaltation of Enthusiasm at the Close of the War." That is, Melville offers the poem as a representation of others' enthusiasm, not as an expression of his own. Melville, moreover, would be aware that enthusiasm was not single, but divided. The *Rebellion Record*, Volume II included, for example, a "Southern War Song" by J. A. Wagener:

Arise! Arise! With rain and might
    Sons of the Sunny clime
Gird on the sword; the sacred fight
    The holy hour doth chime . . .

But the battle to the strong
    is not given
When the Judge of right and wrong
    Sits in Heaven
And the God of David still
    Guides the pebble with his will
There are giants yet to kill
    Wrongs unshriven.

In "A Canticle," as elsewhere, *Battle-Pieces'* energy is invested less in staking out positions than in displaying the rhetoric these positions deploy. None of these voices is necessarily Melville's. Thus, when Melville, in a poem such as "Donelson," italicizes: "Our troops have retrieved the day . . . The spirit that urged them was divine," the line must be placed within the poem's frame of newspaper bulletins, headlines, and reporting. Its divine reference stands as but one claim regarding events among others the poem also incorporates. The poem indeed concludes in a quite different image of a "death-list" flowing "like a river . . . Down the pale sheet." Its final invocation is to "Time" that brings both "wail and triumph to a waste." Similar contradictions emerge between poems, no less than within them. *Battle-Pieces* is not restricted to Northern viewpoints. Southern ones are also represented, in a rhetoric strikingly similar to the North's. "The Battle for the Mississippi" claims God to "appear in apt events . . . the Lord is a man-of-war." But "The Frenzy in the Wake," which describes "Sherman's Advance through the Carolinas, (February, 1865)" is written from the Southern point of view. It no less calls on "Time" to avenge "every woe," and claims for themselves the joy "which Israel thrilled when Sisera's brow / Showed gaunt and showed the clot." This poem is again followed by "The Fall of Richmond" as its "Tidings" are "received in the Northern Metropolis (April, 1865)." There, bells peal and cannons celebrate Richmond's defeat as the fall of "Babylon," the defeat of "Lucifer." Not only rhetoric, but venom, are fully matched, as the Southern-voiced poem curses "Northern faces," the "flag we hate," and the "African – the imp"; while the Northern-voiced poem keeps faith in the "Wilderness" by denouncing the Southern "Hell." The poem's close – "But God is in Heaven, and Grant in the Town, / and Right through might is Law – / God's way adore" asserts not conviction, but only conflict.

The disintegrating voices of *Battle-Pieces* recall Melville's last prose works before he abandoned fiction for verse writing, and especially *The Confidence Man*. Melville's earliest novels such as *Typee*, *Omoo*, and *White-Jacket* had already contained rhetorical set pieces reflecting contemporary American politics. *Redburn*, with its red guidebook that does not guide; *Mardi*, Melville's first achievement of failure, with its multiplying dialogues representing the myriad positions of contemporary places and politics; and *Pierre*, with its dissolving plot and its sustained parody of earthly time against heavenly paradigm; all raise questions regarding rhetorics of promise that, however, finally fail to provide coherent frameworks for integrating events and redeeming them. In *The Confidence Man*, written immediately before *Battle-Pieces*, character and plot further dissolve into serial masquerades, each deploying its own characteristic but uncohesive speaking styles. Melville's poetry takes this disintegration still further. In *Clarel*, the painfully long poem Melville wrote through the ten years following *Battle-Pieces*, he distributes viewpoints among characters. In *Battle-Pieces*, however, rhetorical fragments, piecemeal and discordant, remain uncontrolled by one or even a series of personae. There is no continuous character. And the move into lyric most definitely does not draft Melville himself as the central speaker. Rather, he acts as spokesman for the diverse and competing claims staged by the war itself.

Melville sandwiches the poems of *Battle-Pieces* between a "Preface" and "Prose Supplement," in which he commits himself and his book to a "merciful and healing Reconstruction" requiring "little but common sense and Christian charity." This political stance, for all its defects in potentially mitigating the crime and punishment of slavery, is for Melville a positive commitment. It does not, however, make *Battle-Pieces* into the unity of cohesive voice "making up a whole, in varied amplitude" that Melville, and many readers after him, wish to claim for it. Melville comes closer to the book when he suggests reading it "unmindful" of its "consistency," as "manifold as the moods of involuntary meditation – moods variable and at times widely at variance." As such, the *Pieces* are, as he puts it, the dramatic "poetic record [of] the passions and epithets of civil war," which is to say a record of the way in which "unfraternal denunciations at last inflamed to deeds that ended in bloodshed." That is, the poems above all represent the role of rhetoric in its failure to bind the nation into a common discourse, and indeed in its contribution to national breakdown.

But this is not to say that Melville repudiates America and its promise. What he does suspect, and warn against, is a rhetoric of American destiny grown intolerant, excessive, and absolute in its claims. Especially dangerous are rhetorical patterns based in Biblical prophecy and millennial apocalypse.

In the volume, as in America itself, the Biblical rhetoric of American destiny is set against itself, dispersed and multiplied through the conflicting claims the book portrays. The book explores the way in which American rhetoric, and not least its typology, had itself gone awry, and would only find healing through a rigorous review of the terms of its public discourse. In the context of the poetry of the period, Melville's work is outstanding and almost unique in the step it takes away from contests over interpretation, with each one urging his/her own claims to ultimate truths and vision; and towards a more fundamental skepticism regarding prophetic language as such. He is most unusual among writers of the period in responding to schismatic vision with prophetic restraint. Instead of putting forward his own visions of Biblical, millennial, or historical patterns against those of others, Melville's poetry voices the dangers of appeal to prophetic design altogether. His position emerges as one of self-examination and constraint; resistance to ultimate and sweeping visions; and towards a positive skepticism that, urging the limits of any claim, embraces discourse as an arena of communal exchange, not violent imposition.

3

❦

POETIC LANGUAGES

The career of Henry Wadsworth Longfellow (1807–82) is in many ways contradictory, posing quite a distinctive historical puzzle. His status as both elite and popular; his once extravagant celebrity and now near total eclipse; his shrill enthusiasms and melancholic anxieties; all belie his current reputation as a poet of simple-minded and cheerful satisfactions. Longfellow as a figure attempts to bridge different aspects of American culture, starting with the problem of whether one existed at all. Passionately committed to the birth of a national literature, he devoted himself to establishing and extending an American poetic language. Like Whitman, Emerson, and many other men of letters and society, Longfellow felt called by the Revolution to the creation of a native literature that would do justice to the new American experience and represent its people. In "Our Native Writers" (1825), his graduation address, he called for a poetry that would express "our national character," to be written by those who had "been nursed and brought up with us in the civil and religious freedom of our country." And, in his ambition to speak for a new American people, he largely succeeded. *The Song of Hiawatha* appeared side by side with *Leaves of Grass* in bookstalls in 1855. *Hiawatha* sold 10,000 copies in the first four weeks and 30,000 copies in six months, while most of Whitman's first edition had to be given away. Yet Longfellow's poetry is essentially elegiac. If Longfellow succeeded in expressing America's newly emerging identity, he also records its anxieties and costs. His effort to create a foundational poetry equally registered America's contradictory relations to a cultural past, and yet its need for one; and also its ambivalent relation to a cultural future, not least regarding the place of poetry itself within the emerging American cultural economy.

In attempting to construct a national American literature, Longfellow faced several problems of genealogy. The first involved what language he was to use. As Noah Webster had already demonstrated, defining an American English was in many ways a problematic project. Urging "a national language" as the "band of national union," Webster offered his lexicons of American usage, spelling, and vocabulary as an object "of vast political consequence." His *Blue-Backed Speller*, which sold over a million copies by 1783, was crafted as a weapon in the arsenal of national identity: the author would "throw his mite into the common treasure of patriotic exertions" in order "to promote the honour and prosperity of the confederated republics of America." But his efforts "to dissolve the charm of veneration for foreign authorities which fascinates the mind of men in this country and holds them in the chains of illusion," as he described his first *Compendious American Dictionary*, inevitably assumed just such chains as he wished to dissolve. Webster's lexicon in fact differs little from contemporary British ones. Even he admits American English to be at most a dialect variant. American English could not be wholly invented, since it was already inherited. His call to independence in his *Dissertations on the English Language* (1789) admitted the very dependence it would deny: "Great Britain, whose children we are, and whose language we speak, should no longer be our standard; for the taste of her writers is already corrupted, and her language on the decline."

Longfellow approached this genealogical predicament no less as a linguist, indeed with a genius for languages. Born in Portland, Maine in 1807 and attending (with Hawthorne) the newly founded Bowdoin College rather than the Harvard of his father and grandfather, Longfellow at the age of nineteen was offered the appointment to Bowdoin's new Professorship in Modern Languages on the condition that he go to Europe to learn some. Longfellow accordingly spent three years (1826–9) in Europe, during which he managed to pick up Spanish, Italian, French, and German. A second European tour (1835–6) added Dutch, Danish, Icelandic, Swedish, and some Finnish. Invited at last to Harvard in 1835, he succeeded George Ticknor as Professor of Modern Languages and Literature. There he spent the next nineteen years teaching Romance languages, writing scholarly articles and indeed the textbooks making such linguistic study possible in America, as well as a significant body of translations, which he continued through his years of retirement from Harvard after 1854.

Against this glitter of polyglot talent, American English seemed but a pale resource. On first returning to Brunswick, Maine, he complained to a friend: "nobody in this part of the world pretends to speak anything but English – and some might dispute them even that prerogative." His task, then, as he saw it, in founding an American culture was to incorporate into it that polyglot and multiple range not only located in the European past, but also in his wider American present. This, far from being restricted to English, included, as it had done since the eighteenth century, significant populations of non-English speakers, including Spanish, French Protestants, and especially Germans. Webster groups British English with the "study of ancient and foreign languages" that he decries as substituting for "the improvement of one's own language." But Longfellow undertook to transpose, in many cases to translate, from the Old World to the New.

Such transplantation appeared suspicious even to some contemporaries. Henry James describes Longfellow's as a "large, quiet, pleasant, easy solution" in which his "American consciousness . . . could feel nothing but continuity and congruity with his European." And there is Poe's weirdly energetic "Longfellow War" in which he goes lengthily out of his way to half-accuse Longfellow of plagiarism. But Longfellow's literary continuities first promoted, as they have since compromised, his reputation. And they made available to Longfellow's many students and readers a European culture that he felt must be retained as one foundation for the new American one. Moreover, within his chosen range of formal poetics, Longfellow shows masterful craft through broad experimentation in metrical, stanzaic, and other poetic forms. His readers could therefore find that his verse fulfilled their poetic expectations, remaining readily assimilable, while yet extending and educating them.

Regarding its English and European antecedents, then, Longfellow's work pursues a course of compromise which nevertheless inscribes the tension between new invention and old inheritance. A second genealogical problem works in an opposite, but no less challenging direction. Longfellow's earliest answer to the question of what would make a literature American was the use of American materials. This would include, as he explained in "Our Native Writers," scenery, manners and customs, places and climate. American writing must be one that "hallows every scene, renders every spot classical," so that "every rock shall become a chronicle of storied allusion and the tomb of the Indian prophet be as hallowed as the sepulchres of ancient kings." But this very assertion contains its own subversion. For America does not have a history embedded in landscape such as an English hillock might, where every stone stands as monument to prior events within a communal memory – at least, not for English Americans. Longfellow's gesture towards the "tomb of the Indian prophet" may assert a historical past, but not the one belonging to Longfellow and his ethnic compatriots. Such a native American history could only be acquired through appropriative sleight of hand, as a form of theft.

Longfellow's contending and contentious genealogical projects – the linguistic and the historical – come into conjunction in *The Song of Hiawatha*. *Hiawatha* is, not unlike *Leaves of Grass*, in its way also a language experiment. Longfellow's manuscript notebooks collect not Indian tales and fables, but rather Indian "words and names" – a lexicon of terms culled mainly from Schoolcraft and Tanner's studies of Indian tribes. These word lists, even more than mythical lore and characters, provided Longfellow with the building blocks of his text. The poem is on many levels about the possibilities of an American language and imagination, Longfellow's epic attempt to create a native poem out of a native lexicon. But, of course, the Ojibwa tongue was not native to him. Moreover, even as he wrote, it, and the peoples who spoke it, were under assault by his own national group. The very language studies on which Longfellow based his own were compiled while Schoolcraft was posted as government Indian Agent to Lake Superior, in an ethnographic project that was part of the machinery of Indian removal. Longfellow's translation of Indian words into English linguistic forms, not to mention Finnish-derived tetrameter, may be seen less as a mode of preservation than a mark of extinction. His poem likewise contributes to the preservation of Indian terms and places, but it treats them less as a living culture, than as a dead language.

It is around this figure of dead language that *Hiawatha* turns, not only in its methods of composition, but in its plot. The pivotal canto on "Picture-Writing" presents Hiawatha's gift of writing to his people as the culmination, but also the final act, of his career as culture hero. The remainder of the poem portrays the decline and dissolution of Indian society until its last, gracious vanishing before the coming White Man. That is, writing is presented as a power that commemorates a dead past rather than perpetuating that past into a future. It is inaugurated not as transmission, but as epitaph. What it commemorates, then, is not the continuity, but the passing away of a culture:

> In those days said Hiawatha,
>   "Lo! how all things fade and perish!
> From the memory of the old men
> Pass away the great traditions . . .
> Great men die and are forgotten,
> Wise men speak; their words of wisdom
> Perish in the ears that hear them,
> Do not reach the generations
> That, as yet unborn, are waiting
> In the great, mysterious darkness
> Of the speechless days that shall be!
>   "On the grave-posts of our fathers
> Are no signs, no figures painted;
> Who are in those graves we know not . . .
> And they painted on the grave-posts
> On the graves yet unforgotten,
> Each his own ancestral Totem . . .
> Each inverted as a token
> That the owner was departed,
> That the chief who bore the symbol
> Lay beneath in dust and ashes.

The picture-writing is instituted because "all things fade and perish." Yet it does not so much resist as mark this disappearance. The signs painted on the grave-posts commemorate the dead exactly as "dust and ashes." Describing the graves as "yet unforgotten" may foretell not remembrance, but forgetting itself. Even the gesture to "generations / That, as yet unborn, are waiting" points into silence and erasure, a "great, mysterious darkness / Of the speechless days that shall be."

The Song of Hiawatha is but one outstanding example of pervasive images in Longfellow of language not as a living instrument of renewal or foundational art, but rather as dead. His interest is less in the actual plight of the Indians (although he did once meet one in Harvard Yard) than in Indian language and lore as an anxious figure for American culture itself. His equally popular "The Jewish Cemetery at Newport" (1858) gives Hebrew a similar figural status and function. The poem on the one hand pays homage to America as refuge for the persecuted and commodious home to diverse peoples. On the other hand, the site Longfellow celebrates is a cemetery. The people he commemorates are buried, not reborn into American life.

> How strange it seems! These Hebrews in their graves,
> Close by the street of this fair seaport town,
> Silent beside the never-silent waves,
> At rest in all this moving up and down . . .
>
> While underneath their leafy tents they keep
> The long mysterious Exodus of Death.

The welcoming American seaport and restless movement are there, but as contrast against the final silence of the Hebrews. The Exodus story, far from being a type of deliverance, has become an Exodus of death. Yes, these people with "strange names" came to America to escape European "persecution, merciless and blind"; but their journey is to utter and irrevocable oblivion. The poem ends with a declared finality:

> But ah! what once has been shall be no more!
> The groaning earth in travail and in pain
> Brings forth its races, but does not restore,
> And the dead nations never rise again.

Emma Lazarus, in protest against this ending, tried later in the century to rewrite the poem in terms of a different American-Jewish history. But Jews no more concern Longfellow than Indians do. They instead serve as another figure for cultural pasts that America buries. This is a strange reworking of elements central within American mythology, and especially strange for a poet of national birth. Moreover, as in *Hiawatha*, it is language itself that provides the pivotal images of cultural death:

> No Psalms of David now the silence break,
> No Rabbi reads the ancient Decalogue
> In the grand dialect the Prophets spake . . .
>
> And thus forever with reverted look
> The mystic volume of the world they read,
> Spelling it backward, like a Hebrew book
> Till life became a Legend of the Dead.

What the poem records is the disappearance of an ancient tongue and its works. The Hebrew language itself becomes an image of reversive and erasive time, pointing backwards and spelling history not as progressive realization but as a Legend of the Dead.

What emerges from such texts is a sense of cultural threat and cultural loss. But it is finally Longfellow's own culture which concerns him. In these poems, it is as though Longfellow makes the language of poetry the only site which past cultures can still inhabit. But this makes poetry itself a kind of cemetery, and dead language, in a strange way, a trope for poetry itself. This becomes explicit in one "Elegiac Verse" – a group of poems that to an extent names Longfellow's work as a whole:

> Wisely the Hebrews admit no Present tense in their language;
> While we are speaking the word, it is already the Past.

Hebrew emerges as a reversive, elegiac language, representing the undoing of poetic language itself.

Longfellow's specific commitment, in both his teaching and his writing, had been to a *translatio studii* which would transfer European possibilities into American realizations. His own facility is glimpsed in his translating one canto per day of Dante's *Commedia* for thirty-four days in a row. In his verse, translation appears as a figure closely allied to poetry; and it conjures the same challenges to cultural production and transmission:

> Thou ancient oak! whose myriad leaves are loud
> With sounds of unintelligible speech,
> Sounds as of surges on a shingly beach,
> Or multitudinous murmurs of a crowd;
> With some mysterious gift of tongues endowed,
> Thou speakest a different dialect to each;
> To me a language that no man can teach,
> Of a lost race, long vanished like a cloud.
> For underneath thy shade, in days remote,

> Seated like Abraham at eventide
> Beneath the oaks of Mamre, the unknown
> Apostle of the Indians, Eliot, wrote
> His Bible in a language that hath died
> And is forgotten, save by thee alone.

In this sonnet, "Eliot's Oak," Longfellow returns to the question of Indian language, this time from the viewpoint of translation. John Eliot's Indian Bible was in fact the first Bible printed in America, in 1663, over a century before an American English version was published in 1782 (Webster hoped to displace the King James altogether with an American language version). But here, Eliot's Bible becomes a figure for the defeat of translation. Every line in the sonnet is devoted to linguistic imagery; but every line marks linguistic default. The leaves, though "loud with sounds," amount only to "unintelligible speech." The oak has a "mysterious gift of tongues," speaking in myriad dialects, but as a language that "no man can teach." As for Eliot's translation, for all the devotion of its task, in the end it too is unintelligible, the emblem of a "lost race," monument to a "language that hath died and is forgotten."

This poem, with its image of the "mysterious gift of tongues," seems poised to launch a claim to fabulous poetic power, one able to interpret between worlds and speak to, and for nature. Longfellow in fact has his Emersonian side. *Hiawatha* presents nature as a temple of symbols, with each place and person awakened to figural life and Hiawatha himself a poet-figure of capable imagination. The poem "The Harvest Moon" reads almost like an Emersonian creed:

> All things are symbols: the external shows
> Of Nature have their image in the mind,
> As flowers and fruits and falling of the leaves.

Yet even here, the images for poetry ultimately are empty:

> The song-birds leave us at the summer's close,
> Only the empty nests are left behind,
> And pipings of the quail among the sheaves.

The poetic light of the mind shines only after the harvest is done. And it illuminates no active song-birds, but only their deserted nests. Mental images become modes of negation, of emptiness and banishment.

Longfellow finally lacks confidence in the reality and power of poetic imagination. This is not primarily due to doubts about his own talents – although his sonnet, "Mezzo Cammin," which takes measure of his life in the path of poetry, speaks mainly of his sense of frustration and disappointment, looking back elegiacally on his past as at a "cataract of Death far thundering from the heights." What truly limits poetry, and Longfellow's vision of it, is America itself. For America, in its values and aims, leaves little place for poetic life. In his "Defense of Poetry" (1832) Longfellow calls for a national art, one that would make America's events and mind "visible in its action" and which would express, and help construct, its various historical and political as well as natural histories. But he does so, knowingly, within a culture whose overriding commitment is to "prosperity," "commercial advantages," "profit," "acquisition and pursuits"; in sum, "utility, tangible utility, bare, brawny, muscular utility." Longfellow's own claim in response, is that poetry has utility too, is not "useless," does not "incapacitate us for performing the private and public duties of our life." This is, however, less convincing as a defense of poetry than in showing how much it needed defending.

Santayana specifically had Longfellow in mind in his dismissal of the genteel poet as "grandmotherly in sedate spectacled wonder," an "intellect without will," "female against male," and cut off from America's "aggressive enterprise." But Longfellow recognized the split in America between culture and enterprise before Santayana. He himself became a poet against his father's warning that "a literary life to one who has the means of support may be very pleasant . . . But there is not wealth and munificence enough in this country to afford . . . patronage to merely literary men." Only his unexpected academic appointment rescued him from becoming a lawyer. In the event, he was able to succeed financially as well, cannily marketing his books across upper-, middle-, and lower-class readerships, from leather-bound parlor volumes to cheap paperbacks (as well as through marriage to a wealthy wife). Yet, the poetry he successfully marketed reflects, rather than contests, the marginal place of poetry within American society. As Benjamin Franklin observed in 1763, "After the first Cares for the Necessaries of Life are over we shall come to think of the Embellishments."

Poetry, like "The Children's Hour," effectively comes "Between the dark and the daylight" as "a pause in the day's occupations." The "better life" of poetry begins only at "Night" when

> . . . fade the phantoms of the day,
> The ghosts of men and things that haunt the light,
> The crowd, the clamor, the pursuit, the flight,
> The unprofitable splendor and display,
> The agitations, and the cares that prey
> Upon our hearts, all vanish out of sight.

"Pegasus in Pound," a poem Emily Dickinson admired, recounts how the "poet's winged steed" – unfit for the "daily call to labor" – is imprisoned in the pound, and can only escape by leaving the earth altogether. Poem after poem proposes as its subject poetry's own place within the world of American culture. But the imagery for poetry is recurrently, consistently, figures of displacement, darkness, night, sleep, death. Like "Birds of Passage," the "poet's songs" make their appearance not in the day, but in "star-lit night," and only as they depart the ordinary world. Poetry is read when "The Day is Done." It is under "Curfew," when at end of day, the "book [is] completed" and "Song sinks into silence . . . Sleep and oblivion reign over all." Poetry and death seem increasingly Longfellow's central subjects, and indeed seem to act as images for each other.

That is, they are images of the plight of poetry in America:

> O ye dead Poets, who are living still
> Immortal in your verse, though life be fled,
> And ye, O living Poets, who are dead
> Though ye are living, if neglect can kill,
> Tell me if in the Darkest hours of ill,
> With drops of anguish falling fast and red
> From the sharp crown of thorns upon your head,
> Ye were not glad your errand to fulfil?
> Yes; for the gift and ministry of Song
> Have something in them so divinely sweet,
> It can assuage the bitterness of wrong;
> Not in the clamor of the crowded street,
> Not in the shouts and plaudits of the throng,
> But in ourselves, are triumph and defeat.

The chiasmus which opens this poem on "The Poets" seems to link contemporary American poets to a past but living tradition of immortal verse. But the symmetry breaks down. Poetry cannot live without a social space within a community of readers. And American poets, although alive, are in this sense dead. The sonnet's sestet, despite its decisively positive "Yes," records nothing but displacements and negations, distancing poetry from an America figured as clamor and crowded street. The poetic "errand" is "fulfilled" only where fulfillment is so circumscribed as to cancel the fuller political-communal implications of this loaded American term. Retreating to an inward imagination, the triumph and defeat of the poem's final line are hardly distinguishable.

Longfellow was dedicated, and did much towards creating a native American lore, writing poetry of national myth. Yet he registers deep misgivings about the importance of poetry, and indeed its survival, within the American heritage he is celebrating. Some of his best verses present poetry as an art of erasure, a "palimpsest" in which "we erase . . . the dull commonplace book of our lives" ("Night"); as "footprints" (a characteristic pun on poetic meter) that vanish like those of the "chief of the mighty Omahas" ("To the Driving Cloud"); or as "footprints in the sands" which "The little waves, with their soft white hands, efface" ("The Tide Rises, the Tide Falls"). In the "Fragments" he appended among his last verses, Longfellow almost sums up his whole poetic work as a:

> Neglected record of a mind neglected . . .
> The day with all its toils and occupations
> The night with its reflections and sensations,
> The future, and the present, and the past, –
> All I remember, feel, and hope at last,
> All shapes of joy and sorrow, as they pass, –
> Find but a dusty image in this glass.

The poetic realm, set apart from the day's occupations, threatens to lose its existence altogether – to be no more than a "dusty image" in its own fragile "glass."

American culture had in its initial promise – as all the great mid-century writers insisted – been dedicated to several realms of possibility. What Longfellow records is the narrowing of American culture to a daily occupation that left little room for other pursuits, and to which poetry seemed more and more unreal. His poetry, devoted to establishing American letters, equally doubts its possibility. The shrill assertions of "The Psalm of Life," his first bestseller poem, that "Life is not an empty dream," seems foremostly addressed to convince himself, and not least about the life of poetry. In some sense, in this elegiac work, it is poetry he mourns for. At the very moment of the birth of a national literature, Longfellow laments its lack of place within the conduct of American life.

EDGAR ALLAN POE: REPETITION, WOMEN, AND SIGNS

It is tell-tale that Edgar Allan Poe (1809–49) devoted more of his critical writing to his hatred of Longfellow than to any other purpose. This hatred has a complex structure. It marks a clash of North against South, wealth against poverty, privileged membership against marginality and disownment. It points, in effect, to broad interstices within ante-bellum American life. Poe has often been claimed as a French poet writing in the American language. Translated lavishly by Baudelaire, canonized by Mallarmé and Valéry, he has been adopted by the French poetic tradition much (much) more than by the American. Yet long before becoming recognized as a major impetus to

American modernism; this flower of evil was homegrown. As William Carlos Williams was the first to claim, Poe's is a writing in "a new locality," "the first great burst through to expression of a re-awakened genius of place." And indeed, the counter-worlds that Poe depicts, in what amounts to a counter-language, severely reflect the social and historical world they so strenuously belie.

The ironies are multiple. Like Longfellow, Poe in many ways devoted his career towards the problem of creating an American literature, of writing in a language and tradition not original to America. This problem of originality, reflected not least in Poe's obsession with plagiarism (most notoriously against Longfellow), generally penetrates his whole theory of poetics. He is more-over situated, with his fellows, in the profound divide between any imagined poetic America as against the actual one – commercial, industrial, material – unfolding before his eyes. If one great Romantic project is to recast experience through imagination, to infuse reality with poetic meaning, then Poe's poetry is a measure of its American impossibility. Poe in this sense is a perverse Romantic. But his work points further still, showing the relationship between aesthetics and metaphysics so fundamental to, and also destabilizing within, Romanticism itself. It does so not only in the abstract, but via particular traditions of American religious culture. Poe's poetry thus offers a version not only of American Romanticism but of American religion, as the two mutually and also transformatively mirror each other. In Poe, specific impulses indigenous in America come to a bizarre and often vengeful realization. The result is a poetry of resistance, indeed of negation; carried out in theory and also, concretely, in poetic practice; intentionally defiant, critical, remote, and repudiating – yet also giving strange expression – to American life.

Repudiation largely governs Poe's biography, which traces so disastrous a career as to almost seem a model for Melville's ultimate anti-romance, *Pierre*. Born to actor parents (although his father had come from a respectable Rev-olutionary family of declining fortune), Poe was, at the age of two, doubly abandoned: by his father through desertion and his mother through death by tuberculosis. He was then taken in, but not legally adopted, by Frances Allan and her ambivalent husband John. Poe's earliest life was one of rooming houses, frequent moves, alcohol, and poverty. His next years with the Allans follow a complex and distressing course of ambition and betrayal. John Allan, a merchant with high social ambition, slaveowning but for many years finan-cially uncertain, at last made his way to wealth (including extensive slave and plantation holdings) in 1825 through inheriting a large fortune from an uncle. Poe had been raised liberally and yet also precariously by the Allans, as a gentleman. Educated partly in England, partly in Richmond, he enrolled at the University of Virginia in 1826 at age seventeen, coming into increasing conflict with his foster-father over drinking, gambling, and debts. A quarrel between them in 1827 led Poe to leave the university for the army, followed by an effort, in 1829, to leave army ranks and become an officer at West Point. The death of Frances Allan in 1829, and John Allan's subsequent remarriage in 1830 and death in 1833, left Poe finally disinherited and penniless. Yet this also at last (after his court-martial and expulsion from West Point in 1831) released him from a bourgeois framework of American success, to pursue the writing that had been, since his earliest precocity, his true calling. For the remainder of his life he vainly attempted (again like Melville) to support himself by his art, through what resembles indentured service in both Northern and Southern cities to magazine work – an effort to survive as a writer that equally spelled its defeat in distracting and secondary editorial labor. As he wrote of poetry in his Preface to *The Raven and Other Poems* of 1845: "Events not to be controlled have prevented me from making, at any time, any serious effort in what, under happier circumstances, would have been the field of my choice." In 1836, he married his cousin Virginia, then aged thirteen, who died in 1847 at the age of twenty-four after five years of debilitating tuberculosis. This was followed by a series of duplicating and intercrossing courtships, none brought to consummation. In 1849, Poe was found unconscious on a street of Baltimore on election day, dressed in someone else's clothes apparently to cast, for payment, a bogus ballot at Ryan's 4th ward (voting station) polls. He died four days later of alcoholic poisoning. A headstone at his grave was erected twenty-six years after, attended, among America's literary personalities, by Walt Whitman alone, but marked by Mallarmé's great sonnet on Poe.

Poe's life, made even darker through falsification of his letters and accusations of immorality by his literary executor and first biographer, the indefatigable Rufus Griswold, thus almost shapes a parable of inverse relationship among American identities and promises. It is this inversion or exclusion that marks Poe's poetry, as well as his theorizing about it. Poe is not the only nineteenth-century American poet who can be called self-conscious regarding poetic form. Dickinson, Whitman, and Longfellow each come (differently) to mind. But Poe is the first; and he gives a priority to form that was, as his French inheritors understood, proleptic. "The Philosophy of Composition," in suggesting that composition has a philosophy, is not entirely innovative. Wordsworth had implied the same already in his recollection in tranquility. But Poe suggested further that such philosophy be above all self-reflective, which was to say that composition should be essentially about itself. In opposition to what he calls "*The Didactic*," he writes in "The Poetic Principle," "there exists nor can exist any work more thoroughly dignified – more supremely noble than this very poem – this poem *per se* – this poem which is a poem and nothing more – this poem written solely for the poem's sake."

Didacticism here does not mean only specific claims to "truth" or "moral sense" – a tendency which infuriated Poe, particularly in its Bostonian, aka Longfellowian, practice. Didacticism means in Poe all reference altogether. T. S. Eliot and Aldous Huxley condescendingly suggest that the French craze for Poe was due to their not really understanding English; but this in fact points in important directions. English readers become distracted by attempts to find references for Poe's words, when it is one of Poe's purposeful technical achievements to write in a language structured intently to refute or negate the impulse to reference, among others. This negating – yet within or while retaining the gesture – of reference appears ostentatiously in, for example, "Ulalume," where landscape essentially becomes wordscape:

> The skies they were ashen and sober;
>   The leaves they were crisped and sere –
>   The leaves they were withering and sere;
> It was night in the lonesome October
>   Of my most immemorial year;
> It was hard by the dim lake of Auber,
>   In the misty mid region of Weir –
> It was down by the dank tarn of Auber,
>   In the ghoul-haunted woodland of Weir.

Early critics assumed the name-words here to be nonsense. Further scholarly application, however, unearthed information: that Daniel Auber was a French composer, and/or that there was an Awber river in England; that Robert Weir painted misty landscapes; and that "Mount Yaanek," in the next stanza, denotes Mt. Erebus, the one active volcano in Antarctica. Erebus, of course, would not rhyme with "Titanic" and "volcanic" as "Yaanek" does, just as "Auber" echoes "October." The words are indeed determined by their sound. Yet they are not mere nonsense. For they retain their tie to reference, if only to disrupt it. They hover between nonsense and reference, serving not to dissociate from the latter entirely but rather to confute it. The reference is conjured to be defeated – a gesture fundamental to Poe's theoretics of Beauty exactly in, or as, its (un)relation to concrete reality.

Defeated reference, however, is only one of many techniques of Poesque negation. There is also negation of space. "Dreamland" is "Out of Space – Out of Time." "The City in the Sea" presents a counter-world that "resemble[s] nothing that is ours," constructed as a litany of Noes: "No rays . . . come down,"

"No ripples curl," "No swellings tell," "No heavings hint." Faery-Land" has "dim vales . . . whose forms we can't discover." "The Valley of Unrest," a place where "people did not dwell," is constructed out of "un"s – "unrest," "unquiet," "uneasily" – and by means of what Beckett called "lessness": "restlessness," "motionless," "nameless." Such "lessness" is recurrent in Poe. "Dreamland" has "Bottomless vales," "boundless floods," "seas that restlessly aspire," "Lakes that endlessly outspread." In "To One in Paradise," the poet's spirit hovers "Mute, motionless, aghast." Negation of boundary, of movement, becomes negation of language, accomplished through various retractions and oppositions, and with silence itself a figural center. The "Sonnet – Silence" only highlights a consistent pull in Poe, from "the sound of silence on the startled ear" in "Al Aaraaf" to "The Valley of Unrest's" "silent dell; from the "silent" "solitude" of surrounding "Spirits of the Dead," to Israfel's poetic power defined exactly as the ability to "mute" all other stars.

In terms of affect, a most potent negation is that of time. Poe specializes in loss, nostalgia, regret. This begins when Poe is astonishingly young. Already in the first poem of *Tamerlane and Other Poems* 1827, Poe announces how "The Happiest Day, The Happiest Hour," already "hath flown"; how "The visions of my youth have been," for "they have vanished long, alas!" The most intensive expression of this originary nostalgia occurs in Poe's "Nevermores." One of the many provocative claims Poe makes in "The Philosophy of Composition" is that he came to the "Raven's" refrain of "Nevermore" out of liking the sound of the letters "O" and "R." Poe does like pure sound. But this particular term of negation, with its close cognate "no more," had already appeared frequently in his verse: in "Stanzas" (1827), "Spirits of the Dead" (1827), "Lenore," (1831/1843), "To One in Paradise" (1835, three times), "Sonnet – Silence" (1840), "Sonnet – to Zante"(1845, five times). In "The Raven" "Nevermore" does, however, achieve its fullest implication: not only with regard to time, but to language itself. As "The Philosophy of Composition" attests, the importance of the refrain is not "the pleasure [as] deduced solely from the sense of identity – of repetition," but rather to show how a single "monotone of sound" can carry diverse senses by his continually varying its meanings in context: "that is to say, I determined to produce continuously novel effects, by the variation of the application of the refrain – the refrain itself remaining, for the most part, unvaried." This diversity of application might seem to imply a fullness of language and of a word's possibilities, ever varying through different interpretations in different contexts and indeed showing how interpretation varies with and depends upon context. Yet what these varied senses of "Nevermore" ultimately come to is a kind of collapse of meaning. What occurs from stanza to stanza is an unmooring of the word from any stable content or sense, the multiplication of which also defeats the claim to any particular one, as the ground for any specific interpretation is increasingly undone. The word, that is, instead of becoming full, becomes empty. In meaning anything, it comes to means nothing, a defeat of possible meanings. It becomes, in the theoretical language Poe's work so invites, a signifier whose significance is unanchored rather than released, leading to an ultimate destruction. As "Nevermore" answers every sequent question, all time, past, present, and future, and all hope and desire, become in "The Raven" frozen in an unending darkness, until, at the last line, "my soul from out that shadow that lies floating on the floor / Shall be lifted – nevermore!"

The problem of repetition, dramatized in "The Raven's" "Nevermore," points in Poe in many directions, and indeed, is foundational to his aesthetic. There is, for example, Poe's obsessive concern with plagiarism. This turns out to be the most persistent topic in his magazine essays – the so-called "Longfellow Wars" of accusation, counter-accusation, and self-accusation (1845) alone stretch over more than sixty pages – culminating, most bizarrely, in a pseudonymous piece left unfinished at his death, "A Reviewer Reviewed," in which Poe accuses himself of being a plagiarist. Involved here are enormous anxieties: regarding Poe's own claim to originality, his place in American letters, and the possibility of there being an American literature at all (not to mention the vexed legal question of copyright ownership). Longfellow in this provides a crossroads for various conflicts. There is the problematic link between literary and social standing, as when Poe grumbles how everyone is saying in "private conversation" that "the poetical claims of Mr. Longfellow have been vastly overrated, and that the individual himself would be esteemed little without the accessories of wealth and position . . . Professor Longfellow is the GREAT MOGUL of the imitators." Yet Poe also sees an abstract question regarding the whole relation between imitation and originality. In a *Marginalia* entry again directed at Longfellow, he works his way through a range of subtle distinctions: "Imitators are not, necessarily, unoriginal. Mr. Longellow, decidedly the most audacious imitator in America, is markedly original, or, in other words, imaginative . . . All great poets have been gross imitators. It is, however [not] to infer, that all great imitators are poets."

Repetition in art emerges as the core aesthetic concern in Poe. For Poe extremely and resolutely rejects any sort of mimetic art – any notion that art is imitation of reality. Art, he insists in numberless passages and poetic images, is not accurate representation or repetition. As he wrote first in an 1842 review essay in critique of Longfellow, and then later revised in "The Poetic Principle":

And just as the eyes of Amaryllis are repeated in the mirror, or the living lily in the lake, so is the mere record of these forms and colors and sounds and sentiments – so is their mere oral or written repetition a duplicate source of delight. But this repetition is not poetry. He who shall merely sing with whatever rapture, in however harmonious strains, or with however vivid a truth of imitation, of the sights and sounds, which greet him in common with all mankind – he, we say, has yet failed to prove his divine title. There is still a thirst unquenchable, which to allay he has shown us no crystal springs. This burning thirst belongs to the *immortal* essence of man's nature . . . It is the desire of the moth for the star. It is not the mere appreciation of the beauty before us. It is a wild effort to reach the beauty above. It is a forethought of the loveliness to come. It is a passion to be satiated by no sublunary sights, or sounds, or sentiments, and the soul thus athirst strives to allay its fever in futile efforts at *creation*. Inspired with a prescient ecstasy of the beauty beyond the grave, it struggles by multiform novelty of combination among the things and thoughts of Time, to anticipate some portion of that loveliness whose very elements, perhaps, appertain solely to Eternity.

If Oscar Wilde said of art imitating nature: who needs two of them, Poe might retort: who needs even one. There may be repetition in art, but not as "truth of imitation" (or, as he rewrites in "The Poetic Principle," "truth of description"). Aesthetic repetition instead would involve the removal from natural occasion, as a demonstration of nature's insufficiency. Yet art itself is also insufficient, unable ultimately to represent that "thirst unquenchable," the impossible but impelling "wild effort to reach the beauty above." True vision remains beyond, uncontainable in art and elusive of nature, and indeed, in opposition to these and even destructive of them and to the artist himself: "It is the desire of the moth for the star." Not even its sources are truly of this world, which provides for it "no crystal springs." "It is a passion to be satiated by no sublunary sights, or sounds, or sentiments, and the soul thus athirst strives to allay its fever in futile efforts at *creation*."

The image of the lake which introduces this passage emerges centrally in Poe's verse as a figure for just such aesthetic reflection/removal. From the very early "Evening Star," "Spirits of the Dead," "To the River," and "The Lake – To –"; through such anthologized verses as "The Sleeper" or "Romance" or "The City of the Dead" or "To Helen" or "Annabel Lee," the lake or sea appears as a reflection of consciousness, a mirror of the poet's mind. "To the River" rather straightforwardly sets up a triple reflection between the river, the beloved who looks into it and wherein "her image deeply lies," and the poet, who in the water-reflection becomes joined to both. This poem, for Poe, offers surprising continuity between repetition and source, if also merging of identity and blurring of boundaries. But this is not usually the case. What mostly happens is not positive reflection between image and origin, but negative or counter-transformation, creating oppositions between the images in the lake/mind

and the world presumably reflected there. In "The Sleeper," for example, the
waking world does not generate poetic vision, nor does the sleeping world
reclaim or redeem the world of everyday. The poet stands beside a lake "like
Lethe," where (as in the prose passage above) "The lily lolls upon the wave."
Like both the sleeper and the speaker who witnesses (wills) her, "The lake /
A conscious slumber seems to take, / And would not, for the world awake."
Speaker, sleeper, and lake all unite as images of frozen consciousness, death-like
and silent: "Some tomb from out whose sounding door / She ne'er shall force
an echo more."

The lily in the lake recurs in "Dreamland," again in utter repudiation of any
natural surrounding: "Lakes that endlessly outspread / Their lone waters – lone
and dead, – / Their still waters – still and chilly / With the snows of the lolling
lily." "The Lake – To –" fully treats this negative visionary lake/consciousness:

> In spring of youth it was my lot
> To haunt of the wide world a spot
> The which I could not love the less –
> So lovely was the loneliness
> Of a wild lake, with black rock bound,
> And the tall pines that towered around.
>
> But when the Night had thrown her pall
> Upon that spot, as upon all,
> And the mystic wind went by
> Murmuring in melody –
> Then – ah then I would awake
> To the terror of the lone lake.
>
> Yet that terror was not fright,
> But a tremulous delight –
> A feeling not the jewelled mine
> Could teach or bribe me to define –
> Nor Love – although the Love were thine.
>
> Death was in that poisonous wave,
> And in its gulf a fitting grave
> For him who thence could solace bring
> To his lone imagining –
> Whose solitary soul could make
> An Eden of that dim lake.

What is Poe negating? Here there is interiority, and/as poetic visionary
power, but not as mimetic, or even transformative, of any exterior world with
which it in any way corresponds or illuminates. The poem is situated in
the break between, not the mutual imaging of, interiority and exteriority,
mind and world. It is as if Poe were caught within Romanticism's moment

of negation, when the imagination is freed to effect its changes on the world, but then returns to restore the world in reconciliation with imagination's design. The negation is there but with no return: the poet is cut off from the world, mirrored in a lake "with black rock bound" and "tall pines" enclosing it around. "The Night" blocks out reality when it has "thrown her pall / Upon that spot." And, as in a *Marginalia* entry of 1849, it is this blocking out of nature and reality that releases true imagination. "Art," Poe writes, is not "the mere imitation, however accurate, of what is in Nature," but rather "the reproduction of what the Senses perceive in Nature through the veil of the soul." The veil here does not disclose, but closes off; interposes rather than reveals. Just so the "true beauty of an actual landscape" is doubled if "half closing our eyes when we look at it. The naked Senses sometimes see too little – but then *always* they see too much" (1458).

In the poem, the imaginative moment remains negative both in structure and effect. For it gives rise to experience not as uplifting "melody" but as terror. And yet this terror is itself positive, "not fright, / But a tremulous delight." Poe here goes far towards reversing or inverting ordinary measures or evaluations. Terror is delight exactly because it opposes the world, opposes actual experience. This is "A feeling not the jewelled mine / Could teach or bribe me to define." The "jewelled mine" – at once life's material offerings and, in a pun common in Emily Dickinson, the way the self is constituted through possession – Poe dismisses for something, or rather, for nothing, present in either language or, as he goes on to say, "Love." The strange inversion at the poem's end – "Death was in that poisonous wave" – offers terrifying images as positive. To be in the "gulf" of a "fitting grave" is to be, in Poe, in the right (non)place – the accession of the "lone imagining" of the "solitary soul." It is indeed to make an "Eden of that dim lake."

One of Poe's legacies to Symbolist poetry is this interior reflection as poetic site. The poems are deeply self-reflective, the exterior world an image of interior mind. This self-reflection as poetic process especially impressed Valéry, who focused on the poet's mind as it acts in poetic (and its own) construction. Yet Mallarmé seems truer to Poe when he declares the poem should, in being about itself, be essentially about nothing. The interior processes Poe pursues, in representing poetic process itself, emerge as empty mirror reflecting empty mirror. Poe's "The Haunted Palace," the poem interpolated into "The Fall of the House of Usher," is emblematic. The poem is a self-reflection of the story's protagonist, but also of the narrator, the twin sister, and Poe himself as writer. It constructs, stanza by stanza, the person as house: inhabited by reason – "Thought's dominion"; with a roof of "Banners yellow, glorious golden" as hair, "two luminous windows" as eyes, and the "pearl and ruby glowing" teeth in the "fair palace door" as mouth. This exteriorized interiority, this architecture of the mind, is then dramatically overturned, carrying with it the reader who has, step by step, taken up his/her own habitation in the house as well. In an overthrow of reason and disintegration of selfhood (with imagery again of water – "like a ghastly rapid river"), the eyes become "red-litten windows." Language itself breaks down as the "pale door" mouth lets forth "A hideous throng" of demented utterance and hysteria.

Yet this poetry of the mind in self-reflection – Poe's major legacy to Symbolism – does not fully suggest an autonomy of art and independence of aesthetic experience as it was later to do. Poe is not really French. Art remains, in Poe's work, radically incomplete, pointing not merely to but also beyond itself towards a realm it can never fully grasp. As he writes in "The Poetic Principle," there is "still a something in the distance which he has been unable to attain." "We weep," he continues, not "through excess of pleasure, but through a certain, petulant, impatient sorrow at our inability to grasp now, wholly, here on earth, at once and for ever, those divine and rapturous joys, of which, through the poem, or through the music, we attain to but brief and indeterminate glimpses" (77). Later Symbolism might make art for art a substitute for metaphysical experience, with the poem itself an ultimate object. Poe does not. He instead registers a difficult, disturbed relationship to older metaphysical frameworks, a haunting of its borders as it recedes, leaving behind voided but still impelling spaces. Like Emily Dickinson, he strains to peer over the edge of the world into an afterworld no longer certainly believed in. These are the territories of his stories of the afterlife, or rather, of post-destruction: "Mesmeric Revelation," "The Colloquy of Monos and Una," "The Conversation of Eiros and Charmion," "The Power of Words." Situated after death – the last three situated after the utter apocalypse of the world – they attempt to imagine reports from the Other Side.

What they, and Poe's poetry, show is a disturbed relation between the worlds, which takes on, in Poe, a peculiarly American character or format. Poe was baptized (1812) and confirmed (1825) into the Southern Episcopal Church rather than into the Puritan Calvinist tradition and its offspring, whether liberal or revivalist (although it is worth recalling that Poe's life spans the Second Great Awakening with its wild revivalism). Still, his foster-father, John Allan, had been raised as a Scottish Calvinist, and the general culture in which he participated was still largely Calvinist. The school he attended in England required both morning and evening attendance at services and copious Scripture reading. It was located in a dissenting community, with a nonconformist academy famous for educating Daniel Defoe, Isaac Watts, and Mary Wollstonecraft. In his 1836 review essay of Francis Hawks's *Contributions to the Ecclesiastical*

History of the United States of America – Virginia, Poe defends Hawks's defense of the South and its Episcopal church. "Let not political prejudices, always too readily excited, be now enlisted against the religion we cherish, by insinuations artfully introduced." Poe's references to the Bible are many and learned, including comments on Hebrew grammar in the *Marginalia*, and a list of Hebrew words in his review of John L. Stephens. Allen Tate remarks that "In spite of an early classical education and a Christian upbringing, [Poe] wrote as if the experience of these traditions had been lost"; but this is so only in the sense that Poe is addressing exactly that loss – in the guise, in Tate's further comment, of "a religious man whose Christianity, for reasons that nobody knows anything about, had got short-circuited."

Poe stands in profound connection to two specific modes of American religious imagination: the utopian Kingdom of God, and antinomianism. Indeed, Poe perhaps unintentionally shows how these two are interconnected. As his work dramatizes, an absolute Kingdom turns out to stand in negative relation to the world as it exists. To attempt to achieve the absolute almost entails repudiating earthly norms and conditions – an antinomian identification with an ultimate reality whose main felt attribute is the abnegation of this earthly one. It is this negative implication of apocalypse that Poe underscores – an apocalypse that for him is in any case disjunctive, in being destructive but without rebirth. In Poe, after apocalypse there is no transformation, no new heaven and new earth. At most there is repetition. The drive towards annihilation, expressly announced at the opening of *Eureka*, Poe's cosmological fantasy, repeats an endless recurrence: "In the original unity of the first thing lies the secondary cause of all things, with the germ of their inevitable annihilation."

In the history of religious imagination, there have been a number of possible relations between this world and the next, which can be distinctly charted, even as they also overlap. These can be described as, first, an ascetic relation, where access to the higher world requires renunciation of the lower. Second, there can be a sacramental relation, where access to the higher world occurs by way of ascent from the lower. There can be, third, a sacral relation, where the lower world is radiant with value from the higher. Fourth, there is secularism, where the immediate world is negotiated for its own sake, without reference to any higher world altogether. Finally, there can be an opposition so extreme between ultimate reality and the present world as to project the latter's immolation and destruction as necessary to any higher entry. The relation between the two is then utterly negative, with all earthly norms suspended and repudiated: what has been called, in the American tradition, antinomianism.

Poe's imagination falls into this last category. What he depicts in his poetry is a battle between worlds; an opposition so utter as to make it impossible to see this world as an avenue to a higher one. This is the force of Poe's anti-mimetic theory of art. Mimesis betrays what he calls, from his earliest theoretical "Letter to B—" of 1836 to his late *Marginalia* (1844), "an indefinite instead of a definite pleasure," where the "indefinitiveness" of true art is opposed to any "determinate" concrete specification which would "deprive it of its ethereal, its ideal, its intrinsic and essential character," reducing it to "a tangible and easy appreciable idea – a thing of the earth, earthy." The things of earth cannot represent the realms of ultimacy for which he yearns, which are so radically absolute that nothing in the present world can reflect or conduct to them. Rather, they must be figured as against worldly experience, not rooted in but defiant of it: a "Romance" which opposes rather than completing, elevating, or transfiguring reality, as in his poem (1831) of that title:

> Romance, who loves to nod and sing
> With drowsy head and folded wing,
> Among the green leaves as they shake
> Far down within some shadowy lake,
> To me a painted paroquet
> Hath been – a most familiar bird –
> Taught me my alphabet to say –
> To lisp my very earliest word
> While in the wild wood I did lie,
> A child – with a most knowing eye.
>
> Of late, eternal Condor years
> So shake the very Heaven on high
> With tumult as they thunder by,
> I have no time for idle cares
> Through gazing on the unquiet sky.
> And when an hour with calmer wings
> Its down upon my spirit flings –
> That little time with lyre and rhyme
> To while away – forbidden things!
> My heart would feel to be a crime
> Unless it trembled with the strings.

The poem opens in an apparently Blakean mode of personifying nature as a potent figure. But this proves not to be the case. The "green leaves" turn out not to be in nature, but "Far down within some shadowy lake" of the reflective mind, and with creativity imaged not in response to a natural bird but rather as a fake one. It is from a "painted paroquet" that the poet has learned his "alphabet." The "child" here, similarly, is not a figure in innocent bond with nature, but almost a gnostic figure, born outside of the world and whose "knowing eye" knows an other, alien knowledge altogether. As to the world itself and its time, this is figured as a bird of a different feather, a living Condor who threatens "the very Heaven on high" and whose prey is ultimately the poet himself. Under its threat he can barely escape the tumultuous triumph of time, as it assaults what he describes as "forbidden things," the "lyre and rhyme" that oppose a world that forbids them in turn.

This is not a redemptive art, but an oppositional, negating one. As in "Israfel," true song inheres in a realm utterly removed from our own, "Imbued with all the beauty / Which we worship in a star," far far different from this our world, so inverse that our "sunshine" is the other world's "shadow," which penetrates and betrays our human poetry:

> Yes, Heaven is thine; but this
> Is a world of sweets and sours;
> Our flowers are merely – flowers,
> And the shadow of thy perfect bliss
> Is the sunshine of ours.
>
> If I could dwell
> Where Israfel
> Hath dwelt, and he were I,
> He might not sing so wildly well
> A mortal melody,
> While a bolder note than this might swell
> From my lyre within the sky.

Only removal from this world would elevate poetry to its true fulfillment.

The most brutal poem in this vein is "The Conqueror Worm," inserted into the story "Ligea." This is set up as a stage-performance of earthly life to an audience of angels – an "angel throng" witnessing a copy of a copy. The height of the drama is reached when they

> See amid the mimic rout
> A crawling shape intrude! . . .
> It writhes! – It writhes! – with mortal pangs
> The mimes become its food,
> And seraphs sob at vermin fangs
> In human gore imbued.

The corruption of the body becomes the central fact of human life – the body, as in the oldest traditions of dualism, essentially nothing but corruption. "The play is the tragedy, 'Man,'/ And its hero the Conqueror Worm." Here is the confrontation with suffering, "the tragedy, 'Man,'" which haunts Poe, but for which he has no access to traditional solutions.

For Poe, in repudiating "our" world, does not truly gain entry into a higher realm either. Instead, he presents a war between worlds, draining both of reality. It is as if Poe's loss of metaphysical reality equally undermines his belief in this immediate one. In general the boundaries between reality and unreality, fiction and fact blur in Poe, most blatantly in his Hoaxes or his science fictions; but no less in his poetry. This is expressed in his dream imagery – all is "A Dream within a Dream," as he writes in one dream poem (there are, in various versions, six). At the same time, the world he inhabits takes on, as if by infection, the displaced qualities of his lost absolute realm. What emerges is a reified absolute as our world: a Kingdom not as earthly redemption but as an eternal reign of death. This is the non-place, the frozen, negated reality of "Dream-Land," whose "King . . . hath forbid / The uplifting of the fringèd lid" of the coffin-eye, on a land of

> Bottomless vales and boundless floods,
> And chasms, and caves, and Titan woods,
> With forms that no man can discover . . .
> Mountains toppling evermore
> Into seas without a shore;
> Seas that restlessly aspire
> Surging, unto skies of fire;
> Lakes that endlessly outspread
> Their lone waters – lone and dead.

This is the imploding Kingdom of "The City in the Sea" where "Death has reared himself a throne." There the shrines and palaces that "Resemble nothing that is ours" finally topple:

> But lo, a stir is in the air!
> The wave – there is a movement there!
> As if the towers had thrust aside,
> In slightly sinking, the dull tide –
> As if their tops had feebly given
> A void within the filmy Heaven . . .
> And when, amid no earthly moans,
> Down, down that town shall settle hence,
> Hell, rising from a thousand thrones,
> Shall do it reverence.

This last image seems a reference to Isaiah 14:9: "Hell stirreth up the dead for thee; it hath raised up from their thrones all the kings of the nations." The towers recall Babel, while the poem's reflective sea recalls the Dead Sea, a name Poe surely loved. But here there is no Judgment, nor the particular wickedness of Sodom and Gomorrah, but only spatio-temporal reality in its self-defeat.

What emerges from such visions of earth recast in the image of eternity is an earth become hell-like. This is so whether the realm depicted is ultimate or interior (the two being often traditionally identified). The City in the Sea is mirrored in the "melancholy waters" of a reflecting lake. In "Dream-land," the "lakes that thus outspread / Their lone waters, lone and dead" explicitly open into an interior landscape

> Where dwell the Ghouls, –
> By each spot the most unholy –
> In each nook most melancholy –
> There the traveller meets, aghast,
> Sheeted Memories of the Past – . . .
> White-robed forms of friends long given,
> In agony, to the Earth – and Heaven.

As descent or ascent, the ultimate realm is a death "agony", as is the interior frozen time – "Memories of the Past" – made in its image.

D. H. Lawrence, in his polemical essay on Poe, suggests that Poe "set up his will against the whole of the limitations of nature." Just so, Allen Tate speaks of Poe's as an abrogation of the "discipline of submission to a permanent limitation of man," an "Angelic Imagination" in its attempt towards "unmediated knowledge of essences." What Poe's work discloses is how such revolt against limitation marks a crossing between the antinomian and the utopian, the radical desire for the ultimate as a condemnation of the earthly. This comes out most explicitly in Poe's cosmological fantasy *Eureka*, where a utopian-aesthetic principle of unity renders the cosmos an all encompassing artwork, governed absolutely as a "plot of God" and with every particle subsumed into a single design. But this "Original Unity" entails, as *Eureka* announces at the start, "inevitable annihilation." That is, the reduction to nothingness is revealed as a consequence of the pursuit of unity: "In sinking into Unity, [matter] will sink into that Nothingness which, to all Finite Perception, Unity must be – into that Material Nihility from which alone we can conceive it to have been evoked – to have been created by the Volition of God." This perspective beyond finitude dissolves all reality into dream – or rather, again, dissolves the boundaries between the two. Thus *Eureka* opens with a dedication "to the dreamers and those who put faith in dreams as in the only realities." But its ultimate direction is a will to divinity. That is, the ultimate boundaries that blur are those between any individual being and the divine whole of the universe itself. Thus *Eureka* concludes with a vision of how all "struggles toward the original Unity . . . [such] that no one soul is inferior to another – that nothing is, or can be, superior to any one soul – that each soul is, in part, its own God – its own Creator," conscious "of a final identity with the Divine Being of whom we speak – of an identity with God."

Such vision of unity-as-nothingness positively answers some of Poe's strongest needs. There is a rejection of class difference, against the inferiority of one soul to another, no doubt deeply rooted in Poe's own struggle with social position and Southern Gentlemanhood. There is a powerful drive to answer the problem of evil, to "comprehend the riddles of Divine Injustice," as he goes on to say. "In this view alone the existence of Evil becomes intelligible; but in this view it becomes more – it becomes endurable." Perhaps above all, it answers Poe's need for love. Yet, what Poe shows, intentionally or not, is how such unity is inimical to the conditions of human and earthly life. As D. H. Lawrence put it, "the trouble about man is that . . . he insists on *oneness* . . . and by this means he acquires an ecstasy of vision, he finds himself in glowing unison with all the universe." Yet the impulse, as Lawrence goes on to observe, is a deadly one. And it is directed, above all, towards women; to a unity as love which is also deadly: "carry this too far . . . and a form of death sets in."

There are those who weirdly speak of Poe's figures of women as homage to an "ideal," at least in the poems (it is harder to make this claim for the tales, where the women tend to be luridly murdered, ghoulish, entombed, and/or mutilated). But Poe's mainly dead poetic women are essentially negations, ideal figures only in the way that his ideal generally negates and repudiates human experience. It is, of course, in "The Philosophy of Composition" that Poe announces "the death of a beautiful woman" as "the most poetical topic in the world." This conclusion is closely tied to the aesthetic of unity advanced in this essay, such that, first, all points in a text must be directed to a single intention, determined backwards by the end; second, that there should be a complete "unity of impression." Third, the "impression" or "effect" should be directed toward "Beauty," that "the most intense, the most elevating, and the most pure" pleasure is "found in the contemplation of the beautiful." All these unite in dead women.

The aesthetic of dead women is then more fully clarified in "The Poetic Principle." Poe is not the first poet to make dead women the center of poetic devotion. This tradition reaches back to the troubadors – the "old Bards and Minnesingers" as Poe calls them. There, women, as images of higher aspiration, were made unreachable by marriage and social position rather than by mortality. The Italian inheritors of the troubador minstrels further idealized women by placing them in heaven, which is to say, when they were dead. This helped remove bodily temptation and direct desire upward as an avenue to the divine. The lady thus figured a higher reality, and love for her became converted into love of divine things. In Poe, the lady is dead; but she is a most uncertain conduit to a higher world. Her immortality emerges instead as a reification, an endless death in a world that is not transcended but rather immobilized, fixed into an eternal rigidity.

The difference can be seen in reference to the great source in Western tradition of love as a ladder of ascent, Plato's "Symposium." As Socrates, quoting Diotima, explains of the highest vision of love and beauty:

This is the way, the only way, he must approach, or be led toward, the sanctuary of Love. Starting from individual beauties, the quest for the universal beauty must find him ever mounting the heavenly ladder, stepping from rung to rung . . . until at last he comes to know what beauty is. And if . . . man's life is ever worth the living, it is when he has attained this vision of the very soul of beauty . . . But if it were given to man to gaze on beauty's very self – unsullied, unalloyed, and freed from the mortal taint that haunts the frailer loveliness of flesh and blood – if, I say, it were given to man to see the heavenly beauty face to face, would you call his an enviable life, whose eyes had opened to the vision, and who had gazed upon it in true contemplation until it had become his own forever?

"The Poetic Principle" is Poe's "Symposium." There he too speaks of "a sense of the Beautiful" as "an immortal instinct, deep within the spirit of man."

This it is which administers to his delight in manifold forms, and sounds, and odours, and sentiments amid which he exists . . . [But] it is no mere appreciation of the Beauty before us – but a wild effort to reach the Beauty above. Inspired by an ecstatic prescience of the glories beyond the grave, we struggle, by multiform combinations among the things and thoughts of Time, to attain a portion of that Loveliness whose very elements, perhaps, appertain to eternity alone . . . We weep not through excess of pleasure, but through a certain, petulant, impatient sorrow at our inability to grasp now, wholly, here on earth, at once and forever, those divine and rapturous joys, of which, through the poem . . . we attain to but brief and indeterminate glances. It has been my purpose to suggest that . . . this Poetic Principle itself is, strictly and simply, the Human Aspiration for the Supernal Beauty.

As he writes in the earlier draft on Longfellow: poetry's "first element is the thirst for supernal Beauty – a beauty which is not afforded the soul by any existing collocation of earth's forms – a beauty which, perhaps, no possible combination of these forms would full produce."

As in Plato, Poe describes a longing for supernal beauty, which, as in Plato, means going beyond material reality – in Socrates' words "unsullied, unalloyed, and freed from the mortal taint that haunts the frailer loveliness of flesh and blood"; "no mere appreciation of the Beauty before us" as Poe has it. Still, in Plato, at least in the "Symposium," there is a continuity of ascent from things of this world to the high vision: "Starting from individual beauties, the quest for the universal beauty must find him ever mounting the heavenly ladder, stepping from rung to rung . . . until at last he comes to know what beauty is." In Poe this is not really the case. The "multiform combinations among the things and thoughts of Time" do not finally give us "pleasure," but rather "a certain, petulant, impatient sorrow at our inability to grasp now, wholly, here on earth, at once and forever, those divine and rapturous joys, of which, through the poem . . . we attain to but brief and indeterminate glances." The poem gives glimpses that remain unrealized, a mark of frustration at being unable to possess "now, wholly, here on earth" the ultimate vision.

The dead woman, in this poetic, is accordingly a figure for supernal beauty, but as blocked by actual experience, inaccessible by way of immediate reality, and yet also as displacing the ordinary world. Perhaps the lack of a higher world as accessible also drains the ordinary one of life. The result are Poe's famous scenes of necrophilia: the poet does not rise in vision with his lady to a higher experience but instead becomes fixated with her in a death-vision. Thus, "The Sleeper" in the course of the text is revealed to be not a lady dreaming, but a corpse, whose "closed and fringed lid" is both eye and coffin, whose hair has continued to grow after death ("Strange, above all, thy length of tress"), and who is now reduced to pure body, vulnerable to decay as "the worms about her creep." These disturbed crossings between death and life, the other world and this, are characteristic of Poe. In "To One in Paradise" (which William Carlos Williams named Poe's best poem), desire is shown to be desire for total possession ("and all the flowers were mine"), doomed and voided by the lady's death ("No more – no more – no more –"). "The Raven" of course remains transfixed on the lost, dead Lenore, who may be "within the distant Aidenn," but leaves the poem's speaker in eternal shadow.

This is rather far from Socrates' vision of ascent, as are also Poe's most famous "love" poems, "To Helen" and "Annabel Lee." In the first, the voyage Helen inspires is not to a loved woman, nor even to a historical Greece or Rome, but rather into the speaker's own interiority – the "native shore" of himself via a water-journey "oe'r a perfumed sea." The last stanza, as H. D.'s later rewriting of the poem makes explicit, shows the high cost of Poe's adoration:

> Lo! In yon brilliant window-niche
>   How statue-like I see thee stand,
> The agate lamp within thy hand!
>   Ah, Psyche, from the regions which
> Are Holy Land!

Helen is transformed, first, into an art-object: a statue, frozen in place, as good as dead. And second, into Poe's own interior space. The lamp is his own reflective consciousness; the Psyche, his own soul.

There is, in short, no woman here at all; certainly not an independent being (at most she is evoked by body-parts: hyacinth hair, classic face). Rather, there is a self-reference, in which woman collapses into speaker who creates and possesses her in his own image, with both out of life, but rather located in the rigid realm which represents Poe's displaced "Holy Land." This reification is still more pronounced in "Annabel Lee." This widely sung ballad is among Poe's creepiest. His absolute realm, at once ultimate and self-reflective in the mirror of water, is here "a kingdom by the sea." His unity of love is here absolute possession: "This maiden lived with no other thought than to love and be loved by me." Here we find his gnostic child, alien rather than innocent to the world. Here we find the dire opposition between the higher world and the human one, as child and child love "with a love that the wingèd seraphs of heaven / Coveted her and me."

> The angels, not half so happy in heaven,
> Went envying her and me –
> Yes! – that was the reason (as all men know,
> In this kingdom by the sea)
> That the wind came out of the cloud by night,
> Chilling and killing my Annabel Lee.
>
> But our love it was stronger by far than the love
> Of those who were older than we –
> Of many far wiser than we –
> And neither the angels in heaven above,
> Nor the demons down under the sea,
> Can ever dissever my soul from the soul
> Of the beautiful Annabel Lee.

The children's antinomian love clashes with human society, as heaven clashes with earth, the other world with this one. Yet it is as a kind of other world, reified, rigid, frozen, that the love is concretized, in an unending embrace of living turned dead, of dead inhabiting the living. Total unity of soul to soul is oddly imaged in a word of bodily violence – "dissever." The final stanza announces love-bed as crypt, wedded love as necrophiliac possession, all in watery self-reflection:

> And so, all the night-tide, I lie down by the side
> Of my darling – my darling – my life and my bride,
>   In the sepulchre there by the sea,
>   In her tomb by the sounding sea.

The world is turned into a grave. Afterlife becomes eternal death. Love is the gateway not to a higher or redemptive experience, but to a macabre reification on earth.

Poe's "idealized" women turned into death-effigies may be a hyperbolic exaggeration, carrying to an extreme traditional feminine idealization as an intentional strategy on Poe's part to undo and expose rigid gender types rather than adopting them. Poe, that is, may be demonstrating and exposing rather than enacting and adopting traditional attitudes towards women – attitudes with perhaps, as Allen Tate suggests, a specifically Southern context, where his is "an exalted idealization of Woman . . . only a little more humorless, because more intense, than the standard cult of Female Purity in the Old South." Yet it is difficult to find irony in Poe's statements in his essays regarding "the faculty of ideality" as "the beautiful, the sublime, the mystic." And whatever his intention, whether he means to embrace or expose idealized beauty, certainly Poe's women draw on a tradition of the ideal, and his treatments make us generally wonder about it. This is no merely personal imp of the perverse (although Poe's poetic dead women must surely recall his actual ones, in lingering tubercular deaths: his mother, his foster-mother, his wife). What Poe shows are the implications of the tradition itself: the place of women in imagining ideals and the sorts of ideals thereby imagined. Poe's interest is not in the woman as body or nature. On the contrary, these he sets out to repudiate in an exaggerated spiritualization. As he insisted in a late love letter to "Annie": "with what horror I would have shrunk from insulting a nature so divine as yours, with any impure or earthly love." Yet the result remains one of reification, a reduction to body. And the dedication to purity has deadly result. Whether in adoration or exposure, idealized women lead Poe to a dead end: a failure to provide him with either a viable avenue of ascent or a redemptive imagined desire.

The result, again, has large implications for Poe's aesthetic, and specifically as this takes shape as a language theory. Poe's women are essentially words, with a special importance of being Helen. Poe generally liked names with ls and ns and lots of vowels: Eulalie, Lenore, Ulalume, Annie, Annabel Lee, Helen. He in fact wrote two "To Helen" poems, to two different women, neither of whom, strictly speaking, was named Helen. The first "To Helen" was written of Jane Stanard, the mother of a boyhood friend who died insane at age twenty-eight, and whom he weirdly names "Helen Stanard" in his letter accompanying the poem, which he sent to the second "To Helen," named Sarah Helen Whitman. "For Annie," a poem in which he imagines being dead as a rescue from the "fever called 'Living'" (after, sadly, an attempted suicide), was written to Mrs. Nancy Richmond. Even "Ligeia," the name of the deadly Poe lady in the tale of that title, first appears as a nonsense word in the poem "Al Aaraaf."

Annabel Lee provides an especially intriguing case. Poe adored cryptograms. While working for *Alexander's Weekly Messenger*, he famously challenged any comer to send in a code he could not break. He wrote encoded poems to a number of his final true loves: "An Enigma" and "A Valentine" each spell out the name of his (different) beloved: as he explains in a note, "the first letter in the first line, the second in the second, and so on." Annabel Lee follows next. Could it also be an anagram or cryptogram? One of Poe's favorite words is "analytically." In one *Marginalia* (1846) he comments on "Anastasis" as the Doctrine of the Resurrection of the Body. Elsewhere he praises "Anacreontic" verse, and in another *Marginalia* (of 1849, the same year as "Annabel Lee") he commends Anacreon as a poetic model for whom "Verse has been found most strictly married to music" as "the spirit of antique song." Perhaps Annabel Lee is an anagram, combining the prefix "ana," meaning up, back or through; "belle" as a pun on the French word for "beauty"; and the suffix "ly" to yield: Ana – belle – ly, "anabeautily," "ascent-through-beauty." This would uncannily recall the opening lines of the very early "Al Aaraaf": "O! Nothing earthly save the ray (Thrown back from flowers) of Beauty's eye." The direction is away and up, out of the world to some other realm. As Poe writes in his essays, "In every glimpse of beauty presented, we catch, through long and wild vistas, dim bewildering visions of a far more ethereal beauty beyond." And yet in the poem the conduct is obstructed, the ascent turned in on itself in a reified death-in-life.

In this line of word-play, "The Bells," written in the same year, could also pun on beauty. What would be beautiful, as hinted in the praise of Anacreontic music-verse, would be pure sounds, as in this most extreme exercise in Poesque materiality of language:

> They are neither man nor woman –
> They are neither brute nor human –
> They are Ghouls:
> And their king it is who tolls;
> And he rolls, rolls, rolls,
>   Rolls
> A paean from the bells . . .
> If the bells, bells, bells, bells –
> Bells, bells, bells.

Attention is on the pure body of the word through sound, meter, rhyme, repetition, refrain. These are the main topics of Poe's "Rationale of Verse" and many of his literary essays. Such reduction of language to sound bordering on nonsense, the sort of thing that set Poe up for parody (as with Huxley's famous ones), is of course his most outstanding stylistic marker and

theoretical hint. For it marks a turn to the linguistic "signifier" so important
to much contemporary theory. And yet this turn has its limits in Poe. The
signifier in Poe is not really independent, not really released from a signified to make its meanings through interrelationships with other signifiers.
It still relies on signifieds to make sense, even as these emerge as unavail-
able. Poe's, that is, are blocked signifiers, not free or independent ones. His
words, as we saw, tend to negate a series of references: in time, space, metaphysics. They may strive to point outward or upward, but then recoil back
into pointing to themselves. They are, that is, signifiers not as a process of
meaning but rather as its dearth, its defect; failed signifieds rather than freed
signifiers.

   This is another way in which Poe is caught between worlds, to the negation
of both. The realm Poe inhabits is neither a visionary transmutation into higher
reality, nor a negotiation among earthly counters. In terms of language theory, his is neither an achieved signifier nor an accomplished signified, instead
remaining ultimately ambivalent between the two. As there is a range of relation between earthly and metaphysical reality, so there is a range of relation
between signifier and signified: from conduct between them to mutual repudiation. Poe in his more overt theorizings on language seems to go back and
forth between these. At times he gestures towards a vision of pure signified
that would exceed and indeed undo signifiers. This is the case in one late love
poem "To —— ——":

> Not long ago, the writer of these lines
> In the mad pride of intellectuality,
> Maintained "the power of words" – denied that ever
> A thought arose within the human brain
> Beyond the utterance of the human tongue:
> And now, as if in mockery of that boast,
> Two words – two foreign soft dissyllables – . . .
> Have stirred from out the abysses of his heart
> Unthought-like thoughts that are the souls of thought . . .
> With thy dear name as text, though bidden by thee,
> I cannot write, I cannot speak or think.

The lady again appears as name, as word, "two foreign soft dissyllables,"
("—— ——" is Maria Louise Shew), but one that leads to the end of language:
"I cannot write, I cannot speak or think." Here the notion of "the power of
words" as thought inseparable from language, signified from signifier, is confounded in the experience of love as beyond all expression. The verse seems
to be a poetic corollary to a prose entry in *Marginalia* 1846, in which Poe
explores, on the one hand, how

Whenever I am dissatisfied with a conception of the brain, I resort forthwith to the pen, for the purpose of obtaining, through its aid, the necessary form, consequence and precision. How very often we hear it remarked, that such and such thoughts are beyond the compass of words! I do not believe that any thought, properly so called, is out of the reach of language . . . For my own part, I have never had a thought which I could not set down in words, with even more distinctness than that with which I conceived it.

However:

There is a certain class of fancies, of exquisite delicacy, which are not thoughts, and to which, as yet, I have found it absolutely impossible to adapt language . . . shadows of shadows [that] arise in the soul . . . at those mere points of time where the confines of the waking world blend with those of the world of dreams.

The assertion of the linguistic signifier as necessary and intrinsic to any signified at once equivocates into a dream-land between waking and sleeping, reality and dream, where signified escapes signifier. His "fancies" are "shadows of shadows," between consciousness and trance, beyond time and with no duration. Poe goes on to concede that he does "not altogether despair of embodying in words at least enough of the fancies in question to convey . . . a shadowy conception of their character." This might indeed stand as the project of his verse: a pull between an absolute signified which seems to escape signifiers, and the signifiers that impossibly try to attain it.

This ambivalent linguistic course shapes the enigmatic "Sonnet – Silence":

> There are some qualities – some incorporate things,
>   That have a double life, which thus is made
> A type of that twin entity which springs
>   From matter and light, evinced in solid and shade.
> There is a two-fold Silence – sea and shore –
>   Body and soul. One dwells in lonely places,
> Newly with grass o'ergrown; some solemn graces,
> Some human memories and tearful lore,
> Render him terrorless: his name's "No more."
> He is the corporate Silence: dread him not!
> But should some urgent fate (untimely lot!)
>   Bring thee to meet his shadow (nameless elf,
> That haunteth the lone regions where hath trod
> No foot of man,) commend thyself to God.

The poem is adamantly dualistic, although just what constitutes the dual sides is not entirely clear. Poe passes beyond the traditional doubling of body and soul, matter and spirit, to a dualism inside the incorporeal realm itself. In linguistic terms, the dualism of "matter and light," "solid and shade," "sea and shore" quite traditionally stands first for sound and silence, word and idea. Yet then Poe penetrates into the spiritual realm to discover two types of silence there as well. The first is likened to the world of body, a "corporate Silence," the shadow cast by events as they pass away in Poe's characteristic nostalgia, his "No more." But the second seems like the spiritual world squared; a spirit of a spirit, in absolute removal from any concrete term. Yet this ultimate experience is represented as terrifying and destructive. Language becomes "nameless" in a realm beyond the human and also the poetic, where treads "No foot of man." These lone regions close on the soul in fear and trembling – unless the last line, in a final ambivalence, could be meant as a positive turn to the divine: "commend thyself to God." In each case, however, what is registered is a rupture between, or in a move that comes to the same thing, a collapse of signifier into signified. In one sense Poe struggles with the detachment of signifier from signified, leaving the former without significance. In another, he attempts to enclose signified in signifier, collapsing them into each other. But either way, the poetic result is a language frozen into its own forms. The language, that is, neither encompasses significance through contextual relationships, nor conducts from signifier to signified in a traditional structure, nor is itself a fullness of meaning. Instead of being a site of meaning it becomes empty of meaning, an arabesque of silence.

In such visions of pure language signifying pure language Poe seems as remote as may be from concrete history – in his poetry even more than in his prose. Yet Poe's very repudiations point to the specific American contexts in which they take place. Poe's negations may ultimately be directed against the world as such. But it remains a world with very specific features, and the modes of negation also remain culturally situated, rooted, entrenched. Even William Carlos Williams, claiming Poe as American, does so at least partly by inverse: "Had he lived in a world where love throve, his poems might have grown differently. But living where he did, surrounded as he was by that world of unreality, a formless 'population' – drifting and feeding – a huge terror possessed him." Indeed, Williams's insistence on Poe as American uncannily dovetails with Baudelaire's anti-American Poe. Williams cites Poe's essay on Griswold, where Poe defends Americans against the view that they are "not a poetical people," rehearsing arguments familiar since the founding:

The idiosyncrasy of our political position has stimulated into early action whatever practical talent we possessed. Even in our national infancy we evinced a degree of utilitarian ability which put to shame the mature skill of our forefathers . . . [But] our necessities have been mistaken for our propensities. Having been forced to make rail-roads, it has been deemed impossible that we should make verse.

Here, even if by way of apology, is the inimical world of American material and technological focus. This becomes central to Baudelaire's heroic Poe: "From the womb of a greedy world hungry for material things, Poe soared into dreams." Indeed, Baudelaire goes on to cite Poe's own "Fifty Questions" (wherein Poe himself uses the term "belles"):

The frightfully long money-pouches . . . which have come in vogue among our belles – are not of Parisian origin, as many suppose, but are strictly indigenous here . . . [In Paris], it is money only that women keep in a purse. The purse of an American lady, however, must be large enough to carry both her money and the soul of its owner.

Poe is equally nasty elsewhere. As he writes in the *Marginalia* of 1849: "The Romans worshipped their standards; and the Roman standard happened to be an eagle. Our standard is only one tenth of an Eagle – a Dollar – but we make all even by adoring it with ten-fold devotion." Or, as he writes in "To —": "I wake and sigh, / and sleep to dream till day / Of the truth that gold can never buy – / Of the baubles that it may."

One world Poe is negating, then, is his contemporary America, booming in industry, commerce, and competitive materialism in ways that left writing – and the writer – out. Not that Poe was as immune and single-minded in his resistance to American glitter as Baudelaire would have him be. Griswold at least wrote in his vengeful and damaging memoir: "You could not speak of wealth, but his cheek paled with gnawing envy." At issue seems Poe's own horribly uncertain social standing, his dispossession from expected Southern Gentlemanhood and continued ambivalence about it – also reflected in his at once touchy and pugnacious magazine attacks (his plagiarism war is punctuated with comments on what "gentlemen" ought and ought not to do). Here too may be located his anti-democratic tendencies, his distrust of the crowds that also fascinated him. Certainly, as recent discussion has begun to probe, Poe grew up in a home with slaves – the Allan household had three, although one or more may have been hired; one may also have served as Edgar's Mammy – yet another possible dark/light lady. He lived in a slave society in which the very notions of gentleman and lady were founded on caste, the very idea of liberty founded on subjection. Apocalyptic itself, as has long been argued of "The Fall of the House of Usher," may be in Poe's work an image of the looming fate of the South, about to bring on its own immolation through unwavering commitment to its slave-culture. Yet the North is not spared his ire or critical eye. In a more cultural turn to his persistent fuming against Longfellow, Poe sees Northern materialism as analogue to Southern: "No doubt," he writes in a review of Longfellow's *Poems on Slavery*, it is a very commendable and very comfortable thing, in the Professor, to sit at ease in his library chair, and write verses instructing the southerners how to give up their all with a good grace, and abusing them if they will not; but we have a singular curiosity to know how much of his own, under a change of circumstances, the Professor would be willing to surrender.

Poe's turning away from the material world and yet his inability to embrace a metaphysical one; his dispossession and skepticism of a Southern inheritance and yet his barred entry into and disdain for Northern society; these polarities leave him in a nothingness between, with art as its image. His is an unreformed dualism, but one in which neither term holds firm, while the two deny each other. This is already the case in the very early "Sonnet – To Science" (1829):

> Science! True daughter of Old Time thou art!
> Who alterest all things with thy peering eyes.
> Why preyest thou thus upon the poet's heart,
> Vulture, whose wings are dull realities?
> How should he love thee? Or how deem thee wise,
> Who woulds't not leave him in his wandering
> To seek for treasure in the jewelled skies
> Albeit he soared with an undaunted wing?
> Hast thou not dragged Diana from her car?
> And driven the Hamadryad from the wood
> To seek a shelter in some happier star?
> Hast thou not turned the Naiad from her flood,
> The Elfin from the green grass, and from me
> The summer dream beneath the tamarind tree?

Science here does not really stand for abstract theory, which Poe tended to see as a form of poetry. His essay on Griswold denies "that the calculating faculties are at war with the ideal," insisting instead that "the highest order of the imaginative intellect is always preeminently mathematical, and the converse." Science here instead invokes the "dull realities" of temporal life, of "Old Time" itself, in a world increasingly characterized by utility and the reduction of ends to means. These "peering eyes" distort by calculating only for profit or use. As in "Romance," it is reality as bird of prey devouring the poet, who in contrast seeks different "treasure" in differently "jewelled skies." And yet this other world of poetry also remains unreal. It is a mythology fled, a passing and exotic "summer dream beneath the tamarind tree." As he writes in "Dreams," a "long dream of hopeless sorrow" is opposed against the "cold reality of waking life."

Poe's imagery of dream must surely also be in tension with the increasingly material American one; just as his kingdoms stand in macabre reflection against American utopian fantasy, where apocalyptic fulfillment turns to anti-earthly negation. What is striking and central is that Poe's imagination sees only discontinuity and indeed rupture between realms: between earth and ideal, body and spirit, signifier and signified. One is not an image, or ground, or avenue for the other. There is no reconciliation, only mutual exclusion. Art here is not redemptive. It does not provide for reality a meaning or design in lieu of metaphysical structures or realms that have been lost. As Mallarmé recognizes in his "Tomb of Edgar Poe," Poe's eternity is made in death's image. Yet it is not, for all that, untimely:

> Such as to himself eternity's changed him,
> The Poet arouses with his naked sword
> His age fright-stricken for not having known
> That Death was triumphing in that strange voice!

Devotion to deathlessness is revealed as devotion to endless death; but this eternity takes shape as a specific death-mask of "His age." What is glimpsed in Poe is the destructive-drive of a particular society: a South given over to self-defeating, ruinous "ideals" and a North whose soul was increasingly reified in the image of money. Poe's dislocation thus extends to both South and North, to both this world and the next, to both history and utopia, to both speech and silence. His is not an autonomous language displacing reality, but rather a language of his own displacement from it.

RHETORIC NORTH AND SOUTH

Noah Webster's attempt to institute an American English was founded on a vision of North America as "peopled with a hundred millions of men, all speaking the same language," and looks forward to a "period when the people of one quarter of the world will be able to associate and converse together like children of the same family." Europe may be a Babel of multilingual confusion, a "Continent inhabited by nations, whose knowledge and intercourse are embarrassed by differences of language." We, in contrast, must not "consider ourselves as inhabitants of a particular state only, but as Americans . . . establishing one uniform standard of elegant pronunciation."

Given the multiple languages to be found from the outset in the New World – German in Pennsylvania, Dutch in New York, French in Canada and Louisiana, Spanish in the South and West, as well as the variety of African tribal and Native American languages – it is quite remarkable that what resulted was neither sectionally polyglot nor patois. As President John Witherspoon of Princeton, who coined the term "Americanism," was pleased to observe: "moving frequently from place to place, [Americans] are not so liable to local peculiarities either in accent or phraseology. There is a greater difference in dialect between one county and another in Britain, than there is between one state and another in America." Noah Webster made these linguistic bonds a political issue – "Our political harmony is therefore concerned in a uniformity of language" – as well as a social one: distinctions in speech alarmingly "make a difference between the language of the higher and the common ranks." His *Speller*, *Reader*, and *Dictionary* functioned in ways comparable to the nineteenth century's popular etiquette books. These, alongside a multitude of grammars, guides to correct speech, and the spelling-bee – instituted by Webster as a national rite of public education – made available to the American middle classes the standard of speech which had before been reserved for aristocrats and acquired not in schools or books but in elite social circles.

Within the context of this fundamental uniformity in American English, a certain diversity of language is nevertheless evident within nineteenth-century poetic production. This includes some degree of linguistic regionalism which, within specific geographies and social milieus, reflects local color and custom. But it extends to common words of the American heritage. These acquired different sectional meanings within divergent ideological frameworks. Especially in the poetry around the Civil War, different sections of the country claimed the American language each in its own interpretive interests, engendering variant forms of usage, emphasis, and intention.

What emerges, then, is a language at once surprisingly continuous between South and North, but functioning within sectional differences that give this common language divergent and even opposing meanings. Writers of South and North alike observed the genteel conventions that choked and gagged so much Victorian poetry in America. Economic, intellectual, and political complicity served to integrate the domains of poetic language. The North observed political constraints to sustain commerce with the South. A Philadelphia newspaper, for example, refused to print Longfellow's anti-slavery poems for fear of losing its Southern market. Southern writers reciprocally and ironically depended on the North for publishers, audience, market, and colleagues. The high illiteracy and small expendable income among the great majority of whites in the South, with a sizable black population enslaved, made it a region lacking the means for both literary production and consumption. Henry Timrod (1828–67) complained about the consequent reliance on the North for literature, as indeed for most goods: "We grew fat upon Yankee butter, we plied our daily avocations with Yankee tools, we taught our children in Yankee books on Yankee principles, we amused ourselves with Yankee magazines, and while turning a deaf ear to our own modest litterateurs, we went into ecstasies over Yankee poetry and Yankee romances." Timrod accordingly welcomed "the very blockade that has cut off so completely our supply of Northern and English books," so that "forced to supply ourselves, we have, also, learned to criticize without regard to foreign models." But Timrod's attempt, with poet-friends Paul Hamilton Hayne and William Gilmore Simms, to found *Russell's Magazine* as a Southern equivalent to such journals as the North's *Atlantic Monthly* ended in failure, and with it his hope for a Southern national literature. The South continued in its "scornful indifference" to native writers, exhibiting a "firm conviction that genius – literary genius at least – is an exotic that will not flower in southern soil."

The shared conventions of poetic language between regions in practice acted as a backdrop for the development of distinctive rhetorical fields, such that even common terms take on divergent and contradictory significance within the differing contexts of their deployment. This is especially striking with regard to the shared heritage and mutual claims to central, authorizing myths of American destiny and identity. In poetry, as in political oratory, the South laid claim to its own Revolutionary inheritance, its own Biblical sanction, its own domestic ideal and American destiny. Common terms thus became a scene of competitive usages. Conversely, even competitive claims found strangely similar expression. This is particularly striking within a culture, shared by both North and South, which closely associated oratory with poetry, and ritualized poetry as profoundly occasional.

Such ritualized, occasional poetry is evident in the work of both Henry Timrod and Oliver Wendell Holmes, Sr. Both, for example, wrote poems commemorating Washington's birthday. The grip of the Washington cult, which had risen to supply America with a ready-made hagiographic devotion, heroic aura, and historical unity, is visible in the way each poet casts his scene as a nativity, with the sacred mother duly figured:

> Who guessed as that poor infant wept
> Upon a woman's knee,
> A nation from the centuries stept
> As weak and frail as he?   (Timrod)

> See the hero whom it gave us
> Slumbering on a mother's breast;
> For the arm he stretched to save us
> Be its morn forever blest   (Holmes)

The community of expression here – the homage to the Founding Father through religious iconography and in a domestic setting – acts as common frame for the quite different senses, and different purposes, each poet intends by them. The Fathers had in fact bequeathed on the nation a splintered inheritance. The Revolution provided America with founding national rituals, marked through 4 July celebrations and orations, and Washington's Birthdays. But the South saw the Revolution as authorizing "liberty" to mean self-determination and rebellion against a tyrannical centralized power, now identified with the federal government; the constitutional protection of slavery; and a hierarchical social structure based on landed property. The North saw the Revolution as guarantee for "liberty" as individual rights; the constitutional protection of the Union; and resistance against despotism, now identified with the South. To each section, then, Liberty, Revolution, and America took on different resonance, reference, and even plain meaning.

This bifurcated rhetoric penetrates Civil War poetry even as it frames the war itself. This is the case in popular songs, such as the "Battle Cry of Freedom" sung both in the Union and the Confederacy, but with different intentions and stanzaic illustrations: "And although he may be poor not a man shall be a slave" (North); "Their motto is resistance to tyrants we'll not yield" (South). And it is the case for poets more or less elite.

Henry Timrod acted as almost official spokesman for Southern discourse. Born in 1828 into a non-patrician family in Charleston, South Carolina, his schooling consisted of the irregular instruction characteristic of the Southern educational system, and concluded with one year at the University of Georgia. He then tried to earn his living as a tutor on various plantations. His tubercular condition made him unable to sustain action either as soldier or journalist during the Civil War. But he managed, after publishing a first book of *Poems* in 1859 (through the Boston publishers, Ticknor and Fields), to emerge as "The Laureate of the South" by writing war poems, including "Carolina," which was adopted in 1911 as the South Carolina State Hymn ("It should never be read except aloud, and it can hardly be sung except standing"). This poem provides a showcase of American terms as deployed through Southern sectional rhetoric, as does his "Ethnogenesis" (the birth of the nation) written on the occasion of the first Confederate Congress, 1861; "The Cotton Boll," an ode to cotton with a fantasy of New York City destroyed; "Carmen Triumphale," celebrating Southern victories; and "Ode," his most popular poem, commemorating the graves of the Confederate Dead at Magnolia Cemetery, Charleston, 1866.

"Ethnogenesis" combines the American sense of special political mission with the religious rhetoric of Biblical typology. Timrod declares the birth of the South as "a nation among nations," "under God":

To doubt the end were want of trust in God,
  Who, if he has decreed
That we must pass a redder sea
    Than that which rang to Miriam's holy glee,
    Will surely raise at need
    A Moses with his rod.

The familiar call to "the Lord of Hosts" here is invoked against the North, which has "set up his evil throne, and warred with God," spreading anti-slavery "creeds that dare to teach / What Christ and Paul refrained to preach." The South, conversely, emerges as millennial "type" whereby "distant peoples we shall bless / And the hushed murmurs of a world's distress."

Timrod cannot be entirely reduced to the role of partisan poet, although his death in 1867 left him little opportunity to advance to other occasions. But much of his rhetoric is closely linked to Southern senses of identity. His "Dedication" appeals to the "Fair Saxon, in my lover's creed / My love were smaller than your mead," in a fantasy of medieval discourse expressing the South's self-representation as chivalric nobility – what Mark Twain called the South's Sir Walter Scottism (although he concedes in *Life on the Mississippi* that "It seems a little harsh toward a dead man to say that we never should have had any war but for Sir Walter"). Even Timrod's attempts to redirect sectional rhetoric often serve instead to confirm it. The poem "Christmas" seems meant as a counter-prayer for

      Peace in the crowded town,
    Peace in a thousand fields of waving grain,
    Peace in the highway and flowery lane,
      Peace on the wind-swept down.

      Peace on the farthest seas,
    Peace in our sheltered bays and ample streams,
    Peace wheresoe'er our starry garland gleams,
      And peace in every breeze.

Even here, however, the American "fields of waving grain" and "highway" are claimed for "our" exclusive Southern "sheltered bays." And he still slips in one

    Shame to the foes that drown
    Our psalms of worship with their impious drum.

A poem dedicated to the "New Theatre at Richmond" similarly attempts to demarcate some space for art free from politics – "A fairy ring . . . From whose weird circle every loathsome thing / And sight and sound of pain / Are banished." But it ends with a call to "Liberty" and a remembrance that "on each hand and head / Rest the dear rights for which we fight and pray," where "liberty" means the defense of slave and plantation property, and "rights" connotes the power of Southern states to secede from the Union.

This rhetoric is matched and mirrored in the war-poetry of Oliver Wendell Holmes, Sr. (1809–94), who is perhaps the ultimate occasional poet. Holmes, whose father had been dismissed as pastor of the First Church of Cambridge in internecine doctrinal warfare between orthodox and Unitarian camps, was staunchly anti-Calvinist and indeed anti-creedal. But even Holmes could not withstand his country's rhetorical need. He thus could write, in a style matching Timrod's "Ethnogenesis," a poem "To Canaan: A Puritan War-Song" with lyrics like:

> We're marching South to Canaan
>   To battle for the Lord! . . .
> The Mighty One of Israel,
>   His name is Lord of Hosts!
>   To Canaan, to Canaan
>   The Lord has led us forth,
>   To blow before the heathen walls
>   The trumpets of the North.

Poem after poem features Fathers, Freedom, and Flag, claiming an almost genealogical relationship between them. Holmes's is a New England banner, "The same our grandsires lifted up, The same our fathers bore." Like Timrod, Holmes appeals to a "fair heritage spotless descended" which "the father's made free and defended," but intends different fathers, different freedoms, and, despite the common words, a different heritage. To Holmes, the "tyrant crew" is the South, which is trying to "Tear down the banner of the free." Appeals to the same symbols, using the same words, bespeak different ideological Americas.

Holmes's war-poetry is continuous with his general body of occasional verse. Active as both a doctor and a poet, Holmes made these professions subsidiary to his most serious vocation, that of Harvard alumnus. His poems are dedicated to Harvard commencements and reunions; to birthdays, personal, literary, and national; to club, embassy, and other official dinners; centennials and July 4ths; with the poetic audience often taking the guise of dinner guests or fellow club members. The "Chambered Nautilus," Holmes's most anthologized poem, is one of his least characteristic. "At the Saturday Club" is far more representative, presenting literary history as the invitation list to a private dinner party: Longfellow as "Poet, Laureate," with "ray serene"; Hawthorne "hid beneath his veil / Like the stern preacher of his sombre tale"; and Emerson the "Concord Delphi . . . Prophet or poet, mystic, sage, or seer." The Revolution itself appears in Holmes as a family affair, conjured through the familiar Boston figure of Major Thomas Melville, uncle to Herman and among the last of the "Indians" of the Boston Tea-Party of 1774; or through Holmes's own grandmother's account of "Bunker-Hill Battle" as witnessed from the belfry.

Occasion acts in Holmes as a conjunction of personal and communal history, giving shape to a poetry whose greatest strength is its sense of language as social identity. If the content of his verse is mainly dinner parties and other gatherings of peers – and food is one of Holmes's liveliest tropes for poetry, as "a stuffing of praise and a basting of wit," "served to order" and meant "to purchase with a loaf of bread a sugarplum of pleasure"; the fabric and implicit subject of his verse is the language spoken by the elite Boston society which Holmes dubbed "Brahmin." Holmes's "Autocrat of the Breakfast Table," a series he contributed to the *Atlantic Monthly*, acutely observes language habits, from the tutor who read so much Latin "that his English half turned into it," to "genteel idiots whose vocabulary had deliquesced into some half-dozen expressions." Poetry becomes social-linguistic representation, with "epithets" determined by "relationships, political, religious, social, domestic." In "A Rhymed Lesson," the section on "Language" presents class difference as language difference, which even education cannot conceal: "Words lead to things; a scale is more precise, / Coarse speech, bad grammar, swearing, drinking, vice . . . One stubborn word will prove this axiom true – / No quondam rustic can enunciate *view*." "Ode for a Social Meeting (With Slight Alterations by a Teetotaler)" mocks a movement like temperance as a form of linguistic censorship: "Then a smile/scowl and a glass/howl and a toast/scoff and a cheer/sneer, / For all the good wine and we've some of it here / For strychnine and whiskey, and ratsbane and beer." A poem delivered at a dinner to President Hayes meditates on issues of title and personal status, against a background of American rebellion against British social-linguistic distinctions:

> How to address him? awkward, it is true:
> Call him "Great Father," as the Red Men do?
> Borrow some title? this is not the place
> That christens men Your Highness and Your Grace;
> We tried such names as these awhile, you know,
> But left them off a century ago.
>
> His Majesty? We've had enough of that:
> Besides, that needs a crown; he wears a hat.

Holmes's linguistic sense consistently registers place, class, and period. His own genteel language itself approaches a regional idiom, and shades into moments of dialect he also introduces. His dinner-party wit is often but a step away from the fuller dialect deployed in the "Deacon's Masterpiece, or the Wonderful One-Hoss Shay." This poem, famous as an attack on Calvinism – figured as the rickety chaise that breaks down – represents the New England idiom no less than its religious heritage, from informal Brahmin to full-blown dialect:

> Now in building of chaises, I tell you what,
> There is always somewhere a weakest spot, –
> In hub, tire, fellow, in spring or thill,
> In panel, or crossbar, or floor, or sill . . .
> And that's the reason, beyond a doubt,
> That a chaise *breaks down* but doesn't *wear out.*
>
> But the Deacon swore (as Deacons do),
> With an "I dew vum," or an "I tell yeou"
> He would build one shay to beat the taown
> 'N' the keounty 'n' all the kentry raoun'
> It should be so built that it could 'n break daown.

Holmes's Cambridge talk suggests genteel language to be a speech form natural to his particular region, where, as he puts it in "Over the Teacups," "certain subjects were banished by general consent from the conversation of well bred people and the pages of respectable literature." Indeed, genteel language becomes less stultifying when presented as a regional speech or a near-dialect, rather than being erected as the norm and arbiter for poetic language in general. His praise for James Russell Lowell as "New England's home-bred scholar" who well "knew / Her soil, her speech, her people, through and through" applies rather more to himself.

In the writing of James Russell Lowell (1819–91) himself, Holmes's comic, regionalizing treatment of the genteel vanishes, or rather, breaks schizophrenically apart. Lowell's inclusion in literary histories seems mainly derived from his having been among the first to write them. Born, bred, and buried at Harvard, Lowell on the whole is far more distinguished as editor of the *Atlantic Monthly* (1857–61) and then of the *North American Review* (1863–8); as Smith Professor of Modern Languages at Harvard (in which post Lowell succeeded Longfellow); and then as Ambassador to Spain (1877–80) and England (1880–5). His poetic work divides into genteel verse, such as "The Vision of Sir Launfal" and "A Fable for Critics," as against his dialect writings in *Biglow Papers*. Each offers a distinct kind of language, without cross-over. About "Sir Launfal" the less said the better. Its excruciating metric is overshadowed only by the incoherence of its structure and its intrusive moralisms. "A Fable for Critics" takes Pope as its model. Its rhymed couplets and satirical wit recall Holmes's "At the Saturday Club" in making literary history into social register. The move to satire is a welcome relief after "Sir Launfal"'s stilted diction. But the whole retains the character of an inside joke for an intimate social/literary circle, all in patient attendance as they wait for Lowell to make good his own literary promise. Emerson, known to Lowell from the days he had been "rusticated" to Concord for infractions of Harvard's undergraduate rules (he wore a brown coat on Sunday instead of a black one), is not unwittily represented as

> A Greek head on right Yankee shoulders, whose range
> Has Olympus for one pole, for t'other the Exchange . . .
> In whose mind all creation is duly respected
> As parts of himself – just a little projected.

Outsiders are admitted only enough to underscore their exclusion, and often in the spirit of tit for tat. Poe ("three-fifths of him genius and two-fifths sheer fudge") is admonished for his attack on Longfellow for plagiarism. Margaret Fuller, who had dared to say that Lowell "is absolutely wanting in the true spirit and tone of poesy . . . and posterity will not remember him," is mocked as "Miranda,"

> The whole of whose being's a capital I:
> She will take an old notion, and make it her own,
> By saying it o'er in her Sibylline tone . . .
> And she may well defy any mortal to see through it,
> When once she has mixed up her infinite *me* through it.

The "Fable" includes some interesting observations on, for example, the question of American as against British literature: "Though you brag of your New World, you don't half believe in it; / And as much of the Old as is possible weave in it." But at best it remains a form of society-verse, like Holmes's, which he praises as "matchless among you for wit," while however presenting itself as arbiter of the kind of serious poetry that Lowell himself longed to write.

Lowell, however, does have a second voice, which he adopts not out of literary vocation, but rather, out of political commitment. In *Biglow Papers*, he drops his high poetic mantle to write dialect as a direct representation of New England's social-political positions. Lowell's marriage to Maria White – herself a poet who died young of consumption, after having witnessed the death of three of her four children – brought him into radical Garrisonian abolitionist circles, and helped him to focus his poetic language with a political energy that alone awakened it. In the "Fable for Critics" Lowell had criticized himself as striving to climb Parnassus "With a whole bale of *isms* tied together with rhyme," but it was just such politicized verse-making that impelled him into his most original language use. *Biglow Papers*, first series, was written as an attack on the Mexican War as an extension of slavery; the second series treats the Civil War. Through the characters of Hosea Biglow and Birdofredum Sawin, Lowell speaks a native idiom that directly renders and manipulates the political rhetoric storming around him. Hosea Biglow, resisting the army recruiter as the "fifer feller" ("guess you'll toot till you are yeller / 'Fore you git ahold o' me"), rejects the nationalist call as Christian duty:

> You've gut to git up airly
> Ef you want to take in God . . .
> But it's curus Christian dooty
> This 'ere cuttin' folks's throats.

Biglow Paper V, first series, contests Southern claims to the Revolution ("Here we stan' on the Constitution, by thunder") and to the Bible by putting a "Debate in the Sennit" into the words of H. Biglow:

> Freedom's Keystone is Slavery,
> thet ther's no doubt on,
> It's suttin' thet's –
> wha' d'ye call it? – divine.

The second series, Number III, includes a sustained satire on Southern viewpoints in a letter from Birdofredum Sawin, who has settled there. His version of Southern "pulpit ellerkence" on slavery reports that "All things wuz gin to man for's use, his sarvice, an' delight; / An' don't the Greek an' Hebrew words thet mean a Man mean White?" Number V remains an amusing parody of political rhetoric ("Speech of Honourable Preserved Doe in Secret Caucus"): "A ginooine statesman should be on his guard, / Ef he must hev beliefs, nut to b'lieve 'em tu hard." The mutual counter-claims over Revolutionary heritage and rhetoric are also represented. Thomas Jefferson

> prob'ly meant wal with his "born free an' ekle,"
> But it's turned out a real crooked stick in the sekle.
> It's taken full eighty-odd year – don't you see? –
> From the pop'lar belief to root out that idee.

"In choosing the Yankee dialect," Lowell writes in one of the many notes appended to the poems in *Biglow*,

I did not act without forethought. It had long seemed to me that the great vice of American writing and speaking was a studied want of simplicity, that we were in danger of coming to look on our mother-tongue as a dead language, to be sought in the grammar and dictionary rather than in our heart, and that our only chance of escape was by seeking it at its living sources.

Only in his dialect verse was Lowell able to make this escape into living language. In his role as poet, he rarely rises above rhymed speech-making, such as his "Commemoration Ode" at Harvard. Of this poetry one can say, as Lowell himself said in *Biglow* of debates in Congress, that he uses an English "ever more pedantic and foreign, till it becomes at last as unfitting a vehicle for living thought as monkish Latin." As he himself sadly wrote in his "L'Envoi" to the Muse: "All of thee but thyself I grasp . . . Thou lithe, perpetual Escape."

When Holmes and Lowell spoke, they did so for their region, but with the assumption that their New England embodied and defined the nation as a whole. This privileged position, for which they paid a heavy poetic price, took its toll on poets of other regions as well. Western poets more or less accepted their marginalization as eccentric local colorists. Yet they also launched new senses of American poetic identity. And their world, like that of later New England local colorists, is largely shaped by post-Civil War conditions. Southern poets found themselves in a particularly compromised position. While accepting Northern genteel norms as their own, they yet lived in fierce opposition to the North as a threat to their indigenous culture. The very need to defend slavery against attacks from other parts of the country gave rise to a specifically Southern rhetoric, while the South's "peculiar institution" organized not only its slave system of labor and land arrangement in plantations, but its traditions, values, and modes of self-representation. Largely shaped by this ante-bellum culture whose determining characteristic was slavery – where slavery itself defined the sectional division of the nation and generated the South's distinctive political, economic, and cultural forms – poetry continued to attempt to reproduce it in the post-war cultural devastation of slavery's removal.

Lowell's unhappy experiment with Arthurian legend in "Sir Launfal" gave way to his more successful figure of the Yankee farmer as archetypal New Englander. But Arthurian lore became a central element in the genteel Southern image of the Cavalier, who would guarantee social order by his grace, honor, and patrician dominance over the lower and slave classes. Archaic language consequently intrudes into the writings of both Timrod and Sidney Lanier. In Lanier, however, it becomes tied to other commitments central to his poetic vision. The first, music, is specific to his own talents. The second, commerce, more generally reflects regional issues and concerns.

Sidney Lanier (1842–81), although born in Macon, Georgia, had for ancestors musicians in the courts of Queen Elizabeth, Charles I, and Charles II. Himself a musical prodigy, his flute-playing both supported him and prolonged a life persistently threatened by the tuberculosis he contracted in a Civil War prison. Lanier nevertheless always hoped for a literary and academic career.

He spent the years 1857–60 studying the German Romantics at Ogelthorpe College, Georgia, only to have his appointment as tutor in the college cut short by the Civil War. In the war's aftermath, broken in health and without secure livelihood, Lanier tried to finance his poetry by music, magazine writing, and teaching. He eventually became both first flutist in the Baltimore Symphony Orchestra, and a lecturer at Johns Hopkins. In his technical critical study of poetry, *The Science of English Verse*, he attempts to correlate English metrics with musical notation, a project he also pursued in his verse writing. He, however, died of tuberculosis soon after completing this project, at the age of thirty-nine.

Lanier at his best writes a language that is stately and richly musical. At his worst, he confuses language with music, archaism with dignity, and his obsession against trade, industry, and commerce with reality. The opening of his ambitious "The Symphony" is perhaps his poetic nadir: "'O Trade! O Trade! would thou wert dead! / The Time needs heart – 'tis tired of head: / 'We're all for love,' the violins said." Lanier's essentially archaic, songlike cadences cannot accommodate the direct social–economic commentary to which he was also dedicated, and unravel under the burden of his trying to make them do so. At the other extreme, he wrote a dialect poetry in Georgia Cracker that does little more than give voice to his obsessions for saving the Southern economy by replacing cotton with corn, thus instituting land reform and liberating the South from a poisonous commercialism threatening the American spirit.

Except for the dialect poems, Lanier's work largely carries on the Southern genteel romance with medieval court forms. His early poem, "The Tournament," is a heavy-handed allegorical joust opposing "Heart" against "Brain" and "Love" against "Hate." Another early work, "The Jacquerie," recounts a medieval peasant's revolt in blank verse, with chivalry providing both structure and material. Later poems are chivalric in imagery, style, and rhythm. The result can be beautiful, but the beauty is rarely sustained, especially in Lanier's longer, ambitious odes: the "Hymns of the Marshes," "The Marshes of Glynn," "Corn," and the "Cantata" commissioned for the Centennial celebration at Philadelphia through the intervention of Bayard Taylor. The most consistently successful of these longer poems is perhaps "The Revenge of Hamisch," whose balladic form and archaic language seem ultimately to be self-critical and exposing. Its tale of a maddened servant turning terrible punishment back on his master almost inevitably turns the South's feudal identity back on itself as well.

Lanier's shorter songs, because less inconsistent and distracted, can reach an achieved loveliness, as in the conclusion of "In Absence": "Crossing, the windage of each other's wings / But speeds them both upon their journeyings."

This language, however remote from anything ordinarily spoken, accords with the world of devotion Lanier here constructs. Poems based in landscape, flowers, and natural features of the South similarly gain from their concreteness, anchoring their language, as in "From the Flats," where Lanier compares Florida (where he hoped to ease his tuberculosis) with Georgia, complaining:

> Inexorable, vapid, vague and chill
> The drear sand-levels drain my spirit low.
> With one poor word they tell me all they know;
> Whereat their stupid tongues, to tease my pain,
> Do drawl it o'er again and o'er again.
> They hurt my heart with griefs I cannot name:
>   Always the same, the same.

Lanier, in a college notebook entry concerned with his possible future profession, asked himself: "What is the province of music in the economy of the world?" In technique as well as theory, Lanier tried to construct a unitary system which would combine and correlate the different realms of his experience: musical, poetic, and social. And yet his art dramatizes the impossibility of such a project. His Southern preoccupations intrude into a poetic language that cannot accommodate them. His theory of the poetic word as musical relation, outlined in his study *The Science of English Verse*, threatens in practice to propel his verse into metrical compulsion. And the beauty of language he does achieve never finds its context outside of an imaginary world in which art and life perfect and fulfill each other, as in the "Psalm of the West" or the conclusion of his "Centennial Cantata":

> O Music, from this height of time my Word unfold:
> In thy large signals all men's hearts Man's heart behold:
> Mid-heaven unroll thy chords as friendly flags unfurled,
> And wave the world's best lover's welcome to the world.

In more homely, less flightly poems, Lanier however does create a musical poetic language, still essentially genteel, but in closer contact with actual worlds. The sonnet form of "The Mocking Bird" allows Lanier a control and detachment that reflects, and even mocks, his own need for poetry to find its basis in the world:

> Superb and sole, upon a plumed spray
> That o'er the general leafage boldly grew,
> He summ'd the woods in song; or typic drew
> The watch of hungry hawks, the lone dismay
> Of languid doves when long their lovers stray,
> And all birds' passion-plays that sprinkle dew

At morn in brake or bosky avenue.
Whate'er birds did or dreamed, this bird could say.
Then down he shot, bounced airily along
The sward, twitched in a grasshopper, made song
Midflight, perched, prinked, and to his art again.
Sweet Science, this large riddle read me plain:
How may the death of that dull insect be
The life of yon trim Shakspere on the tree?

Lanier, like Timrod, worked under the desperate conditions of the South's war devastation, in a struggle for survival that strongly, if mainly by fantastic inversion, marks his verse. But the problem posed by this sonnet, of how poetry's birds are to sustain themselves on the world's grasshoppers, is one that extends beyond the South and beyond immediate questions of livelihood. Lanier is like most of the lesser mid-century writers, who seem perpetually caught in social, political, and cultural rhetorics which become confused in their poetic language. John Greenleaf Whittier (1807–92) may stand as a final case. Like Longfellow, he was acclaimed, admired, and enjoyed by a wide reading public. He was born and lived most of his life in northern Massachusetts, making only short forays into the city world of journalism as part of his anti-slavery agitation. His work is highly regional, speaking directly of New England places and people and representing their religious, economic, and linguistic culture. Moreover, it is always determined through the ideological angle of his Quaker Inner Light theology. That is, his theological/political/social commitments largely control his verse. Up until the time of emancipation, his poetry is centrally a vehicle for abolition. After the war, Whittier turns to local, descriptive pieces, ballads, and hymns. In both periods, poetic force tends to be lost through conformity to stylized verbal forms, either political or social. In a number of poems, however, Whittier succeeds in resisting these pressures, to achieve a language of quiet dignity and natural strength.

Whittier's political verse is a showcase for the Northern rhetorical sense of words such as freedom, justice, America. "The Yankee Girl," courted by a planter promising freedom from daily labor – "thou art too lovely and precious a gem / To be bound to their burdens and sullied by them" – responds with her own declaration of independence: "Yet know that the Yankee girl sooner would be / In fetters with [slaves] than in freedom with thee." In a poem strangely mirroring Lanier's "Revenge of Hamisch," Whittier openly scorns the Southerner's taste for medieval lore, making it a shrill medium for exposing "The Hunters of Men." He repeatedly invokes the Revolutionary heritage of the fathers – "Is this the land our fathers loved, the freedom which they toiled to win"– and especially the Biblical message of the divine image in all men and women, with both betrayed when "God's own image [is] bought and sold / Americans to market driven, and bartered as the brute for gold." At stake is the betrayal of the American political/ religious mission, the American possibility of following that divine presence that "went before / Our fathers in their weary way . . . The fire by night, the cloud by day."

While this verse can be programmatic and overwrought, it does project the predicament of American identity caught in the contradictory inheritance which joined American freedom to American slavery. For Whittier, this implicates the Northerner no less than the Southerner, who equally must "be told his freedom stands / On Slavery's dark foundation." The very founding words of the nation are compromised by contradictory meanings. As the "Song of the Negro Boatman" observes,

> O, praise an' tanks! De Lord he come
> To set de people free;
> An' massa tink it day ob doom,
> An' we ob jubilee.

But Whittier's work finally insists on the restoration of a single, moral linguistic register. There is no question of the true, right meaning of freedom or sin in "Laus Deo" as it celebrates emancipation: "Freer breathe the universe / As it rolls its heavy curse / On the dead and buried sin."

Whittier's later verse, mainly ballads, genre pieces, pictorial poetry, and hymns, often serves functions that are social and pious rather than purely poetic. His language becomes prosaic, or predictably sing-song. Yet he can almost suddenly plunge into an idiom that is native and concrete without being merely picturesque. In "The Prelude" to "Among the Hills," the New England farm family becomes not a static moral emblem but a living place of moral struggle:

> Shrill, querulous women, sour and sullen men,
> Untidy, loveless, old before their time,
> With scarce a human interest save their own
> Monotonous round of small economies . . .
> Saving, as shrewd economists their souls
> And winter pork with the least possible outlay
> Of salt and sanctity.

In such rugged, unadorned language, Whittier wrote the anti-apocalyptic "Abraham Davenport," who against the cries of the people that "It is the Lord's Great Day" replies, "slow cleaving with his steady voice . . . Let God do his work, we will see to ours." "Telling the Bees" treats personal tragedy with all the reticence of the local mourning custom it records. "The Preacher," featuring Jonathan Edwards, offers a sober review of New England's past spiritual excesses that declared "that man was nothing since God was all" and failed to oppose this-worldly wrongs. "Snowbound," Whittier's most enduring text, is often seen as a nostalgic portrait of his own past farm life, but instead makes its domestic celebration into an enactment of poetic power. As in Emerson's "Snow-Storm," from which it takes its epigraph, the hearth fire becomes an image of poetic consciousness, confronting and contesting brute nature through imaginative industry, as Whittier opposes the "art" of building the fire against the "shrieking of the mindless wind."

The genteel writers, North and South, offer a range of responses to America's developing languages and their possibilities. In this they are continuous with the great poets of mid-century, Dickinson and Whitman. Yet, there remains an anxiety concerning poetry's audience, function, and relation to the surrounding culture and its discourses. Far from taking for granted poetry's sacral or elite status, mid-century genteel poetry remains uncertain about its role and position in American culture. F. O. Matthiessen sees the failure of nineteenth-century verse as due to its inability "to distinguish between the nature of the two arts" of poetry and rhetoric. But the problem is not poetry's adulteration with rhetoric, but rather the failure to master it. Poetry, far from being the pure, self-enclosed language demanded by formalist aesthetics, inevitably builds its language out of the discourses of the cultural worlds it inhabits. It is this loss of contact with a living idiom that Mark Twain spoofed in his own ill-fated appearance at the *Atlantic Monthly* dinner for Whittier ("the expression of interest," he comments, "turned to a sort of black frost"). There he pictures Emerson, Longfellow, and Holmes declaiming their poetic lines in a miner's cabin, in contrast with the miner's own language: "Beg your pardon, Mr. Longfellow, if you'll be so kind as to hold your yawp for about five minutes and let me get this grub ready, you'll do me proud." Lowell, among the first to introduce just such dialect idiom into verse, was generally unable to carry it over into his serious attempts at poems. These were straitjacketed by the same linguistic restrictions that kept him from publishing Melville, Thoreau, and Whitman in the *Atlantic Monthly*.

Poetry's challenge, then, is not simply to resist or dissociate from the discourses around it, but rather to command without being overwhelmed by them. But most mid nineteenth-century writers, instead of shaping language through their own visions, were either mastered by the rhetoric they deployed or else divorced from its living idiom. Nonetheless, their work reflects the search for an American language available for, even if not fully or often made into poetry.

STEPHEN CRANE: AMERICAN ECONOMIES

From the moment of their publication in 1895, Stephen Crane's poems have been perplexing, even scandalous. On the one hand, the cryptic texts exert a genuine power, at once and in the memory. On the other, it is difficult to specify just where and how the power resides in such minimalist works. The poems, perhaps even more than the fiction, justify H. G. Wells's 1900 description of Crane's work in the *North American Review* as an "art of certain enormous repudiations." These go beyond the once-racy blasphemies and original art-deco format that printed the poems all in capital letters, untitled. On purely formal grounds, Crane's texts strikingly break conventions to introduce a new poetic idiom answering specifically to American scenes and requirements. Crane undertook his poems between writing fiction and journalism. Apparently conjuring them whole out of his brain after hearing William Dean Howells read an edition of Emily Dickinson's verse, Crane showed up at Hamlin Garland's with a manuscript while assuring him, the story goes, "I have four or five up here all in a little row." The resulting "lines," as he called them, almost completely disregard the then-poetic norms in rhyme, meter, stanza definition, and diction. Like many poets in America, Crane was concerned with the possibility of an American art of language that would distinguish itself from its English antecedents. He succeeded beyond most others. His poetic relies instead on concise and condensed image, dramatized viewpoint, directness of idiom, simplified diction, and potent, unadorned figuration. Crane deploys his central formal technique, lineation, as later poets will, in order to distribute emphasis, mediate suspense, and command stark juxtaposition.

Crane's poetry is overshadowed by his prose writings and complicated by his biography. The fictional work blocks a view to the poems in two converging directions. On the one hand, the poems are seen as reduced versions of mainly thematic and philosophical issues thought to inform the novels. The poems become, most usually, existential and heroic cameos of stoic man, alone and isolated, confronting an indifferent and alien universe. On the other hand, comparison with the fictional contexts further heightens an impression of detachment and remoteness in the poems, making them seem metaphysical and abstract visions thoroughly removed from those historical interests which situate Crane's fictional settings and actions. In either case, what is lost is the poetry's figural resonance as a mode of cultural representation, one which retains important ties to Crane's fictional and journalistic impulses. Crane's verse addresses and represents specific configurations of the American culture surrounding him. The poems are culturally situated, written out of a history and in the name of values deeply American; values, as Crane aggressively insists – in a tradition of dissent itself deeply American – that America was increasingly betraying.

Crane's personal history recalls the brief intensity of his art. Many circumstances remain obscure, and rumor continues to befog fact, as it did during Crane's lifetime. Crane was born in 1871, the fourteenth child (the ninth to survive) of a father who came from an old and distinguished Revolutionary family, and who served as a Methodist elder, teacher, writer, and pastor; and a mother who came in turn from an eminent line of Methodist ministers. Demoted from elder to itinerant preacher through theological quarrels with his wife's family, his father died by the time Crane was nine. The mother, to support her family, lectured and wrote for Methodist and women's reform causes, notably temperance, while the family moved among a number of New Jersey places. She may have suffered a mental breakdown in Stephen's fourteenth year. She died when he was twenty.

Crane's subsequent life worsens. His few years at school seem mainly to have been spent smoking and playing baseball: first at Claverock College, a Methodist preparatory school requiring daily Bible study; then at Lafayette, where he failed to pass any courses; and lastly at Syracuse University, where he gained admittance through family Methodist connections and again failed to complete a semester's work. He had in the meantime already begun writing for newspapers, including a stint at his brother's Asbury Park news agency. There he succeeded in getting not only himself, but also his brother fired, for reporting a parade of the Junior Order of American Mechanics in ways that insulted both the workers – described as "plodd[ing] along, not seeming quite to understand, stolid, unconcerned . . . a pace and bearing emblematic of their lives" – and their employer, "to whom a dollar, when held close to his eye, often shut out any impression he may have had that other people possess rights."

Leaving college, Crane lived in New York with no fixed address and no fixed income, writing for newspapers and completing his first works of fiction. *Maggie*, his first novel, features a girl-heroine seduced, ruined, and turned streetwalker in New York City's slums. Crane had to publish this work at his own expense. But then he achieved sudden and unsettling fame for *The Red Badge of Courage*, aided by the patronage of Hamlin Garland and above all William Dean Howells. Countering their promotional aid, however, were run-ins with the police, scandalous gossip of a dissolute life spent drinking or doping, and a peculiar motif involving prostitutes. Crane's quixotic defense of a "chorus girl" (Dora Clark) who had been arrested is said to have caused the New York Police Department so to persecute him as to make his continued residence in the city impossible. His next years were spent, through the fame of the *Red Badge*, as correspondent for various newspapers: partly out West, but especially wherever he could find war. In 1896, he tried unsuccessfully to reach the Spanish–American War in Cuba (his ship sank and he spent three days at sea, which became the basis for his short story "The Open Boat" and his poem "A man adrift on a slim spar"). He then left for the war in Greece, to return later to Cuba once more. He lived his last years in a country manor house in England, overspending his income with Cora Howarth Murphy Stewart, a former hostess at a brothel whom he had met in Florida. He died of tuberculosis in 1900, before reaching the age of twenty-nine.

This life lived at odds against the given structures of his society, which is to say in purposeful critical relation to them, also frames Crane's poetry. It does so on many different levels, both formally and through the central figures which organize his texts: religion, love, war, art, and not least, money and prostitution. Crane's critique finds its first configuration in what may be called his desert-visions. These poems generally feature emptied landscape – wilderness, high place, highway, sea. They are typically structured as confrontations between self-enclosed subjectivities, each with its own faulty viewpoint:

> I saw a man pursuing the horizon.
> Round and round they sped.
> I was disturbed at this;
> I accosted the man.
> "It is futile," I said,
> "You can never—"
>
> "You lie," he cried,
> And ran on.

This poem seems, first, a confrontation between irreconcilable points of view. And it opens towards options equally irreconcilable. In one reading, the man who pursues appears deluded by his vision, but refuses the enlightenment offered by a disinterested speaker-narrator whose position seems privileged. Yet, perhaps the reverse is the case. Perhaps the man who pursues the horizon remains noble in his quest for some ideal without which life would be empty, a devotion which is simply beyond the speaker-narrator's understanding.

Many Crane texts take shape as such epistemological or existential enigma. Typically, as here, two subjectivities or points of view are brought to bear one upon the other, but without resolution. This lack of resolution itself comprises one of Crane's central commitments, and intentionally extends to the reader. As Crane explains in a letter, "If there is any moral or lesson . . . I do not try to point it out. I let the reader find it for himself." Crane's reader is almost always placed in a difficult, compromised position. Acting as an additional subjectivity, the reader is called upon for a decision the text sets up as impossible to make. But this chastening of any single subjectivity is central to Crane's project. It forces the reader to experience directly a critique of selfhood which is one of Crane's prominent concerns. Crane is not demonstrating man as an entrapped selfhood; rather, he is exposing selfhood as a potential trap. The staging of dramas of isolated selfhood in Crane does not finally present a general existential condition. Its interests, instead, are moral, social, and specifically historical.

For the dilemma in the poem is not only abstract, epistemological, or universally metaphysical. The figure of the man pursuing the horizon presents not only a viewpoint, but a figure of subjectivity itself, suggesting the circle of consciousness as such. Its enclosed round recalls the Emersonian circle, with the man a kind of Emersonian self-reliant. But this selfhood proves not expanding, but isolating, circular in a self-constricting sense. Solipsism emerges as a problem, not a solution. Crane's poem, rather than endorsing or even declaring isolated selfhood, instead shows its limitations.

This Emersonian consciousness is placed in a suitably American setting. The desert, far from being a mere empty, abstract, or existential space, evokes a quite definite cultural-historical location. Crane's wildernesses are at once Biblical and national – indeed, are the sites of intersection between these two in America's inherited senses of vision. The Biblical resonance seems to promise revelation; the American one, calling. But characteristically in Crane, the revelation is confounded. The man's pursuit, whether noble or quixotic, seems delusional. As to calling, in the context of Crane's world, pursuit itself takes on specific connotations. It suggests what had, by the century's end, become the central American obsession: a driving of the self to achievement. This drive, itself emerging as an independent value, nevertheless finds expression in particular symbols:

> A man saw a ball of gold in the sky;
> He climbed for it,
> And eventually achieved it –
> It was clay.
> Now this is the strange part:
> When the man went to the earth
> And looked again,
> Lo, there was the ball of gold.
> Now this is the strange part:
> It was a ball of gold.
> Aye, by the heavens, it was a ball of gold.

Multiple subjectivities are here orchestrated through the man's own changing vision before, during, and after his pursuit, with the reader in turn made to bear witness to each. Again, there is a range of possibility: is the pursuit of the ball of gold merely delusive, or is it, delusive or not, ennobling? The ball of gold may also be a figure for the imagination. Its mere repudiation would only empty the world: as Wallace Stevens will later say of such denial, "The sun, that brave man, is just what you say, have it your way, the world is ugly and the people are sad." But here the pursuit seems inert. Nothing has been transformed, achievement is self-negating rather than imaginatively rich. The round, again, is endless and self-enclosed. And its object, suspiciously, is named as that most seductive item of the Gilded Age, gold, which, instead of standing for imaginative possibility, may displace and betray it.

The self, and its emblem of assertion, money, are two central American institutions Stephen Crane's work treats with suspicion. Another such institution, unsurprisingly for the son of ministers, is religion. Crane's angry attacks on a God who seems only to show Himself in punishment and mockery of created beings were the earliest features of his work to rivet attention. But Crane's interests are not really theological. Crane is not mainly concerned with whether God in His True Nature is wrathful or loving, Old Testament or New, his mother's or his father's, cruel or saving. There is in Crane no sustained metaphysical analysis such as Emily Dickinson undertakes in her work. Crane's concern instead is with the way these images of God direct human effort or, rather, are exploited by it. What his poems portray is the variety of religious claims, as these are instituted through, or support, various structures of power. One such structure he resolutely rejects: that of the God of punishment, and of all those who claim to know and speak for him. Crane skillfully out-debates this God in "A god came to a man," one of the poems his publishers insisted he cut from the original Copeland and Day edition of *Black Riders*, to be published only posthumously. In this text, God, having created the apple, the human desire for it, and the interdict against it, has put Himself in a self-canceling position: "What folly is this? / Behold, thou hast moulded my desires / Even as thou hast moulded the apple . . . I am a greater God than God." The God who visits "the sins of the fathers . . . upon the heads of the children" Crane denounces: "Well, then, I hate Thee, unrighteous picture." Crane's contempt for the "god in wrath" who is "beating a man" is ultimately directed against "All people [who] come running" to praise him as "a redoubtable god."

These assaultive instances are not crises of faith, whose theologies Crane early dismissed in imagery of the circus: "my brother Will told me not to believe in Hell after my uncle had been boring me about the lake of fire and the rest of the sideshows." What rivets Crane is what the word "God" is taken to mean from instance to instance; what vision of the world seems implicit in those who claim to know God, especially in the vindictive way of the "stern spirit" condemning the human devotion of a weeping maid. The figure of God(s) can at times in the poems also function, along with angels, spirits, heavenly voices, and animal figures such as the magpie or the ass, as an additional voice or viewpoint outside or beyond self-enclosed visions, in order to expose them. Or the divine can figure as an inner voice "that whispers in the heart," a "god of his inner thoughts." But religion as such emerges in Crane primarily as a debased social discourse, a sale by "strange peddlers," each

> Holding forth little images, saying:
> "This is my pattern of God.
> Now this is the God I prefer."

Of far more importance to Crane than God is sin. But sin is never in Crane metaphysically determined. Crane's verse insists on the collapse of metaphysical space:

> I stood upon a high place,
> And saw, below, many devils
> Running, leaping,
> And carousing in sin.
> One looked up, grinning,
> And said: "Comrade! Brother!"

Above and below come onto one plane, whose measure is not metaphysical, but moral. And the moral "sin" is exactly the metaphysical architecture that supports self-deluding condescensions, which extend to the reader. When Crane's first publishers insisted he edit out the blasphemy, he protested that this would "cut all the ethical sense out of the book. All the anarchy, perhaps. It is the anarchy which I particularly insist upon." Anarchy stands against hierarchy; and for Crane, anti-hierarchy is an ethical position, one that is not metaphysical but social. What he upholds, instead, is responsibility and responsiveness, which he finds, however, almost everywhere betrayed:

> With eye and with gesture
> You say you are holy.
> I say you lie;
> For I did see you
> Draw away your coats
> From the sin upon the hands
> Of a little child.
> Liar.

Crane takes sides, against those with holy pretensions and fine coats, and for those most sinned against. Here, they are represented by the "little child," a figure at once Christic and realistic. It finds its association in Crane's novel *Maggie*, when she, already ruined and walking the street, appeals to "a stout gentleman in a silk hat and chaste black coat," having "heard of the Grace of God." But he gives "a convulsive movement and save[s] his respectability with a vigorous side step."

What do men pursue besides gold? Women. Now this is the strange part. For all his macho image, Crane, perhaps more than any other nineteenth-century male poet, writes a poetry that is deeply gendered; that is, that recognizes the social experiences of women (and men) as structured through gender divisions. Crane's love poetry is usually and apologetically bracketed away from the rest of his work. But Crane's in many ways is a true poetry of Eros. The imagery of wandering, of seeking, of pursuit is also Eros-longing for the remote beloved. In his own life, Crane's loves tended to fall into categories of the unattainable. His first, youthful, unrequited loves were for women belonging to social classes above him, marked in his work by a poem where "black terror, limitless night," is set against "thou and thy white arms / And the fall to doom a long way." His later gallant protections went to fallen women, whose prior sexual experiences made sole possession impossible – a love, as he wrote of Cora, "always [in] the shadow of another lover," seen through "the ashes of other men's love," hence a "temple" on whose "altar" his self and heart can be sacrificed.

The figure of Eros in Crane concentrates his central cultural commitments and critiques. It does so specifically through imagery of women poor, women abused, and most especially harlots. The exploitation of women, complicated through sexuality, is pivotal to Crane's vision, in ways that implicate his entire project concerning the place of the self in the surrounding world. One emblem is the double standard:

> I.   There was a man and a woman
>   Who sinned.
>   Then did the man heap the punishment
>   All upon the head of her,
>   And went away gayly.
> II. There was a man and a woman
>   Who sinned.
>   And the man stood with her.
>   As upon her head, so upon his,
>   Fell blow and blow,
>   And all people screaming: "Fool!"
> III. He was a brave heart.
>   Would you speak with him, friend?
>   Well, he is dead,
>   And there went your opportunity.
>   Let it be your grief
>   That he is dead
>   And your opportunity gone;
>   For, in that, you were a coward.

In another poem, a lover fails his beloved because of "Man's opinions, a thousand thickets, my interwoven existence, my life." He is called "cold coward." Here, the social contexts of cowardice are developed. The poem proposes a series of progressively implicating options. The first man enjoys a perfect double standard, although the lineation of "Who sinned" points no less to him than to the woman. The second man, in critical contrast, does stand with the woman, and suffers the consequences of social blows. But the satisfaction at martyrdoms, and the security of judging the social world, is then subverted in the third stanza, which destroys the privilege of the reader. It is we, ourselves, who are complicit in these blows. We are the screaming people. The sin devolves from a supposedly sexual one to the betrayal of women in gender hierarchy, a hierarchy then attacked as the reader's own questionable privilege. The term "opportunity," like pursuit in the poem "I saw a man pursuing the horizon," evokes an American code of values, but forces its meaning from economic ambition to ethical obligation.

Crane's commitment to exposing female destitution may be grounded in his mother's work in women's reform causes and temperance, and recalls a tradition of literature and sermons devoted to prostitution and slum-life. Especially, his posthumously published poems turn on scenes of female exploitation and female mercy.

> Bottles and bottles and bottles
> In a merry den
> And the wan smiles of women
> Untruthing licence and joy.
> Countless lights
> Making oblique and confusing multiplication
> In mirrors
> And the light returns again to the faces.
>
> A cellar, and a death-pale child.
> A woman
> Ministering commonly, degradedly,
> Without manners.
> A murmur and a silence
> Or silence and a murmur
> And then a finished silence.
> The moon beams practically upon a cheap bed.
>
> An hour, with its million trinkets of joy or pain,
> Matters little in cellar or merry den
> Since all is death.

The apparent glitter of the brothel-like "merry den" is only the obverse side of death in the cellar. Conversely, the cellar, common and degraded from the point of view of social "manners," is the only site of a loving ministry. As occurs in women's writing of the period, Crane recovers and uncovers the silence and murmur of muted female voices, just as his art acts as multiplying mirror for a culture whose pleasures of spending presume consumption of others. Yet here the sacrifice is not redemptive. The practicality which directs the moon continues to reign over this world, whose upper and nether parts frame a social space that requires no additional metaphysics of hell.

What slavery is to Whitman, prostitution is to Crane: the most extreme case of reduction of one person by another; of aggressive self-assertion at another's expense; of self-interest as particularly expressed through money. But prostitution is only one point on a continuum. A cluster of late texts propose questions of material interests as images of social abuse. "The outcry of old beauty / Whored by pimping merchants" is, after all, only one instance of "The impact of a dollar upon the heart." "Flesh painted with marrow" is only one "trivial bow" bought by "the successful man . . . Slimed with victories over the lesser / A figure thankful on the shore of money." In this world, the "real cross" is "made of pounds, dollars or francs." Friendship, heaven, welfare, and curse all become modes of "crying their wares." Even childhood becomes a competitive scene, with those able to marshal "opportunity and skill" dominating "the feeble." Lord opposes bandit. Poverty opposes wealth across a "chasm of commerce." "Carts laden with food" mock those reduced to alms.

War haunts Stephen Crane's work, but it too is treated in ways surprisingly gendered, and is a figure for a complex conflict of values. The American promise of individual freedom and self-discovery is not one Crane simply repudiates. There are texts where the courage of the self is praised for choosing to "be a toad" rather than to "think as I think"; for seeking a "new road" apart from those who go in "huddled procession," even if dying in "dire thickets"; for not being ranged in rows. Crane is too American to endorse mere conformity or subordination to a collective social group. But he also sees that this individualist value, without restraint or responsibility, becomes destructive, with nothing to contain aggression and appetite. Yet the very impulses, such as religion and love, which might serve to frame the self become implicated in its rapacities. The result is war. The title poem of Crane's second volume of poetry, "War is Kind" (does he also mean, of human kind?) addresses the maiden, the orphaned child, the mother, each enjoined not to weep even as the poem makes their doing so inevitable:

> Do not weep, maiden, for war is kind . . .
>   Hoarse, booming drums of the regiment.
>   Little souls who thirst for fight,

These men were born to drill and die.
The unexplained glory flies above them,
Great is the Battle-God, great, and his Kingdom –
A field where a thousand corpses lie.

War here and elsewhere in Crane's work is the destitution of women, family, community, sanctioned, as more explicitly in Crane's own version of a "Battle-Hymn of the Republic," by a "Battle-God" whose power is registered in dead bodies. This is a betrayal of those very ends for which war was presumably acting as means. It is registered not in heroic self-assertion, but in lives that are devastated, in the "tears of her who loved her son / Even when the black battle rages," in "crimson clash" where "Women wept" and "Babes ran, wondering." As he writes in his "Battle-Hymn," "The chanting disintegrate and the two-faced eagle." There is a coming apart of values, such that the heroic destroys the very world it claims to rescue.

Crane, nonetheless, is not without recourse. To each betrayal, he offers his response. The vision of "the loveliness of her" can displace the wilderness "of snow, ice, and burning sand" as long as gazing does not become possessive desiring. Such "brave deeds of war" as "stern stands and bitter runs for glory" give way to the promise of other, "braver deeds." Against self-assertive self-interest, Crane posits a creature of the desert:

In the desert
I saw a creature, naked, bestial,
Who, squatting upon the ground
Held his heart in his hands,
And ate of it.
I said: Is it good, friend?
"It is bitter – bitter," he answered;
"But I like it
Because it is bitter,
And because it is my heart."

This text presents a complicated and polemical texture in which the Christian image of fallen man is at once invoked and questioned; while the "heart" of inner conversion (Jeremiah, Paul) is equally revoked and recast. Crane in one sense recalls the older Christian suspicion of self-love and in favor of humility. But Crane's is not a Christian humility, as he rejects both its institutional and its metaphysical hierarchies, and above all its required submission to higher authority. Yet there is a profound commitment to self-limitation: a bitterness to be embraced.

This self-limitation is inscribed in the formal structures of Crane's verse. Crane's poems recall, in rhetoric and image, the Biblical tradition of parables.

But this is not to promise clear lessons, predetermined metaphysical structures, or secure inclusions into secrecies of meaning. It is rather a form of taunt, as one poem declares: "Unwind my riddle . . . Scorn hits strong because of a lie." The verses plunge the reader into confusion and indecision, devastating his/her certainties of interpretation. But this is the position of the artist as well. The question of artistic imagination – its purposes, its constraints, and the limitations of the artist-self – is raised in a number of texts, all of which take the form of self-mockery. In one poem, "Three little birds in a row" nudge each other and laugh at a man passing near who "thinks that he can sing." Another declares the poet to have "a thousand tongues," but "nine and ninety-nine lie" and the one left "will make no melody at my will, / But is dead in my mouth." The fine song flies away as birds; the man's song, for all his desire, sounds only as a "clip-clapper of this tongue of wood." In these texts, mutually undercutting viewpoints delimit the artist's claims to accomplishment, in the same chastening of the self which characterizes the desert-visions and which emerges as Crane's central Christian revision, and moral–social commitment.

Crane, in constraining the imagination, is not repudiating it. He is, however, examining its reach and its cultural place. In a parody of Longfellow, he warns that life is not made "sublime" by "dabbling much in rhyme," but he also wishes to reaffirm imaginative art in an America where its displacement is threatened. The underside of Crane's own art is signaled in his imagery of the "red muck" of his heart or the "bastard mushroom / Sprung from a pollution of blood" into which he dips as ink. And it remains centered in the drama of always partial knowledge, with the self, including the reader's self, assaulted and forced to acknowledge multiple interpretations and difficult, self-critical judgments. The texts both depict and enact the dangers of imprisonment in any individual consciousness, while asserting the possibility, and indeed the need, to look beyond it to other, further points of view. In this Crane's vision proves to be strangely and surprisingly social in implication: where the social becomes that space which self-limitation makes available to others, as also a sign of commitment to them.

Crane's variety of figures come together in a text which has unusual extent within Crane's reduced art:

> God lay dead in Heaven;
> Angels sang the hymns of the end;
> Purple winds went moaning,
> Their wings drip-dripping
> With blood
> That fell upon the earth.

It, groaning thing,
Turned black and sank.
Then from the far caverns
Of dead sins
Came monsters, livid with desire.
They fought,
Wrangled over the world,
A morsel.
But of all sadness this was sad, –
A woman's arms tried to shield
The head of a sleeping man
From the jaws of the final beast.

This poem apparently recalls a scene in New York, where a young streetwalker tried to protect her procurer from a beating; Crane called the police, who then arrested the woman. The figure of the woman here situates religious apocalypse and warfare in terms of a complex of abuses. Appetite ("livid with desire"), violence ("They fought"), and competitive struggle ("Wrangled over the world") all intersect and focus in the figure of the fallen, redemptive, yet also piteously vulnerable woman. The end this unveils is of the world betrayed by unquenchable thirsts and unrestrained violence. These are sins, but against community, which a devouring selfhood has consumed, in opposition to an assaulted and desperate image of outcast love.

Crane's reduced scenes and idiom have a peculiarly American resonance. They evoke, in their open deserts and isolated visions, American social structures which privilege a privacy of selfhood as the central norm, both economically and morally. But by the 1890s, perhaps particularly in Crane's city world, the American vision had become increasingly self-directed and solipsistic. The subjectivities Crane both presents and limits, insisting in his very formal construction on their placement within or against other viewpoints, finally suggests a critique of that selfhood which, by his time, seemed overwhelmingly a matter of self-interest at the expense of others. But Crane's moral rigor remains American, calling America back to its own unfulfilled promise, in a language at once figural and historical.

GEORGE SANTAYANA AND HARVARD FORMALISM

There is a good deal of Harvard throughout the nineteenth century. Longfellow, Lowell, and Holmes all were firmly situated there, with Tuckerman more peripheral and even Emerson remaining in eccentric relationship. But in the 1890s, Harvard hosted a peculiar concentration of poetic activity, albeit with a peculiar disappointment of poetic achievement. Genuine poetic departures took place, on the whole, outside it, with Whitman and Dickinson, Paul Laurence Dunbar and Stephen Crane. And yet, 1890s Harvard would prove a matrix out of which emerged a range of the next century's divergent and in many ways conflicting modernisms – oddly, but not exclusively, from among "special," non-metriculating students who passed through without taking degrees: E. A. Robinson (1891–3), Wallace Stevens (1897–1900), and Robert Frost (1897–9). T. S. Eliot, officially resident for the BA and MA from 1906 to 1914 (he declined to return from London to defend his completed doctoral dissertation, thus ceding his PhD) in his own way also reflects and revises the aesthetics of Harvard's end of century.

What connects Harvard's nineteenth-century poets is their commitment to a traditional formal poetics, which intensified to the point of rigor mortis by the century's end. This formalism found its fullest expression in the writings of George Santayana (1863–1952), who was central to Harvard poetry during the 1890s and whose influence can be felt through the diverse modernisms that subsequently developed. Santayana is perhaps most notable as a historian of ideas, whose embrace, however, largely stifled him as poet. It is with reference to long traditions of Western civilization that his poetic failure has special resonance. The point is not even that Santayana was a bad poet, whose faults make a long, easy list: stilted diction, predictable rhyme, strained syntax, garbled sequences, unnatural, unmusical phrasing, derivative imagery and sentiment. What is striking is how much and how deeply he himself embodied the genteel tradition he famously and disdainfully named. In many ways, his most astute critical remarks apply foremostly to himself. And yet, his poetic failure announced aesthetic concerns which set the stage for poetry to come.

Of Santayana in general it may be said: he disliked. He disliked natives and immigrants, the masses and the elite, Jews, women, the devout and the secular. As Van Wycks Brooks sums up, Santayana disliked America. "He was repelled by everything that characterized American life . . . His smiling contempt for the efforts of men to better the world and humanity was reflected in a host of Harvard minds that were reversing the whole tendency of the great New England epoch." This disdain no doubt originated in Santayana's horrible childhood of abandonment and displacement, which was deepened through an adult life of homelessness and suppressed homosexuality. Left behind with his Spanish father when his mother returned to America to raise the children from her first, elite New England marriage, joining her again at the age of eight (having spent three years in the care of a household Santayana later described in *Persons and Places* as "crowded, strained, disunited and tragic," Santayana grew up on the borders of wealth, social position, and religious affiliation. When his mother died in 1912, he gratefully resigned his Harvard Professorship to return to Europe, finally to die in a convent in Rome.

Santayana introduced the notion of the "genteel tradition" in a lecture delivered at Berkeley in 1911, as his wave of adieu to America. Neither there nor elsewhere is Santayana especially rigorous in defining what this phrase means, using it as a general term of disapprobation for a number of American cultural features. Yet, by way of this notion, he does dramatize a problem central for American poets and indeed for America: that is, of a split in American culture in which, as he describes it in "The Genteel Tradition in American Poetry,"

one half of the American mind, that not occupied intensely in practical affairs, has remained, I will not say high-and-dry, but slightly becalmed; it has floated gently in the back-water, while, alongside, in invention and industry and social organization the other half of the mind was leaping down a sort of Niagara Rapids . . . The American Will inhabits the sky-scraper; the American Intellect inhabits the colonial mansion. The one is the sphere of the American man; the other, at least predominantly, of the American woman. The one is all aggressive enterprise; the other is all genteel tradition.

Santayana's gendered language here is neither accidental nor inconsequential. It recurs when, in a later essay on "Genteel American Poetry," Santayana describes the genteel as a "frank and gentle romanticism which attached it to Evangelines and Maud Mullers . . . a simple, sweet, humane, Protestant literature, grandmotherly in that sedate spectacled wonder with which it gazed at this terrible world and said how beautiful and how interesting it was." Santayana points here at Longfellow as the epitome of the genteel. Yet Santayana is himself caught in an anxiety that Longfellow (barely escaping the career of lawyer his father had planned for him) first registered: that poetry in America has no place, that it does not count. This is the pivotal insight around which Santayana's conceptual impulses turn: the dissociation of American sensibility into practical life as opposed to a high culture apparently irrelevant to it. He, like Longfellow, accepts this split as a given, although Santayana does so with something of a vengeance. His characterization of genteel poetry as "grandmotherly," in the sphere of the "American woman," is both telling and ironic. American poetry is, for Santayana, a separate sphere.

But it is not the separation that finally disturbs him. He does not really call for the reassociation of American business and American art, as does Whitman, whom Santayana steadfastly deplores. Instead of regretting the division of American life into a commercial, practical, mass culture as against an elite literary one, Santayana is annoyed that it is the elite culture that lacks power. It is not the separateness of the sphere of poetry, but its powerlessness, that, in his view, feminizes it. He would not mind its being separate and male, like the exclusive Laodicean Club he founded at Harvard, which mirrored and rivaled other exclusive men's clubs (and whose journal, the *Harvard Monthly*, declined to publish special-student E. A. Robinson). But he would substitute poetry for money as the counter of prestige. Santayana endorses elite culture, but he wishes it were effective in ways that in America it is not. His solution, or advocacy, will be to intensify poetry as an elite, separate realm, for which he will make greater and greater claims.

Santayana brought out a collection of *Sonnets and Other Verses* in 1894, incorporating into it poems composed through the previous decade. A second sonnet-cycle was written in 1895 and published in 1896, along with his aesthetic treatise, *The Sense of Beauty*. *Interpretations of Poetry and Religion* appeared in 1900, to be followed by many other prose works, but no poetry, in the new century. These 1890s works are of a piece. In both the poetry and the aesthetics, formalization acquires a special, one might say, dissociated privilege. In Sonnet I, the form itself is the earthly "garden of delight" that he seeks as an isolated "island altar" of ritualized, functionless "prayer":

> I sought on earth a garden of delight
> Or island altar to the Sea and Air,
> Where gentle music were accounted prayer,
> And reason, veiled, performed the happy rite.
> My sad youth worshipped at the piteous height
> Where God vouchsafed the death of man to share;
> His love made mortal sorrow light to bear,
> But his deep wounds put joy to sham'ed flight.
> And though his arms, outstretched upon the tree,
> Were beautiful, and pleaded my embrace,
> My sins were loth to look upon his face.
> So came I down from Golgotha to thee,
> Eternal Mother; let the sun and sea
> Heal me, and keep me in thy dwelling-place.

Santayana's sonnets tend to be repetitive. Already apparent here is his characteristic retention of metaphysical space, but as an empty stage-set which he continues to haunt. The poem is interesting in that it displays Santayana's rejection of Christianity, which he generally conflates with a classical world whose main function remains, however, to focus his nostalgia. "I would I had been born in nature's day," he complains in Sonnet IV. Sonnet XVI at once conjures and negates some Olympian heaven whose unreality is as strong as its lure:

> A thousand beauties that have never been
> Haunt me with hope and tempt me to pursue;
> The gods, methinks, dwell just behind the blue;
> The satyrs at my coming fled the green.

What happens in Sonnet I, as typically in Santayana, is the coming apart of Christian suffering and Christian redemption, while a sense of Christian sin is retained. Divine love fails to lift him above this flawed world, and seems, in his critique, to negate whatever earthly joy is available, while sin prevents him from being redeemed through divine sorrow. Each of these elements in the traditional Christian structure works at cross-purposes with the others. A sense of the self and the world as fallen prevents Santayana from ever really embracing the naturalism indicated here and which becomes a central theme in his later prose writings. "Birth," as he writes in Sonnet XXV, is to him a "great disaster." "Do you suppose the slow, painful, nasty, bloody process by which things in this world grow, is worth having for the sake of the perfection of a moment?" he wrote a friend in 1887. Metaphysical heights and depths remain unreal, despite his contrived gestures, just as the invocation to "Mother Earth" at the conclusion of Sonnet I can never be anything more for him than a literary allusion.

Literary allusion, however, in many ways defines Santayana's poetic terrain. Already in his first sonnet sequence, and more consistently in the second sequence that he wrote after his elaborately named "metanoia" or "change of heart," Santayana's sonnets are shaped by pseudo-Neoplatonist-troubadour-Renaissance Italian tradition as described in his chapter on "Platonic Love in Some Italian Poets" in *Interpretations of Poetry and Religion*. The seriousness of this reference is compromised by the fact that Santayana lacks any impelling Neoplatonic or troubadour Beloved, and that he rejects the Platonist metaphysical ladder of ascent, which lingers on in the poems only as a kind of decor. In Sonnet IX,

> Above the battlements of heaven rise
> The glittering domes of the gods' golden dwelling,
> Whence, like a constellation, passion-quelling,
> The truth of all things feeds immortal eyes.

The unreality of the gods and their battlements is matched by their "passion-quelling" effect. Santayana's is a poetry of Eros without the Eros. One may indeed ask, as he does in Sonnet XXXIX, "What ghostly mistress?" As Santayana himself puts it, he is

> Unmindful of the changing outer skies,
> Where now, perchance some new-born Eros flies
> Or some old Cronos from his throne is hurled
> I heed them not . . .   (Sonnet XIV)

Several sonnets suggest that Santayana's closeted homosexuality may be one source for this stillborn Eros (e.g. XXXVI and XXXVII). It finds its clearest expression in "Chorus," one of the "Various Poems" that are not sonnets and show rather more linguistic flexibility. There he devotes to "Immortal love" a series of items of which he has little experience: an "antelope," a "hornèd bull . . . bellowing to his herd," concluding with an aesthetic image:

> The painted bird
> For thee hath music and to thee addressed,
> And the brief sadness of his dying note
> Is for thy bitter absence and thy pain.

This is a revealing moment. The "painted bird" as aesthetic object is image and product of the death and painful absence of Eros. Santayana described his "metanoia" as a conversion which "rendered external things indifferent," a mode of renunciation where "the whole world belongs to me implicitly when I have given it all up, and am wedded to nothing particular in it." In many ways, he retains a structure of ascetic dualism, which lacking any metaphysical basis, preserves its sacrifices while granting few of its rewards (see Sonnet VI – "Love not as do the flesh-imprisoned men," or VII – "I would I might forget that I am I, / And break the heavy chain [of] the body's tomb"). As "metanoia," what this comes to is less renunciation than repression. And form itself becomes his ultimate image for it. Art is

> A wall, a wall to hem the azure sphere
> And hedge me in from the disconsolate hills! . . .
> Come no profane insatiate mortal near
> With the contagion of his passionate ills
>
> (Sonnet XV)

Santayana's formalism, erected like a wall against passion, ills, and mortality in a kind of facsimile of monastic retreat, becomes an intentional aesthetic.

Even before Santayana, Harvard had other poets of formal commitment if not aesthetic theory: not only the Firesiders, but perhaps especially Frederick

Goddard Tuckerman (1821–73). His sonnet writing seems almost a fore-shadowing of the 1890s Harvard poetry-to-be. Tuckerman, having attended the Episcopalian Bishop Hopkin's School in Burlington, Vermont and then Harvard (where Jones Very was briefly his tutor), graduated as a lawyer. But a rich inheritance saved him from having to choose between the different halves of Santayana's American mind. He was thus freed for culture as amateur botanist, astronomer, and poet. These he pursued as a recluse in Greenfield, Massachusetts, even while he enjoyed literary relationships with Tennyson, Emerson, Hawthorne, Longfellow, and Bryant, to whom he sent gift copies of the several sonnet sequences he published in the 1860s (Emerson published some of them in his *Parnassus* collection of 1880). The death of Tuckerman's wife in 1857 after ten years of marriage plunged him into a grief from which he did not recover, deepening his isolation in life and art.

Tuckerman's greatest distinction is to have had his ode on "The Cricket" named by Ivor Winters as "the greatest poem in English of the century." Tuckerman's sonnets are intricate linguistic structures, densely interwoven with details from a naturalist's notebook. Perhaps most successful is the double-sonnet, "The starry flower, the flowerlike stars that fade," in which minute floral patterns find their counterpart in the cosmological heavens. But Tuckerman's world, like Santayana's, has collapsed the metaphysical. While there is often a Hopkinsesque naming of parts of the world, there is little sense of transcendent logos holding them together. Only the sonnet form itself can attempt to do so.

> Dark fens of cedar, hemlock branches gray
> With trees and trail of mosses, wringing-wet,
> Beds of the black pitchpine in dead leaves set
> Whose wasted red has wasted to white away
> Remnants of rain and droppings of decay,
> Why hold ye so my heart, nor dimly let
> Through your deep leaves the light of yesterday,
> The faded glimmer of a sunshine set?
> Is that in your darkness, shut from strife,
> The bread of tears becomes the bread of life?
> Far from the roar of day, beneath your boughs
> Fresh griefs beat tranquilly, and loves and vows
> Grow green in your gray shadows, dearer far
> Even than all lovely lights and roses are?

Tuckerman introduces some mild experimentation into the strict sonnet form by way of rhyme scheme and meter, but he can hardly be said to break new ground. As is the case here, his poems are mostly addressed to an isolated self: they are concerned with isolation, in a poetic form of self-enclosure. Nature, for all its detail, serves essentially as image and foil for an interiority "shut from strife" as by thick overhanging verdure, cloying and decayed. There is an echo of sacramental language, tentatively posed as a question, but ultimately declining the transubstantiation it recalls: "The bread of tears becomes the bread of life?" What remains at the poem's center are introspective griefs "dearer far / Even than all lovely lights and roses" of exterior reality; griefs that "beat" like the sonnet's own meter, in an inner space "Far from the roar of day," which is in turn an image of the sonnet itself.

The most promising of Harvard's formalist poets was Trumbull Stickney (1874–1904), whose 1890s Harvard association with Santayana's Laodicean Club covers the greater part of a career cut off by his sudden death from a brain tumor in 1904. Stickney's work is poised between the nineteenth and twentieth centuries. Like Santayana, Stickney was both European and American. His father, a professor of classics, privately tutored him as the family moved restlessly between various cities, including Geneva, where he was born, Florence, London, Nice, Paris, and New York. He entered Harvard in 1891, where writing and editing for the *Harvard Monthly* became his main occupation, and its group of poets his social circle: Santayana, Robert Moss Lovett, and William Vaughn Moody, along with Henry Cabot Lodge and Henry Adams. Majoring in the classics, he graduated from Harvard and went on to the Sorbonne, where he became the first American to earn a *Doctorat des Lettres*. For his shorter thesis he prepared an edition, in Latin, of fifteenth-century letters from a Venetian ambassador to Rome, which he had discovered by chance in the library at Lucca. His longer thesis, "Les Sentences dans la poésie grecque," studied gnomic, aphoristic elements in Greek verse. He returned to Harvard in 1903 as an instructor in Greek. He died there the following year, at the age of thirty.

Stickney's poems include *Dramatic Verses* (the only poems he published, in 1902, during his lifetime), and his *Poems*, published posthumously in 1905, along with odes and other occasional verses. His Harvard formalism is perhaps most clearly evident in his sonnets, such as the *Sonnets from Greece*, where he spent three months before leaving Europe for America. Classicism deeply penetrates Stickney's work, whether in subject or in orientation. Dramatic verses are spoken by "Lucretius"; by "Kalypso" to Odysseus. "Oneiropolos" is a kind of dialogue between Indian and Greek cultures, both of which he studied. "In the Past" seems to restage without naming the River Styx, evoked as an interior stagnation:

> There lies a somnolent lake
> Under a noiseless sky,
> Where never the mornings break
> Nor the evenings die . . .
>
> And the hours lag dead in the air
> With a sense of coming eternity
> To the heart of the lonely boatman there:
> That boatman am I.

In "Mnemosyne," a poem especially noticed by nineteenth-century readers, Stickney poses "long sun-sweetened summer days" of memory against a "cold," "empty," "lonely," "dark" present "country" in autumn. But this is less personal nostalgia than historiography. The ancient world is for Stickney a cultural point of view, which his own world seems to have lost.

A poem like "Song," with its refrain: "A cuckoo said in my brain: 'Not Yet'," shows Stickney's promise in lyric music and structure. It is a text at once formal and flexible. But Stickney's senses of loss remain haunting. His "An Athenian Garden" can almost stand for his own work:

> The burned and dusty garden said:
> My leaves are echoes, and thy earth
> Is packed with footsteps of the dead.

When, however, he writes about specific sites in Greece, nostalgia merges into the concrete present, giving his Greek sonnets a clear focus. His sonnet on "Eleusis," revisiting the place of "a thousand years processional / Winding around the Eleusinian bay," provides a glimpse into how the natural world was alive and sacral within Greek experience:

> As then the litanies antiphonal
> Obscurely through the pillars sang away,
> It dawned, and in the shaft of sudden day
> Demeter smiling gave her bread to all.
> They drew as waves out of a twilight main,
> Long genuflecting multitudes, to feed
> With God upon the sacramental grain.

Natural pillars open intrinsically into antiphonal celebration. Past ceremony enriches the present. And mystery penetrates the mundane as "sacramental grain." To this immediate classical experience of the imminent world, Stickney opposes what he condemns (in an essay on "Herakleitos" for the *Harvard Monthly*, February 1895) as the Teutonic "provincialism" of "metaphysical abstractions, investing the world with strange values, elaborating explanations for insane hypotheses."

Reading backwards, it is possible to discern nascently in Stickney, as in Santayana, what later became a sharp drawing of battle lines between Romanticism and Classicism for Eliot, Pound, and T. E. Hulme. Stickney describes his poems as a "revival of self-restraint," a poetry of concrete containment, in contrast to Wordsworth, whose world Stickney describes as a repository of vague powers. This containment is finally realized as aesthetic formalization itself. Stickney's sonnet on "Eleusis," in its imagery of "litanies antiphonal," is self-referential. The sonnet "Sunium" converts the whole scene of mountain and cloud into art-object, as lyre:

> These are the strings of the Aegean lyre
> Across the sky and sea in glory hung
> Columns of white thro' which the wind has flung
> The clouds and stars, and drawn the rain and fire.
> Their flutings now to fill the notes' desire
> Are strained and dubious, yet in music young
> They cast their full-blown answer far along
> To where in sea the island hills expire.
> How bravely from the quarry's earthen gloom
> In snow they rose amid the blue to stand
> Melodious and alone on Sunium!
> They shall not wither back into the land.
> The sun that harps them with his golden hand
> Doth slowly with his hand of gold consume.

The Greek world is presented here as its own becoming-into-art. This transmutation, however, remains an after-image of a lost past. The "flutings" of this world-lyre can be felt "now" only as "strained and dubious," compared to the "music young" that "cast their full-blown answer far along." And the figures of lyre and music establish the poem as an image of itself, as the composition of elements standing against, not inside, the movement of time. Its magnificence is consumed within its own declared moment.

Formalization begins in Stickney to take shape as an enclosed world, containing its own elements in a classical restraint. In Santayana, these impulses become an expressed aesthetic program. Santayana's treatise, *The Sense of Beauty*, devotes a long section to "Form," with form defined as symmetry and unity, in an art "object" increasingly geometric, spatialized, totalized, and static. Beauty is "value positive, intrinsic, and objectified," and form is "the unity of a manifold." Through symmetry, "the parts, coalescing, form a single object [of] unity and simplicity." As he reiterates in his theoretical discussions in *Interpretations of Poetry and Religion*, "human reason and human imagination require a certain totality." Poetry is measure, where measure is a condition of perfection, for perfection requires that order should be pervasive, that not only the whole before us should have a form, but that every part in turn should have a form of its own, and that those parts should be coordinated among themselves as the whole is coordinated with the other parts of some greater cosmos.

As in the High Modernism of the new century, Santayana's emphasis on unity and totality emerges as a polemical attack against Romanticism. Beauty is essentially formal for Santayana: "we can only see beauty in so far as we introduce form." Only an "illusion, proper to the romantic temperament, lends a mysterious charm to things which are indefinite and indefinable." From this unsatisfactory, Romanticized viewpoint, Greek perfection seems cloying; but any work of art "which remains indeterminate is a failure . . . The emotion, not being embodied, fails to constitute the beauty of anything." Romanticism is little more than a "loose and somewhat helpless state of mind," an "example of aesthetic incapacity."

That Santayana's ideal of perfected formal unity is essentially ahistorical and atemporal is another foreshadowing of High Modernism. Symmetry, he writes in *The Sense of Beauty*, must contribute to "the unity of our perception," in a manner that is "instantaneous." History itself is nothing but a collection of "indeterminate material," and only attains value when, "like poetry," it asserts "beauty, power, and adequacy of form in which the indeterminate material of human life is presented." As against the Romantics, he is pleased to "prefer the unchangeable to the irrecoverable." This formalist ahistoricism underlies Santayana's attacks on Walt Whitman. Santayana, it is true, cites Whitman as the one American poet who escapes the genteel tradition, but it is an escape that, for Santayana, registers an aesthetic failure. To Santayana, Whitman represents an "attitude utterly disintegrating." His imagination is nothing more than a "passive sensorium for the registering of impressions" in which "no element of construction remained," leaving only a "lazy, desultory apprehension." "Everything" in Whitman "is a momentary pulsation of a liquid and structureless whole." But Santayana's inability to see in Whitman anything but pure "sensation . . . without underlying structure" is directly tied to Whitman's lack of interest in subsuming temporal sequence into unitary wholeness. Whitman, as Santayana complains, offers "no total vision, no grasp of the whole reality," and Santayana prefers a mind that "does not easily discriminate the successive phases of an action in which it is still engaged; it does not arrange in a temporal series the elements of a single perception, but posits them all together as constituting a permanent and real object."

The configuration which emerges in Santayana's essays, as in his poetic writing, opposes form to history, to time, and is detached from nature as a distinct, alternative world. In a sonnet called "The Power of Art," he contrasts the beauties of nature "that by changing live" against what art produces. Natural beauties "in their begetting are o'erthrown, / Nor may the sentenced minutes find reprieve." But while we may not impart "to our works . . . [the] shifting light of life,"

> Yet may our hands immortalize the day
> When life was sweet, and save from utter death
> The sacred past that should not pass away.

Santayana had explained in *The Sense of Beauty* that the sonnet form offered the best, although still inferior, modern equivalent to classical unity through its interlinkage of rhyme and parts. Such unity is the subject of "The Power of Art." Santayana does not see art as an enduring tribute to natural temporality, as he sees Shakespeare to do, faulting him for failing to present "fragments of experience [as though] fallen together into a perfect picture [in which] the universe is total." Art here is antagonistic to nature's changing beauty. Its immortal "day" transforms the "shifting light of life" into a totality of the lost, "sacred past." Nature is eclipsed in an art that he dedicates to the "eternal Whole."

On one level, Santayana's aesthetic makes increasingly ambitious claims for art. As a unification of its materials, it stands outside of time, representing a totalized culture which he, like Eliot after him, names tradition. This tradition forms an ahistorical context to which the individual artist must "discipline" himself, something Whitman refuses to do. But Santayana's claim for art as an independent realm, self-controlled and absolute, is in the end constructed as an obverse image to the world Santayana felt to be commercial, crass, and victorious – a world which left little room for art, or for him. And yet in the process, it derives from and mirrors that world. In its detachment, its enclosure, its self-sufficiency, Santayana's high culture in effect reproduces the genteel irrelevance it is meant to protest. Like religion, which he absorbs into poetry as a formalized fiction, poetry's cultural place is little more than a holiday "relaxation," with artists performing feast-day functions on the order of "cooks, hairdressers, and florists." In one of his crankiest essays, "Materialism and Idealism," he once again resorts to the gendered language so fundamental to him, and so telling: "What is civilization? Porcelain bath-tubs, et cetera?. . . Civilized means citified, trained, faithful to some regimen deliberately instituted . . . [But] the American intellect is shy and feminine; it paints nature in water-colours; whereas the sharp masculine eye sees the world as a moving-picture – rapid, dramatic, vulgar."

Santayana's aesthetic is itself a product and mirror of that split in the American mind against which he protests. Masquerading as aesthetic autonomy, his conception of art is socially determined. Longing for the "perfect human discipline . . . of a Greek city or of the British upper classes," Santayana is faced instead with the "material restlessness" of "a new type of American . . . the untrained, pushing, cosmopolitan orphan," "Jewish, Irish, German, Italian, or whatever they may be . . . [arriving] not in the hope of founding a godly commonwealth, but only of prospering in an untrammelled one." Not only Whitman's writing, but Whitman's democracy, is "a mass of images without structure," collapsing "all extraordinary gifts of genius or virtue" into "material improvement" and, horrors, "an actual equality among all men." Tradition is thereby demoted to a genteel, feminized margin, mere "academic luxuries, fit to amuse the ladies," and lacking both authority and power.

What Santayana's work suggests is that the other side of the coin of formalism is money. The more rigidly self-constituted, autonomous, and absolute the claims for poetic form, the more it mirrors, inversely, a commercial culture that denies it cultural priority. Some of Santayana's best writing occurs when this cultural confrontation comes to the surface. Of his poems, the most readable are the looser Odes, less straitjacketed than his sonnet writing, and openly opposing "this labouring nation" against an "inward gladness . . . in some Persian / Garden of roses" (Ode I). In Ode II,

> My heart rebels against my generation,
> That talks of freedom and is slave to riches,
> And, toiling 'neath each day's ignoble burden,
>   Boasts of the morrow.
>
> No space for noonday rest or midnight watches,
> No purest joy of breathing under heaven!
> Wretched themselves, they heap, to make them happy,
>   Many possessions.

Ode III frankly names Columbus as villain:

> He gave the world another world, and ruin
> Brought upon blameless, river-loving nations,
> Cursed Spain with barren gold, and made the Andes
>   Fiefs of Saint Peter;
>
> While in the cheerless North the thrifty Saxon
> Planted his corn, and, narrowing his bosom,
> Made covenant with God, and by keen virtue
>   Trebled his riches.

What venture hast thou left us, bold Columbus?
What honour left thy brothers, brave Magellan?
Daily the children of the rich for pastime
    Circle the planet.

Trumbull Stickney likewise wrote a sonnet against Columbus as one who "rash and greedy took the screaming main / And vanished out before the hurricane / Into the sunset after merchandise." Stickney's preferred outcome to this betrayal of culture to money is apocalyptic destruction, in which its world would "Pass before us like a cloud of dust." Santayana too concludes his "Ode to the New World" in apocalyptic dust and almost gnostic denial of the natural world for some remote, inhuman, absolutely composed realm:

Until the patient earth, made dry and barren,
Sheds all her herbage in a final winter,
And the gods turn their eyes to some far distant
    Bright constellation.

In the wake of Santayana, a group of modern writers emerged out of Harvard, each facing the formal and cultural problems reflected in Santayana's work. Edward Arlington Robinson's first volume of poems, published without much notice during the 1890s, restored to formalism some natural language and a dramatic, which is to say more temporalized and historicized focus. Robert Frost, who developed a strong distaste for Santayana beginning at Harvard and lasting all his life – "Santayana," he said, "is the enemy of my spirit" – was able to discover formal power and complex figuration within natural language itself. Wallace Stevens and T. S. Eliot each rejected Santayana's conflation of religion with art: Stevens finally to abandon, Eliot finally to reclaim, metaphysical space. Eliot in particular then developed an aesthetic whose notions of autonomy, discipline, and unity in many ways echo Santayana's, even as he found a new accommodation between formalized and natural poetic language. In Santayana himself, the defense of poetry against his cultural world results in a deadliness of form. In trying to rescue the aesthetic, Santayana reified and entombed it.

4

❦

PLURAL IDENTITIES

LOCAL-COLOR POETRY

Is there a local-color poetry, corresponding to the prose that emerged in the decades following the Civil War? The genre of poetry in itself moves representation away from the realism strongly associated with regionalism. What finds expression in prose as concrete, detailed description and psychologized portraiture, is pushed in poetry towards stylization of character and setting, and a balladic treatment of narrative – with or without dialogue, represented speech, and dialect. This generic difference allows impulses and issues to become visible, which are perhaps obscured in features specific to fiction and discussions of them. The very definition of the "local" and its meanings within post-bellum American culture takes on a distinctive color when approached through its poetic representations.

"Regionalism" seems increasingly partial as a term for the literature(s) of diversity which emerged towards the nineteenth century's end. Yet characterizing this literary diversity is in some sense as challenging as characterizing the diversity of America generally. The term "region" was itself undergoing dynamic change of meaning in the post-Civil War era, within a newly reconceived nationality. But geography stands as only one of a number of differentiations becoming newly evident, or evident in new ways, within American cultural development. These include not only emerging senses of diverse locations, but also of languages, especially dialects, of religious, racial, and ethnic affiliations – both in terms of new immigrations and the newly emerging status of the black freedmen – as well as a new self-consciousness regarding gender definitions.

Readings of local-color writing have for the most part framed its interest in variety within an overriding momentum towards consolidation initiated, if not imposed, by the Civil War. This can be traced as a complex of interrelated movements: demographically, from the country to the city; politically, from the section to a reconstituted and centralized federal government; economically, from agriculture to industry; alongside the revolution in technology, permitting new communications and transport across far-flung areas; and the experience of the Civil War itself, as it brought diverse groups into contact as well as conflict. The overall pattern may be read as a drive to a greater and greater integration in American life, one which, however, also entailed a fragmentation and dissolution of earlier forms of community. "Regional" literature in this way is paradoxically linked to an America emerging from the Civil War into more centralized national organization, a centralization, however, which assaults earlier senses of community while failing to provide a new communal cohesion for those being displaced. The proliferations of regional writing thus look like a new and short-lived freedom to explore increasingly minor and irrelevant differences, no longer politically or even socially of primary significance, and no longer nationally threatening. It also seems closely allied to a sense of loss for an American world that is vanishing. In such readings, regional writing appears as essentially nostalgic, whether with backward-looking regret or in critique of the social forms it records.

But local-color poetry has broader contexts. It finds its configurations not in the progressive submergence of diversity, paradoxically kicking at the pricks of a triumphant federal culture, nor only as a nostalgic longing for a cohesion displaced by social fragmentation. Rather, this post-Civil War literature suggests the exploration of new senses and definitions regarding what constitutes American identity and the structures internal to it. Almost from its beginnings, what might be called the grammar of American identity has been in dispute. Is it singular or is it plural? Both options are present from the first colonizations. The nineteenth century emerges as an increasingly complex stage for these contending grammars of definition. Post-Civil War local-color writing represents a swing towards the sense of identity as plural, in new ways and with new implications than had been the case through most of the nineteenth century. It may be said to foreshadow, or show the first glimmerings, of new senses of pluralism that will emerge much later in the twentieth century.

Within local color's representation, pluralism is not only a relationship between diverse social units. Instead, it is situated within each individual's experience and self-constitution. What local color's literary diversifications suggest is a structure of pluralism that resides not only between different groups, but penetrates into each individual. Identity comes to involve the multiple participation in several differing associations. The literary text becomes a site in which crossing, competing, conflicting, coordinating identities confront each other, including not only geographic, but also ethnic, racial, religious, social-economic, and gendered elements in relation to each other. None of these identities serves as necessarily prior to the others, nor is any one absolutely defining and exclusive. As against efforts to define the self essentially and fundamentally through one, overriding definition, these texts – often in a tentative, indirect, and incomplete fashion – explore and assert a number of distinct modes of self-definition, with identity represented as the inter-crossing negotiation between multiple affiliations. Multiplicity and conflict become felt and expressed not only in terms of, and between, groups, but rather within individuals. The issue is not only, or exactly, a new assertion of marginal figures, as against central ones, but rather a challenge to the whole notion of both the margin and the center. Pluralism itself comes to extend beyond the ante-bellum emphasis on region, while individual identity becomes an arena of pluralist multiplicity, conflict, and negotiation.

Local-color writing was already thought of by its practitioners as a kind of literary pluralism. But the specific balance, or direction, between diversity and unity remained uncertain. William Dean Howells, in his essay on "American Literary Centers," praises the opening of multiple literary centers in a "decentralized literature" that gives "its fidelity to our decentralized life." But it remains unclear whether Howells ultimately approves diversity, or only does so as a fuller expression of a single national consciousness. As he also writes, "as soon as the country began to feel its life in every limb with the coming of peace, it began to speak in the varying accents of all the different sections."

A similar ambivalence can be felt in Edward Eggleston's 1892 Preface to *The Hoosier Schoolmaster*: "The taking up of life in this regional way has made our literature really national by the only process possible." In these dicussions, diversity continues to be thought of mainly in geographic terms, as regional. And the question remains: is the regional a means towards constructing a national sense? or does it make its own claims, redefining the very sense of the national? This question is posed, but not answered, by Hamlin Garland as well. In "Local Color in Art" (a paper first delivered at the 1893 Chicago Exposition), he observes that "the similarities do not please, do not forever stimulate and feed as do the differences." Yet his plea for difference remains in the service of an American literature which "must be national, [although] to be national it must deal with conditions peculiar to our own land and climate." These early discussions do less to assert diversity than to show that notions of it are undergoing transformation.

Among poets, it is James Whitcomb Riley (1849–1916) who perhaps best incarnates local color in its aspect as a regional poetry of nostalgic loss. Riley is the most obvious poetic correlative to such prose writers as Thomas Nelson Page and Joel Chandler Harris in the South, with their dialect impersonations of happy slaves on happy plantations so cruelly disrupted by that inexplicable Civil War. Riley's writing has been collected into eleven volumes of more or less formulaic versification, all wildly popular within his own lifetime. Born in 1849 in the village of Greenfield, Indiana, Riley came to verse writing after a motley career as sign painter, house painter, Bible salesman, traveling medicine salesman, and lawyer. In 1875, he became the local editor for his home town paper, moving on to a journalistic career in which poetry proved to be his best ticket to fortune and fame.

Riley addresses himself to the common man, of whom he said: "It is my office to interpret him." As such, his poetry is peculiarly, if not impersonal, then unindividuated. He speaks for, and indeed as, the communal person. As Harriet Monroe observes in her obituary piece in *Poetry* magazine, "He tells the tale of the tribe." This is reflected in his incorporation of folklore elements and superstitions of the popular imagination, most famously in his poem "Little Orphant Annie" with its "Gobble-uns 'at gits you / Ef you don't watch out." The poem asserts a general conformity and obedience to social norms: of piety (the "Gobble-uns git" the little boy for failing to say his prayers) or of family authority (a little girl is "git" for mocking her "ole folks").

As is fitting for a nostalgic poetry, the figure of the child pervades Riley's work. A sizable portion of it was marketed as children's literature, while the remainder offers adult memories of childhood – a "lament of my own lost youth," as Mark Twain put it, "as no words of mine can do." But the child can be seen as a more generalized figure for an aging America bidding farewell to its earlier worlds. Riley's revisited places are not sites for solitary, Wordsworthian personal reconstitutions through recollection. They are instead crowded social gathering-places. At "The Old Swimmin'-Hole," a Riley favorite, "tracks of our bare feet" merge together and the poet speaks as a collective "we." The pool is a mirror, not for individual consciousness but composite identity – a whole society's joint reflection and regret.

"But the lost joys is past!" What is Riley nostalgic for? There is, first, the threat to rural life posed by new technology, transport, and communications. At "The Old Swimmin'-Hole," "The bridge of the railroad now crosses the spot / Where the old divin'-log lays sunk and fergot." But Riley more generally responds to a new sense of region within a new national structure. At its inception, the country's regional divisions seemed to threaten national unity. Each section even had a separate judicial system from colonial times. The greatest danger to the new Union, Washington had said in his "Farewell Address" (1796), lay in "Geographical discriminations: Northern and Southern; Atlantic and Western; whence designing men may endeavor to excite a belief that there is a real difference of local interests and views." Individual regions were referred to as though separate nations: Benjamin Franklin called Philadelphia his "new country" in the *Autobiography*, while Hawthorne a century later observed:

"We have so much country that we have no country at all . . . everything falls
away except one's native State."

But if regional divisions asserted America's sectional nature, they alterna-
tively projected a national vision, where each section claimed to represent the
entire nation. Each region regarded itself as a synecdoche representing the
American whole. It is this sense of universality and priority in the nation that
weakened with the Civil War. Riley's poem "Old Indiany" parodically recalls
such earlier regional claims to priority:

> Old Indiany, 'course we know
> Is first, and best, and most, also.
> Of *all* the States' whole forty-four: –
> She's first in ever'thing, that's shore!
> And *best* in ever'way as yet
> Made known to man; and you kin bet
> She's *most*, because she won't confess
> She ever was, or will be, less!

Riley's use of dialect emerges in this failure of part to claim to be whole,
which left each region as mere part. James Russell Lowell's *Biglow Papers*
presents its Yankee dialect as the representative of the American Revolutionary
discourse of freedom. Riley's dialect, in contrast, is meant to feel eccentric. Yet
it also has a close relationship to genteel writing. Riley, like Lowell, divided his
work between dialect and standard genteel English, modeled, as he repeatedly
said, on the New England poets and particularly Longfellow. To this "Gentlest
kinsman of Humanity," as Riley writes in one of several poetic tributes to
Longfellow, "Worlds listen, lulled and solaced at the spell / That folds and
holds us." Riley's dialect in many ways shares these genteel suppositions as
to poetry's role, even if he gives up on the earlier claim to represent an elite
American culture. For Riley, too, poetry lulls and solaces, whether as dialect
or genteel. As he advised a younger poet, "Keep 'em all sunny and sweet and
wholesome clean to the core; or, if ever tragic, with sound hopes ultimate,
if pathetic." Riley's dialect is little more than genteel verse spelled funny. It
never establishes itself as a truly distinctive identity, neither does it attempt
to create a nationally resonant poetic language.

Local-color writing by women marks a bolder confrontation with the complexities of identity than Riley's does. Recent discussions have explored the
tie between regional and women's writing, noting that a good deal of local-
color work was in fact produced by women. But the attempt to define local
color as specifically a women's tradition of writing is weakened by the broad
range of local-color writing by men. This is especially apparent if city, and
not only rural, settings are accepted as sites for this literature's diverse locations. The later poetry of Stephen Crane would strongly represent such a city

localism. Edward Arlington Robinson's work likewise fulfills many of the criteria claimed for a specifically female regional tradition, as this is associated with socially marginalized viewpoints. Robinson's Tilbury Town, with its eccentric inhabitants abruptly illuminated, similarly features economic, social, and psychological displacement. Robinson, with other local-color writers, men and women, moves in directions Riley fails to, of exploring localized places and persons as complex figures.

What women's local-color writing does dramatize is a dawning sense of plural as opposed to unitary self-definition. Identity comes to be seen not as single and representative, but rather as containing or negotiating multiple elements. The point is not to subordinate the regional element to gender, but to see how the two are mutually negotiated. Region becomes one factor among others in an ongoing work of defining a self complicated by a consciousness of gender, which emerges into prominence, often alongside a further dimension related to social-economic placement as another element in identity. The question of economic status in fact frames local-color work in several directions. The subjects it depicts often are drawn from an underprivileged economic order – whether in country, village, or city. At the same time, the genre's audience, and market, often consisted of an upper-class, urban, spectator public wanting to consume the country's vanishing locations. Local color tends to handle its economic contexts, however, less as a self-conscious critique of class structure than in terms of a more traditional criticism of material desire within American culture.

Local color as a complex juncture between regional, gender, and economic identities can be seen in the work of women poets such as Lucy Larcom, Alice and Phoebe Cary, or Rose Terry Cooke (who is known more for her fiction). It may be seen to extend to Emma Lazarus, who pushes identity issues towards religious-ethnic expression, and Frances Harper, who adds considerations of race. In Lucy Larcom's work (1824–93), sea, land, and townscapes of her native Massachusetts become articulated through feminized figures. The poem "The Light-Houses (Baker's Island, off Beverly, Massachusetts)" presents the light-houses as "Two pale sisters, all alone." Their "long hopeless gleams" anticipate the grief of as yet "unconscious widows" over lost sailors. They also represent a steadfast, domestic hope, keeping alive "Fireside joys for men." Larcom's most famous poem, "Hannah Binding Shoes," recounts the faithful devotion of a New England woman as she waits twenty years for her husband to come back from the sea.

In some of Larcom's texts, region holds center stage; in others, gender does. Larcom revisits the scenes of Pilgrim landings in "They Said" and "The Lady Arbella." But her emphasis is on the arrival in America as it challenged Pilgrim women and made them, in their reticence and endurance, heroic. In "Mistress

Hale of Beverly," she retells a story of witchcraft accusation, and triumph over it, through the viewpoint of Mrs. Hale, a woman falsely accused. "A Gambrel Roof" makes this characteristic feature of New England architecture the site of a wife's protest (and subterfuge) against her colonel husband's revolutionary demand that she stop having tea-parties. "Goody Grunsell's House" presents the house and its New England setting "On a headland slope / Against the gray of the sea" as imagery for the crossed life of an old woman who is, piece by piece, "burning the house over her head" as she survives, impoverished and embittered.

Larcom's personal biography evokes many of the historical shifts that her writing addresses. After the death of her father, she became a "Lowell girl," working from the ages of eleven to twenty-one in the Lowell Mills' experimental factory system, which gave girls an opportunity to leave home to work while retaining many characteristics of a domestic framework. Larcom published her poems in the *Lowell Offering* newsletter supported by the Mills, continuing to do so during her failed attempt to go West and teach school in Illinois. After her return East, she taught for nine years at the Wheaton Female Seminary. She was eventually able to free herself from onerous teaching by working as an editor and writer in Boston. She collaborated extensively with John Greenleaf Whittier in editing several anthologies, an increasingly popular form during this period of literary diversification.

Larcom's life moves between Eastern and Western viewpoints of America, and through new possibilities for women in education and employment. Never marrying, she wrote poems such as "Unwedded," "The School-Mistress," and "A Loyal Woman's No" which reflect on the self-definition and status of the single woman, typically in a Northern context (the Loyal Woman says No to a man with Southern sympathies). "The School-Mistress" concludes by declaring that she is "Glad to earn a living." Other poems recognize the economic implications of marital status and marriage as an economic institution. In "Getting Along" the man has married for money, and the couple get along only in the most ironic senses, across severe alienation. In "Her Choice," the woman has chosen a farmer-man of her own social class, over what she now recognizes to have been a self-destructive fantasy of marrying a "town-bred curl {with} contempt for the boors who till the land."

The poems of Alice (1820–71) and Phoebe (1824–71) Cary similarly move between geographic, gendered, and economic viewpoints. Born in Cincinnati, Ohio, the Cary sisters moved to New York City in 1850, where they lived together, writing poetry and prose, and presiding over a weekly literary salon. Both sisters wrote poems that recall their Western origins, often combining ballad elements with unsentimental touches exposing the difficulties

experienced by frontier women. In Alice Cary's "The West Country," cabins lie "like birds nests in / The wild green prairie grass," but images of the
"tired hands" of women with "fingers worn and thin" compromise that promise
of freedom. In "Growing Rich," husband and wife lead separate lives as the
man accumulates wealth on the farm while the woman mourns the family from
which she has been separated, and who remain caught in the coal-pit and mill.
"The Washerwoman" depicts the life of toil of a poor woman in a poor village.

While Alice Cary's work suggests a local-color extension of the conventions of female verse writing, Phoebe Cary more unusually ventures into a
sharper, satirical domain. Her work brings into special relief contiguities and
transformations between local-color and genteel writing by way of satire. Poe,
Wordsworth, and Goldsmith ("When Lovely Women") are all treated ironically, with Longfellow something of a specialty. Phoebe Cary's parodies characteristically work through gender shifts. "Annabel Lee" becomes "Samuel
Brown," making Poe's erotics of beautiful, dead women into a calculated war
between classes:

> I was a child, and he was a child,
> In that dwelling down in town . . .
> And this was the reason that, long ago . . .
> A girl came out of her carriage,
> Courting my beautiful Samuel Brown;
> And shut him up in a dwelling-house,
> In a street quite up in town.

Wordsworth's "Lucy" becomes "Jacob":

> A boulder, by a larger stone
> Half hidden in the mud,
> Fair as a man when only one
> Is in the neighborhood.

As to Longfellow, his melancholy poetry about poetry is brought decidedly
down to earth. Various foods substitute for verse as comfort and solace when
"The Day is Done." "The Psalm of Life" becomes a raucous psalm to a wife:
"What the heart of the young woman said to the old maid":

> Tell me not in idle jingle
>   Marriage is an empty dream
> For the girl is dead that's single
>   And things are not what they seem . . .
>
> Not enjoyment and not sorrow
>   Is our destined end or way
> But to act, that each tomorrow
>   Nearer brings the wedding day.

In the work of these women poets, region claims neither to represent the whole or core of American tradition, nor to determine individual identity. Even New England, as Howells observes, ceases "to be a nation unto itself" and has become only another region. If genteel poetry is generalizing, presenting itself as speaking for the American whole (which is then also narrowly defined), then local-color writing speaks from particular positions grouped in various combinations. Regional identity, recognized as partial, takes its place beside a newly self-conscious identity of gender, while both carry further social and economic implications.

Local-color writing emerges in an America increasingly complex in cultural, ethnic, and social composition. Towards the century's end, national origins emerge as a pivotal image of American diversity. The question of American identity as singular or plural becomes increasingly posed in terms of ethnicity or national descent. This was not entirely new to the end of the nineteenth century. Ethnic diversity had characterized the American population from its colonial inception. The early settlers included not only English, but Scottish, Scottish-Irish, German, Dutch, and Swedish peoples, in addition to the Africans brought by force and alongside the populations native to America, with Spanish and French populations across shifting borders. This plural population took shape alongside and in complex alignment with regional differentiation. Immigrant arrivals first congregated in broad geographic areas (the English in New England and Virgina; Dutch and Swedes in the Hudson and Delaware river valleys; Germans in Pennsylvania; Norwegians in Wisconsin and Minnesota; Africans in the South, etc.). Yet the earliest established and dominant cultural model was English: in language, law, religion, and social structures. These continued to dominate (although not without tensions) all other groups and later arrivals. John Jay speaks for this English norm when he describes Americans in *Federalist* 2 as "one united people, a people descended from the same ancestors, speaking the same language, professing the same religion, attached to the same principles of government, very similar in their manners and customs . . ."

Such unitary notions of American identity prevail through most of the nineteenth century. They take, however, several forms, in response to a variety of historical developments – most notably the successive waves of immigration that took place through the course of the century. The first form, or model, for a unitary American identity might be called inclusive singularity. This involves accepting diverse populations, but only as they assimilate to the dominant English culture. John Quincy Adams implies this view in his 1818 letter to a German baron, stating that immigrants are welcome to "accommodate themselves to the character, moral, political, and physical, of this country," which means "cast[ing] off the European skin, never to resume it." Washington, who claimed that "the more homogeneous our citizens . . . the greater our prospect of permanent union," and Jefferson, who praised "manners, morals, and habits [that] are perfectly homogeneous," likewise speak for such an inclusive model. Differences in geographical sections represent, in this model, less the possibility of genuine diversity than competing claims by each area as to which represents the true American heritage.

A second form of singular identity may be called exclusive singularity, which views America as essentially English in culture, but no longer assumes that diverse groups could or should be absorbed and assimilated into it. This exclusive singularity found expression in the nativist movements of the 1850s and 1890s, in response to a shift in the kinds of immigrants arriving on American shores (Catholic, non-Northern European) and to new economic conditions. As land became less available, arrivals clustered in cities, providing needed industrial labor but also alien customs, new social organizations, and competition for resources. Exclusive singularity finally culminated in the immigration restriction laws of the 1920s.

Yet a third form of singularity is implied in the notion of amalgamation or melting pot. Here, the diversity of American population is acknowledged, but instead of conformity to an English norm, what is imagined is a synthesis into what Crevecoeur, in his *Letters*, famously called "this New American" where "individuals of all nations are melted into a new race of men." Emerson, railing in an 1845 journal entry against the Native American Party, likewise prophesies that "in this continent, asylum of all nations, the energy of . . . all the European tribes, – of the Africans, and of the Polynesians, – will construct a new state, a new literature." This boundary between plural and singular, in a kind of composite singularity, remained more a logical than a historical option. The New Americans tended closely to resemble the original, old English ones.

Finally, there is the possibility of multiple identities, whose very diversity is seen as central to the American character. America in this vision is an arena for the toleration and indeed assertion of difference, as contributing to individualist freedom and expression, which are in turn seen to define the essential American promise and polity. Such a vision of multiple identities is implicit in positive ways from the beginnings of the American political tradition, and even unitary or singular conceptions of America presume, if they also resist, pluralist forces that were present from the outset of the American venture. Thus, Madison in *Federalist* 10 makes the counter-balance between interest groups the basis for republican freedom in America. Benjamin Franklin similarly defends party interests as integral to democratic government: "such will exist wherever there is liberty; perhaps they help to preserve it. By the collision of different sentiments, sparks of truth are struck out, and political light is obtained." America from this perspective can be characterized as a complex pluralism, composed of different populations, interest factions, and regional areas, all shifting through continued waves of new arrivals. The historiography of Frederick Jackson Turner at the turn of the century is best known for its theories of the American frontier, but the frontier was itself part of Turner's larger, regional theorizing of American diversity, as a "variety which is essential to vital growth and originality."

Within the nineteenth century, pluralism as a defining force in American social, cultural, and political life emerges in the philosophies of Josiah Royce and William James at Harvard. Their student, Horace Kallen, coined the term "cultural pluralism" to mean "a multiplicity in a unity, an orchestration of mankind." Kallen's vision, however, remains vague, and in many ways assumes a model of descent, making group definitions the basis of identity, so that America is imagined as a "democracy of nationalities." But this is to underestimate the voluntarist nature of ethnic affiliation in the American context (with the notable exception of the color line), as well as exchanges and movements across permeable ethnic boundaries. Indeed, Congress itself had rejected identification between regional and ethnic identity in 1818, when it denied a petition by the Irish for a piece of land in the West.

Local-color literature points to pluralist culture as one in which even ethnic affiliations take their place beside other resources available to Americans for self-definition and social location. As with region, ethnic identity in nineteenth-century local color is not exclusive or determining, and there are no fixed correlations between these various group identities. Instead, local color suggests a notion of pluralist individuality such as has reemerged in late twentieth-century discussions of ethnicity in America. A number of parameters contribute to identity, shifting the conception of pluralism away from group definitions and towards one in which multiplicity is experienced within each individual, who then negotiates among multiple identities. Religion, ethnic nationality, along with geographic, racial, and gendered identities each provides an association in which individuals can participate, even as they also acculturate into American patterns. Such voluntarist participation in multiple affiliations may itself be a specifically American cultural form, as suggested in the recent notion of "pluralist individualism." William James's discussion of "pluralism as the intersection of independent loyalties" suggests a nineteenth-century formulation of such a concept of plural identities.

No single local-color poet emerges in the nineteenth century with the scope and stature of a Mark Twain, whose fiction, with its intersections between region, dialect, and race, retains close ties to regional literature. But a complex conjunction of multiple identities emerges in a poet such as Frances Harper. In her work, ethnic and racial, gendered, economic, and regional self-definitions come together. Their meeting is often contentious and painful, as she confronts an America whose institutions and attitudes may cause these identities to collide against or even exclude one another. Harper's sequence of "Aunt Chloe" poems, which take on the voice and viewpoint of a black freedwoman, present such combination and confrontation. Situated firmly in the South, and tracing a historical progression from before the Civil War into Reconstruction, the poem-sequence matches, but inverts, the nostalgic post-war plantation literature.

The first poem, "Aunt Chloe," records the slave's vulnerability, pain, and also fury at the betrayal and violence of white masters who sell children and destroy families. It does so in an idiom that approaches dialect, limiting sentiment through the craft of a controlled viewpoint and homely language. "The Deliverance" is a long account of the war and emancipation, orchestrated through contrasting viewpoints of master and slave as each oppositely witnesses the Yankee advance. At the poem's center is the clash of black and white responses to emancipation:

> But when old Mistus heard it,
> She groaned and hardly spoke;
> When she had to lose her servants,
> Her heart was almost broke.
>
> 'Twas a sight to see our people
> Going out, the troops to meet . . .
> After years of pain and parting,
> Our chains was broke in two.

"Aunt Chloe's Politics" and "Learning to Read" are placed after the war. The first is a critique of political corruption in buying voters, spoken by a woman who is conscious of her own exclusion from the franchise. The second reflects on the political and cultural meanings of literacy for the black slave and then freedman/woman. The "Rebs," like the masters before them, try to prevent blacks from "book learning" and knowledge. But against them and the mockery that an old black woman should attempt it, Aunt Chloe learns to read:

> [Folks] said there is no use trying,
> Oh! Chloe, you're too late;
> But as I was rising sixty,
> I had no time to wait.
>
> So I got a pair of glasses,
> And straight to work I went,
> And never stopped till I could read
> The hymns and Testament.

This poem is a kind of slave-testimonial portraying the effort of blacks, in the context of black religion and against obstacles, to take their place in the American literate culture envisioned by Noah Webster. In "The Reunion," the final "Aunt Chloe" text, Chloe is reunited with the sons who had been sold away from her in the first poem of the sequence (the son of the white mistress had been killed in the Civil War).

In these texts, refracted through Aunt Chloe's voice, American English moves towards black dialect. But dialect is not presented here as eccentric display, as in Riley's work. Nor yet is it intended as universal and representative. It stands instead as one of many diverse expressions worthy to take its place among other American languages. Harper's is an appeal to an American discourse that accommodates diverse voices. The complexity of Harper's languages, and the tensions of her position between conflicting communities, become central to the poetry of Paul Laurence Dunbar.

Local color is no doubt an inadequate term for the literary emergence of diverse American identities, as composed not only of region, but of ethnicity, gender, and new senses of economic status in American life. And local-color poems often remain partial, hesitant, and limited in their realization. Nevertheless, late nineteenth-century local-color poetry can be seen to offer one emerging expression of a plurality of terms within American identity, as located – and contested – within each individual.

CROSSING LANGUAGES IN PAUL LAURENCE DUNBAR

Since its publication in the 1890s, Paul Laurence Dunbar's (1872–1906) poetry has been considered as two separate types: the poems in dialect, as against those in standard English. His first volumes, *Oak and Ivy* (1893), *Majors and Minors* (1895), and *Lyrics of Lowly Life* (1896) present each linguistic type in separate sections. And this division has continued to complicate Dunbar's place among American poets. Each language has raised questions about the authenticity of Dunbar's poetic voice, and indeed about his having a voice at all. But this restages in terms of poetics a larger cultural predicament: the challenge to African-Americans when their dual identities seem, as W. E. B. Du Bois described it, "two souls, two thoughts, two unreconciled strivings, two warring ideals . . ." Du Bois's "double consciousness" takes on in Dunbar a specifically linguistic aspect. In Dunbar's work, the different aspects of his identity do not, however, simply contend against each other. Instead, Dunbar's poetry explores their mutual relation, resulting in a complex form of poetic expression.

Dunbar's poems in standard English have been consistently undervalued. Written in traditional verse forms just as modernist innovation began to repudiate these conventions, the poems have been dismissed as derivatively literary, "genteel, slightly labored . . . set pieces and imitations." But suspicions concerning their literary value are inseparable from the questions they have raised about Dunbar's authenticity as a black poet representing his community. The dialect pieces in any case overshadowed the poems in standard English from the start. These seemed to offer a more authentic black voice. Yet, the dialect pieces raised their own complex set of questions regarding aesthetic control and representation of identity, and it was difficult to place them within an Anglo-American literary canon. Dunbar's two languages thus have worked at cross-purposes. Neither fits easily into established literary categories, while their dual presence has threatened to break apart Dunbar's poetic voice as lacking a controlling center and unity, rather than serving as a framework for the rich intercultural discourse his poetry offers.

Dunbar's two language modes are in one sense discontinuous, and do attest to painful discontinuities within Dunbar's position in the life of American art, society, and politics – discontinuities intimately involved in Dunbar's self-definition as an artist. However, while Dunbar's languages remain distinct, they are not simply opposed. Instead, they register the cross-cultural context in which both finally are situated. Dunbar's poetic is bivocal not only between, but within the standard English and dialect pieces. Each is an expression of his complex African-American identity. Each addresses and incorporates elements from the other. And each acts as a reflection of the other, exactly across their differences. Seeing the two in stark contrast is finally damaging to interpreting each group of poems, and to seeing Dunbar's work as a whole.

The model of interpreting Dunbar's work as starkly split between languages was inaugurated by William Dean Howells, in ways that were for Dunbar complicated and consequential. Howells launched Dunbar into literary visibility, against all odds for a young black writer. Dunbar was born in Dayton, Ohio, in 1872, to parents who had been slaves in Kentucky – although his father had escaped to Canada through the Underground Railroad and then fought in the Civil War for the 55th Massachusetts Regiment. He was taught to read by his mother (herself self-taught) and from her learned the dual traditions of dialect and standard English. The only African-American in his class at High School, Dunbar was an outstanding student. Nevertheless, he could only find work after graduation as an elevator boy. He managed to publish his first books of poems, however, and attracted enough support to obtain a post in the Library of Congress in Washington, DC. He married Alice Moore, also a writer, in 1898 after several years of courtship, and against the opposition of her family because of Dunbar's "very dark skin and his work with minstrel shows and musicals." The marriage, however, deteriorated with his health, ending in separation in 1902. Dunbar died of tuberculosis in 1906, at the age of thirty-three.

William Dean Howells's review of *Majors and Minors* in *Harper's Weekly*, followed by his "Introduction" to *Lyrics of Lowly Life*, were of considerable service to Dunbar in gaining a national audience. But Howells also established stylistic bifurcation as the framework for interpreting Dunbar, emphasizing the division between Dunbar's standard English, in which he saw little value, and the dialect poems, defined in narrow terms. Howells found nothing "especially notable" in the standard English poems "except for the Negro face of the author." It was the dialect pieces "which would most distinguish him, now and hereafter," but would do so by displaying the "difference of temperament between the races." The temperament of the black race, moreover, was restricted to: "appetite and emotion, with certain lifts far beyond and above it, which is the range of the race. He reveals in these a finely ironical perception of the Negro's limitations . . . [and] it was this humorous quality which Mr. Dunbar had added to our literature." According to Howells, Dunbar, by speaking in dialect, speaks for his people. But this confines him to speaking only of "appetite and emotion." He is "finely ironical," but the fit object of his irony is "the Negro's limitations." Finally, Dunbar's most significant contribution is to be "humorous," a nice enough skill in its way, but hardly intended as a high literary compliment, and one that completely misses the depth of seriousness in Dunbar's work.

What Howells indirectly points to is the difficulty of Dunbar's having a language at all, his voicelessness akin to the invisibility that Ralph Ellison was later to expose. James Russell Lowell could use dialect in *Biglow Papers* as another poetic language available beside, rather than in competition with, his Harvard English. Dialect and standard English each expressed a continuous Yankee identity rooted in the New England village of Cambridge, and ultimately claiming to be generally and authentically American. In Dunbar's case, in contrast, dialect is seen to express a racial identity in tension with established literary language. This dialect remains marginal, indeed subordinate, within American cultural life, and unrepresentative of American identity as a whole. Howells on the one hand denies Dunbar the status of an American poet in standard English. On the other, he denies dialect as a language that can represent American culture on any general or serious level.

Dunbar felt the consequences of Howells's review for the rest of his very short life. Ever after he considered himself typed as a dialect poet. As he told James Weldon Johnson, "I didn't start as a dialect poet. I simply came to the conclusion that I could write it as well, if not better, than anyone else I knew of, and that by doing so I should gain a hearing. I gained the hearing, and now they don't want me to write anything but dialect." The hearing he gained in dialect silenced him in standard English. But in the end, either language Dunbar could choose became suspect. If he wrote in standard English, he could be accused of assimilationist or escapist denial of his own true sources in black history and culture. But black dialect was dismissed as a limited literary instrument. And dialect, too, had become suspect as conforming to white expectations and stereotypes, indeed, as itself a product of historical subordination and oppression. Dialect originated in the suppression and loss of the African tribal languages in the passage to America and enslavement. Once in America, the black peoples had available only a dominant English language to which, however, they had limited access. The anti-literacy laws, and the conditions of slavery itself, made attaining formal English most difficult. Dialect, from this point of view, signaled cultural deprivation.

In a literary sense, dialect had been compromised in other ways. By the end of the nineteenth century, it had already been appropriated by such local-color regionalists as Joel Chandler Harris, whose presentation of black dialect and lore reinforced stereotypes in a nostalgic vision of lost plantation life. Black material was thus subsumed into a value structure that glorified white Southern culture. The stereotypes of plantation literature were then widely disseminated and fixed by the minstrel shows. Thus Dunbar, in turning to his black heritage, was contending with appropriated versions already alienated from black perspectives. This compromised position made subsequent African-American writers such as James Weldon Johnson and Sterling Brown critical of Dunbar's dialect verse. Johnson comes to describe Dunbar as "writing in the conventionalized dialect" and therefore as "dominated by his [white] audience . . . expressing only certain conceptions about Negro life that his audience was willing to accept."

Dunbar's best work does not so much transcend this predicament of language as make it his subject. This is accomplished in a number of ways. Dunbar specifically addresses his divided audiences to further force their mutual acknowledgment. He reclaims stereotypes by dramatizing viewpoints and transforming utterance into self-conscious acts of representation. He adopts and transforms genre forms in dual directions, that is, from black to white and from white to black. And he uses richly resonant figures tied to African and African-American culture, including the mask, black religious modes, spirituals, preaching, and song. These cross-cultural exchanges take place, moreover, in both his standard and dialect poems, whose division itself moves from opposition and contrast to mutual address and transformation. It is worth noting that Dunbar, who learned dialect from his mother but never himself lived in the South, was committed to dialect as a self-conscious literary technique. He approached dialect as a craftsman, polishing his skill through writing exercises in German as a foreign language, in Irish dialect, as well as the Hoosier dialect of James Whitcomb Riley. Critiques of his writing as failing to achieve an accurate representation of spoken dialect therefore miss the point. At issue for him was the need to rescue dialect from its compromised exploitation, in order to recover an African-American history that was precious as well as painful. As he wrote to the poet Alice Moore during their courtship:

> I want to know whether or not you believe in preserving by Afro-American writers these quaint old tales and songs of our fathers which have made the fame of Joel Chandler Harris, Thomas Nelson Page, Ruth McEnery Stuart and others! Or whether you like so many others think we should ignore the past and all its capital literary materials.

Dunbar here acknowledges the danger of using slave lore that has been reduced and commandeered by white nostalgia and racism. But he, like W. E. B. Du Bois, recognizes this lore as an essential element in African-American historical consciousness, a rich and necessary medium for cultural expression and redemption. The challenge was to destabilize stereotypic forms and reclaim his heritage for his own positive creation and identity.

"We Wear the Mask" directly represents the complex dilemma facing Dunbar, not least in its implications for his poetic language:

> We wear the mask that grins and lies,
> It hides our cheeks and shades our eyes –
> This debt we pay to human guile;
> With torn and bleeding hearts we smile
> And mouth with myriad subtleties.
>
> Why should the world be overwise,
> In counting all our tears and sighs?
> Nay, let them only see us, while
>   We wear the mask.
>
> We smile, but, O great Christ, our cries
> To thee from tortured souls arise.
> We sing, but oh the clay is vile
> Beneath our feet, and long the mile;
> But let the world dream otherwise,
>   We wear the mask.

The mask is here a complex and reflexive figure. Its first function is to conceal, by adopting the features expected and projected by white society. In this it represents a certain complicity. But the very act of representation here has potent force. To name the mask is already to expose its concealment, which is to translate complicity into recognition. As with Du Bois's figure of the veil, acknowledging the repression of cultural identity is the first step towards liberating it. And the mask itself has deep cultural resonance as a specifically African religious and aesthetic object. Its appearance here signals not only conformity to white social stereotypes, but also the assertion of unique African-American cultural modes of representation. The mask thus at once encloses and discloses. It prevents the outsider from seeing in, but hints at a secret world for those inside, whose mystery it both points to and yet protects. This complex counterpoint between exclusion and inclusion is enacted in the very language in which the poem is written. Its very high standard English ("myriad subtleties") in one sense is the ultimate mask: both concealing and expressing Dunbar's African-American identity. In its language, the poem thus stands at a crossing-point between the worlds seeing and wearing the mask, at once disguising and revealing the "torn and bleeding hearts," the "tears and sighs."

Standard English here does not merely conform to or assert the sacrifice of identity to white social norms. Rather, Dunbar uses it as a powerful and calibrated vehicle for exploring both conformity and resistance. The figure of the mask, also as a figure for language, attests the continuing survival of African cultural forms within the surrounding society that would suppress them, providing both image and vehicle for their cultural expression. The poem, then, enacts a dual cultural negotiation: African-American identity within, and as, American identity.

But this is also the case for poems in dialect. Dunbar's plantation poems in particular have disturbed readers, who fear they betray Dunbar's commitment to African-American self-representation and instead express complicity with white versions of it. But Dunbar seeks in these poem to recover black history in accordance with his own poetic and cultural intentions. The outstanding feature of these poems is their formal constitution: they are almost entirely cast as dramatic monologues. Dunbar handles this form with a sophistication and mastery that antedates its development by modernists such as Pound and Eliot. By using the represented speech of dramatic monologue form, spoken by characters who are precisely situated in historical time and place, Dunbar is able to control, and reframe, what had become black stereotypes.

In some few pieces, such as "The Deserted Plantation" and "Chrismus on the Plantation," Dunbar projects directly the image of the devoted slave, loyal to master and plantation. Even in these, however, Dunbar is not presenting but rather re-presenting one of many black personae: one of the masks that the slaves displayed to their masters, one of the types within black history and lore. Dunbar here has his black speakers act the way whites think they do, an imitation of an image, his reenactment of an act to which blacks themselves might resort. And his plantation poems focus on black rather than white Southern experience, questioning the hegemony of white culture, if not of white power, in the ante-bellum South. Dunbar, however, by no means evades the fact of slavery. His plantation representations must be placed in a difficult socio-history. Just how to come to terms with slave history was a pressing problem at the turn of the century in the context of the failure of Reconstruction. Intensifying racism, political exclusion, and economic neo-enslavement were disappointing the hopes and promises of emancipation. A desire to put slave history behind combined with the need to face and understand its effects on African-American communal life. Dunbar, again like Du Bois, does not flinch from facing the destructive force of slavery. At the same time, he emphasizes black humanity, endurance, and spiritual gifts even under slavery's dehumanizing anomie. A poem such as "Little Brown Baby," for example, is exquisitely balanced between painful recognition of powerlessness and the strength of human devotion:

> Little brown baby wif spa'klin' eyes,
> Come to yo' pappy an' set on his knee.
> What you been doin', suh – makin' san pies?
> Look at dat bib – you's es du'ty as me . . .
>
> Come to yo' pallet now – go to yo' res';
> Wisht you could allus know ease an' cleah skies;
> Wisht you could stay jes' a chile on my breas' –
> Little brown baby wif spa'klin' eyes.

This poem offers no genteel sentimentality. It is powerful and tense in its tragic contradiction between personal dignity and social powerlessness, as a slave father can never guarantee to his slave baby "ease an' cleah skies," however longingly he desires to do so.

The formal constitution of the dialect poems as dramatic monologues which situate speech acts of specified individuals allows Dunbar to investigate nostalgia rather than asserting it. Some poems, such as "The Old Cabin," explicitly study how memory both conveys and distorts the past. Most dialect pieces are extremely complex structures in which speech acts pick up negative or servile images in order to employ them polemically, subversively, or contentiously, to the disadvantage of the (white) outsider to the discourse. "Signs of the Times," to take one example, presents Thanksgiving feasting not as stereotypic reduction of the slave to appetite but as a ritual of celebration. There are further, ironic levels to the poem. Dunbar asks of Thanksgiving what Frederick Douglass asked about the Fourth of July: what do these American holidays mean to the slave? At the same time, there is an encoded prophecy of vengeance:

> Tu'key gobbler gwine 'roun' blowin',
> Gwine 'roun' gibbin' sass an' slack,
> Keep on talkin', Mistah Tu'key,
> You ain't seed no almanac.

The turkey's obliviousness to Thanksgiving becomes an emblem for the whole Southern regime. The master, apparent owner of the turkey, is shown instead to be in its position: unable to read the Signs of the Times and his own coming doom.

In another recasting and reclaiming of slave history, the poem "Accountability" invokes plantation-literature stereotypes of chicken-thieving slaves. But it becomes embedded in an elaborate argument relativizing all action:

> We is all constructed diff'ent,
>   d'ain't now two of us de same;
> We cain't he'p ouah likes an' dislikes,
>   ef we'se bad we ain't to blame;
> Ef we'se good, we needn't show off,
>   case you bet it ain't ouah doin',
> We gits into su'ttain channels
>   dat we jes' cain't he'p pu'suin'.

This discourse stands somewhere between quotation and ironic deployment of a position in order to defeat its own assumptions. The slave has mastered complex moral argument to represent his own behavior within his own circumstances, something Dunbar's dramatic monologue forms in general set out to accomplish.

The dialect poems conduct an investigation into African-American identity. But so do the standard English poems. What is striking through Dunbar's work is the continuity of intention between the two poetic groups. What Dunbar does is transform a double identity apparently at cross-purposes into a mode of cross-discourse. The black identity that dominates the dialect poems also provides a base matrix in standard English poems. If the African-American identity is dual, then standard English is Dunbar's heritage as much as dialect. It too is a medium of his cultural identity. Dunbar sets out to reclaim the Anglo-American tradition in creative relation to his African-American one, to bring them fruitfully into contact, whether critically or affirmatively, rather than posing them as merely contradictory or disjoined. This he achieves not by trying to eliminate one for the other, through either assimilation or radical separatism, nor by attempting to synthesize them into one discourse. His work instead intercrosses the two languages, keeping each as controversially or contrapuntally interwoven strands of his texts.

Many of Dunbar's best-known poems, such as "We Wear the Mask," are in fact poems in standard English that feature powerful emblems of African-American experience. Standard English with black subjects are also characteristic of Dunbar's public verses such as the "Ode to Ethiopia," "Frederick Douglass," and "Harriet Beacher Stowe." These, however, tend to be less successful in achieving an individualized and controlled poetic medium. Their texture becomes more complicated when they are recognized as polemical answers to white racist assumptions. But they often too closely reenact genteel nineteenth-century rhetoric. Yet Dunbar in other instances successfully reworks European-American modes. This is especially true of his use of Renaissance models, recasting their traditional Anglo-European generic forms through dialect or through African-American materials.

Renaissance lyric in fact provides a much better frame for Dunbar's Anglo-American poetics than does the Romantic tradition which is usually emphasized. Among his earliest verse experiments are such elaborate troubadour forms as the madrigal and roundeau. Especially striking are Dunbar's creations of apparently simple formal songs, which he however then crosses with African material. His "To a Lady Playing the Harp" celebrates a "dusk sorceress of the dusky eyes / And soft dark hair." This insertion of African-American materials often challenges hierarchies assumed in the white tradition. "My Lady of Castle Grand" is, in her "lily-white hand," cold in body and heart, as opposed to the loving scullery maids. "A Winter's Day" makes the white snow an "icy mantle, and deceitful," which attempts to smother the "crusty black" of fecund earth. In "Song," archetypal love lyrics – "My heart to my heart, / My hand to thine" – are sung to "my African maid." This is the text from which Dunbar took the title for his first volume of poetry, *Oak and Ivy*, in an image of intertwining that extends to the traditions within the poem itself: "Rend not the oak and the ivy in twain, / Nor the swart maid from her swarthier swain."

The process of crossing black into Anglo-American material can also be reversed. The slave-song "Parted" casts its dialect lament at being sold "down de stream" into a formal address to "My lady":

> De breeze is blowin' 'cross de bay
>   My lady, my lady;
> De ship hit teks me far away,
>   My lady, my lady;
> Ole Mas' done sol' me down de stream;
>   Dey tell me 't ain't so bad's hit seem,
>   My lady, my lady.

The hierarchy of courtly address is here both subverted and converted into a haunting, powerful intimacy.

This complexity of intercrossing discourses provides the structure of other poems in a highly self-conscious technique. "A Corn Song" poses the master's language and viewpoint against the slaves' work song, going back and forth between them. The master takes the corn song to confirm his position of superiority, as if the singing was for his entertainment. But the repeated refrain of the song gathers strength as lament and stubborn endurance, against the master's understanding:

> And his dreamy thoughts are drowned
> In the softly flowing sound
> Of the corn songs of the field-hands slow returning.
>
> Oh we hoe de co'n
> Since de ehly mo'n;
> Now de sinkin' sun
> Says de day is done.

The remarkable poem "The Spellin' Bee" makes brilliant play between the dialect in which it is written and the Bee itself as an induction into standard English, instituted by Noah Webster as a central American ritual of cultural incorporation (with Webster's *Blue Backed Speller* as Dunbar's "Spellin' Bee" prize).

Above all, bivocalism is consistently made the subject of Dunbar's self-reflexive poems on writing poetry. These are constructed in both dialect and standard English. In both, each language addresses itself to the other. These poems have mainly been interpreted as voicing Dunbar's ambivalence towards dialect, his frustration at being restricted to and by it. Certainly they often voice frustration. But language then serves as trope, not cause, for the social and political barriers which Dunbar encountered, especially in the context of turn-of-the-century disappointed hopes that with freedom, blacks might find their deserved place in American culture. "The Poet," most cited as expressing Dunbar's ambivalence concerning a dialect that caged him, instead directs us to the wider basis of his black voice:

> He sang of life, serenely sweet,
> With, now and then, a deeper note.
> From some high peak, nigh yet remote,
> He voiced the world's absorbing beat.
>
> He sang of love when earth was young,
> And Love, itself, was in his lays.
> But ah, the world, it turned to praise
> A jingle in a broken tongue.

The much quoted "jingle in a broken tongue" is rhetorically positioned in this text to dramatize the way dialect has been received and praised by an audience which sees it in reductive terms, and not Dunbar's own attitude towards dialect. Against such reduction, the poet underscores his own self-definition as artist: that is, his sweet song, in which "he voiced the world's absorbing beat."

It is song that emerges as central trope for Dunbar's relation to his multiple traditions and for his art generally. Song imagery registers not only his exquisite melodic structures but the full resonance of music as cultural emblem within black experience. Dunbar's lyrics are always close to song, whether as ballad, serenade, lullaby, children's song, dirge, hymn, or love song, with Dunbar's special Renaissance quality. This musical element emerges with particular social-historical force in Dunbar's use of the spirituals tradition. The spirituals are in Dunbar a varied and multileveled figure. They frame his complex and at times even skeptical stance towards religion, in which professions of strong faith, more usual to his contemporary black expression, appear alongside critical stances. "A Plantation Melody" and "A Spiritual" come close to a re-creation in dialect of spiritual faith, as do various hymns in standard English. Other dialect refrains of longing to "go 'long home" reiterate the other-worldly dimension of the spiritual tradition, as an indictment against this world of enslavement. But in "Philosophy," the speaker's been "t'inkin' bout de preachah" and is critical of his quietist advice. In "Mare Rubrum," the spiritual is wrought anew in the elaborate construction of a Petrarchan sonnet:

> In Life's Red Sea with faith I plant my feet,
> And wait the sound of that sustaining word
> Which long ago the men of Israel heard . . .
> Why are the barrier waters still unstirred? –
> That struggling faith may die of hope deferred?
> Is God not sitting on His ancient seat?

The central spiritual scene of Moses parting the waters of the Red Sea is revisited. As in the spiritual, the continuous presence of the saving and providential Word through history is invoked. But here, historical disruption as it disperses and challenges this Word's continuity is made overt. The poet hovers between doubt and struggling faith, as he inhabits the empty moment of divine history, in its failure to bring redemption to the immediate present.

In Dunbar's evocation of the spiritual, the division between standard English and dialect is destabilized. Dunbar brings both languages to bear on spirituals material, in poems which often examine the racial duality of American culture as reflected in the syncretist nature of the spirituals themselves. Dunbar shows an acute historical sense of black cultural evolution in America, representing black religious forms as they developed both from and against white norms. He repeatedly plays on distinctions between slave religion and white interpretations of it. He portrays tensions within African-American religious life as it responds to and also resists white religious values. The poems thus recreate the heterogeneous sources of the spirituals, as including not only Christian but also African elements such as dream images suggestive of African traditions of spirit-wandering. Some poems address the controversy over dance and music, in which African-based rhythmic worship was seen as contrary to church decorum. "Deacon Jones' Grievance" voices the complaint of a church leader (of whatever complexion) against music and dance in the church: "Why, it shames the name o' sacred / In its brazen worldliness." "Angelina" is warned off fiddling: "Ef you t'ink you got 'uligion an' you wants to keep it, too, / You jes' bettah tek a hint an' git yo' self clean out of view." Such tensions eventually were resolved into rhythmic worship as adopted by black, and also white religious groups, with strong mutual influences penetrating in both directions.

"An Ante-Bellum Sermon" serves as an outstanding example of Dunbar's historiography, rendered through a stunningly complex linguistic act. This poem recalls and reworks both the slave spiritual and the black sermon traditions. Written in dialect, it conducts an elaborate Biblical exegesis within a dialogical counter-discourse addressing at once slave worshipers and the white masters as they attempt to control black worship and understanding of the Biblical message. The poem's staging as a sermon invokes the further complex figure of the preacher within black American religious history, while its poetic form reaffirms its ties to spiritual song. Like so many spirituals, the "Sermon" takes as its text Moses and the Exodus:

> An we chooses fu' ouah subjic'
> Dis – we'll 'splain it by an' by;
> "An' de Lawd said, 'Moses, Moses,"
> An' de man said, "hyeah am I."

The preacher will "'splain" his subject, i.e. conduct an exegesis. The readings he goes on to offer range through Biblical history from Exodus to Gabriel's Last Trumpet, typologically linking events together – as in the spirituals – through a message of deliverance. God's infinite redemptive power is seen shining through individual historical moments, including, of course, immediate slave history. But the preacher must at once announce and disguise this reference, by orchestrating his discourse into a complex layering. He must direct his message simultaneously to his slave congregation and against the white overseers who are present exactly to make sure no such summons to redemption is delivered.

The result is a virtuoso multiplication of meanings, each directed towards the "Sermon"'s different audiences. Towards the one (slave) audience, there is an obvious call to freedom, asserted through continuity and comparison between the past and present: "Fu' de Lawd will he'p his chillun / You kin trust him evah time." Towards the other (white) audience (and historically, black church gatherings were often supervised to guard against subversive messages), the preacher hastens to deny what he has just proclaimed:

> But I tell you, fellah christuns,
>   Things'll happen mighty strange,
> Now, de Lawd done dis fu' Isrul,
>   An' his ways don't nevah change,
> An' de love he showed to Isrul
>   Wasn't all on Isrul spent;
> Now don't run an' tell yo' mastuhs
>   Dat I's preachin' discontent . . .
>
> So you see de Lawd's intention,
>   Evah sence de worl' began,
> Was dat His almighty freedom
>   Should belong to evah man,
> But I think it would be bettah,
>   Ef I'd pause agin to say,
> Dat I'm talkin' 'bout ouah freedom
>   In a Bibleistic way.

The figure of the preacher in the "Sermon" also evokes some of the ambivalence towards his own position that made Dunbar say near the end of his short life, "I am a black white man." Dunbar's career was deeply pressured by the need for patronage support, as well as by illness, marital breakdown, and his often frustrated search for modes of expression that included novels, librettos, songs, and essays in addition to poetry. Historically, he was uncomfortably caught at the turn of the century between a past heritage in slavery, and hopes for future equality and integration into American political, economic, and cultural life increasingly betrayed by Jim Crow restrictions. As with the preacher he portrays, Dunbar in one sense accommodates his means of expression to an inimical and hostile power structure. And yet, in another sense he exposes and challenges the structures that demand such accommodation, and controls his meanings within and despite their hierarchies of power.

Dunbar's poetry resides within this complex orchestration of audiences and linguistic meanings. "An Ante-Bellum Sermon" represents these complicated, multiple, and interpenetrating frames of discourse through the instrument of dialect. A poem such as "Sympathy" does so in standard English. This is one of many texts where Dunbar, using black emblems and black song tradition, attains a lyric and melodic beauty rare in nineteenth-century American poetry. In the poem, contrary forces of assertion and accommodation, complicity and creative command of language engage each other, often painfully:

> I know why the caged bird beats his wing
> Till its blood is red on the cruel bars;
> For he must fly back to his perch and cling
> When he fain would be on the bough a-swing;
> And a pain still throbs in the old, old scars
> And they pulse again with a keener sting –
> I know why he beats his wing!
>
> I know why the caged bird sings, ah me,
> When his wing is bruised and his bosom sore, –
> When he beats his bars and he would be free;
> It is not a carol of joy or glee,
> But a prayer that he sends from his heart's deep core,
> But a plea, that upward to Heaven he flings –
> I know why the caged bird sings!

Dunbar speaks for African-American experience in the double image of caged bird and beating song. The cage evokes America itself as it prevents and restricts its black citizens, but also standard English, which in one sense constrains the poet. Yet he here makes standard English a vehicle of his own expression, overcoming those who would deny him his voice, both as black and as American. Against constraints and in the face of betrayal, recalling historical scars which are not healed but instead reopened, he beats his song in a tradition of African-American defiance and prayer. In this way he both resists silencing and insists on his experience as part of American identity and culture.

Dunbar's senses of betrayal, difficulty, and mission come together in the poem "Compensation," which he wrote when facing death:

> Because I had loved so deeply
> Because I had loved so long,
> God in His great compassion
> Gave me the gift of song.
>
> Because I have loved so vainly,
> And sung with such faltering breath,
> The Master in infinite mercy
> Offers the boon of Death.

Personal betrayal serves here also as an image of cultural predicament. This poem renders into lyric simplicity the conflict, but also intimate connection, between Dunbar's two identities. The figure of song, in religious invocation, implicitly places this poem in a tradition of African-American experience. Its standard English agonizingly registers Dunbar's sense of his cultural life as defeated, and yet, almost against itself, also transmits and movingly expresses his agonistic life. Dunbar's sense of limitation in this regard becomes an integral element of his mastery. He claims as his own an American language that others would deny him, and on his own terms. His languages thus represent the cultural forces that situate him, but by examining and not merely reproducing the conflict between cultural identities. They become an arena for exposing and indicting, resisting and also negotiating Dunbar's double American experience. His most accomplished poems finally attain a delicate and indeed excruciating balance between promise and betrayal, exclusion and transformation, in which his two languages engage each other: antagonistic and reflexive, mutually confronting, mutually constituting.

EMMA LAZARUS: AN AMERICAN-JEWISH TYPOLOGY

Emma Lazarus (1849–87) was among the first poets specifically to assert ethnic voice in America, indeed ethnic voice as American. In doing so, Lazarus appeals to a typological rhetoric which had served from the time of the Puritan landing as a founding ritual of American national identity. Lazarus's rendering of this foundational rhetoric, however, requires a singular restructuring of its basic terms and their distribution, even as she institutes a no less striking reconstruction of her distinctive Jewish commitments. Puritan Biblical typology thus becomes a scene of mutual transformation between her American and Jewish identities, one made possible by their convergences, but necessary by their disjunctions. This complex interchange comes to focus on the strange, and in many ways volatile, Christ figure which emerges as a center of Lazarus's poetic vision.

"The New Colossus," written to raise funds for the pedestal of the Statue of Liberty, remains Lazarus's most forceful and successful poem. In it, Lazarus's multiple identities achieve an especially intricate representation, through a range of rhetorical strategies that persist throughout her later writings. The poem's female gendering finds antecedents in Lazarus's earlier work. Her poem "Echoes" in particular announces her voice to be a feminine one, conceding herself to be barred from epic and public topics of "the world's strong-armed warriors and . . . the dangers, wounds, and triumphs of the fight." She, as "Late-born and woman-souled," is instead confined to echoes heard in nature as a private, almost domestic space. That this also makes claim to an Emersonian poetics of imagination does not entirely dispel the poem's apologetic rhetoric and restriction to the private realms considered seemly for American female poets: "Misprize thou not these echoes that belong / To one in love with solitude and song."

In "The New Colossus," however, feminine figuration emerges instead as a powerful trope for national identity. Lazarus here retracts the renunciations of her early poem, and firmly places herself in a public discourse. Through a pattern of oxymorons, she asserts a uniquely female power:

> Not like the brazen giant of Greek fame,
> With conquering limbs astride from land to land.
> Here at our sea-washed, sunset gates shall stand
> A mighty woman with a torch, whose flame
> Is the imprisoned lightning, and her name
> Mother of Exiles. From her beacon-hand
> Glows worldwide welcome; her mild eyes command
> The air-bridged harbor that twin cities frame.
> "Keep, ancient lands, your storied pomp!" cries she
> With silent lips. "Give me your tired, your poor,
> Your huddled masses yearning to breathe free,
> The wretched refuse of your teeming shore.
> Send these, the homeless, tempest-tost to me,
> I lift my lamp beside the golden door."

Mighty/woman, imprisoned/lightning, Mother/of Exiles, mild eyes/command, cries/with silent lips: each oxymoron of feminized modest power acts as bridge, like the Statue herself, by which the alien is made native, the outcast made essential, the weak made strong. The poet, too, is projected as both welcoming hostess and guest-refugee.

This intricate tropology of feminized, naturalized American, further represents the specific commitments of Lazarus's Jewish identity. The images for the Statue uncannily recast the Biblical text of Deborah (a preferred figure for many nineteenth-century women writers), who is, not Mother of Exiles, but Mother in Israel; whose prophetic presence empowers the army of *Barak*, the Hebrew word for lightning; and who is named *eshet lapidoth*, the wife of *lapidoth*, which also translates as: woman of the torch (Judges 4). This Biblical subtexture, out of the Hebrew Lazarus had just begun to study in the 1880s, is framed by other Judaic associations. The concluding image of the "Lamp" is repeatedly identified with Jewish consciousness in such other Lazarus poems as "The Choice," "Gifts," "The Feast of Lights," and "In Exile."

More suggestive still is the poem's opening image of the brazen giant. Lazarus intends her "New Colossus" to stand opposed to the ancient Colossus of Rhodes, pagan statue of the sun god. This figure is not only masculine, conquering, and pompous as against the Statue's giant modesty. It is Greek.

But for Lazarus, as for Heinrich Heine, whose writings she had been translating since childhood, the opposing counterpart of Greek Hellenism is Hebraism. That the Greek giant acts in the poem as a figure for Europe then implicitly contrasts America against it as Hebraic. America as asylum not only welcomes the Jews (among others) whom Europe, in a phrase that suggests quotation and not Lazarus's own view, rejects as "wretched refuse." In contrast to Greek-Europe, America itself emerges as Hebraic site, with its history a mode of Jewish history.

Lazarus's American discourse is thus made commensurate with her Judaic one. Yet this is hardly an alien imposition. The Puritans themselves had done no less. As Jew, Lazarus would in fact have found particular entry into the Puritan rhetoric of Biblical typology that identified America as the New Israel and Promised Land, providentially revealed at the very moment of Puritan need and call. Indeed, Lazarus has special recourse to several distinctive, and not entirely congruent, strands in this complex rhetorical tradition. The Puritan venture, figured in typology as a new Exodus of chosen people crossing the sea to found the Kingdom of God, was also undertaken in pursuit of religious freedom, consecrating the New World Canaan as haven for the afflicted, "a refuge," in the words of the Psalmist (9: 9), "for the oppressed." The rhetoric thus supports both asylum and election, a particularist and universalist vision at once. If the Puritans were uniquely chosen, so could others be, with America the Promised Land for all who would see it as such.

To be American is in these senses already to be Hebraic. For Lazarus, as later for Horace Kallen, inventor of the phrase "cultural pluralism," committing herself to America commits her to her own most potent Judaic antecedents. It would be all but irresistible to recognize herself and her people in the Puritan image of the Israelite in Exodus, even as she would embrace the promise of asylum. But if thus far Lazarus's strategies seem mutually confirming and conforming between the Jewish and American traditions, just how complicated and potentially destabilizing the relation between them remains can be seen in the figure of Christ, which indeed stands at the center of all typology and which the poem also evokes.

Israel Zangwill, in his 1908 play *The Melting Pot*, hears in the Statue's "Give me your tired, your poor" the language of the Gospels (Matthew 11: 28): "When I look at the Statue of Liberty, I just seem to hear the voice of America crying: 'Come unto me all ye that labour and are heavy laden and I will give you rest.'" This echo, with its Biblical associations, is confirmed by another Lazarus sonnet, "1492," composed at about the same time as the "Colossus." This second sonnet presents "1492" as a "Two-faced Year" in which the Jews of Spain were expelled, but in which America, again feminized as "virgin world" and unveiled as future asylum, was also discovered. The linkage between these two events effectively makes the discovery of America an event in Jewish history. And here again the "doors of sunset," opening in asylum, say: "Ho, all who weary enter here." Lazarus's conflation of Jewish migration to America, Exodus, and Christ occurs elsewhere as well, perhaps most explicitly in a prose poem she wrote shortly before her death at the age of thirty-eight, called "The Exodus (August 3, 1492)." Opening under "The Spanish noon," it envisions the expulsion from Spain as casting out "dusty pilgrims" then spurned by all the nations; but it also offers a prophetic call to "whisper to the despairing exiles" that, at that very historical moment, "a world-unveiling Genoese" sails "to unlock the golden gates of sunset and bequeath a Continent to Freedom." And among these Jewish exiles, as the very image of their suffering, is a "youth with Christ-like countenance" who "speaks comfortably to father and brother, to maiden and wife," while in his breast "his own heart is broken."

Lazarus here no doubt reenacts a typological ritual shared by many ethnic groups become American, for whom the voice of America merges with the voice of Christ. For Lazarus to adapt typology to her particular consciousness, tradition, and need, however, requires strenuous revision, and even refutation, of premises fundamental to the Puritan tradition. Lazarus could discover in typology her Jewish identity within and indeed as founding her American one. But if Jewish Biblical experience serves as Puritan typological ground, it does so only to support a structure which ultimately subsumes it. Especially in the American Puritan context, typology affirms the Biblical history as founding pattern. But to valorize as pattern is to subordinate as history. History becomes figure, indeed prefiguration of the Christian transformation that is its fulfillment.

In this sense, however, to be fulfilled is to be abolished. No independent historical course outside the pattern of its own subsuming is admissible for the ancient Hebrews. Meaning must pass from the Old Testament to the New One, from Judaic letter to Christian spirit, a passage that itself serves as paradigm for redemptive process. Indeed, to allow Jewish history any meaning independent of this figural, typological transformation is sin. As to the Jews, their validity as model is guaranteed only by their relegation to the remote past. Through subsequent history, they are given the status of resistors and indeed betrayers. Refusing its own figuralization, its typological transformation from historical reality to Christian prediction, Judaism refuses integration into sacral and redemptive revelation. Thus, as ground for Christianity, Judaism participates in its sacred history. But as refusing Christian transfiguration, it is anti-witness, renegade, and sinful.

To assert continuous, valid, autonomous historical life on the part of the Jews is then fundamentally to contest Christian sacral history. At issue is a clash of historical claims, as these in turn implicate spiritual meaning and indeed redemptive possibility. This clash becomes Lazarus's central project through all of her later writings. What a poem such as "1492" represents is Lazarus's discovery of history. The very insistence on the expulsion from Spain already radicalizes the poem's typological structure, introducing a moment in Jewish post-Biblical history as within providential design. This is enforced in the poem's Biblical subtext, which presents the expulsion from Spain in the language of the expulsion from Eden, with Spain driving forth "the children of the prophets" by "flaming sword." Evoked here is the expulsion into history itself, as a significant event in an ongoing, meaningful design.

The discovery of history, figured in "1492," was for Lazarus also the crucial moment of her own self-discovery, marking her transformation from a writer of more or less labored and circumscribed conventional verse into a powerful polemicist. Born in Manhattan in 1849 to wealthy, established, and assimilated Portuguese-German Jews, Lazarus was precocious in languages and letters. At the age of eighteen she published her first volume of poems and translations. Its private printing by her father can serve as an emblem for Lazarus's female decorum on the one hand, which prevented her throughout her life from reading her own work in public (others performed this office), and on the other, her driving literary ambition. Her elite social-literary circle included Edmund C. Stedman, anthologist and editor; Richard Gilder, editor of the *Century Magazine* in which much of her prose writings appeared; Rose Hawthorne, daughter of Nathaniel; Thomas Wentworth Higginson, proctor to Dickinson; and most centrally, Emerson, whom she had met at a party given by Julia Ward Howe's brother, Samuel, in 1866. After their meeting, she sent him verses and volumes, while he in turn offered to act as "your professor, you being required to attend the whole term." Emerson's omission of her poems from his anthology *Parnassus* was the most traumatic event of Lazarus's early literary life, and she protested it directly and accusingly in a letter to him: "Your favorable opinion having been confirmed by some of the best critics of England and America, I felt as if I had won for myself by my own efforts a place in any collection of American poets, & I find myself treated with absolute contempt in the very quarter where I had been encouraged to build my fondest hopes."

Lazarus's subsequent change has all the mystery and prepared suddenness of a conversion experience; but what she converts to is historical vision. It was precipitated by the mass immigration of Russian Jews escaping from pogroms in the early 1880s. Lazarus had shown some consciousness of her

Jewish identity even before these massacres. Among her first poems is her "In the Jewish Synagogue at Newport," a reply to Longfellow's "Jewish Cemetery at Newport," where she tries to confute his "dead nations never rise again" with, if not full resurrection, then at least a continued sacral presence: "Still the sacred shrine is holy yet . . . Take off your shoes as by the burning bush." Through the 1870s, her rabbi, Gustav Gottheil, had tried to entice her to contribute some verses to a Reform prayer book (she reluctantly contributed English translations of German versions of medieval Hebrew hymns). More crucially still, he introduced her to the just emerging German and German-Jewish historiography, the new *Wissenschaft des Judentums*. Finally, he accompanied this elite, decorous young lady to Ward Island, to witness for herself the mass of newly arrived refugees.

It is the new sciences of history that provide Lazarus with weapons for confronting the devastation of "murder, rape, arson, [and] one hundred thousand families reduced to homeless beggary" which she describes in one of her first polemical pieces. Lazarus there is replying to one Mme. Ragozin – collaborator in Putnam's many volumed *The Story of the Nations*, member of the Oriental Society, of the Société Ethnologique de Paris, and of the Victorian Institute of London – who, in an essay called "Russian Jews and Gentiles," had defended the pogroms as the appropriate response to an alien, subversive, heretical Jewish presence in Russian society. Lazarus's own essay, "Russian Christianity vs. Modern Judaism," already in its title alters the historiographic map by which Ragozin had divided all Jewry into "those who followed Jesus, and those who crucified him." Lazarus instead asserts that Jewish history is alive, indeed is "the oldest among civilized nations." This historicist approach to Jewish life had itself been an innovation of the *Wissenschaft* movement, whose original group included the young Heine. Lazarus makes it the center of such poems as "The World's Justice" and "Gifts," which contrast Israel with the long defunct kingdoms of Egypt, Assyria, Greece, and Rome. In prose essays she similarly sets out, as she writes in "The Jewish Problem," to "review" Jewish history "since the Scriptural age, where ordinary readers are content to close it." Lazarus, moreover, addresses her historicized vision to Jews no less than Gentiles, "convinced," as she writes in her *Epistle to the Hebrews*, "that a study of Jewish history is all that is necessary to make a patriot of an intelligent Jew."

The new historiography, both German and Jewish, also provides Lazarus with the basis for rewriting typology. Her task is to find a place for Jews not only in history but in America. But her very assertion of Jewish history contests the position of the Hebrew within American typological configuration. She is thus committed to a historiography that both joins her with and distinguishes her within the American community, and she requires a rhetoric that will allow for both impulses. What Lazarus must do is marshal the power of typological rhetorical patterns, while resisting their historical erasures; must recast the Jew as both antecedent and present, figure and history, type and anti-type.

One strategy in this project is to invoke Hellenism as contrast to Hebraism, as she does with the "brazen giant of Greek fame" in "The New Colossus." In poem after poem, Lazarus adopts a Greek/Hebrew structure which presents Hellenism as an ancient, dead culture in contrast to her living Hebraic one. These poems often feature the Maccabees, the leaders of the second century BCE Jewish revolt against Greek imperialism and Hellenist culture. In this, Lazarus substitutes a fundamentally different schema for the basic typological progression in which the Old Testament prepares for, but is abolished by the New Testament which supersedes it. By displacing the rhetoric of Old to New and instituting Greek and Hebrew in its stead, she alters the configuration of forces defining Jewish identity, exchanging dead letter for living culture.

But Lazarus's most daring and disruptive typological venture concerns the figure of Christ himself. Throughout her later poetry, Lazarus persistently makes Christ the central figure for Jewish history itself. In doing so, she draws on the newly contemporary and still controversial studies of the historical Jesus in his Jewish context. This had become a topic for German and German-Jewish historians alike, beginning with Herman Reimarus's *The Aims of Jesus and his Disciples*, a historical reconstruction of the life of Jesus published by Lessing in 1778, and then elaborated by Jewish figures such as Moses Mendelssohn, Heinrich Graetz, and Abraham Geiger, as well as such Christian scholars as David Strauss and Ernest Renan in his *Life of Jesus* (1863). Lazarus herself wrote an essay for *The American Hebrew* on "M. Renan and the Jews," where she presents Renan's view of Judaism as a prophetic religion which "has done much service in the past [and] will serve also in the future," and which declares Christianity to be "Judaism adapted to Indo-European taste." She also cites, in her *Epistle to the Hebrews*, Mark Antokolsky, a contemporary artist whose *Ecce Homo* portrays Jesus in ancient Jewish costume, with Semitic features, side curls, and a skullcap.

Lazarus is, if not the first, then certainly among the first to represent Jesus in literature in these historicist terms, an image that then becomes important in twentieth-century Jewish literature. Lazarus, moreover, goes beyond reclaiming Jesus as Jew and actor in Jewish history. She makes Christ her defining figure of Jewish identity, with the Jews, as a historical people, themselves the body of Christ. Thus, in "The Crowing of the Red Cock," she asks:

> Where is the Hebrew's fatherland?
>   The folk of Christ is sore bestead;
> The Son of Man is bruised and banned,
>   Nor finds whereon to lay his head.
> His cup is gall, his meat is tears,
> His passion lasts a thousand years.

Jesus's Jewish identity makes the Jews the "folk of Christ." He also, through the figure of "The Son of Man," represents them throughout a history seen as prolonged "passion." "The Valley of Baca" similarly presents Jewish historical travail through the figure of a "youth" whose head is "circled with a crown of thorn." In "The Supreme Sacrifice," Israel, enduring "the scorn of man" for two thousand years, "Bows his meek head" and confesses "Thy will be done." "Raschi in Prague" is "featured like the Christ," and in "The Death of Raschi," the great rabbi, having been martyred by Christians, on the "third day" is said to have risen from the dead, "the life returned," a wonder to be believed "knowing the miracles the Lord hath wrought / In every age for Jacob's seed."

Lazarus here undertakes a significant redistribution of forces within typological construction. She gains entry into typology at a different point. And she reverses its fundamental direction, values, indeed its whole redemptive process and pattern. To identify the Jews with Christ is to lift them out of their anticipatory, prefigural role and place them instead at the very nexus of transfiguration itself, in the position of fulfilling revelation. The truth of this revelation is then not transferred from but rather realized through them. The sacred and indeed divine moment is retained in their continuing nationhood rather than eclipsing it. And Christ becomes an extension of the prophetic figure of the "Suffering Remnant," the "remnant lost," as Lazarus names it in "The World's Justice," confirming rather than displacing Jewish prophecy and providential history.

Christian claims are at the same time severely displaced. Instead of emerging as the people of Christ, Christians become their persecutors through history. The crucified becomes the crucifiers, and those long accused as crucifiers become the crucified. Not Jews, but Christians, betray Christ. Thus Lazarus concludes her translation of *The Dance to Death*, a play depicting the destruction of a German-Jewish community by its Christian citizens during the Black Plague, with a cry of Jewish martyrs to the "cruel Christ" against the Christian "child murderer." As she sums up in "The Crowing of the Red Cock," "When the long roll of Christian guilt / Against his sires and kin is known . . . What oceans can the stain remove / From Christian law and Christian love?"

Lazarus's rewriting of typology here clearly emerges as a species of polemic, the central mode of all her later work. This polemic is implicit generally in historiographical arguments which posed Jesus's historical ties to Judaism against the Pauline theology emphasizing his repudiation of it. Yet Lazarus is fully conscious that her revised version contests and is incompatible with the main tradition she nevertheless attempts to invoke and enlist. This can be seen in a series of poems written through the rhetoric of anti-Semitism, including "The Guardian of the Red Disk," two ballads on Jewish persecution she wrote to complete a project initiated by Heinrich Heine, and, most rigorously, in the poem "Epistle." There, as she explains in a note, Lazarus rewrites a letter to Paulus, a Jewish convert to Catholicism who had achieved high office in the church and become active in its persecutions of the Jews of Seville, a story she had come across in Graetz's multi-volume *History of the Jews* (1853–75). The poem systematically reviews Christian beliefs regarding Christ's mission, contrasting it with a Jewish reading of these beliefs in light of their own history. As she quotes from Graetz: "Christianity gives itself out as a new revelation in a certain sense completing and improving Judaism . . . Where [in Christian history] is the truth and certainty of revelation?"

Lazarus's polemic is enlisted in defense of Jewish identity in history. Yet her position remains a complicated one. The Christic imagery she adopts allows her to negotiate a Jewish identity within American culture. But if she thus rewrites typology, she is also rewritten by it. Christ as encompassing center of history and culminating image is, after all, an odd figure for Jewish identity, not unlike the Christian one. Lazarus's reversals are in this sense unstable. Her work in other ways enacts, without resolving, conflicts within her multiple identity. Lazarus in fact institutes not one typology, but two. Alongside the figure of suffering sacrifice, Lazarus introduces a contrary one of Jewish assertion, awakening, and heroism. This finds its ultimate expression in her vision, adopted from George Eliot, of a Jewish restoration in the national homeland of Palestine. Incipient Zionism becomes a central feature of Lazarus's prose, from "The Jewish Problem," where she declares "all suggested solutions other than this of the Jewish problem [are] but temporary palliatives," through her *Epistle to the Hebrews*, where she repeatedly urges "the signs of a momentous fermentation," and the "prophetic intuition" of the "revival of the idea of a Restoration."

Lazarus's Zionist commitment emerges in poems like "The Banner of the Jew" and "The Feast of Lights," where the Maccabean revolt becomes a call to Israel to "wake" and "recall to-day / the glorious Maccabean rage," to "Chant psalms of victory till the heart takes fire, / The Maccabean spirit leap new-born." Most powerfully, "The New Ezekiel" transmutes the graveyard of two millennia of history into a prophetic scene of national rebirth:

> Yea, Prophesy, the Lord hath said. Again
>   Say to the wind, Come forth and breathe afresh,
> Even that they may live upon these slain,
>   And bone to bone shall leap, and flesh to flesh.
> The Spirit is not dead, proclaim the word,
>   Where lay dead bones, a host of armed men stand!
> I ope your graves, my people, saith the Lord,
>   And I shall place you living in your land.

Lazarus here comes closest to realizing a Hebrew poetics in which history and Biblical text act as ethnic voice, spoken as a prophetic "word" that unites, rather than opposes, "flesh" and "Spirit," history and pattern.

Yet a question remains, even here, as to which land she has in mind: America, or Palestine? For Lazarus does not relinquish her claim on America as the Promised Land. Indeed, she is careful to make clear in her *Epistle* that her Zionist program is not intended for American Jews: "There is not," she assures her readers, "the slightest necessity for an American Jew, the free citizen of a republic, to rest his hopes upon the foundation of any other nationality soever." It is only the problem of the East European Jews that Zionism solves, since "their colonization en masse in the United States is impracticable." Her "plea for the establishment of a free Jewish State has not the remotest bearing upon the position of American Jews," for "wherever we are free, we are at home."

To Lazarus, these two Promised Lands are complementary, not competing. Nevertheless, their several claims lead to rhetorical ambivalence, if not confusion, in her verse. The poem "In Exile" celebrates the journey of refugees from the Egypt of Russia not to Palestine, but to Texas, there to enjoy the "Freedom to love the law that Moses brought" and "to drink the universal air." But in having the refugees "link Egypt with Texas in their mystic chain," Lazarus is unclear whether she intends their journey as one of exile or of Exodus. "The New Year" tells how

> In two divided streams the exiles part,
>   One rolling homeward to its ancient source,
> One rushing sunward with fresh will, new heart.
>   By each the truth is spread, the law unfurled.

Two streams, two homecomings: nonetheless, the journey the poem depicts as the fulfillment of "the Prophet's promise" is the one from the Russian "steppes" to the American "Sierras" (a somewhat confused geography), in a rhetoric that realizes Moses' plea to Pharaoh through a "New Colossus" image of American asylum:

> To snow-capped Sierras from vast steppes ye went,
> Through fire and blood and tempest-tossing wave
> For freedom to proclaim and worship Him,
> Mighty to slay and save.

Lazarus's ambivalence finally derives both from herself and from her America. She firmly articulates an ideal that allows participation in American life while retaining distinctive ethnic identity. As she wrote in her *Epistle*, "To combine the conservation of one's own individuality with a due respect for the rights of every other individuality is the ideal condition of society, but it is a foolish perversion of this truth to deduce therefrom the obligation to renounce all individuality." Yet her work poses questions regarding the extent to which ethnic identity is absorbed, tolerated, or encouraged by American cultural forces, in a society where ethnicity must somehow be different and yet the same, integrated and yet separate. Even "The New Colossus" has a polemical context, to assert as much as to confirm the American welcome to the huddled masses. It was written at a time when the mass immigration from Eastern Europe met intensified nativist opposition – a problem Lazarus acknowledges in her *Epistle*. It was, moreover, only after the restrictive Immigration Act of 1924 had put an end to mass immigration, and in the face of renewed persecutions in Hitler's Europe, that the poem was enshrined at the Statue's entrance, in 1945. The two traditions so carefully intertwined in the poem of asylum and election, universalism and nationalism, remained conflictual in the political history of immigration.

Lazarus herself was no immigrant, but an American expressing her ethnic vision through the rhetoric of her native country. Throughout her career she wrote for both Jewish and American audiences, and resolutely dismissed what she calls, in her essay on Renan, "the whole rotten machinery of ritualism, feasts and fasts, sacrifices, oblations and empty prayers" for a rational, historicized national identity and a prophetic tradition consistent with, and founding, "universal religion." The result is a discourse in which the American and the Judaic remain conjunctive and disjunctive at once. The contrastive pressures of the rhetorics she adopts can be seen when she lauds America as "a society where all differences of race and faith were fused in a refined cosmopolitanism," or when, in her *Epistle*, at the very moment she calls for national restoration in "The Jewish Problem," she hastens to add: "From this statement I exclude American Jews, who have lost color and individuality, and are neither Jew nor Gentile." Here Lazarus reverts to a Pauline language that, while apparently universalist, is highly typological and acts to subsume every identity into the unity of Christ, as it is written: "But now also put off all these . . . And have put on the new man . . . Where there is neither Greek nor Jew, circumcision nor uncircumcision . . . but Christ is all, and in all" (Colossians 3: 8–11). The logic of typological rhetoric carries Lazarus at such moments to an erasure of Jew and Greek within a unified identity that remains, however, essentially Christian, rather than allowing her to assert her distinctive, but related, Hebrew and American identities. It seems relevant here to point out that there is as yet no collected works of Emma Lazarus. Emma Lazarus died in 1887 of cancer. Her sister, Annie, who controlled the copyright of her writings, declined permission when Bernard Richards in 1926 asked to edit a complete works. Having converted to Catholicism, she felt, as she wrote to Richards, that while Emma's

politico-religious poems are technically as fine as anything she ever wrote, they were nevertheless composed in a moment of emotional excitement, which would seem to make their theme of questionable appropriateness today . . . There has been, moreover, a tendency, I think, on the part of some of her public, to overemphasize the Hebraic strain of her work, giving it thus a quality of sectarian propaganda, which I greatly deplore, for I understood this to have been merely a phase in my sister's development . . . Then, unfortunately, owing to her untimely death, this was destined to be her final word.

In general Lazarus tries to sustain in her typology Jewish and Christian readings of Biblical history that share common ground but are also incompatible. The result is a poetic that seems half confused, half prophetic; one which yearns, as Lazarus writes in a poem dedicating herself to the spirit of prophecy ("To Carmen Sylva"), to speak both "for poet David's sake" and also "for his sake who was sacrificed – his brother Christ."

5

❦

WALT WHITMAN: THE OFFICE
OF THE POET

THE POET AS PRESIDENT

Walt Whitman cuts so large a figure that readings of his work seem doomed to be fragmentary. At once accessible and evasive, transgressive and yet also centrally defining within American culture, Whitman's work has been persistently split into contradictory and opposing stances. These are readily familiar, in the guises of Whitman the solitary singer as against Whitman the political journalist; Whitman the imperial self as against Whitman the poet of democracy; Whitman the Romantic and/or antinomian ego as against Whitman the wound-dresser; Whitman the homoerotic radical as against Whitman the defender of the American Way.

These opposing categories, which essentially dissociate Whitman's autonomous as against his social involvements, in fact each and all enter into his texts, whose task, not least, is the mutual negotiation and transfiguration of just these various commitments. This transfigural project is at the center not only of Whitman's poetics, but of Whitman's conception of America. Whitman in his poetic work undertakes to enact and initiate a language of democratic selfhood out of which a habitable American community may be inaugurated. His poetic project is in this sense fundamentally political, and is specifically tied to a republican tradition which defines freedom not merely as the capacity for individual and independent self-determination, but as civic virtue: committed to participation in self-government, with other citizens, towards the common good. Whitman's attempt to further this political vision is, in turn, specifically structured through his adopting and transforming a political model of representation into a poetic voice. Through that voice, he addresses every common reader, in the effort and hope to awaken each to his and her individual place and responsibility within the American polity and possibility. This voice in turn takes its place within a broad project of figural multiplicity, which is Whitman's central and governing poetic technique. Tropes, images, descriptions, and narratives in Whitman's work are structured to participate in multiple levels of meaning and experiences, intricately orchestrated together, mutually corresponding and mutually affirming each other within an America that is itself become the greatest poem.

It must be emphasized, however, that Whitman by no means claims this task to have been already accomplished. His stance towards the self and society as it currently exists is instead severely critical. These are not what he is celebrating. Whitman's heroic and exuberant verse is always conducted through a no less profound critique and skepticism regarding the America that confronts him. This skepticism, far from surfacing sporadically as an anomaly or a kind of bad mood, exerts a continuous pressure throughout Whitman's work. It is instrumental to his structuring of both the figure of the self and the figure of America, and in their mutual relationship. Whitman's self, that is, represents not any attained self smugly proclaiming its own celebration, but rather, offers a promise of selfhood, still to be accomplished, through the very processes the poem inaugurates. Just so, the America of Whitman's poem is not an actual America already realized, but no more (and no less) than a promise of America, an America not yet attained but which the poem attempts to guard from despair. Thus the poetry, while certainly the celebration it asserts itself to be, is celebrating a state not yet achieved, but rather is initiating, or inviting, a mode of conduct towards a self and society still to be accomplished. It is this invitation and possibility, rather than the given reality, that is being celebrated.

The pivotal figure in this undertaking to constitute an America of Promise is Whitman's "Myself." Myself emerges as the first Whitmanian trope of multiple figuration, whose intercrossing functions and senses make it an intensely complex and difficult figure to command. Whitman underscores that Myself is a multiple figure through the varieties of self-nomenclature (Myself, the Me Myself, the Real Me, Actual Me, the other, O Soul, etc.) he repeatedly introduces. But its multiplicity is everywhere implied within the authoritative role Whitman claims for it. Indeed, the basis of Myself's authority, of its offering itself as somehow exemplary or representative, is at once the question, and the project, Whitman sets out to perform. It is of central importance to Whitman's entire enterprise that this authority not be derived from any merely autobiographical history (and many readers have been struck by how little one learns in "Song of Myself" about Whitman in any personal sense. Even his name appears only in the 498th line). Nor is it derived from a gigantic, engulfing imperial ego, either as creative poet or as an authoritarian, propagandist voice of America. Rather, Myself is offered in the role of delegate, exemplar, type, representative, whose senses open out from their center in poetry to extend deeply into American history, political philosophy, and culture.

Perhaps the first, most immediate representative role of Myself is to implicate any self reading and undergoing the poem. Myself does not refer to
Whitman in any exclusive sense, but from the outset takes on a multiplied
reference, by representing each of us, including Whitman as poet and reader. It
does so dynamically through the very process of participation which the poem
impels. The poem, as Whitman repeatedly insists, is a journey, an experience
of transformation which the poet himself inaugurates and conducts (but never
concludes), and in so doing invites and even incites each (my) self to undergo
in his/her own right.

> For us the greatest poet is he who in his works most stimulates the reader's imagination
> and reflection, who incites him the most to poetize. The greatest poet is . . . he who
> suggests the most; he, not all of whose meaning is at first obvious, and who leaves you
> much to desire, to explain, to study, much to complete in your turn.

This fact of the poem as a "process" of self-construction is a given of almost
all Whitman criticism. But Myself is representative in still broader and more
complex ways – a particularly American self that Whitman launches on a
particularly American way. As is, again, immediately apparent, the poem's
journey is in many senses through America, and the poem represents America
by traveling it, registering its immense variety. This sense of Myself as speaking for America takes shape in the central rhetorical strategy of gargantuan
personification, which, however, functions in ways that are not, nor are meant
to be, stable, fixed, and consistent. It is announced in such *Leaves of Grass* titles
as "I Hear America Singing," but is implicit in prominent rhetorical features
such as the catalogue. In these, Whitman's "I" stands not only for Whitman
as an individual or even as a poet, but for the country as a personified figure.
"I" can then claim to include all varieties of American experience because, on
at least one figural level, "I" is America (and not merely Whitman) speaking.
Whitman does not then himself engulf his world megalomaniacally, but rather
presents Myself as delegate for America, representing it, as it were, by election.
This personifying impulse is launched in the 1855 Preface, where the catalogue becomes a technique for elaborating a personified America, spanning
geographical, social, historical, and political configurations:

> A bard is to be commensurate with a people . . . he incarnates [his country's] geography
> and natural life and rivers and lakes . . . He spans between them also from east to west
> and reflects what is between them . . . To him enter the essences of the real things and
> past and present events – of the enormous diversity of temperature and agriculture
> and mines – the tribes of red aborigines – the weatherbeaten vessels entering new
> ports . . . the first settlements north or south . . . the haughty defiance of '76, and

the war and peace and formation of the constitution . . . the endless gestation of new states – the convening of Congress every December, the members duly coming up from all climates and the uttermost parts.

Whitman speaks here not only for, but as, America, as an organizing personification for its geography, its revolutionary and current history, its varieties of inhabitants and enterprises.

The personifying rhetoric that authorizes Whitman to speak so is not one he merely invents or imposes. He is working within specific cultural and political models. Like the Representative to Congress in this catalogue "duly coming up from all climates and the uttermost parts," Whitman wishes to gather together in his text and its speaker all the far-flung reaches of America. Whitman's poet, that is, serves as a figure of the political representative. As such, it derives from but goes beyond Whitman's own pre-history as political journalist and his specific partisan allegiances or programs, to reflect and rework poetically the broad structure of political representation as it was evolving in the ante-bellum period. Whitman's poet (speaker, Myself) evokes and transforms a particular relationship and role between representative and people emerging in Jacksonian America, and which Andrew Jackson himself had made a centerpiece of his own Presidency.

That Whitman's political background is decisive and central to his venture into poetics is a point of biographical record. Born in 1819 in Long Island, New York, Whitman was apprenticed and variously practiced as a printer, although also working intermittently as schoolteacher, builder, and small businessman. But his main professional commitment before poetry was in political journalism: as editor, reviewer, and writer, mainly for Democratic journals. His newspaper writings through the 1840s and 1850s trace his political course from a centrist Democratic position increasingly outward to the margin, finally breaking with mainstream Democratic positions and then out of political journalism into his poetic career. His editorship at the *Brooklyn Daily Eagle*, which he took on in 1844, ended with his dismissal in 1848, apparently over the controversy of slavery extension into the newly acquired Southwestern and Western territories. The *Eagle*'s owner, Van Anden, continued to support the conservative Democratic course of compromise with Southern interests; but Whitman opposed this "Hunker" conservatism, sympathizing with Barnburning opposition to slavery extension and then with Free-Soil democracy's support for the Wilmot Proviso, insisting that new territories remain slave-free. These more radical political commitments are evident in Whitman's attempt to found a Free-Soil newspaper, the Brooklyn

Freeman, in 1848 (thwarted by a Brooklyn fire which burned down its offices and then by the defeat of the Free-Soil Party), but extend beyond newspaper writing into party politicking. Whitman himself delivered a political speech in a New York City park in July 1841, actively campaigned for a New York Barnburner gubernatorial candidate, Silas Wright, in 1846, and participated as a delegate to the Buffalo convention of the newly founded Free-Soil Party in 1848, marking his final break with the Democratic Party.

Slavery in some sense frames Whitman's, as indeed the country's, political pathtaking. But questions remain as to just how radical Whitman was on the slavery issue, and at what moments. On the one hand, ante-bellum Whitman never ventured into a more radical abolitionism (a *Brooklyn Eagle* editorial denounces the "wicked wrong of abolitionist interference with slavery in Southern states"). Whitman, like Lincoln, could not justify intervention in the established institution of Southern slavery, restrained as he was by his commitment to the Constitution, including its safeguard of states' rights. He took his political stand, rather, on the controversy of slavery extension, itself the consequence of ante-bellum territorial expansion, which Whitman strongly supported – unlike Emerson, who wrote in his journals, "Mexico will poison us." Both North and South saw their own fates as tied to the status of the recently acquired territories, with both sides in agreement (however correctly or incorrectly) that without further extension, the South's own peculiar institution could not be sustained. The life and death struggle which ensued can be traced in legislative history on slavery restriction through the Northwest Ordinance, the Missouri Compromise, the Wilmot Proviso, the Compromise of 1850, and the Kansas–Nebraska Bill. Each has its place within a series of legislative maneuvers between sectional interests under increasing pressure from the country's expansion to define and control the national character in political, economic, and cultural terms.

It is Whitman's understanding of the nature of republicanism that frames his evolving response to the slavery issue, which is to say that for him slavery implicates the very heart of the American political character. He initially addresses slavery in terms of his commitment to the white working man and free labor. In this, he displays some conformity with racial assumptions and interests widespread in the North no less than in the South: he opposes slave labor as a threat to white Anglo-American opportunity. But his more general commitment is to the American common man as against an unrepublican Southern system of aristocracy. The struggle over territorial status is, he writes in one editorial, between "the grand body of white workingmen" in opposition to the "interests of the few thousand rich 'polished,' and aristocratic owners of the slaves at the south." And Whitman does not – in his journalistic pieces, his manuscript notes, and least of all in his poetry – express his free labor ideology through a heightened rhetoric of race as does, for example, David Wilmot. Wilmot's Proviso launched and rallied a decade of legislative turmoil over the extension question. But Wilmot's call to "preserve for free white labor a fair country . . . where the sons of toil, of my own race and own color, can live without the disgrace which association with negro slavery brings upon free labor" is racist in a way Whitman is not. If Whitman's prose commitment is more to the working man than to the slave, still, he sees slavery as a great evil, indeed as unAmerican, contradicting his fundamental sense of what America is or should be.

Thus, in one *Brooklyn Eagle* editorial (the "American Workingman vs. Slavery"), he seems less interested in the plight of the slaves themselves than in slavery as an assault on "the respectable working man" and as "destructive to the dignity and independence of all who work, and to [free] labor itself." In another piece, Whitman does claim that, for the black, the "lot in Africa is no worse than in America." But even here he adds that "America is not the land for slaves. The recorded theory of America denies slavery any existence in justice, law, or moral fact." A piece on "Slavers and the Slave Trade" names them the "most abominable means for making money" and "a blot on our humanity." If the Constitution constrains against interference with the laws governing the present slave states, still, slavery extension into new territory must be uncompromisingly opposed, for "slavery is inconsistent with the other institutions of the land." By the time he wrote his 1856 tract "The 18th Presidency!", Whitman is in a state of apoplectic fury. "The Cushions of the Presidency are nothing but filth and blood. The pavements of Congress are also bloody" in their policy of slave-extension, which opposes "against the free people the masters of slaves." While he does not specifically speak for the oppressed slaves, Whitman nevertheless sees slavery itself as "the basest outrage of our times," one which betrays "all the main purposes for which the government was established." Concessions to it hideously preach a "perfect equality of slavery with freedom."

Whitman's opposition to slavery, therefore, goes beyond extension to contest the institution of slavery as such, and is based not only on the narrow interest of white work-claims, but on his deepest, most fundamental and enduring political commitment: slavery is unAmerican and anti-republican. His denunciation of slavery is thus rooted in his basic understanding of American culture, which in turn gives shape to his own political history and finally to his poetic vocation. "What is this American Republic for?" writes Whitman in an early manuscript, using the language of social contract which his notes show he had studied in Rousseau:

You know, and the world knows well, what the bargain of this Confederacy and its government are for, and what their distinct meaning is. It is the meaning and direct purpose of our supreme compact, when not impeded by special State sovereignty (and then always in contempt of their letter and spirit) that the hopple shall fall away from the legs of the slave; that his breast, whether black or white, shall be stained no more with blood from the necklace of spikes of iron; that man can walk the earth untortured by that cankerous anguish with which every proud and sympathetic soul sees his likeness and his fellow degraded among owned brutes.

Though unfortunately protected by constitutional state sovereignty, Whitman considers slavery "in contempt of [the] letter and spirit" of American law. Democratic sensibility demands that every "sympathetic soul" see his likeness and fellowship with the black slave. For slavery, as he goes on to say, is "the greatest undemocratic un-Americanism of all," establishing "the odious distinction of an inferior class, composed of all who are not owners of slaves."

The institution of slavery, for Whitman, is profoundly discordant with the foundational American principles, at the heart of the Revolution, reaffirmed in Jeffersonian republicanism and defended and developed through Jacksonian America: that power must not reside in elite social classes ruling over those below them, through a hierarchical, authoritarian, and fixed social-economic-political structure. In notes on "the true American Character" dating from 1856, Whitman contrasts the employer who is "easy and friendly with his workmen" with "the stern master of slaves" and all who make "ignominious distinctions," and comments:

I say that the idea and practice of all the present relics of imported feudal manners, the taking off of hats in any presence, and all sirring and Mr.-ing with all their vast entourage, and all that depends upon the principle they depend upon are foreign to These States, are to go the same road hence as the idea and practice of royalty have gone.

Slavery, to Whitman, stands as the last, hideous vestige in the New World of this feudal, old European order.

Whitman's poetry, written at a different time and in a different medium than his newspaper prose, extends and clarifies his earlier journalistic intentions. *Leaves of Grass* offers extraordinary haunting figures of slavery that emphasize the essential human equality of person to person: in the runaway slave of "Song of Myself," housed in "a room that enter'd from my own," and fed "next me at table" (Song 10); or in the image of the poet himself as "the hounded slave" – "I wince at the bite of the dogs . . . hell and despair are upon me" (Song 33). Whitman is most subversive and transformative in "I Sing the Body Electric" where he converts the very scene of auction into its own critique: "I help the auctioneer – the sloven does not half know his business." What Whitman displays is the radical personhood of the black man, in that sanctity of selfhood, that epitome of volition, body, sense, and possibility which stands at the center of every human person.

The slave, thus, is the terrible vestige of an oppressive feudal order, in a moral sense, but also as this takes on, in America, specifically political form. Against this Old World oppression Whitman opposes what he repeatedly calls (as do many others, from the *Federalist Papers* through Lincoln) the "experiment" of government by, for, and of the people. Whitman's writings are pervaded by an amazed excitement at the invention of popular sovereignty. Anti-hierarchical in social implication and instituted in representative government, the Revolution conceived sovereign power as inhering not in a ruling class of royal and entitled nobility, but in the common people, who, self-governing, delegated power to officials subordinate to the popular authority. Like de Tocqueville's account of democracy in America but without that writer's self-confessed sympathies with federalist elitism, Whitman's texts stand as testimonies of wonder at this revolutionary relocation of power such that authority resides not in the monarch, with the rights of the common man granted as concessions from above, but rather in the common people themselves, with the government itself nothing more than their delegated authority.

Whitman, in his political origins, education, and alignments was first pledged as a Jacksonian Democrat, as this tradition claimed the program and commitments of Jeffersonian republicanism. Such republican American political theory and practice had been one of reasserting and more firmly institutionalizing the popular power base (alongside the ever increasing and painful anomaly of slavery itself, and of course with no reflection on women's political rights). Its course is marked by the victory of Jefferson over the Federalists in 1800, and then aggressively by Andrew Jackson's Presidency. Jackson had opposed John Quincy Adams exactly on the issue of representative structure. Having lost to Adams in 1824 after winning in the popular vote but not in the electoral college, Jackson vehemently opposed the older conception of deferential and elite politics which Adams still upheld (in his disastrous First Address to the Congress in 1825, Adams exhorted the Representatives "not to be palsied by the will of our constituents"). Jackson's own First Annual Message (8 December 1829) after his election in 1828 calls for the direct, popular election of both President and Vice-President in the name of the "experiment" of the American system of government: "To the people belongs the right of electing their Chief Magistrate . . . Experience proves that in proportion as agents to execute the will of the people are multiplied there is danger of their wishes being frustrated." Jackson went on to propose a roster of changes to strengthen the principle of popular sovereignty and to increase the dependence of Representatives upon constituents: a term limit for the Presidency and broadly for public office; rotation of office; direct election of the Senate; election of judgeships; the revocation of property requirements both for holding public office and for the (white male) suffrage; new popular devices of nomination; new districting procedures; and support for the right of constituents to direct their Representatives by instruction.

Jacksonian politics is best known for its reorganization of the party system, its attack on the Central Bank, and Jackson's expanded use of political journals such as those for which Whitman wrote. But these commitments took shape through an articulated vision of the structure of representative government, affirming a broad electorate and subordinating elected officials to constituents. Jackson based the authority of the Presidency itself on its claim to represent the entire people of the United States, and as the single office to do so. It is Jackson, indeed, who officially stated for the first time that "The President is the direct representative of the American people."

Both Whitman's politics and his art are deeply informed by this liberal-republican structure of political representation. It is fundamental not only to his vision of America, but to his poetics and specifically to the role of his poet. Writing in the Democratic *Brooklyn Daily Eagle* (20 April 1847), he asks:

how many ages rolled away while political action, which rightly belongs to every man whom God sends on earth with a soul and a rational mind, was confined to a few great and petty tyrants . . . Is it too much to feel this joy that among *us* the *whole surface* of the body politic is expanded to the sun and air, and each man feels his rights and *acts* them?

Whitman, when he turns to poetry, offers "Myself" as representative of this political configuration. His transformation from political journalist to poet transfigures just this representational structure. That is, Whitman throughout *Leaves of Grass* and especially in the "Song of Myself" can be seen as adopting a stance of transformed political leadership.

This is one sense in which the "Song's" opening lines should be taken:

> I celebrate myself, and sing myself,
> And what I assume you shall assume,
> For every atom belonging to me as good belongs to you.

To "celebrate" suggests a holiday, especially as a public or national commemoration. And when Whitman opens the "Song" saying, "what I assume you shall assume," he does not mean to impose, but to take on, or take up; and it is not accidental that "assume" is what people do when they take up political office. It is similarly suggestive that throughout his journalistic career Whitman wrote leaders.

Whitman's vocabulary of poetics in fact repeatedly introduces terms resonant with political usage. The most obvious example of this is liberty, central first to the discourse of republican ideology and then to sectional conflict. Whitman makes this (also) a term of poetics, when, as in *The American Primer*, he defines the "Real Grammar" as the "liberty to all to carry out the spirit of the laws" and calls on American writers to "show far more freedom in the use of words." In the 1855 Preface, poets are specifically "the voice and exposition of liberty. They out of ages are worthy the grand idea . . . the attitude of great poets is to cheer up slaves and horrify despots." Whitman's central naming of himself as "a kosmos . . . turbulent, fleshy, sensual . . . whoever degrades another degrades me" (Song 24) similarly makes use of a revolutionary and republican rhetoric associating the common people with just such turbulence in opposition to enslavement and tyranny. In the "18th Presidency!" he pits the "Three Hundred and Fifty Thousand Owners of Slaves" against the "fierce and turbulent races" of America's working people whom "Liberty has nursed in these States," and whom slavery betrays. As to poets, in his Letter to Emerson, Whitman calls on them to walk "freely out from the old traditions, as our poetics has walked out" into an America "agitated and turbulent."

Whitman's key notion of translation has at least one political echo in a speech delivered at the wildly exuberant Free-Soil Convention at Buffalo in 1848, which Whitman attended as delegate from Kings County. Joshua Leavitt there proclaimed: "The Liberal Party is not dead, but *translated*." Perhaps most striking is the way Whitman's famous description of the *Leaves of Grass* as itself a "language experiment" transmutes a signal word for American popular government: from the *Federalist Papers*, which uses the word throughout to denote experiments in government and particularly the "experiment of an extended republic"; through Jefferson, whose first Inaugural Address urges "the honest patriot" not to abandon what has proved a "successful experiment" in government; through Lincoln, in, for example, his Address to the Lyceum at Springfield in 1838, where he recalls how at first the republic "was felt by all to be an undecided experiment; now, it is understood to be a successful one . . . to display before an admiring world, a practical demonstration of the truth of a proposition, which had hitherto been considered, at best no better, than problematical; namely, the capability of a people to govern themselves."

Whitman uses this term equally in its specific political sense. He calls, in his editorial pieces, for the nation to go "onward to the very verge with experiment of popular freedom"; to "throw the doors wider and wider and carry our experiment of democratic freedom to the very verge of the limit";

to continually add "to our great experiment of how much liberty society will bear." In *Democratic Vistas* he describes the nation as one "trying continually new experiments," meaning, specifically, as "choosing new delegations" such that "the average man . . . only is important. He, in these States, remains immortal owner and boss, deriving good uses, somehow, out of any sort of servant in office."

These political meanings are then directly imported into his poetic ones. In "A Backward Glance" he writes: "Behind all else that can be said, I consider *Leaves of Grass* and its theory experimental – as, in the deepest sense, I consider our American republic itself to be, with its theory." The translation from politics to poetics is made explicit in the conclusion of his 1876 Preface, which moves from the "new experiments" of America's revolutionary events to "the experiments of my poems."

Whitman's sense of the American experiment specifically commits him to the double structure of democratic representation, from politics through poetics: that the Representative is both in authority over those he represents and yet is also authorized by them; that he is both in the government and among the governed; is both above and of the people, both independent actor and agent, sovereign and subject; acting by mandate but also, in Edmund Burke's term, as trustee. No longer subjects, but rather citizens, the people rather than monarchic authority become the locus of sovereign power. And the Representative must both reflect the people's will and lead them.

The seriousness and depth of Whitman's study of political theory is quite evident in his prose writing. It can be seen, for example, in an editorial called "New Light and Old": "The recognized doctrine that the people are to be governed by some abstract power, apart from themselves, has not, even at this day and in the country, lost its hold . . . Men must be 'masters unto themselves,' and not look to presidents and legislative bodies for aid." In a piece called "Nationality (And Yet)" Whitman explains: "the theory of this Republic is not that the General government is the fountain of all life and power . . . but that THE PEOPLE are, represented in both, underlying both the General and State governments." As Whitman puts it in the 1855 Preface, "Other states indicate themselves in their deputies . . . but the genius of the United States is not best or most in its executives or legislatures, nor in its ambassadors or authors or colleges or churches or parlors, nor even in its newspapers or inventors . . . but always most in the common people." Public office as Whitman conceives it is founded in this distributive structure. It is a mode of being among the common people, not apart from them, or rather, of being both among and apart. The Representative here represents the common people not only as their deputy, but because he remains one of them.

T. S. Eliot, in his "Observations on Walt Whitman," remarks that "just as Tennyson liked monarchs, Whitman liked presidents." But Whitman's President is more like a republican delegate than a British monarch. And it is the office of the President which Whitman's poet particularly transfigures, as the political model for the poet's own role. It was in the face of the failed Presidencies of Fillmore, Pierce, and Buchanan that Whitman felt impelled to run for his own office of poet. He does so in the name of the double structure of liberal-democratic representation as service, indignantly contrasting "Rulers strictly out of the Masses" with the actual "current officials." (As Whitman puts it in the 1855 Preface, "The President tak[es] off his hat to [the people] not they to him.") "We elect Presidents, Congressmen, &c.," he writes in "Notes Left Over," "not so much to have them consider and decide for us, but as surest practical means of expressing the will of majorities on mooted questions, measures, &c."

Whitman takes this republican leadership structure of public servant rather than sovereign, speaking for the people from among them, if also to the people from before them, as the structure of his poetic leadership. His editorial writings are scattered with intriguing remarks about his evolving ambitions phrased in terms of political and specifically Presidential office. "I have sometimes pictured a nation of loafers," he muses proleptically, adding: "for myself, I have had serious thoughts of getting up a regular ticket for President and Congress and Governor and so on for the loafer community in general." Of his newspaper work he later muses: "There is a curious sort of sympathy . . . that arises in the mind of the newspaper conductor with the public he serves. He gets to *love* them . . . Perhaps no office requires a greater union of rare qualities than that of a true editor." Especially vivid is a piece entitled "Hero Presidents," where he comments: "He is but a poor lawgiver who legislates . . . without remembering that men are also endowed with faculties of imagination" and reminds that in times past "the poet, the priest and the warrior exercise[d] more influence over men's minds than the statesman and legislator." These images of poetic office finally burst forth in the Preface to the first edition of *Leaves of Grass*: "Of all nations the United States with veins full of poetical stuff most need poets . . . Their Presidents shall not be their common referee so much as their poets shall."

The President Whitman has been most closely associated with is Lincoln. But the structure of this relationship is complicated not least by the fact that Whitman essentially foretold Lincoln before his election, that in Lincoln, reality (at last) met Whitman halfway. In the "18th Presidency!" Whitman conjures "the Redeemer President" who "fullest realizes the rights of individuals," and who "is not be exclusive, but inclusive." Whitman's politics match

Lincoln's on many specific points, and particularly in an implacable opposition to the extension of slavery into new territories, while feeling Constitutionally constrained from interfering in the established institution peculiar to the already constituted Southern states, in the name of the Union. But the more profound intersection between them lies in the foundation of these political positions in their shared imagining of the American experiment of representative government. Whitman's politics, that is, stretches from Jackson to Lincoln (across party affiliations), and shares with Lincoln the republican tradition of self-government and its institutions. Whitman's (as Lincoln's) commitment to "Union" is often weighed against that to "Emancipation." Both stances, however, derive from loyalty to the principles of self-government, where the equal right to participation and representation is opposed to what Whitman constantly refers to as caste hierarchy. For Whitman, as for Lincoln, it is just this equal right to participation which is promised and guaranteed by the Declaration of Independence.

No less striking are the shared rhetorical practices and resources deployed by both of these great writers. Whitman's praise of Lincoln's literary skill at "indirections" is subtly self-revealing, recalling Whitman's own figures. The power and resonance of Lincoln's prose, like Whitman's, resides in part in its rhetorical evocation of republican tradition. Like Whitman in the "18th Presidency!", Lincoln persistently through the late 1850s denounced slavery extension as "boldly suggest [ing] that slavery is better than freedom," whereas "this government was instituted to secure the blessings of freedom, and . . . slavery is an unqualified evil of the negro, of the white man, to the soil, and to the State." The conflict between those opposed to slavery as against slaveholders Lincoln names in the final debate with Douglas at Alton to be

the eternal struggle . . . from the beginning of time . . . The one is the common right of humanity and the other the divine right of kings . . . No matter in what shape it comes, whether from a king who seeks to bestride the people of his own nation and live by the fruit of their labor, or from one race of men as an apology for enslaving another race, it is the same tyrannical principle.

In the face of British ambivalence towards the war effort, Lincoln persistently describes the Civil War as "essentially a People's contest . . . a struggle for maintaining in the world that form and substance of government whose leading object is to elevate the condition of men . . . to afford all an unfettered start, and a fair chance in the race of life." Lincoln, in a special 4 July speech to the Congress, 1861, reminds that "Our popular government has often been called an experiment," "a government of the people, by the same people." But the crisis around the secession of the Southern states puts this very possibility into question, as though such "a government of necessity [must] be too strong for the liberties of its own people, or too weak to maintain its own existence."

Whitman takes up these matters of political theory in his tract "The 18th Presidency!" which opens:

Before the American era, the programme of the classes of a nation read thus, first the king, second the noblemen and gentry, third the great mass of . . . all laboring persons. The first and second classes are unknown to the theory of the government of these States; the likes of the class rated third on the old programme were intended to be, and are in fact . . . the American nation, the people.

But this republican order is being betrayed by a "deferential" public which allows itself to "be managed in many respects as is only proper under the personnel of a king and hereditary lords."

Not least, the Presidency is corrupt, imposing itself upon the people in the name of ruling interests, so that "every trustee of the people is a traitor." Against this regressive aristocracy of power Whitman poses the "clean superiority" of "qualified mechanics and young men," making them the ones truly fit for office. In this sense, the call in the "18th Presidency!" for a "Redeemer President" nominates not Lincoln, but Whitman himself, as Presidential candidate. His concluding call to "circulate and reprint this Voice of mine" casts the tract as campaign literature. Polemical tirades cannot conceal Whitman's self-descriptive call to "some heroic, shrewd, fully-informed, healthy-bodied, middle-aged, beard-faced American blacksmith or boatman [to] walk into the Presidency, dressed in a clean suit of working attire, and with the tan all over his face, breast, and arms." Yet it is not to the literal Presidency, but to a poetic one, that Whitman nominates himself. "I seek to initiate my name," he concludes. "I perceive that the best thoughts they [the people] have wait unspoken, impatient to be put in shape."

Whitman, in manuscript notes, is critical of Emerson as somewhat the "gentleman," evading the "grand turbulence in the United States with all its multitudinous noise and practical business and politics and vehement and oceanic crowds" and says of those like him: "endlessly gesticulating and talking in every key especially the loud ones is painful to them." In "Notes Left Over" he similarly associates Emerson with notions of a "select class, superfined, (demarcated from the rest,) the plan of Old World lands and literatures" which is not, however, "the true plan for us, and indeed is death to it." America's instead is "an immense and distinctive commonalty over our vast and varied area . . . a great, aggregated, real PEOPLE . . . made of develop'd heroic individuals." But

Whitman's own notions of poetic representation support and reflect Emerson's. Referring to "the poet's fidelity to his office," already in "The Poet" Emerson declares the poet to be "representative: he stands among partial men for the complete man, and apprises us not of his wealth, but of the common wealth." The relation between the complete man and the partial one is a difference not in kind, but in realization, not least in participation in the commonwealth. In his later *Representative Men*, Emerson declares that "Great men" are not a "caste," but a "promise to virtue" – a promise which all men are called to, but which is marked out by "leaders," who, in one of many Emersonian political puns, "admit us to the constitution of things." "As to what we call the masses and the common man," Emerson writes, "there are no common men – all are at last of a size; and true art is only possible on the conviction that every talent has its apotheosis somewhere." For this apotheosis Emerson uses the language of representative democracy no less than Whitman does: "But also the constituency determines the vote of the representative. He is not only representative, but participant. Like can only be known by like. He knows about them in that he is of them."

Emerson's representative, then, like Whitman's, is finally the common man transfigured, who in turn brings others towards transfiguration. Whitman's, in this sense, is not so much a *vox populi* directly broadcasting a collective voice, but rather offers an individuated, translated voice representing the community. Neither only a common man, nor an authoritative self imposing himself, Whitman is instead both among the common and above them, both one of "the roughs" and leader. It is exactly this double possibility, this positioning within and before the people, that his adaptation and transfiguration of the liberal-republican model of representation offers. He is a figure that speaks both for and to the people, acting as their voice yet also urging them to speak for themselves, in a formative politics directed towards realizing what each has not yet become. Whitman in his 1855 Preface writes: "From the eyesight proceeds another eyesight and from the hearing proceeds another hearing and from the voice proceeds another voice eternally curious of the harmony of things with man. To these respond perfections not only in the committees that were supposed to stand for the rest but in the rest themselves just the same." Biblical modulations here beautifully convey the address of the representative to those he represents: his appeal to "another eyesight" and "another hearing" asserts "perfections" not yet achieved. It is the standpoint of a better world as brought to bear on this one. This never negates the conditions of the world, which Whitman implicitly critiques as requiring transformation. Nor does it transcend ordinary conditions; its spokesman remains one among the "rest," among the common people in their common world. The Representative is thus the voice of the common people and also "another voice," in a structure where society is both confronted and called to transfiguration.

FIGURAL POWER

Whitman offers his Myself as Representative in a transfiguration of American political tradition. But while political concerns run through *Leaves of Grass* as a continual engagement, politics constitutes only one of many levels of figural meaning in *Leaves of Grass*. It is just this creation of multiple, mutually reflecting levels of meaning which is at the center of Whitman's art. Whitman's poetry can look like the "scrapbasket" one early reviewer described it to be, as if he merely wrote down whatever came into his head or caught his eye. Yet this haphazard appearance belies a carefully crafted poetic structure (as his many, many revisions attest). Whitman's poetic has its foundation in his ability to create intersecting, elaborating, enlarging, and echoing levels of interrelated figures, with each a reflection and extension of each. His texts are remarkably able to sustain readings on this multiplicity of levels. Whitman can be read according to any one of these levels, but to do so exclusively is in a sense to betray his poetry to what he calls in "Slang in America" a "bald literalism." Against such literalism Whitman opposes "indirection," as the power to "express itself illimitably, which in highest walks produces poets and poems." Whitman's role as poetic Representative is to educate each reader into such illimitable expression. He is not so much the common man, as representative of his/her promise. He places himself at once among Americans and before them, in service and as standard bearer of each one's potential to interpret the world in this multiple way. It is his to inaugurate each into the exercise of just such figural power, which serves as Whitman's ultimate emblem of both poetic realization and democratic participation.

"Song of Myself 6," on what the grass is, acts not only as a kind of title poem to *Leaves of Grass* but also as a model and method of Whitmanian poetics:

> A child said *What is the grass?* fetching it to me with full hands;
> How could I answer the child? I do not know what it is any more than he.

> I guess it must be the flag of my disposition, out of hopeful green stuff woven.

> Or I guess it is the handkerchief of the Lord,
> A scented gift and remembrancer designedly dropt,
> Bearing the owner's name someway in the corners, that we may see and remark,
>   and say Whose? . . .

> Or I guess it is a uniform hieroglyphic,

And it means, sprouting alike in broad zones and narrow zones,
Growing among black folks as among whites,
Kanuck, Tuckahoe, Congressman, Cuff, I give them the same, I receive them
    the same.

And now it seems to me the beautiful uncut hair of graves.

To answer what the grass "is" would be impossible for Whitman. There is no one essence or definition that he could, according to his poetic commitments, know. Instead, what Whitman offers is a series of figures, potentially endless, each giving rise to the next in a processional energy implicitly able to accommodate further figurations endlessly. The grass is not the "flag" of Whitman's Romantic "disposition" *or* a transmuted Puritan sign as "handkerchief of the Lord," itself imaged through an erotic "scented gift and remembrancer," *or* a democratic "uniform hieroglyphic . . . Growing among black folks as among whites" *or* "the beautiful uncut hair of graves." The grass is each of these, as each stands for each, in a pluralized rather than unified structure whose center is the energy itself able to produce these and countless other figures. The form here of ongoing list – almost a catalogue of figural transformation – marks one of Whitman's core methods in the poem: the stringing on of figure after figure in a linear chain of multiple possibilities.

The "uncut hair of graves" becomes the figure Whitman here more fully elaborates, and he does so in a peculiarly Whitmanian direction:

Tenderly will I use you curling grass.
It may be you transpire from the breasts of young men,
It may be if I had known them I would have loved them,
It may be you are from old people, or from offspring taken soon out of
    their mothers' laps,
And here you are the mothers' laps.

This grass if very dark to be from the white heads of old mothers . . .
Dark to come from under the faint red roofs of mouths.

O I perceive after all so many uttering tongues,
And I perceive they do not come from the roofs the mouths for nothing.

On one level, what Whitman goes on to describe is the grass of graves. But when he says he will "use" this "curling grass" he means he will do so in complexly figural fashion. The grass, quite physically, "transpire[s] from the breasts of young men," from "old people," and "from offspring taken soon out of their mothers' laps." In this sense, the graves physically are "the mothers' laps" from which grass grows. The mythological nuance of the Mother suggested in the curling hair is given a disturbing, almost grotesque physical reality. If the grass is then described in turn as "so many uttering tongues" and hence an image for Whitman's own poetic leaves, it does not thereby lose its elemental sense of having grown not only as an image of, but physically from, "the faint red roofs" of buried, rotting "mouths."

Whitman here makes the body, bodily life and death, fertility and decay, one substratum for poetic reference and interpretation. This is another level of figuration throughout his poems, not so much as a "literal" sense of physical or primary reference, as one of many levels of poetic meaning, in which the body itself is a poetic site and figure.

Whitman's poetry was from the first controversial in its handling of physical life. After the outbreak of the Civil War, Whitman had moved to Washington, DC, taking on part time work with the Army Paymaster's office while volunteering as wound-dresser to care for injured and dying soldiers. He was, however, dismissed in 1865 from his next post in the Department of the Interior for the "indecency" of *Leaves of Grass*, whose first (1855), second (1856), and third (1860) editions had appeared. (He was subsequently employed by the Attorney General's office until leaving Washington for Camden in 1873–4, after having suffered his first paralytic stroke.) This sort of squeamish aggression resurfaced in 1882, when *Leaves* (now in its seventh edition of 1881) was prosecuted by the Society for the Prevention of Vice and banned in Boston. As to Whitman's reaction, he chose to ignore Emerson's prudent advice to excise objectionable material in their famous walk on Boston Common of 1882. Whitman had in fact announced his intentions long before, in his "Letter to Emerson" of 1856 where he spoke of the "divinity of sex" and proclaimed:

Of bards for These States, if it come to a question, it is whether they shall celebrate in poems the eternal decency of the amativeness of Nature, the motherhood of all, or whether they shall be the bards of the fashionable delusion of the inherent nastiness of sex, and of the feeble and querulous modesty of deprivation. This is important in poems, because the whole of the other expressions of a nation are but flanges out of its great poems.

Rejecting the "delusion of the inherent nastiness of sex," Whitman asserts its place in the national literature as a resource among "the whole of the other expressions of a nation."

Such physical and sexual life is decisive and challenging in the extraordinary vision of Song 5:

> I believe in you my soul, the other I am must not abase itself to you
> And you must not be abased to the other.
>
> Loafe with me on the grass, loose the stop from your throat,
> Not words, not music or rhyme I want, not custom of lecture, not even
>   the best,
> Only the lull I like, the hum of your valved voice.

> I mind how once we lay such a transparent summer morning,
> How you settled your head athwart my hips and gently turn'd over upon
>   me,
> And parted the shirt of my bosom-bone, and plunged your tongue to my
>   bare-stript heart,
> And reach'd till you felt my beard, and reach'd till you held my feet,
>
> Swiftly arose and spread around me the peace and knowledge that pass all
>   the argument of the earth,
> And I know that the hand of God is the promise of my own,
> And I know that the spirit of God is the brother of my own,
> And that all the men ever born are also my brothers,
>   and the women my sisters and lovers,
> And that a kelson of the creation is love,
> And limitless are leaves stiff or drooping in the fields.

Song 6 presents Whitman's basic method of consecutive figural extension, in which figure follows figure as in a chain. Song 5 offers another no less fundamental technique basic to his poetic venture: that of dream-vision. Here, multiple figures, instead of being posted consecutively, are overlayed one on the other, in an intensive density rather than extensive imagery. These dream-visions, apparently at the opposite pole from descriptive catalogue, in fact rework them in a different compositional mode. "Song of Myself" goes back and forth between each of these methods, with, for example, the dream-vision of the twenty-eight bathers in Song 11, as against the catalogue technique in, for example, Song 8; and with various combinations of the two. The overlayed triadic images of the later elegies "Out of the Cradle" or "When Lilacs Last in the Dooryard Bloom'd" lean towards the one way; the striding chanting of "Song of the Answerer" or "On Blue Ontario's Shore" pursue the other.

Here, in Song 5, Whitman presents sexual experience as mystical, drawing on long-established, ancient traditions. The imagery of love of God as sexual is as old as mysticism itself. *Song of Songs* (surely one echo in the title "Song of Myself") is one rich source for these mirroring loves, erotic and spiritual, human and divine, then continuing through such early medieval visionaries as St. Bernard of Clairvaux, to its later medieval flowering in, for example, St. Teresa of Avila. The body becomes an avenue upward towards spirit, making sexuality an ecstatic adventure of the soul. But Whitman, rather than accommodating this tradition, here recasts it. He does not simply transcend physical sexuality into the self-canceling image of divine union of mystical tradition, where the elevation of sexuality to spiritual vision negates it as a physical experience. But he does not invert the tradition into a literality of (homo)erotic practice either, making spirit an image of mere material body.

Sexuality and ecstatic religious experience instead reflect and mirror each other, opening into further senses of self and world.

Whitman in fact deploys the power of sexual figuration to represent a breathtaking variety of experience, spanning the sexual, the religious, the aesthetic, and the social. Unpacking the senses of this verse thus requires tracing out almost every Whitmanian topic across almost every Whitmanian tropological field.

> I believe in you my soul, the other I am must not abase itself to you
> And you must not be abased to the other.

The soul's "other" surely evokes the body, whose hierarchies of abasement are here, however, utterly undone. In Whitman, neither body nor soul has precedence, neither merely serves nor is canceled for the other. Yet this (counter) metaphysical reading does not exhaust the passage. Its language is purposefully open. Soul and other can also be read as different aspects or regions within each self, as these in turn become the bases for, or images of, erotic and indeed broadly social interaction. Or the soul's "other" may also be others, in a social vision: although just how far Whitman is truly able to sustain an "other" such as he invokes in this passage, and across what distances and differences, remains a haunting tension within his work.

The social vision is pursued in the last part of Song 5, where "all the men ever born are also my brothers, and the women my sisters and lovers." But the social would not exclude the religious. Each is an image and extension of the other. The Song's incantatory concluding passage relocates religious experience in an imminently societal bond, and the social bond as religious: "the spirit of God is the brother of my own." That "the hand" and "spirit of God" are made an image of "my own" extends beyond, or rather through, Whitman's unique personhood to all those he would represent, exactly by calling them into the visionary experience he here conjures, such that (and not least by this very poetry) ultimately "all the men ever born are also my brothers."

The self, that is, remains tied to community, religious and political. And yet this does not negate an immediate and personal selfhood either. Personal autobiography makes up yet another level of meaning, another ongoing event in the poem, as yet another sustained, haunting, yet non-exclusionary figural level throughout. The sexuality of Song 5 points backwards to mystical tradition, but also directly at Whitman, in an almost irresistible autobiographical pull – one, however, that has never been fully satisfied. Through all the controversies over *Leaves* during Whitman's lifetime, attention was paid to heterosexual imagery only. But the text's homoerotic power has been, then and since, increasingly recognized. Lovingly detailed descriptions of men in Whitman's poetry well outweigh attention to women who, despite Whitman's fine intentions of being scrupulously fair-minded, interest him far less. His work as wound-dresser during the Civil War, his Calamus poems, where he is "Resolv'd to sing no songs to-day but those of manly attachment," various biographical hints and relationships (especially that with Peter Doyle in the late 1860s) attest to his homoeroticism. The vivid etching of Song 5 seems especially to demand some autobiographical reference, some momentous encounter of erotic love, perhaps first revealing to Whitman his own homosexuality. No one specific event has, however, been unearthed. Whitman himself refused directly to address the homosexual implication of his work. Yet his troping, diversionary answer to John Addington Symonds's question, weirdly claiming to have fathered six children (could he mean his own siblings, whom he cared for so parentally?) is not mere coyness. Sexuality is certainly central, and is unmistakably evoked in the homoerotic implication of the "head athwart my hips" of Song 5, but it does not alone determine or enclose the passage's meaning, as neither does the personal or autobiographical.

The poem in practice is and is not autobiographical, or is autobiographical in a peculiarly Whitmanian figural sense. Autobiography takes its place among the diverse figural patterns that Whitman interweaves here and throughout his *Leaves*, where it functions on diverse levels. As Whitman warns in an introductory poem, "Even I myself I often think know little or nothing of my real life, / Only a few hints, a few diffused clews and indirections" ("When I read the Book"). What the poem fully offers is transfigured autobiography as exemplary biography. If, as Whitman reminisces in "A Backward Glance O'er Travel'd Roads," *Leaves of Grass* was "an attempt, from first to last, to put a *Person*, a human being (myself, in the latter half of the Nineteenth Century, in America,) freely, fully, and truly on record," still, his own "personality" is posed as the best answer to this crucial question: "how best can I express my own distinctive era and surroundings, America, Democracy." His is "autobiography in colossal cipher," as Emerson recommends in "The Poet." In *Democratic Vistas*, Whitman calls this "personalism," but as conceived in terms of "thorough infusions through the organizations of political commonality." The poet, he writes in the 1855 Preface, must "flood himself with the immediate age as with vast oceanic tides." He is "himself the age transfigured."

These various levels come together in Song 5's declaration of love: "a kelson of the creation is love." Eros is the bonding-expanding energy in self, poem, and society, with "kelson" a master image as the overlapping timbers that brace a ship's keel. Whitman's love is personal and social, transformatively religious and sexual. And the image of "kelson" includes still another dimension, still another figural level that courses through the poem continuously and crucially. This is the poem as self-describing, as constantly meditating on its own poetic norms, conduct, and processes. For the poem is no less an *ars poetica* than a political, or spiritual, or sexual expression. The imbricating, interlocking "kelson" self-describes Whitman's own core method of figural extension and overlaying, the interlocking of his own multiple levels of meaning. Such poetic self-description occurs in the imagery in Song 5 of "leaves stiff or drooping," which are at once natural and highly sexualized as autoerotic and phallic, and also refer to Whitman's own poetic "leaves" as they unfold in endless, transformative erotic creativity. Body and poem figure each other, as Whitman promises in the 1855 Preface: "Your flesh shall be a great poem and have the richest fluency not only in its words but in the silent lines of its lips and face and between the lashes of your eyes and in every motion and joint of your body." Accordingly, "amativeness of Nature" takes on wildly cosmic, as well as poetic and sexualized force in Song 24, when his poetic creativity spills forth as an orgasmic dawn of "libidinous prongs, seas of bright juice suffuse heaven." (Male) sexuality here represents Whitman's poetics itself (and just how far this masculine admits the feminine remains a question). Or, as he writes in "A Song of the Rolling Earth," "Human bodies are words, myriads of words, / (In the best poems re-appears the body)." Poetry, person, society, and nature all embody "The urge and urge and urge, / Always the procreant urge of the world." In Song 5, the imagery of "grass" and "throat" and "voice" and "tongue" and "leaves" all similarly refer to poetic vision and creativity, as do the "grass" and "tongues", the "hints" and the concluding declaration of Song 6, "all goes onward and outward," a description of the path of the poem itself. The revelation of Song 5, its sense of rendering some moment of ecstatic vision, has then not only a sexual, social, and religious shape but can be seen as an image of origin for Whitman's whole poetic venture, to which the remainder of his poetry bears witness. It is an initiation into visionary experience itself: reality itself revealed in all its figural multiplication, resonating through level after level of significance.

Thus the poem brings together a great variety of experiences, including the poetic itself, with each evoking a particular dimension, and yet, also, equally pointing towards (without canceling) these other dimensions of significance and figuration. This is ideally the case with every Whitmanian image. It is his great poetic, and also American faith, that such correlations can be perhaps limitlessly produced and sustained (although, as we shall see, it is his great skepticism and dissent that such correlations cannot be sustained, but are instead betrayed).

Whitman in this is realizing Emerson's definition of poetry as a "meter-making argument," what Whitman calls in *Democratic Vistas* an "image-making faculty" or "image-making work." Emerson meant, as Whitman realized, that poetry is made not of meter but of figures, of "their analogies, by curious removes, indirections . . . This is the image-making faculty, coping with material creation, and rivaling, almost triumphing over it." "The poetic quality is not marshaled in rhyme or uniformity or abstract addresses to things," he remarks in the 1855 Preface. Prosody is instead itself another figure for the poetic energies that act as "ground out of sight." For both writers, poetry is radically defined as figural language in imaginative creation, rather than as any prescribed formal pattern. Whitman's own poetic conduct is most obviously radical in its formal experimentation, its abandonment of meter and rhyme. Poetry is not reducible to these traditional formal structures as such – although poetry in Whitman, too, is necessarily formal in the sense of arranging words in intricate relationships. The very radicalness of Whitman's poetic experimentation – he repeatedly calls the poem a "language experiment" – forces attention back onto this primary poetic power: to represent and multiply meanings through imaginative connections. On these grounds the extraordinary composition of Whitman's poetic architecture becomes visible – the continuous and ongoing orchestration of these multiple levels of meaning in counterpoint and elaboration one with the other.

But this language experiment never loses its ties with the political and social experiment Whitman sees America to be. In being self-descriptive, the poem does not less describe its world, its society, its politics. In the 1855 Preface, traditionally formal poetics is itself compared to a "dressed up, a fine gentleman, distasteful to our instincts, foreign to our soil." Enforced "rhyme and its measurement-rules of iambic" would merely reiterate a "social etiquette of over-sea feudalism and caste," he writes in "Notes" on "New Poetry." And this poetic revolution is closely connected to other revolutions, in technology, in science, in industry, in communications. "The Muse of the Prairies" must "adapt itself to comprehend the size of the whole people . . . to the modern, the busy nineteenth century (as grandly poetic as any, only different) with steamships, railroads, factories, electric telegraphs, cylinder presses . . . to the dignity and heroism of the practical labor." Poetry too becomes heroic and practical labor, electric (a potent Whitman word for just this confluence of energies) as telegraph or press. All are in mutual relation and inter-transformation (although also in countertension against their divisive pulls), in a poetic method as well as subject of fluid and unfixed measures and rhythms and tropes.

Whitman has his own characteristic terms for this poetics of figuration on its many levels. Key words are: "transfigured," "translucent," "transparent," "transpired," or, as in one of Whitman's most forceful declarations, "translation": "I am the poet of the Body and I am the poet of the Soul . . . The first I graft and increase upon myself, the latter I translate into a new tongue" (Song 21). These various "trans" words signal Whitman's own core practice of transference from level to level in figural conversions, a metaphor of metaphor. "Through me forbidden voices," he writes, "Voices of sexes and lusts, voices veil'd and I remove the veil, / Voices indecent by me clarified and trans-figur'd . . . The spread of my own body, or any part of it, translucent" (Song 24). In Song 5 he speaks of his community of self and others as transparency: "I mind how once we lay such a transparent summer morning." In Song 6 the grass "transpire[s] from the breasts of young men" and Whitman wishes to "translate the hints about the dead young men and women."

Emerson, in "Representative Men," had written: "Each materiality has its celestial side; has its translation, through humanity, into the spiritual and nec-essary sphere." "Translation" here plays upon its traditional religious meaning of direct transport from this world to the next. Whitman takes this up, but extends it both vertically and horizontally, so that material/spiritual transmu-tations become further instances and images for the many mutually impli-cating networks of resonance that Whitman's poetry weaves. In *Democratic Vistas* he speaks of the poet as one whose "power (dearest of all to the sense of the artist) transacts itself." Just so the child-poet born "Out of the Cradle" is launched as "Cautiously peering, absorbing, translating." Body and soul, plea-sure and pain, heaven and hell, Whitman will "translate into a new tongue" (Song 21). The "Song of the Answerer" offers almost a kind of terminological précis when it names the poet to be he who "resolves all tongues into his own and bestows it upon men, and any man translates, and any man translates himself also."

Closely allied to words of translation, transparency, transpiring, transaction is Whitman's peculiar term "tally." This breaks forth in full resonance in the great Lincoln elegy, "When Lilacs Last in the Dooryard Bloom'd," but serves elsewhere as a pivotal term in theorizing poetic activity as envisioned correlation. "Speech is the twin of my vision," he writes in Song 25, "My knowledge, my live parts, it keeping tally with the meaning of all things." The "Notes" on "New Poetry" go on to declare that "poems of the first class, (poems of the depth, as distinguished from those of the surface,) are to be sternly tallied with the poets themselves." "Present literature," he writes in *Democratic Vistas*, "needs tally and express Nature," where

Nature, largely considered, involves the questions of the aesthetic, the emotional, and the religious . . . the whole orb, with its geologic history, the cosmos . . . the physical conscience, the sense of matter, and of good animal health — on these it must be distinctly accumulated, incorporated, that man, comprehending these, has, in towering superaddition, the moral and spiritual consciences . . . New law-forces of spoken and written language . . . tallies life and character, and seldomer tells a thing than suggests or necessitates it.

To tally is to align and amplify each realm of experience through further figural extensions, ever suggestive, never exhausted.

Other terms, too, appear in Whitman for the "translation" or "tally" of correlated experience: "echoes," "hints," "clues," "indirections," "indications," "threads"; also "drift" and "list." In "Kosmos" he generalizes them in the figure of a poet

> Who, out of the theory of the earth and of his or her body, understands
>   by subtle analogies all other theories,
> The theory of a city, a poem, and of the large politics of these States.

This complex figural orchestration may help illuminate Whitman's project of textual revision. His rearrangements, editings, and amendments to *Leaves of Grass* over the last decades of his life may reflect his attempt to rework towards denser or more extensive figural layering the multiple resonances he intends each figure to carry. The revisions may not have been, then, dilution or censorship, but rather a balancing of the forces he wished his poetry to unleash in greater complexity.

Although multiple figuration extends through *Leaves of Grass*, it is not sustained uniformly. The texts turn and shift, now towards one emphasis, now towards another, and with varying intensity. The second section of "Song of Myself" offers an outburst of multiple figuration.

> The smoke of my own breath,
> Echoes, ripples, buzz'd whispers, love-root, silk-thread, crotch and vine,
> My respiration and inspiration, the beating of my own heart, the passing
>   of blood and air through
> my lungs . . .
> The sound of the belch'd words of my voice loos'd to the eddies of the
>   wind,
> A few light kisses, a few embraces, a reaching around of the arms . . .
> The feeling of health, the full-noon trill, the song of me rising from bed
>   and meeting the sun.   (Song 2)

These lines represent or address, simultaneously, a number of different but interrelating levels: sexuality, as "kisses" and "embraces," with "a reaching around of the arms" become a cosmic, even mythological event as "the song of me rising from bed and meeting the sun." Poetic self-reflection is strongly marked, given physical, bodily shape as "The smoke of my own breath."

Whitman names elements and functions at once of his body and of his poetry: its tongue circulating from the soil through the life-spirit of air, its breath moving out to the world and receding back to the poet in a poetic respiration and inspiration. Such ebb and flow of breath recurs repeatedly through "Song of Myself" both as image and as broad movement: "These tend inward to me, and I tend outward to them" (Song 15); "Partaker of influx and efflux I" (Song 22); "One of that centripetal and centrifugal gang" (Song 43); and always at once as a description of the poetry even as of the poetic self. In Song 2, the terms of his poetics are sounded as "echoes," "beating" in physical/poetical rhythm through physically/poetically "belch'd words," then carried and figured in prophetic "wind."

Song 1 directs figural energy in a more specifically biographical direction. Song 1 is in many ways a birthday song, marking Whitman's family genealogy as well as the moment when he was mysteriously born from political journalist into poet:

> My tongue, every atom of my blood, form'd from this soil, this air,
> Born here of parents born here from parents the same, and their parents
>   the same,
> I, now, thirty-seven years old in perfect health begin,
> Hoping to cease not till death . . .

It is as if Whitman's poetic "tongue" has been directly formed from the American soil and air, both body and poem (body as poem) a national emblem. Family history, too, is meant here to represent public life. And indeed, Whitman's family was actively pledged to the revolutionary tradition (one of Whitman's brothers was named Thomas Jefferson; another, George Washington; another, Andrew Jackson). His father knew Tom Paine and Elias Hicks, was a member of the radical Workingman's Party, and admired Frances Wright. Elias Hicks, whom Whitman heard speak, joins together radical politics and radical religion. A Quaker (and Whitman's family had Quaker antecedents), he was committed to an unhierarchical equality among all souls in direct access to divinity through an "inner light." A radical Christianity thus confirms a radical politics of individual value and participation.

This intersection between personal biography, religious tradition, and national figure, recalls Puritan biographies. "Song of Myself" is also a recasting of a long American tradition of spiritual self-examination, turning, as is required within Puritan norms, around a conversion experience, figured in Song 5. These biographies evolved, through a combination with national history and Biblical narrative, into a mode of national biography (although in such cases, the exemplars waited for others to represent them, as Cotton

Mather did for John Winthrop as the American Nehemiah, rather than doing it for themselves). Individuals emerged as models not only of personal recti tude but of national destiny. In this way, their significance unfolded in the public sphere. Their personal history presented an image of communal life, in the promise of God. Ancient Israel provided the original type, as crossing individual leader and personified nation, whose historical course takes on a biographical shape from birth through adolescence and into maturity, and who is variously cast as firstborn and daughter, wife and wayward mistress of the Lord. The importance of biographical shaping for imagining community is thus already at work in the Biblical narratives, and was taken up into American narratives of emerging nationhood, and then by Whitman in his song of self-hood. In Song 1 and throughout *Leaves of Grass*, individual narrative represents the narratives of community and nation. The notion of Biblical type (a potent term in Whitman, invoking print, trope, and Biblical antecedent) which connected the individual to Old and New Testament figures adds yet another dimension to Whitman's notion of representative pattern.

When Whitman, in a June 1857 notebook entry, names his project in *Leaves* to be "The construction of a New Bible," he means also types of the representative self incarnating in a personal course the life of the community. But if the Bible is Whitman's model, it is not his master. In his hands Biblical modes undergo near complete transformation.

> I have heard what the talkers were talking, the talk of the beginning and
>   the end,
> But I do not talk of the beginning and the end.
>
> There was never any more inception than now,
> Nor any more youth or age than there is now,
> And will never be any more perfection than there is now,
> Nor any more heaven or hell than there is now.
>
> Urge and urge and urge,
> Always the procreant urge of the world.
>
> Out of the dimness opposite equals advance, always substance and
>   increase, always sex,
> Always a knit of identity, always distinction, always a breed of life.
> To elaborate is no avail, learn'd and unlearn'd feel that it is so . . .
>
> Clear and sweet is my soul, and clear and sweet is all that is not my soul.
> Lack one lacks both, and the unseen is proved by the seen,
> Till that becomes unseen and receives proof in its turn . . .
>
> Welcome is every organ and attribute of me, and of any man hearty and
>   clean,

Not an inch nor a particle of an inch is vile, and none shall be less
    familiar than the rest.

I am satisfied – I see, dance, laugh, sing
As the hugging and loving bed-fellow sleeps at my side through the
    night.   (Song 3)

It has long been recognized that a major resource for Whitman's experimental
poetics was the Bible, with its rhythmic, parallel repetitions as Whitman's
basic poetic unit of organization. Here Whitman may have a particular passage in view, to transformative purposes. It is presumably John who talks of
the "beginning and the end." But Paul, in Romans 1, speaks of "the wise
and the unwise"; of "heaven against all ungodliness"; of the "invisible things"
that are "clearly seen . . . by the things that are made"; of the "uncleanness
of lusts" to "dishonour their bodies", who are therefore "vile"; going on to
particularly condemn homosexuality. This is in extraordinary confluence with
Song 3, which, however, will not "talk of the beginning and the end," nor
of "heaven or hell"; and instead declares welcome "every organ" as "hearty
and clean," denying that "a particle of an inch is vile." Whitman specifically
celebrates the "procreant urge of the world," "always sex," and specifically the
"hugging and loving bed-fellow." Yet Whitman too speaks of the "unseen"
as "proved by the seen," and to the "learn'd and unlearn'd," he too speaks in
Biblical cadences. This is transmutation rather than mere repudiation. Old
doctrines are boldly translated into new structures. Whitman, as here, particularly marks a shift from other-worldly religious focus to an embrace of this
world as the site of spiritual experience.

Whitman does not sustain his intensity of figural conversion and resonance
equally throughout "Song of Myself" or Leaves of Grass. At times the verse
flattens towards single levels of representation, without a fuller play through
figural multiplications. The catalogue technique hovers between flattened historical or descriptive roster and lyric transformation, although even apparently
narrative lines can be self-descriptive poetically. It is clear that not every catalogue will yield to a unifying figural conversion. Yet even Song 33, where
the poet is "afoot with my vision," crosses in its long lists through the lands,
peoples, and politics ("through the office or public hall") of America. It takes
Biblical-mythological shape ("Walking the old hills of Judea with the beautiful gentle God by my side") and historical urgency. It is here that the poet
speaks as "the hounded slave, I wince at the bite of the dogs." And it is here that
he enters the "great battle-field," to "take part" in war and project the shape
of the heroic leader, who is also himself. This Song also includes the sorts of
meditations on poetic method which even descriptive language so often offers:

"I fly those flights of a fluid and swallowing soul . . . I help myself to material
and immaterial."

Song 8, an early catalogue in the poem, serves to initiate the reader towards
interpretive conversions of the material it presents, in the educative function
of the poem that reaches back towards its revolutionary role in building a
citizenry for self-government.

> The little one sleeps in its cradle,
> I lift the gauze and look a long time and silently brush away flies with
>   my hand
> The youngster and the red-faced girl turn aside up the bushy hill,
> I peeringly view them from the top.
>
> The suicide sprawls on the bloody floor of the bedroom,
> I witness the corpse with its dabbled hair, I note where the pistol has
>   fallen.
>
> The blab of the pave, tires of carts, sluff of boot-soles, talk of the
>   promenaders,
> The heavy omnibus, the driver with his interrogating thumb, the clank
>   of the shod horses on the granite floor,
> The snow-sleighs, clinking, shouted jokes, pelts of snow-balls,
> The hurrahs for popular favorites, the fury of rous'd mobs,
> The flap of the curtain'd litter, a sick man inside borne to the hospital,
> The meeting of enemies, the sudden oath, the blows and fall,
> The excited crowd, the policeman with his star quickly working his
>   passage to the centre of the crowd,
> The impassive stones that receive and return so many echoes,
> What groans of over-fed or half-starv'd who fall sunstruck or in fits,
> What exclamations of women taken suddenly who hurry home and give
>   birth to babes,
> What living and buried speech is always vibrating here, what howls
>   restrain'd by decorum,
> Arrests of criminals, slights, adulterous offers made, acceptances,
>   rejections with convex lips,
> I mind them or the show or resonance of them – I come and I depart.

Journalistic reportage transmutes before the reader's eyes into elements of
Whitmanian poetics: birth, sex, and death; the crowds of society and its dis-
orders, and the constraints of society and its orderers. American life is made a
glittering display of variegated sound, with linguistic and poetic implications.

"Blab," "interrogating thumb," "clank," "shouted jokes," "hurrahs,"
"groans," "exclamations," "offers made," "acceptances," "rejections with con-
vex lips" – the world is remade into poetic sound. And Whitman's poem
is itself "talk of the promenaders," is like "the impassive stones that receive
and return so many echoes." He is himself the instrument of the "living
and buried speech . . . always vibrating here," while his own poem, like the

turbulent crowd of democratic society, balances "howls restrain'd by decorum" and provides "the show or resonance of them."

Poetic self-description thus joins with personal, sexual, religious, national, and political orders. This remains the case, within a broad range of balances and emphases, throughout the poem. The catalogue of Song 15, to take another example, presents Whitman's democratic range of American citizenry, from prostitute to President. It (also) inscribes features of Whitman's personal history – his love of opera, his experience as carpenter, his commitment to loafing, his lunatic-like brother, his profession as printer, his exposure to the slave-market at New Orleans, his career as reporter. The "marksman" who "takes his position, levels his piece" is (also) a poet-figure, as is the printer ("print" persists throughout Whitman as a figure for poetry), and the "conductor" who "beats time for the band and all the performers who follow him." Personal experience becomes social representation, as figural images of each other and images for poetic figuration itself.

Transgressive forces – mob violence, crime, and adultery in Song 8, for example – are not omitted in these texts. It is Whitman's faith, and also anxiety, that discordant elements can be "restrain'd by decorum," can be taken into his account. Different levels of experience can complement, mirror, or extend each other, in a fluid orchestration both poetic and social. This premise of harmony reaches a crescendo in the concluding section of the "Song of Myself," which gathers together Whitman's figural patterns with special intensity, pointing towards his later, masterful "elegies."

> I too am not a bit tamed, I too am untranslatable,
> I sound my barbaric yawp over the roofs of the world.
>
> The last scud of day holds back for me,
> It flings my likeness after the rest and true as any on the shadow'd wilds,
> It coaxes me to the vapor and the dusk.
>
> I depart as air, I shake my white locks at the runaway sun,
> I effuse my flesh in eddies, and drift it in lacy jags.

In the final Song 52 (with one Song available, like Bible chapters, to be read each week of the year) the poet takes macrocosmic shape as cloud-vapor and/or comet ("I depart as air, I shake my white locks at the runaway sun, / I effuse my flesh in eddies, and drift it in lacy jags"), with perhaps some orgasmic suggestion (cf. "you my rich blood! your milky stream pale strippings of my life" in Song 24).

And it projects his own poetic commitments as "barbaric yawp over the roofs of the world." "Drift" too picks up from earlier usages as a sign of Whitmanian figural elaboration, while Whitman's core term, translation, makes a new and transmuted appearance: "I too am not a bit tamed, I too am untranslatable."

However placed in a grand orchestration, each element is also untranslatable, unique, and irreducible. The final lines reaffirm Whitman's poetic leadership as rooted in the common grass, yet ahead and summoning, with a last gesture of figural invitation: "Missing me one place search another."

"Song of Myself" is the first incandescent revelation of Whitman's vision of America. What it promises is a concurrence of diverse experiences, as well as unending imaginative production. The poem concludes with an intense experience of figural procedures into which the poem as a whole initiates the reader and by which it seeks to transform him or her. But Whitman is also aware of the tremendous obstacles and resistances to his enterprise. The levels of experience which he would align threaten to contradict, confound, or displace each other. This is not merely a problem of language and its misalignments. It is a problem of America. Whitman's vision of America is one in which each parameter should reflect and extend the other: physical expansion, economic productivity, technological advance, alongside cultural, moral, and creative flowering. But Whitman knows that as things stand in 1855, this is not the case. First, the American social contract contains, with slavery, its own betrayal; and second, the balance among these different spheres is not, as he will come increasingly to feel, easily kept or sustained. As *Leaves of Grass* pursues its course, it confronts directly forces of disruption, as they threaten to make the poem's figural patterns come undone.

The catalogue technique in *Leaves of Grass* in itself walks this difficult line between integration and dispersion. But this is not only a formal problem. It is equally a social and political problem, in an America of uneasy balance between its competing elements, trends, and commitments. "I Sing the Body Electric" is perhaps especially heroic in facing squarely the central betrayal of American social and political claims, slavery. Drawing on Whitman's three-month stint in New Orleans (his only visit to the deep South) working for the *Crescent* in 1848, the poem's "Body" of course intends the body politic as well, which the poet sets out to "discorrupt." "Electric" is one of Whitman's counters of specially dense interrelation. It evokes at once sexual attraction, spiritual extension, figural connection, scientific energy. "All is a procession, the universe is a procession with measured and perfect motion," section 6 of the poem ecstatically declares. But then we read section 7:

> A man's body at auction,
> (For before the war I often go to the slave-mart and watch the sale,)
>
> I help the auctioneer, the sloven does not half know his business.
>
> Gentlemen look on this wonder.
> Whatever the bids of the bidders they cannot be high enough for it . . .

In this head the all-baffling brain,
In it and below it the makings of heroes . . .

This is not only one man, this the father of those who shall be fathers in
their turns,
In him the start of populous states and rich republics,
Of him countless immortal lives with countless embodiments and
enjoyments.

Whitman commandeers the very language of the auction which would
reduce the human being to a material, economic commodity, and transforms
it into a declaration of illimitable and infinite value. He builds his appeal
out of traditions of the religious, moral sanctity of the individual as created
"wonder," then realized in traditions of a political citizenry each of whom
contributes to "populous states and rich republics." But "rich" here is a subtle
term. What he does not mean, what he is polemically countering, is economic
measure as asserting itself to be the determining value in America, and not
only in terms of slavery. The transmutation of his own, key word of tally or
counting to "countless" signals his own fierce defense of the republican life.
It must be more than mere economic gain and the reductive flattening of the
person to such calculated value, to say nothing of the denial of personhood for
the slave. Earlier in the poem he insisted: "The love of the body of man or
woman balks account, the body itself balks account." Section 7, in a stunning
rhetorical inversion, converts the auction scene of utmost degradation and
reduction to the revelation of the incalculable value of the individual, each one
"the makings of heroes."

The "Sea-Drift" poems are less overtly socio-political than is "I Sing the
Body Electric," but carry forward its painful confrontation with disruptive
forces. "Out of the Cradle" offers at once an intensively figural overlaying in
the manner of Whitman's dream-visions, but in a tense counter-pull against
explosive forces that threaten to disperse and unravel such figural patternings.
The text is intricately constructed. Multiple figuration is enacted phrase after
phrase, embedded in the poem's very grammar. Where Song 6 is an extensive
figural sequence, "Out of the Cradle," like Song 5, performs its sequence
intensively.

Out of the cradle endlessly rocking,
Out of the mocking-bird's throat, the musical shuttle,
Out of the Ninth-month midnight,
Over the sterile sands and the fields beyond, where the child leaving his
bed wander'd alone, bareheaded, barefoot,
Down from the shower'd halo,

Up from the mystic play of shadows twining and twisting as if they
 were alive,
Out from the patches of briers and blackberries,
From the memories of the bird that chanted to me,
From your memories sad brother, from the fitful risings and fallings I
 heard,
From under that yellow half-moon late-risen and swollen as if with tears,
From those beginning notes of yearning and love there in the mist,
From the thousand responses of my heart never to cease,
From the myriad thence-arous'd words,
From the word stronger and more delicious than any,
From such as now they start the scene revisiting,
As a flock, twittering, rising, or overhead passing,
Borne hither, ere all eludes me, hurriedly,
A man, yet by these tears a little boy again,
Throwing myself on the sand, confronting the waves
I, chanter of pains and joys, uniter of here and hereafter,
Taking all hints to use them, but swiftly leaping beyond them,
A reminiscence sing.

The first verse paragraph winds its way as one long sentence whose subject and verb are achieved only at the end, as the poet's self-naming in his poetic utterance: "I . . . A reminiscence sing." The grammatical promise is that this "I" will act as "chanter of pains and joys, uniter of here and hereafter." Yet this union remains open rather than closed, constructed through "Taking all hints to use them, but swiftly leaping beyond them." "Hints," one of Whitman's terms for his own figuration, will be both "used" and leaped "beyond." Experiences are linked together, but never finally; relationships are launched, but never exhausted. The multiplication of figures has always a dispersive effect no less than an organizing one. Images refract each other, phrases spin out into multiple references, grammatical links and antecedents slide into and point outward from each other.

The poem, as occurs in other Whitman elegies, works around a core of basic figures, here the sea, the bird, and the poet, as child and man. (Dis)connections are first effected by the grammatically floating images of this first long sentence, where almost every phrase can apply to a number of different subjects. The structure of prepositions accomplishes this grammatical magic. What comes "Out of the Cradle" (which is also the sea) is the child, in the birth of his awakening, but also the poet's memories, as this current song; also the bird's "musical shuttle" and chantings, a figure for the poet's song as well as for the child's awakening. It is child and bird and song (the birds' and the poet's) and also memory who move "Over the sterile sands," or "Down from the shower'd halo," or "Up from the mystic play of shadows" (with shadows a typical image of images). The "fitful risings and fallings" describe poem and sea and memory and birds and birds' song, all "twittering, rising, or overhead passing." All "start the scene revisiting," all are "Borne hither, ere all eludes me, hurriedly," in a fragile and urgent figural chain that is both binding and fluid, and above all deeply temporal.

These diverse and intercrossing figures are tracked or charted in the poem through a framework of antithetical forces of fertility and sterility, beginnings and endings, births and deaths. "The Word out of the Sea" of the poem's original 1859 title is proleptically announced here as "the word stronger and more delicious than any." That word, as the poem will reveal towards its close, is Death. Yet even now the poem turns to a death-vision: "Two feather'd guests from Alabama" arrive in a mating ritual which becomes an abyss of rupture. Their geographical origin adds to the poem an unmistakable political reference of civil division:

> *Two together!*
> *Winds blow south, or winds blow north,*
> *Day come white, or night come black . . .*
>
> Till of a sudden,
> May-be kill'd, unknown to her mate,
> One forenoon the she-bird crouch'd not on the nest,
> Nor return'd that afternoon, nor the next,
> Nor ever appear'd again.

South or North, white or black, the couplings also of America are torn asunder. But the political disruption is situated through the labor of poetic birth. The surviving male bird becomes the "solitary . . . lone singer," and the child, in the face of this rupture and irretrievable loss, now becomes poet.

> Yes my brother I know,
> The rest might not, but I have treasur'd every note
> For more than once dimly down to the beach gliding,
> Silent, avoiding the moonbeams, blending myself with the shadows,
> Recalling now the obscure shapes, the echoes, the sounds and sights
>   after their sorts,
> The white arms out in the breakers tirelessly tossing,
> I, with bare feet, a child, the wind wafting my hair,
> Listen'd long and long.
>
> Listen'd to keep, to sing, now translating the notes
> Following you my brother.

"My brother" is addressed to, and connects, child and bird, poet and child, poet and reader. The passage is dense with words of Whitmanian poetics: "shapes," "echoes," "sounds," as the child is now born into poet "translating the notes" (both musical and poetic) – the very act of figural conversion to which this poem is devoted and is at this moment enacting.

And yet, this moment of recollection is founded in disruption. The figures of poetry, of memory, of biographical progress from child to poet burst not from fullness and completion but from absence and loss. "The white arms out in the breakers tirelessly tossing" emerges as a figure of drowning (recalling "The Sleepers"). The poet's translating song becomes one of negation:

> Never more shall I escape, never more the reverberations,
> Never more the cries of unsatisfied love be absent from me,
> Never again leave me to be the peaceful child I was before what there in
>   the night,
> By the sea under the yellow and sagging moon,
> The messenger there arous'd, the fire, the sweet hell within,
> The unknown want, the destiny of me.

The refrain of "never" is like Lear's (and Poe's), and is no less urgent. Transformed now into a singer of poetry, what the poet sings are negatives: "cries of unsatisfied love" that will "never . . . be absent from me." The song is born in "unknown want," in lack, in loss. From it, the poem proceeds to its final aria, to the word out of the sea, "final, superior to all," "the low and delicious word death, / And again death, death, death, death."

In *Democratic Vistas* Whitman prophesies that "in the future of these States must arise poets immenser far, and make great poems of death." Death has an essential place in Whitman's grand vision of figural transformation:

America needs, and the world needs, a class of bards who will, now and ever, so link and tally the rational physical being of man, with the ensembles of time and space, and with the vast multiform show, Nature, surrounding him, ever tantalizing him, equally a part and yet not a part of him, as to essentially harmonize, satisfy, and put to rest . . . Surely, this universal ennui, this coward fear, this shuddering at death, these low, degrading views, are not always to rule the spirit pervading future society . . . some great coming literatus, especially poet . . . will compose the great poem of death.

Death takes its part in the Whitmanian tally. Nevertheless, it has a number of effects. Like the oxymorons of "sweet hell" and "unknown want" in "Out of the Cradle," death acts as a motive source of Romantic imagination in endless desire. It is because of and in response to nature's deficits, or even through negation of nature's plenitudes, that imagination makes room for itself and for its marvelous productions. In this sense, death and negation are marks of figural transposition and multiplication within the "vast multiform show" of "Nature." Poetic creativity requires acceptance of displacement, change, difference, loss, as one figure is produced by, but also takes the place of another. Like Emersonian "circles," Whitman's figures progress by "dislocations," are "not fixed but sliding," in a process of "abandonment."

The 1860 "Sea-Drift" poems have often been read as a disruptive fall into doubt and depression from the exuberance and confidence of the 1855 edition of *Leaves of Grass*. But death had been a central Whitmanian figure from the outset. "Song of Myself" specifically places death at the core of its exemplary chain of figures, as an essential moment in the poetic task of endlessly interpreting experience, and endlessly renewing interpretation. In "Out of the Cradle," too, death is not an alien sign of decline or loss of poetic nerve, but is inscribed from the origin within Whitman's very project, as the project of inscription itself.

This is not to say that death is merely integrated into a reconstituted totality and unity. Death in Whitman provides no encompassing sphere, no justified circle, no transcendent space. The full force of interruption and negation is felt. Yet disjunction and negation are accepted as generative within figural transformation, which is at once a chain of abolishment and of production: generation inextricable from abolishment. The price of figural power is, in Whitman, an abandonment of the unchanging, an embrace of difference. As with the productions of time itself (and Whitman declares in the "Song of Myself": "I accept Time absolutely," Song 23), for images to multiply, others must pass away. This is essential not only to his vision of poetry, but to his vision of history. It has particular recourse to his democratic commitment, his sense of America as a space of endless individualities, distinct from each other, multiple participants in a plural world. This figural multiplicity within the very venture and polity of the United States is fundamental to Whitman's often repeated claim that "America is the greatest poem." America, like and indeed as a poem, can (must) be read in its plural figuralism. Whitman's poetry is devoted to inaugurating Americans into this figural power as their inheritance.

Yet there is a darker side as well. Whitman's poetic does not attempt to deny rupture and dislocation. Nor does he attempt to resume them into unitary totality. But even within his figural procedures, which depend upon displacements as part of their generative power, there is a disruptive dislocation that does not generate figural chains within correspondences, but rather threatens to explode them. There is a haunting sense that the different levels of experience may not echo and hint at but may rather subvert each other; that individuals may remain in their separate spheres that fail to join in a multiple venture.

> The past and present wilt – I have fill'd them, emptied them,
> And proceed to fill my next fold of the future . . .
>
> Do I contradict myself?
> Very well then, I contradict myself,
> (I am large, I contain multitudes.)   (Song 51)

Whitman's figural poetic pours into past and present, but also empties them. This may be necessary to fill the next "fold" – perhaps also an image of paper. But it remains a Whitmanian, as indeed an American question, whether these "contradictions" Whitman so exuberantly declares, representing America, can indeed be the basis of that communal life which his poetic also would reflect and effect; whether the poem of America can "contain" its multiple and contradictory energies or will be exploded by them.

SKEPTICISM AND DISSENT IN THE LIBERAL REPUBLIC OF WORDS

Whitman as skeptic is less familiar than the solitary singer or poet of democracy. Yet skepticism haunts Whitman, and not only momentarily and sporadically, but profoundly, pervasively, and as integral to his poetics of America. In this sense, a text such as "As I Ebb'd with the Ocean of Life," with its shore-strewn debris, records not a momentary fit of depression, but rather, the threat of disintegration of the world as a pressure against which Whitman is constantly writing. Nor is the pressure of disintegrative force ultimately resolved either into a sense of some Whole, or some Self, absorbing and annexing the world. Whitman's texts provide moments of almost technical epistemological skepticism. In his unusually autobiographical poem, "There Was a Child Went Forth," for example, he writes:

> The doubts of day-time and the doubts of night-time, the curious
>   whether and how,
> Whether that which appears so is so, or is it all flashes and specks?
> Men and women crowding fast in the streets, if they are not flashes and
>   specks what are they?

This moment of skepticist disintegration stands in sustained and intimate relation with the declaration of integrative poetic function that famously opens the poem: "There was a child went forth every day, / And the first object he look'd upon, that object he became." In poem after poem, Whitman places as the very origin of his poetry disintegrative loss, as in the loss of the beloved in "Out of the Cradle" before the intrusive, erasive challenge of nothingness and death. And to see "Out of the Cradle'"s final embrace of "sweet and delicious death death death" as a gesture of transcendence or reintegration is greatly to underestimate the figure of death as Whitman constructs it. "When Lilacs Last in the Dooryard Bloom'd" is also obviously a disruptive text whose center is the confrontation with death, defeat, dissolution, in both personal and social-historical terms. Indeed, "When Lilacs" underscores the point that Whitman's doubts regarding the disintegration of the world are not just his own private fantasy, and cannot merely be resolved into a unifying self. They no less pertain to his culture, bent as America was in the 1850s on the demolition of its joint national life.

The more apparently exuberant celebratory verses, such as "Song of Myself," may seem remote from disintegrative forces. Its affirmations appear so strident, its confidence so unlimited, that we, as Harold Bloom puts it, come to bemoan the Whitman who affirms and affirms till we wish never to hear anything affirmed again. Yet, the poem's formal and rhetorical construction implicates this optimism at every moment. The catalogues assert, but also suggest limits to Whitman's integrative imagination. Most readers assume that the catalogue form works as an image of Whitman's poetic claim to unite within his vision all kinds of disparate material, if not also of America as uniting all diverse elements. The poet then stands as some common denominator, for both the poem and the country. Whitman's very act of incorporating such diversity into his text seems to assert faith in, if not full realization of, the organizing power of poetic imagination, in turn as emblem for America's own embrace of diversity in the democratic enterprise.

But the catalogues also introduce a dispersive force that careens at the edge of imaginative control and poetic organizing power. They enact not a presumption, but an effort to direct diversity – an effort whose strain also shows. They, and Whitman's poetic generally, in effect challenge and raise questions about the possibility, and mode, of cohesive relationship between diverse materials. These indeed have been the determining questions in assessing Whitman, with consequences for interpreting almost every aspect of his career. Whitman's biography moves from the exuberance of poetic vocation of 1855 to 1860 (interrupted by a further stint at newspaper work in 1858 and by the incursions of doubt in the "Sea-Drift" poems) into the Civil War period, which Whitman spent largely in or near Washington, doing government work and serving as wound-dresser for injured soldiers. He finally retired to what became his court at Camden, New Jersey, after suffering a stroke in 1873, dying there in 1892 as "The Good Gray Poet." This title, bestowed by Douglas O'Connor in an 1866 book defending against accusations of obscenity that had led to Whitman's dismissal from the Washington Indian Bureau, is taken by some as a measure of Whitman's betrayal of his initial poetic originality and rebelliousness, in an increasing acquiescence to the pressures of publishing and social and political conformity, beginning with the Civil War volume *Drum Taps* and continuing until his death.

This parable of betrayal and decline intensifies through controversy over Whitman's almost compulsive textual revisions, his returns to the printing press, endlessly revising. The successive editions of 1855, 1856, 1860, 1867, 1871, 1876, 1882 on through the deathbed edition of 1891–2 have been read almost as progress in corruption of Whitman's poetic and/or sexual and/or ideological purity. The revisions, in this reading, are seen to mark a retreat from Whitman's earlier radicalism, and an attenuation of his poetic powers. This is especially argued by those who see Whitman as progressively closeting his homosexuality, in a process of sexual censorship which led him to blur or excise particularly explicit passages. Yet if censorship had been Whitman's intention, he was markedly inept at it, leaving in as much as he took out and refusing the sorts of compromises that would have prevented the legal action against him for obscenity that finally materialized in 1882. And the argument that Whitman exercises sexual censorship ultimately sees Whitman's true project as one that is in radical opposition to the dominant American culture, which Whitman betrays in conformity to and complicity with American social norms. The central crack running through Whitman studies in effect resurfaces here. The history of revision itself becomes a figure for the Poet of Selfhood in opposition against the Poet of Democracy. The social or public person is seen as an effacement of a true, confessional, private selfhood, while genuine poetry is sacrificed to, or drowned out, in prophecy and oratory.

Whitman is thus posed between resistance to and complicity with American ideology and propaganda, imposed through the forced integration in his work of anomalies and differences. This poetic unification is then identified as his own engorged Selfhood, which has paradoxically lost its distinctive difference as well, finally emerging, as it absorbs the world, into a figure of imperialism. That is, the private and public each collapse into the other, so that arguments for megalomaniac selfhood become one with arguments for megalomaniac nationalism. Attempts to rescue Whitman then try to defend him from such complicity, to situate Whitman as against or outside an American ideology, in opposition to it.

But Whitman remains both within American ideology and critical of it. His critique of America is proposed, that is, from within an American set of values, not in rejection of them, but as accusing America of its own self-betrayal. The model of the radical Whitman against the complicitous one does not acknowledge the peculiarly American forms of dissent which Whitman undertakes. The individual does not become simply opposed to social institutions, nor is it engulfed by them, as their collective and mechanical mouthpiece. Rather, Whitman wishes to construct an individual fully distinctive and unique, within a polity of just such distinctive individuals. The effort to project relationships that both respect and join together unique individuals remains the central hope, and also the central anxiety, for Whitman's poetic creation and for the world of America it variously represents.

In terms of Whitman's poetic venture, his American faith is conducted through the orchestration of figural correlations, while his American dissent is expressed through the interrogation, strain, and skepticism regarding just such figural claims. Will everything submit to figural translation? Will the poet's own mind correspond with the minds of others, or even systematically cohere within itself? Whitman repeatedly claims America to be a poem: "These States are the amplest poem" ("By Blue Ontario's Shore"); "the United States themselves are essentially the greatest poem" (1855 Preface). His poetics of America on the one hand reflect American multiplicity: like a Whitman poem, America is a text of endlessly generative figuration, from "deepest basic elements [to] loftiest final meanings." The "United States today," he writes, are become a "poetry with cosmic and dynamic features of magnitude and limitlessness suitable to the human soul . . . never possible before" ("Backward Glance"). In the course of his exuberant tallying, however, Whitman is aware that even while "politics . . . religious forms, sociology, literature, teachers, schools, costumes, etc., are of course to make a compact whole, uniform, on tallying principles," he must still ask: "For how can we remain, divided, contradicting ourselves, this way?" The question, though Whitman hastens to offer assurances, is far from merely rhetorical. It is enacted in Whitman at once on poetic, philosophical, and political grounds.

On one level, Whitman's extremism in embracing so much disparate material takes to its limit a problem generally implicit in Romantic subjectivism. In his early "Sun-Down" papers written while still an editor at the *Long Island Democrat*, Whitman records a vision in which each person gazes at a temple through "an optical glass" of incongruous shapes. In his philosophical notes, he muses: "As a face in a mirror we see the world of materials, nature with all its objects, processes, shows, reflecting the human spirit by such reflection formulating, identifying, developing and proving it . . . The human soul stands in the centre, and all the universes minister to it, and serve it and revolve round it." Whitman is fully cognizant of the Romanticist discovery of the mind's vision of nature as mediated through, and reflecting, its own configurations. In "A Backward Glance," he names it specifically a Kantian discovery of viewpoint, according to which "the objects in Nature, the themes of estheticism, and all special exploitations of the mind and soul, involve not only their own inherent

quality, but the quality, just as inherent and important of their point of view."
Subjectivity is the "last essential reality, giving shape and significance to all
the rest."

Romanticism's discovery of the mind's creative power to construct its own
world, however, carries its own costs and burdens. For it also implies that
without this creative effort, the world itself would collapse. The extent of
the mind's power also demarcates its limits. Romanticism's confidence is also
its terror. The energy of Whitman's voice projects such anxiety, as with the
somewhat desperate "Noiseless Spider" poem. There his soul is

> Surrounded, detached, in measureless oceans of space,
> Ceaselessly musing, venturing, throwing, seeking the spheres to connect
>   them,
> Till the gossamer thread you fling catch somewhere.

Implicit is the risk that the soul's seeking may fail; that the spheres will
not connect, the fragile gossamer thread will not catch. And without such
intersection through the reflecting soul, the world itself threatens to remain
void, or to disintegrate.

"Song of Myself" is self-consciously built out of such Romanticist self-
reflection: "to me the converging objects of the universe perpetually flow"
(Song 20). It proceeds openly from the premise that "One world is aware and
by far the largest to me, and that is myself." Whitman knows that whatever
he encounters is an image of himself ("In all people I see myself") because
he, after all, is its refractor. What he offers, then, is not mere description but
visionary transformation through the eye of the self. His is a task of active
interpretation, which exhibits above all his own interpretive powers: "All are
written to me, and I must get what the writing means" (Song 20). In this way,
he goes far to elide the strains of his poem's different materials, not only in the
exuberance of his rhetoric, but as a mode of his self-expression.

What occurs in a "Sea-Drift" poem such as "As I Ebb'd with the Ocean of
Life" is the examination of the subversive element in this Romanticist project –
the suspicion that the self, and its rhetoric, may not suffice to join the world's
parts. And these doubts are not a strange anomaly but a continuous agon:

> As I ebb'd with the ocean of life,
> As I wended the shores I know,
> As I walk'd where the ripples continually wash you Paumanok,
> Where they rustle up hoarse and sibilant,
> Where the fierce old mother endlessly cries for her castaways,
> I musing late in the autumn day, gazing off southward,
> Held by this electric self out of the pride of which I utter poems

Was seiz'd by the spirit that trails in the lines underfoot . . .
Chaff, straw, splinters of wood, weeds, and the sea-gluten, . . . there and
    then as I thought the old thought of likenesses
These you presented to me you fish-shaped island,
As I walk'd with that electric self, seeking types.

The poem reworks many key Whitman terms for visionary transformation, exposing their fragile foundation in a subjectivist vision whose claim on the world can be questioned. As he walks poetically "musing," the "old thought of likenesses" loses its hold, the "electric self, seeking types" finds not signs of the world to be intelligibly read, but figures for the defeat of intelligibility. This sense of disjunction is reflected in the debris-images of the shore, as its peculiar negative correspondence. Yet this correspondence only closes the circle of the mind more closely around itself, reflecting its own scattered pieces. And the terms of "types" and the "electric" self undergo a kind of counter-conversion, as does the Whitmanian trope of ocean-water itself. Whitman's poetic style relies subtly but steadily on the gathering of diverse meanings through the re-use of resonant terms. Words intersect from text to text, creating depths and echoes in their figural usage. The "electric self" recalls its intensive intersections of meaning in "I Sing the Body Electric," where it evokes the very power of meaning as intersection. The image of "types" takes up older Puritan resources that Whitman in many ways makes his own for his own purposes. Whitman had from the start assumed for his poetic project its religious implication as a sign of divine meaning and purpose in the world and in history. And of course for Whitman, the printer, "types" evokes the very signs of his own publication. In "As I Ebb'd," these become the "trails in the lines underfoot," a pun on poetic measure which unravels, revealing the unstable abyss beneath Whitman's whole undertaking in imaging the world. Whitman's self-reflective imagery of poetics appears here in the "ripples" and sounds of the sea, now, however, as hoarse, sibilant cries.

The sea itself is recurrently in Whitman the medium of transfigural fluidity, not to mention bursting sexuality: "From Pent-up Aching Rivers" identifies the poet's "own voice resonant" as "singing the phallus." This poem also includes a Whitmanian pun on "list." "The divine list for myself or you or for any one making" evokes the roster of distinct-yet-corresponding levels of Whitman's poetic venture. A nautical meaning is added on in the poem "Spontaneous Me," where "list" combines the sense of ledger with the watery tilt of its figural conveyance: "Beautiful dripping fragments, the negligent list of one after another as I happen to call them to me or think of them." In "I Sing the Body Electric," list transmutes into the poetic call to "listen, count."

In "As I Ebb'd," the "list" of co-relation unravels in a listening uprooted from the world, with poetic power unmasked as a conjuring of absences, of voices not there, designs not there:

> As I wend to the shores I know not,
> As I list to the dirge, the voices of men and women wreck'd,
> As I inhale the impalpable breezes that set in upon me,
> As the ocean so mysterious rolls toward me closer and closer,
> I too but signify at the utmost a little wash'd up drift,
> A few sands and dead leaves to gather,
> Gather, and merge myself as part of the sands and drift.
>
> O baffled, balk'd, bent to the very earth,
> Oppress'd with myself that I have dared to open my mouth,
> Aware now that amid all that blab whose echoes recoil upon me I have
>   not once had the least idea who or what I am,
> But that before all my arrogant poems the real Me stands yet untouch'd,
>   untold, altogether unreach'd,
> Withdrawn far, mocking me with mock-congratulatory signs and bows,
> With peals of distant ironical laughter at every word I have written,
> Pointing in silence to these songs, and then to the sand beneath,
> I perceive I have not really understood any thing, not a single object,
>   and that no man ever can,
> Nature here in sight of the sea taking advantage of me to dart upon me
>   and sting me,
> Because I have dared to open my mouth to sing at all.

The poem openly acknowledges itself as a reflection not of correspondence, but negativity. These now are shores "I know not," haunted by "wreck'd" voices of men and women. Neither self nor world stands coherent, nor even accessible. The "echoes" which elsewhere signify figures – the "loud echoes" and "hints" of "my songs" (Song 18) – here are no more than the tautological "recoil" of a voice that expresses no world, but only itself. Yet without the world, even that self dissolves, "untouch'd," in a defeat of Whitmanian sexuality evoked by the sea that here can only "sting" rather "dash with amorous wet" (Song 22) or "souse with spray" as in the erotic vision of the twenty-eight bathers (Song 11). The "real Me . . . untouch'd, untold" is less a metaphysical figure of ultimate being than the lost possibility of personal and poetic coherence (with "untold" an undoing of tally as telling). The person as a figure for poetic, or any other coherence, is now "Withdrawn far, mocking me with mock-congratulatory signs and bows."

The intensely rich texture of the poem seems to recall, but in a way that cancels or casts doubt on, a wide range of Whitmanian figures: the "mocking" or "mock-congratulatory signs" are reversions of "Out of the Cradle"'s mocking-bird birth of song. "Blab" revokes "Song of Myself"'s exuberant "blab of the pave" (Song 8). "Oppress'd" suggests the whole chain of Whitmanian words of impression (Song 13), or of the printing "press" (Song 33). The recurrent image of "drift" is featured in Whitman's work as an especially resonant word of poetic figuration, as when Whitman urges: "The words of my book nothing, the drift of it every thing" ("Shut Not Your Doors"), or when he describes the movement of the "apple-shaped earth and we upon it" as "drift" ("A Song of Occupations" 3). At the starburst conclusion of "Song of Myself," Whitman takes his prophetic departure as the comet "drift" in "lacy jags" (Song 52). The original opening lines of "As I Ebb'd" suggest this positive implication: "Elemental drifts! / O I wish I could impress others as you and the waves have just been impressing me." But this would anticipate a recovery the poem only promises at the end. There, the "fragments buoy'd hither from many moods, one contradicting each other" seem again to collect in a regained contact between poet and his community. "Whoever you are, we too lie in drifts at your feet" almost suggests a mutual discipleship, with drift as poetic configuration, while also evoking the senses of collapse and directionlessness the poem confronts.

In the main course of the poem, the wish to "impress others" seems overwhelmed by the sense of being "Oppress'd with myself." To "signify at the utmost a little wash'd up drift" discloses the fragility of Romanticist poetic vision, itself shifting as the sea, centered in a self that itself remains vulnerable to shifting moments. What Whitman is describing is the role, and also the limitations, of his visionary poetry. The cast of his "eyes, reverting from the south," locates the poem within his own viewpoint as his act of seeing. But, as is intrinsic to any Romanticist visionary transformation, the point of view may shift, as it does here, dissolving the earlier configuration into alienation and solipsism: "I perceive I have not really understood any thing, not a single object, and that no man ever can." The "merge" in this poem, far from denoting the ingesting of the world into the engulfing poet as master, here dissolves the self into the "sands and drift."

Whitman's "Sea-Drift" poems compare with Emerson's late essay on "Experience," where the transfiguring power of vision is reduced to no more than a "prison of glass." And yet, this curtailment was already implicit in the "transparent eyeball" of "Nature" (which Whitman cited in an 1851 lecture), where Emerson hints at the instability of vision. "Every hour and change corresponds to and authorizes a different state of the mind," while what the eye beholds is at least in some sense its own reflection, "somewhat as beautiful as his own nature." A skepticist subjectivity, then, haunts the very claim to Romantic poetic vision.

This skepticism erupts in "As I Ebb'd," a poem of 1860 (and Whitman reverts his eyes in it "from the south"). The aesthetic and epistemological problems of knowledge which concern Whitman have for him as well a social, cultural, and political reference. The skeptical gap between self and world, self and self, self and others; the tensions between self-referring subjectivities; the problem of building community out of diversity, and the forces of disintegration opposed to it, found their most specific political corollary in the Civil War. But Whitman's sense of crisis extends beyond the specific urgency of secession. His poetry has often been interpreted as a kind of mirror-image of the tension between federalism as against states' rights, with Whitman's unionism enacted through his poems' absorbing powers. The secession crisis obviously took America's centrifugal forces to the furthest extent of nightmare, but the fissures of American culture extend beyond the specific politics of federalism, and continue well after the Civil War's refounding of the Union. "The central idea of secession," Lincoln stated in his First Inaugural Address, "is the essence of anarchy." However, Whitman came to feel that anarchic forces and their potential for civic disintegration were always present within the enterprise of American pluralism and its basis in a complex liberal tradition.

It is telling that Whitman opens *Democratic Vistas* (1871) with reference to John Stuart Mill's essay "On Liberty." Mill's notion of a "truly grand nationality" requires, Whitman writes, "1st, a large variety of character – and 2nd, full play for human nature to expand itself in numberless and even conflicting directions." Whitman lauds these principles of "variety and freedom" as the "greatest lessons also in New World politics and progress." They confirm his vision of American liberalism as rooted in revolutionary and constitutional discourses, in which plural interests are seen as essential for a liberal republic, if also requiring balance and direction. *Federalist* 10 proposes that the new government should "take in a greater variety of parties and interests," in order to provide a "greater security afforded by a greater variety of parties, against the event of any one party being able to outnumber and oppress the rest." The dispersive forces of competing individual or factional interests would be made a positive strength through negotiation between pluralist voices and the participation by all in public institutions. "Ambition must be made to counteract ambition," Madison wrote in *Federalist* 51; "The interest of the man must be connected with the constitutional rights of the place."

Within the Jeffersonian tradition, what would prevent the open contention among individuals and interests from becoming disintegrative of society, would be participation in public life that both defined and safeguarded self-government. Jeffersonian democracy envisions the harmony between private interests and the common good in public participation, in which individual effort realizes itself in serving the political community. At the same time, the best guarantor for individual liberty would be individual participation in the political process. As De Tocqueville, writing in the 1840s, puts it, "political liberty is . . . easily lost; to neglect to hold it fast is to allow it to escape." If "individualism" threatens to "sap the virtues of public life," Americans "have combated by free institutions the tendency of equality to keep men asunder." Elections and legislative processes, both local and national, provide "opportunities of acting in concert for all the members of the community and to make them constantly feel their mutual independence." They bring forward the "close tie that unites private to general interest," and make "political freedom" the "remedy" of that "isolation" and "selfishness" which individualist democracy fosters: "When the members of a community are forced to attend to public affairs, they are necessarily drawn from the circle of their own interests."

Such civic or republican virtue, according to which men in public life would rise above private interests in order to act for the good of the whole, has antecedents in the Puritan, Biblical American heritage. John Winthrop's sermon on "Christian Charity," delivered on the *Arabella*, called on his immediate and future congregants to act

That every man might have need of other, and from hence they might be all knitt more nearly together in the Bond of brotherly affeccion: from hence it appears plainely that noe man is made more honourable then another or more wealthy etc., out of any particular and singular respect to himself but for the glory of his Creator and the Common good of the Creature, Man.

Community norms, imposed through ministerial authority, may have impinged too far on individual autonomy within Puritan life. Still, Puritanism provides a further background for attempting a balance between the two. Individual spirituality remains an ultimate Puritan commitment, while also taking its place within a communal life devoted to the common good – a mutual confirmation between private and public central to the exemplary biography which Whitman in turn reworks in "Song of Myself."

These political and Biblical traditions which, while asserting individual autonomy continued to place it within community life as self-government, joined in turn with a tradition of economic individualism, also present from the start of the Puritan venture in joint-stock companies. The publication in 1776 of Adam Smith's *The Wealth of Nations* is emblematic. Its model of wealth as the outcome of multiple, unregulated, individual initiatives became increasingly realized as the nineteenth century advanced. The political tradition of public participation, moreover, still presupposed a governmental authority based on what Isaiah Berlin has called negative liberty, which Whitman strongly upholds. The "sum and substance of the prerogatives of government" are, in Whitman's newspaper formulation of negative liberty, that "no one's rights [be] infringed upon . . . This one single rule, rationally construed and applied, is enough to form the starting point of all that is necessary in government; to make no more laws than those useful for preventing a man or body of men from infringing on the rights of other men" (26 July 1847). The task of democratic government is to defend the individual from interference, which would in turn open the nation to liberal development for all: "In each modern nation there is a class who wish to deal liberally with humanity, to treat it in confidence, and give it a chance of expanding, through the measured freedom of its own nature and impulses" (21 March 1846). Whitman's *Brooklyn Daily Eagle* editorials sum up this vision of individual rights as freedom from others in the popular Jeffersonian formula that "the best government indeed is 'that which governs least.'"

But, as Whitman himself worried, it is not entirely obvious how a nation of discreet individuals protected from each other are to build a common good. Within American ideology, and specifically within Whitman's understanding of it, individualism took shape out of these diverse backgrounds, but with their variety of impulses often remaining in unspecified relationship. Through the nineteenth century, conflicts between values intensified. The communal, social frame of individual endeavor in both the political and religious traditions came under increasing pressure within a developing libertarian politics and, even more, a liberal market economy.

The potential disjunction between the libertarian independence of the individual and the social, communal life into which individuals are joined, erupts within the heart of Whitman's project of figural transformation. In this project, Whitman undertakes to correlate all strands of American experience. Individual and social, economic and cultural, poetic and scientific all are pledged to correspond with and augment each the other. But in Whitman's very enunciation of these mutual figurings, disruptive fissures emerge. In many senses, Whitman's poetics of America is the measure not of his satisfaction but of his dissent with society as it stands. The America Whitman envisions and calls for is in fact a criticism and not a confirmation of the actual one. And yet, this does not lead him to abandon his American commitments or his grounding in liberal republicanism. The failure of actual politics and actual presidents to fulfill their office in many ways impelled Whitman to take up his own office as poet. But the conversion to poetry remains for him a social-political commitment. As he writes in a letter, he chooses to "leave politics . . . out of faith in my own kind, the common people, as truly representative of new world principles." This is no retreat from public duty, but is, rather, the assumption of a figural mantle of leadership. It dedicates Whitman to the creation of a "prophetic literature of these States," which is "to be . . . the only sure and worthy supports and expressions of the American Democracy." Yet Whitman's poetry registers the difficulty of this undertaking. American democracy was in sore need of support. The urgency with which Whitman feels himself called as poet to himself engage in America's transfiguration is a measure of his despondency in the immediate politics of the situation before him.

Whitman's early poem "Pictures" is, in this regard, instructive. Essentially a catalogue (but clearly situated as picturing the contents, as in a house, of Whitman's own mind), it composes its list in a rhetoric that implies the mutual conformity of all it features. This ranges from personal family history to what Whitman announces as "a historic piece":

> And there a historic piece – see you, where Thomas Jefferson of Virginia
>   sits reading Rousseau, the Swiss, and compiling the Declaration of
>   Independence, the American compact;
> And there, tall and slender, stands Ralph Waldo Emerson, of New
>   England, at the lecturer's desk lecturing,
> And there is my Congress in session in the Capitol – there are my two
>   Houses in session.

The American political tradition, rooted in the social contract theory of Rousseau, as translated by Jefferson into America's founding liberal document, and inherited by Emerson as theorist of self-reliance, achieves triumphant realization in the acting Houses of the United States government. But the lines before and after this passage are less secure:

> And there, in the midst of a group, a quell'd revolted slave, cowering,
> See you, the hand-cuffs, the hopple, and the blood-stain'd cowhide
>   . . .
> And here, behold two war-ships, saluting each other – . . .
> And there, on the level banks of the James river in Virginia stand the
>   mansions of the planters;
> And here an old black man, stone-blind, with a placard on his hat, sits
>   low at the corner of a street, begging, humming hymn-tunes . . .

The poem here juxtaposes elements whose mutual compatibility remains highly questionable, in a way which the catalogue rhetoric leaves unresolved. Just how a Rousseauan–Jeffersonian tradition of social compact, equality, and self-government is to be squared with "the mansions of the planters," flanked on one side by "the hopple, and the blood-stain'd cowhide" of the captured slave and on the other by the begging black blind man is, to say the least, unclear, for all their incorporation into a rhythmic chant. Nor does the striking insertion into the sequence of a declaration at once homoerotic and self-portrait clarify much: "And again the young man of Mannahatta, the celebrated rough, (The one I love well – let others sing whom they may – him I sing for a thousand years!)" The "celebrated rough" of "Mannahatta" inevitably evokes Whitman himself, even as the lines also suggest a homoerotic confession. "Love" here, as nearly always in Whitman, asserts a social-erotics no less than any individual one. But in either sense, can love do its job of adhesiveness? Can it bind these wounds and divisions? The question comes back disturbingly at the poem's conclusion:

> But here, (look you well,) see here the phallic choice of America, a
> full-sized man or woman – a natural, well-trained man or woman

(The phallic choice of America leaves the finesse of cities, and all the returns of commerce or agriculture, and the magnitude of geography, and achievements of literature and art, and all the shows of exterior victory, to enjoy the breeding of full-sized men, or one full-sized man or woman, unconquerable and simple;)

> – For all these have I in a round house hanging – such pictures have I –
> and they are but little.

Whitman's long parenthetical remark contains a characteristic list of divergent areas of experience, implicitly claiming some figural (and national) correlation. But do they correlate? Does the "magnitude of geography" (and Whitman supported Manifest Destiny) confirm the "finesse of cities"? Does Whitman's homoerotic confession have place in a society that rejects it? Does the erotic vision, for which he bids to leave all else, truly encompass these variances? Can the figure of the man stand for, represent, convert into the figure of the woman, especially when the "choice" and song of America are seen so emphatically as "phallic"? Not least, do the "returns of commerce" indeed accord with the "achievements of literature and art"? And does the status of his vision as "pictures" in the house of Whitman's mind compose them in any way beyond his own subjectivity?

These dis-correlations in Whitman's rhetoric register fissures in the fabric of American society. This Whitman knows. Much of *Democratic Vistas* is given to exposing them. Money, especially, refuses the conversion Whitman so desperately wishes. On the one hand, Whitman is, must be, by the force of his own design, committed to American prosperity. "Not the least doubtful am I on any prospects of [American] material success," he insists, which will "outstrip all examples hitherto afforded, and dominate the world." Yet the promise of America must be realized beyond material development and acquisition, and even beyond liberal rights as these frame and support economic possession and initiative. *Democratic Vistas* is essentially launched from this motive: to "alarm and caution even the political and business reader . . . against the prevailing delusion that the establishment of free political institutions . . . with general good order, physical plenty, industry, etc. (desirable and precious advantages as they all are,) do, of themselves, determine and yield to our experiment of democracy the fruitage of success."

Whitman essentially embraces the heady liberal promise of personal independence and endless opportunity, in which "the ulterior object of political and all other government . . . [is] not merely to rule, to repress disorder, etc., but to develop, to open up to cultivation, to encourage the possibilities of all beneficent and manly outcroppage, and of that aspiration for independence, and the pride and self-respect latent in all characters." But he sees the ultimate expression of liberal government and economy in "really grand religious, moral, literary and aesthetic results," which alone mark the true "march with unprecedented strides to empire." All the "objective grandeurs of the world" must be transfigured through "the mind, which alone builds the permanent edifice." Only then "are conveyed to mortal sense the culminations of the materialistic, the known, and prophecy of the unknown."

Such transfiguration, however, is not in evidence. Instead, the vista opening before Whitman from the 1870s onward is the "hollowness" of American life, overwhelmed by the "depravity" of business, which, in its "hectic glow" is "all-devouring." The "cry of sense, science, flesh, incomes, farms, merchandise" are become "victorious." Endowed with a "vast and more and more thoroughly appointed body," America has been "left with little or no soul." For all its "unprecedented materialistic advancement, society, in these States, is cankered, crude, superstitious, and rotten." The "depraving influences of riches" are "everywhere turning out the generations of humanity like uniform iron castings," with only the "tremendous and dominant play of solely materialistic bearings upon current life in the United States." Instead of redemptive conversion, we are threatened with demonic inversion: "Our modern civilization, with all its improvements, is in vain, and we are on the road to a destiny, a status, equivalent, in its real world, to that of the fabled damned."

Material economy and reduction of all other aspects of life to its measure is one central area of resistance to Whitman's project. But there is a disintegrative danger within the basic construction of American liberalism. In the defensive space that surrounds the individual – that "independence" which Whitman defines in *Democratic Vistas* as "freedom from all laws or bonds except those of one's own being" – there is latent a "pride, competition, segregation, wilfulness, and license beyond example" which "brood already among us." The disruptive threat extends from political, social, and economic spheres to

Whitman's imaginative project as such. His very commitment to the creative power of each individual, which his poems attest to and which they are devoted to initiating and awakening in others, carries with it the possibility of solipsistic enclosure of each into his or her separate worlds. If each individual interprets discretely in a negative liberty of imagination, what guarantees mutual participation and community? And yet, Whitman must no less resist an imposition of order and agreement by a hierarchical, autocratic power. His democratic commitments forbid any appeal to "authority and . . . cohesion at all cost," as these have through "political history" been based on "order, safety, caste."

Whitman's great poems variously respond to these rending dilemmas. At times, the poems mute such contradictory and disintegrative impulses, moving to reintegrate them into an affirmed harmony. Even then, however, rupture continues to leave its mark. At times, Whitman's impulse is towards lament, conducted in the mode of prophetic Jeremiad calling the nation to return, condemning the America that is in the name of the America that ought to be. Rarely, there are moments that remain in dissolution, with at most ambiguous conversion or resolution. Finally, rupture may be recognized and expressed, in a homage that does not evade, even as it hopes. "Out of the Cradle" and "When Lilacs Last in the Dooryard Bloom'd" are two such poems.

"Crossing Brooklyn Ferry" emerges, within this range of Whitmanian possibilities, as among Whitman's most integrative efforts. Here, Whitman's commitment to material and technological conversion by poetic means is particularly strong. He insists on the river as a scene of commerce and industry: "On the river the shadowy group, the big steam-tug closely flank'd on each side by the barges . . . On the neighboring shore the fires from the foundry chimneys burning high and glaringly into the night." Yet here, no less, is the full force of Whitmanian Romanticist vision. The poem is

> Flood-tide below me! I see you face to face!
> Clouds of the west – sun there half an hour high – I see you also face to
>   face.
>   . . .
> The impalpable sustenance of me from all things at all hours of the day,
> The simple, compact, well-join'd scheme, myself disintegrated, every
>   one disintegrated yet part of the scheme,
> The similitudes of the past and those of the future,
> The glories strung like beads on my smallest sights and hearings, on the
>   walk in the street and the passage over the river,
> The current rushing so swiftly and swimming with me far away,
> The others that are to follow me, the ties between me and them,
> The certainty of others, the life, love, sight, hearing of others.

The poem opens with an extraordinary, powerful image of radiant individual selfhood. The poet, riding the ferry, looks over the side and sees the "Flood-tide below me . . . face to face." This opening image of reflection, strongly Romanticist, encompasses more and more of the surrounding world, centering ultimately in the poet's own visage, around which all the forces and sights of the world collect. "The glories strung like beads on my smallest sights and hearings" is a stunning image of the poet's own vision as the string on which the lights of city and river come into configuration. The poet, however, refuses to make this visionary act one of either isolation or domination. He is not above, but part of the scene, "myself disintegrated," alongside "every one disintegrated yet part of the scheme." Lines of connection, figured in the "current rushing," tie self to others, past to future, in a Whitmanian celebration of "love."

The radiant self as the focal point of each one's experience reaches apotheosis in the next section, when the poet, reflecting on his image, "Look'd at the fine centrifugal spokes of light round the shape of my head in the sunlit water." This halo concentrates in one luminous figure the religious transformation implicit in the "face to face" of the opening. Whitman's poetry throughout undertakes the transfiguration of a variety of American religious traditions. He persistently deploys religious terms for his poetic venture, with the further realization of American promise as including a religious dimension, alternately called moral, spiritual, prophetic, soul. At the "core of democracy," he writes in *Democratic Vistas*, is "the religious element." The highest, "illustrious . . . stage rising out of the previous ones" emerges (also) as a "sublime and serious Religious Democracy." But Whitmanian religion has its own peculiar features. "Starting from Paumanok" announces that "I too . . . inaugurate a religion . . . I say the whole earth and all the stars in the sky are for religion's sake." It continues:

> I say no man has ever yet been half devout enough,
> None has ever yet adored or worship'd half enough,
> None has begun to think how divine he himself is, and how certain the
> future is.

Whitmanian religion is strongly based on that individualist strain which he admired in Elias Hicks and calls, out of his own Quaker background, the mystical and radical "inner light." It is this that gives divinity to each person. Yet Whitman also recognizes that radically individualist religion can be variously destabilizing: sectarian, antinomian, secularizing. When the "inward Deity-planted law of the emotional soul" of the "true Quaker" is "rigidly, perhaps strainingly carr[ied] out," the result can be "unseemly and insane acts."

"Crossing Brooklyn Ferry" presents Whitman's most prophetic effort to contain these contrary directions. Rigorously anti-transcendent, it envisions the fulfillment and perfection of the world not in another world, but in the transfigural sacralization of earthly life. "Thrive, cities . . . Expand, being than which none else is perhaps more spiritual." It does so, not by focusing on any current state of society, but by projecting itself into a future which the ferry crossing, as a figure for Whitman's own poetic voice, itself enacts. "America," he writes at the start of *Democratic Vistas*, "counts . . . for her justification and success (for who, as yet, dare claim success?) almost entirely on the future." Any anxiety regarding possible future failure emerges in "Crossing Brooklyn Ferry" only in section 6, where "dark patches fall":

> The dark threw its patches down upon me also,
> The best I had done seem'd to me blank and suspicious,
> My great thoughts as I supposed them, were they not in reality meagre?
> Nor is it you alone who know what it is to be evil,
> I am he who knew what it was to be evil,
> I too knitted the old knot of contrariety,
> Blabb'd, blush'd, resented, lied, stole, grudg'd,
> Had guile, anger, lust, hot wishes I dared not speak.

Transformative vision is reduced to that "blank" always potential in it, blinded by darkness. As in "As I Ebb'd," confidence in his poetic calling breaks down, with a kind of confession of personal and sexual sins that threaten social-poetic integration. The "knot of contrariety" here stubbornly blocks the figural "ties" of the earlier section.

But section 6 remains rather self-enclosed in the poem. What emerges with overriding force in "Crossing Brooklyn Ferry" is Whitman's double commitment both to divinized individual selfhood and to a community of love. Making good the poem's earlier promise of "similitudes of the past and those of the future," Whitman enfolds time into the structure of simile, crossing in the ferry "Just as" others will cross, endlessly, into an open-ended future:

> Just as you feel when you look on the river and sky, so I felt,
> Just as any of you is one of a living crowd, I was one of a crowd . . .
> Just as you stand and lean on the rail, yet hurry with the swift current, I
>   stood yet was hurried.

Whitman carefully constructs a figure of "you" to match that of self, in a rhetoric of address that enacts the crossing from self to other, from present to future. This positioning of the "you" is crucial in both Whitman's discourses and discourses about him. Is Whitman's a rhetoric of imposition, forcing his selfhood upon the other, with simile and analogy acting here as coercive uniformity? Or does Whitman construct a linguistic space which, while certainly asserting himself, no less provides a model for others equally to do so, with language an arena in which each can emerge into both self-expression and communication? In "Crossing Brooklyn Ferry," Whitman's fantasy is for the democratic crowd to come into free and personal relationship each to each, with the poise of the current itself a figure describing Whitman's own poetic stance and method. Here "the certainty of others, the life, love, sight, hearing of others" promised earlier is furthered, to be again reaffirmed at the poem's end:

> Consider, you who peruse me, whether I may not in unknown ways be
>   looking upon you,
> Be firm, rail over the river, to support those who lean idly, yet haste with
>   the hasting current;
> Fly on, sea-birds! fly sideways or wheel in large circles high in the air . . .
> Diverge, fine spokes of light, from the shape of my head, or any one's
>   head, in the sunlit water! . . .
> Flaunt away, flags of all nations! be duly lower'd at sunset
> Burn high your fires, foundry chimneys! cast black shadows at nightfall!
>   cast red and yellow light over the tops of the houses!
> You necessary film, continue to envelop the soul,
> About my body for me, and your body for you, be hung out divinest
>   aromas,
> Thrive, cities – bring your freight, bring your shows, ample and
>   sufficient rivers,
> Expand, being than which none else is perhaps more spiritual
> We receive you with free sense at last, and are insatiate henceforward . . .
> We fathom you not – we love you – there is perfection in you also,
> You furnish your parts toward eternity,
> Great or small, you furnish your parts toward the soul.

Extensive list and intensive figuration come together in sustained orchestration. The corrosive potential of material prosperity, evoked in the burning foundry chimneys, becomes nevertheless a kaleidoscope of color. The "cities" and the river's "freight" will "expand" as extensions of the "spiritual." Political flags are flaunted alongside the transfigured individual in a recurrence of the image of the halo, "fine spokes of light," now explicitly extended to "any one's head" and resonating in an image of Emersonian "circles" of the sea-bird. Sexuality, in a continuing sexual dimension conducted throughout Whitman's poems, is asserted in the "divinest aromas" of the body, as an image for both social intercourse and poetic energy ("We receive you with free sense . . . and are insatiate," cf. earlier in the poem, when Whitman writes of ties "Which fuses me into you now, and pours my meaning into you"). Indeed, the whole passage (also) stands as self-description of Whitman's poetic enterprise, as the "I" and "you" face and reflect each other in textual exchange ("you who peruse me"); and, above all, in the image of the river, at once driven and idle, directed and at ease, in business and at leisure, connecting water and land through the "hasting current."

In "Crossing Brooklyn Ferry," commerce, spirituality, sexuality, poetics are multiply and mutually celebrated, within an overarching commitment to time itself as the medium of production, figured in the "hasting current." Whitman confirms his commitment to temporal process, indeed to death, as itself an endless series of figural displacements, "perpetual transfers and promotions," as he writes in "Song of Myself" 49 or as the "ceaseless succession through time" of *Democratic Vistas*. The differentiation of experience into passing moments and the division between people are acknowledged but brought into relation, connected through the powerful address to "you," all "parts toward eternity," in an ever further projected future in "love."

And yet the celebration of the ferry does not finally, or fully, reconcile the divisions so masterfully negotiated through its rhetoric. These reemerge in a poem such as "The Sleepers." This text opens in bewilderment. The "I" of "vision" cannot penetrate beyond its own subjectivity, and is left "Wandering and confused, lost to myself, ill-assorted, contradictory." The poem includes in its catalogues highly discordant, alienated elements: corpses, drunkards, onanists, "gash'd" bodies, the insane, the prisoner, the murderer, the murdered, the money-maker. And while it also moves towards reconciliation of these disparate figures, it does so in ways that remain deeply hesitant and self-doubting. The hallucinatory images become "likened" only "in the dim light" of night and sleep, where differences are more erased than negotiated. The soothing hands of the poet here do not touch, nor do they settle, those who fitfully sleep. The "beautiful gigantic swimmer," which seems to suggest some kind of redemptive, if not Christic sacrifice, is at best ambiguously redemptive. The swimmer could be read as a great, mythopoeic figure for America itself, but his effort "is baffled, bang'd, bruised" and finally defeated in its venture on the "slapping eddies." Here, the circles of Emersonian expansion Whitman so often invokes (as in the sea-gulls' "slow wheeling circles and gradual edging toward the south" in "Crossing Brooklyn Ferry") represent the last bruising "in the cirling eddies." From this death, the poem does not recuperate. At most, it offers what it repeatedly calls dream: "O love and summer, you are in the dreams and in me . . . Elements merge in the night, ships make tracks in the dreams." To "merge" here is, as in "As I Ebb'd," to lose definition, not to claim an encompassing one. And the act of reconciliation apparently remains nothing more than dream, a mere poetic vision.

At issue in some sense is the status of poetic vision altogether. As with other nineteenth-century poets, Whitman's task included not only finding a poetic language and mode to match the emerging American national identity, but also finding a place for poetry in America's developing culture. This had been, for example, Longfellow's challenge too. Longfellow's verse as much reflects his anxiety as his desire that poetry be granted a genuine American place. Walt Whitman dares more. He responds to poetry's threatened displacement by claiming for it an integral part in the American venture – indeed, claiming poetry to be that venture's ultimate expression and result. Whitman offers a poetic interpretation of America, and also a poetic preeminence within it. Both are intended when he calls America the greatest poem.

Whitman's poetic efforts finally focus into an attempt to construct a community of, and through, poetic language. Whitman in his prose writings recurrently takes up the question of an American cultural language, from his unpublished notes called *Rambles with Words*, through his *American Primer*, and his essay, in *November Boughs*, on "Slang in America." Rejecting the "etiquette of salons" where "waiters stand behind chairs, silent, obedient, with backs that bend and must often bend," Whitman in the *American Primer* instead speaks for "the appetite of the people of These States, in popular speeches and writings, [as] for unhemmed latitude, coarseness, directness, live epithets, expletives, words of opprobrium, resistance . . . I like limber, lasting, fierce words. I like them applied to myself, I like them in newspapers, courts, debates, Congress." Whitman as poet represents such a community of living, expanding, democratic language, engages to construct it, and addresses the people through it. But this also means negotiating the division and even violence potential in a liberty that may free individuals from each other and become a competitive battle against each other. While endorsing the "voluntary standards and self-reliance" of American energy, Whitman calls beyond "either self-interest or common pecuniary or material objects" to poetic transmutation "in vast, indefinite, spiritual, emotional power."

The community of poetic language Whitman hopes to construct must acknowledge the conflict and division, and even the displacement of poetry itself, potential within the liberal-individual development of America to which he, however, remains committed. This he undertakes perhaps most movingly on the one hand in "When Lilacs Last in the Dooryard Bloom'd," on the other, in the group of Calamus poems: texts that range from the most public to the most private of his expressions. In both, language is situated, not in an exuberant, incorporative rhetoric, but in disruption and loss. The poems do not repossess this loss into fullness. Instead, they insist upon what is unrecuperable in history, and in the self.

"When Lilacs Last in the Dooryard Bloom'd," the elegy to Lincoln ("O powerful western fallen star!") introduces an interplay of visionary figures – the star, the bird, the sprig of lilac, the poet, the president. These never resolve into any single image. They each play off, sorrowfully, against the other. And, as in "Out of the Cradle," it is death that impels the song:

> In the swamp in secluded recesses,
> A shy and hidden bird is warbling a song.
>
> Solitary the thrush,
> The hermit withdrawn to himself, avoiding the settlements,
> Sings by himself a song.
>
> Song of the bleeding throat,
> Death's outlet song of life, (for well dear brother I know
> If thou wast not granted to sing thou would'st surely die).
>
>   . . .
>
> (Nor for you, for one alone,
> Blossoms and branches green to coffins all I bring,
> For fresh as the morning, thus would I chant a song for you O sane and
>   sacred death . . .)

The fullness of self that overflowed as song ("Walt you contain enough, why don't you let it out then" Song 25) now is emptied, with the poem its strange reflection: "If thou wast not granted to sing thou would'st surely die." The singer is solitary, isolated. His song is cut off from the world. Yet, as in "Out of the Cradle," death as constant dislocation also constitutes time and history's unfolding. The poem, without denying death, commits itself to it: "O sane and sacred death." The death of the President is never recuperated nor justified. But the poetic voice, exactly in its disrupted isolation, ventures forth through disaster to express a communal mourning. In treasuring what has been lost the poet measures its extent; and he recognizes disjunction itself as an inevitable element within historical process and a community of discourse.

"When Lilacs" reworks with further complexity and resonance some of Whitman's most important poetic terms. In section 8, the poet addresses the fallen star, recalling how he

> walk'd in silence the transparent shadowy night . . .
> As the night advanced, and I saw on the rim of the west how full you
>   were of woe,
> As I stood on the rising ground in the breeze in the cool transparent
>   night,
> As I watch'd where you pass'd and was lost in the netherward black of
>   the night,
> As my soul in its trouble dissatisfied sank, as where you sad orb,
> Concluded, dropt in the night, and was gone.

Here "transparent night" does not assert the overcoming of darkness into visibility, but rather has the force almost of oxymoron. It is an image strangely resistant to transmutation, suggesting a disjunction from figure to figure which prevents the transfer from one level to another. The pattern of oxymoron continues. What the poet sees is a fullness of woe. On the rising ground, his own soul "dissatisfied sank." And he addresses what is not there: the star is "gone." Unlike the poem "The Sleepers," any question of a unifying erasure of difference is laid to rest. The star is "lost in the netherward black of the night." The loss is unmitigated, and final.

But the time of loss is, finally, also a moment in an ongoing history. The thrush may sing solitary, but elegy is a public ritual – here, quite factually in the commemorated cortege which carried Lincoln's coffin across the States to its burial place in Springfield. The poet's voice accompanies the "Coffin that passes through lanes and streets" of America, in "processions long and winding" that also describe the poet's voice (section 6). Although singing his private emotion, this voice joins

> With dirges through the night, with the thousand voices rising strong
> and solemn,
> With all the mournful voices of the dirges pour'd around the coffin.

Almost in a trope of Whitman's own career, the poet, facing the destruction of the President, takes up his own role as representative, if first to represent that destruction itself.

The poem, in its remaining sections, proceeds between the solitude of the singer and a visionary history of Civil-War America. Section 11 moves through "Pictures" – recalling Whitman's earlier poem of the mind – but here they are of the land, life, and work of America. Section 15 revisits the battlefields of the war. What connects the visionary and historic, the individual poet and the "thousand voices," is the act of "tallying": "the voice of my spirit tallied the song of the bird"; the battle unfolds "To the tally of my soul."

> Passing the visions, passing the night,
> Passing, unloosing the hold of my comrades' hands,
> Passing the song of the hermit bird and the tallying song of my soul,
> Victorious song, death's outlet song, yet varying ever-altering song . . .
>
> I cease from my song for thee . . .
> Yet each to keep and all, retrievements out of the night,
> The song, the wondrous chant of the gray-brown bird,
> And the tallying chant, the echo arous'd in my soul,
> With the lustrous and drooping star with the countenance full of woe,
> With the holders holding my hand nearing the call of the bird,

> Comrades mine and I in the midst, and their memory ever to keep, for
>   the dead I loved so well,
> For the sweetest, wisest soul of all my days and lands – and this for his
>   dear sake.

The poet passes before, and among, surrounding mourners, representing them, transforming their voices through his tallying. The song is the community's, while the community itself comes into being through the song. This does not declare a full conversion of loss into gain, of isolation into comradeship, of difference into unity. Whitman's, like Lincoln's, is in many ways a "cautious hand" ("This Dust was Once the Man"). The "countenance" remains "full of woe." Yet Whitman is committed to time's motion, the "varying ever-altering song," inseparable from its losses: making this poem and this America also "death's outlet song." Brought together by loss, the poet envisions the nation as "holders holding my hand," in a last rite of "memory" (perhaps recalling Lincoln's own appeal to the "mystic cords of memory" in his First Inaugural Address) that binds each to each. The final note is one of love: not as possession, but as attachment to the "dear sake" of the dead who represented the nation; and for the living left now, each alone and yet bound together, in loss and yet related through this representative image.

This poem, like many of those devoted to the Civil War and the wound-dressing of Whitman's war-service, is hesitant and troubled. The image of Whitman as exultant warmonger and justifier of suffering is, I think, unfounded, although there are certainly such moments in his work. In particular, his rage at the "money-shops" and "countless profit" as engulfing every sense of the American pursuit of happiness seems to him to call for the most radical convulsions, "devouring the whole" ("Song of the Banner at Daybreak"). His war-visions most often have a piecemeal, disconnected quality, as though seen "By the Bivouac's Fitful Flame." And it is not long before the sound of the drum becomes "hollow and harsh" ("Spirit Whose Work is Done") and the drum-tapper turns "Wound-Dresser": "Arous'd and angry, I'd thought to beat the alarum, and urge relentless war, / But soon my fingers fail'd me, my face droop'd and I resign'd myself." Although he has "urged you onward with me," he confesses to doing so "without the least idea what is our destination" ("As I Lay with my Head.")

Whitman, in *Democratic Vistas*, encapsulates his own, and America's, liberal vision of individual integrity as the basis for communal commitment:

I say the mission of government, henceforth, in civilized lands, is not repression alone, and not authority alone [nor] the rule of the best men, the born heroes and captains of the race . . . but higher than the highest arbitrary rule, to train communities through all their grades, beginning with individuals and ending there again, to rule themselves . . . In respect to the absolute soul, there is in the possession of such by each single individual, something so transcendent . . . that, to that extent, it places all beings on a common level, utterly regardless of the distinctions of intellect, virtue, station, or any height or lowliness whatever – is tallied in like manner, in this other field, by democracy's rule that men, the nation, as a common aggregate of living identities affording in each a separate and complete subject for freedom.

Through his life, from the ante-bellum through the post Civil-War period, Whitman saw this delicate balance between the "absolute soul" and its effort to enact a "common aggregate of living identities" more or less constantly threatened by political, social, and economic forces. What he offers, and attempts, in his poetic venture is to "train communities," as he says here, to the fullest realization of each of its members, even while retaining that respect in each as "a separate and complete subject for freedom." His poetry is both an image and an exercise of this training, trying to "tall[y] in like manner" independent selfhood with social venture.

In his poem, "Over the Carnage Rose Prophetic a Voice," Whitman calls to his readers, his country: "affection shall solve the problems of freedom yet." But, like America itself, Whitman neither finally accomplishes this risk-laden task, nor finally resolves the potential contradiction of a society whose commitment to individuality always carries the potential for defeat of community, even as it also forms the basis of community. The Sons of Liberty had declared: "the principle of self Preservation, self love, tend[s] in the highest degree to the general Benefit of the Whole and every Part." Whitman's attempt to balance the American celebration of self with the common good perhaps inevitably suffers the strains of liberalism's own dual commitments.

Nowhere does this strain show more than in the Calamus poems of 1860. This grouping perhaps most provocatively raises questions about Whitman's use of homosexuality as a poetic figure. In these poems he hints he will "tell the secret of my nights and days,"

> That the soul of the man I speak for rejoices in comrades,
> Here by myself away from the clank of the world,
> Tallying and talk'd to here by tongues aromatic.
>
> ("In Paths Untrodden")

Taking up his position in that solitude into which the thrush of "When Lilacs" withdrew itself, Whitman in the Calamus poems seems remote from the public voice of the Lincoln elegy. He is "away from the clank of the world," off at a margin ("In the growth by margins of pond-waters") socially and, as he implies ("Resolv'd to sing no songs to-day but those of manly attachment"), sexually. Sexuality had been throughout *Leaves of Grass* a multiple figure: autobiographic, poetic, social. Yet Whitman's sexual figures tend to be highly phallic. In his prose writings, Whitman consistently urges equality between the sexes, "the perfect equality of the female with the male," as he writes in the 1855 Preface. In his poetry, however, the figure of woman is presented in ambiguous and inconsistent ways. To some extent, his imaginative sphere for women seems to remain quite limited, essentially to motherhood, as in the section on "A woman's body at auction" in "I Sing the Body Electric" ("she is the teeming mother of mothers"). Always less erotic than are male figures in his work, women serve, in the somewhat astonishing poem "A Woman Waits for Me," as the site where he may "pour the stuff to start sons and daughters fit for these states . . . I dare not withdraw till I deposit what has so long accumulated within me." Whatever his ideological intentions, and with whatever variety of figural realization, Whitman's paradigm for creativity is essentially male-orgasmic, the explosive outburst of "pent-up rivers of myself." At issue is not so much Whitman's personal homoeroticism, as his use of it to represent experiences beyond his own, to represent others, across gender boundaries.

The Calamus poems thus appear almost to retreat from Whitman's larger figural project. They often seem situated in a psychical interiority, a personal space, remote from Whitman's public concerns and especially vulnerable to solipsistic threat and subjective self-enclosure. A poem such as "Of the Terrible Doubt of Appearances" makes such solipsism and skeptical challenge its explicit topic:

> Of the terrible doubt of appearances,
> Of the uncertainty after all, that we may be deluded,
> That may-be reliance and hope are but speculations after all,
> That may-be identity beyond the grave is a beautiful fable only,
> May-be the things I perceive, the animals, plants, men, hills, shining
>   and flowing waters,
> The skies of day and night, colors, densities, forms, may-be these are (as
>   doubtless they are) only apparitions, and the real something has yet to
>   be known,
> (How often they dart out of themselves as if to confound me and mock
>   me!
> How often I think neither I know, nor any man knows, aught of them,)
> May-be seeming to me what they are (as doubtless they indeed but
>   seem) as from my present point of view, and might prove (as of course
>   they would) nought of what they appear, or nought anyhow, from
>   entirely changed points of view;
> To me these and the like of these are curiously answer'd by my lovers,
>   my dear friends,

When he whom I love travels with me or sits a long while holding me
    by the hand,
When the subtle air, the impalpable, the sense that words and reason
    hold not, surround us and pervade us,
Then I am charged with untold and untellable wisdom, I am silent, I
    require nothing further,
I cannot answer the question of appearances or that of identity beyond
    the grave,
But I walk or sit indifferent, I am satisfied,
He ahold of my hand has completely satisfied me.

This poem is almost technical in its presentation of epistemological doubt.
All we see dissolves into "colors, densities, forms," mere "appearances," "apparitions." The very world seems to fall apart, "the sense that words and reason
hold not, surround us and pervade us," while what is truly "real," beyond such
mere appearance, "has yet to be known." This epistemological doubt has its
aesthetic corollary in a Romantic subjectivity that both discloses and limits
our experience: all that appears to "my present point of view . . . might prove
(as of course they would) nought of what they appear, or nought anyhow, from
entirely changed points of view." The repetition of "nought," following the
"aught" in the line before, shows how much Whitman considers to be at stake:
the utter nothingness of the world skeptically reduced to "only apparitions."
Nor is the poet's doubt directed only to questions that seem beyond certain
knowledge. Whitman grants a peculiar parity between the question of "identity beyond the grave" and the uncertainty of his grasp of everyday perception,
as though both were equally a matter of faith.

But the poem does not attempt to settle or dispel its terrible doubt of
appearances in philosophical terms. Instead, it turns to "lovers" and "dear
friends" as what "curiously answer[s]" its skeptical doubt. Whitman, in his
skepticism, finally appeals not to abstract epistemology but to social community. When "the sense that words and reason hold not, surround us and
pervade us," Whitman responds by turning back to those who share his world
and words: his lovers and friends, his community, his readers. His response
to disappointment is, one might say, appointment. In some sense this is to
concede limitation. In another, it is to require it. The crisis of skepticism is
also a crisis of isolation whose remedy, or perhaps whose work, would be a
renewed sense of community. This, however, is not to answer the skeptical
question with epistemological certainty. Whitman insists at the poem's end:
"I cannot answer the question of appearances or that of identity beyond the
grave." And, he does not answer. "I am charged with untold and untellable
wisdom, I am silent, I require nothing further."

This line resonates with Whitman's multiply charged figure of telling, closely tied to his central tropes of tallying, counting, and accounting. These are core images for his project of figural multiplication. Yet they also become, at certain moments of apotheosis, images for what is beyond measure: as in the transformation of the slave into sacred person that "balks account" in "I Sing the Body Electric," or in the celebration of unique selfhood "untranslatable" in the conclusion of "Song of Myself." Here, too, the "untellable" signals a special conversion – into a unique self, but one that nonetheless defines itself in relation to companions. In the conclusion of "When Lilacs," the poet turns "With the holders holding my hand" to "Comrades mine and I in the midst." So too here he turns to "he whom I love . . . while holding me by the hand." Homoeroticism here becomes a figure for transgression, recalcitrance, but also commitment, and ultimately transformation of society. Homoeroticism thus enacts issues of conformity and its resistance, through which Whitman addresses the social world and presses it towards transfiguration. It may be that, rather than proposing his personal sexuality as a paradigm for all, he asserts it as that sense of self which is not fully convertible, which takes its place in reference to others across difference and distance, but which can nevertheless enter into a social discourse of mutual commitment.

"Song of Myself" 5 offers "a kelson of the creation is love" as its founding vision. Love serves, here and throughout Whitman, as an emblem of community – not as a unity, but as a commitment among autonomous individuals. "Not that half only, individualism, which isolates," he writes in *Democratic Vistas*, but "another half, which is adhesiveness of love, that fuses, ties, and aggregates." Whitmanian love becomes a form of civic virtue, described in one revolutionary tract as "this endearing and benevolent passion [originating] in that charity which forms every social connection." In the 1855 Preface, Whitman invokes a "self-denial" which, by limiting self, commits each self to the other. The crisis of skepticism, as a crisis of isolation, invites a response that would neither assert nor deny subjectivity, but acknowledge the self as situated within a common world. The American venture, as the poet takes it up, is a venture not only in individualism, but in community. How to create a common good out of diverse individuals is Whitman's, as it is America's, challenge. To sacrifice the radical, sacred individual to any collective or external authority would be to betray its very purpose. But to establish only the self, incorporating all into or excluding all from it, would do so no less.

This applies also to his own self. *Leaves of Grass* is finally Whitman's own self-expression. In it, he does not speak for everyone, in the sense of assuming everyone to speak as he does, swallowed by his voice. Nor is the text itself only a neutral space in which different voices encounter each other. Whitman is not the common man, but his representative, the common man transfigured. The poem is a model of one person, himself, speaking in his own voice, for himself, which invites – indeed incites – each person to take up this task just the same: i.e. each one for, as, himself or herself, to other selves.

The poem's language is privileged in this venture in a number of ways. Its procedures of figural multiplication and displacement, without collapsing into any unitary, imposed meanings or utterance, underscore and enact a multiplicity of individuated meanings. Each sense has its own claim, its own assertion, while nonetheless giving way to, and generating, other senses. This involves an interplay of difference and relation, of assertion and limitation, which gives voice to personal expression, subjectivity, and production while linking these to the production of others. In this the poem serves as both image for the kind of individual realization Whitman was pledged to as the promise of a liberal, democratic society, and also as an arena for it. As Whitman's own expression, the poem represents his own participation in this polity, his contribution to it, as required by all in order to realize liberal democracy's own premises. For language is, since the ancient model of the Greek democracy, specifically the arena in which participation takes place. Whitman's America is to broaden the possibility of such participation, where ideally every individual is called on to contribute to the common polity, in order exactly to safeguard, and express, his very autonomy and integrity. Poetry thus emerges as both image and enactment of participation in a space of language, an *agora* or forum of speaking which is the very foundation of the republic as citizenry participating in common venture. While the poet may, as representative self, stand before and ahead of others, he does so in order to lead them forth into the discourse which founds and provides the arena for a community of unique individuals. This project points not beyond the world, or outside of time into any sort of unity, but within the generations and displacements of time, pointing ahead towards distances to be traveled from the outsetting "Myself" to destinations that are never final, but always still to be achieved, always beckoning and inviting. Whitman thereby confirms, rather than repudiating or transcending, the common and historical world "under your boot-soles," where the representative "I" of "Song of Myself" stops always "waiting for you."

Whitman achieves his most authentic and powerful voice when he speaks out of individual difference, not as the merging into union of separate selves but in a summons to each one. Whitman's poetry undertakes to establish an "I" representing and directed towards a "you," in a poetry of address, as much vocative as personifying, expressing himself but towards others, and ultimately calling each to mutual responsibility and common commitments.

He enacts poetically a Jeffersonian call to individual participation in public life, in the face of ongoing American failures to realize this founding vision of a democratic polity. Rather than instituting unlimited senses of selfhood, *Leaves of Grass* awakens a sense of each self in communal relation to other selves. This represents the further transfiguration possible to each, and to the community as a whole.

6

ॐ

EMILY DICKINSON: THE VIOLENCE OF
THE IMAGINATION

FEMININE FIGURES: IN CRITIQUE OF AMERICAN SELFHOOD

Emily Dickinson seems in many ways at the furthest remove from Walt Whitman. His inclusive, expansive energy poses the most extreme counterpoint to Dickinson's exclusions, retractions, and renunciations. Dickinson's work, however, addresses cultural forces and challenges in ways continuous with Whitman's, although ultimately with a difference in cultural position from his which remains fundamental.

Dickinson's placement in terms of wider cultural concerns has been complicated by a privacy so fine no event seems able to penetrate it. Both as woman and poet, Dickinson seems intractably a figure of isolation. Her biographical seclusion cut her off from direct social intercourse with her surrounding world. Her texts seem to draw a circle around themselves, in momentary and apparently inconsistent expression. Even phrases or words are fragmented and isolated by her idiosyncratic dashes, which substitute for the integrating medium of punctuation. All of these almost compel an image of Dickinson's as a private and autonomous, if also a provisional and fragmentary world.

But Dickinson's work nonetheless reflects and enacts cultural forces and cultural challenges. A resistance to history is certainly suggested by her own severe textual obliqueness, as well as by her riveting refusal either to appear in public or to allow the publication of her work. In another sense, however, Dickinson's texts are scenes of cultural crossroad, situated within and acting as an arena for the many and profound transitions taking place around her. This apparent contradiction between private and public involvements is indeed itself a cultural one. Dickinson, among other things, brings to a kind of great consummation – and also transformation – a developing tradition of nineteenth-century women's writing, in which just such tensions between private and public loom large. The changing, highly dynamic status of women in nineteenth-century America in turn takes its place among other dramatic and dynamic changes. These include the counter-crossing between religious tradition as against secularizing forces, the shifting status of both art and artist, as well as emerging definitions of selfhood through complex intellectual, social, and economic developments. In terms of the biography of the nation, Dickinson may be said to reflect a drama of identity-crisis, in which different strands of cultural origins and intentions are in unstable relation, if not open conflict. In this context, Dickinson's poetry can be seen as a battlefield of clashing and conflicting impulses and commitments. Figure clashes against figure, selfhood against selfhood, claim against claim. These conflicts are not merely private and idiosyncratic. They represent a cultural dissension whose components are often violently at odds with each other.

In Dickinson's work, these cultural transformations and tensions take shape most directly as questions of identity, which almost obsessively concern her. Such questions are multiple. They include her identity as a woman; her identity as a poet; her religious identity, broadly defined to include metaphysical qualms and concerns, and which remained, contrary to many twentieth-century readings, a potent force from which she never completely divested herself. Finally, there is her identity as an American, in terms of changing definitions of selfhood as these have peculiarly taken shape within the developing United States.

In Dickinson's verse, each of these identities comes into complicated and often conflicting relation, whether within individual texts or between different poems. Configurations of gender and art are brought into relation and tension with metaphysical and also social/historical concerns. Not every Dickinson poem brings all of these constructions together or situates them in the same ways. Sometimes gender is the prevailing structure, sometimes art, sometimes metaphysics. History is almost always brought to bear in a tangential fashion, often through an imagery of economy that is surprisingly pervasive. The most powerful poems, however, interweave in contact and collision multiple modes of Dickinsonian identity.

The result is highly structured texts of extreme density. A poem or group of poems will propose a number of figural systems on a number of different levels. These invite or promise a complex orchestration of the different figural levels deployed. The texts seem to set up elaborate metaphorical analogues, reminiscent of the intercrossing figural levels of Renaissance metaphysical poetry. Different levels of experience seem to be images or metaphors for each other, to represent each other in an architectonic structure. However, close attention to Dickinson's language often discloses that the figural levels do not fully correlate with one another. A process of what might be called figural slippage, or mismatch, instead occurs. On the one hand, Dickinson's poems seem to establish a structure which brings their multiple levels into figural relation. She gathers into her texts different engagements, seeming to promise they will serve as figural correlatives for each other. But, instead, they come into collision through ambivalent or contradictory representations in ways that question or undermine their full correlation. The promise of systematic, tight, even highly ornate correspondences is stymied. What is in fact experienced is a resistance to just such alignments. Figural correlation becomes figural slippage.

Dickinson's textual strategies for resisting or defeating the analogical figures she also proposes find many expressions. There are dissonant image systems; skewed syntactic and formal relationships; multiple senses or usages within individual words, each of which acts as a point of conflict between several possible senses; and a discordant range of speaking or rhetorical stances, including that of Child (boy and girl), Wife, Lover, Least One (Nobody), Ecstatic, Skeptic, Martyr, and Dead Person. Reading her work therefore becomes an act of severe textual challenge. Indeed, the longer one works with a poem, the more difficult and opaque it becomes. Neither individual texts nor the relationships between them can be reduced to a single stance or resolution. As many readers have noticed, there is a characteristic doubling, or rather a working at cross-purposes, in which Dickinson seems both to say and unsay; claim and disclaim; desire and decline; offer and retract; assert and deny; defend and attack; gain and lose; define and circumvent definition. Whatever stance a poem seems to pursue, by the end it seems no less to unravel: one reason why Dickinson poems must so often be read backwards. Or, oppositional forces, or commitments, which are brought into headlong confrontation, seem to demand exclusive choices and sacrifices, often painfully, and almost always at great cost.

This textual multiplicity and contradiction, however, is not a detached indeterminacy or open-ended ambiguity, as is sometimes claimed. It deploys and brings into mutual confrontation personal and cultural forces which remain deeply at stake for her. Nor does Dickinson ultimately synthesize her antithetical positions, in a poetry of reconciliation or redemption, as is also claimed, where usually it is somehow the art object itself that is proposed as site of resolution and deliverance. Dickinson's is not a poetry of conversion or transfiguration, whether through art, transcendence, romance plot, or open indeterminate possibility. It is, rather, a poetry of disputation. While some texts do offer moments of ecstatic fulfillment, these remain in counter-tension against the many that do not. Her greatest texts often counterpose warring stances, without stable conversion of one into the other. These contradictory stances in Dickinson's work are by no means merely fragmentary pieces of changing mood or attitude. Rather, they are moments in an ongoing critique which Dickinson never brings to completion. Suspicious of cultural claims, sensitive to cultural contradictions, Dickinson's work explores and exposes, challenges, and contests. Opposing possibilities contend against each other with greater or lesser violence, and each imagined resolution is ultimately judged unsatisfactory.

This dramatic clash of cultural roles and definitions takes place across several fields. Among the most important of them is gender. Dickinson's work is pervasively shaped by gender structures, which she exposes as themselves an arena of conflicting claims, roles, and presuppositions. In Dickinson's work, gender structures finally implicate not only definitions of the female self but of American selfhood in general, both in its hidden gendering and in its fundamental values. The poetry offers a rich range of tropes which are either directly or indirectly gendered or feminized. Among these are: feminine speakers, actors, or figures; sexualized encounters or imagery; domestic imagery; feminized genre associations, such as sketch books, albums, keepsakes, and letters; the treatment of scale and size, especially in her use of diminutives and miniatures; imagery of the female body or clothing; feminized approaches to literary and religious traditions; and rhetorical devices which in her handling take on gendered resonances, such as modes of address, and, not least, modes of self-presentation. This last is deeply shaped by self-masking or self-concealment, evoking the modesty that so marks nineteenth-century female writing. In Dickinson, modesty expands into a general rhetoric of duplicity, entrapment, and assault. In some sense modesty becomes Dickinson's pivotal trope. To hide, to be hidden, is central to both her life and work. But modesty is, in Dickinson, a trope of extreme complexity. It both concedes and contests female self-definition. In her work, its various claims and disclaimers become modes in which Dickinson confronts, reappropriates, and contests cultural paradigms surrounding her.

Dickinson's self-representation in concealment begins, inevitably, with her biography. Emily Dickinson was born in 1830 in Amherst, Massachusetts, into a socially and politically prominent family of lawyers and public servants. Her grandfather had founded Amherst Academy and Amherst College, which remained the town's central cultural institutions. He, however, lost his home and position as treasurer of the college after suffering bankruptcy. Her father, intent on recovering lost ground, established himself as a successful lawyer, treasurer of the college, and restored owner of the homestead where his daughter had been born and into which she later retreated. Active in many civic projects, he was committed to integrating the town into the expanding communications and trade networks then transforming America. His sphere widened through the 1850s into a political career, including terms as a Massachusetts State Senator and then as Representative in the United States Congress. Emily Dickinson herself was educated at Amherst Academy and Mount Holyoke Academy, newly founded by Mary Lyon – an avid evangelical

Christian and one of the most powerful reformers of female education, with its many implications and controversies concerning changing female roles and identity. Dickinson was recalled home after one year of study for reasons that remain unclear. Eventually, she began to exhibit strange behavior. First, she stopped leaving her father's grounds, then his house. She began to converse with visitors only from a different room or from behind a screen; refused to address the envelopes for her large correspondence; dressed only in white; and declined to publish the hundreds of poems she started to accumulate in her upstairs dresser drawer.

Efforts to establish a disappointed romance as the cause of Dickinson's reclusion have proved unsuccessful. Dickinson's sister, Lavinia, who also lived unmarried at home, denied such an explanation, as did her brother's wife, Susan Gilbert Dickinson. A broken heart would, in any case, fail to explain Dickinson's emergence as a major poet. The mere fact of her remaining unmarried in itself cannot be regarded as a unique eccentricity. Marriage and motherhood certainly provided the ideological paradigm for women in the nineteenth-century "cult of true womanhood." Statistics, however, show an increasing number of single women through the nineteenth century. Before 1830, about 13 percent of Massachusetts women did not marry; by 1870 the proportion had risen to almost 18 percent: the highest percentage in the history of America. Unmarriage is especially prevalent among women writers, who largely, although not exclusively, wrote either before or after having been married – often out of (or justified by) financial necessity.

In Dickinson's own case, financial need plays no part. Her refusal to marry is striking mainly in the context of her reclusion, as this served both to safeguard her identity and to complicate it. Arguments for Dickinson's reclusion as a "strategy" by which she gained the autonomous freedom to write poetry as against gender roles urging marriage and motherhood, exaggerate on the side of strength. Arguments describing her reclusion as an evasion born of frustration, anxiety, and madness, make her into a mere victim and exaggerate on the side of weakness. Dickinson's self-enclosure surely gained her a certain degree of control over her world. Yet the very extremity of her withdrawal measures how powerful she felt the uncontrolled forces threatening her to be. In her texts and in her life, the force of the violence from within, in Wallace Stevens's phrase, mirrors the force of the violence from without.

Dickinson's relation to gender roles is problematic and conflictual. While she resisted, in her reclusion, certain gendered norms, such as marriage and motherhood, she fulfilled other norms, such as devoted daughterhood, confinement to domestic space, and modest avoidance of public appearance. Her behavior takes its place within a continuum of normative female models. Nevertheless, to the extent that Dickinson does exhibit conformity, she carries convention to such an extreme as to render its norms visible in a critical and even terrifying way. Dickinson's is modesty with a vengeance. Certainly her mantle of modesty does not perform its prescribed function of preserving a (prospective or actual) husband's honor. Her reclusion is a highly contradictory act of explosive compliance: a challenge in the guise of extreme fulfillment of an expected cultural paradigm. It registers to an acute degree both her profound marking by social norms and her equally severe resistance to them. Dickinson suffers from the restrictions imposed by her culture. Her reclusion does not free her from them, but rather displays their imprint. Yet, in exposing to view, in dramatically exaggerated (and symptomatic) fashion, what her culture demanded as conventional, she also protests against these norms, a protest she was able to turn to creative power through her writing.

The move onto the plane of artistic language is a momentous one. It exposes the role of language itself in forming the very cultural constructions she engages, and it investigates the claims of art within nineteenth-century cultural norms. Nevertheless, Dickinson's art does not offer an escape, transcendence, or resolution to the gender-conflicts she experienced. Her poems instead become scenes of anatomizing, staging, enacting, and exposing these conflicts. What is more, her treatment of gender-conflicts implicates more than sexual roles narrowly defined. Gender is a crucial perspective within Dickinson's verse, but not only regarding female conventions. Male conventions of behavior and general cultural values expressed in them are equally exposed.

Modesty becomes in Dickinson a scene of contest among competing gender roles or possibilities, in their mutual relationship or contradiction, and within broader hierarchies and cultural paradigms. Under modest guise, she anatomizes a variety of gender roles which she, however, shows to be less mutually confirming than is ordinarily assumed, and which ultimately extend beyond social models narrowly defined to implicate broad religious, economic, and other cultural orders:

> I meant to have but modest needs –
> Such as Content – and Heaven –
> Within my income – these could lie
> And Life and I – keep even –
>
> But since the last – included both –
> It would suffice my Prayer
> But just for One – to stipulate –
> And Grace would grant the Pair –

> And so – upon this wise – I prayed –
> Great Spirit – Give to me
> A Heaven not so large as Yours,
> But large enough – for me –

Modesty here is a challenge. Far from conforming to retiring female social roles, the text makes them a basis for their own transgression. It does so in ways that expose the arrangement of social roles in terms of religious ones. The "modest needs" which she so minimally names at once burgeon into a "Content" which can be as large as whatever satisfies, and then into "Heaven." The use of economic imagery of "income" could locate her "needs" as earthly or other-worldly, since economic rhetoric itself has, in the American tradition particularly, also a theological application. This is a rhetorical ambiguity Dickinson's poetry repeatedly exploits. In this poem, it points away from divine to human desire. Indeed, despite or through Dickinson's characteristic syntactic obfuscations, the "Prayer" in this poem is one that competes against rather than complies with traditional supplication. The poet is not, as it turns out, asking for a condescending share in the world-to-come, but rather for an independent "Life" in this one. This, as she calculates, would "include both" what the heavenly has to offer, but in preferred earthly terms. The modest request thus becomes an assertive one for personal independence and earthly satisfaction in competition against, and displacing, a heavenly one: "Great Spirit – Give to me / A Heaven not so large as Yours, / But large enough – for me."

But obfuscation, unfortunately, is a game both can play:

> A Smile suffused Jehovah's face –
> The Cherubim – withdrew –
> Grave Saints stole out to look at me –
> And showed their dimples – too –
>
> I left the Place, with all my might –
> I threw my Prayer away –
> The Quiet Ages picked it up –
> And Judgment – twinkled – too –
>
> That one so honest – be extant –
> It take the Tale for true –
> That "Whatsoever Ye shall ask –
> Itself be given You" –
>
> But I grown shrewder – scan the Skies
> With a suspicious Air –
> As Children – swindled for the first
> All Swindlers – be – infer

The persona in this poem takes on a number of different definitions. She is female in her modesty to a male authority; childish in her appeal to a God, therefore filial to His parental role as Father; and also economically vulnerable to His manipulations, figured as financial. Such multiplicity of levels is characteristic of Dickinsonian texts. Here it reflects, on the one hand, authorized structures of relationship within society, including familial, religious, and economic orders. On the other hand, it refuses to comply with these structures, or at least, exposes and protests against them and against the underlying claims which would justify them. The masculine, wealthy divine here does not benevolently protect, endow, and redeem this supplicant. Rather than delivering on such promises, God mockingly exploits them as false ones. His is a power to withhold, not to bestow; or, it is by withholding that He establishes His power.

Dickinson's response is a loss of innocence that initiates into a kind of adulthood. No longer trusting and childish, she now at least can recognize the swindle for what it is. This recognition or suspicion extends across the various levels the poem has established: the masculine, the divine, and the economic. And it serves to question the claim of each one to benevolently care for the childlike, innocent female, who, although paying the price of dependence, at least receives protection and sustenance in return. Not so, the poem insists. This is no system of mediated need, but a naked power structure ultimately grounded in denial of desire as the means of domination. To some extent, she can return the trick. As she puts it in another poem, "Bashful Heaven – thy Lovers small – / Hide – too – from thee –." And she, too, can deny: that divine, male, economic benevolence is anything other than a "Tale" which she, in the "honest" fictions of her own verse, can unmask as such and assault – if only from behind her own mask of "modest needs."

"I meant to have but modest needs" offers several gender alignments, connecting through masculinity the various authorities of family, religion, and economics as against a female modesty that is childlike but also explosive. It thereby suggests how gender alignments, far from representing stable hierarchies or mutually consistent constructions, instead are comprised of inconsistent and often conflicting claims or positions. Dickinson's poem makes such hierarchies visible. But even more, she questions the assumption that hierarchy serves the function claimed for it: the protection and adequate service of each of the participants in its social chain of being. Hierarchy is denied as a benevolent order distributing the good or goods. Far from accepting its justification as providing for each member, if only in different roles or degrees, Dickinson treats it as a scene of competition and domination. And implicated in this social chain are also economic and theological hierarchies, with each order corresponding to each in a stable distribution of authority. This stability Dickinson's poems rattle: economic against familial, familial against divine, male against female, and particularly contesting the place of gender in these structures which claim to treat it justly or benevolently.

The modesty which resists even while acceding to gender roles locates Dickinson not only with regard to God and/or father, but also to husband/lover figures. As she writes in this poem, one text from her group of "Wife" poems:

> The World – stands – solemner – to me –
> Since I was wed – to Him –
> A modesty befits the soul
> That bears another's – name –

Dickinson's figures of love and marriage are among the most discussed in her work, beginning with the "Master" letters – three passionate love letters that Dickinson wrote to an unknown person – that have kept critics busy for years. But Dickinson's images of love are among the most resistant to interpretation. Readings which construe Dickinson's as a romantic plot or a so-called sentimental religion or typology of love, in which she loses or subordinates herself before a lover who takes the place of God or father, seem to me especially wrong. While there is a romance element, or structure, in Dickinson's work, it is an extremely disrupted and complicated one. Dickinson may refer to sentimental conventions, but they do not contain her. Much truer to the texts are discussions that explore the deep ambivalence by which Dickinson at once woos and wards away a figure whose power she yearns towards even as she fears it will engulf her. In Poem 493, for example, what Dickinson accepts, and what she refuses, what she obtains, and what (and why) she forgoes, become more and more complicated as the poem proceeds:

> A doubt – if it be fair – indeed –
> To wear that perfect – pearl
> The Man – upon the Woman – binds –
> To clasp her soul – for all –
> A prayer, that it more angel – prove –
> A whiter Gift – within –
> To that munificence, that chose –
> So unadorned – a Queen –
> A Gratitude – that such be true –
> It had esteemed the Dream –
> Too beautiful – for Shape to prove –
> Or posture – to redeem.

"A doubt – if it be fair": Dickinson here puns upon questions of beauty and of justice. Wearing "that perfect – pearl" may signal an unfair subjection, a "modesty" that in bearing "another's – name" entails erasing her own (and "pearl" has a suggestion of sexual purity, while "bear" implies burdens and birthing). As the poem goes on, it becomes fairly unclear whether or not she wears this "whiter Gift" at all. For, it is "within," an inner "munificence" that is "unadorned," and not an actual, external condition. Is Dickinson speaking of an inner marriage more "true" than any actual, physical one can be? Or is this a trope for no marriage at all, a refusal of that "Dream" which is "Too beautiful – for Shape to prove–"? As often occurs in Dickinson's work, she seems to take away with one hand what she offers with the other.

In this poem, as characteristically occurs in Dickinson's work, a wide range of issues intersects within a narrow compass, while her work shows them to be mutually implicating. Here, questions of embodiment, of fleshly existence ("Shape," "posture") as against inward states also are at work, as they in turn frame questions of gender, of religion, of ownership, and also of art. Pearl, clasp, gift, adornment, munificence create a lexical base suggesting jewelry, both bestowed on the bride and to which she is reduced as she comes to belong to her groom. Or the whole metaphor of marriage may point towards a religious devotion, spiritual rather than physical and social; or an aesthetic one, and yet no less undermined by the poem's ambivalences.

In each area, what emerges is a multiple structure of desire and defense, pursuit and flight, invocation and apotropaic warding, which is so characteristic of Dickinson through many topics. This conflicted structure can also be applied to Dickinson's whole relation to the literary tradition as established by male writers, who offer problematic models of authorship and of representation, including the representation of women. In her gender difference, Dickinson cannot simply appropriate or identify with a literary tradition she nevertheless wishes to claim as her own and turns to for poetic resources. Her literary desires reenact with regard to aesthetic autonomy and heteronomy distributions of power on social, economic, and theological levels which Dickinson must likewise both negotiate and mitigate.

Dickinson's work contests male authority, but not necessarily in the sense of wishing to claim it for herself. Readings of her as though she is prevented by her gender from attaining a desired male position underestimate the extent to which her work puts such power structures into question. Arguments complaining of female exclusion imply inclusion in masculine models to be the antidote. Dickinson's work, however, points to problems in the conceptions of independence, autonomy, and personal power assumed by men in nineteenth-century culture. Gendered readings of Dickinson's relation to male figures are in any case complicated by a persistent and often unnerving gender slippage. In many poems, female figural systems – of speakers, imagery, attribute, stance, or actor – cross with male ones. In another "Wife" poem, for example, the "wife" and "Woman" are figured as "Czar."

> I'm "wife" – I've finished that –
> That other state –
> I'm Czar – I'm "Woman" now –
> It's safer so –

Dickinson implies here a whole theoretics of quotation. The words of her poem become at once hers and not hers. She invokes a social language without fully making it her own, importing accepted usages and meanings into her text, where she can then complicate them. Here, she purposefully confuses positions and claims to power. It is a paradox of womanhood that to achieve one's full state as "wife" is also to lose it in subordination to a husband. It is to be "Czar" and not "Czar," where the male title at once asserts preeminence and denies it to her. The bid for autonomy, for a woman, is deeply troubled by gender associations. Dickinson's poetry raises questions as to how fully male figures can represent women, and yet, how fully women's roles can do so, either, within conventional social structures.

The gender slippage that occurs in poems placing women in relationship to men is further complicated by the fact that it is far from clear whether some of Dickinson's best-known love poems are addressed to men at all. This is overtly the case in the two versions of a poem which begins either: "Going to Him! Happy letter," or "Going – to – Her! / Happy – Letter." Dickinson's sexuality is somewhat inchoate. Nothing approaches for emotional intensity her passionate letters and poems to Susan Gilbert Dickinson, her beloved friend turned sister-in-law. Perhaps the erotic ghost which haunts Dickinson's work is as much female as male. But this is not to say that Dickinson would have chosen a fulfilled lesbian "Boston" marriage over the rigors of Amherst celibacy. Dickinson's ambi-sexual love poetry is as riddled with retraction and resistance as are poems more specifically heterosexual in structure. Though differences may be perceived between the ways she imagines a "Master" as against a "Sister," in either case Dickinson's is a love of evasion. There is no specific gendering in "There came a Day at Summer's full," when "each was to each The Sealed Church"; but whatever the gender of each and each, the poem traces the retreat from their union. Love is a state of separation in "They put Us far apart" and "I cannot live with You," whatever the genders. Within Dickinson's sexuality, however it is constructed and with whatever consciousness on her part, erotic union is a powerful desire to be put off. As in the inversive rhetoric of the famous "Because I could not stop for Death," it is always unclear in Dickinson whether death is a courtship or courtship is a death. Even if she "could suffice for Him," his inviting her to be "Whole" means a unity at the cost of her own separate identity, and hence, "My syllable rebelled." As many readers have noted, sexuality and death, union and erasure, are closely linked in Dickinson's sensibility.

What seems to be left is a defiant self, isolated, enclosed, self-reliant. Dickinson's work, in its recalcitrant selfhood, refers not only to Emerson's specific writing but to the whole concern with autonomy and individualism so central to American culture. But Dickinson's poetry offers a selfhood that remains extremely problematic. Her poetics of retraction extend no less to her treatments of autonomous unity and self-reliance. Almost any text that seems to assert the power, completeness, and sufficiency of self also questions, exposes, and subverts such assertions. Conversions from enclosure to infinitude, from renunciation to fulfillment or transcendence, are highly problematic, compromised, and often blocked. In this, Dickinson offers a critique of American notions of selfhood as expressed in Emerson and indeed widely in her culture. She further bases this critique in a gendering that American ideologies of selfhood, without acknowledging it, assume.

It is very tempting to see Dickinson's retreat into the self as accession to power, making limitation into expansion, intensity into extension, constrictive circles into infinite circumferences. In a number of poems, she does indeed do this. This model of sacrifice/conversion is one she herself would have liked, in fundamental ways, to accomplish. Yet what occurs most often is the failure, or at least severe qualification, of any such conversion. When

> The Soul selects her own Society
> Then – shuts the Door

(and she does so with puns on electoral politics: hers is a "Majority," which she chooses "from an ample nation") the act may declare her independence. But she also finds her self to be a prison, as "The Valves of her attention" close deathlike, "Like Stone." If "A Prison gets to be a friend," it does so not through expansive transfiguration, but rather because its "narrow Round" exchanges "Hope – for something passiver." "Liberty" in this poem, far from being achieved, is "Avoided – like a Dream." If "The Soul unto itself / Is an imperial friend," it is equally "the most agonizing Spy – / An Enemy – could send." The "Chamber" of the self is "Haunted," a frightening self-enclosure concealing "Ourself behind ourself" in multiplying self-fragmentation, not unity. The "Consciousness that is aware / Of Neighbors and the Sun" is a soul hunted, "condemned to be – attended by a single Hound / Its own identity."

Dickinson in such texts invokes a transformative power which then, however, fails. But we fall into her trap. We see "Renunciation" as "Virtue" rather than as "piercing," and overlook the syntactic obfuscations which make it impossible in this poem to weigh what is gained against what is renounced. It is our stubborn Emersonian/American paradigm that seduces us to see independent, autonomous selfhood as ideal and attainable, even if at a price, blinding us to the disturbing disjunctions Dickinson's poems offer. Nor is the problem only Dickinson's exclusion from autonomous independence because of gender restrictions. Rather, her gender may allow her a critical stance on ideologies of the self that dissociate it from social, cultural, or religious commitments: commitments that in other ways are constitutive of identity and which, while on one level they limit, on others extend the self beyond its own boundaries. The burden of self-sufficiency, as Dickinson shows, can be crushing.

Emerson, whose *Essays: Second Series* (1844) Dickinson read in 1850, uses specifically gendered language in his imagery of self-reliance. In "Self-Reliance" he urges that a "true man belongs to no other time or place, but is at the center of things." "Every true man is a cause, a country, an age; requires infinite spaces and numbers and time fully to accomplish his design." In the circular imagery which Dickinson in turn adopts, Emerson declaims:

The life of man is a self-evolving circle, which, from a ring imperceptibly small, rushes on all sides outwards to new and larger circles, and that without end . . . The heart refuses to be imprisoned; in its first and narrowest pulses it already tends outward with a vast force and to immense and innumerable expansions . . . The instinct of man presses eagerly onward to the impersonal and illimitable.

And he adds: "The only sin is limitation."

The gendering of Emerson's self-reliance is not accidental. As Joyce Appleby remarks, the liberal individual of American ideology is male:

Obviously the liberal hero is male. Less obviously liberalism relied on gender differences to preserve the purity of its ideal type. Dependency, lack of ambition, attachment to place and person – these qualities were stripped from the masculine carrier of inalienable rights and conferred upon women . . . This allowed the unsentimental, self-improving, restlessly ambitious, free, and independent man to hold sway as a universal hero.

In Emerson's work, it is the "true man" who is at the center of things; the "life of man" that "rushes on all sides outwards." And if the "only sin is limitation," it is a peculiarly female sin: by social custom, religious stricture, education, legal rule. Emerson can imagine his "true man" as "at the center of things," freed from all social, historical, and personal relationships in ways that no nineteenth-century "true" woman can be. Here Dickinson is no exception. Unlike Emerson's self-reliant who is called on to "shun father and mother," Dickinson, for all her solitude, remained profoundly enmeshed in family life, in a personal network of friendships, and in the domestic duties of cooking, baking, and sewing. She may, in an often quoted letter, bid "God keep me from what they call households," but, in the event, of course He did not. Yet Dickinson's work can also help recover implications in Emerson's own notions of selfhood, which later developments in American modes of the self have obscured. Emerson still defines "the aboriginal Self" as grounding a "universal reliance," and if he urges us to "sit at home with the cause," he does so by referring "Self-existence" to the "Supreme Cause." Emerson's circle of the self has, after all, a transcendent reference beyond itself, which is variously implied and variously figured. It is able to claim for itself an identity with transcendence that remains complicated for Dickinson, or whose complications Dickinson's work makes visible. The Emersonian, liberal notion of autonomous selfhood contrasts not only with female social realities and roles. It may run counter to fundamental conditions in the world, and fundamental needs of society.

Dickinson's poetry of selfhood, and especially her use of circular imagery that suggests Emerson's, makes strange play on selfhood's gendering. There is often a specifically female gender in poems of self-retreat as self-unraveling, such as

> I felt a Cleaving in my Mind –
> As if my Brain had split –
> I tried to match it – Seam by Seam –
> But could not make them fit.

The circle of the self comes apart in a piecemeal imagery of sewing as mismatched patchwork. In "The Missing All – prevented Me / From missing minor Things," imagery of domestic "work" is placed in near-catastrophic context:

> If nothing larger than a World's
> Departure from a Hinge –
> Or Sun's extinction, be observed –
> 'Twas not so large that I
> Could lift my Forehead from my work
> For Curiosity.

Withdrawal into an enclosed world may block out such "larger" breaks as "a World's / Departure from a Hinge – / or Sun's extinction," but it equally registers the cost of renouncing the greater world, whose destruction may be the consequence of just such withdrawal. Dickinson's sewing of poems into fascicle-booklets itself connects her domestic to her poetic arts. Indeed, the dashes that at once mediate and disrupt her flow of syntax suggest the sewing thread on which she strings her words, yet in doing so dramatize the constant threat of their breakage.

Dickinson's "circumference" images register strange genderings at work behind apparent universals of limitless expansion. In the poem "Crisis is a Hair," circumference is an image of panic as the poet "adjusts the Hair" in a feminized gesture of attendance on the dead – or the living:

> Let an Instant push
> Or an Atom press
> Or a Circle hesitate
> In Circumference
>
> It – may jolt the Hand
> That adjusts the Hair
> That secures Eternity
> From presenting – Here –

Marking the boundary between earthly self and supposed infinities, circumference acts as uncertain and unstable reference between them. Defining the self, it stands in unresolved conflict with a (masculine) "Eternity" that both beckons and threatens:

> Time feels so vast that were it not
> For an Eternity –
> I fear me this Circumference
> Engross my Finity –
>
> To His Exclusion

Attachments within the world of time threaten allegiance to an eternity figured as male, although which one is circumference, and which fear is greater – to lose time or eternity – remains a question enacted in the poem's calculated unclarity. The problem of gendering recurs. "Circumference" is "thou Bride of Awe" in another poem, where it is to be "Possessed of every hallowed Knight / That dares to covet thee." Expansive venture aligns with manly quests and conquests, making Dickinson's own possessing highly problematic.

There are in Dickinson apparently ecstatic poems:

> I saw no Way – The Heavens were stitched –
> I felt the Columns close –
> The Earth reversed her Hemispheres
> I touched the Universe –
>
> And back it slid – and I alone –
> A Speck upon a Ball –
> Went out upon Circumference –
> Beyond the Dip of Bell –

Emerson, in his essay on "Circles," also speaks of "dislocations which apprise us that this surface [of nature as concentric circles] is not fixed, but sliding." He also speaks dizzily of a "sudden rushing from the center to the verge." Dickinson, conversely, will venture daringly, as in this poem, "Out upon Circumference," or, as she writes in a similar poem, will go "beyond the estimate / Of Envy, or of Men –" out "among Circumference." But the two poets stand in something like an inverse ratio: where in Emerson skepticism is sporadic, in Dickinson it is confidence that is intermittent. "I saw no Way" associates the adventure of circumference with Dickinson's more cataclysmic imagery. Emersonian circles become severed demi-spheres, where Heavens are "stitched" in feminized imagery of sewing as scarring. The earth's hemispheres reverse, the universe slides. The self "alone" is nothing more than a "Speck upon a Ball," its solitary self-definition posed against the immensity of a universe that it does not contain, or even represent.

Other Emersonian images of self-reliance undergo similar destabilizing in Dickinson. "The eye" which is Emerson's "first circle" ("Circles"), through which "the currents of the Universal Being circulate" ("Nature"), in Dickinson becomes a disquieting self-mirroring. The poem "Like Eyes that looked on Wastes" has been interpreted as a sisterly text in which Dickinson gazes into the eyes of another woman. But it instead suggests someone looking into the terrible mirror of the self, and there finding a wasteland of isolation and solipsism: a "Blank – and steady Wilderness – Diversified by Night." Emerson's "natural world . . . as a system of concentric circles" proceeding "from the eternal generation of the soul" ("Circles") turns in Dickinson into another aspect of wheels:

> Severer Service of myself
> I – hastened to demand
> To fill the awful Vacuum
> Your life had left behind –
>
> I worried Nature with my Wheels
> When Hers had ceased to run –
> When she had put away Her Work
> My own had just begun.
>
> I strove to weary Brain and Bone –
> To harass to fatigue
> The glittering Retinue of nerves –
> Vitality to clog
>
> To some dull comfort Those obtain
> Who put a Head away
> They knew the Hair to –
> And forget the color of the Day –

> Affliction would not be appeased –
> The Darkness braced as firm
> As all my stratagem had been
> The Midnight to confirm –
>
> No Drug for Consciousness – can be –
> Alternative to die
> Is Nature's only Pharmacy
> For Being's Malady –

It is interesting that Dickinson uses a term – "Service" – that most often denotes (feminized) devotion outside the self, to refer here to self-devotion. Her intensive self-preoccupation is set in response against some "awful Vacuum," figured as a loss through death (or loss figured as death). The circles of Emersonian nature have ceased to run, and her own "Wheels" are discontinuous and antithetical rather than encompassing those of the natural world. Inside her own circle, she finds not infinity but that peculiarly Dickinsonian stoppage of time which denotes not eternity, but fragmented, alienated disjunction.

Retreat into the self in this poem is undertaken in painful response to a world that is beyond the self's control. It is, as Dickinson's renunciation is often said to be, a "stratagem." But it is not a successful one. "Affliction would not be appeased." The stratagem confirms the darkness rather than dispelling it. As to "Consciousness," it does not offer freedom, independence, or self-definition beyond mortal conditions. Dickinson's self does not have access to an Emersonian Universal Being beyond individual limitation and tribulation. She instead questions this possibility.

Dickinson's poems of selfhood communicate at times a heady sense of power and autonomy of the self, by itself, without need or dependence. But they also enact a clash between such American, Romantic, or liberal self-definitions as against the self as defined, and conditioned, through relationships and commitments beyond it: as dramatized here in a female attendance on the dead. This sense of conditioned selfhood no doubt reflects in part Dickinson's exclusion, as female, from the liberal paradigm of self-fulfillment, along with the freedom to pursue it. These do not extend to her as a nineteenth-century woman. But she also questions this paradigm. She is aware of its potential solipsism, and is skeptical of its ability to address "Being's Malady" – an illness so severe that death becomes the only solution for it, the only paradoxical defiance of dissolution. Dickinson's poetry contests the American model of self-reliance not only as gendered male, but as incomplete, untrue to experience, and metaphysically vulnerable. The power of her poems of selfhood resides not in the extent to which they fulfill the dream of American selfhood, but in their contention against this model, whose fissures she exposes.

THE SIGNS OF HISTORY

Emily Dickinson's is a poetry of the religious imagination. This is not to claim that Dickinson is an orthodox religious poet. On the contrary, her work offers a forceful and original critique of traditional metaphysics in ways that recall her near contemporary, Friedrich Nietzsche. However, readings of Dickinson as though she had comfortably settled into a post-Christian enlightenment, substituting art and the powers of her own mind for faith in divine orders and meanings, are both historically anachronistic and untrue to her verse. Historians underscore how religious institutions, hermeneutics, and sensibility continued forcefully to frame nineteenth-century life, especially the lives of women. As the century advanced, religious norms may have been boiling away, but they had by no means evaporated. As to the claim that Dickinson freed herself from Christian orthodoxy while transposing many of its most constitutive structures into aesthetic experience and activity, her work exactly explores just how problematic such transpositions can be. She questions to what extent art can indeed serve as figure for faith, and, conversely, exposes how religious assumptions persist even beyond specific dogmas, to continue to exert pressure on both social and aesthetic ideologies.

Dickinson's religious stance is not that of a determined unbeliever. She is not devout, but she is not secular. She attacks religious claims which continue, however, to keep their hold on her and which she never entirely discards. Dickinson both rejects and requires religious faith. Most writers with Dickinson's religious needs return to faith through some conversion structure, as did, for example, T. S. Eliot. Most writers with Dickinson's religious doubts renounce their faith, or transfigure it through some alternative reference or order, however personal, provisional, or aesthetic. Dickinson remains, unusually, in a state of sustained religious crisis, with an intensity that rivals that of mystical devotion. Her reasons for both asserting and denying a divine order, in constant counter-tension, are rehearsed repeatedly throughout her verse. In this sense, Dickinson's work does not take shape as quest. Rather, it engages in endless disputation, which is endlessly inconclusive. There is a perpetual clash in which different positions challenge each other, with each one found ultimately wanting. In this disputation, religious questions confront religious answers, which do not, however, adequately resolve them. The result is a world that remains unsatisfactory without God, but equally unsatisfactory with the God of her fathers.

Dickinson's contention against God is structured, not least, through gender. Her position regarding Him can never be exactly the same as, say, Emerson's, simply by reason of sexual difference. Emerson's self is not as simply self-enclosed and self-reliant as may first appear. When Emerson acclaims the infinity of selfhood, he implicitly links it to divinity, however defined. The Emersonian self extends beyond itself, acting as a figure for God. "The relations of the soul to the divine spirit are so pure that it is profane to seek to interpose helps," he writes in "Self-Reliance." Emerson is free to "sit at home" because the "Supreme Cause" sits there with him, with his own "Self-existence" an "attribute" of the divine. At the "center" of the Emersonian circle remains God, unbound by any "circumference," and whose "waves . . . flow into" him. This divine center not only defines the self. It also establishes the self's relation to the surrounding world as an "eternal generation of circles" whose "central life contains all circles." Crucially, it is the self and divinity as mutual reflections that empower the self to interpret the surrounding world as its own self-reflection. As Emerson states, using Pauline language: "We learn that God IS; that he is in me; and that all things are shadows of him."

In poems where Dickinson does claim for herself such infinitude of selfhood as Emerson announces, she tends to do so by placing herself in relation to some divine principle, as he does. Her self-enclosure is then not restrictive but all-encompassing. "The Soul's Superior Instants" occur with "Eternity's disclosure . . . Of the Colossal substance / Of immortality." But Dickinson has great difficulty in identifying herself with the divine. Even this apparently ecstatic poem on "Superior Instants" admits: "This Mortal Abolition is seldom." Nor can she directly claim to represent God in quite the way Emerson does. Her position regarding Him is finally eccentric, because of gender. There are charming, reassuring poems announcing how "The Soul that hath a Guest / Doth seldom go abroad," especially when "Upon Himself be visiting / The Emperor of Men." But the relation between Soul and Emperor is not one of simple identity. Rather, it is of hostess to guest — or rather, of "Host," with "Himself" and not herself being visited. This odd gender shift complicates the poetess's claim to direct access or identity with the power s/he is hosting. Similar complications creep into "The Soul should always stand ajar / That if the Heaven inquire." Not only its conditional "if," but odd distributions of "Host" and "Guest" both in gender and in reference, and a tortuous syntax, make it difficult to sort out whether or not the visit has even occurred.

One much discussed poem, "On a Columnar Self / How ample to rely," similarly concludes in syntactic obfuscations regarding grammatical number, antecedent, and sequence, so as to severely complicate what first seemed to be a strong declaration of divine self-identity:

> Suffice Us — for a Crowd
> Ourself — and Rectitude —
> And that Assembly — not far off
> From furthest Spirit — God —

The singular self is referred to in plural, but just who is included and who excluded from its "Crowd" remains a slippery question. Is this inner "Rectitude" grounded in a God who is "not far off," or does it instead declare Him to be outside, as "furthest Spirit"? The lapidary imagery, turning the self into stone column, reminds that Dickinson's poems of self-reliance often involve entrapment, mortuary stifling, and a crowded solitude recalling Samuel Beckett's agonized anatomies of the self locked alone into itself.

Dickinson's "Wife" poems often reenact similar questions about how far a woman can claim to identify herself with God, and through which kinds of relation. "Mine – by the Right of the White Election!" the poet ecstatically exclaims. But even here hers is "the Sign in the Scarlet prison," in painful cost to the elected self. White spirituality stands against scarlet suffering in ways that suggest a troubling image of the body as prison. The "Sign," in any case, marks the wife as separate from the power she signifies. This intrusion of the "Sign," in itself and as body, is crucial. As Dickinson writes elsewhere, she may be "titled," but only in ways that remove her from the source and site of power and hence make her own status derivative:

> Title Divine – is mine!
> The Wife – without the Sign!
> Acute Degree – conferred on me –
> Empress of Calvary!
> Royal – all but the Crown!
> Betrothed – without the swoon
> God sends us Women –
> When you – hold – Garnet to Garnet –
> Gold – to Gold –
> Born – Bridalled – Shrouded –
> In a Day –
> Tri Victory
> "My Husband" – women say –
> Stroking the Melody –
> Is *this* the way?

Had Emerson been the author of this poem, he could have written "Title Divine – is mine!" and stopped there. But Dickinson cannot directly claim this divine title. She can only situate herself towards it as "Wife – without the Sign!" The sign here is the sign of sexuality, of body: to be without it is to be "Betrothed – without the swoon" of sexual contact. This divine title requires (or permits) a transcendence of earthly conditions, a birth into another life which is death for this one – "Born" as "Shrouded." The double valence of this exchange is contained in the pun of "Bridalled," as being betrothed but also reined in. But in either case, the woman remains only wife to some divine image as "Husband" and not the divine power itself. Her title is secondary.

At stake in Dickinson's claiming title – to realms poetic, religious, and/or in economic senses that play a surprising role in Dickinson's verse-textures – is the possibility of interpreting her world at all, within a sign-system and its promise of interpretive coherence. That the world may resist interpretation, that established norms may not in fact prove reliable or valid, does occur to Emily Dickinson. But to Dickinson, unlike such later poets as Wallace Stevens to whom she is so often likened, this prospect is terrifying and ultimately unacceptable. As earlier commentators on Dickinson recognized, she continues to work within an inherited system of figural representation. Its remote origins in Puritan America, urging a figural encoding of events in nature, history, and the self as signs, or types, for ultimate things, could be felt especially in the habits of orthodox, ante-bellum Amherst. But figural structures no less survive in more liberal Boston. The figural or typological impulse did not simply die in the nineteenth century. Rather, it underwent transformations marking not only American Romanticism, with its demons of analogy, but the historical culture at large. The events of America continued to be understood as moments in a universal drama of redemption, even if such redemption was increasingly claimed for history rather than eternity. Dickinson's poems repeatedly operate within such a sign-system and its promise of figural structure and transcendent reference. In her terms, time should represent eternity; earthly experience, even, or rather especially when involving loss and death, should find transfigured meaning within a structure of transcendence. In certain moods, her poems declare just such transfigurations, making hers a "Compound Vision . . . The Finite – furnished / With the Infinite . . . Back – toward Time – / And forward – Toward the God of Him – ."

Dickinson's difficulties with her inherited figural system, however, generally prevent her from enjoying its promises. This penetrates not only her religious expectations, but also her aesthetic ones. Readings of Dickinson that see her poetry as converting limitation to infinity, pain to joy, suffering to redemption, and death to poetic immortality replicate and transfer fundamentally Christian structures to the realm of art. But these basic structures of conversion, whether in religion or in art, appear to her to be faulty. Her poetry repeatedly and painfully attests to misgivings that prevent her from reading her world as signs for any redemptive meaning whatsoever. It traces her resistance to making experiences types for each other in a chain of transferred meanings that point ultimately to some redemptive realm. This does not, however, make the figural system dispensable. In text after text, she returns again to the figural premises and promises; again finding them wanting; again finding them necessary.

Dickinson's scruples regarding transcendental conversion structures are recurrent and consistent. Her work in fact offers a sustained and powerful critique not only of religion, but also of displacements of Christian structures into secular and aesthetic modes – where, however, without their religious underpinnings they founder, returning her once more to the religious or metaphysical premises she had criticized. Regarding metaphysical forms, her first objection is epistemological. For another world, there is no certain evidence:

> "Heaven" has different Signs – to me –
> Sometimes, I think that Noon
> Is but a symbol of the Place –
> And when again, at Dawn,
>
> A mighty look runs round the World
> And settles in the Hills –
> An Awe if it should be like that
> Upon the Ignorance steals – . . .
>
> Itself be fairer – we supppose –
> But how Ourself, shall be
> Adorned, for a Superior Grace –
> Not yet, our eyes can see –

As in another, similar text – "These are the Signs to Nature's Inns" – Dickinson opens in confidence. But she closes in hesitation. "'Heaven' has different Signs – to me" suggests multiple avenues to transcendent glory, but becomes by the end occultation of vision: "Not yet, our eyes can see." Reading backwards, uncertainty begins to undermine even the assertive opening language. "Noon / Is but a symbol" may already qualify it as a sign she invents rather than perceives. The "mighty look" may after all be only her own. The "Awe" of divine sign-language steals upon, or is stolen from, "Ignorance." As to her own eventual "Superior Grace," this is never directly witnessed. The vision that "Signs" may open, they also obscure. If their strength is to point beyond themselves, they themselves nevertheless remain the only evidence directly witnessed, and their further implications may be far from straightforward or certain.

But epistemological doubt alone is not really sufficient to disturb Dickinson. Beyond it, and more pressing, are metaphysical and axiological questions. The other world as redemptive, is, as Nietzsche later claims, no more than an antithetical image of this one. It is constituted as earth's negation. Heaven is constructed in opposition to all that we find painful and threatening in this world. About this Dickinson can be flip and comical, as in her image of heaven as "the fair schoolroom in the sky" where it is always "Sunday" without

"Recess." "Eden" is the place of "new shoes." "Is Heaven a Place — a Sky — a Tree?" she reductively asks. But she is painfully serious in her critique of the other world as a negation of this one, in ways comparable to Nietzsche's sustained critique of metaphysics. Each transcendental value is constructed in opposition, but also negation, to an earthly condition. "The things that Death will buy / Are Room —" that is, infinitude, rather than our actual finite lives; "Escape from Circumstances," that is, the negation of accident, contingency, and the limiting conditions of earthly existence; "And a Name —," that is, immortal identity.

This opposition between a metaphysical heaven and a physical earth makes heaven not only earth's antithesis but also its antagonist. Earth and heaven, this world and the next, time and eternity are meant to stand in complementary and indeed redemptive relation one to the other. But the metaphysical structure in another sense places them at war. The pain of that conflict penetrates every attachment to and in this world, until religion seems not to complete earthly life through a heavenly promise, but rather to demand renunciation of present for ultimate things. The revealing letters Dickinson wrote during the winter of 1850 trace her response to the pressures of religious enthusiasm and revival then raging in Amherst. Her resistance to conversion is phrased in just this sense of exclusive choice. "The path of duty," she writes (and the duties she lists are particularly female: "meekness — and patience — and submission") "looks very ugly indeed — and the place where I want to go more amiable." "Christ is calling everyone here, all my companions have answered . . . and I am standing alone in rebellion." Her rebellion, however, is full of conflict, rebelling also against itself: "I am one of the lingering bad ones, and so do I slink away, and pause, and ponder, and ponder and pause, and do work without knowing why — not surely for *this* brief world, and more sure it is not for Heaven." This brief world versus Heaven: such opposition haunts Dickinson's attempts to find some path from one to the other (it is in this letter, too, that she identifies herself with Satan in the book of Job as one who strays "to and fro" about the world, but this is an image for art, identifying her writing with things of this world). Still earlier, she wrote in a letter from Mount Holyoke, while resisting the call to conversion so powerfully delivered there by no less a person than Mary Lyon: "I am not happy, and I regret that last term, when that golden opportunity was mine, that I did not give up and become a Christian. It is not now too late, so my friends tell me, so my offended conscience whispers, but it is hard for me to give up the world." To gain heaven is to give up the world, a rhetoric of renunciation that will persist throughout Dickinson's career. Or again, earlier still to Abiah Root, she wrote: "I feel I have not yet made my peace with God . . . I have perfect confidence in God and his promises & yet I know not why, I feel that the world holds a predominant place in my affections. I do not feel that I could give up all for Christ, were I called to die." Heaven requires earth's renunciation. To value one, as Nietzsche polemicized, is to devalue the other. To gain the next world Dickinson must "give up" this one. Religion does not redeem experience, but rather requires its erasure.

This discontinuity, implicit within Dickinson's experience of religion, further complicates her relation to it. Renunciation subverts the very ground and possibility of analogy between mortal, earthly experience and the immortality beyond, on which analogy also depends. For it severs the connection between experience and redemption, or bases connection on contradictory mutual opposition. Nowhere is this more evident, or more urgent, than in death. Death is the black hole into which Dickinson endlessly gazes, the subject, as she puts it in no fewer than three poems, that "Not even a Prognostic's push / Can make a Dent thereon –." Death stands for Dickinson as two stark, severe, and irreconcilable possibilities: the absolute dissolution of the self, or its final absolution in immortal self-identity. That Dickinson desperately – i.e. with longing despair – desired the latter seems to me undeniable. Face to face with death she implacably kept herself, in her own variation on traditional religious meditation: through hundreds of poems and countless, often bizarre letters of condolence to mourners known only through newspaper obituaries. Interpreting death describes a good deal of her poetic effort.

> The last Night that She lived
> It was a Common Night
> Except the Dying – this to Us
> Made Nature different
>
> We noticed smallest things –
> Things overlooked before
> By this great light upon our Minds
> Italicized – as 'twere.

Death is Dickinson's special text, through which Nature becomes "Italicized." This textual imagery persists through many Dickinsonian attempts to decipher death: to "read [its] sentence," where "no Signal," however, is forthcoming. Dickinson's rites of mortal interpretation are at once Christian, female, and poetic. She adopts the role of attendance on the dying which in her period remained the task of women at home, the practice of removal to a hospital not yet having been widely instituted. In composing poetry, she also composes herself, through layer on layer of longing and terror, submission and rebellious recoil.

> That Others should exist
> While She must finish quite
> A Jealousy for Her arose
> So nearly infinite –

What is infinite here is neither the other world at whose borders Dickinson so compulsively lingers, nor her faith in it; but rather a competitive "Jealousy" of an other world which so ravenously and mercilessly intrudes its claims against her own present one. Earth and heaven are not complementary, but at odds. Yet Dickinson remains no less at odds with herself in her rebellion. She proceeds through her text of death, waiting, as she goes on to write, for its "notice":

> We waited while She passed –
> It was a narrow time –
> Too jostled were Our Souls to speak
> At length the notice came.
>
> She mentioned, and forgot –
> Then lightly as a Reed
> Bent to the Water, struggled scarce –
> Consented, and was dead –

Negatively recorded is the erasure of language itself ("She mentioned, and forgot –") and the breaking of life's "Reed" – perhaps a pun on writing's instrument. What is at last left to her are those final, female attendances of the body, now bereft of spirit, on which her own spirit gazes in unending perplexity:

> And We – We placed the Hair –
> And drew the Head erect –
> And then an awful leisure was
> Belief to regulate –

Dickinson's art is at once iconic and disintegrative. Death as both absolute certainty and absolutely uncertain remained a problem she could not transfigure. Searching for "Significance," as she writes in another poem, of some "Duplicate" or "Parallel" between earthly erasure and "Resurrection," she longs to know that "Circumference be full." In this effort, faith is not abandoned, nor yet is it adopted. As in "The last Night that She lived," all that is left is an "awful leisure" that "Belief" cannot "regulate," and yet must.

Dickinson's poems are characteristically structured around such interpretive acts. As here, her focus is often on the very attempt to interpret, and its fragility. But death, while urgent in the sense of personal eschatology, takes its place within broader interpretive structures, involving communal, religious, and historical references. These begin at the source, in the Bible, whose exegesis forms the substructure of further figural interpretation. Dickinson's poems on the Bible are among her most consistent texts. They take their place within her ongoing contest between assault and appeal, defiance and desire – with each often a form of the other, while gender provides a central and explosive, but also a subtle and complex element in her approach to religious tradition and authority. Dickinson's view of the Bible as an "antique Volume – Written by faded Men" is inevitably framed by the fact that she is a woman.

Dickinson, however, does not particularly dramatize female Biblical figures. She instead casts herself as a female voice within interpretive structures and religious confrontations. She, like Jacob in the poem "A little East of Jordan," wrestles against apparent Biblical claims and indeed against God Himself. At times she gestures towards redefining Eden or Paradise as a site within the world of human experience. Certainly she rejects hell-damnation and punishment as vengeful and unjust. It is this sense of injustice, of the unfairness of God against His creatures, that particularly rouses her. Moses emerges as a special grievance:

> It always felt to me – a wrong
> To that Old Moses – done –
> To let him see – the Canaan –
> Without the entering –

In many texts, Dickinson approaches and reproaches God as a male figure: father or husband, commanding familial authority as well as economic control. In this specifically Biblical revisiting, gender also enters in: God seems to fasten on Moses "with tantalizing Play – As Boy – should deal with lesser Boy – to prove ability." But the final pronouncement is generalized: "Old Man on Nebo! Late as this – My justice bleeds – for Thee." Dickinson utters her condemnation with universal and moral authority. And yet, she may be speaking from the critical viewpoint of a woman, while the fact that she as a woman claims for herself this power of judgment in itself contests the given assumptions and hierarchical orders which so shaped religion within her experience.

Dickinson's Biblical poems, however challenging to genteel piety, remain dialogically engaged with the sacred texts. She does not abandon the Bible, but uses it against itself, or rather, against the uses characteristically made of it. As with other women writers, poetry becomes a form of exegesis in which protest also asserts attachment. Biblical citation provides occasions for defiance. She quotes, and then questions, New Testament assurances of loving care, as in the poem on "modest needs" where she dismisses Matthew 7: 7–8's promise "that 'Whatsoever Ye shall ask – Itself be given You.'" She defends Old Testament figures against divine power. But in this, she is not unlike the Old Testament figures themselves, who first established contention and rebuke as a mode of addressing God. And Dickinson continues to interpret Biblical figures in relation to her own most immediate needs: including her disappointed hope for full revelation of promised things.

Even more pervasive through Dickinson's work than specific Biblical encounters is her engagement with the hymnal, particularly with the popular and influential *Psalms, Hymns, and Spiritual Songs* of Isaac Watts. The Watts hymnal provided the basis for Dickinsonian poetic form. Her versification, with very few exceptions, is based on the hymnal common, short and long meters. But Dickinson adopts more than prosody from the hymnal. She persistently reworks hymnal language – imagery, rhetorical figures, and tropes familiar from Watts. Indeed, she rewrites specific hymns into her own work. Dickinson's engagement with the hymnal goes beyond parody or irony. As in other areas of her religious sensibility, parody and sincere performance presume and overlap one the other. Dickinson's subversions of the hymnal no less assert her tie to them, making them another arena of religious conflict, and ultimately raising general questions about the powers and claims of language and rhetoric.

Dickinson's rewritings of the hymnal include her poem "Go slow, my soul, to feed thyself / Upon his rare approach," which reworks Watts's: "Stand up my soul, shake off thy fears, / And gird thy gospel armour on." "Heaven is so far of the Mind" echoes Watts's "In secret silence of the mind, / My heaven – and there my God, I find." "The Road to Paradise is plain / And holds scarce one" takes for its text Watts's "Broad is the road that leads to death," which Austin Dickinson called "sufficiently depressing in plain print" and "appalling" when sung. Typically, Dickinson twists and complicates Watts's intentions, and yet at the same time continues to operate in their frame, often subverting her own subversions, and attesting to a continued claim on her. Watts's

> Faith is the brightest evidence
> Of things beyond our sight;
> Breaks through the clouds of flesh and sense,
> And dwells in heavenly light.

becomes in Dickinson the equivocal:

> Faith – is the Pierless Bridge
> Supporting what We see
> Unto the Scene that We do not –
> Too slender for the eye . . .

> It joins – behind the Veil
> To what, could We presume
> The Bridge would cease to be
> To Our far, vacillating Feet
> A first Necessity.

In Dickinson's text (based like Watts's on Hebrews 11), the "Pierless Bridge" that should conduct from the visible to the invisible may be pierless, but it may be without proper support. The other world which "Breaks through the clouds of flesh and sense" for Watts, becomes in Dickinson the "Scene that We do not" see, "Too slender for the eye." Nevertheless, this Dickinsonian counter-hymn at its end moves to retrace its own vacillating feet. If faith does not penetrate the "Veil" of flesh and sense, this is, after all, what distinguishes faith from knowledge. To believe is not to know; it is exactly because one does not know that one is called on to believe. And Dickinson does respond to this call. Faith's "Bridge," far from being simply dismantled here, is instead reclaimed as a "Necessity." But what is necessary? The image of the "Veil" is pivotal. Dickinson's deepest interpretive drives impel her towards figural readings, where the events of experience will yield further significance, standing as signs to some further meaning. As in the hymnal, things of this world are approached as bridges to what stands beyond flesh and sense. The "Veil" is, recurrently in Dickinson as elsewhere, an image for the flesh, the body, acting at once as barrier and as sign for a spiritual world standing beyond it. The "Veil," that is, is one Dickinsonian figure for figuration itself: for how signs in this world of earthly body point beyond themselves – or fail to do so.

Dickinson's treatment of the hymnal is one instance where she inhabits a moment of cultural transition, where assertions that were before accepted as conveying truths come to be seen as rhetorical figures only. Language points not to a spiritual realm beyond, but only to itself. In making use not only of Watts's metrical but also his figural schemes, Dickinson explores and exposes how hymnal tropes themselves structure the divine experiences they are meant merely to convey. Attention is thrown back onto the structures of language, as shaping experience and its interpretation, rather than as referring to religious truths. But for Dickinson, this recognition is frightening. She remains deeply ambivalent about the failure of figural transfer which makes reference recoil back onto linguistic structure. At stake is the very coherence of the world whose interpretation relied traditionally on the power of earthly and linguistic experience to signify beyond itself. And her poems remain painfully and precariously balanced between these two possibilities: working still within the structures of figural transfer while at the same time calling them into question:

> I think to Live — may be a Bliss —
> To those who dare to try —
> Beyond my limit to conceive
> My lip — to testify —
>
> I think the Heart I former wore
> Could widen — till to me
> The Other, like the little bank
> Appear — unto the Sea — . . .
>
> No numb alarm — lest Difference come —
> No Goblin — on the Bloom —
> No start in Apprehension's Ear,
> No Bankruptcy — no Doom —
>
> But Certainties of Sun —
> Midsummer — in the Mind —
> A steadfast South — upon the Soul —
> Her Polar time — behind —

Dickinson here echoes the Watts hymn "There is a land of pure delight" which she elsewhere cites ("Could we but climb where Moses stood" is taken from it). This hymn similarly speaks of a "land" where "Infinite day excludes the night" and where

> Everlasting spring abides,
> And never-withering flowers:
> Death, like a narrow sea, divides
> This heavenly land from ours.

In Dickinson's poem, not the sea to cross, but the "Other" shore is "little." And yet, it too represents her desire for infinite day ("Certainties of Sun"), everlasting spring with never-withering flowers ("No Goblin — on the Bloom"), and a unity without the "Difference" of "Polar time," change, and loss. The call of this "Vision" is in fact difficult to gainsay:

> The Vision — pondered long —
> So plausible becomes
> That I esteem the fiction — real —
> The Real — fictitious seems —
>
> How Bountiful the Dream —
> What Plenty — it would be —
> Had all my Life but been Mistake
> Just rectified — in Thee

Dickinson here crosses hymnal meter and imagery with her own counter-style of syntactic obfuscation. She makes it difficult to tell what is "fiction" and what "real." And even when, through slow wading across grammar and antecedent, it is the "Plenty" of the "Other" world that emerges as "Dream," this is conceded with great pain and continued longing. The poem is a near prayer for just this unmasking of the metaphysical to be "Mistake," while appealing to the faith that she has just denied. The issues are both formal and doctrinal. Dickinson's notion of "fiction" implicates her own writing, its own rhetorical power to construct, rather than to convey, what she both exposes and claims to be a true "Dream" of "Plenty." "Fiction" here is a painful concession, not an exuberant freedom, and is no substitute for actual worlds beyond this one of "Goblin," "Doom," and "Bankruptcy." Just how invested Dickinson remains within the figural schemes she is also doubting, she announces at the poem's start. To "Live" in "Bliss" would be to live "Beyond my limit to conceive" and "My lip – to testify," not within her poetic figures but through and past them, into that "Other" world for which this one is merely prefiguration.

The figural faiths Dickinson here evokes are cultural and communal, as are the Bible and the hymnal. Dickinson is speaking from within paradigms that, although undergoing challenge and transition, remain forcefully at work around her. This communal and historical frame is perhaps most penetrating where it appears least so: in Dickinson's poems of suffering. How to read the signs of events so as properly to construe them into figures of redemption is exactly the undertaking of Christian theodicy, whose central emblem is Christ on the cross. As Thomas à Kempis insisted in *On the Imitation of Christ* – a mystical work Dickinson owned and read carefully – only by suffering Christ's passion can we rise with him in glory.

For Dickinson, the most urgent, and yet most recalcitrant figural conversion is just that which links, and transfigures, suffering into redemption. Her poems obsessively measure gain against loss, but often – although often in obfuscated ways – the account fails to come out even. She attempts, again and again, to reenact an arduous way of the cross from suffering to significance, again and again to founder on it. Sometimes her conversions do succeed, revealing the paradigm she is working from. "Joy to have merited the Pain – / To merit the Release," for example, pretty much outlines and fulfills the basic theodicean pattern making pain the ground for deliverance. "The hallowing of Pain," she writes, "Like hallowing of Heaven / Obtains at a corporeal cost." As she sums up in one two-line poem: "Best Gains – must have the Losses' Test – / To constitute them Gains."

But in many instances, the scale fails to achieve its proper balance. The relations between terms of gain and loss grow increasingly complicated the closer they are scrutinized. Even if "Opposites – entice," this does not grant the "Deformed Men" the "Grace" they "ponder." The "Doomed" may "regard the Sunrise / With different Delight," but this does not reprieve them. The poet may "know" "The stature of the empty nest" better by the bird's disappearance, but this "Contrast Certifying" does not restore the bird. Sometimes, gain, rather than redeeming the loss, only intensifies it: as seeing the "Sun" makes only a "newer Wilderness," or being "denied to drink" makes "Water . . . acuter" but does nothing – or rather, worsens – the "condemned lip." Such texts deploy Dickinsonian twists on the sublime as a mode of denial or renunciation, exposing a continuity between Romantic awe and the tradition of sacrificial metaphysics. It may be that "We see – Comparatively," measuring what we do not have against what we do. But this does not guarantee that our vision is more true. It may instead be distorting. "Perhaps 'tis kindly – done us – / The Anguish – and the loss –," she goes on in the poem to ask. But in the end it remains unclear whether comparison works, either epistemologically or soteriologically: whether suffering and loss can be the basis for redemption – or, indeed, are redeemable at all.

These theodicean questions about suffering and its justification are not Dickinson's private ones alone. They belong to her wider community. It is, oddly, just where poems are most personal in terms of Dickinson's suffering that they are also most culturally engaged. For the problem of suffering is, in the Christian scheme, essentially the problem of history. Attempts to find redemptive responses to the most daunting, violent, historical events would have been, in Dickinson's context, completely current. It is more than a coincidental curiosity that Dickinson began writing intensively, and wrote over half of her poems, during the American Civil War. The Civil War reached levels of carnage before unknown, made possible both by new technology and new strategies of total warfare, in combination with a profound ideological threat to American national claims and self-identity. The Civil War focused Dickinson's own need for interpretive transfiguration, in order to put together a world that was breaking apart – quite literally, in American sectional strife and ideological warfare. The image of Dickinson as incarcerated in her room, cut off from the world raging around her, is highly distorted and may itself be gendered. Her father served as treasurer to Amherst College and Amherst civic leader. In 1838 he was elected as Representative to the General Court of Massachusetts (where he came to know Herman Melville's father-in-law, Judge Lemuel Shaw, whom Dickinson retains in her quarrel with God: "Jove! Choose your counsel – / I retain 'Shaw.'"). He was twice elected Massachusetts State Senator in 1842–3, was a Whig delegate, and was then elected to Congress in 1852. Many of Dickinson's friends were influential and politically active journalists and editors.

Within her work, there are numerous references to the war in her letters and numerous images of war in her poems. Not all of these directly refer to immediate historical events. There is a continuity between martial imagery in political and religious contexts that makes them impossible entirely to separate in her writing. But the same is true for her historical world. The war was widely seen in the North as enacting apocalyptic scenes of punishment and retribution, whereby the nation was judged and cleansed of the sin of slavery. The war witnessed incredible outbursts of organized missionary activity. It was the object of intense prayer in churches throughout the nation. As Dickinson wrote to Thomas Wentworth Higginson, then serving in the South as colonel to the first black regiment: "I trust you may pass the limit of War, and though not reared to prayer – when service is had in Church, for Our Arms, I include yourself." The rhetoric of contest itself resonated with the language of holy war and religious drama. As Dickinson's father put it in a published plea of 1855: "By the help of Almighty God, not another inch of our soil heretofore consecrated to freedom, shall hereafter be polluted by the advancing tread of slavery." Even Lincoln, with his exquisite restraint, could speak on one of the many days of fasting and thanksgiving which made up a public religious ritual throughout the war, of Union victories as "the gracious gifts of the most high God, who, while dealing with us in anger for our sins, hath nevertheless remembered mercy."

Dickinson in one letter devotes her own contribution to the war effort not in terms of the womanly provisioning of soldiers, but in terms of her art: "I shall have no winter this year – on account of the soldiers – Since I cannot weave Blankets, or Boots – I thought it best to omit the season – Shall present a 'Memorial' to God – when the Maples turn." But her "Memorial" is deeply equivocal. The war seemed to her an agony of suffering and love. "Let us love better, children, it's most that's left to do," she ends a letter to her Norcross cousins announcing the death of Amherst's Frazer Stearns. In her next letter to her Norcross cousins, she remarks: "I wish 'twas plainer, the anguish in this world. I wish one could be sure the suffering had a loving side." In 1864 she writes the cousins again: "Sorrow seems more general than it did, and not the estate of a few persons, since the war began; and if the anguish of others helped with one's own, now would be many medicines." These concerns come together in one of Dickinson's specific war elegies, for Frazer Stearns, "It feels a shame to be Alive – / When Men so brave – are dead –":

> The price is great – Sublimely paid –
> Do we deserve – a Thing –
> That lives – like Dollars – must be piled
> Before we may obtain?

> Are we that wait – sufficient worth –
> That such Enormous Pearl
> As life – dissolved be – for Us –
> In Battle's – horrid Bowl?
>
> It may be – a Renown to live –
> I think the Men who die –
> Those unsustained – Saviors –
> Present Divinity –

Public affairs intercross with Dickinson's most private concerns. Her position as a woman on the sidelines, whose participation in the war effort is removed from the front (although the two come oddly together in the image of "Battle's – horrid Bowl," imagining the trenches in near domestic terms), would not in itself result in ideological distance, as is shown by countless other women enthusiasts. To Dickinson, however, as presumed beneficiary to war-sacrifice, the whole enterprise suffers from her general doubts concerning such exchanges. "We that wait" can never, she implies, be "sufficient worth" for the destruction of life's "Enormous Pearl." As to the dead themselves, they are glorious, but in their own right, and almost in opposition against a history which demands their sacrifice.

Perhaps most striking, as well as unexpectedly characteristic, is Dickinson's use of economic imagery for gauging sacrifice and its rewards: "price," "paid," "Dollars . . . piled," "worth." This economic imagery testifies, first, to a surprising and steady awareness on Dickinson's part of the American commercial culture around her, and second, to her sense of its relation to other founding American values. Her general undertaking of weighing gain against loss implicitly and also explicitly assumes economic terms: "Riches" may teach "Poverty"; "Bounty" defines "stint"; and "Wealth" makes "Poverty" possible. This personal and aesthetic measure is also a historical and theological one. In another war elegy, Dickinson sees the "Victory" that "comes late" as losing its value, and she asks:

> Was God so economical? . . .
> God keep His Oath to Sparrows –
> Who of little Love – know how to starve –

Dickinson's rendering of redemptive history, construed through terms of sacrifice and mercy, gives the economy of God, a standard theological concept, a commercial and problematic twist as parsimony.

The use of economy as an imagery for metaphysical values is a rhetoric reaching back, in America, to the Puritan Fathers, as Dickinson clearly knows. In one group of poems, she pursues what she calls the "pretty ways of Covenant," acknowledging the foundational Puritan conception of divine/human relations in terms of legal transaction, and replete with commercial signs of reward. Dickinson thus duly represents God as a "Mighty Merchant" who denies the one thing she asks for; as the "Auctioneer of Parting," whose "'Going, going, gone' / Shouts even from the Crucifix." God is a "Burglar! Banker! Father!"; a swindler; an "Exchequer." "'Rich people' buy" into "Heaven." "Paradise" is an "option" one can "Own in Eden." His economic powers also implicate God as male figure, and such poems often include gender-exchanges in which women are reduced to no more than a commercial value. But this in no way excludes – on the contrary, it underscores – the religious history of this rhetoric. The question of authority, in Dickinson's context and rendering, is one mutually implicating metaphysical and social orders. It is impossible to tell whether her "Bargain," or her "'shares' in Primrose Banks" is to be paid to a divine or human "Sovereign." When she gave "myself to Him / And took Himself, for Pay," the exchange, whether social or religious, is both highly gendered and highly questionable.

But this is Dickinson's point. Theo-economic rhetoric was, perhaps, always unstable. Instead of subordinating material things to sacred ones, it risks doing the reverse. Terms of analogy may, after all, be converted in either direction. That is the risk Dickinson mercilessly exploits. Economic figures for spiritual treasure come to a kind of ultimate implosion in nineteenth-century sentimental religion, where the afterworld is presented almost as an epitome of bourgeois, Victorian, domestic luxury. But the danger of reification lurked within the long tradition of American religious rhetoric, itself closely tied to American material visions of promise and prosperity. Dickinson's peculiar poetic territory is the relationship between these different theological, historical, and economic spheres. Economy is one figure – "our Conceit," as she calls it, intending both aesthetic and delusive senses – for negotiating earthly and heavenly exchanges. Dickinson's difficulty is that she continues to work within these given cultural analogies, while feeling tormented by their inconsistencies, cracks, and failures. Hers is a constant effort to read her world according to the codes available to her, and the constant defeat of her attempt to do so.

Her poems thus become conflictual scenes of promise and revocation, across a whole complex of cultural investments: in redemptive history, material prosperity, personal fulfillment:

> Success is counted sweetest
> By those who ne'er succeed.
> To comprehend a nectar
> Requires sorest need.

Not one of all the purple Host
Who took the Flag today
Can tell the definition
So clear of Victory

As he defeated – dying –
On whose forbidden ear
The distant strains of triumph
Burst agonized and clear!

This text fails to convert negative into positive experience, although it invokes the structure for doing so. It may be that sorest need is required to comprehend a nectar, but this does not assert the need to have been addressed or assuaged. Reward remains detached from cost; fulfillment does not answer the lack that required it.

This failed balance is posed in the poem in general terms. But it is striking that Dickinson chooses military imagery to elaborate it. Although the poem has been dated to 1859, before the outbreak of the Civil War, aggressive and pugilist language was increasingly shrill throughout the final pre-war years. Still, the imagery of victory and defeat is by no means exclusive to military battles. On the contrary, the poem evokes personal and spiritual, no less than historical experience, and the struggle to construe suffering into some meaningful and valid configuration extends to each and all of these levels. A further American sense in the poem lurks in the opening word, "Success." This most supreme of American values, perhaps the master measure of all others, had been privileged alike in the rhetoric of the Puritan Fathers, with their notion of earthly calling as sign of spiritual election, and in an evolving nineteenth-century entrepreneurial rhetoric of promise. Dickinson may intend, using a martial setting and male gender ("he"), something specifically masculine in this measuring of self against success, which is here "counted." The poem that follows it begins with a reference to "Ambition." But in any case, here there is no triumph to offset defeat; but only a dying without immortality, a success "counted" by its utter failure to be achieved. This failure of redemption is, in Dickinson's work generally as in this poem, "agonized," a painful agonistic contention between opposing claims. The resistance of events – personal, historical, spiritual – to interpretation within a coherent design that would give them significance is a condition she cannot deny, but also cannot accept.

LANGUAGE AND THE BODY

Roughly a third of Dickinson's poetry concerns or addresses poetry itself. Hers is a highly self-conscious and reflective art, with theoretical implications for

Romanticism and the sublime, the status of poetry and of language, and sign-systems as structures of meaning. Yet her work challenges the assumption of much twentieth-century literary theory, that poetic language is essentially self-referring and self-enclosed, making the work of art its own primary subject. What her writing instead shows is an essential link between poetic reflections on language, broader metaphysical structures, and historical understanding. In Dickinson's work, aesthetic self-reflection penetrates into both theological and historical domains. Intersections between language, metaphysics, and history mark out Dickinson's poetic territory. Her work makes visible and self-reflexively examines what can be called a metaphysics of language, that is, the metaphysical implications of linguistic structure, as these are embedded in the history of Western cultural norms and conditions. At stake not least is her identity as a poet, which is as conflictual and ambivalent, with terms as unstable, as her other senses of self-definition. These ambivalences and conflicts, with their specific implications for language, come into powerful conjunction in her work through the figure of embodiment.

The body, or rather the problem of embodiment, is a central site, or place of intersection, in Dickinson's poetry. In embodiment, the questions of identity which continue to structure her writing on many levels become focused in all their multiple ambivalence. First, her identity as a woman is profoundly ambivalent, both in the sense of inhabiting a woman's body, and of womanhood as a figure for the body. The broad metaphysical context of her religious identity further situates her within that tradition's long history of ambivalence towards material and temporal embodiment. Her embodiment within the terms of American identity connects her selfhood to notions of possession, property, and ownership – with their own complex relations to her gendered status. Finally, her identity as a poet is highly ambivalent, in terms of the very possibility, or desire for, embodiment in a text and in language.

These different and intersecting identities, in their contesting and colliding interrelationships, telescope into the intense nexus of the body:

> I am afraid to own a Body –
> I am afraid to own a Soul –
> Profound – precarious Property –
> Possession, not optional –
>
> Double Estate – entailed at pleasure
> Upon an unsuspecting Heir –
> Duke in a moment of Deathlessness
> And God, for a Frontier.

Emily Dickinson hardly admitted to reading Walt Whitman, conceding only that she had been "told that he was disgraceful." But this poem seems addressed to Whitman's "I am the poet of the Body and I am the poet of the Soul . . . The first I graft and increase upon myself, the latter I translate into a new tongue" (Song 21). Whitman declares here, with perhaps especially aggressive exuberance, his intention to embrace in a continuous poetic translation every aspect of experience – body and soul, the material and the cultural, self and world. Dickinson, in contrast, works through conflict and division. She invokes the variety of experience in painful awareness of the discrepancies and often violent collisions between them.

In this poem, as so often in Dickinson's work, figural relationships are multiplied, but also progressively misaligned as they prove to be unstable in their correlations. What at first seem architechtonic correspondences come to emerge as mismatched, in the process of figural slippage characteristic of Dickinsonian structure. The (fear of) owning a body and/or soul – and it is important that the soul is not privileged here, that Dickinson does not prefer to own a soul without a body – is first a metaphysical or religious topic. But it is developed in a language that is also economic: property, possession, estate. At the same time, the structure of economy becomes increasingly gendered. Entailment is a specifically male form of inheritance; and "Heir" and "Duke" are both specifically male forms of inheritor. But of course "entailed" is at the same time a philosophical term, continuous with the poem's metaphysical opening, and resumed explicitly in the concluding reference to God.

The poem thus introduces three levels: a metaphysical one, an economic one, and a gendered one. And, in the familiar structure of metaphorical transfer or analogy, we expect that these three will be brought into a relationship of mutual representation. But such correlation or transference does not then occur. The poem's conclusion, for example, is peculiar. It oddly obtrudes spatial imagery for a God that by definition is spaceless, indeed, is utterly without and beyond body. The spatial definition, while seemingly an attempt at locating God or locating the speaker in relation to God, at least in metaphor, in effect is no less dislocating, or dissolving into illocality. The conclusion thus points, as Dickinson so often does, in at least two incompatible directions. God as a frontier in one sense promises consolation, as the boundary or bounding principle giving shape or reference to life. In another sense, this frontier-God or God as frontier may be bounding as a menace – inescapable, limiting, imprisoning. An American usage enters here. The frontier only acquired its meaning of unlimited and expansive possibility in the American context; in Europe it had meant a fixed and inexorable boundary. The poem plays on both senses. The second, limiting possibility recalls that the poem opens in fear as to owning a body and/or a soul, a fear tied to just these questions of imprisonment or definition.

Hesitation between terms then continues through the text, with its sense of "precarious" property, imposed ("not optional"), on one unprepared for it ("unsuspecting"). And yet, this language of hesitation appears alongside, or may itself comprise, expressions of exuberance. The property is also "Profound." In this sense its fragility (as "precarious") may be precious. "Unsuspecting" may suggest something unearned, but therefore all the more gracious, or unhoped for, in humility. These double possibilities come to special focus in the line: "Duke in a moment of Deathlessness." The title "Duke" may be a kind of play on Dickinson's own name, a sign of her nobility. And "Deathlessness" suggests just that immortality or transcendence or sublimity which the property, as precious inheritance, could bestow. And yet: this "Deathlessness" lasts but a moment, and "Duke" is a title beyond Dickinson's gender, and is also alien to American social structures and laws of inheritance. Indeed, the whole structure of property she evokes is one which doubly does not apply to herself: as a woman and as an American.

The poem is in fact rich in economic terms, which play a pivotal role. "Estate" is a metaphysical/material pun; while the property structure implicit in the poem reaches beyond selfhood to ownership, another pun that underscores their intimate relationship, especially in America. It is worth noting that several of the poems immediately surrounding this one in its fascicle-set explicitly center on economic imagery. In one, Dickinson's "letter" from the world reports the stock market's "advance and Retrograde." In another, she again equates her self-"Possession" as "Me" with the "Riches I could own" in "Dollars," an "Earldom," and "Income." The poetic prospect opens towards questions of how far a self owns itself under God, how far a woman owns herself in relation to man, and also, how far identity in America is established through ownership, possession, and inheritance.

Dickinson, here as elsewhere, presents her images in ways that keep them at odds with each other. Economic, religious, and gendered terms all work at cross-purposes. The poem almost encapsulates Dickinson's stance towards her religious inheritance in general, including its hierarchy of body and soul, or soul against body. That is, she is profoundly torn regarding her own inheriting of this tradition. Gender certainly plays its part here. The body and soul she fears and desires to inherit is that of a woman, who cannot be entailed heir to a ducal title. To be born into a woman's body is to be barred from such social resources of power. It is also to be precariously placed in metaphysical tradition; to be, if not barred, then subordinated within hierarchies of spiritual power, within the long association of the female with body and emotion, as against a spirituality and reason represented as male.

But to enter into her embodied estate is generally to come under the liability of death, that frontier Dickinson so perpetually met with face to face, whether defined by God or by nothingness. Against more ordinary usage, "Estate" here is not immortality but mortality. Yet to enter the mortal estate is also a kind of birth. The "Double Estate" is, in effect, nothing other than selfhood, which the terms "Property" and "Possession" also evoke. The self is oneself proper, one's self-possession, one's self as one's own. But this double estate as body and soul situates Dickinson's self precariously indeed. Fear, or ambivalence, at owning a body with a soul resonates with centuries of metaphysical hierarchy, or suspicion, according to which embodiment in the material and temporal world somehow threatens, if it does not betray, essential nature defined as intelligible, or spiritual, or eternal.

Adopting the trope of this poem, Dickinson's position may generally be called a "Double Estate," double and indeed contradictory. It at once asserts both her possession and dispossession within the tradition of her inheritances. The poem expresses Dickinson's agonistic voice, caught between incompatible visions, assertively critical of each of them, unable to resolve their contradictions nor yet to reside comfortably in any of their competing claims. And, as characteristically in Dickinson's work, the levels misalign, working at cross-purposes. To inherit as duke is not to inherit as woman. God is welcomed, but also shunned, as frontier. Sublime or religious immortality is announced, but not necessarily as coherent figures for each other, and elusively, for only a moment; seeming to be produced by language construction, as if "Deathlessness" comes into being through the abstract compounding of its word.

Dickinson in this poem brings together, but also breaks apart, the multiple levels of her identity, in terms of gender, religion, history, and also art. For "I am afraid to own a Body" proposes a further, aesthetic level of figuration as well. The body and soul which Dickinson here on the one hand shies from, but on the other hand longs for, can also suggest her literary inheritance, as it becomes embodied in her language. She hopes to inherit a precious (male) legacy; she fears to inherit a precarious estate. God is a sublime frontier of ever opening possibility or desire; God is a repressive boundary. Just so, language is positive embodiment; and language is betrayal, liability, confinement.

Such imagery of embodiment for her own writing is proposed, obliquely or directly, in many poems. It has a special relationship to gender no less than to Christian metaphysical dualism, interweaving these in turn with her conception of poetry, her poetic, and her implicit language theory. Figures of embodiment, that is, mark her language theory as deeply rooted in her other central engagements: gender, metaphysics, history. The specifically linguistic aspect illuminates and clarifies each of these in their mutual involvement and also betrayal. And it clarifies Dickinson's specific cultural position, as a moment of historical transition which she can neither endorse nor resist.

In one arena, linguistic embodiment bears strong connections with Dickinson's Romantic poetics and especially with the sublime. One strong current running through Dickinson's art is a privileging of the unattained and unattainable. What-is-not has precedence over what is, the unseen over the seen, the illimitable over the limited. This hierarchical structure, which remains in many ways traditional, has specific corollaries in terms of language and the body. It privileges and prefers silence, while it suspects linguistic embodiment – where language is itself a central and traditional figure for the body as such. Silence, in contrast, is a mode of disembodiment: in traditional terms, the life of the spirit, in Romantic terms, of the sublime imagination.

This privileging of silence is concordant with a Romantic sublime. Dickinson's resistance to full realizations in both expression and experience may suggest what she calls a "banquet of abstemiousness," a "Sumptuous destitution." Within the tenets of a Romantic imagination, the sublime infinite exceeds and defies any finite embodiment. Poetry is an endless and constantly deferred dwelling in further "possibility." This structure of Romantic imagination pays homage to an infinite ever unreachable beyond it, making the negation of nature or experience into the ground for poetic creativity. It is a vital force in Dickinson's work. In her work, as essentially in Romanticism, attainment of the object is the end of romance. But Dickinson's poetry further brings out the complicated relation between a Romantic imagination and more traditional metaphysical structures. Romantic imagination continues to privilege an unrealized sublimity over concrete realization or embodiment, including embodiment in language, in ways consistent with Western metaphysical hierarchies and dualism of soul over body, whose ultimate reference is a transcendent, other-worldly, and eternal realm. The Romantic privilege, however, refers not to a divine or dogmatic eternity, but to the further power and potential of the human imagination. The art work stands then as a positive sign to its own further productions, a promise which will never be completely fulfilled but which will ever open into still greater creative possibilities.

Dickinson's verse also invokes and asserts such a Romantic sublimity, in ways that recall, for example, Whitman's. But in her case the possibilities of artistic imagination are chastened, as are its resources in the self, by gender and by metaphysical scruple. This peculiarity of her position within the economy of Romanticism helps to expose assumptions that continue to underwrite Romantic norms, as well as contradictions implicit within them. Her work shows complications between the varying commitments of the sublime.

Dickinson is extremely conscious of the religious residue in Romantic language claims, and of its complicating effects. And she is aware of the uneasy place of women in making certain claims, of tensions in definitions of selfhood in artistic, gendered, and economic senses. Her specific structuring of these issues in her work pushes their contradictions towards exposure. Conversely, her cultural situation and its contradictions penetrate her conception of language:

> To own the Art within the Soul
> The Soul to entertain
> With Silence as a Company
> And Festival maintain
>
> Is an unfurnished Circumstance
> Possession is to One
> As an Estate Perpetual
> Or a reduceless Mine.

This poem shares much textual ground with "I am afraid to own a Body," similarly employing an economic language which connects questions of selfhood with ownership, and making explicit their further connection with art. The "Estate" which the speaker is to "own" in "Possession" is clearly demarcated as an internal one, indeed as allied to a "One" which defines the self to be both unitary and interior – further terms traditionally aligned within metaphysical hierarchy. This dualistic and hierarchical structure then aligns true art, and indeed truth itself, with silence as the sign of spirit as against the body of language. The truly owned art is a "Silence," within the "Soul" and without a body. Its "unfurnished Circumstance" is a mode of nakedness or disembodiment. The poem thus associates selfhood with ownership in a valuable estate, and true art with the unspoken word, as opposed to a language that is told aloud, as body.

Disembodiment is thus a multiple figure: of artistic ultimacy, of spiritual selfhood, of perpetual property, of silence. All come together in the concluding image of "reduceless Mine," a multifaceted pun which tallies what is precious with what is possessed; with the self itself, but as interior; as withdrawn into itself, unexpressed outwardly in either body or language. This pun on "Mine" places this poem within a group of interconnecting texts, each of which plays on the figural relationships intersecting through this image of "Mine." " 'Tis little I" dispenses with mere "Pearls" and "Brooches," for which she (he?) has no need as the "Prince of Mines." In "Some – work for Immortality – / The Chiefer part, for Time –," immortality is figured as the "Everlasting . . . Currency" of "Fame." The poem concludes:

"One's – Money, One's – the Mine." In these poems, material possession and religious calling seem figures for poetic election. Yet each also equivocates: in gender (if the "Mines" of " 'Tis little I" are those of a male "Prince," how do they apply to Dickinson?) or in syntactic alignment (which "One" is which "One" in "Some work"?).

These equivocations are deeply rooted in the image systems themselves. Dickinson characteristically exploits the implicit instability in adopting material imagery for immaterial wealth, which, although traditional, always entailed the danger that the material splendor will eclipse its immaterial promise. The precedence of eternity over time is throughout Dickinson a deeply insecure metaphysical structure; she is skeptical of its truth and uncertain of its value. And for the poet, a hierarchy which places silence above language is severely compromising:

> To tell the Beauty would decrease
> To state the Spell demean –
> There is a syllable-less Sea
> Of which it is the sign –
> My will endeavors for its word
> And fails, but entertains
> A Rapture as of Legacies
> Of introspective Mines –

This poem neatly formulates a romance of the sublime: the desired object is failed – or is failure the object? To attain would be to betray. But here the poem specifically formulates this romance structure in linguistic terms. To be beyond attainment is to be beyond language, inexpressible, where expression, telling, stating, would only "decrease" and "demean." This inexpressibility, true to its metaphysical alignments, is then figured as interior, unbodied selfhood: "introspective Mines"; expressed, as in other poems, in terms of possession and inheritance, as "Legacies." Interior terms of value here become explicitly linguistic, as figures for language and for poetry which is the poem's overt subject. And the failure, which is paradoxically success, is a failure of the word, poetry as silence. Ultimacy can only be paradoxically (un)named by a retraction of language, as a "syllable-less Sea" which relies on the linguistic image it also negates. All that language can hope for is to act as "sign" linking its utterance to the "Rapture" inevitably and necessarily beyond it.

The hierarchies Dickinson observes here have a long history, one which continues to frame Dickinson's language-theory. They would have been available to Dickinson through widespread discussions on language surrounding her in New England, such as Horace Bushnell's *Dissertation on The Nature of Language as Related to Thought and Spirit,* which itself reflects theological treatments of

language going back to Jonathan Edwards and beyond. In terms of modern –
and also ancient – sign-theory, articulated words are signifiers for a signified
meaning that stands before and above them. This distinction between signifier
and signified reiterates a fully constituted metaphysical order, which in turn
implies a specific metaphysic of language:

> The Outer – from the Inner
> Derives its Magnitude –
> 'Tis Duke, or Dwarf, according
> As is the Central Mood –
>
> The fine – unvarying Axis
> That regulates the Wheel –
> Though Spokes – spin – more conspicuous
> And fling a Dust – the while . . .
>
> The Inner – paints the Outer –
> The Brush without the Hand –
> Its Picture publishes – precise –
> As is the inner Brand –
>
> On fine – Arterial Canvas –
> A Cheek – perchance a Brow –
> The Star's whole Secret – in the Lake –
> Eyes were not meant to know.

In this poem, as in the norms of Western metaphysical tradition, inner
determines outer, while the outer serves and points back to the inner. In terms
of sign-theory, the outer as signifier subserves the inner as signified, while
the signified determines the signifier's "Magnitude" and meaning, Duke or
Dwarf. Dickinson in this poem follows a whole series of traditional allocations.
The signified meaning is "Inner," "Central," and "unvarying Axis" – interior,
unchanging, singular, while the signifier is "Outer," a "Wheel" spinning in
the "Dust." The association of dust with body, recurrent through Dickinson's
work, is picked up in the final stanza's imagery of the "Cheek" as a "Canvas" on
which is painted the "inner Brand." Throughout this figural series, the ideal
role of the signifier is not only to be secondary, but ultimately to disappear.
The ideal signifier should become transparent as it refers to the signified, the
meaning which it is the true function of the signifier, through self-erasure,
to convey. But these terms were already fully developed by St. Augustine,
who identifies the signified with God the Father in His pure, eternal, unitary
spirituality. The signifier in turn is incarnate language, temporal, multiple,
and material. The imagery of body implicit in language as incarnation and
materialization becomes overt and central in the doctrine of Incarnation, when

divine Word becomes Flesh, and thus links worldly life to transcendent truth through its condescension into linguistic body.

And yet, in Dickinson's poem, the priorities between Outer and Inner are not quite absolutely established. The only way for seeing the "inner Brand" is, after all, through the published "Picture," which achieves in the poem something like parity with its interior, bodiless ("without the Hand") origin: "precise – / As is the inner Brand." The poem's ending is equivocal as well. What is reflected in the "Lake" – an image of this world as a copy of the supernal one as old as Plato – is the "Star's whole Secret." This conclusion verges into a mystical language of occult revelation and penetration, even transgression. Eyes achieve a knowledge beyond knowledge they "were not meant to know." Within the image structures of the poem, the reflection of the "Inner" and the "Star" in language and world seems almost a betrayal of transcendent secrets into material body, language, and time. Yet it is also there that knowledge, realization, and the poem are achieved.

Dickinson's command of this imagery of language and body in its theological implication is attested in many poems, as are also her equivocations concerning it. Persistently she aligns interiority against exteriority, as spirit against flesh, and silence against language. "Speech is one symptom of Affection / and Silence one–," the poem endorses the one "within": "The perfectest communication / Is heard of none." Here Dickinson helpfully cites 1 Peter 1:8 as her authority: "Behold, said the Apostle, / Yet had not seen." In Poem 976, "The Spirit and the Dust" have a "Dialogue" in death, in which the dust dissolves but the spirit merely lays off its "Overcoat of Clay." Poem 664 reiterates, tracing the dissolution of "Sense from Spirit," when "this brief Drama in the flesh – is shifted" and the "Atom" is released from "lists of Clay." This is also a linguistic movement: "Figures" dissolve as well. Most famously, Dickinson directly invokes linguistic Incarnation when "The Word" is made "Flesh" in poetry.

But if Dickinson in her poetry reproduces the structure of a metaphysics of language, she also complicates it. For she is unsure of her allegiances. Her poems also characteristically equivocate as to just which functions of language she is committed; in terms of sign-theory, whether it is the signified meaning, or the signifier that embodies it, and in just what relationship, that she holds dear. "The Word made Flesh is seldom" may evoke the transcendent Word as the signified that was "Made Flesh and dwelt among us," but it concludes with a moving tribute to her own "loved philology." When Dickinson bids the poet to "Tell all the Truth but tell it slant," her allegiance is given not only to the truth in its abstract light but also to its figural representations: "Success in Circuit lies."

Emily Dickinson's is, in its fundamental construction, a traditional sign-theory. But it is a tradition in crisis. Dickinson is not free from her metaphysical tradition, with its linguistic structure and implication. And yet it no longer works for her. In certain poems, she longs to assert a transcendent meaning, which language would successfully convey as its sign. Death would then not be the terrifying rupture it so often appears, "No Territory new," and "Eternity" would be discernible through "Fundamental Signals." More often, however, her desire that language signal something beyond itself becomes enmeshed in qualms and contradictions. If language is the "sign" for a "syllable-less Sea," it is still remote from this transcendent silence, and compromises it: "To tell the Beauty would decrease." Similarly, she writes: "If I could tell how glad I was / I should not be so glad." And yet, to be unable to "make the Force, / Nor mould it into Word" is also "a sign" of "new Dilemma."

In Dickinson's work, the traditional structure which makes linguistic expression an exterior and secondary conduct to an internal and prior signified meaning encounters a number of difficulties. It becomes caught in doubts about transcendent realities; in conflicting allegiances to her immediate worlds of time and language; and in suspicion that traditional claims about language are self-contradictory and problematic. One response to this dilemma is to attempt to redefine a sign-system so as to establish a different relationship between meaning and expression, signified and signifier. This in turn would register a restructuring of relationship between heaven and earth, metaphysical transcendence and temporal experience, soul and body. In some poems, she accordingly attempts to assert embodiment as positive and necessary, the "Body" as a "Temple" standing always

> Ajar – secure – inviting –
> It never did betray
> The Soul that asked its shelter
> In solemn honesty.

She may attempt to reverse the terms of embodiment, to cross positions and interconnect values:

> I heard, as if I had no Ear
> Until a Vital word
> Came all the way from Life to me
> And then I knew I heard . . .
>
> I dwelt, as if Myself were out,
> My Body but within
> Until a Might detected me
> And set my kernel in.

> And Spirit turned unto the Dust
> "Old Friend, thou knowest me,"
> And Time went out to tell the News
> And met Eternity.

Inner becomes outer, self becomes kernel, spirit and dust are made mutual images of each other, and time and eternity seem in continuous communication. Here, the signifier seems completely fulfilled in its signified, without being sacrificed to it.

And yet, even in this text, where Dickinson is as ecstatic, reconciled, and integrated as she ever becomes, continuities verge dangerously into displacements. The "Body" is "within" only in an unconverted condition, as a perverse recursion from its proper position outside. In the restored, redeemed state, body is again "out," exterior, excluded. In contrast, some true, unbodied "Myself" regains its place as "kernel." Spirit does not embrace dust, but rather, abandons it.

As to language, this poem plainly represents the metaphysics of its structure, with "Vital word" the corollary for "Myself," "kernel," "Spirit," and "Eternity." "Body" remains "out," with "Dust," and "Time," correlating to an unawakened, mundane hearing represented as "no Ear." This is the case whether "Vital word" is a religious figure for poetry or a poetic figure for religion (and the poem in either case adapts the Johannine Logos: "And the Word was God . . . In him was life; and the life was the light of men," John 1: 1–4). That is, even to the extent that this is a poem about poetry, its conception of language and aesthetic commitments – not least regarding the sublime – are still modeled on the older norms, inheriting the older hierarchies. But the tradition works against relocating transcendent value into linguistic orders. The Romantic sublime may displace, but it also appropriates metaphysical structures. Its construction of meaning, and its goals, on the one hand point beyond any signifier; on the other, they destabilize the signified as well. But this is to retain the privilege and priority of signified over signifier, spirit over body, and eternity over time, while at the same time attempting to establish material, temporal, and linguistic experience as the realm of meaning.

Dickinson thus in some way resists a full Romanticist aesthetic, and in some ways exposes it. Romantic imagination as sublime elevates the endless productivity of its own inventions as ultimate, even at the cost of displacement, as figures generate each other. But Dickinson is never able fully to embrace temporalized, displacing process, and the price it exacts of loss and death. She is never able to say, as Whitman does, "O sane and sacred death." And this applies as well to the productions of the imagination, in their displacing sequences.

As in the image of "no Ear," she recognizes the processes of imagination to be based in negation. The "Vital word" may transform the mundane "Ear," but only by reducing it to nothingness.

In terms of her poetics, Dickinson lives on an unstable frontier. She resists granting to poetry the status of an independent aesthetic realm where she can comfortably reside, substituting linguistic orders for ultimate ones. Yet she also resists the privilege of eternal, transcendental realms as the site of meaning. Dickinson is caught between signified and signifier, in the inconsistencies of their metaphysical history and metaphysical claims:

> The Spirit lasts – but in what mode –
> Below, the Body speaks,
> But as the Spirit furnishes –
> Apart, it never talks –
> The Music in the Violin
> Does not emerge alone
> But Arm in Arm with Touch, yet Touch
> Alone – is not a Tune –
> The Spirit lurks within the Flesh
> Like Tides within the Sea
> That make the Water live, estranged
> What would the either be?
> Does that know – now – or does it cease
> That which to this is done,
> Resuming at a mutual date
> With every future one?
> Instinct pursues the Adamant,
> Exacting this Reply –
> Adversity if it may be,
> Or Wild Prosperity,
> The Rumor's Gate was shut so tight
> Before my Mind was sown,
> Not even a Prognostic's Push
> Could make a Dent thereon –

This poem cautiously attempts to rethink the relationship between spirit and body, in terms and by way of language. On one level, it accepts the priority of spirit over flesh, as signified over signifier. On the other, it finds this division and determination inconceivable. The body speaks as the spirit "furnishes," dependent upon and secondary to it. But the converse is also true. "The Spirit lasts – but in what mode?" Without some mode, some embodiment, the spirit itself cannot be conceived.

The poem then proceeds through a series of figures, each of which attempts to retain the priority of spirit-signified over body-signifier, but each finally complicating such a sequence. The spirit is to body as meaning is to speech; as music is to violin, the musical instrument; as the tides are to the sea. But the priority and independence of the first terms fail to hold. What would a tide be, apart from water? What would music be, without being realized somehow, without some instrument of its expression? Our very experience of these as signified depends upon the signifiers which they are supposed to determine. The signifiers are, in experience, prior to the meanings they are supposed merely to convey. This uncertainty of relationship is intensified in the poem by pronouns: "that," "this," "which," "it" become hard to sort out, making the supposedly hierarchical terms just about syntactically impossible to distinguish. When is the "now" in which "that" does "know" – or ceases? The knowledge Dickinson seeks remains, for all her efforts, "Adamant," as does Dickinson's always ultimate question: whether the release from the body in death is "Adversity" or "Wild Prosperity." After her father's death, Dickinson asked in a letter: "Without any body, I keep thinking. What kind can that be?" The poem's phrase "Mind was sown" refers to the Pauline promise: "It is sown a natural body; it is raised a spiritual body" (1 Corinthians 15: 42–4; cf. "Sown in corruption"). But, as so often, this Biblical reference settles nothing. Dickinson suspends her text between unknowable alternatives, whose very terms remain problematic and uncertain.

This state of irresolution has its romance. "Sweet Skepticism of the Heart – / That knows – and does not know" has its "delicious throe – Of transport thrilled with Fear." But skepticism for Dickinson is a contentious and not a detached state. Its complications for language theory and poetic expression erupt in poem after poem. "Ended, ere it begun" presents a life and death struggle between language and its interruption. Earthly existence is represented as a text with "Title," "Preface," and "Story." But it can neither be printed nor read, because of a divine counter-word, "the interdict of God." Another poem begins:

> A single Screw of Flesh
> Is all that pins the Soul
> That stands for Deity, to Mine,
> Upon my side the Veil –

"A single Screw of Flesh" is "all that pins the Soul," where the soul "stands for," signifies, "Deity" as signified. But the self – "my side" – is aligned with body as "Veil," and then, as the poem continues, also with letters: "tender – solemn Alphabet." The passion, here, is enacted through the poet's attempt to hold this "Clay" against all efforts of the gods to tear it from her.

In such poems, flesh ranges itself against soul, time against eternity, earth against heaven, signifying words against signifieds supposed to transcend them. There is no continuity or even coherence between body and spirit, the instruments of expression and their supposed meanings. Instead, there is warfare between them. And the poems offer no reconciliation; the very conflict is tortuous, a passion of pinned flesh. For a poet, this combat is particularly painful. It makes poetic language itself a contradictory "Choosing – Against itself," a martyrdom, at once necessary and betraying. For a woman poet, the predicament is still more intensified. The "Veil" which Dickinson in "A Single Screw" associates with body is elsewhere associated specifically with female body. "A limit like the Veil / Unto the Lady's face" conceals not only her body, but the whole incomprehensible puzzle which the world is to Dickinson. In another poem, the mystery of romance is both established and endangered by its inaccessibility: "The Lady dare not lift her Veil." Language in Dickinson's work is a figure not only of body but of gendered body. Her conflicting commitments to expression and silence, assertion and suppression, find their place not only in age-old metaphysical hierarchies, but in the gendering that raises spirit over flesh as male over female, making flesh and female corollaries. If Dickinson would not "be a Poet –" her hesitation runs across the full range of her involvements, in all their strained asymmetries:

> Nor would I be a Poet –
> It's finer – own the Ear –
> Enamored – impotent – content
> The License to revere,
> A privilege so awful
> What would the Dower be
> Had I the Art to stun myself
> With Bolts of Melody!

In this multiply ambiguous poem, the reasons for not being a poet point in a number of directions. The speaker may first seem to renounce her claim to be a poet in lieu of her role as spectator or reader of another's work. But the text then suggests her refusal to be a poet as a refusal to produce embodiment in language altogether. To realize the object would, as in romance structure, betray it. To truly "own the Ear" is then paradoxically to dispossess it, in an image not of having a body but (as in "I Heard"'s "no Ear") of bodily negation. To be "Enamored" is to be "impotent," to desire without bodily incarnation. The final, rhetorical question or declaration then enacts these contradictory alignments of fulfillment with failure, poetry with its suspension, in imagery at once gendered and not gendered. Is the poet in the position of Zeus or Semele? Are hers "Bolts" of lightning or of cloth, is her "Dower" to be paid or retained?

Dickinson's simultaneous assertion and denial of poetic language registers the many conflicts within and between her identities. As we have seen, the ideologies of selfhood which Whitman or Emerson might pursue are a priori different for Dickinson simply because of her gender. For a woman within nineteenth-century culture, to achieve one's selfhood is also to subordinate it, as daughter and wife (although motherhood seems to me to have its own distinctive structure). This would frame a general ambivalence to achievement, poetic as otherwise, which can be located in restrictive gender roles for nineteenth-century women. This equivocally gendered position also reaches beyond the social into the religious realm. The kinds of identification with the divine possible for Whitman or Emerson are from the outset impossible for Dickinson. Her self cannot be a figure for God in the same way as theirs can, if only by virtue of a differently sexualized relationship, with all that this implies regarding authority and subordination, self-fulfillment and self-denial.

That the body should be a peculiar crossing point for these correlations and collisions accords with its equivocal status within the traditions of Dickinson's culture. This deeply marks not only Dickinson's art, but her biography. Her acts of reclusion – of herself in her house and her white dress, and of her poems, in her refusal to publish them, while nevertheless writing and collecting them in her fascicles – can be seen as acts of profound ambivalence towards owning a body and a soul, a (female) way of both being in the worlds of time and text and yet also of withholding herself from them. These issues and images are reassembled, and also disassembled, in the poem "Publication," which centers on the body, but which makes questions of writing and publication its primary topic:

> Publication – is the Auction
> Of the Mind of Man –
> Poverty – be justifying
> For so foul a thing
>
> Possibly – but We – would rather
> From our Garret go
> White – Unto the White Creator –
> Than invest – Our Snow –
>
> Thought belong to Him who gave it –
> Then – to Him Who bear
> Its Corporeal illustration – Sell
> The Royal Air –
>
> In the Parcel – Be the Merchant
> Of the Heavenly Grace –
> But reduce no Human Spirit
> To Disgrace of Price –

In this poem there is a peculiar gendering. Dickinson on the one hand generalizes her statement in terms of "the Mind of Man," but also includes specifically feminine, biographical markers in her imagery of reclusion in "our Garret" and of being "White," recalling her own habit of white dress. There is also a suggestion of gendering in the poem's imagery of prostitution, which, however, is not restricted to sexual sale. Rather, it becomes part of a second figural level involving economic language, in which selling is a betrayal of purity or fidelity or commitment. This is offered as an imagery of metaphysical alignments, where grace is opposed to the dis-grace of "Price." Dickinson again recalls the American rhetoric of representing divine things in economic terms, which, as persistently in her work, threatens reversal: instead of subordinating material things to sacred ones, it risks doing the obverse. Here, instead of making this world a sign for the next one and material success a sign for spiritual grace, economic gain becomes spiritual betrayal. To sell the "Royal Air" is to debase it.

Economic, gendered, and metaphysical imagery are brought into intense relation through the poem's imagery of the body, developed through the poem's central topic, publication. The poem's major site of ambivalence concerns its own production, or at least its status in a public, as against some private realm. To put her work before the public corresponds in the text's economic imagery to a foul auction; in its gendered imagery, to a kind of prostitution, a (sexual) betrayal of white purity. As Dickinson remarked, "I would as soon undress in public, as to give my poems to the world." This corresponds in turn to a religious imagery aligning publication with a betrayal of the next world (the "White Creator") for this one. And all of these come together in a bodily imagery which is itself highly charged and highly conflicted. Publication is made a figure of embodiment: it is the "Corporeal illustration" of a "Thought" aligned with the spiritual and the divine. Such incorporation hence takes on all the valence of foul betrayal associated with auction, sexuality, and worldliness. But it corresponds also with the poem's own existence, at least as it becomes embodied in the text we are reading.

In this poem, Dickinson mediates these tensions to some extent by leaving open the possibility of some intermediate state between published embodiment and a textuality that is written, but not made public. Her fascicle mode of not-publishing might represent just such a compromise, or mediating effort. Despite this compromise, or rather, in response to its riveting peculiarity, the poem remains precariously balanced between its callings. Dickinson remains torn, and dissatisfied with each of her options. As in the famous poem "I'm Nobody! Who are you?", she must negotiate her way between denial and claim of body, as trope for public emergence and publication. It is as if Dickinson wants both to find linguistic body for her poetry and yet not so to limit it; just as, in her white dress, she wants both to be in the body and to be bodiless; to be gendered and yet to be genderless; to be in the world and yet to be in the spirit, where these two remain in some sense antithetical.

In *Twilight of the Idols*, Friedrich Nietzsche writes: "Concerning life, the wisest men of all ages have judged alike: it is no good." Emily Dickinson's is an imagination in conflict with her world. Her work traces, across a broad range of topics, a profound dissatisfaction with the world as it stands, and with the accounts available to her for interpreting it into meaningful and positive order. But her misgivings are not peculiar to herself. Her analogical slips and figural mismatches are not signs of a loss of linguistic control nor mere contingent play. They, rather, textually enact a kind of cultural slippage in which a female gender complicates or contradicts assertions of an American or Romantic selfhood; material progress in the world subverts or opposes rather than realizing spiritual longings; self-fulfillment contests with self-denial; and body remains in tension against soul, including poetic embodiment as against some pure artistic essence.

These conflicts have a specific historical site in nineteenth-century America, where the various strands of American cultural claims were coming under increasing stress and into increasing conflict with each other. The American Civil War itself represents a highly volatile moment in which such cultural tensions exploded. And Dickinson does not resolve them. There are in Dickinson's work moments of rest: of religious devotion, of sentimental romance, of natural harmony, of aesthetic self-sufficiency. But these moments are not sustained. Hers is not a poetics of resolution. She does not offer, although she explores, solutions through or within poetry. Instead, she enacts scenes of violence, across a range of fields and in varying degrees:

> My Life had stood – a Loaded Gun –
> In Corners – till a Day
> The Owner passed – identified –
> And Carried Me away –
>
> And now We roam in Sovereign Woods –
> And now We hunt the Doe –
> And every time I speak for Him –
> The Mountains straight reply –
>
> And do I smile, such cordial light
> Upon the Valley glow –
> It is as a Vesuvian face
> Had let its pleasure through –
>
> And when at Night – Our good Day done –
> I guard My Master's Head –

> 'Tis better than the Eider-Duck's
> Deep Pillow – to have shared –
>
> To foe of His – I'm deadly foe –
> None stir the second time –
> On whom I lay a Yellow Eye –
> Or an emphatic Thumb –
>
> Though I than He – may longer live
> He longer must – than I –
> For I have but the power to kill,
> Without – the power – to die –

The "Loaded Gun" of what is perhaps Dickinson's best-known poem finally reflects not only her own "Life," but also her culture's, where cultural representation in art threatens to unleash explosive violence. As in Dickinson's most highly wrought and overwrought texts, complex image systems never finally settle into consistent correlations. The poem presents a riddle which can never be fully solved: as female speaker becomes phallic gun, passive gun becomes active killer, ownership entails loss of agency, "cordial" pleasure becomes deadly, (religious) devotion (the poem has also Psalmic resonance) becomes lethal mastery, tender closeness keeps its (sexual) distance (the speaker declines to share "the Eider-Duck's Deep Pillow").

The masterful slippage within this poem makes it at once almost indefinitely suggestive and steadfastly resistant. The poem seems, among other things, to invoke old dialogues between the body and soul, with the gun in the place of bodily agent and instrument, exposing, however, a threat of disorderly rebellion within the figure. Its writing during the Civil War suggests historical violence as one of its contexts. Its highly equivocal ending seems as much to fear power as to claim it, as roles of responsibility and control reverse between the male owner and the gun, and the text seems finally to treasure the mortality it defies. Perhaps above all, the "Loaded Gun" is Dickinson's poetic texts themselves as they "speak." The gun is certainly also a figure for textuality, for the power, danger, and also vulnerability of embodied expression. As loaded text, the constructions of Dickinson's self and her culture are brought into powerful collision: masculine and feminine, metaphysical and linguistic; body and spirit, history and rhetoric.

Dickinson's clashing languages point not only outward to her own culture but forward to ours, not least in its implications for poetic language generally. In Dickinson's work, historical, metaphysical, and aesthetic forces intersect, as these are under extraordinary pressure, when longstanding traditional assumptions regarding the basic frameworks for interpreting the world are challenged to the point of breakage. In Dickinson's work, history and paradigm, metaphysics and world come apart. This is felt in her ruptures of syntax and structure, line and image, in ways that have proved proleptic. Dickinson's writing is among the earliest directly to register the effects on poetic language of such a breakdown of interpretive structures. Her poetry dramatizes the task of language, and the burden on it, to articulate orders through which we understand ourselves and the world. Her writing thus makes visible, as does Nietzsche's and many subsequent twentieth-century writers and theorists, how language presumes even as it projects certain continuities and coherences in our experience; and the linguistic consequences when these come under severe challenge and strain.

Dickinson's work remains a battlefield of contending claims. It brings into explosive confrontation the most pressing, and unresolved, cultural forces surrounding her. There are many entries into Emily Dickinson's verse: psychobiography, Romantic aesthetics, philology, literary theory, history, religion, gender. Her work indeed incorporates each of these. But it does so in ways that expose the complex and often tense relationships between these various arenas. In her poems, her several identities remain at war with each other and with her cultural worlds: gendered, religious, material, aesthetic. The result is a work that remains at once formally explosive and culturally engaged: a poetry not of detachment, but of confrontation.

CHRONOLOGY, 1800–1910

Neal Dolan

	American Poetry and Criticism	American Events, Texts, and Arts	Other Events, Texts, and Arts
1800		Washington, DC becomes capital of the US.	Speenhamland Act in England; government supplements wages for the poor.
		Northwest Territory divided into Ohio and Indiana Territories.	Spain cedes Louisiana Territory to France.
		Library of Congress founded.	Napoleon occupies Italy.
1801	Hugh Henry Brackenridge (1748–1816) "Scots Poems" in *Poems of the Scots-Irishman*		
1807	Joel Barlow (1754–1812) *The Columbiad*	Congress passes Embargo Act.	Sir Humphry Davy discovers potassium and sodium.
		Robert Fulton's 150-ft.-long steamboat the *Clermont* proceeds 150 miles up the Hudson River in 32 hours.	Wordsworth writes "Ode on Intimations of Immortality."
		Washington Irving and James Paulding found *Salmagundi*.	
1809	Philip Freneau (1752–1832) *Poems Written and Published During the American Revolution*	Nonintercourse Act repeals Embargo Act; trade reopens with all countries except Britain and France.	Beethoven composes *Piano Concerto No.5 in E Flat Major* (*The Emperor*).
		Washington Irving publishes *History of New York . . . by Diedrich Knickerbocker*.	Byron writes *English Bards and Scotch Reviewers*.
			Lamarck publishes *Philosophie zoologique*, argues that genetic adaptation is affected by effort.

(cont.)

	Author	Work	American events	World events
1812	Joel Barlow (1754–1812)	"Advice to a Raven in Russia"		East India Company's trade monopoly abolished.
1813	Washington Allston (1779–1843)	The Sylphs of the Seasons	British defeated by US fleet in Battle of Lake Erie. Shawnee Indian Chief Tecumseh killed.	Jane Austen publishes Pride and Prejudice. Shelley publishes "Queen Mab."
1815	Philip Freneau (1752–1832)	A Collection of Poems on American Affairs	Anglo-American commercial treaty ends mutual discriminatory duties between Britain and the US. Robert Fulton launches the Demologos, the first steam-powered battleship. General Andrew Jackson defeats British at Battle of New Orleans.	British and Prussian forces defeat Napoleon at the Battle of Waterloo; Napoleon abdicates and is exiled to St. Helena. Congress of Vienna reestablishes Austrian and Prussian monarchies; forms the German Confederation, the Kingdom of the Netherlands, and a Polish kingdom.
	Lydia Sigourney (1791–1865)	Moral Pieces in Prose and Verse		
1817	Manoah Bodman (1765–1858)	An Oration on Death	American Society for the Return of Negroes to Africa founded in Richmond, VA. Construction of Erie Canal begins.	Coleridge publishes Biographia Literaria.
	William Cullen Bryant (1794–1878)	"Thararopsis"		Hegel publishes the Encyclopedia of Philosophy.

	American Poetry and Criticism		American Events, Texts, and Arts	Other Events, Texts, and Arts
1818	James Kirke Paulding (1778–1860)	*The Backwoodsman*	US–Canadian boundary established at the 49th parallel.	Jane Austen's *Northanger Abbey* and *Persuasion* are published posthumously.
			US troops under Andrew Jackson attack Florida Seminoles.	John Keats publishes "Endymion," devotes himself full-time to poetry.
				Mary Wollstonecraft Shelley writes *Frankenstein*.
				San Martin wins independence for Chile with the defeat of the Spanish royalists at Maipu.
				Scott publishes *The Heart of Midlothian* and *Rob Roy*.
1819	Joseph Rodman Drake (1795–1820) & Fitz-Greene Halleck (1790–1867)	The "Croaker" poems	*McCulloch v. Maryland*	Bolivar is made President of Greater Colombia (present-day Colombia, Venezuela, Ecuador, and Panama).
	Fitz-Greene Halleck (1790–1867)	*Fanny*	Spain cedes Florida to the US in Adams-Onis Treaty; Western boundary of Louisiana Purchase is agreed on.	Byron publishes *Don Juan* (Cantos I and II).
	Richard Henry Wilde (1789–1847)	"Lament of the Captive"	Unitarian Church formed in Boston under leadership of William Ellery Channing.	Peterloo Massacre in England; soldiers fire on crowd attending speeches on parliamentary reform and repeal of the Corn Laws.

	Author	Title		
1820	Maria Gowen Brooks (c.1794–1845)	*Judith, Esther, and Other Poems, by a Lover of the Arts*	Congress passes Missouri Compromise.	Keats publishes volume including "Ode to a Nightingale," "Ode on a Grecian Urn," "Lamia," and other poems.
			James Monroe reelected President.	Portuguese regency overthrown; liberal constitution drafted.
			Washington Irving publishes *The Sketch Book*.	Revolutionary movements active in Spain.
				San Martin moves his armies into Peru.
				Scott publishes *Ivanhoe*.
				Shelley publishes "Prometheus Unbound."
1821	William Cullen Bryant (1794–1878)	*Poems*	James Fenimore Cooper writes *The Spy*.	Bolivar wins the independence of Venezuela with defeat of the Spanish royalist army at Carabobo.
	James Hillhouse (1789–1841)	*Judgment: A Vision*	First public high school founded in Boston.	Greeks take Tripolitsa fortress, massacre 10,000 Turks; Greek war for independence begins.
	James Gates Percival (1795–1856)	*Poems*	John Quincy Adams issues "Report on Weights and Measures."	Guatemala, Mexico, and Peru become independent from Spain.
			New York, following the lead of Connecticut (1818) and Massachusetts (1821), abolishes property qualifications for voting.	Michael Faraday discovers electromagnetic rotation.

(cont.)

American Poetry and Criticism		American Events, Texts, and Arts	Other Events, Texts, and Arts
	1822	Sequoya develops Indian alphabet.	Shelley publishes "Adonais," an elegy for Keats.
James Gates Percival (1795–1856)		Failed rebellion of Negro slaves led by Denmark Vesey in Charleston, SC.	Brazil secures independence from Portugal.
Prometheus			
Lydia Sigourney (1791–1865)		President Monroe suggests recognition of new Latin American republics.	Greeks write liberal constitution; declare independence.
Traits of the Aborigines of America			
Carlos Wilcox (1794–1827)		Water-powered cotton mills begin production in Massachusetts using female labor force.	Haitians win control of all of Hispaniola, form the republic of Haiti.
"The Age of Benevolence"			
			Puskin writes *Eugene Onegin*.
			Turks take Chios, massacre most of the Greek inhabitants; Turkish army invades mainland Greece.
	1823	James Fenimore Cooper publishes *The Pioneers*.	Ferdinand VII revokes Spain's constitution, institutes harshly repressive measures.
Sarah J. Hale (1788–1879)		President Monroe states Monroe Doctrine.	Guatemala, San Salvador, Nicaragua, Honduras, and Costa Rica form the confederated United Provinces of Central America.
The Genius of Oblivion and Other Original Poems			William Wilberforce forms society in England to abolish slave trade and slavery itself in British possessions overseas.

1824	Carlos Wilcox (1794–1827)	"The Religion of Taste"		Czar Nicholas I defeats uprising of the Decembrists.
1825	John Brainard (1796–1828)	Occasional Pieces of Poetry	Congress endorses relocation of Indian tribes in the east to lands west of the Mississippi River.	Bolivia proclaims independence.
	Maria Gowen Brooks (c. 1794–1845)	Zophiël, Canto 1	Creek Indians refuse treaty ceding all lands in Georgia to the US government.	Portugal recognizes independence of Brazil.
	William Cullen Bryant (1794–1878)	"An Indian at the Burial Place of His Fathers"	Erie Canal completed.	Manzoni publishes The Betrothed.
	Fitz-Greene Halleck (1790–1867)	"Marco Bozzaris"	Texas opened to US citizens for settlement.	Pushkin writes Boris Godunov.
	Edward Coote Pinkney (1802–28)	Poems	Thomas Cole founds Hudson River School of landscape painting.	British workers permitted to organize into labor unions.
1826	Samuel Woodworth (1784–1842)	"The Old Oaken Bucket"	James Fenimore Cooper publishes Last of the Mohicans.	Felix Mendelssohn composes Overture to Shakespeare's A Midsummer Night's Dream.
			Senate sends delegates to Panama Congress; they fail to arrive on time.	Ottoman Sultan orders Janissaries murdered in their barracks in Constantinople.
1827	Richard Henry Dana, Sr. (1787–1879)	The Buccaneer and Other Poems	All towns in Massachusetts with 500 or more households required to have a high school.	Georg Ohm publishes significant research on electrical currents.
	Edgar Allan Poe (1809–49)	Tamerlane and Other Poems	John James Audubon begins publication of Birds of America.	In preface to Cromwell, Victor Hugo calls for freedom from confining literary conventions.

(cont.)

American Poetry and Criticism			American Events, Texts, and Arts	Other Events, Texts, and Arts
	Lydia Sigourney (1791–1865)	*Poems by the Author of Moral Pieces*	*Freedom's Journal*, first Negro newspaper, published in New York City. James Fenimore Cooper publishes *The Prairie*.	Jean-Baptiste Corot exhibits "Le Pont de Narni," his first major work.
1828	George Moses Horton (1797–1883)	"On Liberty and Slavery"	Congress passes "Tariff of Abominations"; clash of interest between Northern mercantile and Southern agricultural economies.	Berzelius discovers the element Thorium.
	George Moses Horton (1797–1883)	"On Music"	Democratic Party formed; Andrew Jackson elected first Democratic US President.	Russo-Persian war concluded by the Treaty of Turkmanchai.
	George Moses Horton (1797–1883)	"Slavery"	First recorded strike of textile workers in Paterson, NJ.	Test and Corporation Acts are repealed in England.
	Carlos Wilcox (1794–1827)	"The Age of Benevolence," Books II –IV (fragments), in *Remains of the Rev. Carlos Wilcox.*	Noah Webster publishes *American Dictionary of the English Language.*	
	George Moses Horton (1797–1883)	*Hope of Liberty*	Andrew Jackson introduces spoils system into national politics.	Constitutions of Swiss cantons are revised along liberal lines to include universal suffrage, freedom of the press, and equality before the law.
1829	Edgar Allan Poe (1809–49)	*Al Aaraaf, Tamerlane and Other Poems*	Workingmen's Party formed in New York.	Daniel O'Connell works for repeal of the parliamentary union of Great Britain and Ireland.

1831	Edgar Allan Poe (1809–49)	*Poems*	Georgia's order for the relocation of Cherokee Indians west of the Mississippi River upheld by Supreme Court.	Ottoman Empire is severely weakened by the Russian capture of Andrianople, Kars, and Erzerum; Treaty of Andrianople is signed.
	John Greenleaf Whittier (1807–92)	*Legends of New England*	Nat Turner leads failed Negro slave revolt. William Lloyd Garrison founds *The Liberator*.	Austria suppresses uprisings in Modena, Parma, and the Papal States, but does not succeed in rooting out Italy's nationalist movement. Robert Brown discovers the nucleus of the cell. Extensive political unrest occurs in France. Faraday makes an electrical current by altering magnetic intensity.
1832	John Quincy Adams (1767–1848)	*Dermot MacMorrogh, or the Conquest of Ireland*	Andrew Jackson reelected President. Cyrus McCormick invents reaper. Samuel F. B. Morse designs improved electromagnetic telegraph. South Carolina passes Ordinance of Nullification, voiding the tariffs of 1828 and 1832.	First railroad in Europe is completed. Giuseppe Mazzini founds Young Italy. Reform Bill reassigns seats in the British parliament to more accurately reflect population.
	John Greenleaf Whittier (1807–92)	*Moll Pitcher*		

(*cont.*)

	American Poetry and Criticism	American Events, Texts, and Arts	Other Events, Texts, and Arts
1833	Park Benjamin (1809–64) *Harbinger*	Abolitionist groups found American Anti-Slavery Society in New York and New England.	Balzac publishes *Eugénie Grandet*.
	Maria Gowen Brooks (c. 1794–1845) *Zophiël or The Bride of Seven*	Force Bill, authorizing President Jackson's use of the military to enforce tariff laws, passed by Congress.	English Factory Act outlaws children under nine from working in the textile industry.
	Richard Henry Dana, Sr. (1787–1879) *Poems and Prose Writings*	President Jackson orders channeling of public funds from the Bank of the United States to state banks.	Mendelssohn composes *Italian Symphony*.
			Parliament provides first grant for public education in England.
			Slavery is outlawed in the British empire.
			Tennyson begins work on *In Memoriam* (–1850).
1835	Joseph Rodman Drake (1795–1820) *The Culprit Fay*	Samuel Colt designs first revolver.	Dickens publishes his first book, *Sketches by Boz*.
	Lydia Sigourney (1791–1865) *Zinzendorff and Other Poems*	Seminole Indian War sparked by Seminoles' refusal to move west of the Mississippi River.	Juan Manuel de Rosas becomes dictator of Argentina.
		US takes over Cherokee land in Georgia where gold is discovered.	Mexico establishes strong central government.

	Author	Work		
1836	Oliver Wendell Holmes, Sr. (1809–94)	*Poems*	A plot of land in a good location in Chicago will have increased its value by thirty times between 1833 and this date.	Andres Santa Cruz, President of Bolivia, invades Peru and forms a Peru–Bolivia confederation.
	John Greenleaf Whittier (1807–92)	*Mogg Megone*	Martin Van Buren elected as 2nd Democrat President.	Boer farmers and cattlemen depart from British rule in Cape Colony and found Transvaal, Natal, and the Orange Free State.
			McGuffey's Readers published.	Thomas Carlyle publishes *Sartor Resartus*.
			Texas claims independence; massacre of Texan forces at the Alamo and at Goliad by Mexican troops under Santa Anna; establishment of Texas as an independent republic under President Sam Houston.	
1837	Sarah J. Hale (1788–1879)	*The Ladies' Wreath* (ed.)	Ralph Waldo Emerson publishes *The American Scholar*.	Benjamin Disraeli elected to British parliament.
	George Moses Horton (1797–1883)	*Poems by a Slave*	Nathaniel Hawthorne publishes *Twice-Told Tales*.	Dickens publishes *Oliver Twist*.
	Richard Henry Wilde (1789–1847)	*Hesperia*	John Deere invents plow with steel moldboard, revolutionizing farming on heavy prairie soil.	Direct monarchical government restored in Brazil.
			Seminoles defeated at Battle of Okeechobee by US forces led by Zachary Taylor.	Victoria becomes Queen of Great Britain and Ireland.

(*cont.*)

	American Poetry and Criticism	American Events, Texts, and Arts	Other Events, Texts, and Arts
1838	James Hillhouse (1789–1841) *Sachem's Wood*	"Gag resolutions" against anti-slavery petitions adopted by Congress.	Chartism begins in Great Britain, promotes interests of the working and middle classes, aims for substantial parliamentary reform.
	John Greenleaf Whittier (1807–92) *Poems Written during the Progress of the Abolition Question in the United States*	Cherokee Indians in Georgia relocated to Indian Territory.	Charles Lyell publishes *Elements of Geology*.
		Personal Liberty Laws countering the Fugitive Slave Act passed in some Northern states; Underground Railroad established to help Southern slaves escape to the North.	
		Sarah Grimke publishes *Letters on the Equality of the Sexes and the Condition of Woman*.	
1839	Henry Wadsworth Longfellow (1807–82) *Voices of The Night*	John James Audubon publishes *Birds of North America*.	China forbids importing of opium; first opium war begins.
	Edgar Allan Poe (1809–49) "Longfellow's *Hyperion; a Romance*" (Review, *Burton's Gentleman's Magazine*, October)	Liberty Party holds first national anti-slavery convention in Warsaw, NY.	British parliament denies Chartist petition; riots ensue in Birmingham and around the country.
	Jones Very (1813–80) *Essays and Poems*		Prussia limits child labor to maximum of ten hours a day.
			The Central American Federation breaks down into Guatemala, Honduras, Nicaragua, El Salvador, and Costa Rica.

1840	John Quincy Adams (1767–1848)	"The Wants of Man"		British seize Hong Kong and Chinkiang.
1841	Henry Wadsworth Longfellow (1807–82)	*Ballads and Other Poems*	Death of William Henry Harrison one month after his Presidential inauguration; John Tyler becomes first Vice President to succeed to the Presidency.	First law is passed protecting strikers in France.
	James Russell Lowell (1819–91)	*A Year's Life*	James Fenimore Cooper publishes *The Deerslayer*.	Schumann composes *Symphony No. 1 in B Flat Major* and *Symphony No. 4 in D Minor*.
	Edgar Allan Poe (1809–49)	"Longfellow's *Voices of the Night*" (Review, *Burton's Gentleman's Magazine*, February)	*New York Tribune*, the leading newspaper in the North and the West before the Civil War, published by Horace Greeley.	
	Lydia Sigourney (1791–1865)	*Poems, Religious and Elegiac*	Whigs denounce President Tyler after he twice vetoes bill to create a national bank.	
	Lydia Sigourney (1791–1865)	*Pocahontas and Other Poems*		
1842	William Cullen Bryant (1794–1878)	*The Fountain and Other Poems*	Dorr's Rebellion spurs liberalization of voting requirements in new Rhode Island state constitution.	British defeat the Boers in Natal, South Africa, and regain control.
	Henry Wadsworth Longfellow (1807–82)	*Poems on Slavery*	John Fremont leads exploration of Oregon Trail.	Mine Act in England outlaws women or children working in mines.
	Edgar Allan Poe (1809–49)	"Longfellow's *Ballads and Other Poems*" (Review, *Graham's Magazine*, March)	Massachusetts law limits working hours for children under twelve to ten hours per day.	British parliament rejects second Chartist petition.

(cont.)

American Poetry and Criticism		American Events, Texts, and Arts	Other Events, Texts, and Arts
Edgar Allan Poe (1809–49)	"Longfellow's Ballads and Other Poems" (Review, Graham's Magazine, April)	Northeast boundary dispute resolved in Webster–Ashburton Treaty; US–Canadian border established from Maine to Lake of the Woods.	Tennyson publishes Poems, including "Locksley Hall," "Morte d'Arthur," "Ulysses."
		Seminole Indians forced to sign peace treaty after US armed forces annihilate their villages and crops; Seminoles relocated to Indian Territory.	
1843 William Ellery Channing (1818–1901)	Poems	Beginning of migration wave to Oregon Territory on the Oregon Trail.	Dickens publishes Martin Chuzzlewit and A Christmas Carol.
James Gates Percival (1795–1856)	The Dream of A Day and Other Poems	Edgar Allan Poe publishes "The Murder in the Rue Morgue," "The Pit and the Pendulum," and "The Tell-Tale Heart."	General Espartero is deposed in Spain; Isabella II is declared Queen.
Elizabeth Oakes Smith (1806–93)	"The Sinless Child"		John Ruskin publishes Modern Painters (–1860, 5 vols).
John Greenleaf Whittier (1807–92)	Lays of My Home and Other Poems		Mendelssohn composes music to A Midsummer Night's Dream. Sören Kierkegaard preaches Christian existentialism.
1844 Christopher Pearse Cranch (1813–92)	Poems	Democrat James K. Polk elected President.	Alexandre Dumas, père, publishes The Three Musketeers.
Margaret Fuller (1810–50)	Summer on the Lakes (contains poems)	Iron used for railroad tracks.	Dominicans throw off Haitian rule; Dominican Republic established.

Year	Author	Work		
	Frances Kemble (1809–93)	*Poems*	Secretary of State John C. Calhoun negotiates annexation treaty with Texas government.	Factory Act in England outlaws children under thirteen from working more than six hours a day.
	James Russell Lowell (1819–91)	*Poems*		Friedrich Engels publishes *The Condition of the Working Class in England.*
	Epes Sargent (1813–80)	*The Light of the Lighthouse and Other Poems*		Thackeray writes *Barry Lyndon.*
1845	George Moses Horton (1797–1883)	*Poetical Works of George M. Horton the Colored Bard*	Edgar Allan Poe publishes *Tales.*	France and Britain oppose Rosa's plan to make Paraguay and Uruguay dependent Argentine states.
	Henry Wadsworth Longfellow (1807–82)	*Poems*	Frederick Douglass publishes *Narrative of the Life of Frederick Douglass, an American Slave, Written by Himself.*	Ingres paints portrait of the Countess Haussonville.
	Edgar Allan Poe (1809–49)	*The Raven and Other Poems*	Labor organization Industrial Congress of the United States founded in NYC.	Potato blight causes the Great Famine in Ireland; at least a million people perish, millions more emigrate to the US.
	Edgar Allan Poe (1809–49)	"Longfellow's *Waif*" (Review, *New York Weekly Mirror*, 25 January)	Margaret Fuller publishes *Woman in the Nineteenth Century.*	Wagner composes *Tannhäuser.*
	Edgar Allan Poe (1809–49)	"Reply to Outis" regarding imitation, plagiarism, and Longfellow (*Broadway Journal*, 8 March)	Texas accepts annexation proposal and becomes the 28th state of the US.	

(cont.)

American Poetry and Criticism		American Events, Texts, and Arts	Other Events, Texts, and Arts
Edgar Allan Poe (1809–49)	"Further Reply to Outis" (*Broadway Journal*, 15 March)	US sends envoy to establish Texas boundary with Mexico and to purchase California and New Mexico.	
Edgar Allan Poe (1809–49)	"Third Chapter of Reply to Outis" regarding Longfellow and plagiarism (*Broadway Journal*, 22 March)		
Edgar Allan Poe (1809–49)	"Conclusion of Reply to Outis Regarding Longfellow and Plagiarism" (*Broadway Journal*, 29 March)		
Edgar Allan Poe (1809–49)	"Postscript to Reply to Outis Regarding Longfellow and Plagiarism" (*Broadway Journal*, 5 April)		
Edgar Allan Poe (1809–49)	"Longfellow's *Poems on Slavery, Voices of the Night, Ballads and Other Poems*, and *The Waif*" (Review, *Aristidean*, April)		
Lydia Sigourney (1791–1865)	*Poetry for Seamen*		
William Gilmore Sims (1806–70)	*Grouped Thoughts and Scattered Fancies*		
Frances Ellen Watkins Harper (1825–1911)	*Forest Leaves*	Edgar Allan Poe publishes "The Cask of Amontillado."	Berlioz composes *La Damnation de Faust*.
Henry Wadsworth Longfellow (1807–82)	*The Belfry of Bruges and Other Poems*	Herman Melville publishes first novel, *Typee*.	British government repeals Corn Laws.
Lydia Sigourney (1791–1865)	*The Voice of Flowers*	Mexican War begins.	Dostoevsky publishes *Poor Folk*.

1846

Year	Author	Work		
1847	John Greenleaf Whittier (1807–92)	*Voices of Freedom*	Wilmot Proviso rejected by Congress.	British Factory Act limits working day to ten hours for women and children between thirteen and eighteen years of age.
	Ralph Waldo Emerson (1803–82)	*Poems*	Herman Melville publishes *Omoo*.	Charlotte Brontë publishes *Jane Eyre*; Emily Brontë publishes *Wuthering Heights*; Anne Brontë publishes *Agnes Grey*.
	Henry Wadsworth Longfellow (1807–82)	*Evangeline*	US gains control of all of California.	Thackeray publishes *Vanity Fair* (–1848).
	Epes Sargent (1813–80)	*Songs of the Sea*	US troops defeat Mexicans at Buena Vista, capture Veracruz, and enter Mexico City; beginning of peace negotiations with Mexico.	
1848	Lydia Sigourney (1791–1865)	*The Weeping Willow*		February Revolution brings about abdication of Louis Philippe in France; Prince Louis Napoleon Bonaparte is elected President of the French Republic.
	John Quincy Adams (1767–1848)	*Poems* (Posthumous)	Free-Soil Party established; convention in Buffalo is well attended.	John Everett Millais, William Holman Hunt, and Dante Gabriel Rossetti form Pre-Raphaelite Brotherhood.
	Charles Timothy Brooks (1813–83)	*Aquidneck*	New York legislature passes first law granting property rights to women.	

(cont.)

	American Poetry and Criticism	American Events, Texts, and Arts	Other Events, Texts, and Arts
	James Russell Lowell (1819–91)	Poems: Second Series	Treaty of Guadalupe Hidalgo marks end of Mexican War.	Karl Marx and Friedrich Engels publish The Communist Manifesto.
	James Russell Lowell (1819–91)	Bigelow Papers	Whig Zachary Taylor elected President.	Liberal revolutions occur in Italy, Bohemia, Hungary, Denmark, and Schleswig-Holstein.
	James Russell Lowell (1819–91)	The Vision of Sir Launfal	Women's Rights Convention held in Seneca Falls, NY.	Liberal revolutions occur throughout German states; Frankfurt parliament drafts a constitution for a united Germany.
	James Russell Lowell (1819–91)	A Fable for Critics		Millet paints The Winnower.
	Edgar Allan Poe (1809–49)	Eureka: A Prose Poem		Revolution in Vienna; Emperor abdicates in favor of Franz Josef.
	Lydia Sigourney (1791–1865)	Waterdrops		
1849	Alice Cary (1820–71) & Phoebe Cary (1824–71)	Poems	California adopts anti-slavery constitution and proposes to join the Union.	Courbet achieves new realism with The Stone-Breakers and Burial at Ornans.
	Rufus Griswold (1815–57)	Female Poets of America (ed.)	Elizabeth Blackwell receives first MD in the world awarded to a woman.	Garibaldi fights for Roman Republic against the French; retreats.

1850	Author	Work		
	Henry Wadsworth Longfellow (1807–82)	*The Seaside and the Fireside*	Rufus Griswold publishes slanderous "Memoir of the Author" about Poe.	Led by Louis Kossuth, Hungary declares independence, but again comes under Hapsburg rule when Austrians and Russians beat the Hungarian army at Vilagos.
				Ruskin publishes *The Seven Lamps of Architecture*.
	Henry David Thoreau (1817–62)	*A Week on the Concord and Merrimack Rivers* (contains poems)	Herman Melville publishes *Mardi* and *Redburn*.	
			John Greenleaf Whittier publishes *Leaves from Margaret Smith's Journal*.	
	Washington Allston (1779–1843)	*Lectures on Art, and Poems by Washington Allston*, ed. Richard Henry Dana, Jr.	Clayton–Bulwer Treaty signed.	E. B. Browning publishes *Sonnets from the Portuguese*.
	John Greenleaf Whittier (1807–92)	*Songs of Labor*	Compromise of 1850 passed by Congress.	Frederick William IV suggests Prussian Union plan for confederation of Prussia and the smaller German states.
			Death of President Taylor; Fillmore becomes President.	Herbert Spencer publishes *Social Statistics*.
			Ralph Waldo Emerson publishes *Representative Men*.	Millet paints *The Sower* and *The Binders*.
			Fugitive Slave Act requires the turning in of fugitive slaves in free states.	Rudolf Clausius formulates second law of thermodynamics.
			Herman Melville publishes *White-Jacket*.	
			Nathaniel Hawthorne publishes *The Scarlet Letter*.	

(cont.)

American Poetry and Criticism		American Events, Texts, and Arts	Other Events, Texts, and Arts
1851	Henry Wadsworth Longfellow (1807–82) *The Golden Legend*	2,500 buildings destroyed by fire in San Francisco; estimated loss $12 million. First law authorizing the taxing of town inhabitants to support free libraries passed in Massachusetts. Nathaniel Hawthorne publishes *The House of the Seven Gables*. Henry Rowe Schoolcraft publishes *The American Indians: Their History, Condition and Prospects*. Immigration from famine-struck Ireland reaches one-year-peak of 221,253 people. Herman Melville publishes *Moby Dick*. Sioux Indians cede most of their land in Iowa and Minnesota to the US.	Louis Napoleon executes coup d'état in France. Ruskin publishes *The Stones of Venice* (–1853). General Narciso Lopez leads unsuccessful expedition to free Cuba from Spanish rule. Victoria, Australia is made a separate British colony.

1852	Alice Cary (1820–71)	Lyra and Other Poems	Compromise of 1850 accepted by both Democrats and Whigs.	Cavour, a progressive liberal, becomes Premier of Sardinia.
	Emily Dickinson (1830–86)	"Sic transit gloria mundi 'A Valentine'" (in Springfield Daily Republican, 20 February)	Democrat Franklin Pierce elected President.	Dickens publishes Bleak House.
	Lydia Sigourney (1791–1865)	Olive Leaves	First law passed in Massachusetts requiring children between eight and fourteen to attend school for a minimum of twelve weeks per year.	Matthew Arnold publishes Empedocles on Etna, and Other Poems.
			Harriet Beecher Stowe publishes Uncle Tom's Cabin.	Rosas defeated by Urquiza at the Battle of Monte Caseros, Argentina.
				Second Empire established by plebiscite in France; President Louis Napoleon declares himself Emperor.
				South African Republic is officially recognized by Britain.
				Turgenev publishes Sportsman's Sketches.
1853	Charles Timothy Brooks (1813–83)	Songs of Field and Flood	Baltimore & Ohio Railroad completed to Ohio River, first railroad connection between Chicago and the East.	Crimean War begins.

(cont.)

American Poetry and Criticism

			American Events, Texts, and Arts	*Other Events, Texts, and Arts*
	William Gilmore Sims (1806–70)	*Poems*	New York Central Railroad founded.	First railroad through the Alps from Vienna to Trieste starts running.
	James Whitfield (1822–92)	*America and Other Poems*	US fleet commanded by Matthew C. Perry arrives in Edo Bay and demands the opening of Japanese ports to trade.	Grands boulevards of Paris reconstructed by Haussman.
	John Greenleaf Whittier (1807–92)	*The Chapel of the Hermits and Other Poems*	US purchases Arizona and part of New Mexico from Mexico for $10 million.	Liszt composes *Hungarian Rhapsodies* (–1854).
				Mrs. Gaskell publishes *Cranford*.
1854	Phoebe Cary (1824–71)	*Poems and Parodies*	13,000 immigrants arrive from China, mostly as transcontinental railroad workers; beginning of large-scale Chinese immigration.	Brahms composes *Piano Concerto No.1 in D Minor*.
	Frances Harper (1825–1911)	*Poems on Miscellaneous Subjects*	Anti-slavery emigration to Kansas encouraged by Massachusetts Emigrant Aid Society.	Dickens publishes *Hard Times*.
	Julia Ward Howe (1819–1910)	*Passion Flowers*	Kansas–Nebraska Act repeals Missouri Compromise of 1820.	France and Britain ally with Turkey, declare war on Russia.

(cont.)

	Author	Work	American events	World events
	Lydia Sigourney (1791–1865)	*The Western Home and Other Poems*	Republican Party formed in reaction to Kansas–Nebraska Act.	Tennyson publishes "The Charge of the Light Brigade."
			Henry David Thoreau publishes *Walden; or, Life in the Woods*.	The Orange Free State established by Boers in South Africa.
1855	Alice Cary (1820–71)	*The Maiden of Tiascala*	Armed violence breaks out between pro-slavery and free-state constituencies in "Bleeding Kansas."	Alexander II becomes Czar of Russia.
	Henry Wadsworth Longfellow (1807–82)	*The Song of Hiawatha*	Samuel Kier constructs first American oil refinery in Pittsburgh.	Dickens publishes *Little Dorrit*.
	Maria White Lowell (1821–53)	*The Poems of Maria Lowell*		Tennyson publishes *Maud*.
	Lydia Sigourney (1791–1865)	*Sayings of the Little Ones and Poems for their Mothers*		Turgenev publishes *A Month in the Country*.
	Walt Whitman (1819–92)	*Leaves of Grass*		
	Walt Whitman (1819–92)	*Leaves of Grass*	Continuing acts of violence between Free State and pro-slavery factions in Kansas until Federal intervention.	British declare war on Persia.
1856	John Greenleaf Whittier (1807–92)	*The Panorama and Other Poems*	Democrat James Buchanan elected President.	Crimean War ends with Congress of Paris.
			Ralph Waldo Emerson publishes *English Traits*.	Remains of prehistoric man are found in the Neanderthal Valley near Dusseldorf, Germany.

		American Events, Texts, and Arts	Other Events, Texts, and Arts
		Kansas Territory pro-slavery legislature acknowledged by President Buchanan.	Baudelaire publishes *Les Fleurs du mal*, is fined for offending public morality.
		Senator Sumner's bitter criticism of Senator Andrew Butler and Stephen Douglas incurs a beating from Butler's nephew Preston Brooks in the Senate chamber.	Baudelaire publishes "Notes nouvelles sur Edgar Poe" as preface to *Nouvelles histoires extraordinaires par Edgar Poe*.
1857	Oliver Wendell Holmes, Sr. (1809–94)	140 non-Mormon emigrants massacred by John D. Lee and his Mormon followers in Utah.	Flaubert publishes *Madame Bovary*.
	"Autocrat of the Breakfast Table"	Frederick Law Olmsted and Calvert Vaux design Central Park in NYC.	Mexico adopts liberal constitution; reforms lead to civil war between conservatives and liberals.
	Julia Ward Howe (1819–1910)	Free State legislature elected in Kansas; pro-slavery delegates rig constitution to accommodate slavery in the region.	
	Words for the Hour	Herman Melville publishes *The Confidence Man*.	
		President Buchanan agrees to Lecompton Constitution; Democratic Party splits.	

	Author	Work		
1858	Emily Dickinson (1830–86)	"Nobody Knows this little Rose" (*Springfield Daily Republican*, 2 August)	Supreme Court proclaims Missouri Compromise unconstitutional.	Britain retakes Delhi, puts down Indian Mutiny.
	Oliver Wendell Holmes, Sr. (1809–94)	"The Chambered Nautilus" and "The Deacon's Masterpiece" (contained in *The Autocrat of the Breakfast Table*)	Commencement of stagecoach and mail services between San Francisco, CA and St. Louis, MO.	Treaty of Tientsin concludes war between Britain and China.
	Henry Wadsworth Longfellow (1807–82)	*The Courtship of Miles Standish and Other Poems*	Cyrus W. Field successfully lays first transatlantic telegraph wire.	
			Lecompton Constitution rejected in Kansas.	
			Lincoln–Douglas debates.	
			Religious revival in New York and Pennsylvania spreads throughout the US.	
			US signs treaty of peace, friendship and commerce with China.	
1860	Rose Terry Cooke (1827–92)	*Poems*	30,626 miles of railroad tracks laid by this date; 88,296 miles of surfaced roads; 4,723,000 tons of ocean-going shipping; 462,123 tons of shipping on northern lakes.	British and French armies occupy Peking.

(cont.)

	American Poetry and Criticism		American Events, Texts, and Arts	Other Events, Texts, and Arts
	Joseph Rodman Drake (1795–1820), Fitz-Greene Halleck (1790–1867)	Collected Edition of "The Croakers"	City-dwellers make up one quarter of US population; six of the fifteen leading cities fall west of the Alleghenies: Chicago, Cincinnati, Louisville, New Orleans, San Francisco, and St. Louis.	Garibaldi and his Redshirts conquer Sicily and Naples.
	Henry Timrod (1828–67)	*Poems*	Ralph Waldo Emerson publishes *The Conduct of Life*.	Jakob Burckhardt publishes *The Civilization of the Renaissance in Italy*.
	Frederick Goddard Tuckerman (1821–73)	*Poems*	Fast overland mail service by Pony Express between St. Joseph, MO and Sacramento, CA.	Union with Sardinia voted in plebiscites in Parma, Modena, Romagna, Tuscany, Sicily, Naples, and the Papal States.
	Walt Whitman (1819–92)	*Leaves of Grass*	Republican Abraham Lincoln elected President.	Wilkie Collins writes *The Woman in White*.
	John Greenleaf Whittier (1807–92)	*Home Ballads, Poems and Lyrics*	Secession of South Carolina from the Union.	
1861		"Go Down Moses" printed in *National Anti-Slavery Standard*, December 1861; first Negro spiritual to reach a wide white audience.	3 percent federal income tax on incomes over $800 enacted.	Czar Alexander II frees the Russian serfs.
	Emily Dickinson (1830–86)	"I taste a liquor never brewed" (*Springfield Daily Republican*, 4 May and 11 May)	Alabama, Arkansas, Florida, Georgia, Louisiana, Mississippi, North Carolina, Tennessee, Texas, and Virginia secede from the Union.	Dickens publishes *Great Expectations*.

1862	Emily Dickinson (1830–86)	"Safe in their Alabaster Chambers" (*Springfield Daily Republican*, 1 March)	Confederate States of America founded in Montgomery, AL with Jefferson Davis and Alexander Stephens as President and Vice President.	Manet shows *Spanish Singer*, marks shift from Realism to Impressionism.
			Confederates fire upon Fort Sumter, marking beginning of Civil War.	King of Naples capitulates to Garibaldi at Gaeta; Kingdom of Italy is established.
			Matthew Brady begins photographic record of Civil War.	
			Vassar College founded, giving women access to facilities similar to those in men's colleges.	
	Oliver Wendell Holmes, Sr. (1809–94)	*Songs in Many Keys*	First engagement between ironclad battleships, the Union *Monitor* and the Confederate *Merrimack*.	Hugo publishes *Les Misérables*.
			Pacific Railway Act allows Union Pacific Railroad to build a line from Nebraska to join with the Central Pacific in Utah.	Otto von Bismarck made Prime Minister of Prussia, seeks unification of Germany with Prussia at the head.
	Lydia Sigourney (1791–1865)	*The Man of Uz and Other Poems*	Union army commanded by General Ulysses Grant forces Confederates to retreat in Battle of Shiloh.	Risorgimento annexes Venetia, Rome, and parts of the Papal States to larger Kingdom of Italy.
				Turgenev publishes *Fathers and Sons*.

(cont.)

American Poetry and Criticism

	American Poetry and Criticism	American Events, Texts, and Arts	Other Events, Texts, and Arts
1863	Henry Wadsworth Longfellow (1807–82) *Tales of a Wayside Inn*	Emancipation Proclamation issued by President Lincoln. First Union conscription act.	Ernest Renan publishes *Life of Jesus*. French take over Mexico City; Austrian Archduke Maximillian is named Emperor of Mexico.
		President Lincoln gives *Gettysburg Address*.	Manet paints *Le Dejeuner sur L'herbe*.
			Poles rise in January Revolution; rebellion spreads from Russian Poland to Lithuania and White Russia.
1864	Emily Dickinson (1830–86) "Flowers," (*Springfield Daily Republican*, 9 March and 12 March etc.)	Cheyenne and Arapaho massacre at Sand Creek, CO.	Anton Bruckner composes *Symphony in D Minor and Mass No. 1 in D Minor*.
	Emily Dickinson (1830–86) "These are the Days when birds come back" (*Drum Beat*, 11 March)	First Baptist social union formed in Boston.	Dickens publishes *Our Mutual Friend*.
	Emily Dickinson (1830–86) "Some keep the Sabbath" (*The Round Table*, 12 March)	General Grant becomes Commander-in-Chief of Union troops.	Dostoevsky publishes *Notes from Underground*.
	Emily Dickinson (1830–86) "Blazing in gold" (*Drum Beat*, 29 February; *Springfield Daily Republican*, 30 March and 2 April)	General William Sherman captures Atlanta; his troops wreak destruction throughout Georgia.	John Henry Newman publishes *Apologia pro vita sua*.
	Emily Dickinson (1830–86) "Success is counted Sweetest" (*Brooklyn Daily Union*, 2 April)	Republican Abraham Lincoln reelected as President.	Russians squelch revolts and start "Russification" programs in Poland.

Year	Author	Work		
	John Greenleaf Whittier (1807–92)	*In War-Time and Other Poems*		Leo Tolstoy publishes *War and Peace*.
1865	George Moses Horton (1797–1883)	*Naked Genius*	Twenty-seven states ratify Thirteenth Amendment to abolish slavery.	Lewis Carroll publishes *Alice's Adventures in Wonderland*.
	James Russell Lowell (1819–91)	"Ode: Recited at the Commemoration of the Living and Dead Soldiers of Harvard University"	Cheyenne and Arapaho uprisings suppressed by militia in Colorado.	Manet shows *Olympia*; many critics find it obscene.
	Walt Whitman (1819–92)	*Drum Taps*	General Lee surrenders at Appomattox Court House; end of Civil War.	Peru allies with Chile, Bolivia, and Ecuador against Spain.
			President Lincoln assassinated by John Wilkes Booth in Ford's Theater.	Swinburne publishes "Atalanta in Calydon."
			South and North Carolina razed by General Sherman's army in its northward march.	
			Union Stockyards open in Chicago, the world capital of meat production.	
	Alice Cary (1820–71)	*Ballads, Lyrics, and Hymns*	Civil Rights Act, vetoed by President Johnson, passed by Congress.	Dostoevsky publishes *Crime and Punishment*.
1866	Emily Dickinson (1830–86)	"A narrow fellow in the grass" (*Springfield Daily Republican*, 14 February)	Fourteenth Amendment passed by Congress, insuring the civil rights of Negroes.	Mendel publishes his laws of heredity.
	Herman Melville (1819–91)	*Battle-Pieces*	Freedman's Bureau Bill vetoed by President Johnson, passed by Congress.	Swinburne publishes *Poems and Ballads*.

(*cont.*)

	American Poetry and Criticism	American Events, Texts, and Arts	Other Events, Texts, and Arts
	Walt Whitman (1819–92) "Sequel to Drum Taps"	National Labor Union formed in Baltimore; movement for eight-hour workday led by George McNeill and Ira Steward.	Treaty of Prague calls for Austria to cede Venetia to Italy, allows Prussia to annex Hanover, Hesse, Nassau, Frankfurt, and Schleswig-Holstein.
	John Greenleaf Whittier (1807–92) Snow-Bound: A Winter Idyll	Sioux Indians massacre US troops at Fort Philip Kearny, WY.	Treaty of Vienna concludes Austro-Italian War.
		Steamer Great Eastern lays second transatlantic cable between England and America.	
		Winslow Homer paints Prisoners from the Front.	
1867	Ralph Waldo Emerson (1803–82) May-Day and Other Pieces	Three Reconstruction Acts, vetoed by President Johnson, passed by Congress.	Alfred Nobel patents dynamite.
	Emma Lazarus (1849–87) Poems and Translations	Congress sets up Indian reservations for Cherokees, Chickasaws, Choctaws, Creeks, and Seminoles.	Marx publishes volume 1 of Das Kapital.
	John Greenleaf Whittier (1807–92) The Tent on the Beach	First collection of Negro spirituals, Slave Songs of the United States, published.	

	Authors	Literature	American history and politics	Cultural and world events
	Richard Henry Wilde (1789–1847)	*Hesperia*	Tenure of Office Act, vetoed by President Johnson, passed by Congress; President required to obtain Senate's consent before discharging officials. US purchases Alaska for $7.2 million.	Browning writes *The Ring and the Book*. Darwin publishes *The Variation of Animals and Plants Under Domestication*.
1868	Phoebe Cary (1824–71)	*Poems of Faith, Hope and Love*	Bill for eight-hour working day passed by Congress.	Dostoevsky publishes *The Idiot*.
	Julia Ward Howe (1819–1910)	*Later Lyrics*	Burlingame Treaty encourages Chinese immigration to the US.	Emperor of Japan hands government over to Westernizers, who begin modernization.
	Adah Isaacs Menken (1835–68)	*Infelicia*	Fourteenth Amendment ratified in twenty-nine states. Impeachment of President Johnson. Republican Ulysses Grant elected President.	Queen Isabella of Spain is deposed; provisional government institutes liberal reforms such as universal suffrage and a free press. Skeleton of Cro-Magnon man discovered in France. Wilkie Collins publishes *The Moonstone*.

(cont.)

	American Poetry and Criticism		*American Events, Texts, and Arts*	*Other Events, Texts, and Arts*
1869	Frances Harper (1825–1911)	*Moses: A Story of the Nile*	Completion of first transcontinental railroad line at Promontory, UT.	Cortes establish a constitutional monarchy in Spain.
	Lucy Larcom (1824–93)	*Poems*	Fifteenth Amendment passed by Congress, giving equal voting rights to all citizens regardless of "race, color, or previous condition of servitude."	Dmitry Mendeleyev publishes *Principles of Chemistry*; proposes periodic law, devises periodic table of elements.
	John Greenleaf Whittier (1807–92)	*Among the Hills and Other Poems*	Louisa May Alcott publishes *Little Women*.	Lister develops dramatically successful antiseptic techniques.
			National Woman Suffrage Association and American Woman Suffrage Association founded.	Napoleon III reintroduces parliamentary government in France.
			Noble Order of Knights of Labor organized in Philadelphia.	Opening of Suez Canal.
1870	Helen Hunt Jackson (1830–85)	*Verses*	Bret Harte publishes *The Luck of Roaring Camp, and Other Sketches*.	Bismarck's Ems dispatch provokes France to declare war on Prussia.
	James Russell Lowell (1819–91)	*The Cathedral*	Fifteenth Amendment ratified by twenty-nine states; voting rights given to black men, but denied to women.	England makes elementary education compulsory.

Year	Author	Work	United States	World
	John Greenleaf Whittier (1807–92)	*Ballads of New England*	John D. Rockefeller founds Standard Oil Company of Ohio.	Paraguay is devastated and most of its male population killed in War of the Triple Alliance.
			Population reaches 39.8 million, including 4.9 million freed Negroes and 2.3 million new immigrants in last ten years.	Peaceful revolution in Paris deposes Napoleon III; Third Republic is formed.
1871	Frances Harper (1825–1911)	*Poems*	Apache Indians forcibly removed to reservations in Arizona and New Mexico.	Darwin applies evolution to human beings in *The Descent of Man and Selection in Relation to Sex*.
	Emma Lazarus (1849–87)	*Admetus and Other Poems*	First Civil Service Commission appointed by President Grant.	Dostoevsky writes *The Possessed*.
	Walt Whitman (1819–92)	*Leaves of Grass*	Indian Appropriation Act overwrites previous treaties; all Indians become US wards.	George Eliot writes *Middlemarch: A Study of Provincial Life*.
	Walt Whitman (1819–92)	*Passage to India*	Parts of downtown Chicago destroyed by fire.	Labor unions legalized in Britain.
	John Greenleaf Whittier (1807–92)	*Miriam and Other Poems*	Walt Whitman publishes *Democratic Vistas*.	Radicals in Paris establish the Commune; defeated by French army, communards build barricades, shoot hostages, and burn down the Tuileries Palace. Rimbaud writes *The Drunken Boat*.

(cont.)

	American Poetry and Criticism		American Events, Texts, and Arts	Other Events, Texts, and Arts
1872	Henry Wadsworth Longfellow (1807–82)	Three Books of Songs	Amnesty Act passed by Congress; civil rights restored to most Southern citizens.	Carroll publishes *Through the Looking Glass*.
	Henry Wadsworth Longfellow (1807–82)	Christus	Charles Taze Russell founds Jehovah's Witnesses.	Germany, Austria-Hungary, and Russia form Three Emperors' League.
	Walt Whitman (1819–92)	As a Strong Bird on Pinions Free	Democrat and Liberal Republican presidential candidate Horace Greeley loses election to Republican Ulysses Grant.	Voting made secret for the first time in Britain with the Ballot Act.
	Walt Whitman (1819–92)	Leaves of Grass	Eadweard Muybridge invents zoopraxiscope, predecessor of the movie projector.	
	Ella Wheeler Wilcox (1850–1919)	Drops of Water	Yellowstone established as national park.	
1873	Lucy Larcom (1824–93)	Childhood Songs	Bethlehem Steel Company opens in Pittsburgh.	First Spanish republic created by radical majority in Cortes.
	Henry Timrod (1828–67)	Poems	Coinage Act passed by Congress; gold becomes monetary standard of the nation.	Bruckner composes *Symphony No. 3 in D Minor*.
			Mark Twain and Charles Dudley Warner co-write *The Gilded Age*.	Rimbaud publishes *A Season in Hell*.
				James Maxwell publishes *Treatise on Electricity and Magnetism*.

1874	Ralph Waldo Emerson (1803–82)	*Parnassus* (ed.)	Carpetbaggers' takeover of Arkansas government put down by federal armed forces.	British Factory Act requires 56½ hour work week.
	Henry Wadsworth Longfellow (1807–82)	*The Hanging of the Crane*	Greenback Party organized in Indianapolis by farmers in the South and the West.	Disraeli becomes Prime Minister of England for the second time.
			National Woman's Christian Temperance Union founded in Cleveland.	First exhibition of Impressionist paintings held in Paris.
				Mussorgsky composes *Pictures from an Exhibition*.
1875	Oliver Wendell Holmes, Sr. (1809–94)	*Songs of Many Seasons*	Civil Rights Act passed by Congress, granting Negroes equal rights in public places and the right to be jurors.	Charles Stuart Parnell launches movement for Irish independence in British parliament.
	Henry Wadsworth Longfellow (1807–82)	*The Masque of Pandora*	Thomas Eakins paints portrayal of medical school class, *The Gross Clinic*.	France adopts a republican constitution.
	John Greenleaf Whittier (1807–92)	*Hazel Blossoms*	Elihu Thomson invents first radio in the world.	Prussia abolishes religious orders; Austria separates universities from religious affiliations.
			Refrigerated freight cars used to transport meat from the Midwest to the East.	Tolstoy publishes *Anna Karenina*.
1876	Ralph Waldo Emerson (1803–82)	*Selected Poems*	Alexander Graham Bell patents telephone.	Mallarmé publishes *L'Après-midi d'un faune*.

(*cont.*)

		American Events, Texts, and Arts	Other Events, Texts, and Arts
Emma Lazarus (1849–87)	*The Spagnoletto: A Drama in Verse*	Democrat Samuel J. Tilden beats Republican Rutherford B. Hayes in presidential election by 250,000 popular votes; final vote determined by Congress.	Serbia and Montenegro go to war against the Ottoman Empire.
Herman Melville (1819–91)	*Clarel: A Poem and a Pilgrimage to the Holy Land*	Mark Twain publishes *The Adventures of Tom Sawyer*.	Tchaikovsky composes *Swan Lake*.
Walt Whitman (1819–92)	*Leaves of Grass*	Sioux and Cheyenne Indians kill 264 cavalrymen led by General George A. Custer in Battle of Little Bighorn.	Wagner's *The Ring of the Nibelung* is first performed in Bayreuth.
Walt Whitman (1819–92)	*Autumn Rivulets*		
Ella Wheeler Wilcox (1850–1919)	*Poems of Passions*		
1877 Helen Hunt Jackson (1830–85)	*No Name Series* (ed.)	Electoral Commission's decision to give all disputed returns to Hayes enables him to win election by one electoral vote.	Brahms composes *Symphony No. 2 in D Major*.
		End of Reconstruction era; federal troops withdraw from the South.	Flaubert publishes *Trois Contes*.
Sidney Lanier (1842–81)	*Poems*	First intercity telephone call.	Porfirio Díaz becomes President of Mexico, retains power until 1911.

	Author	Work		
1878	Emily Dickinson (1830–86)	"Success is counted Sweetest" in *A Masque of Poets*	Nez Perce Indians under Chief Joseph forced onto Indian Territory reservation after 1,600-mile retreat through Washington, Oregon, Idaho, and Montana.	Rodin shows *Age of Bronze*.
	Henry Wadsworth Longfellow (1807–82)	*Keramos and Other Poems*	Albert A. Michelson successfully measures speed of light.	Russia declares war on Ottoman Empire, beginning last Russo-Turkish war.
			Democrats win first majority in both Houses since 1858.	Hardy publishes *The Return of the Native*.
	John Greenleaf Whittier (1807–92)	*The Vision of Echard*	Greenback–Labor Party co-founded by labor organizations and supporters of inflation.	Treaty of San Stefano ends Russo-Turkish War, revised at Congress of Berlin; Serbia, Rumania, and Montenegro become independent states.
				Zola publishes *Thérèse Raquin*.
1880	Oliver Wendell Holmes, Sr. (1809–94)	*The Iron Gate and Other Poems*	Alexander Graham Bell sends first wireless message with photophone.	Disraeli resigns; Gladstone takes over as Prime Minister in England.
	Sidney Lanier (1842–81)	*The Science of English Verse*	Joel Chandler Harris uses Negro dialect in *Uncle Remus: His Songs and His Sayings*.	Rodin exhibits *The Thinker*.

(cont.)

American Poetry and Criticism	American Events, Texts, and Arts	Other Events, Texts, and Arts
Henry Wadsworth Longfellow (1807–92) *Ultima Thule*	Population grows to 50.1 million, including 2.8 million immigrants. Republican James A. Garfield elected President.	Tchaikovsky composes the *1812 Overture*, the *Italian Capriccio*, and *Serenade for Strings in C Major*. Zola publishes *Nana*.
1881 Walt Whitman (1819–92) *Leaves of Grass*	1862 institution of federal income tax ruled as constitutional by Supreme Court. Clara Barton organizes the National Society of the Red Cross. Death of President Garfield eleven weeks after being shot in a Washington, DC railway station. Former slave Booker T. Washington founds Normal and Industrial Institute for Negroes. Henry James publishes *The Portrait of a Lady*.	Alexander II of Russia is assassinated. Boers defeat the British at Laing's Neck and Majuba Hill; British grant self-government to Transvaal. Gladstone attempts to meet Irish demands for fair rent, fixity of tenure, and freedom of sale; Parnell imprisoned for favoring the intimidation of tenants.
1882 Emma Lazarus (1849–87) "The Dance to Death" (In *Songs of a Semite*)	Act barring "undesirables" from the US passed by Congress; head tax of fifty cents set on immigrants.	Etienne-Jules Marey invents first motion picture.

	Henry Wadsworth Longfellow (1807–82)	*In the Harbor*	Chinese Exclusion Act passed by Congress after race riots in California, barring Chinese immigrants from the US for ten years.	France makes education compulsory, free, and nonsectarian.
			First hydro-electric plant in the world begins operation in Appleton, WI.	Ibsen writes *An Enemy of the People.*
			Thomas Edison patents three-wire electrical system.	Italy, Austria-Hungary, and Germany form the Triple Alliance.
				Koch identifies bacterium that causes tuberculosis.
				Married women are given the right of separate ownership of property of all kinds by Married Women's Property Act in Britain.
1883	Henry Wadsworth Longfellow (1807–82)	*Michael Angelo*	Circulation of *New York World* increases twelve times in four years under direction of Joseph Pulitzer.	Bismarck initiates health insurance and other social welfare programs to preempt Socialists in Germany.
	James Whitcomb Riley (1849–1916)	*The Old Swimmin'-Hole*	Thomas Eakins paints *The Swimming Hole.*	Nietzsche announces the death of God in *Also Sprach Zarathustra.*
			Mark Twain publishes *Life on the Mississippi.*	

(cont.)

	American Events, Texts, and Arts	Other Events, Texts, and Arts
	Pendleton Act introduces merit system in place of spoils system; Civil Service Commission appointed to select persons for federal jobs.	
1884 Sidney Lanier (1842–81) *Complete Poems* (Posthumous)	Democrat Grover Cleveland elected President.	First volume of *Oxford English Dictionary* is published (–1935).
Lucy Larcom (1824–93) *Collected Poems*	Mark Twain publishes *The Adventures of Huckleberry Finn*.	France establishes protectorates over Tonkin in Northern Vietnam and Annam in Southern Vietnam.
Henry Timrod (1828–67) *Katie*	People's Party formed from Greenback–Labor and Anti-Monopoly parties.	Renoir paints first of *Bather* portraits (–1887).
	Sarah Orne Jewett publishes *A Country Doctor*.	Rodin sculpts *The Burghers of Calais*.
	Supreme Court rules in favor of Negroes impeded from voting by the Ku Klux Klan.	Unions legalized in France by Trade Union Act.
1886 Helen Hunt Jackson (1830–85) *Sonnets and Lyrics*	American Federation of Labor formed in Columbus, Ohio; Samuel Gompers elected President.	Henri Moissan identifies the element fluorine.
Emma Lazarus (1849–87) "The New Colossus" (inscribed on plaque at the base of the Statue of Liberty)	Apache chief Geronimo surrenders; end of Apache Indian wars.	British parliament defeats Gladstone's Home Rule Bill, which would have established a separate Irish legislature.

	Author	Work	Events
	John Greenleaf Whittier (1807–92)	St. Gregory's Guest	Rodin exhibits The Kiss.
			Bomb explodes at labor leaders meeting in Illinois; four workers and seven policemen killed in Haymarket Square riot.
			Seurat paints Sunday Afternoon on the Island of La Grande Jatte.
			Henry James publishes The Bostonians and Princess Casamassima.
			Verlaine publishes Rimbaud's Illuminations.
			Legal "persons" in Fourteenth Amendment defined by Supreme Court as both individuals and corporations.
1887	Oliver Wendell Holmes, Sr. (1809–94)	Before the Curfew and Other Poems	British annex Zululand.
			Charles F. McKim designs Low House in Bristol, RI; shingle-style becomes vogue of residential architecture.
	Emma Lazarus (1849–87)	By the Waters of Babylon	French form Union of Indochina.
			Dawes Act passed by Congress.
			Queen Victoria of England celebrates her Golden Jubilee, fifty years of rule.
			Interstate Commerce Act passed by Congress; Interstate Commerce Commission appointed.
			Michelson–Morley experiment demonstrates the constant speed of light.
			Yellow River floods in China, killing more than 900,000.
1888	Rose Terry Cooke (1827–92)	Complete Poems	Cezanne achieves his mature style in L'Estaque.
			Herman Melville publishes John Marr and Other Sailors.

(cont.)

American Poetry and Criticism		American Events, Texts, and Arts	Other Events, Texts, and Arts
	Thomas Nelson Page (1853–1922), Armistead Churchill Gordon (1855–1931) *Befo' de War*	Kodak manufactures George Eastman's hand camera; beginning of amateur photography.	Heinrich Hertz demonstrates that heat and light are forms of electromagnetic radiation.
	Walt Whitman (1819–92) *November Boughs*	Republican Benjamin Harrison elected President.	Rimsky-Korsakov composes *Scheherazade*.
		US Department of Labor established by Congress.	
1889	Emma Lazarus (1849–87) *Poems*	Anti-trust laws passed in Kansas, Michigan, North Carolina, and Tennessee.	Cecil Rhodes's British South Africa Company is granted wide powers in territory north of Transvaal and west of Mozambique.
		Barnard College for Women founded in NYC.	Emperor Pedro II is deposed; Brazil is declared a Republic.
		Charles M. Hall patents process for cheap production of aluminum.	Gaugin paints *The Yellow Christ* and *Bonjour Monsieur Gauguin*.
		Mark Twain publishes *A Connecticut Yankee in King Arthur's Court*.	Tennyson publishes poems including "Crossing the Bar."
		Oklahoma opened to white settlers.	Van Gogh paints *Starry Night*.
		Singer Company manufactures electric sewing machines.	

Year	Authors (works)	American events	World events
1890	Emily Dickinson (1830–86) *Poems by Emily Dickinson*, ed. Mabel Loomis Todd & T. W. Higginson James Whitcomb Riley (1849–1916) *Rhymes of Childhood* John Greenleaf Whittier (1807–92) *At Sundown*	William Kennedy Laurie Dickson makes *Fred Ott's Sneeze*, America's first Celluloid film. 200 Sioux Indians massacred by US armed forces in Battle of Wounded Knee. Anti-trust laws passed in Kentucky, Mississippi, and South Dakota. William Dean Howells publishes *A Hazard of New Fortunes*. Jacob A. Riis publishes *How the Other Half Lives*. Oklahoma Territory established. Sherman Anti-trust Act passed by Congress. Sherman Silver Purchase Act passed.	Bismarck dismissed as Chancellor of Germany by Emperor William II. Debussy composes *Suite bergamasque* (–1905), includes "Clair de lune." England establishes free elementary education. Ibsen publishes *Hedda Gabler*. Knut Hamsun publishes *Hunger*. Social insurance introduced by Swiss government.
1891	Emily Dickinson (1830–86) *Poems by Emily Dickinson. Second Series*, ed. Mabel Loomis Todd & T. W. Higginson Helen Hunt Jackson (1830–85) *Poems* (Posthumous) Herman Melville (1819–91) *Timoleon and Other Poems*	Charles Ives composes *Variations on America*. Forest Reserve Act gives President authority to create national parks on public lands. Hamlin Garland publishes *Main-Travelled Roads*.	Germany, Austria-Hungary, and Italy renew the Triple Alliance. Hardy publishes *Tess of the D'Urbervilles*. Monet exhibits *Haystacks*.

(cont.)

American Poetry and Criticism			American Events, Texts, and Arts	Other Events, Texts, and Arts
	Walt Whitman (1819–92)	*Good Bye My Fancy*	Land ceded to the US by Fox, Potawatomi, and Sauk Indians opened to white settlers.	Oscar Wilde publishes *The Picture of Dorian Gray.*
			Herman Melville writes *Billy Budd;* he dies five months later.	*Pithecanthropus erectus* discovered in Java.
			Tesla coil invented to generate high-voltage, high-frequency electric current.	Widespread famine in Russia.
1892	Lucy Larcom (1824–93)	*At the Beautiful Gate and Other Songs of Faith*	Ten-year extension of Chinese Exclusion Act.	Gladstone elected Prime Minister of Britain again; seeks Home Rule for Ireland.
	Walt Whitman (1819–92)	*Leaves of Grass*	Charlotte Perkins Gilman publishes "The Yellow Wallpaper."	Health Insurance Law and Old-Age Pension Law enacted by Denmark.
			Democrat Grover Cleveland elected President.	Ibsen writes *The Master Builder.*
			Joel Chandler Harris publishes *Nights with Uncle Remus.*	Kocher's *Chirurgische Operationslehre* published; becomes essential surgical text.
			People's Party advocates graduated income tax, state-run railroads and postal banks, and free coinage of silver.	Rudyard Kipling publishes *Barrack-Room Ballads,* including "Gunga Din" and "The Road to Mandalay."
			Workers at Carnegie steel plant go on strike to protest pay-cuts; ten Pinkerton detectives killed.	Tchaikovsky composes *Nutcracker Suite.*

1893	Paul Laurence Dunbar (1872–1906)	*Oak and Ivy*	Chinese Exclusion Act found constitutional by Supreme Court.	Benz builds a four-wheel car.
	Charlotte Perkins Gilman (1860–1935)	*In This Our World*	Henry Ford builds first successful gasoline engine.	Dvorak composes *Symphony No. 9 (From the New World)*.
	James Whitcomb Riley (1849–1916)	*Poems Here at Home*	Land between Kansas and Oklahoma purchased by government for Cherokees in 1891 is opened to settlement.	France and Russia form a dual alliance to counterbalance the Triple Alliance.
			President Cleveland secures repeal of the Sherman Silver Purchase Act of 1890 in a special session of Congress.	Gladstone's second Home Rule Bill voted down by British House of Lords.
			Stephen Crane writes *Maggie: A Girl of the Streets*.	Kruger reelected President of the South African Republic.
				Sigmund Freud and Joseph Breuer publish *The Psychic Mechanism of Hysterical Phenomena*.
1894	Frances Harper (1825–1911)	*The Martyr of Alabama and Other Poems*	Congress passes first graduated income tax law.	Alfred Dreyfus convicted falsely for treason; case divides France.
	George Santayana (1863–1952)	*Sonnets and Other Verses*	Coxey's Army of unemployed men marches to petition Congress for public works programs for the unemployed.	Diesel invents the Diesel engine.

(cont.)

American Poetry and Criticism	American Events, Texts, and Arts	Other Events, Texts, and Arts
		Nicholas II becomes last Czar of Russia.
	Letters of Emily Dickinson published, edited by Mabel Loomis Todd.	
		Shaw writes *Arms and the Man.*
	Pullman railway cars boycotted by American Railway Union in support of striking Pullman workers; strike broken by federal troops.	
	Riot among striking miners in Pennsylvania kills eleven; other large strikes occur in Ohio, New York, and throughout the Midwest.	Toulouse-Lautrec paints *Au salon de la Rue des Moulins.*
	William Jennings Bryan leads Democratic Silver Convention to adopt free coinage plank.	Turks begin extermination of Armenians.
1895 Stephen Crane (1871–1900) *The Black Riders and Other Lines*	Elizabeth Cady Stanton publishes *Revised Version of the Bible,* also known as "Woman's Bible."	Cuba battles Spain for its independence.
Paul Laurence Dunbar (1872–1906) *Majors and Minors*	Income tax declared unconstitutional by Supreme Court in *Pollack v. Farmers Loan and Trust Company.*	Edward Munch paints *The Scream.*

	James Russell Lowell (1819–91)	*Last Poems*	Sears, Roebuck, and Co. opens a small mail-order business. Stephen Crane publishes *Red Badge of Courage.* Use of injunction as strike-breaking device upheld by Supreme Court.	First movie shown by Auguste and Louis Lumière: *Lunch Break at the Lumière Factory.* Marconi invents wireless telegraph. Röntgen discovers X-rays.
1896	Emily Dickinson (1830–86)	*Poems by Emily Dickinson, Third Series*, ed. Mabel Loomis Todd & T. W. Higginson	William Jennings Bryan gives "Cross of Gold" speech at the Democratic National Convention in Chicago; he is nominated for President by Free-Silver Democrats and the Populist Party.	Turks massacre Armenians. Wilde writes *The Importance of Being Earnest.* British quell revolts by the Matabele and Mashona tribes in Rhodesia.
	Paul Laurence Dunbar (1872–1906)	*Lyrics of Lowly Life*	Thomas Edison invents the fluoroscope and the fluorescent lamp.	British victorious over Ashantis in central Ghana.
	Edwin Arlington Robinson (1869–1935)	*The Torrent and the Night Before*	In *Plessy v. Ferguson* Supreme Court rules that "separate but equal" facilities for whites and blacks are constitutional; "Jim Crow" era of segregation begins.	Italians sign the Treaty of Addis Ababa, acknowledging the independence of Ethiopia.

(cont.)

American Poetry and Criticism	American Events, Texts, and Arts	Other Events, Texts, and Arts
	William McKinley elected President on Republican platform endorsing gold standard.	Moritz Cantor publishes complete history of mathematics from the ancients through 1800.
		Puccini composes *La Bohème*.
1897 Edwin Arlington Robinson (1869–1935) *Children of the Night*	Association of eighteen railroads found in violation of Sherman Anti-trust Act.	Freud defines the "Oedipus Complex."
	Bill requiring literacy tests for immigrants vetoed by President McKinley.	Joseph Thomson discovers the electron.
	Boston completes first subway.	Matisse paints *The Dinner Table*.
	National Monetary Conference endorses gold standard.	Rousseau paints *The Sleeping Gypsy*.
		Somali frontier defined in treaty between Ethiopia and France.
1898 Julia Ward Howe (1819–1910) *From Sunset Ridge: Poems Old and New*	Epinephrine extracted from the adrenal glands of a sheep by John Abel; first hormone to be isolated in a laboratory.	"The Boxers," an anti-foreign organization, is established in China.
	First Food and Drug Act passed.	Chekhov writes *Uncle Vanya*.
	Social Democratic Party, later called the Socialist Party, is formed by Eugene Debs.	Marie Curie discovers polonium and radium, and coins term "radioactivity."
	Spanish–American War begins.	Russian industrial workers form Social Democratic Party.

1899	Stephen Crane (1871–1900)	*War is Kind*	Tolstoy publishes "What is Art?"
	Henry Timrod (1828–67)	*Complete Poems*	Spanish fleet destroyed by Admiral George Dewey at the Battle of Manila Bay.
			Spanish forces defeated by US at Guantanamo Bay, El Caney, and San Juan Hill.
			Spanish–American War ends with Treaty of Paris; US recognized as world power.
			US and Filipino forces capture the city of Manila.
			US forces capture Puerto Rico and Guam.
			US *Maine* blown up in Havana harbor.
			Frank Norris publishes *McTeague*.
			Scott Joplin popularizes ragtime with "Maple Leaf Rag."
			Secretary Hay sets forth Open Door Policy towards China, stressing freedom of trade.
			Treaty of Paris ratified by Congress; Filipinos begin three-year rebellion against US rule.
			Boer War begins.
			Freud publishes *The Interpretation of Dreams*.
			Cipriano Castro makes himself dictator of Venezuela after successful coup d'état.
			Monet begins *Water Lilies* (–1906).
			D'Annunzio publishes *In Praise of Sky, Sea, Earth, and Heroes*.

(cont.)

American Poetry and Criticism		American Events, Texts, and Arts	Other Events, Texts, and Arts
1901	George Santayana (1863–1952)	*Hermit of Carmel and Other Poems*	Oil discovered in Texas.	Chekhov writes *The Three Sisters*.
			Platt Amendment passed by Congress; makes Cuba a US protectorate.	Commonwealth of Australia is created.
			President McKinley killed; Theodore Roosevelt becomes President.	Kipling publishes *Kim*.
			US citizenship given to the Indians of the "Five Civilized Tribes" (Cherokees, Creeks, Choctaws, Chickasaws, and Seminoles).	Queen Victoria dies.
			US concludes military rule in the Philippine Islands.	Russian troops occupy Manchuria.
			Walter Reed finds that yellow fever is caused by a virus, and spread by mosquitoes.	
1902	Edwin Arlington Robinson (1869–1935)	*Captain Craig*	150,000 United Mine Workers in Pennsylvania strike in demand of 20 percent wage increase and an eight-hour day.	Boer War ends with Treaty of Vereeniging.

Trumbull Stickney (1874–1904)	*Dramatic Verses*	Commission appointed by President Roosevelt to decide issues in strike by anthracite coal miners, including demands for union recognition, an eight-hour day, and wage increase.	Conrad publishes *Heart of Darkness*.
		Congress authorizes financing of Panama Canal.	Denominational schools brought into state system by Education Act in England.
		Frank Lloyd Wright completes the first of his "prairie style" homes.	Germany, Austria, and Italy renew the Triple Alliance for another six years.
		Henry James publishes *The Wings of the Dove*.	Independence of China and Korea is recognized by Anglo-Japanese alliance.
		Maryland passes the first workmen's compensation law.	Kipling publishes *Just So Stories*.
		Owen Wister publishes *The Virginian*.	Marie and Pierre Curie determine properties of radium.
1905	Trumbull Stickney (1874–1904)	*Poems*	Edith Wharton publishes *House of Mirth*.	"Bloody Sunday" in Russia: petitioning workers fired upon.
		Industrial Workers of the World founded in Chicago by Eugene Debs.	Albert Einstein proposes special theory of relativity, explains Brownian movement, and suggests the quantum theory of light to account for the photoelectric effect.

(cont.)

American Poetry and Criticism	American Events, Texts, and Arts	Other Events, Texts, and Arts
	President Roosevelt instrumental in concluding Russo-Japanese War; awarded Nobel Peace Prize.	Freud publishes *Jokes and Their Relation to the Unconscious* and *Three Essays on the Theory of Sexuality.*
		Japanese take Port Arthur from the Russians; Treaty of Portsmouth ends Russo-Japanese War.
		Matisse exhibits *Woman With the Hat*, initiates Fauvism.
		Rilke publishes *Das Stunden-Buch.*
1906 Thomas Nelson Page (1853–1922) *The Coast of Bohemia*	Jack London publishes *White Fang.*	Dreyfus exonerated by French Supreme Court of Appeals.
	Meat Inspection Act passed.	Representative assembly meets to reform laws in Russia.
	Pure Food and Drug Act passed.	Spheres of influence in Ethiopia agreed upon by Britain, France, and Italy.
	Supreme Court rules that witnesses in anti-trust cases may be compelled to hand over documents and to testify against their corporations.	
	Troops sent to quell revolt in Cuba.	
	Upton Sinclair publishes *The Jungle.*	

| 1910 | Edwin Arlington Robinson (1869–1935) | *The Town Down the River* | Thirty-eight of forty-six states form conservation committees.

Electric washing machines introduced.

Manns–Elkin Act strengthens Interstate Commerce Commission.

Charles Steinmetz publishes "Future of Electricity," warns of air and water pollution.

Teddy Roosevelt advocates "new nationalism." | 122,000 telephones in use in Great Britain.

E. M. Forster publishes *Howard's End.*

Japan annexes Korea.

Kandinsky paints *First Abstract Watercolor*, writes *Concerning the Spiritual in Art.*

Marie Curie publishes "Traité de radioactivité." |

BIBLIOGRAPHY

This selected bibliography is drawn from lists supplied by the two contributors to this volume. It represents works that they have found to be especially influential or significant. The bibliography does not include dissertations, articles, or studies of individual authors.

Appleby, Joyce. *Capitalism and a New Social Order: The Republican Vision of the 1790s.* New York: New York University Press, 1984.

Ardener, Shirley, ed. *Perceiving Women.* London: Malaby Press, 1975.

Auden, W. H. *The Dyer's Hand and Other Essays.* London: Faber and Faber, 1963.

Auerbach, Erich. *Literary Language and Its Public in Late Latin Antiquity and in the Middle Ages.* Translated by Ralph Mannheim. New York: Pantheon Books, 1965.

Barth, Frederik, ed. *Ethnic Groups and Boundaries: The Social Organization of Culture Difference.* Boston: Little, Brown and Co., 1969.

Baym, Nina. *Feminism and American Literary History.* New Brunswick: Rutgers University Press, 1992.

Bercovitch, Sacvan. *The Puritan Origins of the American Self.* New Haven: Yale University Press, 1975.

   The Rites of Assent: Transformations in the Symbolic Construction of America. New York: Routledge, 1993.

Bhabha, Homi, ed. *Nation and Narration.* London: Routledge, 1990.

Bloom, Harold. *Agon: Towards a Theory of Revisionism.* New York: Oxford University Press, 1982.

   Poetry and Repression: Revisionism from Blake to Stevens. New Haven: Yale University Press, 1976.

   The Ringers in the Tower. Chicago: University of Chicago Press, 1971.

Bordo, Susan. *Unbearable Weight: Feminism, Western Culture, and the Body.* Berkeley: University of California Press, 1993.

Brodhead, Richard H. *Cultures of Letters: Scenes of Reading and Writing in Nineteenth-Century America.* Chicago: University of Chicago Press, 1993.

Bromwich, David. *A Choice of Inheritance.* Cambridge, Mass.: Harvard University Press, 1989.

Buell, Lawrence. *Literary Transcendentalism: Style and Vision in the American Renaissance.* Ithaca, N.Y.: Cornell University Press, 1973.

New England Literary Culture from Revolution through Renaissance. New York: Cambridge University Press, 1986.

Carton, Evan. *The Rhetoric of American Romance: Dialectic and Identity in Emerson, Dickinson, Poe, and Hawthorne.* Baltimore: Johns Hopkins University Press, 1985.

Cavell, Stanley. *Conditions Handsome and Unhandsome: The Constitution of Emersonian Perfectionism.* Chicago: University of Chicago Press, 1990.

Charvat, William. *The Profession of Authorship in America 1800–1870.* Edited by Matthew Bruccoli. Columbus: Ohio State University Press, 1968.

Coben, Stanley, and Lorman Ratner, eds. *The Development of an American Culture.* Englewood Cliffs, N.J.: Prentice-Hall, Inc. 1970.

Colacurcio, Michael. *Doctrine and Difference: Essays in the Literature of New England.* New York: Routledge, 1997.

Cott, Nancy F. *The Bonds of Womanhood: "Woman's Sphere" in New England 1780–1835.* New Haven: Yale University Press, 1977.

Davie, Donald. *Trying To Explain.* Ann Arbor: University of Michigan Press, 1979.

Degler, Carl. *At Odds: Women and the Family in America from the Revolution to the Present.* New York: Oxford University Press, 1980.

Dickson, Bruce, Jr. *Black American Writing from the Nadir: The Evolution of a Literary Tradition, 1877–1915.* Baton Rouge: Louisiana State University Press, 1989.

Douglas, Ann. *The Feminization of American Culture.* New York: Knopf, 1977.

Dowling, William C. *Poetry and Ideology in Revolutionary Connecticut.* Athens, Ga.: University of Georgia Press, 1990.

Du Bois, W. E. B. *The Souls of Black Folk.* New York: Bantam Books, 1989.

Elshtain, Jean Bethke. *Public Man, Private Woman: Women in Social and Political Thought.* Princeton: Princeton University Press, 1981.

Erkkila, Betsy. *Whitman the Political Poet.* New York: Oxford University Press, 1989.

Ferguson, Robert A. *Law and Letters in American Culture.* Cambridge, Mass.: Harvard University Press, 1984.

Fredrickson, George. *The Inner Civil War: Northern Intellectuals and the Crisis of the Union.* New York: Harper and Row, 1965.

Gates, Henry Louis, Jr. *The Signifying Monkey: A Theory of Afro-American Literary Criticism.* New York: Oxford University Press, 1988.

Gates, Henry Louis, Jr., ed. *Black Literature and Literary Theory.* New York: Methuen, 1984.

Genovese, Eugene D. *Roll, Jordan, Roll: The World the Slaves Made.* New York: Pantheon Books, 1974.

Gilbert, Sandra and Susan Gubar. *The Madwoman in the Attic: The Woman Writer and the Nineteenth-Century Literary Imagination.* New Haven: Yale University Press, 1979.

Ginzberg, Lori. *Women and the Work of Benevolence: Morality, Politics, and Class in the Nineteenth-Century United States.* New Haven: Yale University Press, 1990.

Greeley, Andrew. *Ethnicity in the United States: A Preliminary Reconnaissance.* New York: John Wiley and Sons, 1974.

Grey, Robin. *The Complicity of Imagination: The American Renaissance, Contests of Authority, and Seventeenth-Century English Culture*. New York: Cambridge University Press, 1997.

Griswold, Rufus Wilmot. *The Poets and Poetry of America, to the Middle of the Nineteenth Century*. Philadelphia: Carey and Hart, 1850.

Hagenbuchle, R., ed. *American Poetry: Between Tradition and Modernism 1865–1914*. Regensburg: F. Pustet, 1984.

Haight, Gordon. *Mrs. Sigourney, The Sweet Singer of Hartford*. New Haven: Yale University Press, 1930.

Haralson, Eric L., ed. *Encyclopedia of American Poetry: The Nineteenth Century*. Chicago: Fitzroy Dearborn Publishers, 1998. (See especially: "John Quincy Adams," by Guy Woodall; "Washington Allston," by Lorin Stein; "Joel Barlow," by Anita M. Vickers; "Manoah Bodman," by Edward Halsey Foster; "Maria Gowen Brooks," by Geofrilyn M. Walker; "William Cullen Bryant," by Paul Bray; "Christopher Pearse Cranch," by Lisa Honaker; "Richard Henry Dana," by Doreen Hunter; "Ralph Waldo Emerson," by Paul Kane; "Fitz-Greene Halleck," by Nicholas Birns; "James Gates Percival," by William Crisman; "John Pierpont," by Nicholas Birns; "Lydia Huntley Sigourney," by Patricia Crain; "William Gilmore Simms," by George C. Longest; "Henry David Thoreau," by Elizabeth Hall Witherell; "Jones Very," by Helen Deese; "John Greenleaf Whittier," by Christopher Beach; "Carlos Wilcox," by James Hazen; "Richard Henry Wilde," by Edward Tucker.)

Hartz, Louis. *The Liberal Tradition in America: An Interpretation of American Political Thought Since the Revolution*. New York: Harcourt Brace, 1955.

Hatch, Nathan. *The Democratization of American Christianity*. New Haven: Yale University Press, 1989.

Higginson, Thomas Wentworth. *Army Life in a Black Regiment*. East Lansing: Michigan State University Press, 1960.

Higham, John. *Send These To Me: Jews and Other Immigrants in Urban America*. New York: Atheneum, 1975.

Hollander, John. *The Gazer's Spirit: Poems Speaking to Silent Works of Art*. Chicago: University of Chicago Press, 1995.

    Melodious Guile: Fictive Pattern in Poetic Language. New Haven: Yale University Press, 1988.

    Vision and Resonance: Two Senses of Poetic Form. New York: Oxford University Press, 1975.

Homans, Margaret. *Women Writers and Poetic Identity: Dorothy Wordsworth, Emily Brontë, and Emily Dickinson*. Princeton: Princeton University Press, 1980.

Howard, Leon. *The Connecticut Wits*. Chicago: University of Chicago Press, 1943.

Howells, William D. *Literary Friends and Acquaintance: A Personal Retrospect of American Authorship*, ed. David F. Hiatt and Edwin H. Cady. Bloomington: Indiana University Press, 1968.

Johnson, James Weldon. *Along this Way: The Autobiography of James Weldon Johnson.* New York: Viking Press, 1933.

Johnson, Linck C. *Thoreau's Complex Weave: The Writing of A Week on the Concord and Merrimack Rivers, with the Text of the First Draft.* Charlottesville: University Press of Virginia, 1986.

Juhasz, Suzanne. *Naked and Fiery Forms: Modern American Poetry by Women, a New Tradition.* New York: Harper and Row, 1976.

Kasson, John F. *Rudeness and Civility: Manners in Nineteenth-Century Urban America.* New York: Hill and Wang, 1990.

Kerber, Linda. *Women of the Republic: Intellect and Ideology in Revolutionary America.* Chapel Hill, N.C.: University of North Carolina Press, 1980.

Kramer, Michael. *Imagining Language in America: From the Revolution to the Civil War.* Princeton: Princeton University Press, 1992.

Lawrence, D. H. *Studies in Classic American Literature.* New York: T. Seltzer, 1923.

Leary, Lewis. *That Rascal Freneau, a Study in Literary Failure.* New Brunswick, N.J.: Rutgers University Press, 1941.

Levine, Lawrence. *Black Culture and Black Consciousness: Afro-American Folk Thought from Slavery to Freedom.* New York: Oxford University Press, 1977.

Lowell, James Russell. *Literary Criticism of James Russell Lowell.* Edited by Herbert F. Smith. Lincoln: University of Nebraska Press, 1969.

MacPherson, C. B. *The Political Theory of Possessive Individualism: Hobbes to Locke.* Oxford: Clarendon Press, 1962.

McPherson, James. *Battle Cry of Freedom: the Civil War Era.* New York: Oxford University Press, 1988.

McWilliams, John P., Jr. *The American Epic: Transforming a Genre, 1770–1860.* Cambridge: Cambridge University Press, 1989.

Michaels, Walter Benn and Donald Pease, eds. *The American Renaissance Reconsidered.* Baltimore: Johns Hopkins University Press, 1985.

Miller, Perry. *Errand into the Wilderness.* Cambridge, Mass.: Belknap Press, 1956.
Nature's Nation. Cambridge, Mass.: Belknap Press, 1967.

Morgan, Edmund. *American Slavery, American Freedom: The Ordeal of Colonial Virginia.* New York: W. W. Norton, 1975.
Inventing the People: The Rise of Popular Sovereignty in England and America. New York: Norton, 1988.

Newlin, Claude Milton. *The Life and Writings of Hugh Henry Brackenridge.* Princeton: Princeton University Press, 1932.

Newman, William. *American Pluralism: A Study of Minority Groups and Social Theory.* New York: Harper and Row, 1973.

Norton, Mary Beth. *Liberty's Daughters: The Revolutionary Experience of American Women, 1750–1800.* Boston: Little, Brown and Company, 1980.

Onderdonk, James L. *History of American Verse (1610–1897).* Chicago: A. C. McClurg & Co., 1901.

Ostriker, Alicia. *Stealing the Language: The Emergence of Women's Poetry in America*. Boston: Beacon Press, 1986.

Pateman, Carole. *The Disorder of Women: Democracy, Feminism, and Political Theory*. Stanford: Stanford University Press, 1989.

Pearce, Roy Harvey. *The Continuity of American Poetry*. Princeton: Princeton University Press, 1961.

Pease, Donald. *Visionary Compacts: American Renaissance Writings in Cultural Context*. Madison: University of Wisconsin Press, 1987.

Raboteau, Albert J. *Slave Religion: The "Invisible Institution" in the Antebellum South*. New York: Oxford University Press, 1978.

Ruether, Rosemary Radford and Rosemary Skinner Keller, eds. *Women and Religion in America, Vol. 1: The Nineteenth Century*. San Francisco: Harper and Row, 1981.

Ryan, Mary. *Womanhood in America: From Colonial to the Present*. New York: New Viewpoints, 1975.

Sedgwick, Eve Kosofsky. *Between Men: English Literature and Male Homosocial Desire*. New York: Columbia University Press, 1985.

Smith-Rosenberg, Carroll. *Disorderly Conduct: Visions of Gender in Victorian America*. New York: Alfred A. Knopf, 1985.

Sobel, Mechal. *The World They Made Together: Black and White Values in Eighteenth-Century Virginia*. Princeton: Princeton University Press, 1987.

Sollors, Werner. *Beyond Ethnicity: Consent and Descent in American Culture*. New York: Oxford University Press, 1986.

Stanton, Elizabeth Cady. *The Woman's Bible*. New York: European Publishing Company, 1895.

Stuckey, Sterling. *Slave Culture: Nationalist Theory and the Foundations of Black America*. New York: Oxford University Press, 1987.

Sundquist, Eric. *To Wake the Nations: Race in the Making of American Literature*. Cambridge, Mass.: Harvard University Press, 1993.

Tocqueville, Alexis de. *Democracy in America*. Translated by George Lawrence. Edited by J. P. Mayer. New York: Doubleday, 1969.

Trachtenberg, Alan. *The Incorporation of America: Culture and Society in the Gilded Age*. New York: Hill and Wang, 1982.

Turco, Lewis Putnam. *The Life and Poetry of Manoah Bodman: Bard of the Berkshires*. Lanham, Md: University Press of America, 1999.

Turner, Frederick Jackson. *The Significance of Sections in American History*. New York: Henry Holt and Company, 1932.

Tuveson, Ernest Lee. *Redeemer Nation: The Idea of America's Millennial Role*. Chicago: University of Chicago Press, 1968.

Von Frank, Albert J. *The Sacred Game: Provincialism and Frontier Consciousness in American Literature, 1630–1860*. New York: Cambridge University Press, 1985.

Waggoner, Hyatt. *American Poets, from the Puritan to the Present*. Boston: Houghton Mifflin, 1968.

Walker, Cheryl. *The Nightingale's Burden: Women Poets and American Culture before* 1900. Bloomington: Indiana University Press, 1982.

Warren, Joyce W., ed. *The (Other) American Traditions: Nineteenth-Century Women Writers.* New Brunswick, N.J.: Rutgers University Press, 1993.

Warren, Robert Penn. *John Greenleaf Whittier's Poetry: An Appraisal and a Selection.* Minneapolis: University of Minnesota Press, 1971.

Whittier, John Greenleaf, ed. *The Literary Remains of John G. C. Brainard, with a Sketch of his Life.* Hartford: P. B. Goodsell, 1832.

Wilson, Edmund. *Patriotic Gore: Studies in the Literature of the American Civil War.* New York: Oxford University Press, 1962.

Winters, Yvor. *Maule's Curse: Seven Studies in the History of American Obscurantism: Hawthorne, Cooper, Melville, Poe, Emerson, Jones Very, Emily Dickinson, Henry James.* Norfolk, Conn.: New Directions, 1938.

Wood, Gordon. *The Creation of the American Republic,* 1776–1787. Chapel Hill: University of North Carolina Press, 1969.

Yerushalmi, Yosef Hayim. *Zakhor: Jewish History and Jewish Memory.* Seattle: University of Washington Press, 1982.

Ziff, Larzer. *Literary Democracy: The Declaration of Cultural Independence in America.* New York: The Viking Press, 1981.

Writing in the New Nation: Prose, Print, and Politics. New Haven: Yale University Press, 1991.

INDEX